MICK JAGGER

MICK JAGGER

PHILIP NORMAN

HarperCollins*Publishers*

HarperCollins*Publishers*
77–85 Fulham Palace Road,
Hammersmith, London W6 8JB

www.harpercollins.co.uk

First published by HarperCollins*Publishers* 2012

1 3 5 7 9 10 8 6 4 2

© Jessica Productions Ltd. 2012

Philip Norman asserts the moral right to
be identified as the author of this work

A catalogue record of this book is
available from the British Library

HB ISBN 978-0-00-732949-6
TPB ISBN 978-0-00-732950-2

Printed and bound in Great Britain by
Clays Ltd, St Ives plc

TO SUE, WITH LOVE

Photo Credits

CONTENTS

PART II: THE TYRANNY OF COOL

ACKNOWLEDGEMENTS

The great nineteenth-century painter James McNeill Whistler was once asked how long a certain canvas had taken him to complete. 'All my life,' replied Whistler, meaning the years of training and dedication that had given him his abilities. Likewise, I could be said to have worked on this portrait of Mick Jagger since I first interviewed him, for a small north of England evening newspaper, in 1965. Our conversation took place on the cold back stairs of the ABC cinema, Stockton-on-Tees, where the Stones were appearing in what used to be called a pop 'package show'. Mick wore a white fisherman's knit sweater, drank Pepsi-Cola from the bottle and, between answering my questions in a not very interested way, made desultory attempts to chat up a young woman somewhere behind me. That one detail, at least, would never change.

In later years, our paths crossed again from time to time, particularly when I was writing about pop music for *The Times* and *Sunday Times* of London during the 1970s. But it never occurred to me that I might be collecting material for a future book. There was, for instance, the time I found myself in Rod Stewart's dressing room at the State theatre in north London when Mick dropped by after the show. Though he was living apart from Bianca, and clearly at a loose end, that night with Stewart did not turn out as one might have expected. Rock's two greatest Lotharios stood around a piano, chorusing sentimental Cockney songs like 'My Old Dutch'.

I didn't become a conscious Jagger watcher until 1982 when for a *Sunday Times* article (later the prologue to my Rolling Stones biography) I joined the band on tour in America and was granted my first formal interview with Mick since Stockton-on-Tees in 1965. This time it happened at the Tangerine Bowl in Orlando, Florida, while he was doing his customary pre-show warm-up on his backstage jogging track. Even before going out to perform to eighty thousand people for two hours, however, the Jagger business brain never switched off. Without pausing in his workout, he told me he'd just read my Beatles biography, *Shout!*, then proceeded to correct a minor point of fact relating to Allen Klein, the manager the Beatles and the Stones used to share. So much for that often repeated claim that he 'can't remember anything' about his astounding career.

It hardly needs saying that this is not an authorised biography. When I accepted the commission in 2009, I made two approaches to the now Sir Mick for cooperation, first privately through a high-level personal friend of his, then publicly through Baz Bamigboye's show-business column in the *Daily Mail*. I thought that possibly my credentials as a biographer, most recently of his old friend John Lennon, might at least arouse his curiosity. But when no response came back, I can't say I was surprised. Sir Mick talks to writers only when he has something to sell. And then the palpitating hack – for, female or male, old or young, they *all* palpitate – can be relied on to churn out the same old clichés. As his one official biographer discovered, he sees no percentage in telling the truth or having it told, even where it reflects most positively on himself. The millions are all in the mythology. And the millions always come first.

So this has had to be a work of investigation and reconstruction, drawing on sources I've acquired during thirty years of writing about the Stones and the Beatles – who in fact constitute one single, epic story. My thrifty side was tickled to be using the same contacts book in 2009–11 that I had for my Stones biography in 1981–83. Inevitably, I reviewed the many hours of interview I had all those years ago with Andrew Loog Oldham, Marianne Faithfull, Keith Richards, Bianca Jagger, Anita

Pallenberg, Bill Wyman, Ronnie Wood, Paul Jones, Eric Clapton, Robert Fraser, Donald Cammell, Alexis Korner, Giorgio Gomelsky and others. But, as I did with my John Lennon biography, I promised myself never simply to recycle the group portrait into the solo one. Indeed, it will be seen that I've revised my view of Mick even more than I did of John.

I must record my indebtedness to Peter Trollope, a superb researcher who opened many doors – not least on the mystery of 'Acid King David' Snyderman and the sinister background of the Redlands drugs bust of 1967 which put Mick briefly (but still terrifyingly) behind bars. It was through Peter, too, that I made contact with Maggie Abbott, who turned out not only to have been a friend of the elusive Acid King but also Mick's film agent in the era when he might have become as big in movies as in rock. Maggie was endlessly helpful and patient, and the section on Mick's wooing by Hollywood, and all those missed acting opportunities, would have been thin without her.

Special thanks go to Chrissie Messenger, formerly Shrimpton, and Cleo Sylvestre, whose recollections of the young Mick differ so greatly from the image he was given in his late teens. One great stroke of biographer's luck came through Jacqui Graham, whom I first met when she was publicity director at Pan Macmillan publishers and I was one of her authors. Quite by chance, Jackie mentioned that in the early sixties she'd been an avid Stones fan and had kept a diary – a hilarious one, as it turned out – about following them around their early London gigs, on one occasion doorstepping Mick at home in his pyjamas. My other piece of luck was being contacted by Scott Jones, a British filmmaker who has devoted years to investigating Brian Jones's death in 1969. Brian's mysterious drowning and the Redlands drugs raid both took place in the county of Sussex, and some local police officers were involved in both incidents. Scott generously put me in touch with two of the bobbies who collared Mick and Keith.

My gratitude to Alan Clayson, Martin Elliott and Andy Neill for fact-checking the manuscript; to Shirley Arnold, who knows better than most that the real Mick 'has no dark side'; to Tony Calder for vignettes of life with Mick and Andrew Oldham; to Maureen O'Grady for memories of Mick and *Rave!* magazine; to Laurence Myers for background to the Stones' 1965 Decca deal; to Christopher Gibbs, for guidance as invaluable here as in my Stones book; to Michael Lindsay-Hogg for the backstage story of *The Rolling Stones' Rock 'n' Roll Circus*; to Sam Cutler for the new perspective on the Altamont festival; to Sandy Lieberson for the saga of *Performance*; to Bobby Keys for recalling 'one hell of a whopper of a good time' as the Stones' sax player; to Marshall Chess for enlightenment on the Rolling Stones Records and *Cocksucker Blues* era; to fellow biographer Andrew Morton for insights on Mick and Angelina Jolie; to Dick Cavett, America's last great talk-show host, for chatting so vividly about being Mick and Bianca's next-door neighbour in Montauk; to Michael O'Mara for his recollections of Mick's aborted memoirs; to Gillian Wilson for the observation about Charlie Watts's underwear.

Grateful thanks also to Keith Altham, Mick Avory, Dave Berry, Geoff Bradford, Alan Dow, John Dunbar, Alan Etherington, Matthew Evans, Richard Hattrell, Laurence Isaacson, Peter Jones, Norman Jopling, Judy Lever, Kevin Macdonald, Chris O'Dell, Linda Porter (formerly Keith), Don Rambridge, Ron Schneider, Dick Taylor and Michael Watts.

Finally, my continuing appreciation goes to my agents and dear friends Michael Sissons in London and Peter Matson in New York; to Dan Halpern at Ecco, New York, Carole Tonkinson at HarperCollins UK and Tim Rostron at Random House, Canada, for their support and encouragement; to Rachel Mills and Alexandra Cliff at PFD for selling this book in other territories with such enthusiasm; to Louise Connolly for her photo research; and to my daughter Jessica for the author photo – and so very much more.

Philip Norman, London 2012

MICK JAGGER

PROLOGUE

Sympathy for the Old Devil

The British Academy of Film and Television Arts is not normally a controversial body, but in February 2009 it became the target of outraged tabloid headlines. To emcee its annual film awards – an event regarded as second only to Hollywood's Oscars – BAFTA had chosen Jonathan Ross, the floppy-haired, foul-mouthed chat-show host who was currently the most notorious figure in UK broadcasting. A few weeks previously, Ross had used a peak-time BBC radio programme to leave a series of obscene messages on the answering machine of the former *Fawlty Towers* actor Andrew Sachs. As a result, he had been suspended from all his various BBC slots for three months while comedian Russell Brand, his fellow presenter and accomplice in the prank (who boasted on air about 'shagging' Sachs's granddaughter) had bowed to pressure and left the corporation altogether. Since the 1990s, comedy in Britain has been known as 'the new rock 'n' roll'; now here were two of its principal ornaments positively straining a gut to be as naughty as old-school rock stars.

On awards night at the Royal Opera House, Covent Garden, a celebrity-packed audience including Brad Pitt, Angelina Jolie, Meryl Streep, Sir Ben Kingsley, Kevin Spacey and Kristin Scott-Thomas received two surprises outside the actual winners list. The first was that the bad language everyone had anticipated from Jonathan Ross came instead from Mickey Rourke on receiving the Best Actor award for *The Wrestler*. Tangle-haired, unshaven and barely coherent – since movie acting also lays urgent claim to being 'the new rock 'n' roll' – Rourke thanked his director for this second chance 'after fucking up my career for fifteen years', and his publicist 'for telling me where to go, what to do, when to do it, what to eat, how to dress, what to fuck . . .'

Having quipped that Rourke would pay the same penalty he himself had for 'Sachsgate' and be suspended for three months, Ross moderated his tone to one of fawning reverence. As presenter of the evening's pen-ultimate statuette, for Best Film, he called on 'an actor and lead singer with one of the greatest rock bands in history'; somebody for whom this lofty red-and-gold-tiered auditorium 'must seem like one of the smaller venues' (and who, incidentally, could once have made the Sachsgate scandal look very small beer). Almost sacrilegiously, in this temple to pure acoustic Mozart, Wagner and Puccini, the sound system began chugging out the electric guitar intro to 'Brown Sugar', that 1971 rock anthem to drugs, slavery and interracial cunnilingus. Yes indeed, the award giver was Sir Mick Jagger.

Jagger's entrance was no simple hop up to the podium but a lengthy red-carpet walk from the rear of the stage, to allow television viewers to drink in the full miracle. That still-plentiful hair, cut in youthful retro six-ties mode, untainted by a single spark of grey. That understated couture suit, worn in deference to the occasion but also subtly emphasising the suppleness of the slight torso beneath and the springy, athletic step. Only the face betrayed the sixty-five-year-old, born at the height of the Second

World War – the famous lips, once said to be able to 'suck an egg out of a chicken's arse', now drawn in and bloodless; the cheeks etched by crevasses so wide and deep as to resemble terrible matching scars.

The ovation that greeted him belonged less to the Royal Opera House or the British Association for Film and Television Arts than to some giant open-air space like Wembley or Dodger Stadium. Despite all the proliferating genres of 'new' rock 'n' roll, everyone knows there is only one genuine kind and that Mick Jagger remains its unrivalled incarnation. He responded with his disarming smile, a raucous 'Allaw!' and an impromptu flash of Rolling Stone subversiveness: 'You see? You thought Jonathan would do all the "fuck"-ing, and Mickey did it . . .'

The voice then changed, the way it always does to suit the occasion. For decades, Jagger has spoken in the faux-Cockney accent known as 'Mockney' or 'Estuary English', whose misshapen, elongated vowels and obliterated *t* consonants are the badge of youthful cool in modern Britain. But here, amid the cream of English elocution, his diction of every *t* was bell clear, every *h* punctiliously aspirated as he said what an honour it was to be here tonight*tt*, then went on to reveal 'how it all came about*tt*'.

A neat little joke followed, perfectly pitched between mockery and deference. He was here, he said, under 'the RMEP – the Rock Stars–Movie Stars Exchange Programme . . . At this moment, "Sir" Ben Kingsley [giving the title ironic emphasis even though he shared it] will be singing "Brown Sugar" at the Grammys . . . "Sir" Anthony Hopkins is in the recording studio with Amy Winehouse . . . "Dame" Judi Dench is gamely trashing hotel rooms somewhere in the US . . . and we hope that next week "Sir" Brad and the Pitt family will be performing *The Sound of Music* at the Brit Awards.' (Cut to Kevin Spacey and Meryl Streep laughing ecstatically and Angelina explaining the joke to Brad.)

Opening the envelope, he announced that the Best Film award went Danny Boyle's *Slumdog Millionaire* – so very much what people used to consider him. But there was no doubt about the real winner. Jagger had scored his biggest hit since . . . oh . . . 'Start Me Up' in 1981. 'It took a lot to out-glamour that place,' one academician commented, 'but he did it.'

Half a century ago, when the Rolling Stones ran neck and neck with the Beatles, one question above all used to be thrown at the young Mick Jagger in the eternal quest to get something enlightening, or even interesting, out of him: did he think he'd still be singing 'Satisfaction' when he was thirty?

In those innocent early sixties, pop music belonged exclusively to the young and was thought to be totally in thrall to youth's fickleness. Even the most successful acts – even the Beatles – expected a few months at most at the top before being elbowed aside by new favourites. Back then, no one dreamed how many of those seemingly ephemeral songs would still be being played and replayed a lifetime hence or how many of those seemingly disposable singers and bands would still be plying their trade as old-age pensioners, greeted with the same fanatical devotion for as long as they could totter back onstage.

In the longevity stakes, the Stones leave all competition far behind. The Beatles lasted barely three years as an international live attraction and only nine in total (if you discount the two they spent acrimoniously breaking up). Other bands from the sixties' top drawer like Led Zeppelin, Pink Floyd and the Who, if not fractured by alcohol or drugs, drifted apart over time, then re-formed, their terminal boredom with their old repertoire, and one another, mitigated by the huge rewards on offer. Only the Stones, once seemingly the most unstable of all, have kept rolling continuously from decade to decade, then century to century; weathering the sensational death of one member and the embittered resignations of two others (plus ongoing internal politics that would impress the Medicis); leaving behind generations of wives and lovers; outlasting two managers, nine British prime ministers and the same number of American presidents; impervious to changing musical fads, gender politics and social mores; as sexagenarians still somehow retaining the same sulphurous whiff of sin and rebellion they had in their twenties. The Beatles have eternal charm; the Stones have eternal edge.

Over the decades since their joint heyday, of course, pop music's essentials have hardly changed. Each new generation of musicians hits on the same chords in the same order and adopts the same language of love, lust and loss; each new generation of fans seeks the same kind of male idol with the same kind of sex appeal, the same repertoire of gestures, attitudes and manifestations of cool.

The notion of a rock 'band' – young ensemble musicians enjoying fame, wealth and sexual opportunity undreamed of by their historic counterparts in military regiments or northern colliery towns – was well established by the time the Stones got going, and has not changed one iota since. It remains as true that, even though the pop industry mostly is about illusion, exploitation and hype, true talent will always out, and always endure. From the Stones' great rabble-rousing hits like 'Jumpin' Jack Flash' or 'Street Fighting Man' to obscure early tracks like 'Off the Hook' or 'Play with Fire', and the R&B cover versions that came before, their music sounds as fresh as if recorded yesterday.

They remain role models for every band that makes it – the pampered boy potentates, lolling ungraciously on a couch as flashbulbs detonate, the same old questions are shouted by reporters, and the same facetious answers thrown back. The kind of tour they created in the late sixties is what everyone still wants: the private jets, the limos, the entourages, the groupies, the trashed hotel suites. All the well-documented evidence of how soul-destroyingly monotonous it soon becomes, all Christopher Guest's brilliant send-up of a boneheaded travelling supergroup in *This Is Spinal Tap*, cannot destroy the mystique of 'going on the road', the eternal allure of 'sex, drugs, and rock 'n' roll'. Yet try as these youthful disciples may, they could never reproduce the swath which the on-road Stones cut through the more innocent world of forty-odd years ago, or touch remotely comparable levels of arrogance, self-indulgence, hysteria, paranoia, violence, vandalism and wicked joy.

Above all Mick Jagger, at any age, is inimitable. Jagger it was who, more than anyone, invented the concept of the 'rock star' as opposed to mere singer within a band – the figure set apart from his fellow musicians (a major innovation in those days of unified Beatles, Hollies, Searchers et al.) who could first unleash, then invade and control the myriad fantasies of enormous crowds. Keith Richards, Jagger's co-figurehead in the Stones, is a uniquely talented guitarist, as well as the rock world's most unlikely survivor, but Keith belongs in a troubadour tradition stretching back to Blind Lemon Jefferson and Django Reinhardt, continuing on to Eric Clapton, Jimi Hendrix, Bruce Springsteen, Noel Gallagher and Pete Doherty. Jagger, on the other hand, founded a new species and gave it a language that could never be improved on. Among his rivals in rock showmanship, only Jim Morrison of the Doors found a different way to sing into a microphone, cradling it tenderly in both hands like a frightened baby bird rather than flourishing it, Jagger-style, like a phallus. Since the 1970s, many other gifted bands have emerged with vast international followings and indubitably charismatic front men – Freddie Mercury of Queen, Holly Johnson of Frankie Goes to Hollywood, Bono of U2, Michael Hutchence of INXS, Axl Rose of Guns N' Roses. Distinctive on record they might be, but when they took the stage they had no choice but to follow in Jagger's strutting footsteps.

His status as a sexual icon is comparable only to Rudolph 'the Sheik' Valentino, the silent cinema star who aroused 1920s women to palpitant dreams of being thrown across the saddle of a horse and carried off to a Bedouin tent in the desert. With Jagger, the aura was closer to great ballet dancers, like Nijinsky and Nureyev, whose seeming feyness was belied by their lustful eyeballing of the ballerinas and overstuffed, straining codpieces. The Stones were one of the first rock bands to have a logo and, even for the louche early seventies, it was daringly explicit – a livid-red cartoon of Jagger's own mouth, the cushiony lips sagging open with familiar gracelessness, the tongue slavering out to slurp an invisible something which, very clearly, was not ice cream. This 'lapping tongue' still adorns all the Stones' literature and merchandise, symbolic of who controls every department. To modern eyes, there could hardly be a cruder monument to old-fashioned male chauvinism – yet it finds its mark as surely as ever. The most liberated twenty-first-century females perk up at the sound of Jagger's name while those he captivated in the twentieth still belong to him in every fibre. As I was beginning this book, I mentioned its subject to my neighbour at a dinner party, a seemingly dignified, self-possessed Englishwoman of mature years. Her response was to re-create the scene in *When Harry Met Sally* where Meg

Ryan simulates orgasm in the middle of a crowded restaurant. 'Mick *Jag-ger*? Oh . . . yes! Yes, YES, *YES!*'

Sexual icons are notoriously prone to fall short of their public image in private; look at Mae West, Marilyn Monroe or, for that matter, Elvis Presley. But in the oversexed world of rock, in the whole annals of show business, Jagger's reputation as a modern Casanova is unequalled. It's questionable whether even the greatest lotharios of centuries past found sexual partners in such prodigious number, or were so often saved the tiresome preliminaries of seduction. Certainly, none maintained his prowess, as Jagger has, through middle and then old age (Casanova was knackered by his mid-thirties). What Swift called 'the rage of the groin' is now known as sex addiction and can be cured by therapy, but Jagger has never shown any sign of considering it a problem.

Looking at that craggy countenance, one tries but fails to imagine the vast carnal banquet on which he has gorged, yet still not sated himself . . . the unending gallery of beautiful faces and bright, willing eyes . . . the innumerable chat-up lines, delivered and received . . . the countless brusque adjournments to beds, couches, heaped-up cushions, dress-ing room floors, shower stalls or limo back seats . . . the ever-changing voices, scents, skin tones and hair colour . . . the names instantly forgot-ten, if ever known in the first place . . . Old men are often revisited in dreams, or daydreams, by the women they have lusted after. For him, it would be like one of those old-style reviews of the Soviet army in Red Square. And at least one of the gorgeous foot soldiers is among his BAFTA audience tonight, seated not a million miles from Brad Pitt.

By rights, the scandals in which he starred during the 1960s should have been forgotten decades ago, cancelled out by the teeming pecca-dilloes of today's pop stars, soccer players, supermodels and reality-TV stars. But the sixties have an indestructible fascination, most of all among those too young to remember them – the condition known to psychologists as 'nostalgia without memory'. Jagger personifies that 'swinging' era for Britain's youth, both its freedom and hedonism and the backlash it finally provoked. Even quite young people today have heard of his 1967 drug bust, or at least of the Mars bar which figured

so lewdly in it. Few realise the extent of the British establishment's vindictiveness during that so-called Summer of Love; how tonight's witty,
well-spoken knight of the realm was reviled like a long-haired Antichrist,
led to court in handcuffs, subjected to a show trial of almost medieval
grotesquerie, then thrown into prison.

He is perhaps the ultimate example of that well-loved show-business
stereotype, the 'survivor'. But while most rock 'n' roll survivors end up
as bulgy old farts in grey ponytails, he is unchanged – other than facially
– from the day he first took the stage. While most others have long since
addled their wits with drugs or alcohol, his faculties are all intact, not
least his celebrated instinct for what is fashionable, cool and posh. While
others whinge about the money they lost or were cheated out of, he leads
the biggest-earning band in history, its own survival achieved solely by
his determination and astuteness. Without Mick, the Stones would
have been over by 1968; from a gang of scruffball outsiders, he turned
them into a British national treasure as legitimate as Shakespeare or the
White Cliffs of Dover.

Yet behind all the idolatry, wealth and superabundant satisfaction
is a story of talent and promise consistently, almost stubbornly, unful-
filled. Among all his contemporaries endowed with half a brain, only
John Lennon had as many opportunities to move beyond the confines
of pop. Though undeniably an actor, as Jonathan Ross introduced him
to BAFTA, with both film and TV roles to his credit, Jagger could have
developed a parallel screen career as successful as Presley's or Sinatra's,
perhaps even more so. He could have used his sway over audiences to
become a politician, perhaps a leader, such as the world had never seen
– and still has not. He could have extended the (often overlooked) brilliance of his best song lyrics into poetry or prose, as Bob Dylan and Paul
McCartney have done. At the very least, he could have become a first-
echelon performer in his own right instead of merely fronting a band.
But, somehow or other, none of it came to pass. His film-acting career
stalled in 1970 and never restarted in any significant way, despite the
literally dozens of juicy screen roles he was offered. He did no more than
toy with the idea of politics and has never shown any signs of wanting

to be a serious writer. As for going solo, he waited until the mid-eighties to make his move, creating such ill-feeling among the other Stones, especially Keith, that he had to choose between continuing or seeing the band implode. As a consequence, he is still only their front man, doing the same job he was at eighteen.

There is also the puzzle of how someone who fascinates so many millions, and is so clearly super-intelligent and perceptive, manages to make himself so very unfascinating when he opens those celebrated lips to speak. Even since the media first began pursuing Jagger, his on-the-record utterances have had the kind of non-committal blandness associated with British royalty. Look into any of the numerous 'Rolling Stones in their own words' compilations published in the past four decades and you'll find Mick's always the fewest and most anodyne. In 1983, he signed a contract with the British publishers Weidenfeld & Nicolson to write his autobiography for the then astounding sum £1 million. It should have been the show-business memoir of the century; instead, the ghostwritten manuscript was pronounced irremediably dull by the publishers and the entire advance had to be returned.

His explanation was that he 'couldn't remember anything', by which of course he didn't mean his birthplace or his mother's name but the later personal stuff for which Weidenfeld had stumped up £1 million and any publisher today would happily pay five times as much. That has been his position ever since, when approached to do another book or pressed by interviewers for chapter and verse. Sorry, his phenomenal past is all just 'a blur'.

This image of a man whose recall disappeared thirty years ago like some early-onset Alzheimer's victim's is pure nonsense, as anyone who knows him can attest. It's a handy way of getting out of things – something he has always had down to a fine art. It gets him out of months boringly closeted with a ghostwriter, or answering awkward questions about his sex life. But the same blackboard-wipe obliterates career highs and lows unmatched by anyone else in his profession. How is it possible to 'forget', say, meeting Andrew Loog Oldham or living with Marianne Faithfull or refusing to ride on the London Palladium's revolving stage or getting banged up in Brixton Prison or featuring in Cecil Beaton's diaries or being spat at on the New York streets or inspiring a London *Times* editorial or ditching Allen Klein or standing up to homicidal Hell's Angels at the Altamont festival or getting married in front of the world's massed media in Saint-Tropez or being fingerprinted in Rhode Island or making Steven Spielberg fall on his knees in adulation or having Andy Warhol as a child-minder or being stalked by naked women with green pubic hair in Montauk or persuading a quarter of a million people in Hyde Park to shut up and listen to a poem by Shelley?

Such is the enduring paradox of Mick: a supreme achiever to whom his own colossal achievements seem to mean nothing, a supreme extrovert who prefers discretion, a supreme egotist who dislikes talking about himself. Charlie Watts, the Stones' drummer, and the one least affected by all the madness, put it best: 'Mick doesn't care what happened yesterday. All he ever cares about is tomorrow.'

So let's flick through those yesterdays in hopes of refreshing his memory.

PART I

'THE BLUES IS IN HIM'

CHAPTER ONE

India-Rubber Boy

To become what we call 'a star', it is not enough to possess unique talent in one or another of the performing arts; you also seemingly need a void inside you as fathomlessly dark as starlight is brilliant.

Normal, happy, well-rounded people do not as a rule turn into stars. It is something which far more commonly befalls those who have suffered some traumatic misery or deprivation in early life. Hence the ferocity of their drive to achieve wealth and status at any cost, and their insatiable need for the public's love and attention. While awarding them a status near to gods, we also paradoxically view them as the most fallible of human beings, tortured by past demons and present insecurities, all too often fated to destroy their talent and then themselves with drink or drugs or both. Since the mid-twentieth century, when celebrity became global, the shiniest stars, from Charlie Chaplin, Judy Garland, Marilyn Monroe and Edith Piaf to Elvis Presley, John Lennon, Michael Jackson and Amy Winehouse, have fulfilled some if not all of these criteria. How, then, to account for Mick Jagger, who fulfils none of them?

Jagger bucked the trend with his very first breath. We expect stars to be born in unpromising locales that make their later rise seem all the more spectacular . . . a dirt-poor cabin in Mississippi . . . a raffish seaport . . . the dressing room of a seedy vaudeville theatre . . . a Parisian slum. We do not expect them to be born in thoroughly comfortable but unstimulating circumstances in the English county of Kent.

Southern England has always been the wealthiest, most privileged part of the country, but clustered around London is a special little clique of shires known rather snootily as 'the Home Counties'. Kent is the most easterly of these, bounded in the north by the Thames Estuary, in the south by Dover's sacred white cliffs and the English Channel. And, rather like its most famous twentieth-century son, it has multiple personalities. For some, this is 'the Garden of England' with its rolling green heart known as the Weald, its apple and cherry orchards and hop fields, and its conical redbrick hop-drying kilns or oast houses. For others, it conjures up the glory of Canterbury Cathedral, where 'turbulent priest' Thomas à Becket met his end, or stately homes like Knole and Sissinghurst, or faded Victorian seaside resorts like Margate and Broadstairs. For others, it suggests county cricket, Charles Dickens's *Pickwick Papers,* or ultra-respectable Royal Tunbridge Wells, whose residents are so famously addicted to writing to newspapers that the nom de plume 'Disgusted, Tunbridge Wells' has become shorthand for any choleric elderly Briton fulminating against modern morals or manners. ('Disgusted, Tunbridge Wells' will play no small part in the story that follows.)

In the two thousand years since Julius Caesar's Roman legions waded ashore on Walmer Beach, Kent has mainly been a place that people pass through – Chaucer's pilgrims 'from every shire's ende' trudging towards Canterbury, armies bound for European wars, present-day traffic to and from the Channel ports of Dover and Folkestone and the Chunnel. As a result, the true heart of the county is difficult to place. There certainly is a distinctive Kentish burr, subtly different from that of neighbouring Sussex, varying from town to town, even village to village, but the predominant accent is dictated by the metropolis that blends seamlessly into its northern margins. The earliest linguistic colonisers were the trainloads of East End Cockneys who arrived each summer to help bring in the hop harvest; since then, proliferating 'dormitory towns' for city office workers have made London-speak ubiquitous.

Jagger is neither a Kentish name nor a London one – despite the City lawyer named Jaggers in Dickens's *Great Expectations* – but originated some two hundred miles to the north, around Halifax in Yorkshire. Although its most famous bearer (in his 'Street Fighting Man' period) would relish the similarity to *jagged,* claiming that it once meant 'knifer' or 'footpad', it actually derives from the Old English *jag* for a 'pack' or 'load', and denotes a carter, peddler or hawker. Pre-Mick, it adorned only one minor celebrity, the Victorian engineer Joseph Hobson Jagger, who devised a successful system for winning at roulette and may partly have inspired a famous music-hall song, 'The Man Who Broke the Bank at Monte Carlo'. The family could thus claim a precedent for hitting the jackpot.

No such mercenary aims possessed Mick's father, Basil Fanshawe Jagger – always known as Joe – who was born in 1913 and raised in an atmosphere of clean-living altruism. Joe's Yorkshireman father, David, was a village school headmaster in days when all the pupils would share a single room, sitting on long wooden forms and writing on slates with chalk. Despite a small, slender build, Joe proved a natural athlete, equally good at all track-and-field sports, with a special flair for gymnastics. Given his background and idealistic, unselfish temperament, it was natural he should choose a career in what was then known as PT – physical training. He studied at Manchester and London universities and, in 1938, was appointed PT instructor at the state-run East Central School in Dartford, Kent.

Situated in the far north-west of the county, Dartford is practically an east London suburb, barely thirty minutes by train from the great metropolitan termini of Victoria and Charing Cross. It lies in the valley of the River Darent, on the old pilgrims' way to Canterbury, and is known to history as the place where Wat Tyler started the Peasants' Revolt against King Richard II's poll tax in 1381 (so rabble-rousers in the blood, then). In modern times, almost its only invocation – albeit hundreds of times each day – is in radio traffic reports for the Dartford Tunnel, under the Thames, and adjacent Dartford–Thurrock Crossing, the main escape route from London for south-coast-bound traffic. Otherwise it is just a name on a road sign or station platform, its centuries as a market and brewing town all but obliterated by office blocks, multiple stores and even more multiple commuter homes. From the closing years of Queen Victoria's reign, traffic funnelled to Dartford was not only vehicular; an outlying village with the serendipitous name of Stone contained a forbidding pile known as the East London Lunatic Asylum until a more tactful era renamed it 'Stone House'.

Early in 1940, Joe Jagger met Eva Ensley Scutts, a twenty-seven-year-old as vivacious and demonstrative as he was understated and quiet. Eva's family originally came from Greenhithe, Kent, but had emigrated to New South Wales, Australia, where she was born in the same year as Joe, 1913. Towards the end of the Great War, her mother left her father and brought her and four siblings home to settle in Dartford. Eva was always said to be a little ashamed of her birth 'Down Under' and to have assumed an exaggeratedly upper-class accent to hide any lingering Aussie twang. The truth was that in those days all respectable young girls tried to talk like London débutantes and the royal princesses Elizabeth and Margaret. Eva's work as an office secretary, and later a beautician, made it a professional necessity.

Joe's courtship of Eva took place during the Second World War's grim first act, when Britain stood alone against Hitler's all-conquering armies in France and the Führer could be seen gazing across the Channel towards the White Cliffs of Dover as smugly as if he owned them already. With summer came the Battle of Britain, scrawling the sunny Kentish skies with white vapour-trail graffiti as British and German fighters duelled above the cornfields and oast houses and gentle green Weald. Though Dartford possessed no vital military installations, it received a constant overspill from Luftwaffe raids on factories and docks in nearby Chatham and Rochester and on London's East End. The fact that many falling bombs were not aimed at Dartford, but jettisoned by German planes heading home, made the toll no less horrendous. One killed thirteen people in the town's Kent Road; another hit the county hospital, wiping out two crowded women's wards.

Joe and Eva were married on 7 December 1940 at Holy Trinity Church, Dartford, where Eva had sung in the choir. She wore a dress of lavender silk rather than traditional bridal white, and Joe's brother, Albert, acted as best man. Afterwards there was a reception at the nearby Coneybeare Hall. This being wartime – and Joe wholeheartedly committed to the prevailing ethos of frugality and self-sacrifice – only fifty guests attended, drinking to the newlyweds' health in brown sherry and munching dainty sandwiches of Spam or powdered egg.

Joe's teaching job and work in resettling London evacuee children exempted him from military call-up, so at least there was no traumatic parting as he was sent overseas or to the opposite end of the country. Nor, conversely, was there the urgency to start a family felt by many service people briefly home on leave. Joe and Eva's first child did not arrive until 1943, when they were both aged thirty. The delivery took place at Dartford's Livingstone Hospital on 26 July, the birthday of George Bernard Shaw, Carl Jung and Aldous Huxley, and the baby boy was christened Michael Philip. As a possibly more significant omen, the town's State Cinema that week was showing an Abbott and Costello film entitled *Money for Jam.*

His babyhood saw the war gradually turn in the Allies' favour and Britain fill with American soldiers – a glamorous breed, provided with luxuries the British had almost forgotten, and playing their own infectious dance music – preparatory to the reconquest of Fortress Europe. Defeated though Nazism was, it possessed one last 'vengeance weapon' in the pilotless V-1 flying bombs or doodlebugs, launched from France, that inflicted heavy damage and loss of life on London and its environs during the war's final months. Like everyone in the Dartford area, Joe and Eva spent many tense nights listening for the whine of the V-1's motor that cut out just before it struck its target. Later, and even more terrifyingly, came the V-2, a jet-propelled bomb that travelled faster than the speed of sound and so gave no warning of its approach.

Michael Philip, of course, remained blissfully unaware as a bombed, battered and stringently rationed nation realised with astonishment that it had not only survived but prevailed. One of his earliest memories is watching his mother remove the heavy blackout curtains from the windows in 1945, signifying no more nighttime fear of air raids.

By the time his younger brother, Christopher, arrived in 1947, the family was living at number 39 Denver Road, a crescent of white pebble-dashed houses in Dartford's genteel western quarter. Joe had exchanged day-to-day PT teaching for an administrative job with the Central Council of Physical Recreation, the body overseeing all amateur sports associations throughout Britain. Accomplished track-and-field all-rounder though he still was, his special passion was basketball, a seemingly quintessential American sport that nonetheless had been played in the UK since the 1890s. To Joe, no game was better at fostering the sportsmanship and team spirit to which he was dedicated. He devoted many unpaid hours to encouraging and coaching would-be local teams, and in 1948 launched the first Kent County Basketball League.

Tolstoy observes at the beginning of *Anna Karenina* that, whereas unhappy families are miserable in highly original and varied ways, happy families tend to be almost boringly alike. Our star, the future symbol of rebellion and iconoclasm, grew up in just such fortunate conformity. His quiet, physically dynamic father and ebullient, socially aspirational mother were a thoroughly compatible couple, devoted to each other and their children. In contrast with many postwar homes, the atmosphere at 39 Denver Road was one of complete security, with meals, bath- and bedtimes at prescribed hours, and values in their correct order. Joe's modest stipend and personal abstinence – he neither drank nor smoked – were enough to keep a wife and two boys in relative affluence as wartime rationing gradually disappeared and meat, butter, sugar and fresh fruit became plentiful once more.

There is an idealised image of a little British boy in the early 1950s, before television, computer games and too-early sexualisation did away with childhood innocence. He is dressed, not like a miniature New York street-gangster or jungle guerrilla but unequivocally as a boy – porous white Aertex short-sleeved shirt, baggy khaki shorts, an elasticised belt fastening with an S-shaped metal clasp. He has tousled hair, a broad, breezy smile and eyes unclouded by fear or premature sexuality, squinted against the sun. He is Mike Jagger, as the world then knew him, aged about seven, photographed with a group of classmates at his first school, Maypole Infants. The name could not be more atmospheric in its suggestion of springtime and kindly fun, of pure-hearted lads and lasses dancing round a beribboned pole to welcome the darling buds.

At Maypole he was a star pupil, top of the class or near it in every subject. As was soon evident, he possessed his father's all-round aptitude for sports, dominating the school's miniature games of soccer and cricket and its egg-and-spoon or sack-racing athletics. One of his teachers, Ken Llewellyn, would remember him as the most engaging as well as brightest boy in his year, 'an irrepressible bundle of energy' whom it was 'a pleasure to teach'. In this seven-year-old paragon, however, there was already a touch of the subversive. He had a sharp ear for the way that grown-ups talked, and could mould his voice into an impressive range of accents. His imitations of teachers like the Welsh Mr Llewellyn went down even better with classmates than his triumphs on the games field.

At the age of eight he moved on to Wentworth County Primary, a more serious place, not so much about maypole dancing as surviving in the playground. Here he met a boy born at Livingstone Hospital like himself but five months later; an ill-favoured little fellow with the protruding ears and hollow cheeks of some Dickensian workhouse waif, though he came from a good enough home. His name was Keith Richards.

For British eight-year-olds in this era, the chief fantasy figures were American cowboy movie heroes like Gene Autry and Hopalong Cassidy, whose Western raiment was flashingly gorgeous, and who would periodically sheathe their pearl-handled six-shooters and warble ballads to their own guitar accompaniment. In the Wentworth playground one day, Keith confided to Mike Jagger that when he grew up he wanted to be like Roy Rogers, the self-styled 'King of the Cowboys', and play a guitar.

Mike was indifferent to the King of the Cowboys – he was already good at being indifferent – but the idea of the guitar, and of this little imp with sticky-out ears strumming one, did pique his interest.

However, their acquaintanceship did not ripen: it would be more than a decade before they explored the subject further.

At the Jaggers', like every other British household, music was constantly in the air, pumped out of bulky valve-operated radio sets by the BBC's Light Programme in every form from dance bands to operetta. Mike enjoyed mimicking American crooners he heard – like Johnnie Ray blubbing through 'Just Walkin' in the Rain' and 'The Little White Cloud That Cried' – but did not attract any special notice in school singing lessons or in the church choir to which he and his brother Chris both belonged. Chris, at that stage, seemed more of a natural performer, having won a prize at Maypole Infants School for singing 'The Deadwood Stage' from the film *Calamity Jane*. The musical entertainments that appealed most to Mike were the professional Christmas pantomimes staged at larger theatres in the area – corny shows based on fairy tales like *Mother Goose* or 'Jack and the Beanstalk', but with an intriguing whiff of sex and gender blurring, the rouged and wisecracking 'dame' traditionally played by a man, the 'principal boy' by a leggy young woman.

In 1954, the family moved from 39 Denver Road and out of Dartford entirely, to the nearby village of Wilmington. Their house now had a name, 'Newlands', and stood in a secluded thoroughfare called The Close, a term usually applied to cathedral precincts. There was a spacious garden where Joe could give his two sons regular PT sessions and practise the diverse sports in which he was coaching them. The neighbours grew accustomed to seeing the grass littered with balls, cricket stumps, and lifting weights, and Mike and Chris swinging like titchy Tarzans from ropes their father had tied to the trees.

For the Jaggers, as, for most British families, it was a decade of steadily increasing prosperity, when luxuries barely imaginable before the war became commonplace in almost every home. They acquired a television set, whose minuscule screen showed a bluish rather than black-and-white picture, allowing Mike and Chris to watch *Children's Hour* puppets like Muffin the Mule, Mr Turnip and Sooty, and serials like Frances Hodgson Burnett's *Secret Garden* and E. Nesbit's *The Rail-*

way Children. They took summer holidays in sunny Spain and the South of France rather than Kent's own numerous, cold-comfort resorts like Margate and Broadstairs. But the boys were never spoiled. Joe in his quiet way was a strict disciplinarian and Eva was equally forceful, particularly over cleanliness and tidiness. From their youngest years, Mike and Chris were expected to do their share of household chores, set out in a school-like timetable.

Mike pulled his weight without complaint. '[He] wasn't a rebellious child at all,' Joe would later remember. 'He was a very pleasant boy at home in the family, and he helped to look after his younger brother.' Indeed, the only shadow on his horizon was that Chris seemed to be his mother's favourite and he himself never received quite the same level of affection and attention from her. It made him slow to give affection in his turn – a lifelong trait – and also self-conscious and shy in front of strangers, and mortified with embarrassment when Eva pushed him forward to say 'hello' or shake hands.

The year of the family's move to Wilmington, he sat the Eleven Plus, the exam with which British state education pre-emptively sorted its eleven-year-olds into successes and failures. The bright ones went on to grammar schools, often the equal of any exclusive, fee-paying institutions, while the less bright went to secondary-moderns and the dullards to 'technical schools' in hope of at least acquiring some useful manual trade. For Mike Jagger, there was no risk of either of these latter options. He passed the exam easily and in September 1954 started at Dartford Grammar School on the town's West Hill.

His father could not have been better pleased. Founded in the eighteenth century, Dartford Grammar was the best school of its kind in the district, aspiring to the same standards and observing the same traditions that cost other parents dear at establishments like Eton and Harrow. It had a coat of arms and a Latin motto, *Ora et Labora* (Pray and Work); it had 'masters' rather than mere teachers, clad in scholastic black gowns; most important for Joe, it placed as much emphasis on sports and physical development as on academic achievement. Its alumni included the Indian Mutiny hero Sir Henry Havelock, and the great novelist Thomas Hardy, originally an architect, had worked on one of its nineteenth-century extensions.

In these new surroundings, however, Mike did not shine nearly as brightly as before. His Eleven Plus results had put him into the 'A' stream of specially promising pupils, headed for good all-round results in the GCE O-level exams, followed by two years in the sixth form and probable university entrance. He was naturally good at English, had something of a passion for history (thanks to an inspirational teacher named Walter Wilkinson), and spoke French with an accent superior to most of his classmates'. But science subjects, like maths, physics and chemistry, bored him, and he made little or no effort with them. In the form order, calculated on aggregate marks, he usually figured about half way. 'I wasn't a swot and I wasn't a dunce,' he would recall of himself. 'I was always in the middle ground.'

At sports, despite his father's comprehensive coaching, he was equally inconsistent. Summer was no problem, as Dartford Grammar played cricket, something he loved to watch as well as play, and under Joe's coaching he could shine in athletics, especially middle-distance running and javelin. But the school's winter team game was upper-class rugby football rather than proletarian soccer. Fast runner and good catcher that Mike was, he easily made every school rugger side up to the First Fifteen. But he hated being tackled – which often meant crashing onto his face in squelching mud – and would do everything he could to avoid receiving a pass.

The headmaster, Ronald Loftus Hudson, sarcastically known as 'Lofty', was a tiny man who nonetheless could reduce the rowdiest assembly to pin-drop silence with little more than a raised eyebrow. Under his regime there were myriad petty regulations about dress and conduct, the sternest relating to the fully segregated but tantalisingly near-at-hand Dartford Grammar School for Girls. Boys were forbidden to talk to the girls, even if they happened to meet out of school hours at places like bus stops. The head also used corporal punishment, as most British educators then did, without legal restraint or fear of parental pro-test – between two and six strokes on the backside with a stick or gym

shoe. 'You had to wait outside [his] study until the light went on, and
then you'd go in,' the Jagger of the future would remember. 'And everybody else used to hang about on the stairs to see how many he gave and
how bad it was that morning.'

All the male teachers could administer formal beatings in front of
the whole class and most, in addition, practised a casual, even jocu-
lar physical violence that today would instantly land them in court for
assault. Any who showed weakness (like the English teacher, 'sweet,
gentle Mr Brandon') were mercilessly ragged and aped by Jagger, the
class mimic, behind their backs or to their faces. 'There were guerrilla
skirmishes on all fronts, with civil disobedience and undeclared war;
[the teachers] threw blackboard rubbers at us and we threw them back,'
he would recall. 'There were some who'd just punch you out. They'd slap
your face so hard, you'd go down. Others would twist your ear and drag
you along until it was red and stinging.' So that line from 'Jumpin' Jack
Flash', 'I was schooled with a strap right across my back,' may not be as
fanciful as it has always seemed.

At number 23 The Close lived a boy named Alan Etherington, who
was the same age as Mike and also went to Dartford Grammar. The
two quickly chummed up, biking to school together each morning and
going to tea at each other's house. 'There was a standing joke with us
that if Mike appeared, he was trying to get out of chores his parents had
given him, like washing up or mowing the lawn,' Etherington remembers. House-proud Eva could be a little intimidating, but Joe, despite his
'quiet authority', created an atmosphere of healthy fun. When Etherington dropped by, there would usually be a pick-up game of cricket or
rounders or an impromptu weight-training session on the lawn. Sometimes, as a special treat, Joe would produce a javelin, take the boys to the
open green space at the top of The Close, and under his careful supervision allow them to practise a few throws.

Having a father so closely connected to the teaching world meant
that Mike's daily release from school was not as complete as other boys'.
Joe knew several of the staff at Dartford Grammar, and so could keep
close watch on both his academic performance and his conduct. There

also could be no shirking of homework: he would later remember getting up at 6 A.M. to finish some essay or exercise, having fallen asleep over his books the night before. But in other ways Joe's links with the school were an advantage. Arthur Page, the sports master – and a celebrated local cricketer – was a family friend who gave Mike special attention in batting practice at the school nets. Likewise as a favour to his father, one of the mathematics staff agreed to help him with his weakest subject even though he wasn't in the teacher's usual set.

Eventually, Joe himself became a part-time instructor at Dartford Grammar, coming in each Tuesday evening to give coaching in his beloved basketball. And there was one game, at least, where Mike's enthusiasm, and application, fully matched his father's. In basketball one could run and weave and catch and shoot with no risk of being pushed into mud; best of all, despite Joe's patient exposition of its long British history, it felt glamorously and exotically American. Its most famous exponents were the all-black Harlem Globetrotters, whose displays of almost magical ball control, to the whistled strains of 'Sweet Georgia Brown', gave Mike Jagger and countless other British boys their earliest inklings of 'cool'. He became secretary of the school basketball society that evolved from Joe's visits, and never missed a session. While his friends played in ordinary gym shoes, he had proper black-and-white canvas basketball boots, which not only enhanced performance on the court but were stunningly chic juvenile footwear off it.

Otherwise, he was an inconspicuous member of the school community, winning neither special distinction nor special censure, offering no challenge to the status quo, using his considerable wits to avoid trouble with chalk-throwing, ear-twisting masters rather than provoke it. His school friend John Spinks remembers him as 'an India-rubber character' who could 'bend every way to stay out of trouble'.

By mid-1950s standards, he was not considered good-looking. Sex appeal then was entirely dictated by film stars, of whom the male archetypes were tall, keen-jawed and muscular, with close-cut, glossy hair – American action heroes such as John Wayne and Rock Hudson; British 'officer types' such as Jack Hawkins and Richard Todd. Mike, like his father, was slightly built and skinny enough for his rib cage to protrude, though unlike Joe he showed no sign of incipient baldness. His hair, formerly a reddish colour, was now mousy brown and already floppily unmanageable.

His most noticeable feature was a mouth which, like certain breeds of bull-baiting terriers, seemed to occupy the entire lower half of his face, making a smile literally stretching from ear to ear, and Cupid's-bow lips of unusual thickness and colour that seemed to need double the usual amount of moistening by his tongue. His mother also had markedly full lips – kept in top condition by the amount she talked – but Joe was convinced that Mike's came from the Jagger side of the family and would sometimes apologise, not altogether jokingly, for having passed them on to him.

As the boys in his year reached puberty (yes, in 1950s Britain it really was this late) and all at once became agonisingly conscious of their clothes, grooming and appeal to the opposite sex, small, scrawny, loose-mouthed Mike Jagger seemed to have rather little going for him. Yet in encounters with the forbidden girls' grammar school he somehow always provoked the most smiles, blushes, giggles and whispered discussions behind his back. 'Almost from the time I met Mike, he always had girls flocking around him,' Alan Etherington remembers. 'A lot of our friends seemed to be much better looking, but they never had anything like the success that he did. Wherever he was, whatever he was doing, he knew he never needed to be alone.'

At the same time, his maturing looks, especially the lips, could arouse strange antagonism in males; teasing and taunting from classmates, sometimes even physical bullying by older boys. Not for being effeminate – his prowess on the sports field automatically discounted that – but for something far more damning. This was a time when unreformed nineteenth-century racism, the so-called colour bar, held sway in even Britain's most civilised and liberal circles. To grammar school boys, as to their parents, thick lips suggested just one thing and there was just one term for it, repugnant now but back then quite normal.

Decades later, in a rare moment of self-revelation, he would admit that during his time at Dartford Grammar 'the N-word', for 'nigger', was thrown at him more than once. The time was still far off when he would find the comparison flattering.

THOUSANDS OF BRITISH men who grew up in the 1950s – and almost all who went on to dominate popular culture in the sixties – recall the arrival of rock 'n' roll music from America as a life-changing moment. But such was not Mike Jagger's experience. In rigidly class-bound postwar Britain, rock 'n' roll's impact was initially confined to young people of the lower social orders, the so-called Teddy Boys and Teddy Girls. During its earliest phase it made little impression on the bourgeoisie or the aristocracy, both of whose younger generations viewed it with almost as much distaste as did their parents. Likewise, in the hierarchical education system, it found its first enraptured audience in secondary modern and technical schools. At institutions like Dartford Grammar it was, rather, a subject for high-flown sixth-form debates: 'Is rock 'n' roll a symptom of declining morals in the twentieth century?'

Like Spanish influenza forty years previously, it struck in two stages, the second infinitely more virulent than the first. In 1955, a song called 'Rock Around the Clock' by Bill Haley and the Comets topped the sleepy British pop music charts and caused outbreaks of rioting in proletarian dance halls, but was plausibly written off by the national media as just another short-lived transatlantic novelty. A year later, Elvis Presley came along with a younger, more dangerous spin on Haley's simple exuberance and the added ingredient of raw sex.

As a middle-class grammar school boy, Mike was just an onlooker in the media furore over Presley – the 'suggestiveness' of his onstage hip grinding and knee trembling, the length of his hair and sullen smoulder of his features, the (literally) incontinent hysteria to which he aroused his young female audiences. While adult America's fear and loathing were almost on a par with the national Communist phobia, adult Britain reacted more with amusement and a dash of complacency. A figure like Presley, it was felt, could only emerge from the flashy, hyperactive land of Hollywood movies, Chicago gangsters and ballyhooing political conventions. Here in the immemorial home of understatement, irony and the stiff upper lip, a performer in any remotely similar mode was inconceivable.

The charge of blatant sexuality levelled against all rock 'n' roll, not merely Presley, was manifestly absurd. Its direct ancestor was the blues – black America's original pairing of voice with guitar – and the modern, electrified, up-tempo variant called rhythm and blues or R&B. The blues had never been inhibited about sex; *rock* and *roll* were separate synonyms for making love, employed in song lyrics and titles ('Rock Me, Baby', 'Roll with Me, Henry', etc.) for decades past, but heard only on segregated record labels and radio stations. Presley's singing style and incendiary body movements were simply what he had observed on the stages and dance floors of black clubs in his native Memphis, Tennessee. Most rock 'n' roll hits were cover versions of R&B standards by white vocalists, purged of their earthier sentiments or couched in slang so obscure ('I'm like a one-eyed cat peepin' in a seafood store') that no one realised. Even this sanitised product took the smallest step out of line at its peril. When the white, God-fearing Pat Boone covered Fats Domino's 'Ain't That a Shame', he was criticised for disseminating what was seen as a contagiously vulgar 'black' speech idiom.

As a Dartford Grammar pupil, the appropriate music for Mike Jagger was jazz, in particular the modern kind with its melodic complexities, subdued volume and air of intellectualism. Even that played little part in daily school life, where the musical diet was limited to hymns at morning assembly and traditional airs like 'Early One Morning' or 'Sweet Lass of Richmond Hill' (the latter another pointer to Mike's remarkable future). 'There was a general feeling that music wasn't important,' he would recall. 'Some of the masters rather begrudgingly enjoyed jazz, but they couldn't own up to it . . . Jazz was intelligent and people who wore glasses played it, so we all had to make out that we dug Dave Brubeck. It was cool to like that, and it wasn't cool to like rock 'n' roll.'

This social barrier was breached by skiffle, a short-lived craze pecu-liar to Britain which nonetheless rivalled, even threatened to eclipse, rock 'n' roll. Skiffle had originally been American folk (i.e., white) music, evolved in the Depression years of the 1930s; in this new form, how-ever, it drew equally on blues giants of the same era, notably Huddie 'Leadbelly' Ledbetter. Leadbelly songs like 'Rock Island Line', 'Mid-night Special' and 'Bring Me Little Water, Sylvie', set mostly around cotton fields and railroads, had rock 'n' roll's driving beat and hormone-jangling chord patterns, but not its sexual taint or its power to cause disturbances among the proles. Most crucially, skiffle was an offshoot of jazz, having been revived as an intermission novelty by historically minded bandleaders like Ken Colyer and Chris Barber. Its biggest star, Tony Donegan, formerly Barber's banjo player, had changed his first name to Lonnie in honour of bluesman Lonnie Johnson.

British-made skiffle was to have an influence far beyond its barely two-year commercial life span. In its original American form, its poor white performers often could not afford conventional instruments, so would use kitchen utensils like washboards, spoons and dustbin lids, augmented by kazoos, combs-and-paper and the occasional guitar. The success of Lonnie Donegan's 'skiffle group' inspired youthful facsimi-les to spring up throughout the UK, rattling and plunking on home-spun instruments (which actually never featured in Donegan's line-up). The amateur music-making tradition, in long decline since its Victorian heyday, was superabundantly reborn. Buttoned-up British boys, never previously considered in the least musical, now boldly faced audiences of their families and friends to sing and play with abandon. Overnight, the guitar changed from obscure back-row rhythm instrument into an object of young-manly worship and desire surpassing even the soccer ball. Such were the queues outside musical-instrument shops that, evoking not-so-distant wartime austerities, the *Daily Mirror* reported a national guitar shortage.

Here Mike Jagger was ahead of the game. He already owned a guitar, a round-hole acoustic model bought for him by his parents on a family trip to Spain. The holiday snaps included one of him in a floppy straw hat, holding up the guitar neck flamenco-style and miming cod-Spanish words. It would have been his passport into any of the skiffle groups then germinating at Dartford Grammar and in the Wilmington neighbourhood. But mastering even the few simple chord shapes that covered most skiffle numbers was too much like hard work, nor could he be so uncool as to thump a single-string tea-chest 'bass' or scrabble at a washboard. Instead, with the organisational flair already given to programming basketball fixtures, he started a school record club. The meetings took place in a classroom during lunch hour and, he later recalled, had the atmosphere of an extra lesson. 'We'd sit there . . . with a master behind the desk, frowning while we played Lonnie Donegan.'

As bland white vocalists grew famous with cleaned-up R&B songs, the original black performers mostly stayed in the obscurity to which they were long accustomed. One notable exception was Richard Penniman, aka Little Richard, a former dishwasher from Macon, Georgia, whose repertoire of window-shattering screams, whoops and falsetto trills affronted grown-up ears worse than a dozen Presleys. While obediently parroting rock 'n' roll's teenage gaucheries, Richard projected what none had yet learned to call high camp with his gold suits, flashy jewellery and exploding liquorice-whip hair. Indeed, his emblematic song, 'Tutti Frutti', ostensibly an anthem to ice cream, had started out as a graphic commentary on gay sex (its cry of 'Awopbopaloobopalopbamboom!' representing long-delayed ejaculation). He was the first rock 'n' roller who made Mike Jagger forget all middle-class, grammar school sophistication and detachment, and surrender to the sheer mindless joy of the music.

The numerous media Cassandras who predicted rock 'n' roll would be over in weeks rather than months found speedy corroboration in Little Richard. Touring Australia in 1958, he saw Russia's Sputnik space satellite hurtle through the sky, interpreted it as a summons from the Almighty, threw a costly diamond ring into Sydney Harbour and announced he was giving up music to enter the ministry. When the story reached the British press, Mike asked his father for six shillings and eight pence (about thirty-eight pence) to buy 'Good Golly Miss Molly' because Richard was 'retiring' and this must be his farewell single. But Joe refused to stump up, adding, 'I'm *glad* he's retiring,' as if it would be a formal ceremony complete with long-service gold watch.

In America, a coast-to-coast network of commercial radio stations, motivated solely by what their listeners demanded, had made rock 'n' roll ubiquitous within a few months. But for its British constituency, to begin with, the problem was finding it. The BBC, which held a monopoly on domestic radio broadcasting, played few records of any kind, let alone this unsavoury one, in its huge daily output of live orchestral and dance-band music. To catch the hits now pouring across the Atlantic, Mike and his friends had to tune their families' old-fashioned valve wireless sets to Radio Luxembourg, a tiny oasis of teen tolerance deep in continental Europe whose nighttime English language service consisted mainly of pop record shows. Serving the occupying forces braced for nuclear attack by Communist Russia, there were also AFN, the American Forces Network, and the US government's 'Voice of America', both of which sweetened their propaganda output with generous dollops of rock and jazz.

Seeing American rock 'n' rollers perform in person was even more problematic. Bill Haley visited Britain only once (by ocean liner) and was greeted by cheering multitudes not seen since the coronation three years earlier. Elvis Presley was expected to follow hard on his heels but, inexplicably, failed to do so. For the overwhelming majority of UK rock 'n' roll fans, the only way to experience it was on the cinema screen. 'Rock Around the Clock' had originally been a soundtrack (to a film about juvenile delinquency, naturally). No sooner was Presley launched than he, too, began making movies, further evidence to his detractors that his music alone had no staying power. While most such 'exploitation' flicks were simply vehicles for the songs, a few were fresh and witty dramas in their own right, notably Presley's *King Creole*, and *The Girl Can't Help It*, featuring Little Richard with new white heartthrobs Eddie Cochran and Gene Vincent. For Mike, the epiphany came in the companionable darkness of Dartford's State cinema, with its fuzzy-faced luminous clock and cigarette smoke drifting across the projector beam: 'I saw Elvis and Gene Vincent, and thought, "Well, *I* can do this."'

Such American acts as did make it across the Atlantic often proved woefully unable to re-create the spellbinding sound of their records in the cavernous British variety theatres and cinemas where they appeared. The shining exception was Buddy Holly and his backing group, the Crickets, whose 'That'll Be the Day' topped the UK singles charts in the summer of 1957. As well as singing in a unique stuttery, hiccupy style, Holly played lead guitar and wrote or co-wrote songs that were rock 'n' roll at its most moodily exciting, yet constructed from the same simple chord sequences as skiffle. Bespectacled and dapper, more bank clerk than idol, he was a vital factor in raising rock 'n' roll from its blue-collar status in Britain. Middle-class boys who could never hope or dare to be Elvis now used Holly's songbook to transform their fading-from-fashion skiffle groups into tyro rock bands.

His one and only British tour, in 1958, brought him to the Granada cinema in Woolwich, a few miles north of Dartford, on the evening of 14 March. Mike Jagger – already skilled at aping Holly's vocal tics for comic effect – was in the audience with a group of school friends, all attending their very first rock concert. Holly's set with the Crickets lasted barely half an hour, and was powered by just one twenty-watt guitar amplifier, yet reproduced all his record hits with near-perfect fidelity. Disdaining musical apartheid despite hailing from segregated west Texas, he freely acknowledged his indebtedness to black artists like Little Richard and Bo Diddley. He was also an extrovert showman, able to keep the beat as well as play complex solos on his solid-body Fender Stratocaster while flinging himself across the stage on his knees, even lying flat on his back. Mike's favourite number was the B-side of 'Oh Boy!', Holly's second British hit fronting the Crickets: a song in blues call-and-response style called 'Not Fade Away', whose quirky stop-start tempo was beaten with drumsticks on a cardboard box. The lyrics had a humour previously unknown in rock 'n' roll ('My love is bigger than a Cadillac / I try to show it but you drive me back . . .'). This, Mike realised, was not just someone to copy, but to *be*.

Yet still he made no attempt to acquire the electric guitar needed to turn him into a rock singer like Buddy Holly, Eddie Cochran or Britain's first home-grown rock 'n' roller, the chirpily unsexy Tommy Steele. And though attracted by the idea, along with countless other British boys, he did not seem exactly on fire with ambition. Dartford Grammar, it so happened, had produced a skiffle group named the Southerners who were something of a local legend. They had appeared on a nationwide TV talent show, *Carroll Levis Junior Discoveries,* and then been offered a recording test by the EMI label (which lost interest when they decided to wait until the school holidays before auditioning). Easily managing the transition from skiffle to rock, they were now a washboard-free, fully electrified combo renamed Danny Rogers and the Realms.

The Realms' drummer, Alan Dow, was a year senior to Mike, and in the science rather than arts stream, but met him on equal terms at the weekly basketball sessions run by Mike's father. One night when Danny and the Realms played a gig at the school, Mike sidled up to Dow backstage and asked if he could sing a number with them. 'I was specially nervous that night, because of appearing in front of all our school mates,' Dow recalls. 'I said I'd rather he didn't.'

He had no better luck when two old classmates from Wentworth Primary, David Spinks and Mike Turner, started putting together a band intended to be more faithful to rock 'n' roll's black originators than its white echoes. Mike suggested himself as a possible vocalist, and auditioned at David's home in Wentworth Drive. Much as the other two liked him, they felt he neither looked nor sounded right – and, anyway, lack of a guitar was an automatic disqualification.

His first taste of celebrity did not have a singing or even a speaking part. Joe Jagger's liaison duties for the Central Council of Physical Recreation included advising television companies about programmes to encourage sports among children and teenagers – implicitly to counter the unhealthy effects of rock 'n' roll. In 1957, Joe became a consultant to one of the new commercial networks, ATV, on a weekly series called *Seeing Sport.* Over the next couple of years, Mike appeared regularly on the programme with his brother

Chris and other hand-picked young outdoor types, demonstrating skills like tent erecting or canoeing.

A clip has survived of an item on rock climbing, filmed in grainy black-and-white at a beauty spot named High Rocks, near Tunbridge Wells. Fourteen-year-old Mike, in jeans and striped T-shirt, reclines in a gully with some other boys while an elderly instructor soliloquises droningly about equipment. Rather than studded mountaineering boots, which could damage these particular rock faces, the instructor recommends 'ordinary gym shoes . . . like the kind Mike is wearing'. Mike allows one of his legs to be raised, displaying his virtuous rubber sole. For his father's sake, he can't show what he really thinks of this fussy, ragged-sweatered little man treating him like a dummy. But the deliberately blank stare – and the tongue, flicking out once too often to moisten the outsize lips – say it all.

At school he continued to coast along, doing just enough to get by in class and on the games field. To his teachers and classmates alike he gave the impression he was there only under sufferance and that his thoughts were somewhere infinitely more glamorous and amusing. 'Too easily distracted', 'attitude rather unsatisfactory' and other such faint damnations recurred through his end-of-term reports. In the summer of 1959 he took his GCE O-level exams, which in those days were assessed by marks out of 100 rather than grades. He passed in seven subjects, just scraping through English literature (48), geography (51), history (56), Latin (49) and pure mathematics (53), doing moderately well in French (61) and English language (66). Further education being still for the fortunate minority, this was when most pupils left, aged sixteen, to start jobs in banks or solicitors' offices. Mike, however, went into the sixth form for two more years to take A-level English, history and French. His headmaster, Lofty Hudson, predicted that he was 'unlikely to do brilliantly in any of them'.

He was also made a school prefect, in theory an auxiliary to Lofty and the staff in maintaining order and discipline. But it was an appointment that the head soon came to regret. Though Elvis Presley had originally cast his disruptive spell over girls, he had left a more lasting mark on boys, especially British ones, turning their former upright posture to a rebellious slouch and their former sunny smiles to sullen pouts, replacing their short-back-and-sides haircuts with toppling greasy quiffs, 'ducks' arses' and sideburns. The Teddy Boy (i.e., Edwardian) style, too, was no longer peculiar to lawless young artisans but had introduced middle- and upper-class youths to ankle-hugging trousers, two-button 'drape' jackets and Slim Jim ties.

Mike was not one to go too far – his mother would never have allowed it – but he broke Dartford Grammar's strict dress code in subtle ways that were no less provocative to Lofty's enforcers, sporting slip-on moccasin shoes instead of clumpy black lace-ups; a pale 'shorty' raincoat instead of the dark, belted kind; a low-fastening black jacket with a subtle gold fleck instead of his school blazer. Among his fiercest sartorial critics was Dr Wilfred Bennett, the senior languages tutor, whom he had already displeased by consistently performing below his abilities in French. Matters came to a head at the school's annual Founder's Day ceremony, attended by bigwigs from Dartford Council and other local dignitaries, when his gold-flecked jacket marred the otherwise faultless rows of regulation blazers. There was a heated confrontation with Dr Bennett afterwards, which ended with the teacher lashing out – as teachers then could with impunity – and Mike sprawled out on the ground.

Perhaps more than any other pastime, music forges friendships between individuals who otherwise have nothing whatsoever in common. Never was it truer than in late 1950s Britain, when for the first time young people found a music of their own, only to have it derided by adult society in general. A few months from now, this feeling of persecuted brotherhood would initiate, or rather revive, the most important relationship of Mike's life. The prologue, as it were, took place in his last two years at school when, somewhat surprisingly, the genteel kid from Wilmington chummed up with a plumber's son from Bexleyheath named Dick Taylor.

Dick's consuming passion was not rock 'n' roll but blues, the black music that had preceded it by something like half a century and provided its structure, its chords and its rebellious soul. For this esoteric taste he had to thank his older sister Robin, a hard-core blues fan while her friends swooned over white crooners like Frankie Vaughan and Russ Hamilton. Robin knew all its greatest exponents and, more important, knew where to find it on AFN or Voice of America, where the occasional blues record was played for the benefit of black GIs helping to defend Europe from communism. Dick, in turn, passed on the revelation to a small coterie at Dartford Grammar that included Mike Jagger.

This was unconventionality on an altogether more epic scale than shorty raincoats. Liking rock 'n' roll with its concealed black subtext was one thing – but this was music wholly reflecting the experience of black people, which few musicians but black ones had ever authentically created. In late-fifties Britain one still very seldom saw a black face outside London, least of all in the bucolic Home Counties: hence the unimpaired popularity of Helen Bannerman's children's story *Little Black Sambo*, Agatha Christie's stage play *Ten Little Niggers* and BBC TV's *Black and White Minstrels*, to say nothing of 'nigger brown' shoe polish and dogs routinely named 'Blackie', 'Sambo' and 'Nigger'. Nor was there any but the most marginal, patronising awareness of black culture. Mass immigration until now had come mainly from former colonies in the Caribbean, furnishing a new menial class to staff public transport and the National Health Service. The only generic black music most Britons ever heard was West Indian calypsos, full of careful deference to the host nation and usually employed as a soundtrack to first-class cricket matches.

There might seem no possible meeting point between suburban Kent with its privet hedges and slow green buses, and the Mississippi Delta with its tar-and-paper cabins, shanty towns and prison farms; still less between a genteelly raised white British boy and the dusty black troubadours whose chants of pain or anger or defiance had lightened the load and lifted the spirits of untold fellow sufferers under twentieth-century servitude. For Mike, the initial attraction of the blues was simply that of being different – standing out from his coevals as he already did through basketball. To some extent, too, it had a political element. This was the era of English literature's so-called angry young men and their well-publicised contempt for the cosiness and insularity of life under Harold Macmillan's Tory government. One of their numerous complaints, voiced in John Osborne's play *Look Back in Anger*, was that 'there are no good, brave causes left'. To a would-be rebel in 1959, the oppression of black musicians in pre-war rural America was more than cause enough.

But Mike's love of the blues was as passionate and sincere as he'd ever been about anything in his life, or perhaps ever would be. In crackly recordings, mostly made long before his birth, he found an excitement – an empathy – he never had in the wildest moments of rock 'n' roll. Indeed, he could see now just what an impostor rock was in so many ways; how puny were its wealthy young white stars in comparison with the bluesmen who'd written the book and, mostly, died in poverty; how those long-dead voices, wailing to the beat of a lone guitar, had a ferocity and humour and eloquence and elegance to which nothing on the rock 'n' roll jukebox even came close. The parental furore over Elvis Presley's sexual content, for instance, seemed laughable if one compared the pubescent hot flushes of 'Teddy Bear' and 'All Shook Up' with Lonnie Johnson's syphilis-crazed 'Careless Love' or Blind Lemon Jefferson's nakedly priapic 'Black Snake Moan'. And what press-pilloried rock 'n' roll reprobate, Little Richard or Jerry Lee Lewis, could hold a candle to Robert Johnson, the boy genius of the blues who lived almost the whole of his short life among drug addicts and prostitutes and was said to have made a pact with the devil in exchange for his peerless talent?

Though skiffle had brought some blues songs into general consciousness, the music still had only a tiny British following – mostly 'intellectual' types who read leftish weeklies, wore maroon socks with sandals and carried their change in leather purses. Like skiffle, it was seen as a branch of jazz: the few American blues performers who ever performed live in Britain did so through the sponsorship – charity, some might say – of traditional jazz bandleaders like Humphrey Lyttelton, Ken Colyer and Chris Barber. 'Humph' had been bringing Big Bill Broonzy over as a support attraction since 1950, while every year or so the duo of Sonny Terry and Brownie McGhee attracted small but ardent crowds to

Colyer's Soho club, Studio 51. After helping give birth to skiffle, Barber had become a stalwart of the National Jazz League, which strove to put this most lackadaisical of the arts on an organised footing and had its own club, the Marquee in Oxford Street. Here, too, from time to time, some famous old blues survivor would appear onstage, still bewildered by his sudden transition from Chicago or Memphis.

Finding the blues on record was almost as difficult. It was not available on six-shilling and fourpenny singles, like rock and pop, but only on what were still known as 'LPs' (long-players) rather than albums, priced at a daunting thirty shillings (£1.50) and up. To add to the expense, these were usually not released on British record labels but imported from America in their original packaging with the price in dollars and cents crossed out and a new one in pounds, shillings and pence substituted. Such exotica was, of course, not stocked by record shops in Dartford or even in large neighbouring towns such as Chatham or Rochester. To find it, Mike and Dick had to go to up to London and trawl through the racks at specialist dealers like Dobell's on Charing Cross Road.

Their circle at Dartford Grammar School included two other boys with the same recondite passion. One was a rather quiet, bookish type from the arts stream named Bob Beckwith; the other was Mike's Wilmington neighbour, the science student Alan Etherington. In late 1959, during Mike's first term in the sixth form, the four decided to form a blues band. Bob and Dick played guitar, Alan (a drummer and bugler in the school cadet force) played percussion on a drum kit donated by Dick's grandfather, and Mike was the vocalist.

Their aim was not to earn money or win local fame, like Danny Rogers and the Realms, nor even to pull girls. Mike in particular – as Alan Etherington recalls – already had all the ardent female followers he could wish for. The idea was simply to celebrate the blues and keep it alive amid the suffocating tides of commercial rock and pop. From first to last, they never had a single paid gig or performed to any audience larger than about half a dozen. Dartford Grammar gave them no opportunities to play or encouragement of any kind, even though they were effectively studying a byway of modern American history;

Alan Etherington recalls 'a stand-up row' with the school librarian after requesting a book by blues chronicler Paul Oliver as background reading for the quartet. They existed in a self-created vacuum, making no effort to contact kindred spirits in Kent or the wider world – hardly even aware that there were any. In Dick Taylor's words, 'We thought we were the only people in Britain who'd ever heard of the blues.'

CHAPTER TWO

The Kid in the Cardigan

Mike Jagger seemed living proof of the unnamed band's determination to go nowhere. He remained firm in his refusal to play a guitar, instead just standing there in front of the other three, as incomplete and exposed without that instantly glamorising, dignifying prop as if he'd forgotten to put on his trousers. The singing voice unveiled by his prodigious lips and flicking tongue was likewise an almost perverse departure from the norm. White British vocalists usually sang jazz or blues in a gravelly, cigarette-smoky style modelled – vainly – on Louis 'Satchmo' Armstrong. Mike's voice, higher and lighter in tone, borrowed from a larger, more eclectic cast; it was a distillation of every Deep Southern accent he'd ever heard, white as much as black, feminine as much as masculine; Scarlett O'Hara, plus a touch of Mammy from *Gone with the Wind* and Blanche DuBois from *A Streetcar Named Desire* as much as Blind Lemon Jefferson or Sonny Boy Williamson.

Unencumbered by a guitar – mostly even by a microphone – he had to do something while he sang. But the three friends, accustomed to his cool, non-committal school persona, were amazed by what he did do. Blues vocalists traditionally stood or, more often, sat in an anguished trance, cupping one ear with a hand to amplify the sonic self-flagellation. When Mike sang the blues, however, his loose-limbed, athletic body rebutted the music's melancholic inertia word by word: he shuffled to and fro on his moccasins, ground his hips, rippled his arms and euphorically shook his shaggy head. Like his singing, it had an element of parody and self-parody, but an underlying total conviction. A song from his early repertoire, John Lee Hooker's 'Boogie Chillen', summed up this metamorphosis: 'The blues is in him . . . and it's *got* to come out . . .'

Practice sessions for the non-existent gigs were mostly held at Dick Taylor's house in Bexleyheath or at Alan Etherington's, a few doors along from the Jaggers. Alan owned a reel-to-reel tape recorder, a Philips 'Joystick' (so named for its aeronautical-looking volume control) on which the four could preserve and review their first efforts together. The Etherington home boasted the further luxury of a Grundig 'radiogram', a cabinet radio-cum-record-player with surround sound, an early form of stereo. Dick and Bob Beckwith did not have custom-built electric guitars, only acoustic ones with metal pickups screwed to the bodies. Beckwith, the more accomplished player of the two, would plug his guitar into the radiogram, increasing its volume about thirtyfold.

At Dick's, if the weather was fine, they would rehearse in the back garden – the future lord of giant alfresco spaces and horizonless crowds surveying a narrow vista of creosoted wood fences, washing lines and potting sheds. Dick's mum, who sometimes interrupted her housework to watch, told Mike from the start that he had 'something special'. However small or accidental the audience, he gave them his all. 'If I could get a show, I would do it,' he would remember. 'I used to do mad things . . . Get on my knees and roll on the floor . . . I didn't have inhibitions. It's a real buzz, even in front of twenty people, to make a complete fool of yourself.'

Though Joe and Eva Jagger had no comprehension of the blues or its transfiguring effect on their elder son, they were quite happy for his group to practise at 'Newlands', in either his bedroom or the garden.

Eva found his singing hilarious and would later describe 'creasing up' with laughter at the sound of his voice through the wall. His father's only concern was that it shouldn't interfere with his physical training programme. Once, when he and Dick Taylor were leaving for a practise session elsewhere, Joe called out, 'Michael . . . don't forget your weight training.' Mike dutifully turned back and spent half an hour in the garden with his weights and barbells. Another time, he arrived for band practice distraught because he'd fallen from one of the tree ropes at home and bitten his tongue. What if it had permanently damaged his singing voice? 'We all told him it made no difference,' Dick Taylor remembers. 'But he did seem to lisp a bit and sound a bit more bluesy after that.'

Building up a repertoire was a laborious process. The usual way was for Mike and Dick to bring a record back from London, and the four to listen to it over and over until Bob had mastered the guitar fills and Mike learned the words. They did not restrict themselves to blues, but also experimented with white rock and pop songs, like Buddy Holly's, which had some kinship with it. One of the better performances committed to the Philips Joystick was of 'La Bamba', whose sixteen-year-old singer–composer Ritchie Valens had died in the same plane crash that killed Holly in February 1959. Its Latino nonsense words being impossible to decipher, no matter how often one replayed the record, Mike simply invented his own.

The Joystick's inventory dramatically improved with their discovery of harder-edged electric blues, as played by John Lee Hooker, Lightnin' Hopkins, Memphis Slim and Howlin' Wolf. A discovery of almost equal momentousness was that many of these alluring names could be traced to the same source, the Chess record label of Chicago. Founded in the 1940s by two Polish immigrant brothers, Leonard and Phil Chess, the label had started out with jazz but become increasingly dominated by what was then called 'race' music – i.e., for exclusively black consumption. Its most notable early acquisition had been McKinley Morganfield, aka Muddy Waters, born in 1913 (the same year as Joe Jagger) and known as 'the father of the Chicago Blues' for tracks like 'Hoochie

Coochie Man', 'I Just Want to Make Love to You' and his theme song, 'Rollin' Stone'. His album *At Newport 1960*, capturing his performance at the 1960 Newport Jazz Festival, was the first album Mike Jagger ever bought.

In 1955, Chess signed St. Louis-born Charles Edward Anderson – aka Chuck – Berry, a singer-songwriter-guitarist who combined the sexiness and cockiness of R&B with the social commentary of country and western, the lucid diction of black balladeers like Nat 'King' Cole and Billy Eckstine, and a lyrical and instrumental nimbleness all his own. Soon afterwards Berry made an effortless crossover from 'race' music to white rock 'n' roll with compositions such as 'Johnny B. Goode', 'Sweet Little Sixteen' and 'Memphis, Tennessee' that were to become its defining anthems. Long before he ever heard a Chuck Berry song, Mike's voice had some of the same character.

After a long and fruitless search for Chess LPs up and down Charing Cross Road, he discovered they could be obtained by mail order directly from the company's Chicago headquarters. It was a gamble, since prepayment had to be enclosed and he had no idea whether he'd like the titles he ordered – if they ever materialised at all. But, after a lengthy wait, flat brown cardboard packages with American stamps began arriving at 'Newlands'. Some of the covers had been badly chewed up in transit and not all the music lived up to his expectations. But the albums in themselves were splendiferous status symbols. He took to carrying around three or four at once tucked under one arm, a fashion accessory as much as his gold-flecked jacket and moccasins. Alan Dow, who'd rejected him as a vocalist for Danny Rogers and the Realms, witnessed one such almost regal progress across the school playground.

In summer 1961, he sat his A-level exams, passing in English and history but, surprisingly, failing in French. He considered becoming a schoolteacher in his father's – and grandfather's – footsteps, and toyed with the idea of journalism and (unmentionably to his parents) disc-jockeying on Radio Luxembourg. Leafing through the pop music papers one week, he spotted an advertisement by a London record producer named Joe Meek, inviting would-be deejays to submit audition tapes.

He clipped the ad and kept it, but – perhaps fortunately – didn't follow it up. Meek later produced several British pop classics, all from his small north London flat, but was notorious for trying to seduce the prettier young men who crossed his path.

Instead, somewhat against expectations, Mike Jagger joined the 2 per cent of Britain's school leavers in that era who went on to university. Despite those clashes over uniform, his headmaster, Lofty Hudson, decided he was worthy of the privilege and, in December 1960, well before he had sat his A-levels, supplied a character reference putting the best possible gloss on his academic record. 'Jagger is a lad of good general character,' it read in part, 'although he has been rather slow to mature. The pleasing quality which is now emerging is that of persistence when he makes up his mind to tackle something. His interests are wide. He has been a member of several School Societies and is prominent in Games, being Secretary of our Basketball Club, a member of our First Cricket Eleven and he plays Rugby Football for his House. Out of school he is interested in Camping, Climbing, Canoeing, Music and is a member of the Local Historical Association . . . Jagger's development now fully justifies me in recommending him for a Degree course and I hope you will be able to accept him.'

Though in no sense hyperbolic, the head's letter did the trick. Conditional on two A-level passes, Mike was offered a place at the London School of Economics to begin reading for a BSc degree in the autumn of 1961. He accepted it, albeit without great enthusiasm. 'I wanted to do arts, but thought I ought to do science,' he would remember. 'Economics seemed about halfway in between.'

At that time, Britain's university entrants were not forced to run themselves into debt to the government to pay for their tuition, but received virtually automatic grants from local education authorities. Kent County Council gave Mike £350 per annum, which at a time of almost zero inflation was more than enough to cover three years of study, especially as he would continue living at home and travel up each day by train to the LSE's small campus in Houghton Street, off Kingsway. Even so, it was clearly advisable to earn some money during the long summer holiday between leaving school and starting there. His choice of job sheds interesting light on a character always thought to have been consumed by selfishness, revealing that until his late teens at least he had a caring and altruistic side that made him very much his father's son.

For several weeks that summer, he worked as a porter at a local psychiatric institution. Not Stone House – that would have been too perfect – but Bexley Hospital, a similarly grim and sprawling Victorian edifice locally nicknamed 'the Village on the Heath' because until recently, in the interests of total segregation, its grounds had included a fully functioning farm. He earned £4.50 per week, not at all a bad wage for the time, though he clearly could have chosen an easier job, both physically and emotionally. He was to be remembered by patients and staff alike as unfailingly kind and cheerful. He himself believed the experience taught him lessons about human psychology that were to prove invaluable throughout his life.

It was at Bexley Hospital, too, by his own account, that he lost his virginity to a nurse, huddled in a store cupboard during a brief respite from pushing trolleys and taking round meals: the furthest possible extreme from all those luxury hotel suites of the future.

A STUDENT AT the London School of Economics in 1961 enjoyed a prestige only slightly below that of Oxford or Cambridge. Founded by George Bernard Shaw and the Fabians Beatrice and Sidney Webb, it was an autonomous unit of London University whose past lecturers had included the philosopher and pacifist Bertrand Russell and the economist John Maynard Keynes. Among its many celebrated alumni were the Labour chancellor of the exchequer Hugh Dalton, the polemical journalist Bernard Levin, the newly elected president of the United States, John F. Kennedy, and his brother (and attorney general) Robert.

It was also by long tradition Britain's most highly politicised seat of learning, governed largely by old-school right-wingers but with an increasingly radical student population and junior staff. Though its heyday as a cauldron of youthful dissent was still half a dozen years in the future, LSE demonstrators already took to the streets on a regular basis, protesting against foreign atrocities like the Sharpeville Massacre in South Africa and supporting their elder statesman Bertrand Russell's Campaign for Nuclear Disarmament. One of Mike's fellow students, the future publisher and peer Matthew Evans, had won his place despite passing only one A-level and with a far more modest cache of O-levels, including woodwork. More important was that he'd taken part in the famous CND protest march to the nuclear weapons research establishment at Aldermaston, Berkshire.

On the same BSc degree course was Laurence Isaacson, in later life a highly successful restaurant tycoon who would quip that if he'd sung or played an instrument his future might have been very different. Born in Liverpool, he had attended Dovedale Primary School like John Lennon and George Harrison and then, like Lennon, gone on to Quarry Bank High School; now here he was actually sitting next to another future legend of rock. The two were doing the same specialist subject, industry and trade, for the second paper in their finals. 'That meant that if Jagger missed a lecture, he'd copy out my notes, and if I missed one, I'd copy out his,' Isaacson says. 'I seem to recall he used to do most of the copying.'

Like Evans, Isaacson remembers him as 'obviously extremely bright' and easily capable of achieving a 2:1 degree. At lectures, he was always quiet and well mannered and spoke 'like a nice middle-class boy . . . The trouble was that it still all felt a bit too much like school. You had to be very respectful to the tutors and, of course, never answer back. And the classes were so small that they always had their eye on you. I remember one shouting out, "Jagger . . . if you don't concentrate, you're never going to get *anywhere!*"'

Barely two years into a new decade, London had already taken huge strides away from the stuffy, sleepy fifties – though the changes were only just beginning. A feeling of excitement and expectation pulsed through the crusty old Victorian metropolis at every level: from its

towering new office blocks and swirling new traffic overpasses and
underpasses to its impudent new minicars, minivans and minicabs and
ever-lengthening rows of parking meters; from its new wine bars, 'bis-
tros' and Italian trattorias to its sophisticated new advertisements and
brand identities and newly launched, or revivified, glossy magazines like
Town, Queen and *Tatler*; from its young men in modish narrower trousers, thick-striped shirts and square-toed shoes to its young women in
masculine-looking V-necked Shetland sweaters, 1920s-style ropes of
beads, black stockings and radically short skirts.

Innovation and experimentation (once again the merest *amuse-
bouche* from the banquet to come) flourished at new theatres like Bernard
Miles's Mermaid and Joan Littlewood's Theatre Royal, Stratford East;
in the plays of Arnold Wesker and Harold Pinter; in mould-shattering
productions like Peter Cook, Dudley Moore, Alan Bennett and Jonathan
Miller's *Beyond the Fringe* and Lionel Bart's *Oliver!* The middle-aged metropolitan sophisticates whose posh accents always ruled London's arts
and media now began to seem laughably old-fashioned. An emergent
school of young painters from humble families and provincial back-
grounds – including Yorkshire's David Hockney, Essex's Allen Jones
and Dartford's Peter Blake – were being more talked and written about
than any since the French Impressionists. *Vogue* magazine, the supreme
arbiter of style and sophistication, ceased employing bow-tied society
figures to photograph its model girls, instead hiring a brash young East
End Cockney named David Bailey.

Only in popular music did excitement seem to be dwindling rather
than growing. The ructions that rock 'n' roll had caused among mid-
fifties teenagers were a distant, almost embarrassing memory. Elvis Presley had disappeared into the US army for two years, and then emerged
shorn of his sideburns, singing ballads and hymns. The American music
industry had been convulsed by scandals over payola and the misadventures of individual stars. Buddy Holly and Eddie Cochran were dead;
Little Richard had found God; Jerry Lee Lewis had been engulfed in
controversy after bigamously marrying his thirteen-year-old cousin;
Chuck Berry had been convicted on an immorality charge involving a

teenage girl. The new teenage icons were throwbacks to the crooner era, with names like Frankie and Bobby, chosen for prettiness rather than vocal talent, and their manifest inability to hurt a fly (or unbutton one). The only creative sparks came from young white songwriters working out of New York's Brill Building, largely supplying black singers and groups, and from the black-owned Motown record label in Detroit: all conclusive proof that 'race' music was dead and buried.

Such rock idols as Britain had produced – Tommy Steele, Adam Faith, Cliff Richard – had all heeded the dire warnings that it couldn't possibly last and crossed over as soon as possible into mainstream show business. The current craze was 'Trad', a homogenised version of traditional jazz whose bands dressed in *faux*-Victorian bowler hats and waistcoats and played mainstream show tunes like Cole Porter's 'I Love You, Samantha' and even Rodgers and Hammerstein's 'March of the Siamese Children'. The wild, skirt-twirling rock 'n' roll jive had given way to the slower, more formal Stomp, which involved minimal bodily contact between the dancers and tended to come to a respectful halt during drum solos.

In short, the danger seemed to have passed.

BARELY A MONTH into Mike's first term at LSE, he met up with Keith Richards again and they resumed the conversation that had broken off in the Wentworth County Primary playground eleven years earlier.

The second most important partnership in rock music history might never have happened if either of them had got out of bed five minutes later, missed a bus, or lingered to buy a pack of cigarettes or a Mars bar. It took place early one weekday on the 'up' platform at Dartford railway station as they waited for the same train, Mike to get to Charing Cross in London and Keith to Sidcup, four stops away, where he was now at art college.

Since their discussion about cowboys and guitars as seven-year-olds, they had remained vaguely in each other's orbit without being friends. When the Jaggers lived on Denver Road in the centre of Dartford, Keith's home had been on Chastillian Road, literally one street away. Their mothers were on casually friendly terms, and would exchange family news if ever they chanced to meet around town. But after Wentworth their only further encounter had been one summer day outside Dartford Library when Mike had a holiday job selling ice cream and Keith, recognising him, stopped and bought one. That time, their conversation had been even briefer, albeit punctuated by a prophetic lapping tongue.

As eighteen-year-olds, waiting among the diurnal wage slaves at Dartford Station, they could not have looked more different. Mike was a typical middle-class student with his beige wool cardigan and black-, purple- and yellow-striped LSE scarf. Keith, though also technically a student, did his utmost not to resemble one with his faded blue denim jeans and jerkin and lilac-coloured shirt. To 1961 eyes, that made an unpleasing cross between a Teddy Boy and a beatnik.

Keith instantly recognised Mike by the lips, as Mike did Keith by the almost skull-bony face and protruding ears that had barely changed since he was in short trousers. It also happened that Mike was carrying two albums he had just received from the Chess label in Chicago, *The Best of Muddy Waters* and Chuck Berry's *Rockin' at the Hops*. 'To me,' Keith would recall, 'that was Captain Morgan's treasure. I thought, "I know you. And what you got under your arm's worth robbing."'

The upshot was that when their train pulled in, they decided to travel together. Rattling through the Kentish suburbs, they found they had other idols in common, a crowd almost as dense as the newspaper-reading, strap-hanging one around them: Sonny Boy Williamson . . . John Lee Hooker . . . Howlin' Wolf . . . Willie Dixon . . . Jimmy Reed . . . Jimmy Witherspoon . . . T-Bone Walker . . . Little Walter . . . Never one to stint on melodrama, Keith would afterwards equate the moment with the blues' darkest fable – young Robert Johnson keeping a tryst with the devil and, Faust-like, bartering his soul to be able to play like an angel. 'Just sitting on that train . . . it was almost like we made a deal without knowing it, like Robert did.' When the train pulled into Sidcup, he was so absorbed in copying down the serial numbers on Mike's albums that he almost forgot to get off.

Keith not only had music in his blood (where it was destined to be severely jostled by other, more questionable additives) but guitar wood almost in his bones. Once again, Kent could claim little of the credit. On his mother's side, he was descended from French Huguenots, Protestants who had fled Catholic persecution in their own country and found asylum in the Channel Isles. The music was infused largely through his maternal grandfather, Theodore Augustus Dupree, who led a succession of semi-professional dance bands and played numerous instruments, including piano, saxophone, violin and guitar. One of Keith's great childhood treats — all in all somewhat fewer than Mike Jagger enjoyed — was to accompany his 'Grandfather Gus' to the Ivor Mairants music store in London's West End, where guitars were custom-built on the premises. Sometimes he would be allowed into the workshops to watch the fascinating silhouettes take shape and inhale the aromas of raw rosewood, resin and varnish; despite stiff competition, the headiest narcotic he would ever know.

An only child, he had been raised by parents who in every way were the opposite of Mike's. His father, Bert Richards, a dour, introverted character, worked punishingly long shifts as a supervisor in a lightbulb factory and so had little energy left over to be an authority figure and role model like Joe Jagger. In equal contrast with Eva Jagger, Keith's mother, Doris, was a sunny-natured, down-to-earth woman who spoiled him rotten, loved music, and had an eclectic taste ranging from Sarah Vaughan to Mozart. As she washed up his dirty dishes with the radio blaring, she'd call out to him to 'listen to that blue note!'

Doris's refusal ever to make Keith toe the line had withstood every sanction of mid-fifties state schooling and resulted in an intelligent, perceptive boy being branded an irredeemable dunce. By the age of thirteen, he was regarded as an academic no-hoper and had been consigned to Dartford Technical School, hopefully to acquire some honest artisan trade. The school was in Wilmington, which meant he unknowingly crossed paths with Mike every morning and evening as Mike went to and from Dartford Grammar. At Dartford Tech, he was as inattentive and disruptive as at school, and was expelled after two years without a single plumbing or bricklaying certificate to his name.

Sidcup Art College was the bottom of the heap. In this era, even the smallest British town usually had its own college or school of art built in Victorian mock-Gothic style, a civic amenity as familiar as the library or the swimming baths. All were open to school leavers with the faintest artistic bent, which as a rule meant misfits who had not reached university standard but lacked the drive to go out and find a job. Since the fifties, a secondary role of art schools had been giving shelter to young men whose obsession with rock 'n' roll music seemed destined to take them nowhere. Keith had joined an unwitting brotherhood that also included, or would include, John Lennon, Peter Townshend, Eric Clapton, Ronnie Wood, Ray Davies, Syd Barrett and David Jones, later Bowie.

As a working-class teenager, he felt the full impact of rock 'n' roll's first wave, rather than waiting around like bourgeois Mike for it to clean up its act. The national guitar fever unleashed by Elvis Presley had infected him long ago, thanks to Grandfather Gus and the craftsmen at Ivor Mairants's. His adoring mum bought him his first guitar for seven pounds, out of her wages from working in a Dartford baker's shop. Though he could sing – in fact, had sung soprano in the massed choirs at the Queen's coronation – his ambition was to be like Scotty Moore, the solo guitarist in Presley's backing trio, whose light and jaunty rockabilly riffs somehow perfectly set off the King's brooding sexual menace.

At Sidcup Art College he did little on a creative level, apart from developing what would become a near genius for vandalism. Musically speaking, however, the college provided an education which he devoured like none before. Among its students was a clique of hard-core blues enthusiasts, as usual acting like a resistance cell in an occupied country. Their moving spirit, Dick Taylor, had lately arrived from Dartford Grammar School, where he had belonged to an identical underground movement with Mike Jagger. Dick converted Keith to the blues just as he'd converted Mike a year earlier. In the process, he sometimes mentioned playing in a band, but so vaguely that Keith never realised his old primary schoolmate was also a member. He had in fact been longing to join but, says Taylor, was 'too shy to ask'.

After their chance reunion on that morning commuter train, Mike and Keith met up again at Dartford's only cool place, the Carousel coffee bar, and were soon regularly hanging out together. Keith brought along his guitar, an acoustic Hofner cello model with F-holes, and Mike revealed that, despite his college scarf and well-bred accent, he sang blues. They began making music together immediately, finding their tastes identical – blues, with some pop if it was good – and their empathy almost telepathic. 'We'd hear something, we'd both look at each other at once,' Keith would later write in his autobiography, *Life*. 'We'd hear a record and go "That's wrong. That's faking it. That's *real*."' As with two other total opposites, John Lennon and Paul McCartney, who had met in Liverpool four years earlier, their character differences only seemed to cement the friendship. '[Mike] liked Keith's laid-back quality, his tough stance, his obsession with the guitar,' says Taylor, 'and Keith was attracted to Mike's intelligence, his dramatic flair.'

Mike was all for bringing Keith into the unnamed blues band that still somehow struggled along. But aside from Taylor, there were two other members to convince. Although Bob Beckwith and Alan Etherington had also now left Dartford Grammar School, both still lived at home, in circumstances as irreproachably middle class as the Jaggers'. Keith was not simply their social inferior, but hailed from very much the wrong side of the tracks: he lived in a council house on the definitely rough Temple Hill estate in east Dartford, and was known to hang out with the town's most disreputable 'Teds'. However, one band practice session was enough for Beckwith and Etherington to agree with Taylor's estimate of Mike's mate as 'an absolute lout . . . but a really nice lout'. The line-up obligingly rearranged itself so that Keith could alternate on lead guitar with Beckwith.

Chuck Berry was Keith's real passport into their ranks. For Berry had done what no schoolteacher or college lecturer could – made him pay attention and apply himself. The gymnastic electric riffs with which Berry punctuated his vocals were still way beyond most of his young British admirers. But Keith, by listening to the records over and over, had nailed every last note and half chord in 'Sweet

Little Sixteen', 'Memphis, Tennessee', even the complex intro and solo to 'Johnny B. Goode', where Berry somehow single-handedly sounded like two lead guitarists trying to outpick each other. Mike's voice, if it resembled anyone's, had always sounded a bit like Berry's; in this authentic instrumental setting, he now became Chuck almost to the life.

With Keith's arrival, the band finally acquired a name, Little Boy Blue and the Blue Boys. His guitar had the name 'Blue Boy' inside it, and 'Little Boy Blue' was a pseudonym of the blues giant Sonny Boy Williamson. There was also a hint of giggle-making *double entendre* ('Little Boy Blue, come blow up your horn') and an ironic nod to *The Blue Boy*, Thomas Gainsborough's eighteenth-century portrait of an angelic youth in sky-coloured satin. In other words, they could not have dreamed up anything much worse.

Away from the band, not all Mike's friends were quite so accepting of Keith. Alan Etherington recalls that in their wider ex-Dartford Grammar School circle, there would sometimes be parties to which Mike's Teddy Boy friend was pointedly not invited. That used to upset Mike, showing his bandmates a more sensitive, caring person than they previously had taken him for. He adopted a protective attitude towards Keith – who was not nearly as tough as he pretended, and in many ways a rather sensitive, vulnerable soul – while Keith, in return, followed him with almost dog-like devotion.

Mike, for his part, crossed over to Keith's side of the tracks without any problem. The Richardses' cosy, untidy council house on Spielman Road was the pleasantest possible contrast to the spotless and regimented Jagger home in The Close. Keith had no vigorous dad around to insist on weight training or team washing up, and Doris was motherly and easygoing in a way that Eva Jagger, for all her sterling qualities, had never been. When the Richardses went away for the weekend to Beesands in Devon that summer, Mike accompanied them in their battered old Vauxhall car. Keith took his guitar, and the two friends entertained customers at the local pub by playing Everly Brothers songs. Otherwise, Doris Richards remembered Mike being 'bored to tears' and repeatedly moaning, 'No women . . . no women.' On their marathon return journey, the car battery failed and they had to drive without lights. When finally they drew up outside the Jagger house four or five hours late, a tight-lipped Eva showed little sympathy.

Mike had always soaked up other people's accents and manner-isms, usually in a mocking spirit, sometimes in an admiring one. Now, outside of college – and home – he abandoned his rather goody-goody, stripe-scarfed student persona and began to dress and carry himself more like Keith, no longer speaking in the quiet, accentless tone of a nicely brought-up middle-class boy, but in brash Kentish Cockney. Around Keith, he ceased to be known as 'Mike', that name so redolent of sports cars, Harris-tweed jackets, and beer in pewter mugs at smart roadhouses on Sunday mornings. Now, instead, he became 'Mick', its defiantly proletarian butt end, redo-lent only of reeking public bars and mad-drunk Irishmen. It was the tough-nut prefix for which 'Jagger' seemed to have been waiting all these years; joined together, the three syllables were already practi-cally smashing windows.

While Keith's arrival in the band widened their repertoire and gave their sound an extra bite, it did not make them any more ambitious or purposeful. They continued to practise together in a vacuum, still not trying to find live playing gigs or acquire a manager who might do so for them. Early in 1962, at Alan Etherington's house, they used the Philips 'Joystick' recorder to tape Mike's – or Mick's – better Chuck Berry take-offs with Keith on lead guitar: two versions apiece of 'Beautiful Delilah', 'Little Queenie' and 'Around and Around', and one each of 'Johnny B. Goode' and 'Down the Road Apiece', plus Billy Boy Arnold's 'I Ain't Got You' and Ritchie Valens's 'La Bamba'. The tape was not submitted to a record company or talent agent, however, but simply analysed for instrumental and vocal faults, then forgotten – until thirty years later, when it was put up for auction as a unique glimpse of a superstar and supergroup in embryo, and sold for a fortune.

*

ON 15 MARCH 1962 Little Boy Blue and the Blue Boys discovered
they were not alone after all. Scanning that Thursday's edition of *Melody
Maker*, they lit on an advertisement for what was described – wholly justifiably, in their view – as 'The Most Exciting Event of This Year'. In two
evenings' time, a club dedicated to blues music would open in the west
London suburb of Ealing.

The club's founder, Alexis Korner, was the first in a succession of
characters from exotic regions far outside Kent who would assist Mike's
transfiguration into Mick. Born in Paris of an Austro-Russian father
and a Greco-Turkish mother, Korner spent his infancy in Switzerland
and North Africa before growing up in London and attending one of its
most exclusive schools, St Paul's. He became addicted to the blues as
a schoolboy, rejecting all his various heritages to learn boogie-woogie
piano, banjo and guitar, and feeling – much like our Dartford schoolboy
in later years – an almost sacred mission to keep the music alive.

As a result, thirty-three-year-old Korner, a genial man with a shock
of Afro hair before its time and an uneroded public school accent, now
led Britain's only full-time blues band, Blues Incorporated. The name
had no twenty-first-century big-business associations, but had been
inspired by *Murder Inc.*, a Humphrey Bogart film about American gangsters – which, indeed, was very much how Korner's musical contemporaries viewed him.

In 1962, any popular musician who wanted to make it in Britain had
first to make it in Soho. The maze of narrow Georgian streets at the heart
of London's West End contained what little music industry the capital
could yet boast, harbouring song publishers, pluggers, talent scouts,
agents and recording studios – plus almost all the live venues that mattered – among its French restaurants, Italian groceries, cigar shops and
seedy strip clubs. Rock 'n' roll and skiffle had each been launched on the
nation from Soho, and anyone in search of pop stardom, as well as of
a flash of naked breasts, an espresso or *coq au vin*, instinctively headed
there.

Since the Trad jazz boom, however, Soho was no longer a centre of musical pioneering but of entrenchment and prejudice. It was now where 'pure' jazz enthusiasts gathered – nowhere more fervently than at the National Jazz League's own Marquee Club, a cellar designed (by the surrealist photographer Angus McBean) to resemble the interior of a tent. In this siege atmosphere, the blues was no longer recognised as a first cousin to jazz, but looked down on as disdainfully as was Trad, or even rock. Alexis Korner had formerly played banjo with the Barber band, which made his decision to put syncopated music behind him, and form a band essentially playing only twelve bars and three chords, all the more reprehensible.

Despite repeated rejections from Soho club managements – the brusquest from the Marquee's manager, Harold Pendleton – Korner remained convinced there was an audience for blues who were at present totally excluded from London's live music scene and would beat a path to Blues Incorporated's door, if he could just provide them with one. Hence his decision to open his own club in the hopefully friendlier environs of the suburb where he'd grown up.

Like Dartford, Ealing had never previously been regarded as a crucible for the blues. It was an affluent, sedate and almost wholly 'white' residential area, best known for its eponymous film studios – maker of British screen classics like *Kind Hearts and Coronets* and *Passport to Pimlico* – and for having a 'Broadway' rather than just an ordinary High Street. Korner's Ealing Club (a name more suggestive of golf or bridge than visceral music) was situated almost directly opposite Ealing Broadway tube station, underneath an ABC bakery and tea shop. Local matrons being served afternoon tea by frilly-aproned waitresses little suspected what was brewing beneath their feet.

Little Boy Blue and the Blue Boys' excitement over the new club was somewhat dampened by the inaccessibility of its location, twenty-odd miles to the north west of Dartford and a tricky journey, whether by road or public transport. Owing to prior commitments, they were not present at Korner's opening night on 17 March. But the following Saturday the five of them set off for Ealing, packed into Alan Etherington's father's car, an appropriately named Riley Pathfinder.

First impressions were hardly promising. The club premises consisted of a shabby staircase and a single room, smelling dankly of the adjacent River Thames, with a central bar and a makeshift stage at one end. The kindred spirits waiting for showtime, no more than a couple of dozen strong, were equally uninspiring. Mick of the future would remember them as 'trainspotters who needed somewhere to go . . . just a bunch of anoraks . . . and the girls were very thin on the ground'.

Excitement barely quickened when Blues Incorporated took the stage. The three main figures in the line-up, all men in their early thirties (advanced middle age by 1962 standards), were attired conventionally in white shirts with sober ties, baggy grey flannel trousers and black lace-up shoes, and had a serious, preoccupied air better suited to some chamber orchestra. But when they started playing, none of that mattered. The music was Chicago-style instrumental blues, a leisurely tag match between guitar, saxophone and harmonica that by rights should only have worked on a Roy Brown or Champion Jack Dupree live album soaked in the rotgut gin and cheap neon of the Windy City's South Side. Yet astonishingly here it was, conjured up with near-perfect fidelity by a clump of square-looking Englishmen under a cake shop on Ealing Broadway.

The band was jointly fronted by Korner on guitar – usually seated on a chair – and his long-time playing partner, Cyril Davies, a burly metalworker from Harrow (the suburb, not the illustrious school) who had somehow turned himself into a virtuoso on blues piano, harmonica and twelve-string guitar. Their only other regular sideman was the tenor-sax player Dick Heckstall-Smith, a black-bearded agriculture graduate from Cambridge University. Otherwise, Korner used a roster of much younger musicians, mostly not yet even semi-pro, who looked up to him as a teacher and mentor and so required mercifully little payment. Among this floating population were nineteen-year-old classically trained double bassist Jack Bruce, one day to play bass guitar with the supergroup Cream, and a twenty-one-year-old drummer and erstwhile art student from Wembley named Charlie Watts.

It was Korner's reputation for giving newcomers a break that awoke the first definite glimmer of ambition in Mick. He found out Korner's address and, a few days later, posted him a tape of Little Boy Blue and the Blue Boys performing Chuck Berry's 'Reelin' and Rockin'' and 'Around and Around', Jimmy Reed's 'Bright Lights, Big City' and 'Go on to School' and Bobby Bland's 'Don't Want No Woman'. Korner heard nothing of compelling interest on the tape (then lost it, to his eventual huge regret) but, as ever, was willing to give a chance on the bandstand to anyone. Without prior audition, Mick was offered a spot the next Saturday, backed by Keith and Korner himself on guitars and Jack Bruce on double bass.

Mick took the stage looking the picture of respectability in his chunky student cardigan, white shirt and Slim Jim tie. As an opener, he and Keith picked what they thought was their best Chuck Berry impersonation, 'Around and Around', one of Berry's several hymns of praise to music itself ('Well, the joint was rockin' . . . goin' round and round . . .'). Even for the broad-minded Korner, it was a bit too perilously close to rock 'n' roll: after the first jarring chords, he conveniently broke a guitar string and remained preoccupied with changing it until the song was safely over. He later recalled being struck less by Mick's singing than by 'the way he threw his hair around . . . For a kid in a cardigan, that was moving quite *excessively.*'

It was not in any way what the club was supposed to be about, and the performance met with frigid silence from the men of Korner's age whom he had previously regarded as his target audience. 'We'd obviously stepped over the limit,' Mick would remember. 'You couldn't include Chuck Berry in the pantheon of traddy-blues-ists.' But Korner, glancing up at last from that troublesome guitar string, saw a different reaction from the younger men present – and a very different one from their girlfriends, wives and sisters. Until now, women had never been considered a significant factor in blues appreciation. The kid in the cardigan, with his flying hair, had suddenly changed that.

When Mick came offstage, certain he had blown his big chance, Korner was waiting for him. To his astonishment, he was offered another spot next week, this time with Blues Incorporated's full heavyweight line-up of Korner, Cyril Davies and Dick Heckstall-Smith. Blues Incorporated remained predominantly an instrumental band and to start with Mick was only a brief, walk-on feature, rather like megaphone-toting crooners in 1920s orchestras. 'It was a bit of a scramble to get onstage with Alexis,' he would recall. 'For anyone who fancied themselves as a blues vocalist, that was the only showcase, that one band. I wouldn't ever get in tune, that was my problem, and I was often very drunk, 'cause I was really nervous.' As Korner recalled, he seldom sang more than three songs in a night. 'He learned more, but was only really sure of three, one of which was Billy Boy Arnold's "Poor Boy" – and he used to sing one of Chuck's songs and a Muddy Waters.'

Some time before the Ealing revelation, he had accepted that an authentic bluesman couldn't just stand there but had better play some kind of instrument. Feeling it too late to start learning guitar or piano, he had settled for harmonica – what musicians call a 'harp' – and had been struggling to teach himself from records by American virtuosi like Jimmy Reed, Little Walter and Sonny Boy Williamson.

Fortuitously, Blues Incorporated had Britain's finest blues harp player in Cyril – aka 'Squirrel' – Davies, who carried his collection of harmonicas around in a bag like a plumber's tools. When the band played *sans* Jagger, Mick would haunt the stage front as avidly as any future Mick worshipper, watching the big, ungainly man coax the most delicate melodies as well as the most wickedly rousing rhythms from his tiny silver mouthpiece. However, the prickly, insecure and fiercely anti-rock 'n' roll 'Squirrel' felt none of Korner's zeal to help younger musicians. 'He was very gruff, almost to the point of rudeness,' his would-be pupil would recall. 'He told me to fuck off, basically. I'd ask, "How do you bend a note?" and Cyril would say, "Well, you get a pair of pliers..."'

Nor was Alexis Korner's hospitality limited to the Ealing Club stage. At his London flat, in Moscow Road, Bayswater, he and his wife, Bobbie, kept open house for his young protégés as well as for the occasional blues maestro visiting from America. Mick and the other Blue Boys would go back there after closing time to sit in the kitchen – where Big Bill Broonzy had once slept on the floor – drinking instant coffee and talking until dawn came up over the cupolas of nearby Whiteley's department store. The Korners found Mick always quiet and polite, though by now more than a little influenced by the LSE's in-house radicalism. On one occasion, he described the blues as 'our working-class music' and expressed surprise that a former public schoolboy like Korner should be involved with it. Keith always seemed consumed by shyness, never pushing himself forward as a musician or a person, just happy to be around Mick.

On the club's second night, yet another Korner find had made his début there. He was a short, stocky twenty-year-old, dressed at the height of fashion in a grey herringbone jacket, a shirt with one of the new *faux*-Victorian rounded collars and elastic-sided Chelsea boots. He had a mop of fair hair almost as ungovernable as Mick's, and even more silkily clean, and a smile of shining choirboy innocence. His name was Brian Jones.

Two evenings later, the Dartford boys walked in to find him onstage, playing Robert Johnson's 'Dust My Broom' on 'bottleneck' or 'slide' guitar – not holding down individual strings but sliding a steel-jacketed finger back and forth along all six at once in extravagant sweeps to produce quivering metallic mayhem. It was a style, and song, identified with one of the Blue Boys' greatest Chicago idols, Elmore James; the newcomer did not merely sound like James but was billed under a pseudonym, 'Elmo Lewis', clearly designed to put him on the same level. This hubris excited Keith, in particular, almost more than the music. 'It's Elmore James, man,' he kept whispering to Mick as they watched. 'It's fuckin' Elmore *James* . . .'

Brian was a blues pilgrim from even farther afield than Dartford. He had been raised in Cheltenham, Gloucestershire, a bastion of stuffy propriety rivalling Kent's Tunbridge Wells. His background was as solidly middle class as Mick's and his educational background almost identical. The son of a civil engineer, he had attended Cheltenham Grammar School, distinguishing himself both in class and at games, though hampered in the latter by chronic asthma. Both his parents being Welsh, and his mother a piano teacher to boot, he was instinctively musical, easily mastering the piano, recorder, clarinet and saxophone before he had left short trousers. He could pick up almost any instrument and, in a minute or two, coax some kind of tune from it.

Like Mick, he turned into a rebel against middle-class convention, but in his case the process was considerably more spectacular. At the age of sixteen, while still at Cheltenham Grammar, he fathered a child with a schoolgirl two years his junior. The episode devastated his upright Welsh parents, scandalised Cheltenham (especially sensitive to such issues because of its world-renowned 'Ladies' College'), and even reached Britain's main Sunday scandal sheet, the *News of the World*. After matters with the girl's family had been resolved and the baby given up for adoption, most young men would have learned an unforgettable lesson — but not this one. By the age of twenty he had sired two further children with different young women, each time failing to do the decent thing by marrying the mother and accepting responsibility for the child. Long before there were rock stars as we have come to know them — motivated only by music and self-gratification, oblivious to the trail of ruined lives in their wake — there was Brian Jones.

Leaving school with two more A-levels than Mick, he could easily have gone on to university, but instead drifted from one tedious office job to another while playing alto sax with a rock 'n' roll group (aptly named the Ramrods). He had met Alexis Korner in Cheltenham while Korner was still in the Chris Barber band; with Korner's encouragement he'd migrated to London soon afterwards, hotly pursued by the latest young woman he had got 'up the duff' with their baby son. In the meantime, he taught himself to play slide guitar well — brilliantly — enough for Korner to put him into the Blues Incorporated line-up at the Ealing Club.

He was only a little older than Mick and Keith, but seemed vastly more mature and sophisticated when they talked to him following his Elmore James imposture. As a guitarist, his rapport was initially with Keith. But Mick was equally impressed by his soft, lisping voice with no trace of West Country bumpkin; his super-chic clothes and hair; his knowledge of music across the whole spectrum from pop to jazz;

his surprising articulateness and literacy and wicked sense of humour; above all, his determination not to let his chaotic private life hinder him from, somehow or other, becoming a star.

Thereafter, when the Dartford boys drove to Ealing, they would make a lengthy detour to pick up Brian from his flat in Notting Hill Gate. He was supporting himself – and, to a minor extent, his girl-friend and third child – with day jobs in shops and department stores that usually ended when he was caught stealing from the cash register. Despite a seeming total lack of scruples, he had a knack of endearing himself to honest people with what Alexis Korner termed 'a beauti-ful mixture of politeness and rudeness'. Whereas Mick was merely a visitor to the Korners' flat – not always appreciated for his left-wing stridency and his patronising way of calling thirty-something Bobbie Korner 'Auntie Bobbie' – Brian treated the place virtually as a second home.

By now, the Ealing Club's open-mic policy had produced other young blues singers, all similarly white and bourgeois, to challenge the kid in the cardigan. Brian – who, despite his Welsh antecedents, did not possess a singing voice – worked as a guitar/vocal duo with a sometime Oxford University student named Paul Pond (later to find fame as Paul Jones with the Manfred Mann band and, still later, as an actor, musical comedy star and radio presenter). On some nights the vocal spot with Blues Incorporated would be given to 'Long' John Baldry, a hugely tall, sandy-haired former street busker whose father was a police officer in Colindale; on others it went to a long-faced Middlesex boy named Art Wood whose kid brother Ronnie was among the club's most devoted members, though not yet old enough to be served alcohol.

Occasionally, two or more vocalists at once took the stage in an implied talent contest that did not always seem to come out in the kid's favour. Both Paul Pond and Long John Baldry had more rec-ognisably 'soulful' voices, while Long John, towering over him in a shared rendition of Muddy Waters's 'Got My Mojo Workin'', brought his lack of inches into uncomfortable relief. Yet Mick was the vocal-ist Korner always preferred. The waspish Long John – openly gay at a time when few young Britons dared to be – dismissed him as 'all lips and ears . . . like a ventriloquist's dummy'.

Korner also began using Mick on Blues Incorporated gigs outside the club, paying him 'a pound or ten bob [fifty pence]' per show. Some of these were for débutante balls at posh London hotels or country houses, in Buckinghamshire or Essex, whose front gates had porters' lodges almost as big as the Jagger family home and front drives that seemed to go on forever. As far as Mick – or anyone in his social bracket – knew, the aristocracy had never taken the slightest interest in blues or R&B. But these young men in dinner jackets, Guards mess tunics or even kilts, proved as susceptible to Muddy, Elmore, T-Bone and Chuck as any back in proletarian Ealing; the girls might have double-barrelled surnames and horsey accents, but were no less putty in his hands when he threw his hair around. Despite the wealth all around, the gigs seldom earned him more than a few shillings – but at least he always got fed well.

The most memorable was a grand ball given by the youthful marquess of Londonderry at his ancestral home, Londonderry House in Park Lane, shortly before its demolition to make way for the new London Hilton Hotel. Among the guests was the future interior designer and super-socialite Nicky Haslam, then still a pupil at Eton. Though America's legendary Benny Goodman Orchestra was the main musical attraction, Blues Incorporated had an early-evening spot fronted, as Haslam's memoirs recall, 'by a hired-in singer . . . a skinny kid named Mick something'. Haslam's companion, the future magazine editor Min Hogg, later reported the skinny kid had been sure enough of himself to make overtures and even 'paw' at her strapless pink satin evening gown. From the ABC bakery to the upper crust: he had found the milieu where from now on he would be happiest.

THE EALING CLUB had started with just one hundred members; now, only two months later, it boasted more than eight hundred. When it was crowded to capacity, and beyond, the heat rivalled that of a similar subterranean space called the Cavern in far-off Liverpool. So much condensation dripped from the walls and ceiling that Korner had to hang a tarpaulin sheet over the stage canopy to stop the already precarious electrical connections from shorting out.

Korner's real triumph was a phone call from Harold Pendleton, manager of Soho's Marquee Club, who had so loftily banned the blues from his stage at the beginning of the year. Worried by the numbers who were defecting from the Marquee to Ealing Broadway – and by an upsurge of younger blues musicians in rival Soho clubs – Pendleton had undergone a rapid change of heart. It happened that in his weekly programme, the Thursday-night spot had fallen vacant. This he offered to Blues Incorporated, starting on 19 May.

There was, of course, no question of the band appearing without a regular vocalist as it had mostly done in Ealing. Korner wanted Mick but – atypically nice man that he was – hesitated to split up the band Mick still had with Keith. However, Keith was happy for his friend to jump at this big chance. 'I'll always remember how nice he was about it,' Bobbie Korner recalls. 'He said, "Mick really deserves this and I'm not going to stand in his way."'

Disc magazine made the announcement, a first droplet of newsprint oceans to come: 'Nineteen-year-old Dartford rhythm and blues singer Mick Jagger has joined the Alexis Korner group Blues Incorporated and will sing with them regularly on their Saturday dates in Ealing and at their Thursday sessions at the Marquee.'

Brian Jones was also heading for the West End. His stage partner Paul Pond, the vocalist he needed to set off his slide guitar riffs, had decided to resume studying at Oxford (and would do so until being recruited into Manfred Mann as Paul Jones). Korner's move back to Soho, taking Mick along, spurred Brian into forming a blues band of his own whose centre of gravity would be there rather than provincial Ealing. The fact that he was unknown in Soho did not deter him. He placed an ad in *Jazz News*, the most serious of all London's music trades, inviting prospective sidemen to audition in the upstairs function room of a pub called the White Bear, just off Leicester Square. When its

management caught him pilfering from the bar, he was forced to relo-
cate to another pub, the Bricklayers Arms on Broadwick Street.

His original plan had been to poach the two most talented members
of a well-regarded band called Blues by Six, lead guitarist Geoff Bradford
and vocalist Brian Knight. Soon after the move to the Bricklayers Arms,
however, Mick Jagger and Keith Richards turned up, accompanied by the
other most serious musician from the Blue Boys, Dick Taylor. There was
nothing to stop Mick singing with Brian's band as well as Blues Incorporated if he chose, but that spot already seemed to have been taken
by Brian Knight. Fortunately for him, the instrumental mix as it stood
simply did not work. Geoff Bradford wished only to play the authentic
blues of Muddy Waters and his ilk and was offended by Keith's Chuck
Berry licks — as well as nervous of Brian's kleptomania. After a couple of
practice sessions, Bradford bowed out, loyally accompanied by his friend
Knight, so leaving the way open for Mick and Keith.

The only other worthwhile recruit was a burly, pugnacious-looking
youth named Ian Stewart, a shipping clerk with the Imperial Chemical
Industries corporation who arrived unpromisingly wearing too-brief
leather cycling shorts and munching a pork pie, but who could play stride
and barrelhouse piano as if he'd grown up around the New Orleans
bordellos rather than in Ewell, Surrey. Just as appealing were his plain-
spoken manner, dry wit and refusal to show his prospective bandmates
the slightest reverence. 'Stu' was not only welcomed into the line-up but
recognised as a natural friend and ally even by the cautious Mick — in
his case, perhaps the only one who would always talk to him as an equal,
refuse to flatter him and be unafraid to tell him the truth.

Brian had now filled every spot in his blues band except that of
drummer. It was the vital ingredient for any kind of 'beat' music, marking out the serious from the strum-along amateur. Drummers tended
to be slightly older men with daytime jobs well paid enough for them to
afford the £60 which a new professional kit could cost. Even mediocre
players were as sought after as plumbers during burst pipe season and
could take their pick from among the best Trad or rock 'n' roll bands.
Although Soho had a whole street of drummers for hire (Archer Street,

where pro and semi-pro musicians congregated seeking work), none was likely to be tempted by a gaggle of young blues apostles without money, management or prospects. The Bricklayers Arms auditions did produce one promising candidate in Mick Avory, who sat in with the line-up a couple of times and seemed to fit in well enough. But he could see no future in playing behind this other Mick, and refused to commit himself permanently.

There was also the question of what to name the band. Brian, whose prerogative it was, had endlessly agonised about it, rejecting all suggestions from Mick and Keith while thinking of nothing suitable himself. The problem was only resolved when he decided to advertise for gigs in *Jazz News* and had to come up with a name while dictating the small ad over the telephone. His impromptu choice of 'the Rolling Stones' was a further debt to Muddy Waters – not only Waters's 1950 song 'Rollin' Stone' but a lesser-known EP track, 'Mannish Boy', which includes the line 'Oh, I'm a rollin' stone.'

To British ears it was an odd choice, less evocative of a blues master's raunchy potted autobiography than of the sententious proverb recommending stagnation over adventure: 'A rolling stone gathers no moss.' Mick, Keith, Stu and Dick all protested that it made them sound halfway between a classical string quartet and an Irish show band, but the die was cast – and, after all, it *was* Brian's group.

Their big break was the end result of a rather brutal slap in the face for Mick. Alexis Korner's success at the Marquee Club had by now not only galvanised Soho but come to the notice of the British Broadcasting Corporation in Portland Place, three-quarters of a mile to the north. As a result, completing Korner's sense of vindication, Blues Incorporated were offered a live appearance on BBC radio's Thursday night *Jazz Club* programme on 12 July. It was an opportunity not to be missed, even though it clashed with the band's regular weekly show at the Marquee. So as not to disappoint their club audience, Long John Baldry, the Ealing Club's queenly blond giant, was lined up to deputise for them.

For this hugely important exposure on national radio, Korner did not want Mick to be his band's sole vocalist but to perform in alternation with Art Wood, elder brother of the still-unknown school-boy Ronnie. However, the parsimonious BBC would not pay for two singers on top of five instrumentalists. So Korner, figuring that Mick's appeal was more visual than vocal, and thus of doubtful impact on radio, decided to drop him in favour of Art Wood. (In the end Art did not appear either, and the vocals were left to Cyril Davis.)

As a consolation prize for Mick, Korner arranged that the band in which he'd been moonlighting should play their first-ever gig on the same night as the broadcast, filling the Marquee's intermission spot between Long John Baldry's sets for a £20 fee. They even received a mention in *Jazz News*'s preview section, on equal terms with all Soho's most illustrious jazz names, Chris Barber, Ken Colyer and the like.

By rights, the paper should have sought details from the loquacious and articulate Brian, but instead, because of the Korner connection, it contacted Mick. Consequently, he rather than Brian seemed like the leader of the band as he listed its personnel and showed a twinge of unease lest its new name should offend the Marquee's purist blues audi-ence. Brian, for some reason, had decided to revert to his slide-guitar alter ego for the occasion, so was not even identified: 'Mick Jagger, R&B vocalist, is taking a rhythm and blues group into the Marquee tomor-row night while Blues Inc. is doing its Jazz Club gig. Called "The Rolling Stones" ["I hope they don't think we're a rock 'n' roll outfit," said Mick], the line-up is: Jagger (vocals), Keith Richards, Elmo Lewis (guitars), Dick Taylor (bass), "Stu" (piano) and Mick Avory (drums).'

So that night of 12 July 1962, under the pink-and-white canvas awning of the Marquee stage, Mick sang with the Rolling Stones for the very first time. To set off his cord trousers, he wore a horizontally striped matelot jersey, common enough among young men in the South of France but in London chiefly identified with girls or sexually ambigu-ous 'chorus boys' in West End musicals. As blues-singing attire, it was as daring as the white frilly dress he would select for an open-air show at the other end of Oxford Street seven years later.

The hour-long set consisted mostly of irreproachable blues and R&B standards by Jimmy Reed, Elmore James and Billy Boy Arnold, with the odd Chuck Berry like 'Down the Road Apiece' and 'Back in the USA' ('New York, Los Angeles, oh, how I yearn for you . . .'). As Mick Avory did not, after all, play drums that night, the sound had considerably less attack than usual. Even so, many hard-core blues Marqueesards could not dissociate the word *stones* from *rock;* the applause was muted and at times almost drowned by whistles and boos.

Among the crowd that night was Charlie Watts, the drummer who occasionally played for Blues Incorporated but more regularly for Blues by Six, the band that was supposed to have given the Rolling Stones both a lead guitarist and a vocalist. Charlie was the epitome of the superior drummer class, immaculately dressed and barbered, with the almost tragically serious face of a latter-day Buster Keaton. True to form, he showed no outward emotion as the stripe-jerseyed figure onstage blew the 'harp' passages in Jimmy Reed's 'Bright Lights, Big City' as if it were an erotic rite rather than a religious one. But, as he would recall, the highly esteemed blues and jazz musicians of his acquaintanceship all suddenly seemed like 'eccentric old men' compared with Mick.

Afterwards, collecting their £4 apiece (enough in these days to buy three LPs, dinner for two at an Angus Steakhouse or a pair of boots from the modish Regent Shoe store), Brian, Mick, Keith, Dick and Stu felt they had connected with the Marquee crowd at least enough to be offered further regular work there. But Harold Pendleton still considered them to be infected with rock 'n' roll virus, if not in their repertoire then in the energy of their sound and the body language and flying hair of their front man. He would use them only as an interval band and with the worst possible grace, muttering that they were 'bloody rockers' and their R&B idols were 'rubbish'.

Brian's adverts in *Jazz News* and ceaseless touting for work brought a few gigs at other Soho clubs in transition from jazz to blues: the Piccadilly, Ken Colyer's Studio 51 and the Flamingo in Wardour Street – the latter attracting a mainly black clientele, made up of West Indian immigrants and American servicemen. Here, it took real nerve for a white teenager to walk in and buy a drink, let alone get onstage and sing a Muddy Waters song, especially the way Mick did it.

Whereas Little Boy Blue and the Blue Boys used to shrink away from gigs, the Rolling Stones under Brian were positive gluttons for work. When Soho could not provide enough, they lit out for the suburbs once again, travelling in an old van that belonged to Ian Stewart – and trimming their name of its g to make the roll sound smoother. Following Ealing's example, quiet Thames-side boroughs like Twickenham and Sutton also now had thriving blues clubs, in local church halls or bucolic pubs whose loudest sound had once been ducks on the river. In places where no club yet existed, the band would create their own ad hoc one, renting the hall or pub back room for a Saturday or Sunday night, putting up posters and handing out flyers: 'Rhythm 'n' blues with the Rollin' Stones, four shillings [20p]'.

At this stage, Mick's organisational talents were not much to the fore: Stu acted as driver and roadie and Brian was the self-appointed leader and manager (in which capacities he would secretly negotiate an extra payment from promoters or just take it when they were handling the money themselves).

While rehearsing at the Bricklayers Arms, they had taken an informal oath to keep their music pure and never 'sell out' to any commercial agent or record label should the possibility arise. But this resolution did not last long. Early in October, once again chivvied on by Brian, they went to Curly Clayton's recording studios in Highbury, close to the Arsenal football ground, and recorded a three-track demo consisting of Jimmy Reed's 'Close Together', Bo Diddley's 'You Can't Judge a Book by Its Cover' and (despite its fate-tempting potential) Muddy Waters's 'Soon Forgotten'.

The demo was sent first to the huge EMI organisation, owner of prestigious labels such as Columbia and HMV, which returned it without comment. Undaunted, Brian tried Britain's other main label, Decca, and this time at least received some feedback with the rejection: 'A great band,' Decca's letter said, 'but you'll never get anywhere with that singer.'

CHAPTER THREE

'Very Bright, Highly Motivated Layabouts'

The Rollin' Stones' far-flung work schedule was making it increasingly hard for Mick to get back to his own bed in Dartford each night. Besides, at nineteen he was too old to be ordered to do washing up or weight training any longer. So in the autumn of 1962 he left his spotless, well-regulated home and moved up to London to share a flat with Brian Jones at number 102 Edith Grove in the World's End district of Chelsea. Originally, the *ménage* also included Brian's girlfriend, Pat Andrews, and their toddler son, Julian, but after a few days Pat and Julian departed without explanation, and Keith Richards moved in instead.

Chelsea at this time was a backwater whose days as a resort of hard-drinking, drug-taking artists and bohemians seemed long gone. Situated at the western extremity of King's Road, on the frontier with romance-free Fulham, World's End was a sleepy area of still mainly working-class homes, shops, cafés and pubs. Edith Grove ranked as perhaps its least attractive thoroughfare, terraced by shabby mid-Victorian houses with pilastered front porches, and shaken by traffic to and from Knightsbridge and the West End.

The flat, which came already furnished, was on the first floor of number 102. The rent was £16 per week excluding electricity, which had to be paid for as it was used by inserting one-shilling coins into a battleship-grey iron meter. Mick shared the only designated bedroom with Keith, while Brian slept on a divan in the living room. There was an antiquated bathroom with a chipped and discoloured tub and basin and taps that yielded a reluctant, rusty dribble. The only toilet was a communal one on the floor below.

Deeply unattractive to begin with, the place quickly descended into epic squalor that would later be unwittingly re-created in the classic British film *Withnail and I*. Beds stayed permanently unmade; the kitchen sink overflowed with dirty dishes and empty milk bottles encrusted with mould. The ceilings were blackened by candle smoke and covered with drawings and graffiti, while the windows were so thick with grime that casual visitors thought they had heavy curtains, permanently closed. When an extra flatmate materialised in a young printer named James Phelge, his surname proved curiously anagrammatic: he won the others' approval by his skill at 'gobbing', or spitting gobbets of phlegm up the wall to form a horrible pattern in lieu of wallpaper.

It might be wondered how the famously fastidious Mick could ever have endured such conditions. But in most nineteen-year-olds, the urge to react against parental values tends to be overwhelming. There was also the sense of roughing it like a real bluesman, even though few of these might have been spotted in the vicinity of Chelsea's Kings Road. Besides, while enthusiastically joining in the trashing of the flat, he was never personally squalid but – like Brian – remained conspicuously neat and well groomed, just as young officers in the Great War kept their buttons bright amid Flanders mud. Brian somehow managed to wash and dry his fair hair every single day, while Mick (so Keith would later recall in one of their recurrent periods of mutual bitchiness) went through 'his first camp period . . . wandering around in a blue linen housecoat . . . He was on that kick for about six months.'

All of them were in a state of dire poverty which the few pounds from Rollin' Stones gigs barely alleviated. Brian had just lost yet another job, as a sales assistant at Whiteley's department store, for thievery, while Keith's only known shot at conventional employment, as a pre-Christmas relief postal worker, lasted just one day. The sole regular income among them was Mick's student grant from Kent County Council; as the only one with a bank account, he paid the rent by cheque and the others gave him their share in cash. Once, he jokingly wrote on a blank cheque: 'Pay the Rolling [*sic*] Stones £1 million.'

He and Keith survived mainly by adopting Brian's little ways – stealing the pints of milk that were left on other people's doorsteps each morning, shoplifting potatoes and eggs from the little local stores, sneaking into parties being given elsewhere in the house or in neighbouring ones, and making off with French loaves, hunks of cheese, bottles of wine or beer in the new outsize cans known as 'pins'. Brian doctored the electric meter (a criminal offence) so that it would work without shillings and the power would remain on indefinitely, rather than plunging them into darkness at the end of the usual costly brief span. A serious source of income was collecting empty beer bottles, the sale price of which included a two-penny deposit repaid when they were returned to the vendor.

Ian Stewart also played a part in supporting the trio he regarded as 'very bright, highly motivated layabouts'. In Stu's day job at ICI the perks included luncheon vouchers: certificates exchangeable for basic restaurant meals. These he would buy up cheap from dieting co-workers and pass on gratis to the layabouts. However, Mick, who had always been notably fond of his stomach (as if those large lips needed stoking with food twice as often as normal-size ones) would frequently eat alone and at a slightly higher level than his flatmates. There was, for instance, a Wardour Street café, felicitously named the Star, which offered a superior set lunch for five shillings (twenty-five pence). Mick was a regular customer, known to staff only as 'the rhythm-and-blues singer'.

Each morning, he would go off to LSE, and the non-musician flatmate James Phelge to a printing works in Fulham, leaving Keith and

Brian to sleep late between their foetid sheets. Their afternoons were spent mainly in guitar practice, with Brian coaching Keith. Often after a gig, the teacher would tell the pupil his playing had been 'bloody awful' and, back at the flat, would make him go over his fretboard fluffs again and again until they were cured. Many was the night when the pair fell asleep where they sat, cigarettes still smouldering in their mouths or wedged in the top of their guitar fretboards. Brian also taught himself to play blues harp, taking only about a day to reach a level that had taken Mick months, then forging on ahead.

It clearly could only benefit the band, and Brian was equally willing to help bring on Mick's instrumental skills, showing him new harmonica riffs, even persuading him finally to take a few cautious steps on guitar. But Mick felt uneasy about the bond being forged between Brian and Keith during the day. In the evening when he returned he would sulk or pointedly not speak to Keith while showing overweening friendliness to Brian.

As well as immeasurably raising the others' musical game, Brian kept them laughing when there might not seem much to laugh about. Like Jim Dixon in Kingsley Amis's *Lucky Jim,* his response to moments of stress was to pull a grotesque face he called a Nanker. The flat's walls being now spattered with the marks of Phelge's 'gobbing', Brian gave each a name according to its colour – 'Yellow Humphrey', 'Green Gilbert', 'Scarlet Jenkins', 'Polka-Dot Perkins'. He and Mick competed in coining supercilious nicknames for their fellow World's Enders. Their flat was owned by a Welshman who operated a small grocery shop, so a Lyons Individual Fruit Pie bought (or filched) from him was known as a 'Morgan Morgan'. Any male conspicuously devoid of their own cool and *savoir faire* was an 'Ernie'. The local greasy-spoon café – whose clientele marked them down at once as gays, or 'nancy boys' – was The Ernie. The flat above theirs belonged to a hostile elderly couple known as 'the Offers' after Mick described them as 'a bit off'. Brian discovered where the Offers kept a spare latchkey and, one day while they were out, led a raiding party into their flat to ransack the fridge.

Despite their poverty, Mick, Brian and Keith managed to make the two-hundred-mile journey north to Manchester that October for what was billed as 'the First American Folk-Blues Festival', featuring Memphis Slim, John Lee Hooker, T-Bone Walker, Willie Dixon, and Sonny Terry and Brownie McGhee. The trio made the long trip north in a beaten-up van with a group of fellow fanatics from Ealing and Eel Pie Island (including a boy guitarist named Jimmy Page, one day to become the co-godhead of Led Zeppelin). Mick took along a copy of Howlin' Wolf's *Rocking Chair* album, hoping that Wolf's songwriter Willie Dixon would autograph it. One track in particular obsessed him: a flagrant piece of sexual imagery entitled 'Little Red Rooster'.

Amid the Victorian splendour of Manchester's Free Trade Hall, he saw all his greatest idols finally made flesh: tall, austere John Lee Hooker singing 'Boogie Chillen'', the song that could have been describing that former well-spoken Dartford schoolboy ('The blues is in him . . . and it's *got* to come out'); dapper Memphis Slim with a skunk's-tail streak of white through his hair; Willie Dixon, the blues' great backroom boy, almost as big and bulky as his stand-up bass; jokey T-Bone Walker, playing his guitar behind his head in the way Jimi Hendrix would 'invent' a few years later. There was no security in the modern sense, and afterwards the bluesmen were freely accessible to their fans, onstage below the hall's massive pipe organ. One of the lesser names, 'Shaky Jake' Harris, presented the London boys with a harmonica, which became the proud centrepiece of a blues singsong on the long drive home. Mick, Keith and Brian were supposed to reimburse the van's owner, Graham Ackers, for petrol and other incidental costs – amounting to 10s 6d, or about 52p each – but never did.

If the Rollin' Stones' gigs still paid only peanuts, there was another reward which their blues masters in Manchester had never known. Increasingly, after the night's performance, they found themselves being mobbed by teenage girls, whose excitement their faithful interpretation of John Lee or T-Bone only partially explained. Most sought only autographs and flirtation, but a good few made it clear – clearer than young British women had done since the bawdy eighteenth century – that a deeper level of musical appreciation was on offer. Though

Mick and Brian were the main objectives, Keith, Stu, Dick Taylor, even Phelge, as their occasional assistant roadie, shared in the unexpected dividends. Most nights, a bevy of these proto-groupies would accompany them back to 102 Edith Grove for what, due to space restrictions, was a largely open-plan sex session. Some were deemed worthy of a second invitation, for example a pair of identical twins named Sandy and Sarah partial to Mick and Phelge – neither of whom could tell one from the other, or bothered to try.

He would later become legendary for his apparent callousness towards females – yet among the Edith Grove flatmates it was Mick who showed the most awareness of how young and often vulnerable many of their visitors were to be with older men so late at night. One girl, after having had sex with two of his flatmates in succession, broke the news that she'd run away from home and the police were looking for her. The others were all for getting rid of her as soon as possible, before police officers came knocking at the door. But Mick, showing himself his father's son once again, took the trouble to talk to the runaway at length about her problems at home, finally persuading her to telephone her parents and arrange for them to come and collect her.

THE WINTER OF 1962–3 turned into Britain's worst for one hundred years, with arctic temperatures setting in long before Christmas and London hit as heavily by snow as the remotest Scottish Highlands. At 102 Edith Grove, it was almost as cold inside as out. Mick could escape to centrally heated lecture theatres and libraries at LSE, but Brian and Keith had to spend all day huddled over one feeble electric fire in skimpy 'shorty' overcoats, rubbing their hands and blowing their fingernails like penurious Dickensian clerks. The household was further enlarged by a Cheltenham friend of Brian's named Richard Hattrell, a simple soul who did everything Brian told him and believed everything he said. One night when the Stones were out on a gig, Hattrell crept into Brian's bed to snatch a little warmth and rest. Brian awoke him, brandishing two amplifier leads and threatening to electrocute him. The credulous Hattrell fled into the snow wearing only underpants. Not until he started to turn blue from exposure would the others let him back inside.

At the end of each week, Mick, Brian and Keith bought, borrowed or stole the music trades and scanned the pop charts, never thinking for one second they might ever figure there. America's immemorial dominance was maintained by white solo singers like Neil Sedaka, Roy Orbison and Del Shannon. Black artists scored mainly by pandering to the white audience, as in novelty dance numbers like Chubby Checker's 'Let's Twist Again' and Little Eva's 'The Locomotion'. Britain seemed capable of producing only limp cover versions and wildly uncool Trad jazz. The one exception was an oddball minor hit called 'Love Me Do' by a Liverpool group with funny, fringed haircuts and the almost suicidally bizarre name of the Beatles. Rather than the usual slick studio arrangement, it had a rough R&B feel, with harmonica riffs very much like those Brian and Mick played in the clubs every night. They felt like their pockets had been picked by these insectoid upstarts from the unknown far north.

In October, Dick Taylor, the last of Mick's old school friends still playing with him, had won a place at the Royal College of Art and decided to leave the band. There was some idea that Richard Hattrell might take over on bass guitar, but a course of lessons with their Ealing Club colleague Jack Bruce showed Hattrell to be totally unmusical. He returned to Tewkesbury and, worn down by his life with the Stones (a syndrome to be oft-repeated in the future) suffered a burst appendix and almost died. At the same time, their latest temporary drummer, Carlo Little, moved on to a better gig with Screaming Lord Sutch's backing band, the Savages. There were thus two vacancies to be filled, this time with Mick and Keith as Brian's co-judges. Auditions took place on a cold, slushy December day at a Chelsea pub called the Wetherby Arms.

The first spot was quickly filled by Tony Chapman, an experienced drummer with a successful semi-pro band called the Cliftons, who'd become bored by their conventional rock repertoire. Having got the gig, Chapman suggested that the Cliftons' bass guitarist should also come and audition at the Wetherby Arms. He was a hollow-cheeked, unsmiling Londoner, even shorter and bonier than Mick, who held his instrument at an odd near-vertical angle. He had been born William Perks but used the stage name Bill Wyman.

Here, the fit seemed more problematic. At twenty-six, Bill was seven years older than Mick and Keith, a married man with a small son and steady day job on the maintenance staff of a department store. Furthermore, he lived in Penge, a name which British sophisticates find eternally amusing, along with Neasden, Wigan and Scunthorpe. Added to his seeming advanced age, archaic backswept hairstyle and south London accent, it instantly condemned him in Mick and Brian's eyes as an Offer and an Ernie. He possessed one major saving grace, however, in the form of a spare amplifier, roughly twice as powerful as the band's existing ones, which he told them they were free to use. So, notwithstanding the satirical nudges and Nanker grimaces of the ex-grammar school duo behind his back, working-class Wyman was in.

He for his part had serious misgivings about joining a group of scruffy arty types so much his junior – especially after seeing their domestic arrangements. '[The flat] was an absolute pit which I shall never forget – it looked like it was bomb-damaged,' he would recall. 'The front room overlooking the street had a double bed with rubbish piled all round it [and] I've never seen a kitchen like it . . . permanently piled high with dirty dishes and filth everywhere . . . I could never understand why they carried on like this . . . It could not just have been the lack of money. Bohemian angst most likely.'

Despite having left school at the age of sixteen, Bill was just as intelligent and articulate as Mick or Brian. He soon realised that although the Rollin' Stones might not be going anywhere in particular, their singer definitely was – if not necessarily in music. While Keith merely seemed like 'a Teddy Boy who'd spit in his beer to ensure nobody drank it' and had 'no plans to work', and Brian regarded music as an irreplaceable vocation, Mick talked often of becoming a lawyer or perhaps a journalist, as the LSE graduate Bernard Levin had done with spectacular success. At times, he did not even seem quite comfortable with his new first name. 'He *hated* being called Mick,' Bill remembers. 'In his own eyes he was still Mike.'

He was keeping up his LSE studies despite the late nights and distractions, and that previous June had sat part one of his BSc degree, achieving just-respectable C grades in the compulsory subjects of economics, economic history and British government and the optional ones of political history and English legal institutions. Behind the mask of coolness and indifference, he worried that he was not making the most of his opportunities or justifying the investment that Kent County Council had made in him. His vague hankering for some kind of literary career was sharpened, that autumn, when his father became the Jagger family's first published author. As the country's leading authority on the sport, Joe edited and partially wrote a manual entitled *Basketball Coaching and Playing* in a series of how-to books issued by the prestigious house of Faber & Faber (which Mick's fellow economics student Matthew Evans would one day run). B. Jagger's opening chapter, 'The Basketball Coach', written in simple but forceful prose, set out principles his son would later employ in a somewhat different context. The successful coach, wrote B. Jagger, 'must definitely possess . . . a sense of vocation, a dedication to the game, faith in his own ability, knowledge and enthusiasm'. Without these qualities, the team would be 'an ordinary run-of-the-mill affair, rising to no great heights and probably keeping warm the lower half of some league table . . .' The coach must train himself to develop 'a keen analytical sense' and view each game as 'an endless succession of tactics' dictated solely by him. 'The players are for the whole time examples of [his] skill and ability . . . He must quickly eradicate weaknesses and use to the full the strong points of his players . . .'

The greatest pressure on Mick, as always, came from his mother. Eva Jagger still could not take his singing seriously, and protested with all her considerable might at its deleterious effect on his studies – and the high-level professional career that was supposed to follow. The Edith Grove flat so appalled her that she couldn't bear to set foot inside it (unlike Keith's down-to-earth mum, who came in regularly to give it a good clean-up). When Mick remained obdurate about continuing with the Stones, Eva telephoned Alexis Korner and in her forthright way demanded whether 'Michael', as she firmly continued to call him, really was anything special as a singer. Korner replied that he most definitely was. The unexpectedly public-school voice at the other end of the line pacified Eva but still did not convince her.

At LSE, Mick's absences from lectures and tutorials were becoming more frequent, his need to copy fellow student Laurence Isaacson's notes more urgent. Though only dimly aware of his other life with the Rollin' Stones, Isaacson could not but notice the changes coming over that once-typical middle-class student. 'He was still very quiet and unobtrusive when he did appear at college. But one day when he turned up, he'd had his hair streaked. He was the first bloke I ever knew who did that.'

WHEN CLEOPATRA SYLVESTRE caught Mick's eye at the Marquee Club, she was seventeen and still attending Camden School for Girls. The paradox of these clubs dedicated to black music was that very few actual black people frequented them – and those who did tended to be predominantly male. More often than not, Cleo would find herself the only young black woman in the Marquee's audience. Anyway, she was an eye-catcher: tall and lovely in an American rather than British or Caribbean way, and always wearing something outrageous like a pink leather miniskirt she had made for herself, or a bright orange wig.

Though she lived in a council flat in Euston, Cleo's background was richly cosmopolitan. Her mother, Laureen Goodare, a well-known West End cabaret dancer during the Second World War, had had a long-time affair with the composer Constant Lambert. Her godfathers were Lambert and the MP, journalist and notorious homosexual Tom Driberg. Her close friend and frequent companion around the blues clubs was Judith Bronowski, daughter of the mathematician, biologist and television pundit Dr Jacob Bronowski.

Cleo had first seen Mick when he was still with Blues Incorporated;

he would smile and say hello, but it wasn't until after the Rollin' Stones started that he came over and spoke to her. Still experimenting with their sound and look, the band had thought of using black female back-up singers like Ray Charles's Raelettes and Ike and Tina Turner's Ikettes. Mick asked Cleo if she could find two black friends and audition as a backing trio, to be known as the Honeybees.

The audition, at the Wetherby Arms pub in Chelsea, was a disaster. Cleo could find only one other candidate for the trio, a clubbing companion named Jean who proved to be tone-deaf. Though Cleo herself had a good voice, the idea of a nine-strong, mixed-race-and-gender Rollin' Stones progressed no further. But from then on she became a special friend to the band and, increasingly, a very special one to Mick.

She and Jean were their most faithful followers – *groupies* would be too crude – trailing them from places they now easily packed, like the Ealing Club, to those where they still struggled against anti-rock 'n' roll prejudice, like Ken Colyer's Studio 51 Club in Great Newport Street. 'Sometimes when they played to only about nine people, Brian would literally be in tears,' Cleo recalls. 'But Mick was always the optimistic one, who said they had to keep going and they'd win everyone over in the end.'

She and Mick began dating with all the conventionality – and chasteness – that word used to imply, during the brief intervals between his college hours, her school ones and the Stones' nightlife. 'We'd go to the cinema,' Cleo remembers. 'Once, Mick got tickets for the theatre, but for some reason we never made it there. He rang me up one day and asked me to join Keith and him in a boat on the lake in Regent's Park. A few times, I met him at LSE, where he used to work in the library.' Unluckily, she already had a boyfriend, who could not but know what was going on since he shared a flat with Mick's sometime stage colleague, Long John Baldry. Their break-up was an early example of the threat Mick would later pose to so many men's masculinity. When Cleo went to her ex's flat to collect some records she'd left there, he was pressing clothes on an ironing board. He thrust the hot iron into her face so it burned her forehead, and hissed, 'When you next see Mick, give him that for me.'

Cleo was formidably bright as well as beautiful, and remembers 'quite heavy' discussions with Mick about politics and current affairs. He even suggested that when she left school, as she was soon to do, she should try to get into LSE so that they could see more of each other. She remembers his sense of humour and love of mimicking people, like the West Indian staff on the Underground shouting 'Mind the doors!' 'Bill Wyman had just joined the band, and Mick used to laugh about him coming from Penge.' The later stories of his stinginess are baffling to Cleo. 'He was always so generous to me. Once, he bought me a huge box of chocolates that he'd spent all his money on, even his bus fare, so he had to walk all the way home to Chelsea.'

He was also welcomed into the Euston council flat where Cleo lived with her mother, Laureen, the Blitz-era cabaret dancer, and their fluffy black-and-white cat. 'My mum thought he was great, even though the neighbours used to mutter about his long hair. I'd come home to find the two of them nattering away together. Mick used to practise his stage moves in front of our mirror.' Cleo, on the other hand, paid only fleeting visits to 102 Edith Grove – and never stayed overnight. Her main memory of his domicile is 'trying to scrape the laboratory cultures out of the milk bottles'.

Cleo's home became a refuge for the whole band, with Brian making himself at home in his usual way and competing with Mick for the fascinating Laureen's attention. 'Brian used to love having our cat on his knees and stroking it,' Cleo recalls. 'When he left, his velvet suit used to be covered in white hairs, so my mum would run the Hoover over him as he stood there. One morning after an all-nighter, I took Mick and Brian back to our place for breakfast and my friend took Keith to hers. But my friend's dad was a Nigerian and a bit militant. He said, "Get outa my house, white man," took a spear down from the wall, and chased Keith with it.'

Chronically hard up as they were, the Rollin' Stones never turned down any job, however low-paying and hard to reach through the snow and slush. One night their Marquee audience included a Hornsey School of Art student named Gillian Wilson (in later life to become curator of the Getty Museum in California). 'At the interval,' she recalls, 'I went up to this character with outsize lips and asked if they'd play at our Christmas dance. "'Ow much?" he said. I offered fifteen bob [seventy-five pence] each and Mick – though I didn't know his name then – said "Okay."'

The Stones' performance at Hornsey School of Art – which Gillian Wilson remembers lasting 'something like four hours' – featured yet another drummer. Tony Chapman had gone and Charlie Watts, the dapper jazz buff with the Buster Keaton face, had yielded to Brian and Mick's pleas and joined what he still regarded as just an 'interval band' (leaving a vacancy in Blues Incorporated that was filled by a carroty-haired wild man named Ginger Baker). Despite his large wardrobe and impressive day job with a West End advertising agency, Charlie still lived at home with his parents in a 'prefab' rented from the local council in Wembley, Middlesex. With Bill Wyman on bass, this made the rhythm section solidly working class, in contrast with the middle-class, upwardly mobile tendency of the two main front men. At the time such things seemed of small importance compared with scoring an extra amp and a drum kit.

From that grim British winter, too, emerged another of the exotic non- or half-Britishers to whom the Stones – Mick especially – would owe so much. In January 1963, the suppliers of blues music to unwary outer London suburbs were joined by Giorgio Gomelsky, a black-bearded twenty-nine-year-old of mixed Russian and Monegasque parentage, brought up in Syria, Italy and Egypt and educated in Switzerland. By vocation a filmmaker, blues-addicted Gomelsky had managed various Soho music clubs as a sideline but, like Alexis Korner before him, had wearied of the jazz lobby's hostility and decided to seek a new public farther up the Thames. With Ealing already taken, Gomelsky targeted Richmond, where a pub called the Station Hotel had a large, mirror-lined back room for dinners and Masonic functions. This he rented for a Sunday-night blues club named (after a Bo Diddley song) the Crawdaddy.

Gomelsky never intended to give a home to the Rollin' Stones, whom he had seen die the death in front of about eighteen people when he ran the Piccadilly Jazz Club back in central London. The Crawdaddy's original resident attraction were the, to his mind, far more competent and reliable Dave Hunt Rhythm & Blues Band (featuring Ray Davies, later of the Kinks). But one Sunday, Hunt's musicians could not make it through the snow and Gomelsky, yielding to Brian Jones's entreaties, gave the Stones a shot instead. Their fee was £1 each, plus a share of the gate. So few people turned up that Gomelsky had to go into the adjacent pub and recruit extra heads by offering free admission.

In the event, they astounded Gomelsky, who was expecting the same 'abominable' performance he had witnessed at the Piccadilly. Their saturnine new drummer and chilly-looking new bass player seemed to have had a transforming effect; while still evangelising for Jimmy Reed and Muddy Waters, their style was no longer reverential but brash, aggressive, even provocative. Indeed, their two principal members now offered contrasting studies in how simultaneously to delight and goad an audience – Brian, barely moving but staring fixedly from under his fringe as if ogling every female and challenging every male in the room; Mick, mincing and head tossing in his off-the-shoulder matelot-striped sweater and new white Anello & Davide boots.

Gomelsky did not make them give back the spot to the Dave Hunt band. And from then on, Richmond on Sunday nights ceased to be a silent zone of shuttered shops and winking traffic lights. Early-sixties teenagers were desperately short of Sabbath amusements; consequently, the hundreds that descended on the Station Hotel were not just blues enthusiasts but of every musical and stylistic allegiance: 'Rockers' in black leather and motorcycle boots; 'Mods' in striped Italian jackets and rakish trilby hats; jazzers in chunky knits; beatniks in polo necks; rich kids from opulent riverside villas and mansion blocks; poor kids from back streets and council estates; and always girls, girls and more girls, with hairstyles across the board, from bob to beehive. As they streamed through the nondescript pub into its red-spotlit rear annexe, they shed factionalism with their winter coats and simply became Stones fans.

The club closed at ten-thirty, the same time as the pub, but by then the glasses in the nearby bars would literally be shaking. From the start, Gomelsky encouraged his members to forget the usual restraint of blues worship and to express themselves as uninhibitedly as Mick did onstage. A special Crawdaddy dance evolved, based on the Twist and Hully Gully, where partners were not needed (in fact were superfluous) and males rather than females competed for attention, wagging their heads and hips Jaggerishly or leaping up and down on the spot in a punk-rock Pogo fourteen years too early. The finale, in which everyone joined, was two Bo Diddley songs, 'Do the Crawdaddy' and 'Pretty Thing', spun out to twenty minutes or more and floor-stompingly loud enough to wake the Tudor ghosts at Hampton Court Palace across the river. Yet, for now at least, excitement never turned into violence or destruction. The Stones in this glass house left it completely unscathed, the multi-mirrored walls suffering not even a crack.

Returning to his first love, Gomelsky began shooting a 35mm film of the Stones onstage at the Crawdaddy and, partly as a source of extra footage, arranged for them to cut further demos at a recording studio in Morden. During this era, according to rock folklore, a demo tape was sent to *Saturday Club,* BBC radio's main pop music programme, which responded that the band was acceptable but not the singer, as he sounded 'too coloured'. However, the show's host, Brian Matthew – still broadcasting in the twenty-first-century – denies ever having been party to such a judgement; in any case, the whole point about Mick's voice was that it *didn't* sound 'coloured'.

Their only other contact with the recording industry was a friend of Ian Stewart's named Glyn Johns, who worked for a small independent studio called IBC in Portland Place, owned by the BBC orchestra leader Eric Robinson. Johns was allowed to record any musicians he thought promising, and at his invitation the Stones taped five numbers from their stage act at IBC. In return, he received a six-month option to try to sell the demo tape to a major label.

Giorgio Gomelsky became the band's de facto manager yet, with extraordinary selflessness, never tried to put them under contract or even keep them all to himself. Continuing the fishy theme ('crawdaddy' is Deep Southern slang for crayfish or langoustine), they also began playing regularly on Eel Pie Island, situated on a broad stretch of the Thames at Twickenham. The island's main feature was a dilapidated grand hotel with a ballroom whose sprung wooden floor had been famous in the Charleston and Black Bottom era. Here, a local antiques dealer now put on weekend blues marathons, featuring the Stones in rotation with other superstars of the future, then unrecognisable as such. They included a Kingston Art College reject named Eric Clapton – at this stage so nervous that he could only play guitar sitting down – and a raspy-voiced trainee gravedigger from north London named Rod Stewart.

Gomelsky, besides, had other fish to fry. One of early 1963's few talking points outside of the weather was that eccentrically barbered Liverpool band the Beatles, who had followed their mediocre début single with a smash hit, 'Please Please Me', and were whipping up teenage hysteria unknown since the early days of Elvis Presley. Gomelsky had first seen them playing seedy clubs in Hamburg a couple of years previously, and even then had thought them something way out of the ordinary. When 'Please Please Me' became a hit, he approached their manager, Brian Epstein, with the idea of making a documentary film about them.

Though the film proposal fell through, Gomelsky grew friendly enough with the Beatles to get them out to the Crawdaddy one Sunday night when the Rollin' Stones were playing. Despite the enormous difference in their status, the Liverpudlians and the southern boys immediately hit it off – and, surprisingly, discovered musical roots in common. The Beatles had played American R&B cover versions for years before John Lennon and Paul McCartney began writing original songs; they had also been just as edgy and aggressive as the Stones onstage before Epstein put them into matching shiny suits and made them bow and smile. Lennon, never comfortable about paying this price for success, appeared positively envious of the freedom Mick, Brian and Keith enjoyed as nobodies.

Later, the Beatles visited 102 Edith Grove, pronouncing it almost palatial compared with their own former living conditions behind the screen of a porno cinema in Hamburg's red-light district. The rock 'n' roll-obsessed Lennon turned out to know almost nothing about the Stones' blues heroes, and had never heard a Jimmy Reed record until Mick played him Reed's 'I'll Change My Style'. When, a few days later, the Beatles appeared in a BBC-sponsored 'Pop Prom' at the Royal Albert Hall, they invited Mick, Keith and Brian to come along and visit them backstage. To avoid having to pay for tickets, the three borrowed guitars from the Beatles' equipment and passed themselves off as roadies. For the only time in his life, Mick found himself in a crowd of screaming fans who were completely unaware of his presence.

MOST YOUNG MEN of this era, whatever their calling, expected to be engaged by their late teens and married by the age of twenty-one. And in the beautiful, bright and fascinatingly connected Cleo Sylvestre nineteen-year-old Mick thought he had already found the woman for him. There would, of course, be huge problems in taking their presently casual (and still platonic) relationship to a more permanent level. Inter-racial matches were still exceedingly rare in Britain, particularly among the middle class, and heavy opposition could be expected from both his family and Cleo's. However, he was prepared to face down any amount of disapproval and prejudice. As a first step, he wanted Cleo to come to Dartford and meet his family, certain that even his mother would be instantly captivated by her.

But Cleo did not feel nearly ready for such a commitment. She had only just left school and was about to begin studying at a teacher-training college near Richmond. She also had an inbuilt nervousness about marriage – and men – having witnessed stormy and at times vio-lent rows between her own parents before their separation. 'I told Mick it had nothing to do with how I felt about him,' she recalls. 'It was just that the time wasn't right. I wanted us still to be friends, but he said he couldn't bear for it to be just on that level.'

The heartbreak, though real enough, was not to be of long duration.

One night in early 1963, the Rollin' Stones were playing yet another Thames-side blues club, the Ricky-Tick, hard by the battlements of the royal castle at Windsor. When Mick launched into Bo Diddley's 'Pretty Thing' ('let me buy you a wedding ring / let me hear the choir sing . . .'), his bandmates knew exactly whom it was aimed at.

Her name was Christine – aka Chrissie – Shrimpton; she was seventeen years old, but very different from the usual schoolgirl blues fan. Her older sister, the fashion model Jean Shrimpton, was growing increasingly famous through appearances in once-stuffy *Vogue* magazine, photographed by the young East Ender David Bailey. While Jean's looks were coolly patrician – more fifties, in fact, than sixties – Chrissie was a quintessential young woman of now with her Alice-banded hair, ethereally pale face and thick black bush-baby eyes. The impassive pout essential to this look was enhanced by unusually wide and full lips, albeit not quite on the same scale as Mick's.

Despite a noticeably posh accent and aura, Chrissie Shrimpton was less upper class than she appeared – and also more of a natural rebel than Mick had ever been. Her father was a self-made Buckinghamshire builder who had used his wealth to realise his dream of owning a farm in the high-priced countryside near Burnham. Though brought up with every luxury and given an expensive private education, Chrissie was an unruly spirit, constitutionally unable to submit to rules or authority. When she was fourteen, her convent school gave up the unequal struggle and asked her parents to remove her.

While fashion modelling took her sister Jean steadily up the social ladder, Chrissie consciously went the other way, dressing down like a beatnik and seeking out the raucous, proletarian R&B set. By day, she followed the only course open to young women without educational qualifications, training to be a shorthand typist at a secretarial college – her third – on London's Oxford Street. At night, she roamed far from the Shrimptons' Buckinghamshire farmhouse, becoming a regular at Eel Pie Island and the Crawdaddy, where she got to know both Rod Stewart and Eric Clapton well before first setting eyes on Mick and the Stones.

The various printed accounts of their first meeting are always set at the Windsor Ricky-Tick, with seventeen-year-old Chrissie – who sometimes cleared away glasses there in exchange for free admission – brazenly taking the initiative. In one version, she accepts a dare from a girlfriend to go up to Mick on the bandstand and ask him to kiss her; in another, the place is so packed that she can reach him only by crawling across the decorative fishing nets above the dance floor, helped along by people below in an early instance of crowd surfing.

Chrissie herself is unsure now whether the two of them first seriously locked eyes at the Ricky-Tick, at a nearby pub where the Stones sometimes played upstairs on Sunday afternoons, or at a place called the International Club, frequented by foreign au pair girls in nearby Maidenhead. 'I was attracted to Mick originally because he looked like an actor named Doug Gibbons,' she remembers. 'At least, Doug was a prettier version of Mick. And I remember that when we first spoke his Cockney accent was so thick I could hardly understand him.'

After serenading her with Bo Diddley's 'Pretty Thing' a few times, he asked her for a date, naming an afternoon the following week and suggesting Windsor, with its castle and fluttering Royal Standard, as their most convenient common ground. 'It was the day of my grandmother's silver wedding party, and I explained I'd have to go to that first. I remember meeting Mick on the street in Windsor because that was when I first saw him in daylight and realised one of his eyes was two colours – the left one was brown and green.'

For their next date, he took her down to Dartford by train, as she thought, to meet his family. After her father's substantial Buckinghamshire farm, the Jagger family home struck her as 'very ordinary'. Neither Mick's parents nor his brother turned out to be there, and Chrissie realised he was hoping – or, rather, expecting – to have sex with her. But the seeming wild child was not the pushover he expected. 'I was very worried about it and I wouldn't stay,' she recalls. 'So I had to come back again on the train on my own.'

Mick forgave the rebuff, however, and a week or so later, after an early-ending gig, Chrissie took him home to Burnham by train to meet her parents, Ted and Peggy, also inviting Charlie Watts and her friend

Liz Gribben, to whom Charlie had taken a shine. 'My parents were slightly appalled by the way Mick looked, but they were impressed by the fact that he went to LSE, and my dad liked him because he was so bright and into money. I don't think my mother ever really liked him – even before everything that happened – but Dad could always see how sharp he was and what a success he was going to be, whatever he ended up doing.'

Mick became a regular overnight visitor at the Shrimptons', always occupying a separate room from Chrissie's, as any well-brought-up young man in that era would be expected to do. After breakfast he would catch the same 8:42 commuter train from Burnham that Chrissie took to her secretarial school. 'My sister Jean by that time was going around with a lot of debby *Vogue* types who'd sometimes be on the same train,' she remembers. 'I used to hear them whispering "Poor Chrissie . . . her boyfriend's so ugly."'

Chrissie, by contrast, spent little time in the bosom of the Jagger family, though that was a consequence of Mick's desire to get away from home more than any mutual antipathy. She remembers her surprise on discovering that, unlike their elder son, neither Joe nor Eva had any trace of a Cockney accent and that both were 'quite intellectual people, which my parents weren't, though we had more money. Mick's mother was quite simply a domestic slave, devoted to looking after the males of the household. She was one of those garrulous women, and Mick was often very irritated by her and very dismissive of her. And his father was very formal and – to me – charmless and rather alarming. But I did get on very well with his brother, Chris, who at that time was mostly away at school. We were the two Chrisses, the younger siblings of the more successful older ones.'

Very soon after that initial refusal, Chrissie began sleeping with Mick – something that for a genteelly raised, convent-educated seventeen-year-old in 1963 was still far from routine. The first time was at the Shrimpton family home while her parents were away, since she couldn't bring herself to enter his bed at the squalid flat he shared with Keith, Brian and the 'gobbing' printer Phelge at 102 Edith Grove. 'I

hated it . . . it was so dirty,' she recalls. 'The spitting and the Nankering
. . . and they'd got notes that girls had sent them pinned up all over the
wall. It was an all-blokes place, where I was always made to feel like an
intruder.'

Keith she remembers as 'just a weedy little boy, who was very sweet
and shy and upset about his parents having recently got divorced . . .
Brian was very bright, and it was obvious that he and Mick didn't get
on at all. He tried to pull me a couple of times, but only to spite Mick.
When it happened I can remember thinking "This is ridiculous because
you're half my size."'

Mick had been seeing Chrissie only about two weeks when – out of
nowhere – the Stones' fortunes suddenly began to improve. A whole-
page feature article on the Crawdaddy Club in the local *Richmond and
Twickenham Times* gave them a laudatory plug. Then Giorgio Gomelsky
persuaded a leading music trade journalist, Peter Jones of the *Record Mirror* – who had filed the first-ever national story on the Beatles – to come
to the Station Hotel on a Sunday lunchtime and watch the Stones while
Gomelsky shot further documentary footage of them onstage. 'I met
them in the bar, before they started playing,' Jones remembers. 'Mick
was amiable and well spoken, but he stayed pretty much in the background. I thought Brian was the leader because he was the pushiest one,
waving their single press cutting under my nose.'

Peter Jones was 'knocked out' by the set that followed, but cautiously
said he wanted his paper's in-house R&B enthusiast, Norman Jopling,
to give a more knowledgeable assessment. Nineteen-year-old Jopling
turned up at the Crawdaddy's next Sunday session, but without great
expectations. 'British bands who tried to play the blues all had this kind
of worthy, post-Trad feel, so I expected them to be rubbish. But as soon
as Mick opened his mouth, I realised how wrong I was. All I remember
thinking as the Stones played was "This stuff doesn't only belong to
black guys in the States any more. White kids in Britain can play it just
as well."'

When the band talked to Jopling afterwards, Brian again took the
lead, quizzing him at length about what he could do for them in print.

Mick was 'a bit distant', as if he resented his colleague's assertiveness. 'He knew Brian had started the band and was the leader, but he knew *he* was the guy people were looking at.' Later, Jopling rode with them in Stu's van to the house of a record producer, where Keith initiated an earnest discussion about Motown music and how disappointing Mary Wells's latest single had been. 'I remember that there were a lot of musical instruments lying around, Brian was picking them up and just playing them with that instinctive talent of his. But Mick was playing some, too – and I don't mean only percussion instruments.'

Jopling's article in the next week's *Record Mirror* was the stuff of which careers are made:

> As the Trad scene gradually subsides, promoters of all kinds of teen-beat entertainments heave a sigh of relief that they've found something to take its place. It's Rhythm and Blues, of course. And the number of R&B clubs that have sprung up is nothing short of fantastic . . . At the Station Hotel, Kew Road, the hip kids throw themselves around to the new 'jungle music' like they never did in the more restrained days of Trad. And the combo they writhe and twist to is called the Rolling Stones. Maybe you haven't heard of them – if you live far from London, the odds are you haven't. But by gad you will! The Stones are destined to be the biggest group in the R&B scene if that scene continues to flourish . . .

After engineering such a triumph, Giorgio Gomelsky might have expected formal ratification as the band's manager in time to handle the consequent surge of interest from record companies and talent agents. But all Gomelsky's unselfish work on their behalf was suddenly forgotten. Before the Norman Jopling article had even appeared, Brian asked Jopling's *Record Mirror* senior Peter Jones whether he'd consider taking on the Stones' management. Jones was not interested – but once again proved a crucial catalyst. A couple of days later, he happened to run into a business acquaintance, a young freelance PR man whose naked ambition was a byword throughout the music trade press. If the young PR man cared to check out the Crawdaddy Club's house band, Peter Jones suggested, he might find something of interest. And until the *Record Mirror*'s rave appeared, the field would be clear. When Mick had played Jimmy Reed's 'I'll Change My Style' to his new Beatle friend John Lennon, he little imagined how prophetic the title would be.

CHAPTER FOUR

'Self-Esteem? He Didn't Have Any'

L ong before the Rolling Stones turned into a new kind of band and Mick into a new kind of singer, Andrew Loog Oldham was a totally new kind of manager.

Before Oldham, managers of pop acts – a pool of talent then 99.9 per cent male – had been older men with no interest in the music beyond what it might earn them, and no empathy with their young charges or with teenagers generally. Most in addition were homosexuals, which explains why so many early boy rock 'n' rollers had the same rough-trade fantasy look of flossy blond hair, black leather, tight jeans and high-heeled boots. Andrew Oldham was the first manager to be the same age as his charges, to speak their language, share their outlook, mirror their rampant heterosexuality and seem motivated by their collective ideals as much as by financial gain. While engineering managerial coups that, at the outset, seemed little short of magical, he was naturally and undis-putedly one of the band.

Managers of the traditional kind had been content to stay in the shadows, counting their percentages. Oldham, however, craved star-dom in his own right and, from the earliest age, possessed all the drive, ruthlessness and shamelessness necessary to win it. He was ahead of his time in nurturing such ambition despite possessing no abilities whatsoever as either a performer or musician and, indeed, no quantifiable talent in any direction. The talent he did have – one of the very highest order – would emerge only when he began managing the Stones, which at the outset he saw primarily as a means of projecting himself into the spotlight.

The other two most celebrated managers in pop history, Colonel Tom Parker and Brian Epstein, both had little real comprehension of the artists under their control. With the Stones – particularly their singer – Oldham very quickly realised exactly what he had found and what to do with it. In all the annals of huckstering and hype, no one has possessed a shrewder understanding of both his product and his customers.

It is a familiar music-business cliché to give the name 'Svengali' to any manager who radically remoulds a performer's appearance or persona. Svengali is one of the scarier figures in Victorian gothic literature, a music teacher with a black beard and a hypnotic stare, combining the auras of Dracula and the Phantom of the Opera. In George du Maurier's 1894 novel, *Trilby*, the eponymous heroine, an innocent young artist's model, allows Svengali to take her over, heart and soul, in exchange for transforming her into a world-famous operatic diva.

The analogy is always made with both Colonel Parker and Epstein, even though the managerial reshaping of Presley and the Beatles was purely cosmetic, impermanent, and reached neither their hearts nor their souls. In pop's premier league, the Svengali–Trilby scenario has actually been played out just once: when Andrew Loog Oldham met Mick Jagger.

When it happened, it would stir yet more foreign influences into the making of Mick. Oldham's arrestingly hybrid name commemorated his father Andrew Loog, a Dutch-American air-force lieutenant, shot down and killed while serving in Britain during the last years of the Second World War. His mother, born Cecelia Schatkowski, was the daughter of a Russian Ashkenazi Jew who, like Mick's mother's family, had emigrated to New South Wales in Australia. After arriving in Britain aged four – the same age Eva Jagger did – Cecelia became known as Celia and, like Eva, preferred to draw a veil of pukka Englishness over her origins.

Born in 1944, after his father's death and out of wedlock, Oldham grew up in the literary-bohemian north London suburb of Hampstead and attended a first-rank private school, Wellingborough. Like his future Trilby, he possessed a keen intelligence but resolutely refused to live up to his academic promise, instead hungering for glamour and style and choosing the unlikeliest possible role models for a boy of his background. In Oldham's case, these were not venerable blues musicians but the amoral young hustlers who swindled and finger-snapped their way through late 1950s cinema – Tony Curtis as Sidney Falco, the sleazy Broadway press agent in *Sweet Smell of Success*; Laurence Harvey as Johnny Jackson, the prototype 'bent' British pop manager in *Expresso Bongo*.

When London first began to swing, Andrew Loog Oldham – by now a strawberry-blond nineteen-year-old with an educated accent and a killer line in suits and tab-collared shirts – was perfectly placed to hop aboard the pendulum. He became an odd-job boy at Mary Quant's Bazaar boutique while working nights as a waiter at Soho's Flamingo Club (where he could easily have sighted Mick but somehow never did). Given his mania for attention seeking, it was inevitable he should end up in public relations, a field until then also dominated by much older men and therefore largely uncomprehending of teenage music and culture.

Among Oldham's earliest PR clients from the pop world, one left a lasting impression. This was America's Phil Spector, the first record producer to become as famous as the acts he recorded, thanks to his trademark 'Wall of Sound' technique, the total artistic control on which he insisted, and his already legendary egotism and neurosis. Most fascinating to his young English minder was the simultaneous image of a maestro and hoodlum Spector cultivated, wearing dark glasses whatever the weather or time of day, travelling in limousines with blacked-out windows, and surrounding himself with more bodyguards than most current heads of state. If being a backroom boy could be like that, who needed the front parlour?

Oldham's primary ambition was to be working with the Beatles, whose records now instantly topped the UK charts on release and who were showing themselves to be far more than just another pop group with their Liverpudlian charm and wit. Their breakthrough had allowed their manager, Brian Epstein, to successfully launch a whole troupe of 'Mersey Beat' acts, so destroying London's historic anti-northern snobbery at a stroke and becoming the most successful British pop impresario ever.

Oldham soon talked himself into a freelance PR role with Epstein's NEMS organisation and forged a good personal relationship with all four Beatles. Ambition-wise, though, it was a blind alley, since the possessive Epstein handled all their PR himself in tandem with fellow Liverpudlian Tony Barrow, and would allow Oldham to publicise only second-rank NEMS names like Gerry and the Pacemakers. He had decided to move on and was just reviewing his not very numerous options when his *Record Mirror* contact Peter Jones advised him to check out the house band at the Richmond Station Hotel.

For Oldham, walking into the Stones' jam-packed, mirror-multiplied lair was like seeing 'rock 'n' roll in 3-D and Cinerama for the very first time'. His cracklingly entertaining autobiography, *Stoned*, records the visual shock of their front rank like a James Joyce epiphany: Keith's 'black as night, hacked hair . . . atop a war-rationed baby body . . .'; Brian's 'pretty-ugly shining blond hair belied by a face that already looked as if it had a few unpaid bills with life . . .'; Mick, 'the boy from the railway towpath . . . the hors d'oeuvre, the dessert and meal in between . . .' After the cute Liverpudlian harmonies currently clogging the Top 10, that raw, sour, southern solo voice was like a dash of icy water in the face. 'It wasn't just a voice, and it was much, much more than a rendition, a mere lead vocal . . . It was an instrument . . . a declaration, not backed by a band but a part of a band . . . their decree.'

Oldham, in fact, caught the Stones at a low-energy moment, when they had reverted to being serious bluesmen seated on a semicircle of bar stools. Even then, Mick 'moved like an adolescent Tarzan plucked from the jungle, not comfortable in his clothes . . . a body still deciding what it was and what it wanted . . . He was thin, waistless, giving him the human form of a puma with a gender of its own . . . He gave me a look that asked me everything about myself in one moment – as in "What are you doing with the rest of my life?" The lips looked at me, seconding that emotion.'

In the brief interlude before *Record Mirror*'s story brought every London talent scout flocking to Richmond, Oldham persuaded the Stones he should be their manager. It was a pitch of finely tuned brilliance, in which the nineteen-year-old presented himself simultaneously as a street-smart metropolitan tycoon with more experience of life than all of them put together, and a kindred spirit who shared their love of the blues and sacred mission to preserve it. Actually, he would confess in *Stoned*, '[the blues] didn't mean dick to me. If it had, I might have had an opinion about it and missed the totality of what had hit me.' The clincher was the tenuous connection with Brian Epstein and the Beatles, now made to sound as if John, Paul, George and Ringo barely made a move without his say-so. The cautious Mick could not help but be as impressed as the fame-famished Brian. 'Everything to do with the Beatles was sort of gold and glittery,' he would recall, 'and Andrew seemed to know what he was doing.'

For all his hubris, Oldham was realistic. As a small-fry freelance PR, without even an office, he knew he was in no position to launch into management on his own. Bearing in mind the main plank of his sales pitch to the Stones, his first move was to approach Brian Epstein and offer Epstein a half share in them in return for office space and facilities. But Epstein, feeling he already had more than enough artists, declined the opportunity that would have put the two biggest bands of all time in his pocket. Trawling the lower reaches of West End theatrical agents, Oldham next hit on Eric Easton, a former professional organist whose middle-of-the-road musical clients included guitarist Bert Weedon and the pub pianist Mrs Mills, and who also hired out electronic organs to theatres, cinemas and holiday camps.

Despite being an archetypal 'Ernie', according to Mick and Brian's private argot, Easton realised how the British pop market was explod-ing and readily agreed to become the Stones' co-manager and financial backer. However, a potentially serious obstacle existed in Giorgio Gomelsky, who had given the band their Crawdaddy residency, got them eulogised by *Record Mirror* and was their manager in every way other than writing. Oldham brought an incognito Easton to the Station Hotel to see the Stones perform and meet their acknowledged leader, Brian Jones. A few days later – during Gomelsky's absence in Switzerland following the sudden death of his father – Brian and Mick attended a meeting with Oldham and Easton at the latter's office.

It was a scene that had already been played in hundreds of other pop-managerial sanctums, and would be in thousands more – the walls covered with signed celebrity photos, framed Gold Discs and posters; the balding, over-genial man at a desk cluttered by pictures of wife and children (and, in this case, electronic organs), telling the two young-sters in front of him that, of course, he couldn't promise anything but, if they followed his guidance, there was every chance of them ending up rich and famous. The only difference was the sceptical look on one youngster's face and the penetrating questions he put to both his older and younger would-be mentors. 'Mick asked me to define this "fame" I kept talking about,' Oldham recalls. 'I breathed deeply and said, "This is how I see fame. Every time you go through an airport you will get your picture taken and be in the papers. That is fame and you will be that famous."'

True to his altruistic nature, Giorgio Gomelsky made no trouble about having the Stones filched from him in this devious manner, sought no financial compensation for all he had done to advance them, and even continued to offer them bookings at the Crawdaddy. In May 1963, Brian Jones signed a three-year management contract with Old-ham and Easton on behalf of the whole band, setting the duo's com-mission at 25 per cent. During the grooming process, each Stone would receive a weekly cash retainer, modest enough but sufficient to lift the three flat-sharers out of their previous abject poverty. Unknown to Mick and Keith, Brian negotiated an extra £5 per week in his capacity as leader.

Svengali lost no time in setting to work, though his original aim was to package the Stones pretty much like other pop bands, i.e., as Beatle copies. Their piano player, Ian Stewart, was dropped because Oldham thought six too cumbersome a line-up in this age of the Fab Four – and besides, chunky, short-haired Stu looked 'too normal'. Good friend as well as fine musician though he was, neither Mick nor Brian protested, and there was general relief when he agreed to stay on as roadie and occasional back-up player. Keith deeply disapproved of Stu's treatment – as he had of Giorgio Gomelsky's – but felt his subordinate position ('a mere hireling') did not entitle him to take a moral stand. He was equally docile when Svengali gave a moment of attention to him, ordering him to drop the s from 'Richards' to give it a more showbizzy sound, as in Cliff Richard.

As an experienced entertainment agent, as well as a substantial investor, Eric Easton had a voice that must also be heeded. And, so far as Easton was concerned, the Stones had one possibly serious weak link. He wondered whether Mick's voice could stand the strain of nightly, often twice-nightly, appearances in the touring pop package shows that were every band's most lucrative market. There was also the question of whether the crucially important BBC would still bar him for sounding 'too coloured'. Group leader Brian Jones was brought into the discussion, and readily agreed with Easton that, if necessary, the Stones' vocalist would have to go the same way as their pianist.

A couple of days after the contract signing, Oldham telephoned a young photographer friend named Philip Townsend and commissioned the Stones' first-ever publicity shoot. The only brief Townsend received was to 'make them look mean and nasty'. He posed them in various Chelsea locations: on a bench outside a pub, mingling with oblivious King's Road shoppers, even sitting kindergarten-style on the road outside 102 Edith Grove, ferociously casual and cool with their corduroy jackets, polo necks and ever-smouldering cigarettes, but, to twenty-first-century eyes, not mustering a shred of meanness or nastiness between them. Mick stands out only for his lighter-coloured jacket with raglan lapels; if anyone seems the star of the group, it's sleek, enigmatic-looking Charlie Watts.

Having been dubbed the next big thing by London's most influential music trade paper, the Stones were as good as guaranteed a contract with a major record label. Theoretically, of course, they were still bound to IBC studios by the demo tape on which they had given Ian Stewart's friend, Glyn Johns, a six-month option. Eric Easton's advice was that the agreement would have no validity if they could get back the tape's only copy. Adopting Brian's habit of bare-faced lying, they therefore told Johns they'd decided to break up the band but would like to keep the tape as a souvenir. An unsuspecting Johns handed it over in exchange for its recording cost: £109.

Among Britain's few record labels in 1963, the mighty Decca company was the Stones' almost inevitable destination. Having dominated the UK music market for thirty years, Decca had seen its arch-rival, EMI, achieve the equivalent of a Klondike gold strike with the Beatles. To compound the agony, Decca's head of 'artists and repertoire', Dick Rowe, had had first chance to sign the Liverpudlians but had passed on them. So desperate was Rowe to rescue his reputation that the Stones (whose demo tape his department had also rejected a few months earlier because of Mick's vocals) walked into Decca without the customary studio audition.

A well-worn procedure now lay ahead, which even the otherwise mould-breaking Beatles had followed – and continued to follow. The new signees would go into their record company's own studios in the charge of a staff producer, who would choose the material they recorded and specify how it should be performed. Though Rowe, in his thankfulness, offered a significantly higher royalty than EMI had given the Beatles (it could hardly have been lower), the Stones would still receive only a tiny fraction of the sale price of each record, and that at a far-distant date, after labyrinthine adjustments and deductions.

Andrew Oldham had other ideas, absorbed from his American entrepreneurial idol, Phil Spector. The artists who helped constitute Spector's Wall of Sound were recorded privately by the producer at his own expense and free from any interference by third parties. The master tapes were then leased to the record company, which manufactured, distributed and marketed the product but had no say in its character or creative evolution and, crucially, did not own the copyright. In Britain's cosily exploitative record business, a tape-lease deal had never before been proposed – let alone in the airily arrogant way Oldham proposed it. Such was Decca's terror of losing another next big thing that they complied without a murmur.

Again following Spector's lead, Oldham appointed himself the Stones' record producer as well as co-manager, undaunted by his indifference to their sacred music – or by never having set foot in a recording studio other than as a PR minder. Decca were already agitating for a début single to catch the ever-rising tide of hysteria around the Beatles and beat groups generally. With no clue what that début should be, Oldham simply told his charges to pick out their five best R&B stage numbers and they would make the choice democratically between them. A session was booked at Olympic Sounds, one of central London's only three or four independent studios, on 10 May. Mick arrived straight from a London School of Economics lecture with a pile of textbooks under one arm.

The decision about the single's A-side – the one to be submitted for radio play and review in the trades – proved problematic. The Stones' best live numbers were uncommercial blues like Elmore James's 'Dust My Broom' or Chuck Berry anthems like 'Roll Over Beethoven', which by now had become the staple of many other bands, not least the Beatles. Finally they chose Berry's 'Come On', a serio-comic lament about a lost girlfriend, a broken-down car, and being rudely awoken by a wrong number on the telephone. Released two years earlier as the B-side to 'Go Go Go', it had made little impact in Britain, and had a slightly more pop feel than Berry's usual output.

There was little time for any radical reinterpretation of the track at Olympic Sound. Oldham, using Eric Easton's money, had booked the studio for three hours at a special rate of £40, and was under strict orders from his co-manager not to run over time. That sense of haste and compromise permeated the Stones' 'Come On'; indeed, Berry's languid vocal was so speeded up by Mick, it sounded more like some tongue-twisting elocution exercise. With an eye to the mass market, he also toned down the lyrics (an act of self-censorship never to be repeated), singing about 'some stupid guy tryin'' to reach another number rather than 'some stupid jerk'. Brian Jones's musicianship was limited to a harmonica riff in place of Berry's lead guitar, and a falsetto harmony in the chorus. Even with a key change to spin it out, the track lasted only one minute and forty-five seconds. For the unimportant B-side, the band could return to their comfort zone with Willie Dixon's 'I Want to Be Loved'.

The session wrapped in just under three hours, so sparing Eric Easton a £5 surcharge. As the participants left, the single engineer – whose services were included in the price – asked Oldham what he wanted to do about 'mixing'. Britain's answer to Phil Spector did not yet know this to be an essential part of the recording process. Still fearful of being charged overtime, he replied, 'You mix it and I'll pick it up tomorrow.'

Everyone involved realised how unsatisfactory the session had been, and there was neither surprise nor protest when Decca's Dick Rowe judged both the tracks to be unreleasable in their present form and said they must be re-recorded at the company's West Hampstead studios under the supervision of a staff producer, Michael Barclay. The wisest thing would have been for Mick to start afresh with a new A-side, but instead he continued trying to pummel some life into his hepped-up yet watered-down version of 'Come On'. The infusion of technical expertise and extra time made so little audible difference that Decca's bureaucracy decided to stick with the Olympic Sound version, and this was duly released on 7 June 1963.

To drum up advance publicity, Oldham took his new discoveries on an exhaustive tour of the newspaper and magazine offices to which he had easy access thanks to his former connection with the Beatles. As well as the trade press, these included magazines catering to a female teenage audience, like *Boyfriend*, whose Regent Street offices were just around the corner from Decca. 'After Andrew first brought them in, the Stones just used to turn up – usually at lunchtime,' recalls former *Boyfriend* writer Maureen O'Grady. 'I remember Mick and Brian going round the office, trying to cadge a sandwich from our packed lunches. They were obviously ravenous.'

When it came to getting television exposure, the 'Ernie' Eric Easton proved to have his uses. Among Easton's more conventional clients was Brian Matthew, the host of British television's only significant pop performance show, *Thank Your Lucky Stars*. Transmitted in black-and-white early each Saturday evening from ABC-TV's Birmingham studios, it featured all the top British and American chart names lip-synching their latest releases and, in this era of only two UK television channels, pulled in a weekly audience of around 13 million. Six months earlier, while Mick, Brian and Keith were shivering at Edith Grove, the show had broken the Beatles nationally, sending their second single, 'Please Please Me', straight to No. 1.

Easton spoke to Brian Matthew, and as a result *Thank Your Lucky Stars* booked the Stones to perform 'Come On' on the show to be recorded on Sunday 7 July and aired nationally the following Saturday. The catch was that they would have to look like a conventional beat group, in matching black-and-white-checked bumfreezer jackets with black velvet collars, black trousers, white shirts and Slim Jim ties. Mick and Keith protested in outrage to Andrew Oldham their supposed soul mate, but to Oldham exposure on this scale far outweighed a little compromising clobber; if they wanted the spot, they must wear the check.

Thus did Britain receive its first sight of Mick Jagger – far down a bill headlined by the teenage songstress Helen Shapiro and introduced by Brian Matthew in the kind of cut-glass BBC tones that traditionally commentated on Royal funerals or Test cricket matches. By today's standards, it was hardly a provocative début. The Stones in their little checked jackets appeared on a two-sided set formed of giant playing cards, with Mick standing on a low plinth to the rear of Brian and Bill, and Keith and Charlie shown in profile. Merely lip-synching 'Come On' removed any involvement Mick had ever felt with the song, reducing him to the same tailor's-dummy inanimation as the other four. For nobodies like these, the track was not allowed even its pitifully short ninety-second running time, prematurely fading amid the (artificially induced) screams of the studio audience.

It was long enough to cause horror and revulsion in living rooms the length and breadth of Britain. Earlier that year, a nation that immemorially equated masculinity – and heterosexuality – with the army recruit's stringent 'short back and sides' had been appalled by the sight of four young Liverpudlians with hair slabbed over their foreheads like the twenties Hollywood vamp Louise Brooks. Closer inspection, however, had revealed the Beatles' mop-tops to be no more than that, leaving their necks and ears as neatly shorn as any regimental sergeant major could wish. But here were pop musicians whose hair burst through those last frontiers of decorum and hygiene, curling over ears and brushing shirt collars; here in particular was a vocalist (if one could call him that), the blatant effeminacy of whose coiffure carried on into his marginally twitching torso and unsmiling, obscurely ungracious face.

Out there, of course, nobody knew who he was: almost no band members' names were yet known but John, Paul, George and Ringo. The telephone calls that flooded ABC-TV's switchboard were to protest about the 'scruffy' group who had disfigured *Thank Your Lucky Stars*, and to urge the producers never to invite them back.

Nonetheless, 'Come On' proved a rallying cry in vain. After the muddle over the recording, Decca seemed to lose interest, spending almost nothing on promotion and publicity. Reviews in the music trades were no more than tepid. 'A bluesy, commercial group who could make the charts in a small way,' commented *Record Mirror*. Writing as guest reviewer in *Melody Maker*, fellow singer Craig Douglas was scathing about Mick's vocal: 'Very ordinary. I can't hear a word [he's] saying. If there were a Liverpool accent it might get somewhere.'

The national press failed to pick up on the *Thank Your Lucky Stars* furore and would have ignored the Stones altogether but for the unflagging generosity of the manager they had just rudely dumped. Giorgio Gomelsky knew the tabloid *Daily Mirror*'s rather elderly pop correspondent, Patrick Doncaster, and persuaded Doncaster to devote his whole column to the Crawdaddy Club, the Stones and a new young band named the Yardbirds whom Gomelsky had found to take his ungrateful protégés' place. The good turn backfired when the beer brewery that owned the Station Hotel read of the wild rites jeopardising its mirror-lined function room and evicted the Crawdaddy forthwith.

In 1963, the procedure for getting a single into the Top 20 charts published by the half-dozen trades, and broadcast each Sunday on the BBC Light Programme and Radio Luxembourg, was quite straightforward. The listings were based on sales by a selection of retailers throughout the country. Undercover teams would tour these key outlets and buy up the 10,000 or so copies needed to push a record into the charts' lower reaches and to pole position on radio playlists. At that point, in most cases, public interest kicked in and it continued the climb unaided.

Decca being unwilling to activate this mechanism for 'Come On', Andrew Oldham had no choice but to do it himself. To help him, he brought in a young freelance promotion man named Tony Calder who had worked on the Beatles' first single, 'Love Me Do', and who, as a former Decca employee, knew the whole hyping routine backwards. But even with Calder's bulk-buying teams behind it, 'Come On' could be winched no higher than No. 20 on the *New Musical Express*'s chart. To blues-unaware pop-record buyers, the name 'Rolling Stones', with its echo of schoolroom proverbs, struck almost as bizarre a note as 'the Beatles' initially had. And Mick's over-accelerated vocal removed the crucial element of danceability.

He was never to make that mistake again.

OUTSIDE OF MUSIC, Chrissie Shrimpton occupied Mick's whole attention. They had been going out for more than six months and were now 'going steady', in this era the recognised preliminary to engagement and marriage – though *steady* was the least appropriate word for their relationship.

Chrissie, now eighteen, had left secretarial college and moved up to London, ostensibly to work but really to provide a place where she and Mick could find some privacy. With her friend Liz Gribben, she lived in a succession of bed-sitting-rooms which, though 'very grim', were still more conducive to romance than 102 Edith Grove. However, she still could not break it to her parents that she was sleeping with Mick; on their visits home to Buckinghamshire to stay with Ted and Peggy Shrimpton, they continued virtuously to occupy separate bedrooms.

One of Chrissie's first secretarial jobs was at Fletcher & Newman's piano warehouse in Covent Garden – at that time still the scene of a raucous daily fruit and vegetable market. 'It was only a few minutes' walk from the London School of Economics and Mick would come and meet me for lunch. One day as we walked through the market, a stallholder threw a cabbage at his head and shouted, "You ugly fucker."'

In fact, he hugely enjoyed showing Chrissie off to his fellow LSE students, not only as a breathtakingly beautiful 'bird' but as sister of the famous model Jean. Only Matthew Evans, the future publisher and peer, went out with anyone on the same level, a girl named Elizabeth Mead. 'That amused Mick,' Evans recalls. 'We used to sit and discuss how similar Elizabeth and Chrissie were.'

When Andrew Oldham first saw Mick, in the passageway to the Crawdaddy Club, he was with Chrissie and the pair were having a furious argument – this only a couple of weeks after they met. 'We were always together,' Chrissie says, 'and we rowed all the time. He'd get upset about something that hadn't been my fault – like I'd been meant to turn up at a gig and then the bouncers wouldn't let me in. I always stood up for myself, so we did have huge rows. They'd often end in physical fights – though we never hurt each other. Mick would cry a lot. We both would cry a lot.'

Though she found him 'a sweet, loving person', his evolution from club blues singer to pop star began to create a barrier between them. 'We'd be walking down the street ... and suddenly he'd see some Stones fans. My hand would suddenly be dropped, and he'd be walking ahead on his own.' Yet their rows were always devastatingly upsetting to him, especially when – as often happened – Chrissie screamed that she never wanted to see him again, stormed out of the house and disappeared. Peggy Shrimpton grew accustomed to late-night phone calls and Mick's anguished voice saying, 'Mrs Shrimpton ... where *is* she?'

With the Stones now launched as a pro band, however precariously, there clearly could no longer be two members with parallel occupations. Charlie Watts must leave his job with the advertising agency Charles, Hobson & Grey, and Mick his half-finished course at LSE. In truth, his attendance at lectures was by now so erratic that Andrew Oldham's new associate, Tony Calder, barely realised he went there at all. 'I knew Charlie had a day job that sometimes affected his getting to gigs,' Calder remembers. 'But with Mick, it was never an issue.'

By all the logic of the time, it seemed pure insanity to sacrifice a course at one of the country's finest universities – and the career that would follow – to plunge into the unstable, unsavoury, overwhelmingly proletarian world of pop. The protests Mick faced from his parents, especially his voluble, socially sensitive mother, only articulated what he himself already knew only too well: that economists and lawyers were sure of well-remunerated employment for life, while the average career for pop artists up to then had been about six months.

One afternoon, when the Stones were appearing at Ken Colyer's club in Soho, he told Chrissie that his mind was made up and he was leaving the LSE. 'I didn't get the feeling that he'd agonised very much about it,' she remembers. 'He certainly didn't discuss it with me – but then my opinion wouldn't have meant that much. I do remember that it was very upsetting to his father. To his mother, too, obviously, but the way it was always expressed was that "Joe is very upset."'

The decision became easier when it proved not irrevocable. For all his recent lack of commitment, the LSE had clearly marked him down as something special and, with its traditional broad-mindedness, was prepared to regard turning pro with the Stones as a form of sabbatical or, as we would now say, gap year. After a 'surprisingly easy' interview with the college registrar, he would later recall, he was allowed to walk without recrimination or financial penalty, and reassured that if things didn't work out with the Stones he could always come back and complete his degree.

It was not the best moment to be competing for British pop fans' attention. That rainy summer of 1963 saw the Beatles change from mere teenage idols into the objects of a national, multi-generational psychosis, 'Beatlemania'. Their chirpy Liverpool charm a perfect antidote to the upper-class sleaze of the Profumo Affair – for now, Britain's most lurid modern sex scandal – they dominated the headlines day after day with their wacky (but hygienic) haircuts, the shrieking hysteria of their audiences and the 'yeah yeah yeah' chorus of their latest and biggest-ever single, 'She Loves You'. Politicians mentioned them in Parliament, psychologists analysed them, clerics preached sermons on them, historians found precedents for them in ancient Greece or Rome; no less an authority than the classical music critic of 'top people's paper' *The Times* dissected the emergent songwriting talent of John Lennon and Paul McCartney with a seriousness normally devoted to Mozart and Beethoven.

For the national press, which hitherto had virtually ignored pop music and its constituency except to criticise or lampoon, the Beatles were a circulation booster like nothing ever before. As a result, Fleet Street entered into an unspoken pact to print nothing negative about them, to keep the cotton-wool ball rolling as long as possible. Before the year's end, they would top the bill on television's prestigious *Sunday Night at the London Palladium* and duck their mop-tops respectfully before Queen Elizabeth the Queen Mother at the Royal Variety Show.

While the Beatles headed for the Palladium and the royal receiving line, the Rolling Stones, with only half a hit to their name, continued playing their circuit of little blues clubs, with the occasional débutante ball, for fees between £25 and £50. While the Beatles were fenced off by increasing numbers of police and security, the Stones still performed close enough to their fans for any to reach out and touch them. Among the newest of these was a Wimbledon schoolgirl named Jacqui Graham, in future life the publicity director of a major British publishing house. Fifteen-year-old Jacqui charted her developing obsession with twenty-year-old Mick in a diary that – rather like a 1960s version of Daisy Ashford's *The Young Visiters* – combines eagle-eyed observation and the innocence of a bygone age:

How fab can anyone be! . . . I have just seen the Rolling Stones and they
are endsville! Mick Jagger is definitely the best. Tall [sic], very, very thin,
with terribly long hair he was gorgeous! Dressed in a shirt, a brown wool
tie which he took off, brown cord trousers and soft squidgy chukka boots.
He (or I'm pretty sure he did) kept looking at me – I was just in front of
him so he couldn't help it – & I wasn't quite sure what to do! Keith Richard
is marvellous-looking but he didn't join in much, he only seemed human
when one of his guitar-strings broke. He wore very long and tight grey
trousers, shirt and black leather waistcoat. Brian Jones had lovely colour
hair & was rather nice. Didn't think much of Bill Wyman. Charlie Watts
had a rather interesting face. Oh but when Mick and Keith looked at me
– I'm sure they did. Must see them on Sunday. They really are good – my
ears are still buzzing.

One August night when the Stones appeared at Richmond Athletic
Ground – the Crawdaddy Club's new, much-enlarged home – a production team from London's Rediffusion TV company was there, recruiting
audience members to take part in a new live Friday-evening pop show
called *Ready Steady Go!* Its co-presenter was to be a twenty-year-old fashion journalist, and über-Mod, named Cathy McGowan, who belonged
to the Stones' regular Studio 51 following. And, after the show's talent
scouts had watched them at Richmond, they were booked for the show's
second broadcast, on 26 August.

Ready Steady Go! was a mould-breaking production, designed in every
way to give a musical mould-breaker his first significant national exposure. Whereas previous TV pop shows like *Drumbeat* and *Thank Your Lucky*
Stars had kept the young studio audiences firmly out of shot, this one made
them integral to the action, dancing the newest go-go steps on a studio
floor littered with exposed cameras and sound booms or mingling with
the featured singers and bands as if they were all guests at one big party.
London's new allure was captured in the slogan flashed on-screen with
the opening credits – 'The Weekend Starts Here.' Coincidentally, the programme was made at Rediffusion's Kingsway headquarters, just around
the corner from the London School of Economics.

The Rolling Stones on *Ready Steady Go!* showed Britain's youth the real band behind that odd name and rather spiritless début single. Even though dressed in a kind of matching uniform – leather waistcoats, black trousers, white shirts and ties – and lip-synching to a backing track, they connected with their audience as instantaneously as at Richmond or on Eel Pie. Indeed, the resultant party atmosphere in the studio was a little too much even for *RSG*'s lenient floor managers. After the Stones' brief spot, so many shrieking girls waited to waylay them that they couldn't leave the building by any normal exit. Instead, Mick's *alma mater* provided an escape route, across the small back courtyard Rediffusion shared with LSE and into the student bar where so recently he'd sat in his striped college scarf, discussing Russell and Keynes and making a half pint of bitter last a whole evening.

Also in accordance with the beat-group style book (rule one: take all the work you can while it's going), the Stones were launched on a series of one-nighters at the opposite extreme from the comfortable residencies to which they were accustomed. Distance was no object, and they frequently faced round-trips of two hundred miles or more in Ian Stewart's Volkswagen van: no joke in an era when motorways were still a rarity and even two segregated traffic lanes were an occasion. These journeys often took them up north, the Jagger family's original homeland – not that Mick ever showed any sign of nostalgia – through redbrick towns where streets were still cobbled, factories still hummed, coal pit-head wheels still turned and long-haired Londoners were gawped at like just-landed aliens.

The gig might be at a cinema, a theatre, a Victorian town hall or corn exchange; one was a kiddies' party whose guests, expecting more conventional entertainment, pelted them with cream buns. The Britain of 1963 had no fast-food outlets but fish-and-chip shops and Wimpy hamburger bars: but for these and Chinese and Indian restaurants, a certain ever-hungry mouth would have seen little action the livelong night. Local promoters who had booked the Stones sight unseen reacted with varying degrees of incredulity and horror at what turned up. After one show to a near-empty hall in the industrial back-of-beyond, the promoter docked them their entire fee for being 'too noisy', then saw them off the premises with the help of a ferocious Alsatian guard dog and wearing boxing gloves for good measure.

At the beginning, Mick and Keith still saw themselves as missionaries, preaching R&B to the unenlightened as they had dedicated themselves to doing back in Dartford. They discovered, however, that dozens of other bands around the circuit, especially northern ones, had undergone the same conversion and felt the same proselytising zeal. The difference was that, while the others played only Chuck Berry's 'Roll Over Beethoven', the Stones knew Berry's entire œuvre. Mick observed, too, that northern bands in particular felt a common affinity with old-fashioned music-hall comedy and, following the Beatles' example, 'turned into vaudeville entertainers onstage'. That was a trap he was determined never to fall into. Graham Nash from the Hollies, the north's second most successful band, couldn't help admiring these unsmiling southerners' refusal to conform to type: 'They didn't seem to be copying anybody – and they didn't give a fuck.'

The word that increasingly went ahead of them, based solely on the length of their hair, was *dirty*. Nothing could have been further from the truth. Mick was utterly fastidious about personal cleanliness, and one of those fortunate people who do not show dirt; Brian washed his eye-obscuring blond helmet so religiously each day that the others nicknamed him 'Mister Shampoo'; Bill Wyman as a small boy used to do his mother's housework for her; the Hornsey Art School student Gillian Wilson, who had a fling with Charlie Watts, remembers his underwear being cleaner than hers. They had now given up any semblance of a stage uniform and went onstage in the same Carnaby motley in which they'd arrived at the theatre. Though all of them were clothes-mad and cutting-edge fashionable, this revolutionary break with tradition added a reek of BO to the implied dandruff and head lice. Their manager took every opportunity to circulate the double slander, adding a third for good measure: 'They don't wash much and they aren't all that keen on clothes. They don't play nice-mannered music, but raw and masculine. People keep asking me if they're morons . . .'

For Oldham had finally seen with the clarity of a divine vision where to take them – and, in particular, Mick. As the Beatles progressively won over the older generation and the establishment, and were unconditionally adulated by Fleet Street, many of their original young fans were feeling a sense of letdown. Where was the excitement – the rebellion – in liking the same band your parents or even grandparents did? He would therefore turn the Rolling Stones into anti-Beatles; the scowling flip side of the coin Brian Epstein was minting like a modern Midas. It was a double paradox, since the angelic Fab Four had a decidedly sleazy past in Hamburg's red-light district, whereas the bad boys Oldham now proposed to create were utterly blameless, none more than their vocalist.

Indeed, the Jagger image at this point could well have gone in the very opposite direction. Early press stories on the Stones still gave his Christian name as Mike, resurrecting that bourgeois aura of Sunday-morning pubs, sports cars and driving gloves. There was also PR mileage to be extracted from his intellectual achievements. Until now, only one British pop star, Mike Sarne, had experienced further education (coincidentally also at London University).

As Tony Calder remembers, Mick was profoundly uneasy over the master plan that Oldham outlined to him – and not just for its gross misrepresentation of his character. 'He said he'd bide his time and see if it worked out or not. But there were so many times when he'd turn up at the office, Andrew would call for two cups of tea and shut the door. He'd be in there alone with Mick for a couple of hours doing one thing – building up his confidence. Self-esteem? He didn't have any. He was a wimp.'

A famous colour clip of the Stones onstage at the ABC cinema, Hull, filmed by one of Britain's last surviving cinema newsreels, shows them playing 'Around and Around' for the umpteenth time, against a barrage of maniacal screams. They seem to be doing remarkably little to encourage this uproar: Bill playing bass in his odd vertical style, Keith lost in his chords, Brian almost street-mime motionless, with an odd new electric guitar shaped like an Elizabethan lute. Mick, in his familiar matelot-striped shirt – and almost glowing with cleanliness – seems least involved of all. Even in this paean to the liberating joy of music, his well-moistened lips barely stir, giving the words an edge of sarcasm ('Rose outa my seat . . . I just had to daynce . . .') reflected in his veiled eyes and occasional flamenco-style hand clap. In the guitar solo he does a stiff-legged dance with head thrust forward and posterior stuck out, ironically rather like the vaudeville 'eccentric' style, then still preserved by such veterans as Max Wall and Nat Jackley.

Since the onset of Beatlemania, young girls at pop shows had screamed dementedly whatever acts were served up to them, male or female, but until now had always stayed in their seats. With Rolling Stones concerts came a new development: they attacked the stage. These were the days when security at British pop concerts consisted of theatre staff checking tickets at the door, and the only barrier between performers and audience as a rule was an empty orchestra pit. During a performance in Lowestoft, Suffolk, on 6 September, half a dozen demented girls began trying to tear off the band's clothes and grabbing for souvenirs. (Bill later discovered a valuable ring had been wrenched off his finger.) Mick's athleticism proved an unexpected asset: as one invader rushed at him, he swept her up in a fireman's lift, carried her offstage, then returned to continue the number.

The next day brought a 200-mile drive from coastal Suffolk to Aberystwyth, north Wales, then another of 150 miles south to Birmingham for a second appearance on *Thank Your Lucky Stars*. Also on the bill was Craig Douglas, who had panned Mick's 'Come On' vocal in *Melody Maker*. Before becoming a pop singer, Douglas had been a milkman on the Isle of Wight; in revenge for his hostile review – and with unendearing social snobbery – the Stones dumped a cluster of empty milk bottles outside his dressing room door.

On 15 September they were opening in a show called *The Great Pop Prom* at London's Royal Albert Hall, with the Beatles as top of the bill. Five months earlier, Mick, Keith and Brian had walked into the Albert Hall anonymously, disguised as Beatle roadies; now the Chelsea boot was well and truly on the other foot. The Stones' support-band spot unleashed such pandemonium that John Lennon and Paul McCartney were seen peeping through the curtains, nervous of being upstaged for the first time since their Hamburg days. *Boyfriend* magazine was unequivocal in naming the night's real stars: 'Just one shake of [that] overgrown hair is enough to make every girl in the audience scream with tingling excitement.'

Two weeks later, the Stones set out on their first national package tour, as footnotes to a bill headed by three legendary American names, Little Richard, the Everly Brothers and Bo Diddley. As a mark of respect to their third-biggest R&B hero – and perhaps a tacit admission that their singer was not as brazenly confident as he seemed – the band dropped all Bo Diddley songs from their stage act during the month-long tour. In fact, as well as being flattered by their reverence, Diddley was impressed by their musicianship, later using Bill and Charlie as his rhythm section on a BBC radio appearance. For Mick, the main benefit was seeing Diddley's virtuoso sideman, Jerome Green, play lollipop-shaped maracas, two in each hand. From now on, he, too, shook maracas in the faster numbers, albeit only one per hand – and even that with a hint of irony.

Touring meant staying in hotels, which for such a bottom-of-the-bill act meant grim establishments with dirty net curtains, malodorous carpets and electricity coin meters in the bedrooms, all in all not much different from home back in Chelsea. It emerged, however, that one Edith Grove flatmate was not having to endure it. As well as his leader's £5-per-week premium, Brian had secretly arranged with Eric Easton to stay in a better class of hotel than the others.

Before long, the tour's American headliners were facing the Beatles' recent problem at the Royal Albert Hall. Little Richard remained oblivious, entertaining his audience with an extended striptease, then going for a ten-minute walkabout through the auditorium with a forty-strong police guard. But the Everly Brothers' tender harmonies became increasingly drowned out by chants of 'We want the Stones!' In the end, the emcee had to go out and plead for Mick's heroes of yesteryear to be given a break.

By autumn, the Stones' word-of-mouth reputation was sufficient for them to be voted Britain's sixth most popular band in *Melody Maker*'s annual readers' poll. Yet their future on record was anything but secure. Unless their inexperienced young manager–record producer could concoct a far bigger hit single than 'Come On', Decca would be looking for excuses to circumvent their contract and dump them. And the stock of likely hits in the R&B canon was shrinking all the time as other bands and solo singers dipped into it.

After a flick through R&B's back catalogue, Andrew Oldham chose an overt novelty number, Leiber and Stoller's 'Poison Ivy', originally recorded by the Coasters with voices teetering on the edge of goonery. As the B-side, weirdly, he prescribed another quasi-comedy song, Benny Spellman's 'Fortune Teller'. For a time Mick seemed headed for exactly the vaudeville kind of pop he so despised. However, a recording session with Decca's in-house producer, Michael Barclay, on 15 July revealed the whole band to be deeply uncomfortable with Oldham's choice. And, having scheduled the two tracks for release in August, Decca then ominously cancelled them.

Salvation came unexpectedly while Oldham and the Stones were at Ken Colyer's Studio 51 Club in Soho, trying out other potential A-sides and getting nowhere. Escaping outside for a breath of air, Oldham chanced to run into John Lennon and Paul McCartney, fresh from receiving awards as Show-Business Personalities of the Year at the Savoy Hotel. Told of the Stones' problem, John and Paul good-naturedly offered a song of theirs called 'I Wanna Be Your Man', so new that it wasn't even quite finished. The duo accompanied Oldham back to Studio 51 and demo'd a Liverpudlian R&B pastiche that their rivals could cover without shame or self-compromise. Their gift thankfully accepted, they added the song's final touches then and there, making it all look absurdly easy.

On 7 October the Stones went straight into Kingsway Sound Studios, Holborn (just down the road from LSE), and recorded a version of 'I Wanna Be Your Man' needing virtually no production and only a couple of takes. The B-side was a cobbled-up instrumental, based on Booker T. and the MG's' 'Green Onions' and entitled 'Stoned' – to most

British ears, still only something that happened to adulterous women in the Bible.

'I Wanna Be Your Man' was released on 1 November, three weeks before the Beatles' own version, sung by Ringo Starr, appeared on their landmark second album, *With the Beatles*. While the northerners could not stop themselves adding harmony and humour, the Stones' treatment was raw and basic, just Mick's voice in alternation with Brian's molten slide guitar; not so much sly romantic proposition as barefaced sexual attack. 'Another group trying their chart luck with a Lennon-McCartney composition,' patronised the *New Musical Express*. 'Fuzzy and undisciplined . . . complete chaos,' sniffed *Disc*. Indiscipline and chaos seemed to be just what Britain's record buyers had been waiting for, and the single went straight to No. 12.

At year's end, BBC television launched a new weekly music show called *Top of the Pops*, based solely on the week's chart placings, that would run without significant change of format for the next forty years. The Stones featured in the very first programme, their vocalist adding a further twist to that un-Beatly Beatles song still rudely disrupting the Top 20. Motionless and in profile, buttoned into a tab collar as high as a Regency hunting stock, he seemed as detached and preoccupied as the lyric was hot and urgent. The downcast eyes and irritably drooping mouth suggested something rather tedious being spelled out to an unseen listener who was either slow-witted or deaf. To the studio audience surging round him, the clear message came straight from his recently aborted version of 'Poison Ivy': 'You can look but you better not touch . . .'

Everyone knew now it was Mick, not Mike, and that – even though they might have attended the same seat of learning – he was nothing whatsoever like Mike Sarne.

CHAPTER FIVE

"'What a Cheeky Little Yob,"
I Thought to Myself'

Saturday 14th December, 1963: Beatles at [Wimbledon] Palais, Stones at [the Baths] Epsom. Went down to Palais but saw nothing but police & more police. Got to Epsom early & when we saw 'admission by ticket only' thought we might as well go home. Stayed for a little while chatting to 2 mods however & then that darling DARLING doorman let us in. Got right to the front & wow! Leaning up on the stage gazing into the face of Mick and he looked at me – he did! Keith glanced once, Charlie never & I don't know about Brian & Ghost [Bill Wyman]. Mick kind of looks at you in a funny way – shy? impersonal? sexy? cold? I don't know but it's certainly cool & calm . . . as usual [he] commanded all the attention. He was in a pink shirt, navy trousers, Cuban [heeled] Chelsea's & brown Chelsea cord waistcoat with black onyx cufflinks. He looked thin, cool and haggard. His hair hung in long ginger waves & his sharp sideways glances down at the audience (no – me!) made him look even more fright [crossed out] aloof and somehow witchlike . . . After the Stones had gone off, the curtains were drawn across but we got underneath them & watched the Stones standing around at the side, talking . . . Couldn't get backstage worst luck!

– from Jacqui Graham's diary

C helsea had lost Mick, for now anyway. Under Andrew Oldham and Eric Easton's management, the Rolling Stones received around £20 each per week, the same as most top British soccer players of that era. The three Edith Grove flatmates therefore could move on from the squalid pad where they had frozen and half starved – but also shared an idealism and camaraderie that were never to be revived.

Treading his usual fine line between sex addict and sex offender, Brian Jones had impregnated yet another teenage girlfriend. The mother of this, his fourth child by different partners – due to arrive in summer 1964 – was a sixteen-year-old trainee hairdresser named Linda Lawrence. In a surprising reversal of his usual tactics, Brian did not instantly desert Linda but showed every sign of standing by her and the baby and, still more surprisingly, went to live with her at her family's council house in Windsor, Berkshire, where Mick had first wooed Chrissie Shrimpton. So fond of this prospective son-in-law did the Lawrences become that they named the house 'Rolling Stone' in Brian's honour and also gave board and lodging to a white goat he bought as a pet and liked to take out for walks through Windsor on a lead.

It went without saying that Mick and Keith would continue living together. However, treading his usual fine line between authority figure and honorary bandmate, Andrew Oldham put forward the idea, or instruction, that he should join them. Svengali needed to be as close as possible to the Trilby he was moulding day by day.

Trilby, as a result, migrated from trendy Chelsea to the more prosaic north London district of Willesden. The new flat was a modest two-bedroom affair on the first floor of 33 Mapesbury Road, a street of identical 1930s houses with even less charm than Edith Grove – though immeasurably cleaner and quieter. Mick and Keith were the official tenants, while Oldham came and went, staying part of the time with his widowed mother in nearby (and more desirable) Hampstead.

Rock musicians' neighbours are usually condemned to purgatorial nuisance, but with Jagger and Richard, Mapesbury Road got off lightly. For much of the time the pair were away on tour, and when they returned they would sleep for twelve or fourteen hours at a stretch. Their fans had no idea where they were living, and none yet possessed the gumption to find out. There were no riotous all-night parties, no revving cars or motorbikes or onslaughts of deafening music, not even the tiniest tinkle of breaking glass. There was no drug taking whatsoever at this stage, or even very much drinking. 'A half bottle of wine in that place,' Oldham would remember, 'was a big deal.'

Since Mick had been swept up into his new pop-star life, his parents back home in Dartford had hardly seen him and, apart from the increasingly unflattering stories they read in the press, had no idea where he was or what he was doing. When Oldham commandeered the Stones, he did not have to sell himself as a responsible manager to their respective families the way Brian Epstein had, painstakingly, to the Beatles'; Oldham, indeed, had not even met Joe and Eva Jagger, and initially left all dealings with the couple to his associate Tony Calder. 'One day,' Calder remembers, 'a call came through to the office, and this very polite voice said, "My name's Joe Jagger. I understand that my son is getting rather famous. If you need help of any kind, just let me know." I took calls from so many angry, hysterical people every day . . . I couldn't believe I'd just been talking to somebody who was polite.'

Liaison with Joe and Eva improved when Oldham employed seventeen-year-old Shirley Arnold, a long-time loyal Stones supporter around the club circuit, to organise their fast-growing national fan club. Shirley joined the small Oldham enclave inside Eric Easton's office in a Piccadilly office block called Radnor House. Also among the staff was Easton's elderly father-in-law, a Mr Boreham, who advised clients on long-term financial planning. Shirley remembers Mr Boreham's amazement after a consultation session with Mick. 'He said Mick had asked him what he thought the pound would be worth on the currency markets in a few years' time. That was something no one in the music or entertainment business thought about in those days.'

Henceforward, Shirley kept Joe and Eva fully updated about their son, finding them 'lovely people' who never made the slightest demands on their own account or expected to profit from his success. 'Eva was the dominant one in the marriage, very conscious of what other people thought, and to begin with she wasn't sure what to make of all the head-lines. But Mick's dad was always totally laid-back about it all.'

Brian Jones might cut a dash with his pet goat on the streets of Wind-sor, but elsewhere he was finding it increasingly hard to win the atten-tion he craved. Ironically, the Stones' takeover by professional manag-ers that he had wanted so desperately had eroded almost all his former power and status as the band's founder, chief motivator and creative driving force. While they were still struggling to break through, Brian had a certain value to Oldham and Easton as an ally within their ranks, and so could wangle preferential treatment in pay or hotel accommoda-tion. But now that they had made it his doom was effectively sealed.

Knowing in his own mind what a star he was, he could not under-stand why Oldham should be devoting such time and trouble to Mick, or why audiences responded to the results with such fervour. 'Brian would come into the office to collect his fan mail,' Tony Calder remem-bers, 'and there it would be in a little pile, with a dirty great pile next to it. "Who's that other lot for?" he'd say. "They're for Mick," I'd say. Brian would storm out in a fury, not even taking his own fan mail.'

One way of fighting back would have been to compete against Mick in onstage showmanship, as lead guitarists often did against vocalists. But with curious perverseness – the same that made him go and live with his girlfriend and goat in Windsor rather than at least try to pre-serve the old solidarity of Edith Grove – Brian in performance struck none of the melodramatic or flamboyant poses that normally went with his role. Throughout the Stones' set, he stood rooted to the stage with his lute-shaped Vox Teardrop guitar, as innocent-looking as some Eliza-bethan boy minstrel, giving out nothing but an occasional enigmatic smile. It was a technique that seldom failed him with individual females in intimate one-to-one situations, but in front of eight or nine thousand going crazy for Mick's duckwalk, it was an ill-advised tactic.

The erosion of Brian's leadership did not end there. Until now, he had always been the spokesman for the band in the quiet, cultured voice which, unlike Mick, he never slurred into *faux* Cockney. But Oldham considered him long-winded and – as an inveterate hypochondriac –

too prone to ramble on about his latest head cold. So, with great reluc-
tance at first, Mick began to do the talking as well as the singing (Keith
being regarded, in both areas, as totally mute). 'If Andrew told Mick,
"You've got two interviews today," his response would always be "Are
you sure they want me?"' Tony Calder remembers. 'Andrew rehearsed
him in talking to journalists just like he rehearsed him in how to perform.' Under the rules of early-sixties pop journalism, this generally
meant no more than reciting a press release about the Stones' recording and touring plans. It also meant showing a deference scarcely in his
nature to interviewers whom Oldham particularly needed to cultivate.
When the *New Musical Express*'s editor Derek Johnson turned up in person, a well-briefed Mick shook his hand and said, 'Nice to meet you, sir.'

The music press, of course, voiced no criticisms of the Stones' hair
and personal hygiene, though their lack of stage uniforms still excited
spasmodic wonder. Nor did the canny Oldham yet try to sell them as
direct challengers to the Beatles. Rather, he peddled the line that they
were standard-bearers for London and the south against the previously
unchecked chart invasion from Liverpool. Mick delivered the perfect
quote: proudly territorial without slighting the Liverpudlian songwriters who had recently done his band such a good turn, competitive but
not unfriendly, ambitious but not arrogant. 'This Mersey Sound is no
different from our River Thames sound. As for these Liverpool blokes
proclaiming themselves better than anyone else, that's a load of rubbish.
I've nothing against the Mersey Sound. It's great. But it's not as new and
exclusive as the groups make out. I can't say I blame them for jumping
at this sort of publicity, though. If we came from Liverpool, we'd do the
same. But we don't, and we're out to show the world.'

At first, Oldham sat in on every interview, poised to jump in with
corrections or contradictions where necessary. But Mick proved so reliable at giving journalists what they wanted without giving anything
away that he was soon allowed to go solo. 'Andrew would prime him to
do ten minutes,' Tony Calder says. 'But he'd expand it into twenty-five
. . . then forty-five, then an hour.' While other pop musicians frater-
nised with their interviewers, chatting over a pint at the pub or a Chi-

nese meal, he always preferred the neutral ground of an office; while unfailingly polite, he had an air of detachment and faint amusement, as if he couldn't understand all this fuss over the Stones – and him. 'I still haven't grasped what all this talk of images is about,' he told *Melody Maker*. 'I don't particularly care whether parents hate us or not. They may grow to like us one day . . .' It was a trick that never failed [in the perceptive Bill Wyman's words] 'to portray himself as indifferent whereas in fact he cared very much.'

But the most revealing encounter with Mick in this era was not recorded by any professional journalist. It appears in the diary kept by Jacqui Graham, the fifteen-year-old from Wimbledon County Grammar School for Girls who had switched allegiance from the Beatles to the Rolling Stones in late 1963, and now devoted her leisure hours to getting close to them. In the innocent time before security checks, backstage passes, Neanderthal bodyguards and dressing rooms turned into royal courts, that could be often be extraordinarily close.

Jacqui's diary greets 5 January as a 'brilliant Stoning start to 1964' after a show at the Olympia Ballroom, Reading, which (in a portent of things to come) begins one and a half hours late. This time, it is Keith, with his 'lovely hair', and Charlie Watts who captivate her, while Mick 'seem[s] not to be his usual bright self' and is rather less 'gorgeous' than at Epsom three weeks before: 'I noticed his gold cufflinks & his identity bracelet,' the diarist says with her usual unsparing eye for detail. 'He has rather repulsive fat lips and a wet, big tongue!'

On 11 January, when the Stones return to Epsom Baths, Jacqui and some other girls are waiting by the stage door and manage to follow them all the way into their dressing room. 'Fabulous Keith' with his 'lovely, lean, intelligent face', does not mind being watched while he dabs on acne cream, even allowing Jacqui to hold his Coke bottle and Mod peaked cap during the operation. Brian is observed, presciently, to be 'not looking madly happy', and to have 'a very clipped and well-spoken voice . . . and a lovely slow, tired smile'. Charlie is 'dreamsville but much smaller than I had imagined' and Bill is 'sweet, small, dark, very very helpful'. But Mick proves 'a big disappointment & a big head

. . . [he] thought he was *it* in his usual blue suit, brown gingham shirt and tartan waistcoat & he looked at us as tho' we were something that the cat had brought in, although I did look up once to find him eyeing me up and down in a rather sly way. Still – although the worst – he is still fab! . . . then (damn & sod) home at 11.25.'

Friday, 24 January, which for the diarist 'started off being puke', turns into 'the most fabulous day ever . . . Mick, Keith and Charlie relaxed, friendly & TALKING – yes REALLY TALKING TO US!' With the Stones on again at Wimbledon Palais, she and her friend Susan Andrews manage to sneak into their empty dressing room and hide out there until they arrive. Once again, the intruders are allowed to hang around while the band prepares to go onstage. There is no sexual ulterior motive; they are simply resigned to goggling school-age girls being part of the furniture. This time, Jacqui finds Mick 'very friendly . . . he smiled at me and seemed interested in what I had to say'. Only Brian seems reticent, possibly because his 'secret wife', Linda Lawrence, is also there. The two girls squeeze themselves into corners, watching the ebb and flow of official visitors, including an ad man who wants to put the Stones in a TV commercial for Rice Krispies. Mick relaxes so far as to strip off his shirt and put on another. 'He made crude remarks like "must cover me tits up" etc.,' the diarist records, 'but I liked him.' She is equally unfazed, later in the evening, to see both Mick and Keith wish Charlie good night by kissing him full on the mouth.

By mid-February, Jacqui and Susan have learned via the fans' grapevine (or gape-vine) where Mick and Keith live and found out their home phone number. When the girls pluck up courage to ring it, Keith answers. Not in the least annoyed at being thus run to earth, he apologises that Mick isn't in and stays on the line chatting for some time. This spurs the pair to an adventure which will later fill several pages of Jacqui's diary, laid out with dialogue and stage directions like a film script:

MONDAY 17TH FEBRUARY. Fate held in store a 15 min conversation in Mick's hall.

We set off with the spirit of adventure strong within us & at great length found 33 Mapesbury Road NW2. Not knowing which bell to ring we knocked and asked for Mick Jagger. Several minutes passed & then this old woman appeared & behind her I could see Micky standing on the stairs, arms folded with a queer sort of smile on his face. He looked like a sort of pale blue pole in the dim light because he was in his pyjamas – pale blue, dark blue trimmings & white cord. The jacket was open & the pyjama trousers falling down but he seemed quite oblivious & stood there in his bare feet just looking. I felt incapable of walking in but we did & once more our conversation was friendly but I got the feeling he was faintly amused at us for his expression, a vague sort of genial smile, remained unchanged throughout.

   This is a rough idea of the conversation:

SILENCE

   J: 'Good morning'

   S: "   "

M: "   "

   S: 'We phoned you up'

   J: 'Yes, I hope you don't mind us coming round here like this, you remember we phoned you up about that party.'

M: 'Yes, I remember'

   J: 'Well, we went to it & then went to another one over at Black-heath – the second one was at Blackheath, wasn't it?'

   S: 'Yes'

   J: 'Anyway, we landed up at Hampstead station this morning & we knew you lived round this way so we thought we'd pop in. I hope you don't mind. I s'pose it's a bit of a cheek really but it's typical of us, we're always doing mad things.'

M: 'How did you know my address?'

   J: 'Oh we've known it for ages. I've forgotten who gave it to us.'

   S: 'Which is your bell, you haven't got your name on it.'

M: (evading question) 'Oh, we always put different funny names on it.'

   J: 'I think you thought we were Bridget before, you know, about the long skirts.'

M: 'Oh, I knew you weren't Bridget – I thought you might be
some of her friends. Someone sent me 2 dolls the other day, with
long skirts on – very nice. I appreciated it.'

Crosses over to mirror having got up from sitting on stairs.

'I must look awful, haven't shaved or anything. A bloke came to
see me once & took a picture of me like this.'

Arranges hair.

'Sent them to me afterwards. I looked terrible – it was the
flash.'

J: 'I'd kill anyone if they did that to me.'

M: 'Oh, we've got to go away again soon.'

S: 'Where to?'

M: 'Oh, Sunbury or some stupid place like that. We're playing at
Greenford tonight.'

Comes over to us.

'Gosh, aren't I small? Why aren't you at work or anything.'

J: 'Oh we got the day off, hadn't got much to do. Where's Keith, is
he upstairs?'

M: 'Yes, he's, uh, busy' (laughs)

Phone rings

'Excuse me.'

Answers it.

'Hallo, hallo, hallo – press Button A – git. Hallo, who's there?'

Puts it down

M: 'You were saying?'

J & S: Inordinate mumbles

M: 'I thought you were the bloke coming to see me s'morning
about some script.'

J: 'Oh, is that for the Rice Krispies advertisement?'

M: 'No, but how did you know about that?'

J: 'Oh we were there when that bloke asked you.'

S: 'We were in your dressing room at Wimbledon.'

J: 'Yes, it was Brian that wanted to do it, wasn't it?!'

No answer. Various other topics of conversation, then

M: 'What's the time?'

J: 'Twenty past twelve.'

M: 'Oh, he'll be here soon. I've got to go & have a bath & get some clothes on. I'd invite you up but it's a bit awkward – you do understand.'

Giggles

J & S: 'Yes, we understand.'

M: 'And I've only got a little room to myself. Can't very well invite you in there, people might get ideas.'

J & S: 'Uh ... yea.'

Shows us the door

M: 'Oh well, give us a ring sometime, when we're at a theatre or dance hall & come and see us.' Mumble Mumble 'Come into the dressing room. Cheerio.'

J & S: 'Cheerio.'

Exit

Door slams shut.

We trail around Willesden miserably – we return to Wimbledon & make dinner at around 3.30. We feel choked up & a bit silly.

GOING OUT WITH Jean Shrimpton's younger sister was not Mick's automatic passport into the upper echelons of Swinging London. Jean had always done her best to keep Chrissie at arm's length and, besides, was still far from certain about the 'ugly' young man who sometimes decorously occupied her bed at her parents' home in Buckinghamshire while she was away. Far more important to Mick's initial social rise was David Bailey, the East End photographer who had put Jean into *Vogue*, made them both international celebrities and was now going out with her. Bailey, indeed, was to become a friend outlasting the era of both Shrimpton sisters; perhaps his closest ever outside music.

When the two first met, they could not have been much more unequal, one a nineteen-year-old LSE student, the other five years older and at a seemingly unsurpassable peak of celebrity. Mick was frankly awestruck by the glamour and sophistication of Bailey's lifestyle – the Lotus Elan sports cars, mews studios and cowboy boots he had made a photographer's essential accessories in place of potted palms, black cloths and 'watch the birdie!' Of no small influence either was the delighted frisson Bailey's unreformed (and totally genuine) Cockney accent created among the debs and high-born female magazine editors who lionised him. Such was Mick's admiration that he even allowed Bailey to tease him, as few others dared to do openly, about his appearance. When Eva Jagger took him shopping as a boy, Bailey used to joke, there would have been no problem about going into places where small children weren't welcome. She could leave him outside, securely clamped to the shop window by his lips.

Early in their friendship, rather like Pip with Herbert Pocket in Dickens's *Great Expectations,* Mick asked Bailey to take him to a posh restaurant and teach him how to conduct himself. They went to the Casserole on King's Road, not far from the World's End village where three hard-up Stones had so recently subsisted on stolen milk and stale fruit pies. Mick paid the bill – not an act to be much associated with him – but jibbed at Bailey's suggestion that he should also leave a tip. Finally, he put down a pre-decimal ten-shilling (or 'ten-bob') note, equivalent to fifty pence today, with a 1964 purchasing power of £10. But as they left, Bailey saw him slip it back into his pocket.

Bailey soon picked up on Andrew Oldham's influence over Mick, one that reminded him of a worldly-wise older brother with an awestruck younger one, and made his own moulding of Jean Shrimpton as a couture icon seem superficial by comparison. At the few Stones gigs he attended, he also found himself an uncomfortable witness to Brian Jones's decreasing influence in the band and continual attempts to claw some power and status back. The photographer's eagle eye for nuances noted that, while Mick was happy to zoom around with Jean and him in an unpretentious Mini-Minor, Brian drove a bulky Humber saloon, 'the kind of car a vicar would use'. At the end of a gig, Bailey recalls, Mick and Keith would be like unkind children, playing an obviously habitual game of 'let's get away from Brian'.

Chrissie Shrimpton, too, recognised Oldham's power over Mick, although at her tender age — she was still not yet nineteen — it represented unfathomably deep waters. Chrissie now spent most nights with Mick at 33 Mapesbury Road while officially sharing a bedsit with her friend Liz Gribben for the sake of appearances with her parents. When Jacqui Graham or other schoolgirl fans rang up the flat, a terse female voice would answer, discouraging them from further surprise appearances on the front doorstep.

For all the Stones' growing fame, Mick still felt it a huge feather in his cap to be going out with Jean Shrimpton's sister, even though Chrissie refused to capitalise on her surname or her own spectacular looks, and continued to work as a secretary, now at the Stones' record company, Decca. 'I still wanted to be with him all the time,' she remembers. 'The trouble was that my life was going on mostly in the daytime and Mick's mostly went on at night.' And Oldham's rival stake in him was something she could only characterise as 'powerful and frightening'.

The explosive, sometimes physically violent quarrels she and Mick had always had increased exponentially as the Stones' fame did and he became more aware of himself as their star attraction and more prone to shove her out of sight whenever female fans materialised. Mortifyingly, to someone who valued coolness and self-possession above all, the blow-ups with Chrissie increasingly tended to happen in front of other people, at gigs, parties or new clubs like the Ad Lib. 'They once had a terrible one at Eric Easton's office,' Shirley Arnold remembers. 'It ended with Chrissie kicking Mick down the stairs.'

The fans who thought him so untouchable would have been astonished by his distress after Chrissie had stormed off into the night, and repeated phone calls to her mother could not locate her. Andrew Oldham would receive an anguished SOS and would go and meet him, usually at a bench on the Thames Embankment as far as possible from other prying eyes and ears. As Oldham recalls in *Stoned*, Mick would pour out his side of the story and almost tearfully recount how Chrissie had gone for him with her fists. (She herself now says firmly that she never used fists and 'he wasn't a victim of domestic abuse'.) The heart-to-hearts with Oldham would often last the rest of the night, ending at dawn with a walk through the deserted West End and breakfast at a taxi drivers' café.

Oldham writes in *Stoned* that during this period he and Mick were 'as close as two young men could probably become' – and there has been endless speculation ever since about the extent of that closeness. Oldham certainly was not homosexual – indeed, had lately begun going out with a Hampstead girl named Sheila Klein (a surname to have large resonance in another context later in this story) whom he was soon to marry. At the same time, with his homing spirit for all outrage, he sought out the company of notable gay men in the music business – in particular the composer of *Oliver!*, Lionel Bart – and added their gestures and speech mannerisms to his repertoire of devices for amusing his friends and disconcerting his foes.

At all events, rumours began to fly around that in the extremely crowded quarters of 33 Mapesbury Road Mick and Oldham's closeness extended to sharing the same bed. One must hasten to add that, in purer-minded 1964, that did not necessarily signify what it would today. Young men could still have platonic friendships in the Victorian mode, sharing flats, rooms and even beds (as pop band members often did on tour) without the slightest homoerotic overtones. Oldham's own memoirs recall a night when the two of them ended up at his mother's flat in Netherhall Gardens, Hampstead, and, rather than struggle home to Willesden, decided to crash out there. When Mrs Oldham looked into his room the next afternoon, she found them both squeezed into his single bed, still dead to the world.

According to Chrissie, Oldham's soon-to-be fiancée, Sheila Klein, was also vexed by these rumours and – on a different occasion, at Mapesbury Road – suggested that the two of them should investigate for themselves. '[Sheila] got me to wait all night with her to see if Andrew and Mick slept in the same bed and they did ... We found them asleep, facing the same way, and I can remember thinking how sweet they looked. Sheila said, "There, I knew they were!" and I still didn't know what she meant.'

ON 7 FEBRUARY 1964 the Beatles had crossed the Atlantic for the first time, touching down in New York amid scenes of juvenile hysteria that made European Beatlemania seem muted by comparison and ending American dominance of pop music with a single appearance on the nationwide *Ed Sullivan* TV show. They were Britain's most successful export since Shakespeare and Scotch whisky, ambassadors of seemingly boundless charm and good manners whose once-controversial hair was now regarded back home as a precious national asset. During a reception for them in Washington, DC, a woman guest produced some nail scissors and playfully snipped a lock or two from the back of Ringo Starr's neck. For the attendant British media, it was an outrage tantamount to defacing the Crown Jewels.

While the Beatles conquered America, the Rolling Stones had to be content with conquering the American act meant to have headlined their second UK package tour. This was Phil Spector's black female vocal trio the Ronettes, whose tumultuous 'Be My Baby' was a UK hit single currently far outselling 'I Wanna Be Your Man'. They were also sexy in a way no female pop group had ever been, with their beehive hair, brazen eye makeup and slinky, chiffon-sleeved trouser suits. Even that could not save them from the same fate as the Everly Brothers, two months previously. Before the tour even began, the Stones replaced them as top of the bill.

Spector, the trio's manager as well as record producer, was already fixated on lead singer Veronica – 'Ronnie' – Bennett (whom he would later subject to a gothic horror story of a marriage). Having received an advance character sketch of the top three Stones from his would-be British counterpart, Andrew Oldham, he sent them a stern collective telegram saying 'Leave my girls alone'. This did not stop both Mick and Keith from making a beeline for Ronnie's beehive at a party at deejay

Tony Hall's Mayfair flat which John Lennon and George Harrison also attended on the eve of their departure for America. *Boyfriend* magazine's correspondent, Maureen O'Grady, remembers the atypical tension between the Dartford chums as they competed for Ronnie's attention, and Mick's sulky pique when she proved immune to his charms and went off with Beatle George.

With 'I Wanna Be Your Man' barely out of the Top 10, the insatiable pop music machine was already slavering for a third Rolling Stones single. And this time there would be no friendly Beatles to help out. Instead, the Stones looked beyond the over-ransacked R&B back catalogue to the one white American performer who counted as an equal influence on them all. The unanimous choice was 'Not Fade Away', the B-side to Buddy Holly's 1957 hit 'Oh Boy', which Mick had seen Holly play live at the Woolwich Granada cinema during the one British tour he managed before his premature death. Serendipitously, the Stones–Ronettes show would appear at the same venue.

'Not Fade Away' was recorded at Regent Sound Studios during a brief interlude between early tour dates. To lighten an initially rather tired, grumpy atmosphere, Oldham turned the session into a booze-fuelled party, inviting various other pop personalities along to lend a hand. The American singer Gene Pitney, a former PR client of Oldham's, contributed extra percussion and an outsize bottle of cognac. Graham Nash and Allan Clarke of the (highly appropriate) Hollies dropped by to watch while the great Phil Spector, who had formerly produced Pitney's records, shook maracas.

Buddy Holly and the Crickets' 'Not Fade Away' had been an almost hymn-like chant of a cappella voices, whose only beat was drumsticks tapping on a cardboard box. But the Stones' cover version was as full-on and aggressive as 'I Wanna Be Your Man', with Keith's rhythm guitar turned up to maximum for the first – but not last – time in the staccato, seesaw beat invented by their late tour companion Bo Diddley. Mick's vocal made no attempt to replicate Holly's subtlety and charm, but stuck to the same snarling sexual challenge as before. In counterpoint to Keith's rhythm-led chords, Brian supplied a throbbing harmonica bottom line that made the others, temporarily, forgive him everything. The result might not exactly be a Wall of Sound on the Phil Spector level, Andrew Oldham commented, but it certainly was a Wall of Noise.

With nothing to put on the B-side, and tipsiness now firmly in control, Spector and Mick together cobbled up a song called 'Little by Little', an outright copy of Jimmy Reed's 'Shame Shame Shame'. At a later session, two further tracks were put on tape, both obviously unreleasable for commercial purposes. 'And Mr Spector and Mr Pitney Came Too' was a free-for-all instrumental featuring a wicked Mick take-off of Decca Records' elderly boss Sir Edward Lewis. 'Andrew's Blues' was a pornographic monologue by Phil Spector, dedicated to his British disciple-in-chief, featuring Allan Clarke and Graham Nash on back-up vocals.

When 'Not Fade Away' was released on 21 February few among the target audience even recognised it as a Buddy Holly homage. In its raw belligerence it seemed quintessentially Rolling Stones, which by now meant quintessentially Mick. For Jacqui Graham and her ilk, the accompanying vision was not of a bespectacled young Texan, dead too soon, but of ironic eyes and overstuffed, well-moistened lips slurring Holly's original 'A love for real will not fade away' to a barely grammatical 'Love is love and not fade away'; turning wistful hope into a sexual *fait accompli*. The single raced up every UK chart, peaking at No. 3, while Mick was still out on the road, upstaging, if not upending, Ronnie of the Ronettes.

With so many readers – or, at least, readers' offspring – converted to the Stones, Britain's national press now had to find something positive to say as well as recoiling like a Victorian maiden aunt from their hair and 'dirtiness'. And the line from Fleet Street could not have been more perfect if Andrew Oldham had dictated it himself. 'They look,' said the *Daily Express*, 'like boys whom any self-respecting mum would lock in the bathroom . . . five tough young London-based music-makers with doorstep mouths, pallid cheeks and unkempt hair . . . but now that the Beatles have registered with all age-groups, the Rolling Stones have taken over as the voice of the teens.' Maureen Cleave of the *London*

Evening Standard – who had been among the first national columnists to interview the Beatles – wrote about the Stones in a tone of repugnance more valuable than five-star adulation: 'They've done terrible things to the music scene, set it back, I would say, about eight years . . . they're a horrible-looking bunch, and Mick is indescribable.'

The rest of Fleet Street tumbled over itself to follow Oldham's script, depicting the Beatles – without circulation-damaging *lèse-majesté* – as just a teensy bit staid and conventional and the Stones as their unchallenged successors at the cutting edge. The two bands' followings were made to seem as incompatible and mutually hostile as supporters of rival soccer teams (though in truth there was huge overlap), one side of the stadium rooting for the honest, decent, caring North, the other for the cynical, arrogant, couldn't-give-a-shit South; the family stands applauding tunefulness, charm and good grooming, the hooligan terraces cheering roughness, surliness and tonsorial anarchy. A few months earlier, schoolboys all over the country had been suspended for coming to class with Beatle cuts; now one with a Jagger hairdo was excluded until he had it 'cut neatly like the Beatles'.

The *raison d'être* of all male pop stars, back through the Beatles and Elvis to Frank Sinatra and Rudy Vallee, had been sex appeal. Oldham's greatest image coup for the Stones was to make them sexually menacing. In March, the (predominantly male) readers of *Melody Maker* were confronted with a banner headline he had skilfully fed the paper: WOULD YOU LET YOUR SISTER GO WITH A ROLLING STONE? The *Express* helpfully amplified this to WOULD YOU LET YOUR DAUGHTER MARRY A ROLLING STONE?, thereby conjuring up hideous mental pictures in respectable homes throughout Middle England. Nor did it need specifying which Rolling Stone most threatened the virtue of all those sisters and daughters. It was hard to think of a comparable bogeyman-seducer since Giacomo Casanova in eighteenth-century Italy.

On the road – travelling from gig to gig in a manner still totally law-abiding and unobtrusive – the band were publicly insulted and mocked, barred from hotels, refused service in restaurants, pubs and shops, at times even physically attacked. In Manchester, after their first *Top of the*

Pops show, they went to a Chinese restaurant, were served pre-dinner drinks, but then sat for an hour without any food arriving. When they got up to leave, having scrupulously paid for their drinks, the chef burst out of the kitchen and chased them with a meat cleaver. On the Ronettes tour, their show at Slough's Adelphi Theatre ended so late that the only restaurant still open in the area was the Heathrow Airport cafeteria. As they ate their plastic meals, a big American at the next table began yelling insults. Mick, impressively, went over to remonstrate and received a punch in the face that knocked him backwards. Keith tried to come to his aid, but was also felled. These being days long before airport security, Fleet Street never heard of the incident.

'Not Fade Away' ramped up the mayhem at Stones' concerts – a strange outcome for Buddy Holly's quiet little prairie hymn. It proved their best live number to date, not so much for Mick's vocal as Brian's harmonica playing. The former blond waxwork seemed to gain new energy, hunched over the stand mike with fringed eyes closed and shoulders grooving, as if literally blowing life into the embers of his leadership.

British pop's notional North–South conflict reached a climax with its very own Battle of Gettysburg, a 'Mad Mod Ball', televised live from the Wembley Empire Pool arena and pitting the Rolling Stones against the cream of Merseybeat acts including Cilla Black, the Fourmost, the Searchers and Billy J. Kramer and the Dakotas. When the Stones arrived, they found they were expected to perform on a revolving rostrum in the midst of some eight thousand already demented fans. The set-up terrified Mick, who was convinced he would be pulled off the stage before the end of his first song and that someone might actually be killed. To reach the stage, he and the others had to run through an avenue of police and stewards, implausibly miming song words while one of their tracks was played over the loudspeaker system. The cordon immediately gave way against the weight of the crowd, leaving the Stones submerged among mad Mods while their music echoed round a bare rostrum.

After their set, they were marooned onstage for a further half hour, fighting off would-be boarders, while a contingent of Rockers, the Mods' motorbike-riding arch-foes, staged a counter-riot out in the street that resulted in thirty arrests. Unlike the real Gettysburg, it was a night of unstoppable victory for the South over those and all other rivals but one. 'In mass popularity,' wrote *Melody Maker*'s chief correspondent, Ray Coleman, 'the Stones are second only to the Beatles.'

THAT POSITION, HOWEVER, could not be maintained simply by doing live shows. To stay ahead of Merseybeat and offer the Beatles any real challenge, the Stones had to come up with a new single as big as 'Not Fade Away' and – such was the rate of the pop charts' metabolism – keep coming up with them at a rate of one roughly every twelve weeks. And the search for songs they could cover without compromising their ideals as a blues band or their carefully cultivated bad-boy image was growing ever more problematic.

Their options had been further reduced by using up four potential singles at once on an EP (extended play) record: Chuck Berry's 'Bye Bye Johnny', the Coasters' 'Poison Ivy', Barrett Strong's 'Money' and Arthur Alexander's 'You Better Move On', the latter always introduced by Mick as 'our slow one' and sung in atypically soulful, even plaintive mode, though its underlying message was still 'piss off'. Produced in small 45-RPM format, with a glossy picture sleeve, EPs were as important a UK market as albums, and had their own separate chart. The Stones' first not only went straight to the top of this but also made No. 15 on the singles charts.

The obvious solution was to give up covering other artists' songs and write their own, as the two main Beatles did with such spectacular success. Thanks to John Lennon and Paul McCartney, songwriting was no longer the sacred preserve of Moon-and-June-rhyming Tin Pan Alley hacks, but something at which all young British pop musicians, however untrained, were entitled to have a shot. If it worked, it was insurance against that seemingly inevitable day when the pop audience tired of them as performers and they could fall back on writing full-time. Even

Lennon and McCartney, at their America-conquering apogee, drew comfort from that safety net.

Until now, Mick had never for one moment visualised himself as a songwriter, let alone as one half of a partnership that would one day rival Lennon–McCartney's. The idea came from Andrew Oldham and was not motivated by a desire to advance Mick. The fact was that, while Oldham's management-PR side remained absorbed in the daily challenge of maintaining the Stones' disreputability, his would-be Phil Spector side was growing bored by working in the recording studio with just a 'covers band' – and resentful of having to pay copyright fees and royalties to the composers whose songs were covered.

In February, he had grandiosely informed *Record Mirror* that by autumn he would be 'Britain's most powerful independent record producer'. Since the Stones alone did not justify his assuming that title, he was actively scouting round for other artists to shape in the recording studio *à la* Spector – and had already found one. This was Cleo Sylvestre, who had auditioned as a back-up singer with the Stones eighteen months earlier, then gone on to have a platonic love affair with Mick which he took with so much the greater seriousness. Mick, in fact, recommended her to Oldham as a potential talent, even though he was still too upset by their break-up to be friends with her.

Oldham recorded Cleo singing the old Teddy Bears' hit 'To Know Him Is to Love Him', which had been Phil Spector's first writing and producing success. The B-side was an instrumental entitled 'There Are but Five Rolling Stones', played by the Stones but grandiosely credited to 'The Andrew Oldham Orchestra'. Cleo's pop-singing career failed to take off, but she went on to an award-winning career as an actress, notably with a one-woman show about Mary Seacole, the Crimean War's 'black Florence Nightingale'.

The domestic arrangements at 33 Mapesbury Road – and Brian's absence in Windsor – meant that the songwriters within the Stones more or less had to be Mick and Keith. Likewise, Keith's skill at playing hypnotic chords – as on 'Not Fade Away' – and Mick's verbal fluency dictated which of them would write the lyrics and which the tune. Both agreed it was a good idea, but were too much intimidated by the competition all around to sit down and try. Oldham exerted every fibre of PR persuasiveness to change their minds, insisting that it could not be that difficult – witness the speed at which John and Paul had dashed off 'I Wanna Be Your Man' that afternoon at Ken Coyler's club – and spinning extravagant visions (hugely underestimated, it would turn out) of the publishing royalties they could earn. Even that could not tempt Mick to have a go.

Finally, one November night in 1963, Oldham resorted to simple coercion, locking the pair in the flat's kitchenette, having previously removed all food and drink from it, then going off to spend the evening with his mother in Hampstead. If they wanted to eat that night, he shouted, they'd better have written a song when he came back. Returning a couple of hours later, he opened the front door quietly, tiptoed halfway upstairs and heard them hard at work. He went down again, slammed the door, and shouted 'What have you got?' A resentful, hungry Mick – those lips long-unstoked – 'told me they'd written this fucking song and I'd better fucking like it'.

That first effort, unconsciously reflecting Oldham's pressure, was entitled 'It Should Be You' and sounded enough like a real song to make them try again – and again. Fortuitously, the Stones were just leaving on a third national tour – this one including British pop's only other ex–college student, Mike Sarne – which provided live models to copy and hours of boredom, backstage or in Stu's van, when thinking up tunes and lyrics came as a positive relief. In a short time, Mick and Keith had accumulated around half a dozen songs, the most promising of which they recorded as rough demos at Regent Sound during quick trips back to London. The whole batch showed a romantic, even feminine side to the composers which made them quite unsuitable as Stones tracks, some indeed being specifically targeted at female artists: 'My Only Girl', 'We Were Falling in Love', 'Will You Be My Lover Tonight?' To hold their copyrights and receive any royalties they might earn, Oldham set up a publishing company called Nanker Phelge Music, a name as deliberately grotesque as the Beatles' Northern Songs company was quietly

traditional. A Nanker was Brian Jones's name for his *Lucky Jim* facial con-
tortions while Phelge was the Edith Grove flatmate who used to 'gob' so
colourfully up the walls.

Oldham's search for artists to cover these first Jagger–Richard songs
was confined to the lower reaches of British pop and even there met with
only modest success. 'Will You Be My Lover Tonight?' was recorded by
a mutual friend of Oldham and the Stones named George Bean and
released on Decca in January 1964, sinking without a trace. 'Shang a Doo
Lang', an unashamed knock-off of the Crystals' 'He's Sure the Boy I Love',
went to a sixteen-year-old newcomer named Adrienne Posta and was
produced by Oldham with Spectoresque Wall of Sound effects. By far the
most prestigious catch was Gene Pitney, a major American name whose
fondness for London pop low life had led him to play back-up percussion
at the boozy 'Not Fade Away' session. Pitney, it so happened, needed a
follow-up to his recent massive hit with Bacharach and David's '24 Hours
from Tulsa'. Oldham persuaded him to make it Jagger and Richard's 'My
Only Girl', retitled 'That Girl Belongs to Yesterday'. Though Pitney substantially rewrote the song, Mick and Keith's credit survived when it
made the UK Top 10 and even sneaked into the US Hot 100.

Adrienne Posta was the daughter of a wealthy furniture manufacturer who intended to make her a pop star by hook or by crook. When
Decca released Adrienne's version of Jagger and Richard's 'Shang a Doo
Lang' in early March, Oldham persuaded Mr Posta to hold a launch
party at his flat in Seymour Place, Bayswater. The party was to witness
a momentous meeting, though not the one Oldham originally had in
mind. Deciding it was time Keith Richard 'started going out with something other than a guitar', Oldham asked his girlfriend Sheila Klein
to bring along someone for Keith. She chose a friend with the happily
coincidental name of Linda Keith, a former assistant at *Vogue* who had
progressed to modelling.

Launch parties for records were unusual in 1964, and an impressive posse of Swinging London insiders turned up to wish Adrienne's
single Godspeed and partake of her father's hospitality. They included
Peter Asher from the singing duo Peter and Gordon, the latest act to

benefit from Lennon–McCartney songs. Asher brought his actress sister Jane and her boyfriend, Paul McCartney, who lodged at the Asher family home in Wimpole Street, Marylebone. With them came an old Hampstead friend of Oldham's named John Dunbar and his seventeen-year-old girlfriend, Marianne Faithfull.

The name that always seemed too perfect for the young woman it adorned – 'Faithfull' with two *l*'s, suggesting a double portion of innocent steadfastness – was not a publicist's invention, as many people later assumed. Marianne's father was an academic named Robert Glynn Faithfull who served with British intelligence during the Second World War, then went on to receive a doctorate in psychology from Liverpool University. Nothing about this seemingly quintessential English rose hinted at a background that was also more exotically foreign than any of the crucial people in Mick's life had been, or would be.

Her mother, Eva, was an Austro-Hungarian aristocrat, Baroness Erisso, whose family, the Sacher-Masochs, dated back to Emperor Charlemagne. Eva's great-uncle Leopold von Sacher-Masoch was the author of the nineteenth-century novel *Venus im Pelz* in which he gave his own name, 'masochism', to pleasure derived from self-inflicted pain. Brought up in Hapsburg grandeur, Eva had become an actress and dancer with the Max Reinhardt company in Vienna during the 1930s and, but for the war, might have followed Reinhardt to America and a career in Hollywood. Instead, she married the British intelligence officer Robert Faithfull and settled with him in Britain, where Marianne, their only child, was born in 1946.

The couple separated in 1952 and the Austrian baroness relocated to – of all places – Reading, the unexciting Berkshire town best known for Huntley & Palmer's biscuits and Oscar Wilde's *Ballad of Reading Gaol*. Here she acquired a small house in the poorest district and worked variously as a shop assistant, coffee-bar server and bus conductress while still managing to imbue her daughter with a sense of patrician superiority. Marianne was educated on semi-charity terms at a Catholic convent school, St Joseph's, under a regime so strict that the girls had to bathe in underslips to avoid the sin of looking at their own nude bodies.

She grew up to be a stunning combination of beauty and brains, mistily innocent-looking, yet with a voluptuous figure; shyly and refinedly spoken, yet with an inquiring intellect and a rich mezzo-soprano singing voice. She had no doubt that life would lead her into the theatre or music – possibly both – and by the age of sixteen was already working as a folk singer around Reading coffee bars. Early in 1964, she visited Cambridge to attend an undergraduates' ball, and met Andrew Oldham's friend John Dunbar, then studying fine arts at Churchill College. Oldham was looking to expand his managerial empire beyond the Stones, and asked Dunbar if he knew any girl singers. 'Well, actually, yes,' Dunbar replied.

At Adrienne Posta's launch party, the other female guests wore butterfly-bright 'dolly' dresses with the new daringly short skirts. Mari-anne, however, chose blue jeans and a baggy shirt of Dunbar's that was sexier than the most clinging sheath. Tony Calder, standing near the door with Mick, Oldham, Chrissie Shrimpton and Sheila Klein, still remem-bers her entrance: 'It was like someone turned the sound down. It was like seeing the Virgin Mary with an amazing pair of tits. Andrew and Mick both said together, "I want to fuck her." Both their girlfriends went, "What did you say?" Mick and Andrew went, "We said we want to record her."'

Marianne at this point thought the Rolling Stones were 'yobbish schoolboys . . . with none of the polish of John Lennon or Paul McCart-ney'. By her own later account, she wouldn't have noticed Mick if he hadn't been in the throes of yet another row with Chrissie, 'who was crying and shouting at him . . . and in the heat of the moment, one of her false eye-lashes was peeling off'. The person who most interested her was Andrew Oldham, especially when he came over ('all beaky and angular, like some bird of prey'), brusquely asked his friend John Dunbar for her name – no female equality for years yet! – and, on learning it genuinely was Marianne Faithfull, announced that he intended to make her a pop star.

Within days, to her amazement, Marianne had a contract with the Stones' label, Decca, and an appointment to record a single with Old-ham as her producer. The A-side was to have been a Lionel Bart song, 'I Don't Know How (To Tell You)', but when she tried it out it proved totally unsuited to her voice and to the persona her Svengali intended to create. Instead, Oldham turned to his in-house team of Jagger–Richard, giving them precise instructions as to the kind of ballad he required for Marianne: 'She's from a convent. I want a song with brick walls all round it, high windows and no sex.'

Though the result bore a joint credit, Tony Calder remembers its conception to have been entirely Mick's, working with session guitarist Big Jim Sullivan. The monologue of a lonely, disillusioned older woman – harking back to Alfred Lord Tennyson's 'Lady of Shallot' and foreshadowing the Beatles' 'Eleanor Rigby' – it was a glimpse of the sensitivity and almost feminine intuition Mick was known to possess but so rarely showed. The original title, 'As Time Goes By', became 'As Tears Go By' to avoid confusion with pianist Dooley Wilson's famous cabaret spot in the film *Casablanca*.

With hindsight, Marianne would consider 'As Tears Go By' 'a Françoise Hardy song . . . Europop you might hear on a French jukebox . . . "The Lady of Shalott" to the tune of "These Foolish Things"'. She still concedes that for a songwriter so inexperienced it showed remarkable maturity – clairvoyance even. 'It's an absolutely astonishing thing for a boy of twenty to have written a song about a woman looking back nostalgically on her life. The uncanny thing is that Mick should have written those words so long before everything happened . . . it's almost as if our whole relationship was prefigured in that song.'

For this second recording session, Marianne travelled up from Reading to London chaperoned by her friend Sally Oldfield (sister of the future *Tubular Bells* wizard, Mike). Oldham's production stuck to the 'high brick walls and no sex' formula, toning down her usually robust mezzo-soprano to a wispy demureness, counterpointed by the mournful murmur of a *cor anglais*, or English horn. Mick and Keith watched the proceedings and afterwards gave the two girls a lift back to Paddington station by taxi. On the way, Mick tried to get Marianne to sit on his lap, but she made Sally do so instead. 'I mean, it was on that level,' she recalls. '"What a cheeky little yob," I thought to myself. "So immature."'

Within a month, 'As Tears Go By' was in the UK Top 20, finally peaking at No. 9. British pop finally had a thoroughly English female singer, or so it appeared, rather than just would-be American ones. And the media were confronted with a head-scratching paradox: two members of a band

notorious for dirtiness, rawness and uncouthness had brought gentility –
not to say virginity – into the charts for the very first time.

The success of 'As Tears Go By' might have been expected to start a
wholesale winning streak for the Jagger–Richard songwriting partnership that would finally benefit their own band rather than ill-assorted
outsiders. But, strangely, having their name on a No. 9 hit acted more
like a brake. Mick had no idea where the song had come from and, after
weeks of racking his brains with Keith, began to despair of writing anything else a fraction as good.

Certainly, when the Stones' first album appeared, on 17 April, it was
still far from clear that they had a would-be Lennon and McCartney in
their ranks. Recorded at Regent Sound in just five days snatched from
the Ronettes tour, this was almost completely made up of the cover versions from which Oldham had struggled to wean them – Chuck Berry's
'Carol', Bo Diddley's 'Mona (I Need You Baby)', Willie Dixon's 'I Just
Want to Make Love to You', James Moore's 'I'm a King Bee', Jimmy Reed's
'Honest I Do', Marvin Gaye's 'Can I Get a Witness?', Rufus Thomas's
'Walking the Dog', Bobby Troup's 'Route 66'. The only Jagger–Richard
track thought worthy of inclusion was 'Tell Me (You're Coming Back)',
an echoey ballad in faintly Merseybeat style. The album, in fact, was like
a Stones live show (much as the Beatles' first one had been), its imme-
diacy heightened by Regent Sound's primitive equipment and Andrew
Oldham's anguished eye on the clock. At the session for 'Can I Get a
Witness?', Mick realised he couldn't remember all Marvin Gaye's words,
and neither could anyone else present. A hurried phone call had to be
made to the song's publishers on Savile Row for a copy of the lyrics to
be hunted out and left in reception. The usefully athletic vocalist ran a
half mile from Denmark Street to collect them, then back again. On the
track he is still audibly breathless.

The album was entitled, simply, *The Rolling Stones* – in itself an act of
extreme Oldham hubris. The Beatles' first album had followed custom
in bearing the name of a hit single, 'Please Please Me', and even their
ground-breaking second, *With the Beatles*, still had a whiff of conventionality. But Oldham did not stop there. In defiance of Decca Records'

entire marketing department, he insisted that *The Rolling Stones'* front cover showed neither name nor title – just a glossy picture of the five standing sideways with heavily shadowed, unsmiling faces turned to the camera. Mick was first, then dapper Charlie, a squeezed-in Bill and barely recognisable Keith, with Brian – the only one in their old stage uniform of leather waistcoat and shirtsleeves rather than varicoloured suits – symbolically at the back and out of line.

On its reverse, the cover returned to wordy normality, with track listings, studio credits and a pronouncement that seemed like yet more Oldham hubris: 'The Rolling Stones are more than a group – they are a way of life.' Little did even he imagine that, almost half a century later, at the BAFTA film awards, an audience of the world's most glamorous people would still be hungering to lead it.

Advance orders for *The Rolling Stones* exceeded 100,000 as against only 6,000 for the Beatles' album début, *Please Please Me*. Better still, as it climbed the UK album chart to No. 1 it passed *With the Beatles*, finally on the decline after six months in the Top 20. The Stones, Oldham crowed delightedly, had 'knocked the Beatles off' in their home market. Now for America.

CHAPTER SIX

'We Spent a Lot of Time Sitting in Bed, Doing Crosswords'

For any British band, the supreme challenge, and greatest thrill, is to 'crack' America. And few have failed quite so comprehensively as the Rolling Stones on their first US tour, in June 1964. The country would notice Mick soon enough, for better or worse, but during most of this initial three-week visit he was a barely distinguishable face among five, taking his equal share of disappointment and humiliation.

The Stones were not only following the triumphal footsteps of the Beatles four months earlier; they were also well to the rear in the so-called British Invasion of other UK bands who had stampeded after John, Paul, George and Ringo across the Atlantic and into the US charts. On the American edition of their first album, they were billed as 'England's Newest Hitmakers', bracketing them with 'soft' pop acts they despised, such as Gerry and the Pacemakers, Billy J. Kramer and the Dakotas and the Dave Clark Five.

When the Beatles had arrived in New York in February, it was with an American No. 1 single, 'I Want to Hold Your Hand'. But the Stones could offer no such impressive calling card. Their Beatle-bestowed UK hit, 'I Wanna Be Your Man', had been released on the London label, Decca's US affiliate, but then abruptly withdrawn because its B-side was called 'Stoned', which in America meant drunk. It had then been rere-leased, coupled with 'Not Fade Away', but even in a market supposedly ravenous for all British bands had barely scraped into *Billboard* maga-zine's Top 50.

Thanks to Andrew Oldham, their transatlantic hosts had been primed to welcome them like a new strain of herpes. 'Americans, brace yourselves!' warned the flash circulated to newspapers and broadcast media by the Associated Press. 'In the tracks of the Beatles, a second wave of sheepdog-looking, angry-acting Britons is on the way . . . dirtier, streakier and more disheveled than the Beatles . . .' The Fab Four had flown off, carrying the whole nation's hopes and even prayers like Nev-ille Chamberlain bound for Munich or a Test cricket team for Austral-asia. Before the Stones left Heathrow Airport on 1 June an MP in the House of Commons expressed fears that they might do real harm to Anglo-American relations.

Even with this advance word-of-badmouth, it proved impossible for Oldham to whip up any major media coverage on the American side. Turndowns came from the NBC and CBS TV networks and, most slightingly, from *The Ed Sullivan Show,* which had clinched the Beatles' conquest by beaming them to a national audience of more than 70 mil-lion. Paradoxically, the splashiest print coverage came from a quarter not normally interested in dirtiness and scruffiness – *Vogue* magazine. Diana Vreeland, the legendary editor of *Vogue*'s American edition, agreed to publish a David Bailey photograph of Mick that every British maga-zine had rejected, despite never having heard of him or his band. 'I don't care who he is,' she told Bailey. 'He looks great, so I'll run it.'

While calling the Stones 'scruffier and seedier than the Beatles', *Vogue* summed them up more pithily than any UK publication thus far, and with a hint of ladylike moist gussets that probably did Mick's image more good in the long run than NBC, CBS and Ed Sullivan put together:

'To the inner group in London, the new spectacular is a solemn young man, Mick Jagger, one of the five Rolling Stones, those singers [*sic*] who will set out to cross America by bandwagon in June. For the British, the Stones have a perverse, unsettling sex appeal, with Jagger out in front of his teammates. To women he's fascinating, to men a scare . . .'

Since the Beatles' reception by three thousand banner-waving fans, spilling over observation terraces and buckling plate-glass windows, the arrival of British pop bands at New York's John F. Kennedy Airport had become a routine story to the city's media. For the Stones, London Records laid on a markedly cut-price version of the now-familiar procedure, enlisting a few dozen teenage girls to scream dutifully as the band descended the aircraft steps after their economy-class flight, hiring a couple of Old English sheepdogs to represent kindred spirits, and providing a cake for Charlie Watts's twenty-third birthday. At the press conference which followed, there was surprise, even some disappointment, when they proved to be politer and better spoken than most of the invaders who had come before. Who was the leader? one reporter asked. 'We are . . . all of us,' Mick lisped in his best LSE accent, without a frisson of Cockney.

The Beatles had spent their first New York landfall with their manager and considerable retinue in interconnecting luxury suites at the top of Manhattan's grandest hotel, the Plaza, at Fifth Avenue and Central Park. The Stones spent theirs at the far-from-grand Hotel Astor in Times Square, bunking two to a poky room with their retinue (i.e., roadie Ian Stewart). To save money – an urgent consideration throughout the tour – Oldham slept on the office sofa of his friend and role model, Phil Spector.

Once his charges had checked into the Astor (which, miraculously, offered no objection), Oldham managed to feed the British press a story that, in true Beatle style, they had caused riots in midtown Manhattan and were imprisoned in their hotel by shrieking mobs. Unfortunately, agency photos which arrived home at the same time showed them exploring the Times Square district without a single hysteric in sight.

That is not to say that they went unnoticed. They had come to a land where every 'manly' man, from President Lyndon Johnson downwards, had hair cropped as close to the scalp as a convict's but for a little tooth-brushlike crest. The Beatles had been let off their hair because of some vague correlation with British classical theatre – Laurence Olivier as Richard III or Hamlet. But Rolling Stone hair meant only homosexual-ity, which – save in certain enlightened parts of Greenwich Village – was regarded as even more unnatural and detestable than it was in Brit-ain. What should have been a magical first experience of New York for Mick and the others was marred by the typically forthright comments of passing New Yorkers: 'Ya fuckin' faggot!' or 'Look at that goddamn faggot!' The fact that to English ears *faggot* still meant a rissole, or meat patty, did not make the experience any pleasanter.

The city's welcome grew several degrees warmer after they met up with Murray 'the K' Kaufman, the WINS radio deejay who had gen-erated huge publicity for his show, and himself, by hooking onto the Beatles back in February. Now he adopted the Stones in the same way, escorting them to nightspots like the Peppermint Lounge – where the Twist had been born and was now in its death throes – and introducing them to useful New York music-biz cronies like Bob Crewe, songwriter and producer to the Four Seasons.

The Stones privately thought Murray the K a ludicrous figure, but he did do them one huge favour. It happened at a party at Crewe's apart-ment, in a gloomy Central Park-side pile known as the Dakota where, sixteen years later, the Beatles' story would come to a horrific full stop. During the evening, Murray gave Andrew Oldham an R&B single, 'It's All Over Now', written by Sam Cooke's guitarist Bobby Womack and recorded by Womack and his three brothers as the Valentinos. It would be a perfect song for the Stones to cover, the deejay insisted. And the rights could be picked up here in New York from Womack's manager, an accountant-turned-pop impresario named Allen Klein.

For Mick and Keith, the main point of being in New York was to visit the Apollo Theater, Harlem's famous showplace for black music, which had launched the careers of Billie Holiday, Ella Fitzgerald, Aretha Franklin and Stevie Wonder among many others. Harlem was still a no-go area for unaccompanied whites, so they had to ask Ronnie Spector of the Ronettes – on whom Keith still had a huge crush – to be their guide. Because of the difficulty of getting cabs back to Midtown late at night, which, anyway, they couldn't afford, they had to sleep on the floor at Ronnie's mother's apartment in Spanish Harlem. In the morning, she would cook them bacon and eggs, and they would thank her with punctilious good manners.

To add to the thrill, it happened to be James Brown Week at the Apollo. Known as 'the Godfather of Soul', Brown had a mesmerising stage act that combined R&B and soul with Barnum-esque showmanship: backed by his vocal group the Famous Flames, he never stopped moving for a second, boogieing as if on an invisible Travelator (two decades before Michael Jackson's Moonwalk), hurling himself onto his knees or into the splits, finally suffering a make-believe seizure, when two minders would rush from the wings, wrap him in a cloak and half carry him away. Four or five of these operatic cardiac arrests would be simulated before the curtain finally fell.

Such was Mick's awe of the Godfather that he never had covered any of Brown's great showstoppers: not 'Papa's Got a Brand New Bag', or 'Please Please Please' or even 'It's a Man's Man's World', much as he might applaud the sentiment. Now, in the Apollo's marijuana-scented dark, he took careful note of every dance move Brown made, to be practised later in front of a full-length mirror. When Ronnie sneaked him and Keith into Brown's dressing room, he beheld an almost monarchical figure, surrounded by servants and sycophants, who took care of business as assiduously as he did music, watched every penny and imposed strict discipline on his musicians, fining anyone who was late or went onstage with dirty shoes. Here, too, were important lessons for the future.

From New York, the Stones flew to Los Angeles to make their one nationwide TV appearance. This was not on a prestigious show like Ed Sullivan's, but *Hollywood Palace*, a mixed-bag variety programme emceed that week by Dean Martin. When they turned up at the studio, the producer was aghast that they weren't in matching suits and, unavailingly, offered them money to go out and buy some. They did not meet the great 'Dino' himself during rehearsals, when a stand-in was used; only during transmission did they realise they had been set up as stooges to their host's boozy humour. 'Now here's something for the youngsters,' Martin announced with an air of intense long-suffering. 'Five young musicians from England . . . the Rolling Stones. I've been rolled a few times when I was stoned myself. I dunno what they're singin' about, but here they are . . .' A few moments of Mick singing 'I Just Want to Make Love to You', and their tuxedo-clad host was sniping at them again. 'The Rolling Stones! Aren't they great? [Exaggerated eye roll] People talk about these long-haired groups but it's really an optical illusion. They just have smaller foreheads and higher eyebrows.'

The tour that followed had been planned by the American agency GAC, seemingly with some of the same malevolence. There was a good opening show in San Bernardino, California, where a capacity crowd roared enthusiastic response to the name check their home town received in Mick's version of 'Route 66'. After that, a series of economy-class internal flights took the band on a transcontinental wander far off Route 66: San Antonio, Minneapolis, Omaha, Detroit, Pittsburgh and Harrisburg. Their support was the American balladeer Bobby Vee, whose backing musicians wore matching mohair suits, collars and ties just like the ones they themselves had lately escaped. At some stops, they found themselves appearing at state fairs in company with carni-val midways, rodeos and circus acts, including a baby elephant and a troupe of seals. Thanks to wildly uneven advance publicity, audience sizes varied between a rapturous two or three thousand and an apa-thetic few dozen among whom the dominant element were homophobic red-necked cowboys.

The Stones' heyday as arrogant kings of the American road were still far in the future. Surrounded by gun-toting, crop-headed and resentful police, they all did their utmost not to step out of line. In one cheerless, raw-brick dressing room, Mick and Brian were drinking rum and Coca-Cola while Keith, atypically, made do with plain Coke. A policeman walked up and screamed at them to empty their glasses down the toi-let. When Keith protested, the cop drew his gun. Also in contrast with later trans-American journeys, Keith would recall, 'it was almost impossible to have sex . . . In New York or LA you can always find something, but when you're in Omaha in 1964 and you suddenly feel horny, you've had it.'

The itinerary, however, included something of importance far outweighing these petty – and short-lived – setbacks. In Chicago, Oldham had booked the Stones to lay down some tracks (hopefully including their next British single) at Chess Records, the mythic label on which Chuck Berry, Muddy Waters, Willie Dixon and just about every other major R&B and blues giant had transfigured Mick's prim boyhood. Other than counselling him, against all his instincts, to become wicked, it was probably the greatest service his Svengali ever did him.

This nonpareil black music label had in fact been started by two white men, Polish immigrants named Leonard and Phil Chess, who had changed their surname from Czyz. Leonard's twenty-two-year-old son, Marshall, had worked for the company since the age of thirteen and, during a spell in the postroom, used to send off albums to an unknown blues fanatic in England named Mike Jagger. Normally, Chess did not allow outsiders to record in its studio – especially young, white, British ones – but Marshall knew about the blues scene in London, so he persuaded his father and uncle to make an exception for them.

The band spent two days in Chess's studios at 2120 South Michigan Avenue, working with the label's most-sought-after engineer, Ron Malo. (Having delivered them there, Oldham had the good sense not to put on airs as their producer, but stayed discreetly in the background.) Malo treated the awestruck young Britons like musicians as legitimate as any others; their response was to work hard and harmoniously, finishing fourteen tracks during the two day-long sessions.

Top of the list was that gift from Murray the K, 'It's All Over Now'. The Valentinos' version had hovered on the edge of burlesque, with a hermaphrodite lead vocal and a tempo lifted from Chuck Berry's 'Memphis, Tennessee'. Ron Malo turned it into a guitar-jangly pop track with a growling bass riff that was instant jukebox fodder, yet preserved the Stones' essential roughness and hinted at the myriad influences of the blues mecca around them. While all the band sounded better than they ever had, the main advance was in Mick's voice, now refined to a punk-Dixie snarl and hovering between self-pity ('Well, I used to wake 'n mawnin', git ma brek-fusst in ba-a-id . . .') and yah-boo triumph ('Yes, I used to looeerve her, bu-u-rd it's awl over now . . .'). Bobby Womack's original lyric spoke of the errant girlfriend's having 'spent all my money . . . played the high-class game', which Mick amended to 'half-assed game'.

Marshall Chess was amused to see Mick, Brian and Keith behave in the studio as they thought their blues masters did, 'swigging Jack Daniel's from the bottle, where our guys would've poured it into a glass and sipped it'. Partly, this was nerves; they expected real Chicago blues-men to tear them to pieces for their presumption. But in fact they were met with nothing but friendliness. During the first day's session two of their greatest heroes, Willie Dixon and Buddy Guy, both dropped by Malo's studio to listen and bestow compliments and encouragement. On their second morning they found themselves walking in through Chess's front lobby beside an immaculately dressed man with the face of a merry black Toby Jug – none other than Muddy Waters, without whose catalogue (not least 'Rollin' Stone') they would never have got started. Muddy carried himself as regally as a king but, on seeing roadie Ian Stewart struggling with the Stones' equipment, picked up an amp and carried it into the studio for them.

At the end of their second day, the great Chuck Berry himself drove in from his country-estate-cum-hotel, Berry Park, to take a look. Though never noted for philanthropy to young musicians, he could not but be softened by the Stones' devotion – and the number of his songs they were covering that would pay him royalties. 'Swing on, gentlemen,' he told them in flawless Berry-ese. 'You are sounding most well, if I may say so.'

Keith was always to remember a beyond-brilliant Chess session musi-cian named Big Red, a huge black albino with a Gibson guitar that looked 'like a mandolin' in his hands. During breaks from their own session, Mick, Keith, Charlie and Stu used to creep into the next-door studio and listen to Big Red, but could never pluck up courage to ask him to sit in with them. 'We just thought we were terribly lucky to be there, so let's learn what we can,' Keith would recall. 'It was like being given extra tuition.'

And Mick? Before leaving Britain, he'd told an interviewer with unusual candour, and passion, that his main objective in America was to meet as many of his blues idols as possible, and that even 'to see and hear them work in person will be a big thing for me'. What happened with Chuck and Muddy and Willie and Buddy and Big Red in Chicago was, by a long way, the most thrilling experience of his life thus far. But afterwards it was to be swallowed up by all-enveloping Jagger amnesia. 'I don't remember going to Chess,' he would claim. 'It's just something I read about in books.'

Back in New York, things decidedly improved with a better hotel, the Park Sheraton (albeit still in shared rooms), and two sold-out concerts, like the Beatles', at the city's illustrious Carnegie Hall. After the second show, there was a party at the hotel with guests including the *New York Post* pop correspondent, and Bob Dylan's close friend, Al Aronowitz. 'The first thing we saw when we walked in,' Aronowitz recalled, 'was Mick sitting on a bed, surrounded by a flock of elegantly styled chicks, fluttering as if they all wanted to rub his body . . . Okay, Mick'd discovered room service.'

There was also a first glimpse of the Jagger attitude to women that we will come to know so well. At one point, Gloria Stavers, the influential editor of *16 Magazine,* approached him among his seraglio to tell him how much she'd enjoyed the show. 'Should I be flattered?' he replied.

With the release of the Stones' 'Merseybeat' song 'Tell Me' as a US single increasing album sales, and a general sense of making some headway at last, it was clearly vital for them to extend their visit beyond its scheduled three weeks. Instead – bafflingly to new American converts like Aronowitz and Murray the K – Oldham whisked them home as scheduled. The excuse he gave out was that they had to honour a booking to play at the summer ball of Magdalen College, Oxford. The truth was that he couldn't afford to keep them in America a moment longer. In contrast to later forays there, he calculated the tour had earned them ten old shillings, or fifty pence, each.

*

ARRIVING BACK IN Britain during the music press's awards season
did much to restore everyone's self-esteem. In the *New Musical Express*
readers' poll, the Stones came second to the Beatles as Top British Vocal
Group with 'Not Fade Away' only just losing out to 'She Loves You' as
Year's Best Single. *Record Mirror* named them Top British Group and
Mick – underlining his still unusual non-guitar-playing role – as Top
British Group Member. Nor was it long before the American nightmare
was totally vindicated. On 26 June 'It's All Over Now' was released,
with advance orders of 150,000, and took only two weeks to become
their first British No. 1.

No hype from Tony Calder was needed – nor even help from the
amendment to the Valentinos' original lyric which Andrew Oldham had
expected to create such a furore. Rendered in Mick's Dixie drawl, 'half-
assed game' was widely mistaken for 'high, fast game', as in some poker
school on a Mississippi paddleboat. Anyway, *ass* is much less vulgar to
British ears than the good old Anglo-Saxon *arse*. At all events, no objections were made and the single played uncensored on the BBC.

What made 'It's All Over Now' irresistible was its dishevelled, slightly
off-register sound, so unlike the high gloss of the Beatles' Abbey Road
Studios, and glimpses of seamy real life compared with wholesome
Beatle heaven: Mick getting his 'brekfusst [and who knew what else] in
ba-a-id', his 'achin' ha-id' no doubt partly due to a hangover. It was not
quite the first grown-up-sounding single ever to challenge the infantil-
ism of the UK pop charts; the Animals had just got there first with 'The
House of the Rising Sun'. Its new dimension was the hint of loucheness
– something that most British women didn't yet know they liked.

The backlash came from fans of pure blues and R&B, especially
those who had followed the Stones up through the clubs and now felt
personally betrayed by what was seen as a sell-out to commercial pop.
(Only an enlightened few were aware that 'It's All Over Now' had been
recorded at R&B's epicentre, Chess Records, or that Bobby Womack and
the Valentinos, its writer and original performers, were as 'pure' as could

be.) To make matters worse, the single it had booted from the No. 1 spot was 'The House of the Rising Sun', a classic blues song rendered in uncompromising blues style.

This was an era, unlike later, in which Mick was unafraid to stick his head above the parapet. When controversy erupted around 'It's All Over Now', he was already in hot water for having publicly called a new group called the Zephyrs 'a load of rubbish', so violating an unwritten rule that British pop bands were always generous towards each other. Now he told *Melody Maker* intemperately (for the Stones knew the Animals well) that 'people shouldn't kid themselves "House of the Rising Sun" is R&B . . . it's no more R&B than how's your father . . .' It brought him a stern reproof in the next week's paper from reader Keith Temple of East Croydon: 'Who is to blame for this misconception of R&B? Mick Jagger. One and a half years ago, Jagger's proud boast was that the Stones played pure R&B – the music they loved. On being accused of going commercial, Jagger denies this. Yet the Stones reached number one with 'It's All Over Now', a rock song. Don't kid yourselves, readers, that there's R&B in the chart with "It's All Over Now". It's no more R&B than "House of the Rising Sun".'

The front-page lead in the same edition, accompanied by a caricature head of Mick, was an unwontedly humble and ingratiating apology for his previous rudeness about the Zephyrs: 'I don't want [them] to be angry or anything. I didn't like their record but I didn't mean to cause offence . . . In fact, [it] was no worse than our first record, "Come On" . . . I'd like to meet 'em all and tell 'em how I feel personally.' 'JAGGER ATTACKED AGAIN,' said a flash at the foot of the column, 'See Letters, back page.' The letters page was headlined 'R&B? NOT ON YOUR LIFE' below a strap line 'IT'S ALL THAT JAGGER'S FAULT.'

Most of the criticism was defused, however, by a second Stones EP, *Five by Five*, containing a quintet of irreproachably R&B tracks from the Chess sessions, including Jay McShann's 'Confessin' the Blues' and Wilson Pickett's 'If You Need Me', and with liner notes by Andrew Oldham, pointing out that the Stones' first album, packed with authentic R&B, had stayed at No. 1 on the UK chart for thirty weeks (it had actually been twelve). Purist Stones fans breathed easier, reassured that Keith's growly rock tremolo and the glimpse into Mick's bedroom had been a momentary aberration.

By mid-summer 1964 a surfeit of real-life attempts to see Mick's bedroom had broken up the flat-sharing ménage at 33 Mapesbury Road. The fans who had followed Jacqui Graham's pioneer trail to his Willes-den hideaway possessed little of Jacqui's considerateness, staking out number 33's front gate around the clock, ringing the doorbell at all hours and invading the garden to peer through windows and steal flowers, even blades of grass, as souvenirs. The three original flat-sharers' per-sonal circumstances had also changed, with Oldham now married to Sheila Klein and Keith going steady with the *Vogue* model Linda Keith, as Mick was with *Vogue* supermodel Jean Shrimpton's sister, Chrissie.

While Oldham set up home with Sheila, Mick and Keith moved together to 10a Holly Hill, Hampstead, a sought-after area then, as now, where every other house seems to bear a blue plaque commemorating some former resident celebrated in the arts or sciences. Their flat, in estate agent's language, was 'chalet-style with a long living room and a sunken bedroom', and (farewell, Edith Grove!) enjoyed the regular services of a cleaner. Chrissie Shrimpton moved in with Mick, though, for appearances' sake with her family, she kept on her bed-sitting room with her friend Liz in Olympia, west London.

Outed as Mick's steady girlfriend some months previously, Chris-sie was regularly pictured by his side with her flicked-up, Alice-banded hair, enormous black eyes and matching full-lipped pout, her famous surname giving that intriguing extra twist to his own accelerating fame. Along with Paul McCartney's similarly 'classy bird', Jane Asher, she was the envy of almost every young woman in Britain.

In reality, Chrissie hated the life she now found herself leading as the consort of a pop star. 'The fans used to attack me and throw things at me, and it was often really frightening. I can remember being in cars and having to hold the roof up because there were girls piling on it and we thought we were going to be crushed.' Under her wild-child exterior was a deeply conventional person who had slept with Mick as a seventeen-year-old only because she genuinely believed she would marry him and start a family. 'As far as I was concerned, it was total love and I'd be with him for the rest of my life. I hated all the fan hysteria stuff and I wasn't really interested in running around the clubs and everything rock chicks are supposed to do. All I wanted was to have babies and be normal.'

Still resolutely refusing to be drawn into the couture world after Jean, Chrissie continued to work as a secretary, latterly with the Stones' record company, Decca, and thus to have a daytime routine out of synch with Mick's nocturnal one of performing, recording and partying. Even after her existence became known to his female followers, Oldham still felt it inadvisable to parade her too much at Stones' gigs and public appearances. 'As a girl in those days, you were a second-class citizen. You were on your honour to stay in the background and keep your mouth shut.'

Just as her sister kept her at arm's length from the Bailey–*Vogue* set, so she met few of the musicians with whom Mick consorted, on the road or at their chosen club, the Ad Lib. One exception was 'the Duchess', the glamorous young black woman in a skin-tight gold lamé cat-suit who played guitar in Bo Diddley's band. Another was Mickie Most, the young singer-turned-producer responsible for the Animals' 'House of the Rising Sun' that Mick had so ungraciously slagged off. 'Mickie's wife was also named Chrissie, so we were two Mickie-and-Chrissies.'

Her main ally within the Stones' circle was Charlie Watts's steady girlfriend, Shirley Shepherd, a sculpture student at the Royal College of Art, to whom Charlie became engaged in April 1964. A strong-willed, outspoken character, in utter contrast to his mildness and politeness, Shirley refused to accept the vow of anonymity imposed on Chrissie and other Stones' women. Since Mick found Charlie the most restful of all his bandmates and Chrissie got on well with Shirley, the four went on holiday together to Ibiza during a brief respite from touring that summer. When they arrived at their hotel, Shirley found she and Chrissie were expected to register separately so that lurking paparazzi would not link them with the two Stones. 'A photographer tried to take a picture of our names in the hotel register,' Chrissie remembers. 'So Mick hit him. And when we left, Shirley and I were told we had to come home on different flights from Mick and Charlie. I went along with it, of course, but Shirley absolutely refused to be bullied by Mick.'

Shirley was also one of the few around Mick who ever dared find fault with his appearance. 'Neither of our boyfriends looked good on the beach,' Chrissie recalls. 'Mick was terribly skinny and Charlie had a fat tummy and used to keep his socks on when he sunbathed. I remember Shirley saying, "They don't show up well in the sun. They look better in the evening."'

From that point, Shirley defied the *diktats* that streamed from Mick and Oldham almost on principle. 'The firm rule was always "no girls on tour", but Shirley would nearly always go because Charlie simply refused to get up or wash if she didn't,' says Chrissie. 'We weren't supposed to go into the studio while the band was recording, but she decided she was going and took me with her. Mick was absolutely furious and ordered us out, but Shirley hissed at me, "Don't *move!*" So we just sat there with Mick pulling Nankers [faces] at us through the control room glass. If he ever came into the dressing room and found girlfriends there, he'd glare so much that the girls did Nazi salutes and went "Heil Jagger!"'

Although Chrissie's parents in Buckinghamshire believed her to be leading a life of barely imaginable decadence, it mostly wasn't at all like that. Drugs, for instance, still barely figured in the UK pop scene. The Stones had always taken (quite legal) amphetamine uppers to stay awake and in America had already been offered marijuana, historically the narcotic of choice for blues and jazz musicians, but only Brian and Keith indulged in either to any serious degree. Mick certainly drank, but had no real head for alcohol; after one Bo Diddley concert at Hammersmith he was so far gone that Chrissie needed help from one of Diddley's musicians to keep him on his feet. However, an image of hard drinking had to be cultivated as part of the Stones' outlawry. One day, Mick's old Dartford Grammar School friend and fellow Blue Boy Alan Etherington happened to bump into him in central London. 'He had a Ford Zephyr car with a bottle of whisky in the back,' Etherington remembers. 'I said, "That's not like you, Mick," and he muttered something about it being just for publicity.'

As Chrissie discovered, he had a conventional, even old-fashioned side that very much reflected the values of his father, Joe. 'He was very very strict with me. I was always being told how to behave and what to say. There was one of my girlfriends who was known to be promiscuous and Mick didn't like me having anything to do with her.'

She was in effect going out with two people: the public, image-conscious Mick who hastily dropped her hand and strode ahead whenever any fans appeared, and the utterly different, often endearing private one. 'He wasn't horrible to me. A lot of the time he was very nice to me. We had a very ordinary life in spite of his other life. We spent a lot of time, if you can believe it, sitting in bed, doing crosswords, or Mick reading James Bond books. I always had strong opinions and I think originally that was what he liked because we used to talk a lot and discuss things. He was always very interested in sociology and economic issues like monopolies and capitalism – I remember him talking once about the monopoly of the ice creams sold in cinemas. That's what he wanted with me: I was his security. He used to say he was only at home when he was with me.'

Such interludes grew more infrequent as Mick and the Stones prepared for a return American tour that would wipe away the bad taste of the first, and meanwhile concentrated on jeopardising Britain's relations with some closer neighbours. European countries that were traditionally a sluggish market for UK pop now witnessed the worst outbreaks of youth violence since Bill Haley and the Comets had first brought rock 'n' roll from America a decade earlier. In The Hague, Holland, an opera house where the Stones played was almost rent apart; in Belgium, the interior minister unsuccessfully tried to ban their appearance at the Brussels World's Fair ground, and later had the dubious satisfaction of saying 'I told you so' in both French and Flemish; after their show at L'Olympia theatre in Paris (where the Beatles had been booed), rioting youths fought street battles with gendarmes, breaking shop windows, overturning pavement café tables and vandalising newspaper kiosks.

For the return to New York just two days later, on 23 October, there was no more 'England's Newest Hitmakers' claptrap or niche marketing to *Vogue*. The advance publicity picture showed all five Stones in a state of (entirely cosmetic) scruffiness and unshavenness, with the super-fastidious Mick affecting to scratch under one arm like a baboon. 'The Rolling Stones, who haven't washed for a week . . .' began the accompanying press release.

Paradoxically, back in Britain they seemed to be making a move towards family-friendliness with their first TV commercial, the one for Kellogg's Rice Krispies of which Jacqui Graham had received an early inkling. However, they provided only its soundtrack, with Mick giving the product's child-appealing 'snap, crackle and pop' the same sarcastic edge he did to faithless girls who played half-assed games: 'Wake up in the morning there's a snap around the place . . . wake up in the morning there's a crackle in your face . . . wake up in the morning there's a pop that really says . . . Rice Krispies for you . . . and you . . . and you!'

To follow up on 'It's All Over Now' – which had just left *Billboard*'s Top 100 after peaking at No. 26 – a second American album, *12 x 5*, had been put together for release on the day of their first New York concert. Its cover was a David Bailey shot of the band in close-up, moody and hirsute but now sartorially irreproachable. Brian Jones's gold fringe and immensely deep-collared blue shirt dominated the foreground, with Mick slightly craning his neck at the back. Bailey had put him there deliberately to avoid any accusations of favouritism.

As well as recycling 'It's All Over Now', the album contained everything from their British EP, *Five by Five*, plus other material from the Chess sessions and two Jagger–Richard compositions, 'Grown Up Wrong' and 'Congratulations' – the second not in any way to be confused with the Cliff Richard song later ceremonially performed on Queen Elizabeth the Queen Mother's birthday. The stand-out track was Irma Thomas's 'Time Is on My Side', a yearningly soulful Mick vocal, slightly marred by a talking bit which seemed to metamorphose him into the scolding black housekeeper in Tom and Jerry cartoons: 'And I know . . . I KNOW . . . like I tol' you so many times BEFAW . . . you're gonna come back, baby, 'cause I KNOW . . . yeah, knockin' right on my DAW!' Ad-libbing would never be his forte.

Whereas England's Newest Hitmakers had slipped into Manhattan almost unnoticed, Europe's Newest Shitmakers received a welcome from an American fan club, now numbering 52,000, that made the Beatles' look almost tame by comparison. Mindful of recent events in The Hague, Brussels and Paris, New York's police department had forbidden any mass demonstration when they returned to JFK Airport; even so, some 500 shrieking, banner-waving girls were waiting, corralled by an almost equal number of cops and security men. Dozens broke through barriers and human cordons, but were restrained with a ferocity at which even Parisian gendarmes might have balked. That was nothing to the scenes at the Stones' hotel, where a task force of police and Pinkerton detectives had been unable to prevent mass infiltration from the howling masses outside. To reach their ritually uninformative press conference, the band had to be brought down from their rooms in a service lift, then ushered through the hotel kitchens by guards who looked considerably more threatening than any intruder.

The visit kicked off with two live shows at the New York Academy of Music, staged by the Beatles' promoter Sid Bernstein. Among the more conventional reviews was one by 'Baby' Jane Holzer, a bohemian socialite whose reputation as the 'muse' of Andy Warhol could hardly have been a faster track into Mick's presence. 'They look divine!' gushed Baby Jane. 'You know what Mick said to me? He said "Come on, love, give us a kiss." How can one express it? Look at [him] at the centre of the stage, a short, thin boy with a sweatshirt on, the neck of his shirt almost falling over his shoulders, they are so narrow. All this surmounted by this enormous head with hair puffing down over the forehead and ears. This boy has exceptional lips, particularly gross and extraordinary red lips. They hang off his face like giblets. Slowly his eyes pore over the horde and then close. Then the lips start spreading into the most languid, confidential, wettest, most labial, concupiscent grin imaginable. Nirvana!'

This time, there was no question of their not appearing on CBS's *Ed Sullivan Show*, which, for the Beatles and Elvis before them, had been the gateway to a transcontinental audience. After the Stones' booking became public, CBS tried to take anti-riot measures, refusing to allocate places in the studio audience to unaccompanied teenagers, but a sizeable contingent got around the ban simply by making their parents apply for tickets on their behalf. With crowds also besieging CBS's Broadway studios, the Stones were cooped up there for ten hours, rehearsing in the afternoon, then doing the single live transmission that evening.

Their two brief spots (first with 'Around and Around', then 'Time Is on My Side') have passed into legend for the hysteria they supposedly unleashed on the studio floor – wilder than either the Beatles or Elvis had caused before them – and for the horrific spectacle of shaggy surliness they brought to America's hearth and home. But the grainy video record tells a different story. Sullivan, notorious for mangling his guests' names, announces, 'The first appearance by . . . the *Rollingstones!*' then throws up both arms as if physically beating them off. The Stones, all in dapper jackets and ties but for Bill's leather waistcoat and Mick's crew-neck sweater, play it utterly straight and poker-faced. Mick himself (his hair admittedly lanker and greasier-looking than the others') does Irma Thomas with maximum soul but minimum theatrics. Cutaways to the audience show mainly grown-up faces, set in slightly glassy smiles, though here and there a proscribed female fan breaks cover, bobbing up and down in her seat, half screaming, half weeping and stuffing a fist or handkerchief into her mouth to avoid attracting the ushers' attention.

Innocuous as it all looks now, CBS's switchboard that night lit up with viewer complaints from coast to coast. With the insecurity that haunts so many of television's great ones, Sullivan disclaimed all responsibility for booking the Stones, blaming his production staff and saying he'd expected nice, clean-cut types like the Dave Clark Five. 'It took me seventeen years to build this show and I'm not going to have it destroyed in a matter of weeks,' he fulminated to a Canadian journalist. 'I promise you they'll never be back.'

On the West Coast, the Stones were booked for further recording sessions at RCA studios and an appearance in a filmed pop concert for cinema release called Teenage Awards Music International, or TAMI, shot at Santa Monica Civic Auditorium and billed as 'the Greatest, Grooviest, Wildest, Most Exciting Beat Blast Ever to Pound the Screen'. Out here five months ago, Mick had competed for audience attention with tractors and trained seals; now he and the band found themselves headlining over top American acts, both black and white: the Beach Boys, Chuck Berry, Bo Diddley, Smokey Robinson and the Miracles, Jan and Dean, the Supremes, Lesley Gore, Marvin Gaye and James Brown.

The Stones felt uncomfortable to be given seniority over so many of their own musical heroes, Mick as much as anyone, and steeled themselves for heavy resentment backstage. But the very opposite happened. Chuck Berry proved as friendly as in Chicago, while Marvin Gaye – the super-cool Motown star, destined to be shot dead by his own father – was paternal in a thoroughly good way, almost patting Mick's head as he advised them not to be nervous but just to go out there and do their best.

Most disquietingly, their spot in the TAMI film came immediately after James Brown, the Godfather of Soul, at whose feet Mick and Keith had worshipped at the Harlem Apollo back in June. The Godfather could not have failed to note how many of his stage moves Mick had absorbed meantime, and was on record as saying once he'd done with them on TAMI, 'the Rolling Stones will wish they'd never come to America'.

Because of the filming process, there was a half-hour interval between each act, so the Stones did not have to try to compete with Brown's soul heart attack. When they finally struck up, a British journalist in the wings rather cringed to see Mick follow 'the Godfather' with his 'paraplegic funky chicken' routine. But his by his final song, aptly entitled 'I'm Alright', he'd found his feet again. As the other artists came onstage for the finale, Brown was first in line to shake his hand and congratulate him.

★

MICK'S TROUBLES WITH the law began in November 1964, when he was pulled over for three minuscule traffic offences while driving his car near Tettenhall, Staffordshire. He attended the court hearing in person, wearing a sober dark suit, white shirt and tie, to plead guilty and be fined a total of £16. His solicitor pleaded that the length of his hair should not be an aggravating factor in the case, pointing out that in the eighteenth century shoulder-length, curly wigs had been the norm for British noblemen, including the nation's greatest military commander: 'The Duke of Marlborough had hair longer than my client's and he won several battles. His hair was powdered, I think because of fleas. My client has no fleas . . .'

Trivial though the proceedings were, they had the essential features of far graver ones, three years ahead. Here was first articulated the idea, contrary to every principle of British justice, that Mick's being a shaggy, disreputable Rolling Stone could make him liable to harsher penalties than usually prescribed for the offence in question. Here, too, deployed in his defence, was the same condescending facetiousness that would later characterise his prosecution.

On record, by contrast, he continued to get away with murder. The Stones' UK follow-up single to 'It's All Over Now', released that same month, was Willie Dixon's 'Little Red Rooster'. Already famously covered by Howlin' Wolf and Son House, it seemed like an apology to the purist followers they had recently so offended; it also happened to be the most overtly phallic blues song since Blind Lemon Jefferson's 'Black Snake Moan' in the 1920s. Against a muted, somnolent beat, broken only by shivering thrusts of Brian Jones's slide guitar, Mick's vocal made every trouser-snake metaphor unmissable. 'I am the little red rooster . . . too la-a-azy to crow for days . . . Keep ever'thing in the farmyard . . . upset in ever' way . . .'

This seemingly perverse return to unashamed niche music after a pop smash like 'It's All Over Now' dismayed everyone around the Stones – except the manager who usually preached commercialism like an evangelist. Not that Andrew Oldham cared 'dick' for blues music any more now than when he first met them. To Oldham, 'Little Red Rooster' was a demonstration of the band's power, under his tutelage, to make the punters buy anything they chose to put out. As with 'half-assed games', the massed censors of British broadcasting proved strangely unalert, totally missing the connection between *rooster, red, cock* and the Top 20's supposed arch-cocksman (though in America the track was refused radio airplay and the less suggestive 'Heart of Stone' was released instead). Thanks mainly to loyal bulk buying by the Stones' fan club, the single made No. 1, for just a week, in December 1964. Mick had thus finally fulfilled his boyhood ambition to bring the blues to Britain the way St Augustine had once brought Christianity.

If Britain's moral custodians were deaf to the nuances of 'Little Red Rooster', American TV producers proved quicker on the uptake. Mick's performance on the *Shindig!* pop show in May 1965 was an erotic black-and-white horror movie in miniature, with scary overture music and mock-medieval gates creaking open to reveal him in his lair, a proto-punk Dracula, twirling a silver mouth organ in one hand as if to heighten the beat's mesmeric spell. On a rival US show, *Shivaree,* that same month, the camera zoomed in on his face until only the lips remained in vision, like the disembodied mouth that narrates Samuel Beckett's play-monologue *Not I*. When the time came for his harp solo (actually played by Brian Jones on the record), it was not blown so much as fellated.

'Little Red Rooster' was hardly less a starring vehicle for Brian than for Mick. Both his harmonica and slide-guitar playing won him praise throughout the British music press and admiration from musicians in rival bands, even the cerebral, super-cool Manfred Mann. Its chart success also stemmed – for the present – his complaint that Mick and Keith were diverting the Stones from their blues roots and towards commercial pop. But unfortunately, Brian on an upswing was even more of a liability to the band than Brian on a downer.

Whatever the aggravation they faced from the outside world – either engineered by Andrew Oldham or wholly genuine and spontaneous

— Brian always managed to ratchet it up a few more notches. His co-stardom on 'Little Red Rooster' rekindled his delight in goading already crazed audiences, with little tambourine shakes or air kisses from his choirboy mouth, to a pitch of aggression that Mick's more obvious moves never could. He was agreed to have been the main instigator of the Stones' worst-ever British concert riot, in Blackpool, when an audience consisting largely of drunken Glaswegians on holiday had begun spitting at them *en masse* as they played. After Keith retaliated by sinking a pointed boot toe into a gobbing stage-front face, they were lucky to escape with their lives.

The band's schedule was continually disrupted by Brian's health problems, many just hypochondriacal attention seeking but some spectacularly real. As a chronic asthmatic, he had chosen the worst possible work environment; a performance in a hall or cinema drained of oxygen by thousands of overworked lungs would leave him gasping, wheezing and fumbling for the inhaler he always carried. During the Stones' second US tour he missed three shows after suffering an attack of acute bronchitis and was rushed to hospital, where he became delirious and had to be fed intravenously. His absence from the stage line-up provoked rumours that he intended leaving the band, or had already left.

His reckless consumption of alcohol, amphetamines – and now marijuana – fed his long-festering grievance about the way, so he believed, the band he'd created had been taken over. He was always complaining to Bill Wyman and Charlie Watts, or anyone else who would listen, that Mick and Keith, with Oldham's connivance, were plotting to undermine him or oust him altogether. At the same time he would alienate Bill and Charlie by displays of pop-star petulance that had not yet even crossed Mick's mind. When they were travelling by road in the States and stopped to eat at a wayside diner, Brian would say he wasn't hungry and stay in the car. Then, when the others came back and the convoy was ready to move off, he'd say he *was* hungry now, stroll into the diner and consume a steak or burger at a deliberate snail's pace.

Once, his behaviour goaded the monumentally patient and good-humoured roadie Ian Stewart to pick him up by the throat and shake him, 'Why do you always want to drag everyone down, you little bag of shit?' bellowed Stu in rhythm with the shakes. 'Why? *Why?*' At the same time he could still be irresistibly well mannered and charming, especially to fans, elderly people and Andrew Oldham's office staff. 'We all used to love it whenever we saw Brian's beautiful golden hair,' Shirley Arnold remembers. 'It was like the sun coming out.'

The greatest potential trouble lay in a carnal appetite far larger than the public's most lurid conception of Mick's. For behind the golden fringe and lisping *faux-naïf* charm lay complex sexual hang-ups and a strain of sadomasochism which booze and drug-fuelled insecurity and paranoia could bring out in highly unpleasant ways. At one American stop-over the young girl who'd spent the night with Brian emerged from their motel cabin next morning with a blackened eye and a face covered in bruises. A member of Eric Easton's staff travelling with the Stones was so incensed that he gave Brian a retaliatory beating up, which cracked two of his ribs and obliged him to wear a remedial corset for some days afterwards. A story was given to the press that he'd hurt himself while 'practising karate' with his bandmates beside the pool.

Witnesses from the time all agree that Mick felt no personal animosity towards Brian, but was simply concerned about the effects of his unreliability and instability on the Stones' increasingly big business. If Mick and Oldham did conspire against him at this stage, it was in damage limitation for the good of the whole band. According to Bill Wyman, at the height of the 1964–65 media tsunami, yet another young woman came forward claiming to be pregnant by Brian and threatening to sell the story to the newspapers. Oldham and Mick dealt with the complainant without reference to Brian, drafting a lawyer's letter in which she agreed to drop her allegations for a one-off payment of £700. The money was then deducted from Brian's wages without his knowledge.

On 19 January 1965 the Stones set out on their first tour of Australia and the Far East, flying – still economy class – from Los Angeles via Hawaii and Fiji. At Sydney Airport the scenes of mob hysteria and chaos put even New York's JFK into the shade. Before the Stones' plane even landed there was a mini-disaster when the combined force of several hundred shrieking girls caused a high-level metal barrier to collapse and, according to Bill Wyman, 'the bodies piled up six deep'. One resourceful group of five managed to get through security onto the tarmac and were hiding behind a mobile staircase as the band disembarked. Three managed to reach Mick, Bill and Charlie before being dragged away by police.

For Mick, it was a first visit to the country where his mother had spent her early childhood – and whose accent she had tried so hard to banish in suburban Kent. During the Stones' time in Sydney, he was under strict orders to see Eva's sister, who had returned to live there in the 1950s, and several cousins he had never met. Hearing that his aunt was to attend one of the Stones' shows at the city's Agricultural Hall, Eva wrote to her, with a characteristic tone of faint put-down: 'I solemnly advise you to take earplugs because after the last concert I saw my doctor had to treat me for perforated eardrums.'

Australia was still a ragingly macho society with a huge inferiority complex towards Britain, its former colonial ruler. Much more to almost every reviewer's taste on the tour was the Stones' American co-headliner, Roy Orbison. And the effect of such 'Pommie poofters' on the nation's young womanhood – from whose eager throngs at every stop they could choose sexual partners like diners selecting live crustaceans from a tank at a seafood restaurant – inspired the most scandalised headlines yet. 'SHOCKERS! UGLY LOOKS! UGLY SPEECH! UGLY MANNERS!' almost retched a *Sydney Morning Herald* banner.

In fact, the nearest to ugly speech or manners on the entire journey came when the Stones passed through Invercargill, New Zealand, and Mick forgot his usual press conference blandness to complain about their accommodations. 'There are twenty-eight rooms in this hotel and only two baths,' the so-called dirty pop star marvelled. 'The last meal ends at 7 P.M.' Forty years later, the discovery of a scrawled 'MICK JAGGER' on a back-stage wall at the Civic Theatre indicated that he hadn't spent his whole time there in an unwashed, unfed strop.

Back in Britain, a second Stones album, *The Rolling Stones No. 2*, was already in the shops. Once again, the intention seemed to be to reassure their purist following with a menu of almost unadulterated R&B, re-using several tracks from the *12 x 5* album released in America the previous October, and with the same David Bailey cover shot. The only wobble towards pop was Jagger–Richard's 'Off the Hook', already heard as the B-side of 'Little Red Rooster', another dispatch from Mick's bedside, this time in the sarcastic-comic vein at which he was proving rather good.

All in all, the album had seemed rather second-hand and lacklustre until Andrew Oldham found a way to juice it up a little. Oldham's favourite book was *A Clockwork Orange*, Anthony Burgess's vision of a near-future Britain (all too accurate, as it would prove) terrorised by gangs of boys committing random, unprovoked acts of violence and rape. The narrator, Alex, leads a group of four known as 'droogs' on a thrill-seeking rampage until caught by the police, imprisoned and subjected to an aversion-therapy technique that scares the devilment out of him. First published in 1962, the novel seemed a parable of young males' growing empowerment and arrogance as the decade progressed – though to most of Swinging London's carefree rude boys the idea of being persecuted by officialdom and thrown in jail still belonged to the realm of science fiction.

For Oldham, the parallel was irresistible: the band of rampaging droogs were the Stones, with his Trilby morphed into the amoral, sexually rapacious (and rather well-spoken) Alex. On *The Rolling Stones No. 2*, David Bailey's moody front cover shot gave them a markedly droog-like air, even if Brian, with the blue dagger points of his shirt collar, looked more a ringleader than last-in-line, head-craning Mick. On the back cover were liner notes by Oldham, pastiching Alex's 'Nadsat' jargon, and commending his promiscuous ultra-violence to British record buyers: 'It is the summer of the night London's eyes be shut tight all but six hip malchicks who prance the street. Newspaper-strewn and grey which waits another day to hide its dingy countenance the six have been sound ball journey made to another sphere which pays royalties in eight months or a year . . . This is the Stones' new disc within. Cast deep in your pocket for loot to buy this disc of groovies and fancy words. If you don't have the bread, see that blind man, knock him on the head, steal his wallet and lo and behold, you have the loot. If you put in the boot, good. Another one sold.'

In the hyper-sensitive twenty-first century such comments would touch off an instant media hurricane. But back in 1965 the taking-offence industry was still in its infancy. The 'disc of groovies and fancy words' had been on sale a full month before the first protesting voice was heard, from the estimable but scarcely high-profile Bournemouth Blind Association. 'They [the Stones] are horrible,' said spokesperson Mrs Gwen Matthews. 'It's simply putting ideas into people's heads. I'm writing to Decca to ask them to change it.' With that, Fleet Street finally creaked into sanctimonious life. Bowing to the headlines, if not Mrs Matthews, Decca called back several thousand copies of the album and reshipped them in new covers with the offending passage deleted. In the House of Lords, a former Conservative minister demanded that the Director of Public Prosecutions be asked to investigate 'what seems a deliberate incitement to criminal actions'. All of which was promotion that money couldn't buy: *The Rolling Stones No. 2* contradicted its title by reaching No. 1 in the UK album charts, staying in the Top 20 for twelve weeks.

By the time the Stones left Australia they had four tracks in the national singles chart, including Mick's rather wobbly version of the Drifters' 'Under the Boardwalk'. Stopping off in Singapore for two final shows, they received an official welcome very different from in the previous outpost of empire: the British deputy high commissioner invited them to lunch and gave them a guided tour of his garden. After the sell-out performances at Badminton Stadium, the local promoter threw them a drinks party and, by way of a bonus, offered them a choice of twelve ravishing hookers of various ethnic origins, to be enjoyed in adjacent bedrooms. Unused to sex with paid companions, even though someone else might be paying, they were initially paralysed with shyness; then, as Bill Wyman recalls, 'Andrew got the ball rolling, followed by Mick and me . . .'

The tour was book-ended by sessions at RCA Studios, Hollywood, with another gifted engineer, Dave Hassinger, which brought many nights of brain cudgelling by Mick and Keith at their chalet-style London flat to a final resolution. Although the pair had had considerable success in writing songs for other people – notably 'As Tears Go By' for Marianne Faithfull – they somehow could not come up with a hit track for their own band. An answer finally emerged with a gospel song, originally recorded by the Staple Singers, called 'This May Be the Last Time', later adapted by James Brown into 'Maybe the Last Time'. Mick changed the gospel message to sneery heartbreak in a few simple, slipshod couplets (rhyming 'mind' and 'time'; 'please me' and 'easy') though still echoing Pop Staple's original vocal with its dying fall of 'May be the last time . . . Ah don' kna-a-o-ow . . .' The killer new element was a seesaw guitar riff, played by Brian Jones, not just an intro but tolling through the whole song like a malevolent metronome.

Released as 'The Last Time' on 26 February 1965, it became the Stones' third UK No. 1 single and their first to penetrate the American Top 10, reaching No. 9. Because it had no listed composer, but was categorised as 'traditional', Jagger and Richard were free to claim it as an original composition. If not quite that, it was the first recognisable Rolling Stones track in a formula that, with a few deviations, quickly rectified, would see them through the next half century.

In London, Mick's domestic circumstances had changed yet again without becoming much more stable. It had taken the fans only a few weeks to locate his and Keith's Hampstead hideaway and to make any normal life there impossible. And now that Keith's relationship with Linda Keith had settled into the same apparent permanence as Mick's with Chrissie Shrimpton, they could hardly continue being roommates in the sloppy, studenty fashion of the past two years. So writing (or rewriting) 'The Last Time' at 10a Holly Hill had been prophetic in more ways than one.

While Linda and Keith easily found a flat in nearby St John's Wood, Mick was not so easily pleased. For a time he shared Keith's temporary base at the London Hilton hotel, then moved in with his friend David Bailey, enjoying the succession of stunning models who paraded through Bailey's studio. At that point, an unlikely Good Samaritan stepped forward in Lionel Bart, creator of *Oliver!* and putative composer of Marianne Faithfull's record début. Though Bart's offering had been rejected in favour of 'As Tears Go By', he bore the song's co-composer no ill will and, on hearing that Mick was temporarily homeless, offered sanctuary in his flat in Bryanston Mews, Marylebone. Abandoning all remaining pretence of a separate address, Chrissie took up residence there, too.

As a bolt-hole from intrusive fans, it was not ideal: Ringo Starr of the Beatles had a flat a couple of doors away which was under round-the-clock siege more intense than either of Mick and Keith's previous addresses. When news of Mick's presence leaked out, Stones' fans poured into the narrow mews to join the Beatles' ones, and there were frequent clashes between the two factions. Soon after Chrissie's arrival, she was leaving the house, a step behind her lord and master as usual, when one of Ringo's female pickets jumped her. Mick came to the rescue, prising the assailant off Chrissie's back and dismissing her with a kick up the rear. 'I was only wearing plimsolls, so I didn't hurt her much,' he said afterwards. 'In fact I got the worst of it because she gave me a few clouts.' In 1965 the episode rated only a few newspaper paragraphs; today, giant headlines would shriek of assault charges and claims for damages.

Mick and Chrissie were now engaged, and expected by both their families to be married in the next few months. Eva Jagger had taught Chrissie to make pastry — for Eva, one of the first essentials of good-wifeliness — while Chrissie's father, the builder-turned-farmer, kept an eye out for properties close to the Shrimptons' Buckinghamshire home where the newlyweds could live. On the one hand, it impressed Ted Shrimpton hugely that Mick could buy a substantial house outright; on the other, as someone who'd worked long and hard for his own money, he felt that wealth acquired with such apparent ease was not quite legitimate.

Chrissie still wanted nothing but to be Mick's wife, even though her one glimpse of pop-star matrimony had not been encouraging. The two had recently been houseguests at John Lennon's mock-Tudor mansion in the Surrey Stockbroker Belt, where Lennon's wife, Cynthia, lived in child-rearing purdah while he practised multiple infidelities out and about with the Beatles. During the visit, Mick and Chrissie watched the film *Citizen Kane* in Lennon's private cinema, then he insisted they should all play Risk, the board game in which each player has a different-coloured army and competes to conquer the world. 'Cynthia was winning, and John started getting so nasty that she just gave up the game and went to bed,' Chrissie says. 'I remember thinking, "She's so much under his thumb that she doesn't even dare to win a silly game."'

Though the Beatles had seemed to penetrate every part of the British press, there was one sector – the society pages – that never printed a word about them. Of these, the most assiduously read was the *Daily Express*'s William Hickey column, whose past editors had included Tom Driberg, the homosexual MP (and godfather of Mick's old flame Cleo Sylvestre). As the sixties reached their halfway point, hostesses drawing up guest lists for the coming season received a surprising new tip on etiquette. 'It's no disgrace these days to know a Rolling Stone,' announced William Hickey, '[and] some of their best friends are fledglings from the upper classes.'

'Fledglings from the upper classes', in fact, had always been an essential component of Swinging London. Rebels that they were in embracing 'trade' to become boutique owners or restaurateurs, they usually preferred the rebellious Stones to the charming Beatles. And there was no doubt which particular Stone headed this new inverted social register. A few months previously, Mick had merely been part of the cabaret at London débutante balls; now engraved invitations arrived for 'Mr Michael Jagger and Miss Christine Shrimpton' to attend a gala dance for Jane Ormsby-Gore, given by her father, the fifth Lord Harlech, a direct descendant of William the Conqueror and Mary Tudor.

Chrissie, who at that stage still had her token bedsit in Olympia, spent hours there trying to put together an outfit grand enough for the occasion. When Mick arrived to collect her, he agreed sympathetically that it didn't really work and told her to wear the catsuit she usually did around the clubs. At the gala, they found themselves seated at the table next to the Queen's younger sister, Princess Margaret, and her friend comedian Peter Sellers. And this time at least, Mick showed that Chrissie meant more to him than social mountaineering. 'Princess Margaret asked for Mick to be brought over, and I was just left, sitting there on my own,' she remembers. 'So I went up to him while he was chatting to Princess Margaret, and I just said, "I'm leaving." I started to walk out and Mick stood up so suddenly that it shook the whole table and made everything rattle. He came after me and we ran out into the street, laughing. That was one of the happiest times.'

Chrissie was more worried by other new friends that Mick was attracting. Lionel Bart, whose roof they now shared, was ostentatiously gay and, despite the draconian anti-homosexuality laws, made no secret of a buccaneering sex life. Prominently displayed throughout the flat were tubes of K-Y lubricating jelly which Chrissie in her innocence mistook for hair gel. One of Bart's closest cronies was Lord Montagu of Beaulieu, who had spent a year in jail for homosexual offences in 1954 (following a famous police raid). 'He was always trying to persuade Mick to go and stay at his country house. I objected to all these people being after my boyfriend, but I wasn't really aware why.'

Chrissie now worked for Andrew Oldham at his new offices, a flat on a Marylebone mansion block called Ivor Court. Here at the centre of the Rolling Stones' world – often putting through telephone calls from the office switchboard – she continued to hear troubling rumours about Oldham's relationship with Mick. These were hardly assuaged when the pair appeared on *Ready Steady Go!* performing Sonny and Cher's 'I Got You Babe' as a duet and stroking each other's hair. According to Chrissie, an actual showdown once trembled briefly on the horizon, thanks to a young male TV star who had fallen in love with Oldham and felt bitter because his affections were unrequited. 'Andrew came to me and warned me that – was going to tell me that he and Mick were having an affair. That never happened and I never knew anything for certain. But they were definitely in love. I can remember the two of them holding hands.'

Among Mick's growing store of posh male friends, two in particular would make major contributions to his cultural development – and, coincidentally, both would be witnesses to the most traumatic episode of his life. The first was Robert Fraser, twenty-eight-year-old son of a Scottish merchant banker who had become Swinging London's foremost art dealer thanks to prescient sponsorship of American pop artists like Andy Warhol and Jim Dine. Fraser introduced Mick to his fellow Old Etonian Christopher Gibbs, a Chelsea antiques dealer whose uncle was the colonial governor of Rhodesia (later Zimbabwe) and whose social circle included the photographer, aesthete and friend to Royalty Cecil Beaton. Meeting Mick at a party among the littered artworks of Fraser's Mayfair flat, Gibbs was instantly captivated. 'He was very charming, very funny, and he had a way of flirting with one that had no erotic charge but wasn't the least bit patronising either. And I'd never imagined a pop musician who could be so sharp and well informed. Here was someone who read the *New Scientist* every week and who could talk intelligently about everything in it.'

Mick had already told Fraser about his engagement to Chrissie and so far unsuccessful search for a marital home. 'We must find this boy a house,' Fraser told Gibbs, though the 'we' proved a misnomer: it was the good-natured Gibbs who scanned estate agents' brochures and organised car trips to likely properties, some with Chrissie along, some tête-à-tête with Mick that became as much about visiting historical or architectural landmarks *en route*. 'He was always a delightful companion, and interested in everything. If I said we'd got to go up that hill to look at a certain church, it was okay with him. He got a lot from his father, who was a bit of an antiquarian, particularly keen on Kentish history. I get very annoyed when I read stories that I "educated" Mick. No one needed to do that.'

House-hunting and church-visiting with Christopher Gibbs was interrupted by the Stones' third American tour in eleven months, this one spilling over for the first time into even more shockable Canada. Barely two months after 'The Last Time', Mick and Keith also had to come up with a new song to maintain their hard-won place in the US singles charts. And, unlike the last time, there was no helpful old gospel song on hand to be topped and tailed and served up as their own work.

In Los Angeles, the Stones reappeared on *Shindig!*, the nationally popular TV show staged by the gifted British producer Jack Good. Again, the cast featured one of their great heroes, the bluesman Howlin' Wolf (whom the punctilious ex-public schoolboy Good was uncertain whether to address as 'Mr Wolf' or just 'Howlin''). During a break from rehearsals came a moment destined to stay even in Mick's sieve-like memory: Howlin' Wolf led him into the studio audience to meet a little, gnarled old man in faded blue denims, incongruously seated among a group of children. It was Son House, the seminal Delta bluesman whose version of 'Little Red Rooster' had most influenced the Stones' – and who might have been expected to resent its conversion into a chart hit by upstart white boys. But instead he was all graciousness. 'Don't you worry 'bout copying "Little Red Rooster,"' he told Mick, ''cause I wasn't the first one to do it.'

The tour had reached Clearwater, Florida, when Keith woke up with a bass-string guitar riff running through his head – not unlike the one Brian had played on 'The Last Time' – together with a line from Chuck Berry's 'Thirty Days', 'If I don't get no satisfaction from the judge . . .' He made a tape cassette of the riff, then passed it and the guide phrase 'I can't get no satisfaction' over to Mick, at this stage visualising no more than a makeweight album track and intending his guitar intro to be played by a horn section.

For a time, Keith's low opinion of the track seemed justified. When the Stones stopped off in Chicago to record it at Chess Studios, the usual Chess magic refused to work: they could manage only a vaguely folksy arrangement reminiscent of the Rooftop Singers' 'Walk Right In'. Not until they reached RCA Hollywood and engineer Dave Hassinger did the production come together, with Keith's bass riff fed through a

Gibson fuzz box that made it sound less like a guitar than some diabolic pipe organ.

'Satisfaction' was released in America in June 1965, almost three months ahead of Britain. In six weeks it jumped sixty-seven places in the *Billboard* chart to become the Stones' first US No. 1 single.

Before a note had been heard, the song created the greatest scandal since Elvis Presley had first curled his lip and swivelled his hips exactly a decade earlier. 'Satisfaction' may once have been what young noblemen sought by fighting duels at dawn, but by 1965 its meaning had become explicitly sexual – and implicitly solitary. What else could those thrice-dreadful Rolling Stones have contrived, therefore, but a hymn to mas-turbation, vocalised by the one among them seemingly least in need of it? 'Ah try . . . and Ah try . . . and Ah TRY . . . and Ah *TRY*!' The 'vice' still believed by many to cause blindness, heart disease and hair to sprout on the palms was being blatantly advocated, even simulated, on a million rotating vinyl discs.

Its sexual daring apart, 'Satisfaction' was a pop musical landmark as significant as Presley's 'Heartbreak Hotel' – more so than any Beatles track yet. Over the previous couple of years, the charts had increasingly featured so-called protest songs against nuclear bombs, racial persecu-tion in the American South and the accelerating horrors of the Vietnam War. Whereas pop had once given young people only intoxicating noise, it now gave them a voice which, to adult ears, was becoming ever louder and more threatening. The opening riff of 'Satisfaction' was its most ominous manifestation to date.

Not that any hint of morality or altruism leaked into this particular protest song. It was about nothing but the singer himself; not his fail-ure to achieve orgasm but his frustration and ennui with a life palpably mirroring Mick's own, 'ridin' round the world, doin' this and signin' that', while the electronic media and advertising industry competed in fatuity for his attention and his money. If the title wasn't enough, its third verse contained the first direct reference to sex in any pop song ('tryin' to make some girl') and the first indirect one to menstruation ('Baby, better come back, maybe next week / 'Cause you see I'm on a losin'streak.'). Pure blues fans would be outraged, of course, but in a way this *was* a blues song, albeit turned upside down; a *cri de cœur* from the luxury penthouse, a lament for having just too damned much of every-bloody-thing.

No song was ever more perfectly matched to a voice – or, rather, a mouth – from the almost girlish cooing of those four scandalous syl-lables at its start to the raucous 'Hey! Hey! Hey! That's what I say!' at its multiple climax. Nor was a voice ever more perfectly in synch with a body in performance than this one with the moves recently appro-priated from James Brown – the tossing head, the rippling arms, the staring eyes and Travelator feet; the employment of a heavy stand micro-phone with a trailing lead like the mute partner in a ballet or Apache dance, grabbed around the neck and dragged down almost to the floor or tilted vertically into the air.

Andrew Oldham's associate Tony Calder has three separate memo-ries of cracking America at last, and for good. The first is driving on LA's Pacific Coast Highway with Oldham and Mick in a red Ford Mustang, punching all five buttons of its radio in turn and getting 'Satisfaction' every time.

The second is flying back to New York with the pair and being but-tonholed in the first-class cabin by a young woman with some 'useless information' that came as news to all of them. 'You guys smoke dope, right?' she said. 'That bit in the song where Mick sings "Hay! Hay! Hay!" he's really talking about grass.'

The third is walking with Oldham, Mick and Keith along Broadway near the CBS theatre – where of course *The Ed Sullivan Show* had now welcomed back the Stones with open arms. 'As we passed this bloke on the sidewalk, he spat at Mick and Keith. "That's just what we want," Andrew said. "That means we've *really* made it over here." Dead chuffed he was.'

CHAPTER SEVEN

'We Piss Anywhere, Man'

O n 12 June 1965 the Beatles gained total acceptance by the British establishment when each was awarded a minor deco- ration, the MBE (Membership of the Most Excellent Order of the British Empire) in the Queen's Birthday Honours list. Three weeks later, a case at East Ham magistrates' court in east London brought home yet again the difference between this national treasure and an ever-worsening national disgrace.

Charles Keeley, manager of the Francis petrol station in nearby Rom- ford, testified that, late in the evening of 18 March, a chauffeur-driven limousine had pulled onto his forecourt and a 'shaggy-haired monster' (Bill Wyman) had got out and asked 'in disgusting language' if he could use the toilet. When Mr Keeley refused, 'a group of eight or nine youths and girls' including Mick Jagger and Brian Jones had emerged from the car and Mick had allegedly pushed him aside, saying, 'We piss any- where, man.' The others had echoed the words in 'a gentle chant' with one of the females swaying in time. As a climax to this drunken scene straight out of *A Clockwork Orange*, Mick, Bill and Brian were said to have urinated in a row against the forecourt wall.

In vain did the Stones' solicitor offer a less droog-like scenario: on the night in question they were returning from a show at Romford's Odeon cinema, where rioting fans had necessitated a quick escape without any chance to use the backstage facilities. At the service station, Bill had made his request politely, but Mr Keeley had gone berserk and started screaming 'Get off my forecourt!' None of the car's passengers had drunk anything all evening but tea and Coca-Cola, and the urinating had not taken place on the floodlit forecourt but some way up a dark side road.

Once again, no credibility could be given to shaggy-haired monsters: Mick, Brian and Bill were found guilty of 'insulting behaviour likely to cause a breach of the peace', fined £5 each with 15 guineas (£15.75) costs, and reprimanded as if it were the mid-nineteenth rather than mid-twentieth century, for 'behaviour not becoming young gentlemen'. An additional charge against Bill of using insulting language was not pursued.

The police had not been involved on the night of the incident, and showed little interest until Keeley and an onlooker with the suitably fragrancing name Eric Lavender threatened to bring a private prosecution if there were no official one. A judicious grovelling apology to the two outraged citizens might easily have smoothed everything over; instead, Andrew Oldham and his associate Tony Calder had fed the story to Britain's two main news agencies (each receiving a fee as freelance journalists, according to Calder) with the result that police action had to follow.

However, Oldham's creation of an anti-Beatle Antichrist demanded one major tweak to the facts. The only person in the group actually taken short had been Bill and the only one to provoke the garage manager (with mock-hysteric cries of 'Get off my foreskin!') had been Brian. The notion of super-cautious Mick elbowing someone aside and saying 'We piss anywhere' was as far-fetched as that of super-fastidious Mick publicly unzipping and doing it against a wall. Yet somewhere between Messrs Keeley and Lavender's complaint and the formal summons, Oldham managed, in his own words, to '[transfer] the credit as piss-artist from the bass line to the lead vocalist'.

Oldham himself at the time would have been a far more unwelcome visitor to any garage forecourt. As Britain's answer to Phil Spector – that is, combining the auras of a recording genius and a gangster – Oldham now employed a permanent bodyguard to drive him around in his white American Lincoln Continental, shield him from the crush at the Stones' concerts, and wreak summary vengeance on anyone who aroused his displeasure. The bodyguard in question was a blond young Cockney named Reg King, known as 'Reg the Butcher' for an alleged prowess with flick knives and razors (though his offensive weapon of choice was actually a walking stick). What was known as *that* side of Andrew' worried friends like John Dunbar. 'If another driver even cut across them in traffic,' Dunbar recalls, 'Reg would take off after him.'

On one level, Oldham seemed quite happy to be closer to his 'boys' than any other manager ever had been or would be; the undisputed sixth Stone who went everywhere with them, roomed, ate, got drunk and laid with them, bore the insults hurled at them, and (with or without Reg the Butcher's help) joined in the physical confrontations that often followed. On the road, he had the same fuck-'em-all attitude that Keith did and Mick so conspicuously didn't: when the Stones visited Ireland in January 1965, Oldham and Keith each bought a handgun and shoulder holster which they wore under their jackets on the flight home and through UK Immigration.

At the same time the only just ex-'teenage tycoon-shit' regarded himself as the star and the Stones, along with a growing roster of other acts and projects, as mere pawns in the heady game he was playing with the music business, the media and the public. To be sure, in his egotism, arrogance, grandiosity, self-indulgence and lack of self-control he was far more like a modern rock star than any of them, Mick especially.

His excesses and eccentricities were becoming the stuff of legend: how on visits to Los Angeles he kept two limos on standby around the clock . . . how he'd once got the Stones out of trouble in a British roadside 'greasy spoon' full of threatening lorry drivers by having a fried egg served to every customer, so the truculent truckers had no choice but to smile and say thank you . . . how on one day he might impulsively give an expensive suede jacket he was wearing to a young employee, and on the next personally trash the office of another employee he wanted rid of . . . how he'd bought a whole-page ad in the *NME* to praise Phil Spector's latest production, 'You've Lost That Lovin' Feelin'' by the Righteous Brothers, despite having had no financial interest in promoting it . . . how the only way he could come down from his permanent high on drink, pills and success was to disappear to a north London clinic and be put to sleep for a couple of days . . . how he'd taken against an American producer offering lucrative new business because at lunch the man cut his bread roll with a knife.

If all this were not enough to be going on in one twenty-one-year-old, there was also the extravagant campness (a word only just entering general British usage) that kept rumours about his relationship with Mick constantly simmering. It was not only his habit of addressing males and females alike as 'darling' or 'dear' and his fascination with celebrity mega-queens like Lionel Bart. His office staff always contained a high quotient of pretty young men, the most likely recipients of expensive suede jackets; even his bodyguard, the sinister Reg the Butcher, was a predatory gay with tastes verging on the paedophilic.

In fact, no one around Oldham thought for a second that he was genuinely homosexual. Some speculated that because London's other foremost pop managers were, like the Beatles' Brian Epstein and the Who's Kit (aka 'Kitty') Lambert, he felt it gave him more credibility; others saw it merely as another symptom of 'being Andrew', never happy unless shocking people and living on the edge. But while camping it up among colleagues and friends, he tolerated no slur on his heterosexuality from outsiders. Once when he was lunching with David Bailey, a man at a nearby table wolf-whistled at them. Oldham went over, grabbed the whistler's head and rammed it down into his plate.

Despite his oft-expressed notion of pop management as first and foremost a cultural crusade, no one on the London music scene was hungrier for profit or more adept at wringing it from the unlikeliest sources. When he was producing Marianne Faithfull's 'As Tears Go By', the B-side Oldham had chosen was 'Greensleeves', which not only suited

Marianne's virginal image but (having been written by King Henry VIII five centuries earlier) was also comfortably out of copyright. A few slight changes thus turned it into an 'original' composition on which he now controlled the publishing. On the Stones' live EP *Got Live If You Want It*, one track consisted only of a theatre audience chanting 'We want the Stones!' This, too, Oldham listed as a song, eligible for royalties from radio play and available for cover versions.

In 1964 had come a typical act of hubris and hopeful revenue raising, the so-called Andrew Oldham Orchestra, which went on to release four all-instrumental albums on Decca. The Orchestra recruited London's best classical session musicians; individual Stones – including Mick – played anonymously in its ranks; and Oldham himself took the baton, wearing a black beret like some punk Stravinsky. The repertoire combined easy-listening versions of Jagger–Richard songs like 'The Last Time' with the bereted maestro's self-written mini-symphonies: 'Funky and Fleopatra', 'There Are 365 Rolling Stones' and 'Theme for a Mod Summer Night's Ball'.

And yet somehow, after two hit-studded years in these hyperactive hands, the Stones' capital worth still came nowhere near that of their main rivals. For the Beatles' next American tour, kicking off at New York's Shea Stadium, one million dollars was known to be on the table. The Stones, by contrast, had received only £10,000 into their collective company, Rolling Stones Ltd, for the year ending June 1965, and still had not been paid for their UK tour the previous year. When Oldham could not extract the money from the tour's promoter, Robert Stigwood, Keith Richard confronted Stigwood at the Scotch of St James club and beat him up in front of a sizeable crowd including the *NME* journalist Keith Altham. 'Why do you keep hitting him, Keith?' Altham asked. 'Because he keeps getting up,' Keith replied.

By far the greatest obstacle to affluence was Decca Records, which had signed the Stones for a reasonable enough royalty – roughly three times the pitiful rate the Beatles first received from EMI – but which settled accounts with elephantine slowness, two years or more in arrears. The band's contract with Decca was due to expire in July 1965;

their co-manager Eric Easton had convinced them to re-sign with the same label and was in the process of negotiating new and significantly better terms: 24 per cent of wholesale price or the equivalent of four pence on every record sold. The deal was all but done when Allen Klein happened along.

Klein was a thirty-three-year-old New York accountant-turned-entrepreneur who specialised in obtaining large advance payments for recording artists – a concept still unknown in Britain – as well as ferreting out royalties that had been withheld from them, through either inefficiency or guile, and freeing them from oppressive contracts. His success in combating previously complacent and unchallengeable record companies on behalf of put-upon performers like Buddy Knox, Bobby Vinton and Sam Cooke had earned him the nickname 'the Robin Hood of Pop' (though some in retrospect would consider the beady-eyed Sheriff of Nottingham a better comparison). The popularity of British bands in America brought him to London, where he signed up Mick and Keith's friend Mickie Most, an astute talent spotter as much as a producer. As a result, Most's whole roster, including major names like the Animals and Herman's Hermits, passed into Allen Klein's control.

His first dealings with Andrew Oldham had been over the Stones' cover version of 'It's All Over Now', written by his client Bobby Womack and controlled by his company, ABKCO. That minor publishing transaction led to talks about the Stones' poor financial yield, despite having had so many hits, and their still-to-be-finalised new recording contract with Decca. Klein's real ambition was to bag the Beatles, but until he could pull off that supreme coup he saw no harm in bagging the Beatles' main rivals. He offered to take Oldham on as a client, becoming the hard-nosed moneyman in the background that he already was for Mickie Most while the young genius concentrated on being creative. And, as a first priority, he would sort out the Stones' finances the way he had those of so many grateful chart-toppers in America. Needless to say, no role was envisaged for Oldham's present management partner, Eric Easton.

Initially, only Mick and Keith out of the five Stones were let in on the plan and called to meet Klein at the Scotch of St James club. Though

Klein's background was devoutly Jewish, his strong-arm negotiating style with formidable American record bosses, like the Roulette label's Morris Levy, had inspired rumours of connections to the Mafia. That, indeed, was his main appeal to Oldham: a boardroom Reg the Butcher. But while Keith was equally amenable to the notion, Mick presented a serious obstacle. With two hugely overblown and humiliating court appearances already on his record, he would scarcely fall over himself to embrace organised crime. Besides, Klein was so comprehensively *not* Mick's type: a podgy man who still combed his hair into a greasy fifties cowlick, wore none-too-clean white turtleneck sweaters, talked like Leo Gorcey from the Bowery Boys films and smoked a malodorous pipe.

At the meeting, however, Klein played his hand perfectly, not only spinning visions of the vast wealth the Stones would enjoy under his protection but showing a mastery of percentages and high-multiple mental arithmetic that held the former economics student transfixed. In addition, he knew all the Stones' music by heart and proved as adept at flattery as a Japanese geisha. While keeping the Mafia act going for Oldham and Keith, since that was what they transparently wanted, he massaged Mick's ego – one bystander would later recall – 'like a chick'. By the evening's end, Mick was in Klein's pocket along with the other two.

The whole band then met Klein at the brand-new London Hilton hotel on 26 July, coincidentally Mick's twenty-second birthday. Brian, Bill and Charlie were similarly dazzled by Klein's promises, but balked at the idea of dropping Eric Easton, who had backed them financially when no other agent would and whom, in spite of his desperate naffness, they all rather liked. But the Oldham–Jagger–Richard axis prevailed. The next day, without any prior warning, Oldham informed Easton that he should no longer consider himself the Stones co-manager, and simply walked away from their joint company, Impact Sound. The Stones' affairs were transferred to Klein's London accountants, Goodman Myers, and, as a taste of the riches to come, Oldham received a Rolls-Royce Phantom V.

The new contract with Decca currently on the table had been negotiated by Easton with the company's financial department. But Klein announced he would talk only to Decca's chairman, and major stock-holder, Sir Edward Lewis. As Laurence Myers, one of the Stones' newly appointed accountants, recalls, the elderly, gentlemanly Sir Edward was totally unprepared for what followed. When Klein arrived for the meet-ing, all five Stones – Mick included – followed him into the room like trustful ducklings. 'Good afternoon, Mr Klein' was Sir Edward's cour-teous opening. 'Would you like some tea?' Klein ignored both greeting and question, then dismissed the Stones – Mick included – and barked, 'The Rolling Stones won't be recording for Decca any more.' 'But we have a contract,' Sir Edward protested. 'You may or may not have a contract,' Klein replied, 'but the Stones won't be recording for you any more. *Now* I'll have some tea.'

By the end of that brief meeting, a dazed Sir Edward had committed Decca to pay the Stones $1.25 million in advance royalties – about £3 million by modern values. It was not only the first advance ever paid to a British pop act, but also, by some way, larger than any Klein had previously extracted from an American label. Press reports of the deal (which in those days included no informed financial analysis or investi-gation) put the band's collective earnings over the next five years as high as $3 million. Klein's 20 per cent commission might be double what British managers usually received, but even Mick had to admit that on the strength of his performance so far he looked like being well worth it.

'That was the mistake the Stones made,' says Laurence Myers, their accountant for the next couple of years. 'They thought they were giving Allen 20 per cent of theirs. They didn't find out until years later that in reality he was giving them 80 per cent of *his*.'

KLEIN HAD MOVED in at a fortuitous moment, just when 'Satisfac-tion' was topping the American charts and climbing towards eventual sales of 1.5 million. Before the ink on his contract was dry, he hastened to capitalise on the situation, ordering the rush release on 30 July of the Stones' fourth American album, *Out of Our Heads*. Though little more than a remarketing of 'Satisfaction' bulked out by blues and soul covers, it took only days to become their first No. 1 album in the United States. A month later, the scandalous single itself finally went on sale in Britain, having been held back since June by the negotiations with Decca. On home ground, too, it juddered instantly into the No. 1 spot, selling 250,000 copies and nauseating almost everyone over thirty.

The media's outrage at its lyrics and condemnation of the mouth that uttered them were fuelled further by – of all non-masturbatory things – a wedding. In the week of its release, David Bailey married the young French film star Catherine Deneuve, with Mick as his best man. Though the ceremony took place at a London registry office, tradition demanded that the two male principals should dress with a certain formality: instead, Bailey turned up in a sweater and Mick in an open-necked button-down shirt. The fact that the bride (who smoked throughout the ceremony) had recently starred in a film called *Repulsion* was, for Fleet Street's headline writers, the rancid icing on the cake.

Having given Decca a mauling, Klein applied himself to making the Stones a cinema attraction like their arch-competitors. The Beatles had already made two critically acclaimed feature films, *A Hard Day's Night* and *Help!*, which, while not earning them much as actors, had each spun off a hugely profitable soundtrack album. Film-making was still regarded as an essential step for flimsy pop stars whose success in the charts might evaporate at any moment. In Mick, it wasn't hard to see someone whom the film camera would love as ardently as did his concert audiences and who could redefine the screen idol for the sixties as radically as he'd redefined the pop idol one. Besides, in his present role didn't he prove himself a brilliant actor almost every hour of every day?

The problem was that the happy-go-lucky on-screen romps that usually constituted a pop film would not do for the Stones, Mick least of all. Thus far, the most interesting alternative had been offered by David Bailey, who, having reached the pinnacle of still photography, now hankered to try film producing and directing. Bailey spent much time and effort in trying to set up a screen version of Anthony Burgess's *A Clockwork Orange*, starring his erstwhile best man as the vicious, amoral (but finally prison-tamed) lead droog, Alex. Bailey's efforts came to nothing, even though Burgess himself commended Mick for the role as 'the quintessence of delinquency'.

Rumours of a Stones film appeared periodically in the music press, but nothing definite ever seemed to happen while the Beatles mopped up at the box office and lesser chart acts like the Dave Clark Five made successful screen débuts. Earlier in 1965, Keith had told the *NME* of yet another project, not so far scripted or titled: 'Mick will play Ernie who's a kind of hero and I play his right hand buddy . . .' Klein had no sooner joined Oldham in the driving seat, and seized the wheel, than it was announced the Stones would make 'five feature films over the next three years' with funding to be provided largely by Decca (which turned out to be news to Decca).

Klein fancied himself as a movie mogul in the David O. Selznick mould, and already had a seemingly ideal first project in his desk drawer. This was a novel entitled *Only Lovers Left Alive* by a north country schoolteacher named Dave Wallis, portraying a nightmare vision (not a million miles from *A Clockwork Orange*) of a world inhabited only by warring, vandalous and promiscuous teenagers (not a million miles from a Stones audience). 'SMASHING, LOOTING, KILLING, LOVING – THE TEENAGERS TAKE OVER THE WORLD!' said the book's cover in unconscious echo of Andrew Oldham's liner notes for *The Rolling Stones No. 2*. 'A NOVEL EVEN MORE SHATTERING THAN *LORD OF THE FLIES.*'

Mick was strongly attracted to the project and, together with Oldham, met several leading British film directors, including Michael Winner and Bryan Forbes, to discuss how they might handle it. There was also an unhappy encounter with Nicholas Ray, who had directed James Dean, the first and everlasting icon of rebellious youth, in *Rebel Without a Cause* exactly a decade earlier. Now in his sixties, Ray claimed never to have heard of the Stones or Mick and was patronising and dismissive; as they left the meeting, Mick told Oldham never again to put him through such an experience. So no Jimmy Dean for the sixties came to pass.

After this, *Only Lovers Left Alive* fell by the wayside; nor did any of the four other supposedly Decca-funded film projects announced by Klein take its place. Instead, Mick found himself back with the Stones on the relentless live-show treadmill through autumn until early December: the UK and Ireland, followed by their second North American tour that year to back up a second US album in six months, *December's Children (and Everybody's)*, and a new single, 'Get Off of My Cloud'.

To whet the appetites of prospective feature film producers, the documentary maker Peter Whitehead was hired to travel with them on the Irish leg and shoot a black-and-white *cinema verité* record much as the American Maysles brothers had done on the Beatles' first American tour. Whitehead unfortunately disregarded the band's usual pecking order, dwelling at such length on Charlie Watts – who came across as far the most interesting as well as best-looking, like a monosyllabic Oliver Reed – that the documentary was eventually titled *Charlie Is My Darling*.

Brian, typically, regarded himself as the central figure, and spoke to camera with a hushed earnestness that had his bandmates falling about satirically behind his back. 'Let's face it,' he mused at one point, little knowing what sombre truth he spoke, 'the future as a Rolling Stone is very uncertain . . .' The best bits with Mick revealed his talent as a mimic: at different times, he took off Elvis Presley, the voice-over on a BBC bird-watching programme, and the guitar intro to the Beatles' 'I Feel Fine'.

The previous year had seen Britain's already crowded fan-magazine market joined by a new full-colour weekly called *Rave* (a word then suggesting harmless enthusiasm rather than drug-crazed rioting). Among its contributors was Maureen O'Grady, who had worked for the more down-market *Boyfriend* when a ravenous Mick used to come around her office at lunchtime cadging leftovers from the secretaries' packed lunches. Mick, in fact, had helped her get the job with *Rave* and she was considered to have a special in with him. With *Out of Our Heads* at number two in the British album charts, behind the Beatles *Help!*, her editor tasked her with compiling '10 New Facts About Mick Jagger'. The compiler being blond and extremely good-looking, *Rave*'s readers received a – for him – unusual dose of specificity:

1. Mick, who bought his girlfriend Chrissie a white Mini for her birthday, is now getting one for himself, probably in grey – or a Bentley.
2. His latest and most favourite buy: a pair of white suede lace-up shoes.
3. Mick is now living apart from Keith in his own flat in London NW1.
4. Mick now has his hair cut about every two months. He likes it long at the back and quite short at the front, 'so it doesn't hang in my eyes when it gets wet while I'm onstage'.
5. Mick shares a tiny kitten with Chrissie, his first real pet. Its name? Sydney.
6. These days the only ready-made things that Mick buys are socks and jackets. All his shirts, trousers and shoes are specially made for him.
7. Mick doesn't go to the Cromwellian Club any more. 'Too many of my friends have been barred.' He goes now for the Scotch club in St James's where he likes to meet the 'Fab Four'.
8. Mick no longer likes dancing much. 'One two-minute dance in one evening is enough. I'd rather sit and watch.'
9. Mick is mad about Swedish Ingmar Bergman. His latest 'good' film being 'Compulsion' [sic] with Catherine Deneuve who, by the way, is married to Mick's good friend David Bailey.
10. All Mick's conversations are punctuated with 'Help!' Asked if it was because of the Beatles, Mick said, 'Funny, I thought I was saying that before they existed.'

Rave's front covers were provided by the huge tribe of young male pop stars Britain now boasted, each photographed in close-up, purified of his facial blemishes, and tinted a livid brown and pink. Three in particular appeared so often it became almost like a rota – Mick, Paul McCartney and Scott Walker of the Walker Brothers, the vocal trio whose 'Make It Easy on Yourself' finally ended 'Satisfaction's' reign at the top of the UK charts. Walker (real name Scott Engel) was a fey-looking American whose deep baritone could make the tritest pop lyric seem profound. Mick regarded him as an arch-rival almost equalling the Beatles, the more so because Andrew Oldham harped on continually about Walker's voice and stage presence. 'One night when I was at the Scotch, someone started flicking things at my table . . . cigarette ends and peanuts,' Maureen O'Grady remembers. 'It was so dark, I couldn't see at first who was doing it. Then I saw Mick sitting across the way in a booth with Chrissie Shrimpton, and realised it was him. He was annoyed because he thought Scott Walker got more *Rave* covers than he did.'

Sandwiched between September concerts in Douglas, Isle of Man, and Finsbury Park, north London, was a six-day visit to West Germany and Austria, the bomb-dealing enemies of Mick's babyhood, now transformed into Western Europe's front line against nuclear onslaught from Russia. Backstage at Munich's Circus-Krone-Bau arena, he warmed up by doing a Nazi goose step in time to 'Satisfaction', which proved such a good match that he continued it out in front of the audience. The resultant mayhem destroyed forty-three rows of seats and damaged 123 cars outside, but produced relatively little comment and no real censure from the British press. In those days, sending up the Third Reich was as permissible for a Rolling Stone as for any other entertainer; certainly, on the scale of offensiveness it ranked far below peeing on a garage forecourt or appearing tieless at a wedding.

Allen Klein's drive to release the maximum possible Stones product in America was reflected in the new album coinciding with their pre-Christmas return on tour. *December's Children (and Everybody's)* was mainly just another grab bag of covers that none of the band felt happy about releasing. There were, however, two solid Jagger–Richard compositions, 'Get Off of My Cloud', the current new single, and the band's own version of 'As Tears Go By', which Mick and Keith – mainly Mick – had written to order for Marianne Faithfull a year earlier. Such a soft, ladylike ballad was the last thing anyone expected from the barbarously macho Stones. And Mick, that supposedly superhuman stud and masturbator, somehow managed to sound even more shyly virginal than had Marianne.

With Klein directing operations, everything in America this time around was done on a vastly more impressive scale. The release of *December's Children (and Everybody's)* was announced to New York by a billboard picture of Mick and the Stones at their shaggiest and moodiest, towering a hundred feet above Times Square. 'The sound, face and mind of today,' ran the accompanying message (written by Andrew Oldham – who else?), 'is more relative to the hope of tomorrow and the reality of destruction than the blind who cannot see their children for fear and division. Something that grew and related. Five reflections of today's children. The Rolling Stones.'

For the first time, the Stones were to have their own private tour aircraft rather than taking interminable scheduled flights, with all the waiting around, being pestered for autographs by fans, hassled by police and officials and insulted by fellow travellers which that entailed. In their growing entourage, too, they now had their own personal photographer, Gered Mankowitz, nineteen-year-old son of the playwright Wolf Mankowitz, who had caught Oldham's eye with his recent portfolio of Marianne Faithfull.

In reality, things were rather less glamorous than promised. The tour aircraft was no luxury jet but a twin-propeller Martin whose gimcrack cabin had all the stage equipment piled amidships. Flights between shows were mainly overnight, leaving little opportunity for sexual adventure. 'In fact, the only one I remember getting lucky wasn't Mick or even Bill but Ian Stewart, the roadie,' Gered Mankowitz says. 'And that was only because he took the precaution of chatting up the stewardess.'

Throughout the tour's five-week duration, Allen Klein came and went in a selection of knitwear that caused even more covert hilarity among Oldham, Mick and Keith than Brian's to-camera soliloquies in Ireland. During Klein's absences, his interests were watched over by his Italian-American associate Pete Bennett, who looked and spoke like a cartoon mafioso but did undoubtedly possess formidable powers of persuasion. The previous July, when Mick and Keith were in New York for talks with Klein, Bennett had asked casually if they fancied seeing the Beatles' concert at Shea Stadium, the New York Mets' baseball ground, later that day. As a result of a single phone call, they had found themselves watching the show from the players' dugout.

Gered Mankowitz recalls how, during a meal stop on one of the tour's road journeys, Brian played his familiar trick of waiting in the limo while the others ate, then strolling into the diner after they'd finished, sitting down and scanning the menu at leisure. When the others' protests as usual produced no response but a dreamy smile, Pete Bennett lifted him off his seat by the scruff of the neck and carried him bodily out to the car.

In 1965, as far as most Britons were concerned, drugs had not been a part of everyday life for a good half century. Only the oldest could recall how in unregulated Victorian times chemists' shops used to sell opium as children's cold remedies, upper-class women (supposedly including the Queen herself) would relieve menstrual pains with cannabis, and English literature's greatest superhero, Sherlock Holmes, could mainline cocaine without fear of his frequent visitor, Inspector Lestrade. Since then, the 'dope fiend' had been the least threatening of social evils and – for all but a very few in the upper reaches of the aristocracy and the lower ones of show business – recreational drugs had come to mean a straight choice between nicotine and warm, flat beer.

The country was therefore totally unprepared for the upsurge in drug taking, this time among the modish young, which first became noticeable about halfway through 1965. For the newspapers, initially it meant no more than a random series of quasi-humourous stories in the Just Fancy That mould – garden centres having to be cleared of morning-glory flowers when their seeds were found to possess hallucinogenic properties if chewed, or newly prevalent mauve-coloured pep pills being nicknamed Purple Hearts after one of the highest decorations for American soldiers in the current Vietnam War.

Little more consternation at first greeted the reported resurgence of marijuana, dried cannabis leaves otherwise known as pot or grass, hand-rolled into a working-class cigarette paper, and smoked as what – like the historic roast beef of Old England – was called a joint. Pot had been illegal since the 1920s, but since almost nobody knew what it looked or smelled like, it could be smoked quite openly in pubs and clubs, even on plane journeys, its distinctive fragrance passed off as Turkish cigarettes. The police were equally unschooled in recognising the telltale fumes. One night when Mick and Chrissie arrived at a film première with Andrew and Sheila Oldham in Oldham's new Rolls-Royce, the constable who opened the car door for them received a billow of pot smoke full in the face. He merely coughed and wished them a pleasant evening.

In youth-speak, the meaning of *stoned* had changed from being drunk to being under the influence of this new manifestation of Swinging Britain. And of all alluring advertisements for it, none seemed more potent than a band whose second name was a variant of *stoned* and whose first no longer suggested inability to gather moss, but rolling a joint. With an album called *Out of Our Heads* and a single called 'Get Off of My Cloud' simultaneously topping the charts on both sides of the Atlantic, the Stones were seen as pop's first public converts to the pot-smoking fad and Mick as its first, unignorable mouthpiece. (In reality, neither title had been meant to suggest pot: they were out of their heads only through music, and 'Get Off of My Cloud' was just another Jagger way of saying 'Look but don't touch.')

In early 1966, the British press was intrigued, but again not especially alarmed, by reports from America of an entirely new drug, a laboratory-made hallucinogen named lysergic acid diethylamide, whose initial letters were also the symbols of Britain's old pounds, shillings and pence currency – LSD. Known for short as acid, it was said not to fuddle the senses, like pot, but to create 'mind-expanding' powers of perception and imagination in the user. Because of LSD's previous use in psychiatry, it had not yet been made illegal and, indeed, was preached as a kind of secular gospel by bohemian intellectuals like the Harvard academic Dr Timothy Leary, the poet Allen Ginsberg and the writer Ken Kesey.

Musicians were, of course, the first and most willing targets in this crusade, both domestic and visiting ones from across the Atlantic. On 5 December, after the Stones played their final date of the tour at the Los Angeles Sports Arena, Brian and Keith attended one of Ken Kesey's regular LSD parties, or acid tests, listened to Kesey's sermon on the new consciousness and creativity it could unlock in them, and then tested it on themselves. For both, the experience fully lived up to expectations, and they urged Mick to try it without delay. But the cautious, health-conscious Mick – so unlike the out-of-his-head vinyl one who floated on clouds and saw 'little men dressed up like Union Jacks' – preferred to hold back a while.

If acid was a future threat to the Stones' existence, another one, no less alluring and deadly, was already in their midst. Three months earlier, on the night of the Jagger goose step in Munich, a rangy blonde fashion model named Anita Pallenberg had talked her way backstage and magnetised the Stone whose hair colour matched hers. Three months on, she was living with Brian at his flat in Elm Park Lane, Chelsea, and already creating havoc with the band's internal politics.

The exotic European influences that had always nurtured the plain English Stones, and their Kentish commuter-belt Casanova in particular, were back again with a bang. Twenty-one-year-old Anita had been born in Sweden of German-Swiss ancestry (including the nineteenth-century neoclassical painter Arnold Böcklin), had spent her childhood between Germany, Spain and France, and had studied art in Rome and New York before settling in London as a model and occasional film actress. She already knew Mick's art-world friends Robert Fraser and Christopher Gibbs, but had felt no curiosity about him or his band until she chanced to be in Munich on a fashion shoot when they were playing at Circus-Krone-Bau.

The immediate effect was to send Brian's shaky self-esteem rocketing into the stratosphere – for not even Mick had ever managed to pull a bird like this. Anita was stunningly beautiful in the crop-haired, snub-nosed, long-legged way that perfectly suited skimpy sixties fashion, but with an extra, almost feral quality, 'like a cheetah', John Dunbar recalls. She was formidably intelligent, fluent in four languages, and knowledgeable about art and the obscurer byways of German and European literature. She also had a recklessness and appetite for devilment that would cause more than one of her new rock 'n' roll friends to suspect her of being a witch. In Munich, she had picked out Brian as the Stone seemingly most like herself, so was taken aback when he begged her to stay with him because he couldn't bear to be alone, and spent much of the subsequent night in tears.

As a further boost to Brian's spirits, Anita seemed immune to Mick's supposedly irresistible sex appeal and, indeed, showed the same tendency to challenge and even tease him that Charlie Watts's wife, Shirley, did. He in turn made clear his view – to prove so very far-sighted – that no good would come of her involvement with the Stones, and ordered Chrissie Shrimpton to have nothing to do with her.

From being an outnumbered outsider, Brian now found himself one half of Swinging London's most famous couple, prototypes of the soon-to-be-dubbed Beautiful People. By early 1966, modish young men's clothes had become scarcely distinguishable from women's – ruffled-fronted blouses, huge floppy-brimmed hats, figure-hugging crushed-velvet bell-bottom hipsters with outsize belts, trailing fur boas and knee-high suede boots. The hippie flower-child culture, blowing in from America's West Coast, added even more gender-unspecific caftans, headbands, and multilayers of beads, bangles and amulets. With their matching gold heads and virtually interchangeable wardrobe, Brian and Anita often looked less like lovers than identical twins.

However, their relationship was primarily and overwhelmingly physical. At the outset, their love-making sessions could go on for days at a time, another cause of Brian's lateness for Stones recording sessions or shows. In the bedroom, Anita was in every way different from the shy English girls he had made such a career of impregnating. She was quite happy to indulge his existing sexual fantasies by tying him to their Moroccan bed and whipping him, and introduce him to new ones by making him up with her lipstick and cosmetics or dressing him (and herself) in the World War II Nazi SS uniforms which somehow or other had crept into their combined wardrobe.

The two seldom enjoyed absolute privacy, since Brian was always inviting friends, or even chance acquaintances, to crash out at the flat and live there at his expense for as long as they liked. Among these floating tenants was a young Scots film student named Dave Thomson, whom Brian had met in Glasgow when the Stones were playing there. In collaboration with Thomson, he was supposedly writing a feature film script to be shot in Scandinavia and the French Camargue – although, when talking about it in the *Charlie Is My Darling* documentary, he'd been unable to provide any coherent synopsis.

A side of LSD downplayed by its advocates was its power to focus on the weak spots in its user's psyche and expand these into visions of peculiar customised hellishness. As such, it became the worst trigger yet to Brian's insecurity and paranoia about his situation in the Stones. Allen Klein's arrival, engineered largely behind his back, seemed yet another dastardly ploy to throw his lost leadership in his face and strengthen Mick and Keith's new power base (though there was no evidence thus far that Klein regarded him as a problem). Even his triumph at winning Anita rapidly soured to dread that she would tire of him and – as might have been expected in the first instance – make a play for Mick. Once the first lovers' idyll had passed, they began to have rows, far surpassing any of Mick's with Chrissie, in which Brian's penchant for violence soon resurfaced. Anita would appear publicly with a black eye under the blonde urchin cut or bruised arms inside the jewel-studded Afghan coat, which, like most victims of domestic violence, she blamed on falling over.

After Brian's first meeting with Dave Thomson in Glasgow, Thomson had seen him listening at the keyhole of a hotel bedroom where, he suspected, Mick, Keith and Andrew Oldham were plotting against him. To his young Scots lodger he poured out the piteous tale of how, having stolen away his band and perverted its blues ideals, 'They' were now trying to get rid of him altogether. Thomson also received worried representations from Charlie Watts and Bill Wyman, the Stones' second division, who were untouched by any of these internecine feuds and pressures, but worried at the career threat they presented. Charlie told Thomson of an American doctor's chilling diagnosis on the band's 1964 tour when Brian had to be hospitalised in Chicago: if he carried on drinking his present two bottles of Scotch per day, never mind all the drugs, he'd be dead inside two years.

Paranoia soared almost off the graph in January 1966 when the Sunday *News of the World* published revelations about the child Brian had sired by his Cheltenham girlfriend, Pat Andrews, before making his way to London. A week later another Sunday scandal sheet, *The People*, weighed in with a story about Linda Lawrence, from the Windsor–Edith Grove era, and the second unsupported baby to whom he'd quixotically given the name Julian. This was not publicity that even Oldham wanted for the Stones, and it automatically branded all the others with something of which they were totally innocent. In particular, wherever the dread name 'Rolling Stones' was spoken or written – as had been proved by the pissing incident – most people thought first and exclusively of Mick.

Brian's discovery of LSD did have one seemingly beneficial side effect. It brought him closer to Keith than they had been since the Edith Grove days – which by definition meant shutting out Mick to an unusual and exhilarating degree. The fact that he and Keith had sampled acid first in each other's company made them feel like fellow pioneers venturing into the unknown, and gave them a new, consuming interest in common. Acid was the first sociable drug, which explained its special appeal to America's flower children: users were encouraged to have an experienced friend or friends nearby to provide encouragement, reassurance, or actual rescue in the event of a bad trip. So Brian and Keith continued to take it together, see its marvellous visions or endure its periodic horrors together, and have obsessive discussions about the experience from which Mick was excluded.

As it happened, Keith had just been dumped by his first real girlfriend, Linda Keith, and was in a broken-hearted state that no one who saw him onstage, putting the boot in to rioting Glaswegians, could have imagined. Rather than pick a new girl from the hundreds available, he sought the solace of old mates. Since his oldest mate was still deep in a relationship (in fact, engaged to be married), he gravitated to Brian, back in their old common stomping ground of Chelsea. He became one of the most regular visitors to Brian and Anita's new flat in Courtfield Gardens, to take acid, listen to music or simply hang out. Brian was pathetically pleased by this return to the old atmosphere of 102 Edith Grove and – in the worst mistake of his short life – encouraged Keith to get to know Anita better and Anita to consider Keith as great a mate as he did.

In June 1966 Mick moved on from his temporary billet with Lionel Bart but, surprisingly, opted to stay in north London rather than follow Brian back to Chelsea, where so many of the Stones' up-market friends were also to be found. For £50 per week he rented a fifth-floor flat in Harley House, an Edwardian mansion block on Marylebone Road, the busy traffic artery connecting King's Cross, Euston, Marylebone and Paddington rail stations. Across the road was Harley Street, with its exclusive private doctors, dentists and clinics; to the rear lay Regent's Park. Living in this grand but rather impersonal environment, far from trendy SW4, seemed to underline how the new Brian–Keith–LSD alliance had consigned him, however temporarily, to the margins.

Number 52 Harley House was supposed to have been where Mick and Chrissie set up home as newlyweds. After finding the flat, however, he informed her that he no longer wanted to get married, just to live with her there. It was, perhaps, not such a surprising decision for a young man, not yet twenty-three, at whom half the girls in the Western Hemisphere were now hurling themselves like moths at a fluorescent tube. Chrissie was devastated by this change of heart, and made her feelings known in her usual fiery fashion. But as a sixties dolly-bird, she accepted having no real say in the matter; if she wanted to keep him she must do what he wanted.

The price she had to pay was a heavy one. Until now her cohabitation with Mick had been diplomatically concealed from her parents by a supposed bed-sitter and female roommate in Olympia. But doing so openly with him without first becoming Mrs Jagger was what many British people in 1966, including Ted and Peggy Shrimpton, still termed 'living in sin'. So shaming a prospect was it to Chrissie's father that he told her if she went through with it she'd no longer be welcome at the family's Buckinghamshire home. She still has a letter from her mother, less intransigent but no less subservient to male authority: 'Daddy says

Mick can't live as a married man and not be married . . . You're being used . . . I wish I could wave a magic wand and make it all right for you.'

Chrissie would have ample time to reflect as much on the vanished dream of coming to Harley House as a bride as on her banishment from her family. For Mick's continual absences with the Stones meant that she spent weeks, even months, there alone.

To begin with, at least, he seemed to find the separations as hard as she did. Photographer Gered Mankowitz remembers him talking constantly about Chrissie, and how much he missed her, on the (largely sex-free) *December's Children* American tour. She herself recalls how he would telephone her at every opportunity – a complicated process across the Atlantic in those days – send her telegrams and write her 'hundreds' of letters. Even from distances of thousands of miles, she says, 'he was very controlling, very paternalistic, very caretaking. I used to go to the Scotch [of St James club] every night when he was on tour. He arranged for a car to be sent for me at three in the morning and I'd be taken home. And then he would ring me as soon as I got in to make sure I was there.'

Having never been especially close to Mick's parents, Chrissie did not feel they were particularly grief-stricken to lose her as a daughter-in-law. The highly respectable Joe and Eva Jagger did not care for this alternative arrangement any more than did the Shrimptons, but even Joe no longer had any control over his older son's behaviour. Chrissie's one seeming ally was Mick's brother, Chris, with whom she felt a certain affinity, both in their names and in their situations as younger siblings of stars. Now eighteen, Chris looked very much like Mick and had a good, albeit more conventional, singing voice, but he nurtured no ambitions to capitalise on his surname by going into music, preferring to develop interests in acting and writing. The brothers still had as good a relationship as when they used to play cricket or climb ropes as small boys; despite Mick's exalted state, he took care to stay in touch with Chris, and would often have him to stay at Harley House, where Chrissie was expected to look after him.

So that she wouldn't be lonely, Mick bought her a Yorkshire terrier she named Dora and a collection of cats that eventually numbered six, even though (despite *Rave*'s story about the kitten named Sydney being his 'first pet') he himself hated cats. 'He couldn't stand them,' Chrissie remembers. 'They used to drive him mad. They'd pee on his shirts.' A certain Romford service-station manager named Charles Keeley might have considered this proof of justice in heaven.

Nonetheless, knowing how much Chrissie wanted to add a white Persian kitten to the menagerie, Mick nobly went off alone to buy her one as a surprise twenty-first-birthday present. 'He had a new midnight-blue Aston Martin, and he brought the kitten home in that – without a travelling basket. He came in and said, "It's in the car . . . I can't get it out. It's under the seat." I was expecting a little white ball of fluff and I put my hand under the seat and was clawed by this skinny little rat-like thing. It was a Siamese . . . he'd got the wrong breed. It was terrified, and you know how they scream. This one even screamed when it was eating. So we took it back and swapped it for another in the litter, a girl. I called her Grace.' Her other twenty-first present from Mick, not an ideal mix with her cat pack, was a Victorian birdcage with three singing birds, 'because I loved the dawn'.

Chrissie was by now, despite herself, something of a celebrity. Finally yielding to pressure to emulate her older sister, she had been photo-graphed by David Bailey modelling the first collection of a new young designer named Ossie Clark for *Vogue*'s Young Idea section. In America, *Mod* magazine featured a Chrissie Shrimpton column, 'From London with Luv', concocted by the Stones' office without her permission (or, indeed, her knowledge) and filled with rose-tinted chitchat about home life with Mick. 'I think Stevie Winwood is the best singer we have. (Ouch! Mick had just hit me!) Recently I had my twenty-first birthday. Mick gave me a huge rocking horse which I named Petunia . . .'

Yet Mick and she were never a famous couple like Brian Jones and Anita Pallenberg. Even when they were engaged and planning to marry, Mick continued metaphorically dropping Chrissie's hand in public, refusing to talk about her to the media or admit they were seri-ously involved, taking time during the most insignificant interviews far outside London to denounce 'all those stories about me and Chrissie Shrimpton'. On the rare occasions when he was photographed at their

Harley House flat – lounging against a décor lifted whole from Terence Conran's new Habitat store or disdainfully sipping coffee from 'an out-size cup of Cantonese design', as one caption writer breathlessly noted – Chrissie was nowhere to be seen.

Once he was out of Chrissie's sight, any attractive young female was fair game and supposedly panting to surrender to him, though it didn't always happen that way. *Rave* magazine's Maureen O'Grady remembers being alone with him in a dressing room and finding herself the target of a pointed come-on. 'He asked me whether the trousers he had on were too tight round the buttocks and crotch. "No, they're fine, Mick," I told him. "Are you sure?" he kept saying. "What about here . . . and here . . . and *here*?"'

Not long afterwards she met the Stones in Scotland for a *Rave* photo shoot during their current tour with the Hollies. Unable to afford the plush Gleneagles Hotel, where the band was staying, she asked her photographer to find her a cheap local B&B. The photographer reported back that nothing was available, whereupon Mick offered her the spare bedroom in his suite. 'I said "no thank you" and went out and found a perfectly nice place nearby,' Maureen remembers. 'Later, the photographer told me that Mick had asked him to say there were no B&Bs in the neighbourhood so that I'd have no alternative but to stay in his suite. It made things even more difficult for me that I knew Chrissie . . . in fact, she phoned me while we were there to check on what Mick was up to.'

For her own peace of mind, Chrissie did not inquire too deeply into what went on on the road and, in this era before paparazzi and tabloid kiss-and-tell, could remain – mostly – in blissful ignorance. 'I think I only knew he was unfaithful to me about three times, though I know there must have been many more times when I didn't find out. And when I did, he would be *so* regretful. I remember him playing "I've Been Loving You Too Long", the first time I heard that beautiful song – which I still find hard to listen to – after I'd found out about something. And I can remember him lying on the floor and crying all over my feet because I'd threatened to leave him.'

His long absences on tour in America brought the worst such forebodings, despite his blizzards of phone calls, letters and telegrams. Nor were matters really helped when she would be flown across to meet him at some stop on the tour route, usually New York or Los Angeles. 'I think I've still got a list he made for me of things I had to do when I was going to the airport . . . "Don't speak to any reporters . . . Have you got your passport? Make sure you keep it in your handbag . . ." I have to say I rather liked all that.' But joining Mick in the bosom of the Stones was always horribly uncomfortable. 'They'd obviously been up to loads of things that the girlfriends weren't supposed to know about. It felt like coming into a room when you know people have just been talking about you and everything suddenly goes quiet.'

Despite all those evenings alone at the Scotch of St James, she was unfaithful to Mick only once, before the move to Harley House, with a performer briefly notorious for even tighter trousers and sexuality far more blatant than his. This was P. J. Proby, a fruity-voiced Texan in a Tom Jones ponytail whose performances included the ritual splitting of his velveteen breeches. While Mick was away, she received a rhyming telegram from Proby which she can still recite by heart: 'I'm sitting here, drinking beer / Wishing that old Mick was queer / If he was, I wouldn't fret / 'cause he might forget you yet.'

At the time Chrissie was back at her former bedsit staying with her friend Liz Gribben, as she often did for company while Mick was overseas. When she returned there after spending the night with Proby, she found Mick had sent her the white Mini Minor car mentioned by *Rave* magazine – even though she hadn't yet learned to drive. 'Liz said, "He's been phoning and phoning from America, you're in trouble . . . and there's a new white Mini outside."'

Another time when she was at Proby's house, a pair of heavies turned up with expressions promising to split more than his trousers. 'These two blokes said, "Mick wants you" – so I just went,' Chrissie remembers. 'I was taken away and put on a plane to join him in Ireland.'

Chrissie was only aware of LSD insofar as Mick, in his controlling, almost paternalistic way, told her she mustn't try it. 'Just around that time, the Beatles were first getting into acid. I remember Paul McCartney coming round to see Mick at Harley House . . . because he brought me a sweetheart plant as a present. The way he talked about acid worried me because I didn't think he and the others knew what they were getting into or what effect it would have on the people who regarded them as role models. I felt he should have thought about it more.'

That spring of 1966 brought a blue-blooded social event to delight Mick's heart. Chrissie's posh friend Camilla, who also worked for Andrew Oldham, knew Tara Browne, fourth son of Lord Oranmore and Brown and the Irish brewing heiress Oonagh Guinness. Mick, Chrissie, Brian and others from the Stones' inner circle were invited to Tara's twenty-first-birthday party at his family home, Luggala Castle, high in the Wicklow Mountains. Before the year's end, this seemingly most blessed of young men would die when, for no apparent reason – but probably on an acid trip – he ran a Chelsea red light in his Lotus Elan sports car and crashed into a truck, afterwards gaining immortality as 'the lucky man who made the grade' in John Lennon's song 'A Day in the Life'.

Tara's twenty-first was a sumptuous bash featuring a private performance by the Lovin' Spoonful and all the acid a young rock star or Irish noble could desire. At one point during the revels, the Stones' photographer friend Michael Cooper went into hallucinations so extreme that he was terrified by the sound of an Alka-Seltzer tablet fizzing in a glass of water.

According to Chrissie, it was here that Mick sampled acid for the first time, taking a 'sparkle' with unusual incaution just before driving her and Camilla down the narrow winding mountain roads from the castle to the airport. The trip set in during the journey, and he became convinced that a medieval pike had materialised inside the car and the Duke of Edinburgh's severed head was grinning at him from the end of it. At the time a sheer drop of several hundred feet yawned below; as Chrissie recalls, 'Camilla and I kept very quiet and just went along with what he was saying in case he ran the car over the edge.'

★

APRIL 1966 HAD brought the first Rolling Stones album to dispense with cover versions and consist entirely of Jagger–Richard songs, so completing their metamorphosis from idealistic bluesmen to the most mercenary rock band the world would ever know. The collection's original title, *Could You Walk on the Water?*, had been vetoed by Decca as a sacrilegious reference to the most spectacular of Christ's miracles; it was left to John Lennon to equate his band with Jesus and unleash a worldwide storm of protest and abuse. Instead, the Stones' album was named *Aftermath*, the very thing from which their God-fearing record bosses may well have saved them.

Aftermath and the Beatles' *Revolver* are the two albums that most vividly evoke Swinging London at its apotheosis, during the uncharacteristically glorious summer of '66, which culminated with England's victory against West Germany in the final of the football World Cup. Musically, too, it was the one and only time when the Stones seriously competed with the Beatles and – now and again – even surpassed them.

Mick's lyrics showed him still experimenting with different personae like someone trying on a succession of outfits at a Carnaby Street boutique. For 'Lady Jane', he transformed himself into a virginal, deferential Elizabeth pageboy, serenading a succession of mistresses in the old, non-carnal sense of the word, as if butter wouldn't melt even in that capacious mouth. 'Paint It Black' (on the album's US version only) was funereally self-flagellating with its unlikely vision of the singer turning away from young girls 'until my darkness goes' like some tortured young seminarian in James Joyce's Ireland. 'Mother's Little Helper' was a satire about amphetamine addiction among those whom it was still permissible to call 'housewives', as sociologically spot-on as anything being written at the same time by the Kinks' Ray Davies.

In 1966 the term *male chauvinist* was still three years way from being coined, and laddish triumphalism had been part of every rock idol since Elvis; nonetheless, the streak of contemptuous condescension towards women running through Mick's *Aftermath* songs was noticed by everyone with half a brain cell who reviewed the album, and terminally alienated several important female pop columnists, notably the London *Evening Standard*'s Maureen Cleave.

There had been a foretaste back in February with the single '19th Nervous Breakdown', his mocking psychoanalysis of the pushy yet neurotic (and usually upper-class) females who were always coming on to him at parties. In Maureen Cleave's subsequent interview piece for the *Standard,* gussets stayed resolutely dry. 'For some unaccountable reason, Mick Jagger is considered the most fashionable, modish man in London, the voice of today. Cecil Beaton paints him and says he reminds him of Nijinsky. Mick is also reported to be a friend of Princess Margaret. He has said nothing – apart from a few words on the new single – to suggest he is of today, yesterday or any other day. He remains uncommunicative, unforthcoming, uncooperative . . .'

Now here was *Aftermath* with a track called 'Stupid Girl' (chorus: 'Looka' that stoopid ge-*erl*!'). Here was 'Out of Time', with a patronising sympathy that was somehow even more objectionable: 'Yaw obsolete, mah baby . . . mah paw old-fashioned bay-*buh* . . .' Here was 'Under My Thumb' with its clear reference to Chrissie, the former sharp-clawed 'Siamese cat of a girl', now 'the sweetest pet in the world' who 'does just what she's told' and 'talks when she's spoken to'.

However questionable their sentiments, most of the songs were at a technical level Mick and Keith had never previously reached. But none would have worked half so well without Brian Jones's uncanny ability to pick up almost any musical instrument and immediately coax a tune from it. His self-confidence on an upswing again thanks to Anita – and getting Keith back in his gang – Brian contributed a bravura range of instrumental effects to *Aftermath*. On 'Paint It Black' and 'Mother's Little Helper,' he played Indian sitar with a brio that made George Harrison on the Beatles' 'Norwegian Wood' sound fumbly. On 'Lady Jane' he complemented Mick's pageboy innocence with the lute-like rippling of an Appalachian dulcimer. On 'Under My Thumb' he played marimba (African xylophone) in a slightly off-register, soft-pawed descant that would keep it on radio playlists long after its words had become the height of political incorrectness.

Some months earlier, in another seeming step away from wholehearted commitment to the Stones, Andrew Oldham had set up his own independent record label. It was called Immediate (something its creator required all forms of gratification to be) and, in tune with the new hippie love-and-peace ethos, loftily declared itself 'Happy to Be a Part of the Industry of Human Happiness'. In no time, the new label's performance lived up to its name: it struck gold by UK-releasing an American smash-hit single, the McCoys' 'Hang on Sloopy', and acquired a roster of soon-to-be brilliant new acts including Fleetwood Mac, Rod Stewart, the Nice and the Small Faces.

Bound as the Stones were by that million-dollar Decca contract, they could not sign up with Immediate. But they were umbilically linked with the label, not least because its headquarters and their management office were both in Oldham's Marylebone flat. A visitor remembers getting lost in the warren of little rooms and opening a door to find Mick in front of a mirror practising his James Brown moves. 'He just said "Hi" and continued, like a stick insect in some weird mating dance.'

If the Stones were not available to Immediate, the Jagger–Richard songwriting partnership was. Also in the label's first batch of signings was Chris Farlowe, a big-voiced young blues singer looking to make a Jagger-like transition into mainstream pop. Oldham's answer was to hand him 'Out of Time' from *Aftermath* and get Mick to produce it – one of the few times a recording artist has supervised a cover of his original track. Far from diluting its misogyny, the version he concocted with Farlowe pumped up the contempt for that 'obsolete' and 'poor old-fashioned baby' almost to the point of nausea. It reached No. 1 in the cloudless July week when England's soccer players triumphantly proved themselves *not* out of time, snatching the World Cup from West Germany with two goals in extra time.

In August, after barely three years as a world-class stadium attraction, the Beatles gave up touring and withdrew into the recording studio to concentrate their creative energies wholly on making albums. That left the Stones as kings of the live performance circuit, a position they still have not yielded half a century later.

The band's fifth American tour that summer of 1966 was across

a country much changed from the one to which they had followed
the Beatles so dispiritingly in 1964. The escalating Vietnam War had
led to mass conscription, and this in turn to wholesale unrest in the
nation's immemorially tranquil schools and colleges and conversion
to the hippie creed of pacifism, long hair and drugs. It was a genuine
revolution, but one strangely without leaders or demagogues; instead,
to articulate their fury and stiffen their resolve, the insurgents turned
to music. So, in medieval times, might Holy Land crusaders have taken
their cue not from Richard the Lionheart but from Blondin, his lute-
plucking minstrel.

Spurred on by the Beatles, American pop music had taken huge
strides, and there were now many fine domestic bands standing shoulder to shoulder with the hippies and bringing the protest song coruscat-
ingly up-to-date. Yet somehow, wherever young Americans vandalised
their alma mater, burned their military draft cards or obliterated their
once clean-cut faces with apostle-length hair and beards, the only possible mental soundtrack was 'The Last Time', 'Get Off of My Cloud',
'(I Can't Get No) Satisfaction' or maybe that extraordinary six-minute
name check from the revolution's troubadour in chief, Bob Dylan's 'Like
a Rolling Stone'. 'The Beatles want to hold your hand,' wrote the radical journalist Tom Wolfe, 'but the Stones want to burn your town,' and
hundreds of thousands were ready to line up behind them with extra
kerosene.

No matter that the Beatles in earlier times had not been averse to a
little arson, whereas the only matches that ever tempted the Stones were
cricket ones. No matter that, via their cautious mega-mouthpiece, they
never uttered a word calculated to whip up anti-war or anti-government
feeling or threaten public order in any way. On the contrary, for the rampaging boys who now competed with screaming girls as their core audience, narcissistic self-absorption – personified by Mick above all – was
precisely what gave them overwhelming superiority to preachier American bands like the Byrds or Buffalo Springfield. The Stones were about
nothing but being the Stones, just as their music boiled down at last to
the bulge in their singer's trousers. Their only crusade was against the

TOP LEFT
Mick at Dartford Grammar School; already cooler than any of his classmates and a magnet to girls.

—

TOP RIGHT
The India Rubber Boy, dressed for cricket; it would remain a lifelong passion.

—

BOTTOM
Mick's parents, Joe and Eva. How could such nice, normal people have produced a rock superstar?

TOP LEFT
The unknown Stones, just after
Andrew Oldham and Eric Easton
took them over, sitting in the road
outside Mick, Keith and Brian's
squalid flat in Edith Grove, Chelsea.
The photographer was under
instructions to make them look 'nasty'.

ABOVE
Onstage at Soho's Studio 51 club.
–

BOTTOM LEFT
Backstage photo with Mick just
getting a look-in. In those days,
many regarded Brian as the
band's star.

BEAT
MONTHLY

OCTOBER, 1963

1/6d

TOP RIGHT
Black-leather-clad poster boys for
Beat magazine. Brian still looks
like their leader.

—

TOP CENTRE
Posing in the matching houndstooth-
check jackets they wore for their
first UK TV appearance. Clean
cut as they look now, the studio
switchboard was jammed
with complaints.

—

BOTTOM RIGHT
Mick and Keith in early studio days
with Andrew Oldham and their friend
and supporter Gene Pitney, one of the
first to cover a Jagger-Richards song.

TOP LEFT
Mick and Chrissie Shrimpton at the Shrimpton family farm after announcing their engagement
–

BOTTOM LEFT
Mick and Marianne arrive in Australia in July 1969 for the filming of *Ned Kelly*. In a few hours, Marianne will try to kill herself.

TOP CENTRE
Hair-netted Mick being prepped for a TV appearance.
–

BOTTOM CENTRE
Mick in the era when every rock star's home resembled a Moroccan souk.

TOP RIGHT
Stones-mania USA. One American fan described them as 'so ugly, they're attractive'.
–

CENTRE RIGHT
Mick chats to Cathy McGowan on the set of *Ready, Steady Go!*, the TV show that gave him his best early (and surly) exposure.

BOTTOM RIGHT
Keith with Anita Pallenberg, the bewitching – some said, witching – model and actress who started out with Brian and later made love to Mick on the cinema-screen.

TOP LEFT
Manacled Mick en route
to Brixton Prison after his
conviction.

–

BOTTOM LEFT
Robert Fraser, the art dealer
who was busted along with
Mick and Keith – but did not
have their get-out-of jail card.

ABOVE CENTRE LEFT
Keith with 'Acid King David'
Snyderman on the beach at
West Wittering, shortly before
Snyderman shopped him and
Mick to the Sussex police.

BELOW CENTRE
Mick and Michele Breton in
the pot-in-the-bath scene from
Performance. The film's horrified
distributor complained that
'even the bathwater is dirty.'

ABOVE CENTRE RIGHT
The execution scene from
Ned Kelly (which the film critics
also slaughtered).
–

TOP RIGHT
Mick in the *Performance
– Rock 'n' roll Circus* era.

BOTTOM RIGHT
The Stones–Beatles entente
lasted throughout the Sixties.
Here John Lennon and Yoko
Ono appear as a support-act
in the Rolling Stones' *Rock 'n'
roll Circus* – a virtuoso Jagger
appearance destined not to be
seen for decades afterwards.

TOP
Publicity shot for *Beggars Banquet*, the album that restored the Stones' reputation after Mick's misguided detour into psychedelia with *Their Satanic Majesties Request*.

—

CENTRE LEFT
After Brian Jones's mysterious death in 1969, Mick introduces the band's new lead guitarist, the cherubic (but not for long) Mick Taylor.

—

CENTRE RIGHT
One of the career highs Mick prefers not to recognise: making 250,000 people at the Brian Jones memorial concert shut up and listen to poetry.

—

BOTTOM
Hell's Angels run amok at the ghastly Altamont festival, for which Mick took much of the blame. In fact, he behaved with great courage.

norms of good taste and restraint; their only cause that of having a good time and not giving a fuck.

Their September single, a new Jagger–Richard composition rather than one of the several unexploited *Aftermath* tracks, was equally provocative to student arsonists, proto-feminists and defenders of good taste. Long-windedly entitled 'Have You Seen Your Mother, Baby (Standing in the Shadow)?', it featured Mick once again in mocking psychoanalytical mode – now managing to patronise two female generations at once – and a chaotic backing with the nakedly Beatle-ish touch of a brass section. Accompanying its US release was a publicity picture of the band in drag, grouped around Bill Wyman in a wheelchair – the one and only time Bill ever took centre stage. As a nod to anti-war *zeitgeist*, he and Brian wore American female military uniforms, but otherwise the effect was pure pantomime dame with Keith in flyaway spectacles like Dame Edna Everage before her time and Mick, swathed in moth-eaten fur, pouting from beneath a blowsy blond wig.

The real-life Stones and Beatles were not only total contradictions of Tom Wolfe's *aperçu*; they were also as intricately linked as old European royal houses. In November, newly liberated from touring, John Lennon went to a show at a small London art gallery called Indica which Paul McCartney had helped to fund, and there had his first encounter with the Japanese conceptual artist Yoko Ono. Indica's founder and director, John Dunbar, was an old Hampstead crony of Andrew Oldham's, a friend of the principal Stones as much as the principal Beatles, and now husband of Marianne Faithfull.

CHAPTER EIGHT

Secrets of the Pop Stars' Hideaway

I n the two years since Marianne had recorded Mick's first successful song, there had been no whisper of the love affair which would
scandalise the sixties even more than John and Yoko's.

'As Tears Go By' had given her a successful career in the persona
Andrew Oldham invented for her: one step in driven-snow purity
behind the Singing Nun. Managed first by Oldham, then by Tony
Calder, she had released a handful of further singles and two albums
and crisscrossed the country on pop package tours. At a time when British female pop artists mostly sang in *faux*-American soul accents and
had little individual character, Marianne's delicate beauty, polite-posh
English voice and intimations of both breeding and brains gave her a
niche to herself. As one PR handout put it, 'She likes Marlon Brando,
Woodbine cigarettes and going to the ballet, and she loves wearing long
evening dresses.'

On tour, as on record, Marianne was a figure apart, her air of innocent refinement mixed with a certain grandeur inherited from her Austrian baroness mother. Her fellow performers being almost wholly male
and raveningly randy, she travelled with a chaperone and, on journeys

between gigs, could usually be found sitting quietly at the back of the bus, absorbed in a Jane Austen novel or poetry by Wordsworth or Keats. In reality, her air of innocence could be misleading and the chaperone not infallible: she had brief affairs with the Stones' friend Gene Pitney and Allan Clarke from the Hollies (but turned down the great Bob Dylan when he tried to seduce her by writing poetry to her).

All this time, despite constant contact with Oldham and Calder, she met up with Mick again only once, at a party given by the *Ready Steady Go!* TV show. The impression he made was not a great advance on the 'cheeky little yob' who'd offered her his lap in the car after the 'As Tears Go By' session. Exceedingly drunk (something that never became him), he talked to her in a facetious copy of Oldham camp, then deliberately slopped champagne down the front of her dress.

In May 1965, now aged eighteen, Marianne seemed to take a deliberate step away from the pop scene – and any prospect of further liaisons with its male power figures – by marrying John Dunbar, who at that point was still reading fine arts at Churchill College, Cambridge. ('Only a goddammed student!' a disappointed Bob Dylan lamented.) She was three months pregnant and the following November gave birth to a son, Nicholas.

The marriage proved of brief duration, a fact that had nothing whatever to do with Mick. Dunbar was too immersed in setting up the Indica gallery to have much time to be a husband or father, and Marianne found herself the main breadwinner from her pop earnings. Their flat in Lennox Gardens, Knightsbridge, swarmed with Dunbar's artist friends, many of whom were hardened druggies; used needles would lie on the same kitchen worktop where baby Nicholas's bottles were prepared. Though Dunbar himself had been into LSD long before it became chic or illegal, he had the same paternalistic attitude to Marianne that Mick did to Chrissie Shrimpton, and forbade her to try so much as a joint.

Marianne, however, was determined to try everything, and quickly gravitated to Swinging London's most beautiful couple, Brian Jones and Anita Pallenberg, who were more than willing to abet her. The pair still lived in Courtfield Gardens, Chelsea, in a cavernous flat halfway between a medieval manor house and a Moroccan souk. On every available surface and much of the floor were strewn clothes, his, hers or, most likely, theirs, either freshly brought from nearby King's Road (whose boutiques were more than happy to give away merchandise to a Rolling Stone and his 'old lady'), worn once and then discarded, or clammy from being worn too many times without a wash. Amid this opulent squalor were signs of Brian's nerdy side, such as books about London buses, a model train layout and a collection of vintage Dinky cars. With no prospect yet of unwelcome surprise visits by the law, pot and pills lay around in full view.

With their matching golden heads and floor-length robes, Brian and Anita seemed to Marianne 'like two children who had inherited a decrepit palazzo'. Having both exotic European ancestries and intellectual curiosity in common, Marianne and Anita got on well, though Marianne always professed herself 'terrified' by the sardonic beauty who at one moment was Brian's dominatrix, at the next a seemingly helpless victim of his physical abuse. Like others at their court, she pretended not to notice when Anita's hippie finery was topped off by brutally bruised arms or a black eye.

Usually Marianne would find Brian absorbed in efforts to catch up with the Jagger–Richard songwriting partnership, scribbling lyrics in notebooks or putting embryo songs on tape, then erasing them because they never seemed good enough. The flat had no front doorbell; instead visitors had to stand in the street and shout until their host or hostess appeared on a first-floor balcony. One day while Marianne was there, the mother of one of Brian's two illegitimate children named Julian appeared, hoping to shame him into paying maintenance. She stood in the street, holding the baby up entreatingly with both arms while Brian and Anita looked down from the balcony, laughing like tsarist nobility at comical peasants.

For all Brian's pot-fumed hilarity, Marianne noticed how 'a doomed look had begun to set on his face. Inner demons had started eating that Renaissance angel's head . . .' On acid, his paranoia increased to the point where he heard voices plotting against him even in gurgling water pipes or the fizz of electrical wiring, and, with yet more horrible fore-sight, he was painting a mural of a graveyard on the wall above his and Anita's bed.

Keith would almost always be there, too, 'exuding lonely bachelor-hood' since his break-up with Linda Keith, having walked the four miles to Chelsea from St John's Wood. Mick put in only occasional appear-ances from far-distant Harley House, somewhat like a boss checking on his workforce, and soon departed, unnerved by all the drug use and appalled by the squalor of the kitchen.

By the winter of 1966, Marianne and Dunbar had separated and Marianne and baby Nicholas were on their own at the Lennox Gar-dens flat. Disillusioned by the superficiality of her pop career, Mari-anne wanted to progress to acting but recently had had to turn down a plum offer, playing opposite Nicol Williamson at the Royal Court The-atre in John Osborne's *Inadmissible Evidence*, because her management said it paid too little. One day, Andrew Oldham dropped by to see her, accompanied by Mick. Despite all Mick's recent sneering at women, she noticed how he took in the chilly basement with its single small electric fire, and sensed his genuine sympathy for her predicament.

Early in October, Keith and Brian invited Marianne to a Stones con-cert, with Ike and Tina Turner as support act, at the Colston Hall in Bristol. Backstage, she found Mick in a corridor being taught by Tina Turner, the sexiest dancer in the Cosmos, to do the 'sideways Pony'. As she watched him being bossed around by Tina – told he was useless, in fact, but taking it good-humouredly – she still had not the smallest inkling of what lay ahead.

AFTER THE COLSTON Hall show came the usual hanging out back at the Stones' hotel, with Keith, Brian and trusted courtiers like the pho-tographer Michael Cooper. As Marianne recalls in her autobiography, *Faithfull,* she smoked joint after joint until she was 'speechless and unable to move'. Gradually the others drifted away, leaving only her, Mick and one of the Ikettes, Ike and Tina Turner's backing dancers, who hoped to be Mick's companion for the night and took an annoyingly long time to realise that three was a crowd.

By now it was getting on for morning, and despite the October chill Marianne proposed a walk in the park next to the hotel. To discover if Mick was anything more than the rude little yob of their previous encounters, she gave him a *viva voce* test in the Arthurian legends, so many of which are rooted in Bristol's West Country hinterland. He not only answered every question correctly but proved himself a modern Sir Lancelot when they returned to his room by unlacing her dew-soaked boots and placing them on a heater to dry before they got down to making love. Marianne was 'completely moved by his kindness'.

For both of them, however, it initially seemed no more than just another casual fling. With a failed marriage behind her, Marianne was in no hurry to commit herself again. And if she did so with anyone, she wanted it to be Keith Richard. To her bookish mind, especially in the dazzle of LSD, Keith resembled the poet Byron, 'the injured, tormented, doomed Romantic hero with wild hair and gaunt visage . . . an eruptive, restless presence . . . a fusion of decadence and surging energy'. Yet in all those acid-dropping nights together at Courtfield Gardens, she had never dropped any hint of how she felt about him. Partly this was because she sensed his own inadmissible fixation on the girlfriend of his new best mate. He clearly worshipped Anita Pallenberg and longed as devoutly as any Camelot knight errant to rescue her from Brian's ill treatment, but was constrained by loyalty to a brother Stone from making the slightest move.

Mick, too, seemed to have his sights set elsewhere. After ending things with Chrissie Shrimpton – a moment that everyone around him, bar Chrissie, now knew to be imminent – he had ambitions to date British cinema's sexiest new face, Julie Christie. But that night at the Ship Hotel, Bristol, with its quiz about Guinevere, Mordred and Excalibur, proved impossible to forget. When the tour ended, he telephoned Marianne and, from that moment, began secretly visiting her at her Lennox Gardens flat.

For Marianne, he was a welcome change in every way from John Dunbar, the only other man with whom she'd ever been in a serious relationship. Whereas Dunbar had been too cool and hip to show her the affection she demanded, Mick continued to be as loving, kind and considerate as when he'd saved her boots from the foggy, foggy dew. Whereas Dunbar had been deeply into drugs, Mick was only marginally and manageably so; where Dunbar was ascetic, Mick's love of luxury, refinement and shopping almost matched Marianne's own; whereas Dunbar had been vague and disorganised, Mick was decisive and effective; whereas Dunbar had an artist's indifference to money, Mick was rich and – especially in the first flush of romance – munificently generous. Marianne's son, Nicholas, now aged one, acquired a variety of expensive new toys, and electric heaters glowed throughout the once-chilly little Knightsbridge flat. 'I needed a friend,' Marianne recalls. 'Mick was a friend who happened to be a millionaire.'

In *Faithfull* she would write that, from the very beginning, she 'realised in some part of my mind that Mick was bisexual' and sensed the 'sexual undercurrent' between him and Andrew Oldham. Indeed, his more feminine qualities of sensitivity and intuition were part of his appeal after the one-dimensionally macho males to whom she was accustomed. She would later claim that one night when they were in bed together he even confessed to a fantasy of performing oral sex on Keith (who happened to be asleep in the next room). Here, Marianne could wholeheartedly concur: in *Faithfull* she would confess that throughout her whole time with Mick she remained secretly lusting after Keith.

In the run-up to Christmas 1966, she departed with Nicholas and his nanny for a holiday in Positano on Italy's Amalfi coast. With her she took a copy of the Stones' just-released compilation album *Big Hits: High Tide and Green Grass*, whose tracks included Mick's version of 'As Tears Go By' – his feminine side at its most delicate and sensitive. Whenever she played the album, it seemed, the phone would ring and it would be Mick surreptitiously calling her from London. Torn between his seductive wooing and Keith's Byronic decadence, she even sought advice from the Stones' business manager, Allen Klein:

the only known occasion when that hawk-eyed money-man was asked to play agony aunt. Klein told her that if she did manage to pair off with Keith it would 'destroy' Mick.

On returning to London, she headed straight for Brian's flat, where she found Keith and the doomed young Guinness heir Tara Browne, the latter now just days away from 'blowing his mind out in a car'. There was no sign of Anita or any other female, and as Marianne dropped acid with Brian, Keith and Tara it was plain that the trio thought sex with her would be part of the trip. Two of them, however, quickly became too stoned to do any such thing, while even the priapic Brian managed only a brief grope while the others slumped, insensible, nearby. The party then dispersed, but a few hours later Marianne and Keith met up again and spent the night together at the Mayfair Hotel – 'the best night I've ever had in my life', she would later say, implicitly including the thousand and one with Mick that were to follow. However, the next morning all Keith wanted to talk about was how smitten Mick was with her.

A couple of days later, she and Mick went out shopping together; he bought a tricycle as a Christmas gift for Nicholas at Harrods and they had a late, long lunch at the San Lorenzo restaurant in Beauchamp Place. If they'd wanted to be seen by friends of Chrissie Shrimpton, they couldn't have planned it better.

Until this moment, all Chrissie knew was that Mick had become increasingly remote and strange in his manner towards her. 'With hindsight, I don't blame him,' she says. 'You can't help going off people, and we were both very, very young. I knew the reason why he was getting fed up with me; it was because I wasn't cool. He was taking acid by that time, and I was always scared to try it. It was also when Anita Pallenberg had just come on the scene, and these orgies started happening over at Brian's. When I was first with Mick, I wasn't allowed to look at anyone else or even be friends with girls he considered tarts. Now he wanted everyone to sleep with everyone else, and I refused to be a part of that. I remember him calling me "uncool" and it being the most terrible insult.'

Pent up with her dog and six cats on the fifth floor at Harley House, still tortured by thoughts of the wedding and babies that might have been, and guilt-ridden over her estrangement from her father, Chrissie felt herself perilously near the state Mick had had such fun with in '19th Nervous Breakdown'. Mick suggested she should see a psychiatrist, of whom an abundance were to be found just across the road on Harley Street. She paid a couple of visits to an unsympathetic middle-aged shrink, who seemed mainly concerned to know whether her sex life with Mick was still healthy. A deeply embarrassed Chrissie said that it was. The shrink requested to see Mick also, then reported back to her that Mick was definitely still in love with her.

On 15 December, the day of Mick's shopping trip with Marianne, he and Chrissie had been due to go to Jamaica on holiday. When Chrissie telephoned the office, she discovered that their flights had been cancelled.

But she still had no idea that he was seeing Marianne. 'I remember thinking "He doesn't want me and I can't live without him."' Alone at the Harley House flat with her dog, six cats and three songbirds chirruping in their Victorian cage, Chrissie took an overdose of sleeping pills. 'It wasn't just attention seeking or a cry for help,' she says. 'I really wanted to die. I thought my life was over.'

She believes it was Mick who found her, though she has never been completely sure. When she regained consciousness, she was in St George's Hospital, Hyde Park Corner. The nurses tending her called her by a name she didn't recognise. To prevent the story leaking out to the newspapers, she had been checked in under an alias.

From there on, Chrissie says, less attention seemed to be given to her physical and mental state than to hushing up the fact that Mick Jagger's girlfriend had attempted suicide. From St George's, she was taken 'in a wheelchair, in the back of a lorry' to a private clinic in Hampstead, where, without any choice in the matter or even explanation, she was given some kind of sleep therapy. 'The basement where they put me was so damp that I remember, as I lay in bed, my feet were wet. Every time I came round, I was put back to sleep. I asked to see my psychiatrist, but when I tried to ask him what was happening, he stuck a needle into my arm while I was speaking and knocked me out again.'

Finally, she managed to struggle to a pay phone and contact her

mother in Buckinghamshire. The long estrangement with Ted Shrimpton over her cohabitation with Mick was instantly forgotten. 'I'll always
remember that when my father arrived at this clinic, he was in tears —
something I'd never seen before.' She also sent a plea to Mick to bring
her her Yorkshire terrier, Dora. 'He did bring the dog . . . and when he
arrived, he was wearing a black fur coat and full makeup. Again, I don't
blame Mick for any of this. The way I was treated was probably thought
to be the best, and no doubt cost a lot of money — and it was all semi
out of his hands. But it was very frightening and very scarring.' Mick
subsequently did speak to her mother, admitting that he'd been responsible for a radical change in her personality, and he didn't like what she'd
become. 'From being strong and feisty and good fun, I'd turned into a
neurotic mess.'

Only after Chrissie was released from the hospital, and recuperat-
ing at home in Buckinghamshire, did she learn from the newspapers
about Mick and Marianne. When at last she nerved herself to return to
Harley House to collect her possessions and six cats, she found the flat's
front-door lock had been changed and she had to telephone the Stones'
office and make an appointment. There was no further discussion or
contact with Mick; instead, she had to deal with his brother, Chris, the
near namesake to whom she'd always felt close, but who now treated
her with icy indifference. 'That was horrible, because I'd been so fond of
him. He let me know I certainly didn't have any right to be back there.'

Nowadays, no major rock star dumps a long-term girlfriend with
impunity. As his partner or common-law wife, she can claim to have
contributed to his success and, as such, to be entitled to a substantial
part of his fortune. Should this tactic fail, she can make a lucrative book
deal for her memoirs, sell interviews at high prices to tabloid newspapers and magazines, haunt the TV talk-show circuit, and in general be a
rankling embarrassment forever afterwards. But for twenty-three-year-
old Mick, all such things were still mercifully far in the future; he could
cast off Chrissie with as little difficulty as a once-worn satin shirt.

Marianne had returned to Italy with Nicholas and her backing
guitarist, Jon Mark, to appear in the San Remo Song Festival. On an

impulse, she telephoned Mick and asked him to join her. They met at Cannes Airport, and to escape the press Mick chartered a boat with a skipper and crew, and they spent an idyllic week with Nicholas cruising along the Riviera coast. Though the Mediterranean mostly stayed millpond smooth, there was one day when a heavy swell blew up and the boat began to pitch and roll alarmingly. When Nicholas started to cry, Mick climbed into the bunk with Marianne and him, cradled them both in his arms, and was comforting and reassuring.

In San Remo, the two gave an interview to the *Daily Mirror* journalist Don Short, tacitly admitting they were now together. There, too, in a local discotheque, Marianne bought some mild uppers from the deejay so that she and Mick could keep dancing until dawn.

The news that the wicked, unkempt chief Rolling Stone and the young woman who'd brought virginity and refinement to the pop charts were now an item caused less of a media furore than might have been expected. Marianne was separated from her husband, so there was no question of enticement by a sex-mad fiend, and she had a one-year-old child, which dealt with the virginity issue. Moreover, the news blackout around Chrissie's attempted suicide had been 100 per cent effective. There was little for journalists to write other than that Beauty and the Beast had been reincarnated in Swinging London.

When they returned from San Remo, Mick wanted Marianne to move into Harley House with Nicholas without delay. Marianne agreed, despite some squeamishness about occupying rooms he had so recently shared with someone else – which, indeed, still contained some of Chrissie's possessions, including Petunia, the rocking horse he'd given her for her twenty-first birthday. Christopher Gibbs, the Stones' antique-dealer friend, was brought in to remove all traces of uncool 1965 and give the place a mystic Moroccan makeover like Brian and Anita's. Anything Marianne wanted, for herself or her son, she could have. Even so, she felt it a wise precaution to keep her old flat in Knightsbridge.

Few types of romance are more exhilarating than those between total opposites – at least in the rosy beginning, as the lovers introduce each other to their alien worlds and take on the added mystique of all-knowing teachers and guides. And from its genesis in a spot test about Camelot, this affair between an Austrian baroness's intellectual daughter and a Dartford gym teacher's son had a certain schoolroom flavour. Marianne, whose musical tastes had hitherto tended towards the twee and folksy, now received a crash course in Mick's blues and soul idols, from Robert Johnson and Slim Harpo to Smokey Robinson and the Miracles. Mick, whose literary adventures thus far had not gone much beyond James Bond, was inducted into Marianne's numerous favourite books, both ancient and modern, and also her passion for mythology, magic and the occult.

Literature was not the only area in which Beauty far outdistanced the Beast. Despite unrelenting peer pressure on every side, Mick still did almost no drugs beyond the occasional 'little smoke' that seldom seemed to affect him much – though he remained as bad as ever at handling alcohol. When he did take acid, Marianne noticed, he remained impressively in control; unlike Brian, he seemed to have no deep-seated fears or insecurities for the drug to ferret out and blow up to big-screen size. For their first trip together at Harley House, five floors above the hurtling Marylebone Road traffic, they both donned their finest hippie clothes and Mick put on a record of an Indian raga. As the acid took hold, he began to dance – not the sexual strutting and posturing of his stage shows but with 'pure beauty and exaltation . . . He had become Shiva. I hadn't realised until then that I was living with somebody who at odd moments could turn into a god.'

The mystical mood evaporated when Andrew Oldham's new recording protégés the Small Faces unexpectedly showed up with their guitars and asked Mick to join them in a jam session. But as interruptions went, it could have been worse.

NINETEEN SIXTY-SEVEN, THAT most horrifically memorable year of Mick's life (whatever he may say), kicked off with a flurry of small scandals that in the coming months – along with every previous scandal – would pale into insignificance.

To start with, there was the continuing fall-out from Brian's pre-Christmas appearance on the cover of West Germany's *Stern* magazine, wearing a black Nazi SS uniform and red swastika armband, with one jackbooted foot planted on a small, naked plastic doll. Nor was it hard to guess the instigator of the stunt: Anita Pallenberg had been in Munich at the time, making a film called *Mord und Totschlag* (*A Degree of Murder*) for her director friend Volker Schlöndorff, with Brian in tow. To allay Brian's paranoid jealousy of Schlöndorff, and give him some creative status outside the Stones, she had arranged for him to write the film's score. His wide-eyed assertion that the *Stern* cover was 'an anti-Nazi protest' convinced no one.

Then on 13 January the Stones released a new single entitled 'Let's Spend the Night Together', a solo Mick composition plainly inspired by Marianne and the Ship Hotel, Bristol. There had, of course, been innumerable previous pop songs about nocturnal trysts, from Johnnie Ray's 'Such a Night' to Elvis Presley's 'One Night', but never one with so barefaced an invitation between the sheets. The furore was even greater than over 'Satisfaction', especially in America's Puritan belt: when the Stones previewed the song in New York on *The Ed Sullivan Show*, Mick was forced to change the crucial phrase to 'Let's spend some time together', though the rest of his heavy-breathing lyric ('I'll satis-fah yo' ev-ery need / And now Ah know you'll satis-fah me . . .') went out unedited. Yet on the flip side, this aural phallus could be heard back in virgin choirboy mode, singing Keith's ballad 'Ruby Tuesday' as if his heart would break while Brian, so recently seen as a baby-crushing SS *Obergruppenführer*, piped a nursery-innocent descant on the recorder.

The next weekend, the Stones were back in London to top the bill on Britain's most popular television variety show, *Sunday Night at the London Palladium*. The show had been the making of the Beatles, but the Stones had never yet appeared on it; their inclusion was implicitly a chance win over the nation's parents even at this late stage. All such hopes vanished during Sunday-afternoon rehearsals at the theatre for the 8 P.M. live airing. By hallowed tradition, headliners appeared last, then joined the other acts to wave good-bye from a revolving podium with giant letters spelling out SUNDAY NIGHT AT THE LONDON PALLADIUM. Mick, however, informed the producer that the Stones would not get onto the podium and wave. So, close to transmission time, tempers quickly flared with the producer threatening to drop them from the bill and Mick doggedly refusing to become 'part of a circus'.

Andrew Oldham was called to the Palladium to intercede, together with the Stones' new UK booking agent, Tito Burns. In a reversal of all known precedent, Oldham told them to bow to custom and ride the podium with the comedians, jugglers, trampolinists, puppeteers and high-plumed dancers as every *Sunday Night* star from Frank Sinatra to Buddy Holly had uncomplainingly done before them. But Mick would not yield: Trilby was defying Svengali and thinking for himself at last. Instead, a compromise finale was devised, with the Stones off the podium but still – Mick especially – somehow managing even to wave good-bye with an edge of sarcasm and disrespect.

January also brought a new Stones album, *Between the Buttons*. Since *Aftermath*'s creative breakthrough nine months earlier, they had toured almost non-stop with little time to spare for recording or for Jagger–Richard to write anything else as strong as 'Let's Spend the Night Together' and 'Ruby Tuesday'. If the album lacked its predecessor's Beatle-challenging colour, energy and satirical bite, there were still a few good things: 'She Smiled Sweetly', afterwards covered by the Love Affair, 'Yesterday's Papers', covered by Mick's protégé Chris Farlowe, and 'Something Happened to Me Yesterday', partly sung by Keith rather than Mick (though in a voice much like Mick's) against a Trad-jazzy backing which, a few years earlier, would have caused them far more anguish than the London Palladium's revolving podium.

With hindsight, this last lighthearted track seems eerily prophetic of the 'something' so soon to happen to them both. 'He's not sure what it was,' sings Keith's Mick-clone lightheartedly, 'Or if it's against the law … What kind of joint is this? . . .' At the end, real arch-mimic Mick chips in with a spoken passage mocking the type of avuncular British bobby, epitomised by television's *Dixon of Dock Green*, whose main function until now has been helping old ladies across roads, giving directions to lost tourists, and making sure bicyclists show enough light after dark. 'If you're out tonight, don't forget . . . if you're on your bike, wear white . . . *Eve*nin' all.'

OVER THE PRECEDING year, Britain's attitude to drugs had received what nowadays would be described as a wake-up call. Young people, it had become clear, used narcotics in ever-increasing numbers, in the form of cannabis (which could be grown domestically as a houseplant), amphetamine uppers or LSD. And the main conduit for this nationwide epidemic was plain to see – or, rather, hear. Pop music, both American and domestic, teemed with references to drugs and celebrations of the ecstatic and elevated states of mind they supposedly induced. The buzzword of the hour was *psychedelic*, a term originally coined by LSD's American apostles to describe its sensory effects, but now applied to the muzzy, free-form style of avant-garde rock, the bands who played it, and the head-swimmingly brilliant fluorescent colours of 'in' fashion and décor. One way or another, it seemed half the country was getting stoned.

Yet the police, largely conforming as they still did to *Dixon of Dock Green*'s benign stereotype, were woefully unprepared to deal with all this. Even in London, the Metropolitan Police's drug squad, based at Scotland Yard, had just one inspector with an operational staff of six to cover the whole capital. Most regional police forces did not yet possess dedicated anti-narcotics units; instead, general-purpose detectives and uniformed officers received hasty instruction in the appearance and smell of cannabis and where it was most likely to be found – i.e., among young people with very long hair, playing music very loudly.

The situation was a gift to Britain's popular press, at this time a sector of Fleet Street quite separate and distinct from serious broadsheets like the *Daily Telegraph*, the *Guardian* and the august *Times*. For Sunday papers in particular – traditionally the nation's most widely read and sensational – pop stars and drugs in tandem provided a heaven-sent combination of circulation-boosting celebrity coverage with sanctimonious moralising. And, to be sure, the moral issue did carry some weight. Was it not only right that young pop musicians who were role models to millions should be held to account for promoting and glamorising drugs rather than using their enormous influence to help combat the problem?

For the present, no offensive was planned against the Beatles, whose recent music had positively reeked of pot, but who – despite their retirement from touring and John Lennon's 'bigger than Jesus' gaffe – remained inviolate. Instead, the pious indignation of the gutter press focused on the Beatles' nearest rivals, a band who from their inception had set out to affront polite society; who were still at it as tirelessly as ever, whether urinating over petrol stations or being impolite on *Sunday Night at the London Palladium;* and who therefore just had to be involved in this new and most reprehensible of all pop-star vices up to their badly barbered necks.

The great bonus for Sunday scandal sheets, not to be found in the Beatles or any other pop band, was the raw sex the Rolling Stones' front man had been peddling since long before drugs came along. Who was it who had put both fornication and masturbation at the top of the charts? Who, in his slight frame, awoke all Britain's worst phobias about effeminacy while at the same time conveying the macho sexual threat of a beardless Bluebeard? Whose unnaturally large mouth and livid red lips in themselves almost ranked as a case of public indecent exposure? Who, come to think of it, had swooped down and carried off that inno-cent little songbird Marianne Faithfull? Above all, who was long, long overdue to be taken down a peg or three?

The British Sabbath's leading purveyor of sanctimony and scandal was the broadsheet *News of the World,* popularly known as 'the news of the screws' and commanding a six-million circulation that enabled it to boast 'world's largest weekly sale' on its archaic banner masthead. The paper presented itself as a tireless crusader against vice in public life, and specialised in sting operations by teams of undercover reporters, forerunner of today's secret filming and phone hacking, at the climax of which the targets condemned themselves out of their own mouths.

Traditionally these exposes had dealt with fraud or prostitution, but on 5 February 1967 new territory was broached. A double-page spread, headlined 'SECRETS OF THE POP STARS' HIDEAWAY', identified a house in Roehampton, Surrey, alleged to have been used for LSD parties by various leading names from the charts, including members of the Moody Blues and Mick Jagger of the Rolling Stones.

The remainder of the article was exclusively about Mick. The *News of the World*'s investigators described tracking him to a London club, Blaises, in Kensington, asking point-blank whether he took LSD, and being rewarded with full disclosure, not only about that but other types of drug also. 'I don't go much on [acid] now the cats have taken it up,' he was quoted as saying. 'It'll just get a dirty name. I remember the first time I took it. It was on our first tour with Bo Diddley and Little Richard . . .' The report continued: 'During the time we were at Blaises, Jagger took about six Benzedrine tablets. "I just wouldn't stay awake at places like this if I didn't have them," he said . . . Later at Blaises, Jagger showed a companion and two girls a piece of hash and invited them to his flat for a "smoke".'

Apart from the spelling of Mick's surname, the account had not one iota of truth. He had not even been at Blaises Club when the *News of the World* team visited it, let alone unburdened himself in this wholly uncharacteristic way. The investigators had not been young journalists, knowledgeable about the pop scene, but old foot-in-the-door men to whom all Rolling Stones looked the same. They had certainly talked to a Stone that night, but one who was the utter opposite of Mick in his approachability, garrulity and pathetic pleasure at finding someone to listen to him, let alone in the colour of his hair. Even the untrendiest *NoW* reporters might have been expected to recognise Brian Jones after the paper had unearthed two of his illegitimate children a year earlier. But they hadn't.

The irony wasn't just that Mick indulged in drugs so little compared with Keith and, especially, Brian. Lately he had become increasingly worried about the extent of their consumption and their vulnerability to just such a retribution as this. 'It's all getting out of hand,' he'd muttered forebodingly to his art-dealer friend Robert Fraser just a few days earlier. 'I dunno where it's going to end.'

On the evening of 5 February the Stones were booked to perform on the Eamonn Andrews television show, with Mick joining fellow guests (comedy actor Hugh Lloyd and the singer of 'Bobby's Girl', Susan Maughan) in a panel discussion afterwards. When the subject of that morning's *News of the World* story came up, he said it was all lies and that he'd be issuing a libel writ against the paper. The other panellists treated him frigidly, and Eamonn Andrews, normally the blandest of TV hosts, asked if he didn't feel some responsibility to give his fans moral leadership. 'I don't think I have any real responsibility at all,' he replied. 'They will work out their own moral values for themselves.'

The article was prima facie libel, fulfilling the law's definition of bringing Mick 'into hatred, ridicule or contempt', with no possible defence of truth, justification or publication in the public interest, and showing a clear element of malice. Even so, canny legal advisers might have cautioned him against rushing into litigation. They could have cited the case of the playwright Oscar Wilde – as controversial a figure in the 1890s as Mick was in the 1960s – who had taken the witness stand to deny a specific, untrue accusation of homosexuality despite being demonstrably homosexual, and had consequently wrecked both his career and his life.

They might also have cautioned that for a paper like the *News of the World* there was a well-tried way to avoid being held up to public ridicule for an idiotic mistake and having to pay whopping damages. The blunder at Blaises would not matter if could be proved that, although Mick may not have bragged about taking drugs to the *NoW* team that night, he nonetheless did take them in less public places, so the story was justified retrospectively. He would therefore have to drop his action or face humiliation in court. Unfortunately for him, such wise counsels did not prevail, and at the beginning of the following week a writ for libel was served at the *News of the World*'s then offices in Bouverie Street, just off Fleet Street.

For someone always so cautious and coolly calculating, Mick's next step was one of bewildering stupidity. The very next weekend he and Marianne went off to the Sussex countryside to take LSD with Keith Richard.

In fairness, acid was not the primary purpose of the trip. 'Lonely bachelor' Keith had recently bought a house – a half-timbered cottage called Redlands, bizarrely at odds with his rock 'n' roll vagabond image – near the small West Sussex seaside resort of West Wittering. Mick and Marianne were to spend the weekend there with their two closest establishment friends, Christopher Gibbs and Robert Fraser, plus the photographer Michael Cooper. Brian and Anita had also been invited, but Brian said he was too immersed in his film score, though he'd try to join them on the Sunday. Keith's incurable susceptibility to hangers-on had added two further houseguests, neither of them trusted insiders like the others. One was Nicky Cramer, a fey and rather solitary young man from the fringes of the Chelsea set; the other was a personage destined to pass into rock mythology as 'Acid King David'.

While Cramer was at least a friend of friends, almost nothing was known about this twenty-four-year-old American whose lean face and shortish curly hair gave him slightly the look of some American art-house movie actor, a younger John Cassavetes or Ben Gazzara. His surname was Snyderman, though over the weeks to come it would be rendered in legal depositions and court reports as 'Schneiderman' or 'Snidermann'. He had arrived in London from California only a couple of weeks previously, but in that time somehow became friendly with all the front-rank Stones, and of particular indispensability to Keith. As his nickname implied, Acid King David possessed one sovereign virtue – an encyclopaedic knowledge of all the newest strains of LSD combined with an almost magical ability to procure them. Christopher Gibbs later recalled him as 'an up-market flower child' constantly dazzling the Stones' inner circle with ever more exotic chemical come-ons: 'What? You mean you've never heard of dimethyl tryptomine?'

The highlight of the Redlands weekend party was to be a new California-made variety known as 'Sunshine', said to provide a more tranquil and relaxing kind of trip than usual, which Acid King David had promised to give out to Keith's guests. If Mick could not see the folly in such a plan, just at the moment when the *News of the World* would be gunning for him, one might expect a highly intelligent, clear-minded man like Gibbs to have done so. 'All I can say,' responds Gibbs, 'is that, to all of us at that time, the English countryside seemed like a safe place to be.'

ON THE NIGHT of Friday 10 February, Mick, Marianne and Keith were at Abbey Road studios, watching the Beatles work on the new album that had been evolving since their withdrawal from touring six months previously. The track being recorded was 'A Day in the Life', a John Lennon song partly inspired by the death of Tara Browne and peppered with seemingly blatant drug invitations, from its drawn-out wail of 'I'd love to turn you on!' to its chaotic unscored orchestral passages suggestive of acid-induced delirium. The recording of these orchestral parts in Abbey Road's cavernous Studio 1 was a gala occasion, to which the Beatles invited other pop A-listers like Donovan and Mike Nesmith of the Monkees along with the two Stones and the chief Stone's new lady. To heighten its merry atmosphere, the forty classical musicians involved wore evening dress embellished with carnival novelties like clowns' red noses, rubber gorilla paws, false moustaches and funny hats including – in another unwitting prophecy – miniature police helmets.

The taping lasted into the early hours of Saturday; then Keith and his weekend guests – Mick, Marianne, Robert Fraser, Christopher Gibbs and Acid King David Snyderman – drove in convoy the fifty miles down to his West Sussex cottage. Alongside Fraser in his white van – normally used for transporting artworks – sat his young Moroccan manservant, Mohammed, who was to act as cook. Other than possibly Brian and Anita the next day, no other guests were expected. It was to be a traditional country-house weekend in every respect save that the participants wore caftans and beads rather than Barbour-oiled coats and green wellies.

Sunday morning at Redlands was spent sleeping late, drinking, eating, smoking, listening to music and basking in the synthetic Sunshine which Acid King David had brought along in a businesslike attaché case. There was also plenty of genuine sunshine, though the weather was cold, and in the afternoon – once more true to country weekend routine – the party decided to blow away the cobwebs by going out for a drive in Robert Fraser's van. Not far away was a house which had once belonged to the surrealist art collector Edward James and was open to the public. As part of Mick's cultural education, Marianne wanted to show him a sofa which James had commissioned from Salvador Dalí in the shape of movie goddess Mae West's lips – the sexiest ones ever known pre-Jagger.

The Edward James house turned out to be closed, so instead the two Stones, two art connoisseurs, one girlfriend, one photographer and two hangers-on went for a long walk through the neighbouring woods and along West Wittering's shingle beach (where Michael Cooper took a photograph of Keith and Acid King David in an affectionate man-hug). On returning to the cottage, they found two surprise visitors: George Harrison and his wife, Pattie. However, the low-key atmosphere was not to George's taste and he soon left in his customised Mini, taking the acquiescent Pattie with him. By a similar stroke of good fortune, Brian Jones had still not turned up with Anita.

At around 5 P.M. Detective Constable John Challen answered the telephone at West Sussex Regional Police Headquarters in Chichester, just six miles from West Wittering. A voice on the line informed him that a 'riotous party' was going on at Redlands and drugs were being used. The informant, a man, declined to give his name and hung up before DC Challen could extract any further details.

Like most other regional forces, West Sussex did not have a dedicated drugs squad. Their nearest to a narcotics expert was a Detective Sergeant Stanley Cudmore, who had recently been diagnosed with a brain tumour and been given light office duties with the Crime Intelligence Unit while receiving hospital outpatient treatment. Detective Sergeant Cudmore had used the time to read up on the various illegal substances now said to be circulating; in the whole West Sussex Criminal Investigation Department, he was thus the only officer who could distinguish between LSD, heroin, cocaine, cannabis and marijuana, and he knew what the ones that had a smell smelled like.

Redlands was already known by the police to belong to a Rolling Stone, though no breath of a complaint against Keith had ever been made before. Detective Sergeant Challen immediately contacted Chichester's divisional commander, Chief Inspector Gordon Dineley, who, like most of his command at that somnolent winter Sunday hour in a low-crime rural area, was at home with his family. With commendable speed, Dineley mustered a task force numbering eighteen, both uniformed and plainclothes, including the invaluable Detective Sergeant Cudmore and three female officers for the searching of women suspects. It was the first drugs raid ever to have been mounted in West Sussex, and to mark its importance, on the direct orders of the chief constable, Thomas Williams, Dineley led it personally, wearing a chief inspector's full-dress uniform with white-braided peaked cap and military-style cane.

Dineley's hasty briefing gave little idea of what to expect at the 'riotous party' or how to conduct this entirely new kind of operation. Another of the plainclothes officers involved, Detective Constable Don Rambridge, recalls that he and his colleagues were instructed simply to 'grab one person each and hold on to them' until a methodical search could be organised. The force then packed into seven vehicles for a journey of some ten minutes. As they turned off the main Chichester road into the lane leading to Redlands, they passed George Harrison's Mini, heading back towards London. According to rock folklore, the police did not dare bust a nationally sacred Beatle, so deliberately held back until George was safely out of the way. But neither DC Rambridge nor DS Challen heard his name mentioned prior to the raid or knew at the time that the car was his.

Unlike twenty-first-century rock-star hideaways, this one had no electric perimeter fence, speakerphone entry or patrolling security guards with dogs. The occupants of Redlands did not hear the seven police vehicles draw up outside or notice anything amiss until a female detective's face peered through the leaded window of the big, high-raftered living room, where they all happened to have gathered. Even then, she was thought to be just a Stones fan who, like many before, had got onto Keith's property without difficulty and would be appeased by a friendly word and an autograph. It took thunderous knocking at the front door – rather than the routine forced entry of today's armed, shrieking SWAT teams – to reveal Chief Inspector Gordon Dineley, resplendently uniformed and brandishing his search warrant.

If Mick and the others felt shock and disbelief at the surge of police officers, the raiders themselves were almost equally at a loss. Straight-forward Sussex coppers whose usual beat was the seaside or Chichester Harbour, they had none of them ever been inside a rock star's home before. Challen and Rambridge both recall being momentarily disori-ented by the scene in Keith's living room – the rubble of bottles, ash-trays, guitars, record albums, cassette tapes, flickering candles and smouldering joss sticks, among which long-haired, long-robed figures of not instantly determinable gender reclined on outsize Moroccan floor cushions. Even Keith's choice of paintwork to set off the old oak beams, not healthy-minded white or cream distemper but dark matte shades of purple, brown and orange, struck the officers as incriminatingly 'weird' (Rambridge) and 'strange' (Challen).

And, as somewhat of an anticlimax, no riotous party was going on. After their strenuous country walk that afternoon, the weekenders' only wish was to chill out. In what Christopher Gibbs would describe as 'a scene of pure domesticity', they had just been served a Moroccan buffet supper by Robert Fraser's manservant and were settling down to watch a film on television (*Pete Kelly's Blues*, starring Jack Webb) while a Bob Dylan track played on the stereo.

One decorative detail above all mesmerised constable and chief inspector alike. On returning from the afternoon's ramble, Marianne had gone upstairs for a bath and, rather than put the same muddy clothes back on (and surprisingly lacking any alternative outfits) had rejoined the others swathed in a fur rug pulled from one of the beds.

The straitlaced cops thus beheld a young woman attired like some pin-up from *Razzle* or *Tit-Bits* magazine seated on a couch next to the young man they recognised as the most notorious in Britain. Detective Sergeant Cudmore 'formed the impression' – as police jargon has it – that Mick was wearing makeup.

The Stones' reputation for conduct beyond the pale had prepared the police for verbal abuse, if not physical violence, from the band's two chief members when their sanctum was breached, especially if drugs were involved. Instead, to their surprise, Mick and Keith behaved with utter politeness and reasonableness. 'They weren't morons like we'd expected them to be,' Challen remembers. 'Both very intelligent, very pleasant . . . nothing untoward about either of them.'

As instructed, each plainclothes officer collared an individual house-guest to search while the uniformed element guarded the exits. There was some initial confusion when woman detective constable Evelyn Fuller approached the King's Road flower child, Nicky Cramer, who also wore makeup as well as exotic silk pyjamas, and mistook him for a female. Meanwhile, West Sussex Constabulary's nearest approach to a sniffer dog, Detective Sergeant Cudmore, was inhaling the air around Marianne like seaside ozone for what he alone could recognise as the tell-tale odour of cannabis. While this was going on, Cudmore later attested, Marianne was in 'a merry mood' and seemingly quite unconcerned by the heavy influx of strange men into the room. Indeed, her behaviour was almost tantamount to obstructing a police officer in the course of his duty, as from time to time she would deliberately let her fur rug wrap slip down around her shoulders, showing 'portions of her nude body'.

The exasperated Cudmore ordered one of the three female officers, Detective Constable Fuller, to take Marianne upstairs and search her in the privacy of one of the bedrooms. Since she had nothing on under the fur rug, this was self-evidently pointless, and as she climbed the open-plan staircase with the grim-faced policewoman, Marianne says, theatricality got the better of her. Stopping halfway, she turned to her audience below, let the rug fall, and in her best Sarah Bernhardt voice said ringingly, 'Search me!' Detective Constable Challen was on the upper landing at the time but received only a rear view. Challen later testified that her words made Mick roar with laughter.

The first finds were made on Acid King David: a small tin box and an envelope containing what Cudmore recognised as cannabis, plus a 'ball of brown substance' he could not identify. But a much more spectacular discovery seemed imminent. In plain view was the attaché case which Acid King David had used to transport his LSD to Redlands and which, despite its popularity, still contained an ample supply. Yet as the police executed their search warrant to the utmost, rummaging minutely through every cupboard and drawer, none of them seemed to notice the attaché case. After some time, it finally did catch the attention of a young detective constable, but as he bent to examine it Acid King David shouted that it was full of unexposed photographic film which would spoil if subjected to light. The officer swallowed this unlikely tale without a murmur and made no attempt to open the case.

DS Challen, meanwhile, had searched an upstairs bedroom, evidently Mick and Marianne's, which, he remembers, had 'little strings of coloured bulbs, like Christmas lights, blazing away even although no one was there'. On the bed – minus its usual cover – he found the outfit Marianne had discarded: 'some pink ostrich feathers, a pair of black velvet trousers, a white blouse, a black cloak, a large sombrero-type hat and a single ladies' boot' (the other of which lay on the floor nearby). There was also a man's jacket of an extravagant cut and in a shade of green velvet which, until recently, only a woman would have worn. Going through its pockets, Challen found a phial of four white tablets. They were the remains of the amphetamine uppers Marianne had bought from the disco deejay during the Mediterranean cruise at the start of her affair with Mick. At some point, she had slipped them into his jacket pocket, then had forgotten about them.

Challen took the garment downstairs and Mick identified it as his. Shown the four tablets, he said they had been prescribed for him by his doctor, whom he named as Dr Dixon Firth of Wilton Crescent, Knightsbridge. What did he need them for? Challen asked. 'To stay awake and work,' Mick replied.

Despite the resources expended on it and its dramatic staging, the raid ended with not one single arrest. Robert Fraser, a habitual heroin user, was found in possession of twenty-four heroin jacks but told DC Rambridge they were insulin tablets needed for a diabetic condition. For now, all that could be done was send half of the jacks for analysis by Scotland Yard's laboratories in London, together with Mick's alleged prescription, Acid King David's tin box, envelope and 'ball of brown substance', and two carved wooden pipes and a china pudding basin from the cottage which had aroused Detective Sergeant Cudmore's suspicions. Keith was formally cautioned that if any of the confiscated items proved to contain illegal substances, he would face prosecution for allowing their use in his home. The police convoy then departed, leaving Acid King David's attaché case still undisturbed in the middle of the living room.

There seemed little doubt that the raid's main target had been Mick and that the *News of the World* was up to its well-known entrapment tricks. In the search for evidence to neutralise his libel action, the paper must have learned about the Redlands weekend, guessed that drug taking would feature, and tipped off the police. This in turn meant that – unless Mick had been bugged by techniques far beyond his hero, James Bond – one of the other houseguests had been a *NoW* informer. Since Fraser, Gibbs and Michael Cooper were above suspicion and Mohammed the Moroccan had to be absolved on linguistic grounds, the only two possible suspects were Nicky Cramer and Acid King David. The list quickly shrank to one, thanks to the muscle with which the Stones now surrounded themselves. A heavy friend of Mick and Keith's named David Litvinoff visited the inoffensive Cramer, accused him of being a traitor, and, with scientific precision, began beating him up. When he did not confess even after being battered to a pulp, he was pronounced in the clear.

That left Acid King David, whom the police had relieved of a small quantity of cannabis, but whose stash of acid had been so mysteriously ignored. But, alas, there was no opportunity of 'doing a Nicky Cramer' on him. Straight after the raid, he had hitched a ride back to London with Robert Fraser and left Britain the same night.

His disappearance concentrated the others' minds on how little had ever really been known about Acid King David before he entered Mick's orbit. And with hindsight some things about him struck a distinctly odd note. Even the surname they'd known him by – Snyderman? Snidermann? Schneiderman? – now seemed suspiciously vague, if, indeed, it was genuine. Michael Cooper recalled a moment at Redlands when, searching through Acid King David's luggage for hash, he'd noticed a passport in the name 'David English'. Later, as the two chatted by themselves, the subject matter had unexpectedly segued from new LSD varieties into spying and espionage. Cooper remembered how the 'upmarket flower child's' manner had become serious, even menacing, 'like he was into the James Bond thing, you know . . . the whole CIA bit.'

The following Sunday brought apparent conclusive proof of everyone's suspicions. The *News of the World* splashed the raid exclusively on its front page, naming no names – since criminal charges had yet to be formally brought – but accurate in every detail: as a result of a police swoop on 'a well-known pop star's country home, one nationally-known star' had been found in possession of suspect pills, 'bottles and an ashtray' had been seized, and as a result 'two nationally-famous names' were likely to be charged with drug offences. The paper even knew that a third 'nationally-famous name' (George Harrison) had left the scene in the nick of time and that 'a foreign national' (Acid King David) was being watched for at air- and seaports. Every line suggested a quid pro quo from the police for passing on such a prime piece of intelligence.

Even so, Mick looked to be facing the very smallest of narcotic raps. The tablets discovered in his jacket were not an illicitly compounded route to oblivion but a proprietary travel-sickness aid named Stenamina whose amphetamine content did not breach any European country's drug laws but Britain's. For such a technical offence the worst penalty he should have expected was a fine. And if the Stenamina was a doctor's prescription, as he had said, to help him stay awake and alert through nights of recording with the Stones, he would not be charged at all.

A few days after the raid, the officer who had found the tablets, Detective Constable John Challen, travelled up to London with

Detective Sergeant Stan Cudmore to interview the alleged source of the prescription, Dr Raymond Dixon Firth of Wilton Crescent, Knightsbridge. Dr Firth had been Mick's doctor since 1965 and was also a personal friend whose parties he sometimes attended. And what he had told Challen seemed to be true. According to Dr Firth, Mick had telephoned 'some time before February' saying he needed the Stenamina to help him cope with 'a period of intense personal strain' (which the change-over from Chrissie to Marianne undoubtedly was). Dr Firth said he could take the pills, as long as it was only in an emergency. In the doctor's view this verbal agreement had the same validity as any written prescription presented at a pharmacist's counter.

If the tip-off about the Redlands gathering had come from the *News of the World*, none of the rank-and-file coppers involved in the raid was aware of it. John Challen, who'd answered the phone to the anonymous male caller, had no sense of talking to a journalist or of typewriters clattering in the background. And significantly, when rumours of the paper's complicity began to circulate, Challen was ordered to check them out. After interviewing Dr Dixon Firth, he and Sergeant Cudmore went to the *News of the World*'s offices in Bouverie Street and asked an editorial executive whether the call had been made from there. They were told emphatically that it hadn't.

THE CHARACTER WHO might have been expected to hog the limelight in the unfolding drama would in fact remain offstage and uncharacteristically silent. When Andrew Oldham learned of the raid, he left London before the press could reach him for comment and, in his own words, 'went missing in California'. The first SOS call was to Allen Klein, who immediately flew from New York to coordinate Mick and Keith's defence, avowing that 'their problems are mine'.

Oldham's detachment was a far cry from the one-time sixth Stone who used to pride himself on sharing every tribulation his boys went through. Mick in particular might reasonably have looked for help from that Svengali-PR brain which had done so much to create the predicament in which he now found himself. But over the past few months, and especially since the London Palladium incident, there had been a growing coolness between them. Everyone around the Stones noticed how Mick, that once-docile and malleable Trilby, no longer went to Oldham for guidance, but took decisions about both himself and the band on his own, then presented Svengali with a *fait accompli*.

Oldham, on his side, disapproved of Mick's new upper-class social circle, blaming 'the Robert Frasers and Anita Pallenbergs' for making the Stones' internal politics and sexual tensions even more byzantine than when he himself had had a hand in them. His response to the Redlands bust was not to revel in the headlines, the way the old Andrew Oldham would have done, but to berate the victims for their recklessness, effectively saying it served them right. According to the second volume of his memoirs, *2Stoned*, he had another reason for his low profile during the next four eventful months: he was terrified of being next in line to be busted.

Oldham's withdrawal from running the Stones day to day had in any case been happening by degrees for some time. In his place as their press and media spokesman, he had hired someone who at first sight seemed to confirm how depressingly corporate he now was. However, events were to prove the middle-aged, grey-suited Les Perrin an inspired choice. A PR of the old school, Perrin was liked and trusted equally by his clients and by journalists, whom he encouraged to telephone him at home at any hour of the day or night if need be. Utterly straight in every sense, he would turn out to be the best mouthpiece Mick and Keith could possibly have in their coming ordeal – as well as one of the few people ever able to keep Mick in order.

For a time it seemed as if the trouble might be bought off, the way trouble around the Stones often was. A fixer within their circle – variously identified as a drug-dealer friend of Keith's named 'Spanish' Tony Sanchez and a shyster lawyer friend of Oldham – claimed to have contacts in the Metropolitan Police who could arrange for the various substances confiscated at Redlands to be lost before they reached

Scotland Yard's laboratory for analysis. With only a small technical offence in prospect, and that conceivably avoidable through evidence from his doctor, Mick had no need to risk charges of bribing a police officer, conspiracy or attempting to pervert the course of justice. He went along with the idea for the sake of Keith and Robert Fraser, both of whom had much more to lose when the Yard's chemists got to work.

According to Spanish Tony's memoirs, published in 1979, the bribe demanded was $12,000. According to Robert Fraser, it was £7,000 – about £50,000 by today's values – of which Mick and Keith were to pay £2,500 each, while he, with considerably more hardship, scraped up the remaining £2,000. Keith has always believed the money was handed over by Spanish Tony to his Met contact in a Kilburn pub and that the subsequent unimpeded analysis of the substances just proved how doubly 'bent' some British coppers could be. According to Marianne, however, Allen Klein got wind of the plan and wisely killed it.

Klein's advice was that Mick and Keith should get out of Britain for a while, to avoid harassment by the media while the police deliberated when and with what to charge them. They decided on Morocco, a country still comparatively remote and unspoiled – despite having influenced Swinging London décor almost as much as India had – and with mythically liberal attitudes to drugs and sex. Brian and Anita had gone there the previous year with Christopher Gibbs to buy ornaments and clothes in the souks, smoke hash and listen to the indigenous music that fascinated Brian. His return with a bandaged hand had been attributed to a mountain-climbing accident: actually, he had gone to hit Anita in their hotel room, but missed and slammed his fist into a metal window frame.

In the end, a party of eight gathered in Morocco in March 1967 in what would prove a vain attempt to take the heat off Mick and Keith. Brian and Anita were invited, along with two other Redlands bust victims, Robert Fraser (in a state of dire anticipation over the analysis of his 'insulin' tablet) and photographer Michael Cooper. To allay any press suspicions that the two main bustees were bolting from the UK together, Mick and Marianne flew to Tangier while Keith travelled overland in his new blue Bentley Continental, chauffeured by his driver, Tom Keylock, with Brian, Anita and a mutual friend named Deborah Dixon.

This four-day road trip down through France and Spain was to prove fateful and, for one of the car's occupants, fatal. At Toulon, Brian developed pneumonia — probably a combination of acid and his chronic asthma — and had to be admitted to a hospital. With atypical selflessness, he insisted that Anita should not wait around for him to recover, but that she and Keith should continue the journey together by themselves (Deborah having also dropped out). Keith did not mean to take advantage of the situation, but during the drive through Spain Anita gave him a blow job in the back of the Bentley while chauffeur Keylock kept firmly eyes-front. The pair spent that night together, but agreed to treat it as just a fling, since Keith did not want to mess up his new understanding with Brian. Afterwards Keith went on to Morocco alone while Anita returned to meet Brian and start the journey afresh from London, this time by air.

In Tangier first, then Marrakesh, the Stones' party fell in with a group of expatriate celebrities, most of whose drug consumption made even Brian's seem mere toe dabbling by comparison. These included the venerable American novelist William S. Burroughs, author of *Junkie* and *Naked Lunch*, and the English writer and artist Brion Gysin, who contributed a recipe for 'marijuana fudge' to the cookbook written by Gertrude Stein's lesbian lover Alice B. Toklas. Pop stars with drug charges hanging over them could have picked wiser company.

They also encountered the legendary royal photographer and stage designer Cecil Beaton (sixty-three at the time and known as 'Rip Van With-it') who spent a night enjoyably slumming it with the 'ragged gypsies' and made a date to take pictures of Mick and Keith by their hotel pool the next day. Beaton's famously bitchy diaries describe sitting next to Mick at dinner, his skin of 'chicken-breast white', 'inborn elegance' and 'perfect manners . . . He has much appreciation and his small, albino-fringed eyes notice everything . . . He asked "Have you ever taken LSD? Oh, I should, It would mean so much to you: you'd never forget the colours . . . One's brain works not on four cylinders but four thousand . . .'" Meeting him again in the next morning's harsh sunlight for their poolside photo session, Beaton could hardly believe it was the same person: 'his face a white podgy, shapeless mess, eyes very small, nose very pink, hair sandy dark . . . He is sexy yet completely sexless. He could nearly be a eunuch.' Mick, however, was to take an unaccustomed back seat during the events of the next seventy-two hours, observing rather helplessly, in his normal voice rather than the hushed, soulful one assumed for Cecil Beaton's benefit, that 'things are gettin' fuckin' heavy'.

They were. Brian guessed that some hanky-panky had gone on between Keith and Anita after they'd left him in the hospital in Toulon, but could not bring himself to confront Keith about it. Instead, he took it out on Anita to a point where she began to fear for her life. The crunch came when he returned to the hotel with a pair of tattooed Berber whores he had picked up, and tried to force Anita into a group-sex session with them. (In *Faithfull*, Marianne claims to have already hired a local prostitute for a three-in-a-bed session with Mick.) The incident finally spurred Keith into becoming Sir Galahad, with a blue Bentley Continental in place of a white horse. Next day, Brion Gysin was deputed to take Brian off to shop and listen to the open-air musicians in Jemaa el-Fnaa, Marrakesh's teeming city square. While he was out of the way, Keith and Anita fled together in the Bentley back to Britain.

On 18 March the *Daily Mirror* splashed the story that Mick Jagger and Keith Richard were to be charged with drug offences. Two days later, the formal summonses arrived. Mick – his address given as 'New Oxford Street, London W1,' actually the office of the Stones' new PR, Les Perrin – was charged with possessing four tablets containing amphetamine sulphate and methylamphetamine hydrochloride contrary to the Dangerous Drugs (Misuse of) Act 1964. Keith was charged in his real surname, Richards, with 'knowingly' allowing Redlands to be used for cannabis smoking. The cases, together with those of Robert Fraser and the vanished Acid King David, were to come before Chichester magistrates in May.

Meanwhile, the Rolling Stones were committed to a three-week European tour between 25 March and 17 April, taking in Sweden,

West Germany, Austria, Italy, France, Poland, Switzerland, Holland and Greece. Amazingly, the tour went ahead and kept every date on its schedule, despite conditions more nightmarish than any rock band had ever faced before – or has since. Mick and Keith's bust had been headline news in every country the Stones were to visit; at every frontier, as a result, they faced stringent searches by customs officers with far more expertise than West Sussex Police for the further sackfuls of drugs they were presumed to be carrying. Bill Wyman and Charlie Watts, those law-abiding, acid-free 'other ranks', fell under the same dark suspicion and suffered the same rough handling as their officers.

At Malmö Airport in Sweden, they were turned over to an elite customs unit known as 'the Black Gang', who grabbed the unfortunate Bill for the same detailed strip search they gave Mick, then became highly excited over a heavy equipment chest for which the key could not be found. Mick was ordered to unscrew its back – a new kind of screwing on tour for him. The absence of any trace of drugs in the band's luggage only seemed to increase trans-European officialdom's hostility. At Paris–Le Bourget, a simple misunderstanding over passport procedure caused a scuffle between their driver, Tom Keylock, and immigration officials.

In addition, the audiences in each country were wilder than the band had ever seen before – screaming almost in exultation that, after all the ambiguities surrounding Mick, he had proved himself a true Rolling Stone after all – and the crowd-control measures adopted by police and security guards more brutal. Even in historically neutral and well-behaved Zurich, a demented boy knocked Mick over, then started jumping on him.

If all this wasn't enough, the band's rhythm guitarist had just enticed away the girlfriend of its lead guitarist and his best friend, yet there hadn't been time to resolve the matter before the tour began. After Keith and Anita's exit from Marrakesh, a hysterical Brian had made his way to friends in Paris, then returned to London, determined to win Anita back but still reluctant to sever his relationship with Keith. Somewhat hedging her bets, Anita had gone off to make another film, Roger

Vadim's *Barbarella*, leaving the two rivals for her hand to swap guitar licks onstage, one irradiating embarrassment, the other broken-hearted reproach. As Mick went through his moves, there was almost as much psychological tension behind his back as hysteria at his feet.

His own situation with Marianne Faithfull – for the present – seemed stable by comparison. There had been no awkwardness with Marianne's husband, John Dunbar, from whom she had been separated for some time before she and Mick got together. Indeed, Dunbar was along on the European tour, one of the select few permitted 'access all areas'. As a sideline to his Indica gallery, he had started a stage-lighting company with a young Greek electronics wizard named Alexis Mardas (later to find fame with the Beatles as 'Magic Alex'). Mick had asked the pair to create a sequence of special effects for the Stones and come on the road to operate them personally. So each evening John Dunbar found himself putting the man now living with his wife in the best possible light.

Marianne herself was back in London, looking forward to a year that promised only to fulfil her long-held ambition to become a straight actress. Despite her much greater familiarity with drugs than Mick's, and Detective Sergeant Cudmore's pointed sniffing of the air around her, she had not been charged after the Redlands raid or mentioned by name in the subsequent press reports. While Mick and the Stones struggled round Europe, she was preparing for her stage début in Chekhov's *Three Sisters* at the Royal Court Theatre, in a stellar cast including Glenda Jackson. Her role as the sweet, innocent youngest sister, Irina, who marries a baron and yearns to go to Moscow, was exactly what the British public expected of her.

When the Stones reached Italy, Marianne found herself missing Mick so much that she decided to fly out to Genoa and surprise him at his hotel after the night's show. It was an experience that cured her of ever wanting to go on the road with him again. The Genoa show was a particularly violent and chaotic one, and when Mick came into the hotel room where she waited in bed, 'he was possessed, as if he had brought in with him whatever disruptive energy was going on at the concert . . . he walked over to the bed and began slapping me across the face'. Her first thought was that he'd found out about her one-night stand with Keith at the Mayfair Hotel weeks before. But the violence ceased as abruptly as it had started, and neither of them ever mentioned it afterwards.

All the time, a stream of negative reports came back to Britain, casting the Stones as *agents provocateurs*, with no mention of the hassles to which they were subjected, and creating the very worst atmosphere for Mick and Keith's court appearance on 10 May. In Dortmund, West Germany, they happened to share a hotel with the Olympic long-jump champion Lynn Davies, who complained to reporters that a 'stream of obscenities' from their table during breakfast had made him feel 'sick and ashamed to be British'. Mick's response, to a Paris press conference, was unusually quotable, albeit hardly calculated to please his gym-teacher father: 'The accusations are disgusting and completely untrue. I deny that we were badly behaved. I cannot remember when we have behaved better. We hardly used the public rooms at this hotel. They were crammed with athletes, behaving very badly.'

Ironically, the Stones were also acting as ambassadors for Britain, taking rock to Poland, a Communist-bloc country where even mild pop-sters like Cliff Richard were regarded as symbols of capitalist decadence. At Warsaw's forbidding Palace of Culture, the band found themselves playing to two thousand of the party faithful and their children, seated in rows and applauding timorously – rather as speeches by Stalin used to be – while several thousand disappointed fans ran amok outside, and police responded with armoured cars, tear gas and water cannons. Afterwards the musicians tried to make amends by driving through the city, throwing bundles of albums through their car windows. In Athens their show took place four days before the Greek royal family was overthrown by a cabal of fascist army officers. Such was the anticipatory paranoia at Panathinaikos football stadium that the audience was kept back forty feet from the stage and Mick couldn't perform his new end-of-set trick, tossing out red roses from a bowl.

On the way back to London, he said he'd had it with live shows and never wanted to tour America again. His wish would very nearly be granted.

CHAPTER NINE

Elusive Butterfly

In the coming court ordeal, there was an option for Mick that his lawyers were not slow to point out. The four amphetamine uppers he was charged with possessing technically belonged to Marianne; she had bought them at an all-night disco during their romantic escape to San Remo, slipped them into a side pocket of his green velvet jacket without his knowledge, then forgotten about them. She was more than willing to testify as much, but Mick wouldn't hear of it. Ever the chivalrous knight, and his father's son, he said his career as a rock star could withstand a drug bust but hers as a serious actress could not, and he wasn't about to let her be 'thrown to the wolves'. A vain hope, as it would prove.

The preliminary hearing took place before Chichester magistrates on 10 May. Mick, Keith and Robert Fraser pleaded not guilty to the charges against them and were bailed in the sum of £100 each to appear at West Sussex Quarter Sessions for trial by jury the following month. Magistrates at this time had no power to impose reporting restrictions if media coverage seemed likely to prejudice the trial in the higher court. So, while Mick and the other two reserved their defence, journalists could report the prosecution's account of the police raid in full with all its insinuations and innuendoes. The sole restriction concerned the fourth defendant – named in the indictment as David Schneidermann [sic] – who had fled Britain with his charmed attaché case of LSD on the night of the bust and afterwards seemingly vanished into thin air. Because Acid King David was not in court, the magistrates ruled it would be 'unfair' for his name to be made public.

At four o'clock that same day, Scotland Yard's drugs squad raided Brian Jones's Chelsea flat. They found Brian, dressed in a Japanese kimono, sitting among the debris of an all-night party. The sole remaining guest was a twenty-four-year-old Swiss nobleman and aspiring pop singer, Prince Stanislaus Klossowski de Rola, known for short – rather unfortunately in this instance – as Stash. More focused and knowledgeable searchers than their West Sussex colleagues, the Yard team quickly turned up eleven incriminating items, including a pile of hashish, some methedrine and a glass phial containing traces of cocaine. When the latter was shown to him, Brian reacted with seemingly genuine horror. 'No, man, that's not mine at all,' he protested. 'I'm not a junkie.'

The synchronisation of the raid with Mick and Keith's court appearance in Chichester made clear that Britain's anti-drug agencies, such as they were, had declared open season on the Rolling Stones. And this time there was no doubt about police collusion with the press. A crowd of journalists watched the raiders go in, and Brian and Stash being taken away for questioning at Chelsea Police Station on the otherwise carefree, swinging King's Road. There Brian was charged with possessing cocaine, hashish and methedrine and Stash with possessing cannabis – even though none had been found in his pockets or around the divan where he'd been sleeping. Next morning, the pair appeared at Great Marlborough Street magistrates' court, around the corner from carefree, swinging Carnaby Street, and were bailed in the sum £250 each until 2 June. At that hearing, both elected trial by jury and their case was set down for Inner London Sessions on 30 October with the same bail conditions.

For a young man who had been pampered and flattered as Mick

had these past five years, it was salutary to realise how urgently he now needed friends and allies – and how thin on the ground they suddenly became. The Stones' UK record label, Decca, refused to lend the slightest help or support despite the millions of records they had sold. Thanks to Andrew Oldham's tape-leasing deal, Decca regarded the band as freelancers rather than in-house artists as the Beatles were to EMI; sour memories also still lingered of the $1.25 million advance which Allen Klein had bludgeoned out of them in 1965.

With Oldham still inexplicably absent from the battlefront, it fell to Klein to organise solicitors for Mick and Keith in the lower court and procure a top Queen's Counsel to represent them at West Sussex Quarter Sessions. This was Michael Havers, a future Conservative attorney general and lord chancellor and father of the actor Nigel Havers. The Stones' publicist, Les Perrin, also proved invaluable by lobbying his contacts in Parliament about the inequities that the case had already thrown up. And to be sure, Mick and Keith's treatment was already causing disquiet among those not usually considered their natural allies. On 19 May Home Office minister Dick Taverne opined that unrestricted reporting of magistrates' court hearings risked creating prejudice against the defendants at their later jury trial, and cited the Jagger–Richard case as a recent glaring example.

Coincidentally, in the run-up to their trial a new kind of pop music experience took place 5,000 miles away in Monterey, California. An open-air festival on the lines of the jazz one staged at Newport, Rhode Island, it had one radical innovation: the star-studded bill of Jefferson Airplane, Simon and Garfunkel, Country Joe and the Fish, Scott McKenzie, the Mamas and the Papas, Eric Burdon and the Animals, the Who, Otis Redding and Janis Joplin that performed for the 55,000-strong audience all gave their services for free. Well organised, laid-back and peaceful – unlike almost all its successors – the Monterey festival established the idea of American and British rock musicians as a kind of hippie high command, abolishing the music's exploitativeness at a plectrum stroke, promoting hysteria and violence no more, but benign coexistence. Its afterglow seeped across America, then the Atlantic, to become the first, and quintessential, event in what would come to be known as the Summer of Love.

Andrew Oldham was one of the festival's organisers (it was where he had 'gone missing in California'); Mick was a non-executive member of its planning board, along with Paul McCartney, and in normal circumstances the Stones might have been expected to join its headliners. However, with Mick and Keith about to go into court on drug charges, there was no hope of either being granted an American visa. With his trial less imminent, Brian did manage to get one, and took the stage at Monterey to introduce a young black singer–guitarist in an orange ruffled shirt named Jimi Hendrix, whose sexual showmanship made Mick seem almost decorous by comparison. Later, with his usual awesome imprudence, Brian joined Hendrix in sampling STP, a hallucinogen whose trips could last up to seventy-two hours.

Britain staked its own claim to the Summer of Love on Sunday 25 June when the Beatles' new single, 'All You Need Is Love', was unveiled on a TV programme called *Our World*, broadcast by the BBC from London over the new satellite broadcasting system to a global audience of 400 million. The studio audience included Mick, Keith and Marianne, seated hippie-style on the floor with Eric Clapton, Jane Asher and Keith Moon. The sequence was supposed to represent everything Britain could show off most proudly to the world telly-watching community, and at the last minute it was realised this label might not be best applied to two Rolling Stones due in court on drug charges forty-eight hours later. But the Beatles might have refused to do the broadcast if their friends had been excluded, so rather than risk disappointing 400 million viewers Mick and Keith were left in.

Their trial, like the Monterey festival, lasted three days, and attracted a global audience like *Our World*'s, even if its content wasn't quite so wholesome. With the caprice of a British summer, weather as gloriously sunny as California's prevailed throughout. The ancient cathedral town of Chichester became almost a festival site on its own, with hysterical fans, jostling journalists, craning TV cameras, sweating police, hot dog wagons, T-shirt and souvenir vendors and ice cream vans. But spiritually speaking, the Summer of Love was halted at the town limits, frisked and turned away.

It was not quite the full majesty of the law ranged against Mick on that Tuesday morning, 27 June. Under a court system that had lasted since medieval times, and would not be reformed until the early 1970s, quarter sessions (i.e., convened four times per year) dealt with only middle-rank offenders, leaving the most serious cases to the regional assizes. Although West Sussex's midsummer quarter sessions were under the charge of a fully qualified judge, sixty-one-year-old Leslie Block, he presided in his capacity of wealthy local squire, chairing a panel of three lay magistrates and exchanging his accustomed shoulder-length wig and red robes for a plain dark suit. Even out of Gilbert and Sullivan costume, however, Justice Block would prove himself at one with the era that had pilloried Oscar Wilde. The judge's surname, in short, was an all too accurate pointer to the consistency of his head.

Mick was first to be called, wearing a light green jacket, olive-coloured trousers, frilled shirt and multi-striped tie – formal attire by his standards, but a string of extra offences against the worn brown woodwork of the dock. His appearance brought a suppressed shriek from the young women in thigh-high mini-dresses who filled most of the forty-two public seats, prompting the first of many exasperated calls for order from Judge Block. Not since R&B club days, when Jacqui Graham used to record the minutiae of his cufflinks, had fans been allowed this close.

Only here there was to be no vocal. Apart from confirming his full name to be Michael Philip Jagger, his address to be New Oxford Street, London, W1, and his plea to be 'not guilty', Mick, as was his right, did not utter a word. His counsel, Michael Havers, outlined his defence – that possession of the amphetamines had been legalised by a verbal prescription from his doctor – but did not question him directly, thus sparing him cross-examination by prosecution counsel Malcolm Morris QC. The only oratory required from Havers concerned the triviality of the offence; how, although illegal in Britain, the pills were a proprietary travel-sickness remedy sold in pharmacies throughout Europe, and any respectable person returning from holiday with a toilet bag of foreign medicines could end up in the same predicament.

The entire hearing lasted barely thirty minutes. Detective Sergeant Stanley Cudmore took the stand to testify that, after Detective Constable (since promoted to sergeant) John Challen had found the tablets in the green velvet jacket, Mick had said they were his and that he needed them 'to stay awake and work'. Cross-examined by Michael Havers, Cudmore agreed that Mick's conduct throughout the raid had been 'thoroughly adult and co-operative'. The sole witness for the defence was Dr Raymond Dixon Firth, who repeated what he had told Challen when the two West Sussex detectives visited him after the raid: that he'd given Mick verbal permission to take the tablets and, in Dixon Firth's view, this was a legitimate prescription.

Judge Block hardly seemed to be listening. After a whispered exchange with the lay magistrates beside him – two local farmers and a Worthing shopkeeper – he turned to the jury of eleven men and one woman. 'These [Dixon Firth's] remarks cannot be regarded as a prescription,' he said. 'I therefore direct you that there is no defence to the charge.' The jury retired for six minutes before returning the prescribed guilty verdict. Rather than sentence Mick there and then, Block deferred the moment until after Keith and Robert Fraser's trials, so keeping him in suspense for at least another twenty-four hours. His counsel's application for bail was refused, and he was remanded in custody.

Robert Fraser was dealt with just as speedily, and inconclusively. Following the analysis of his 'insulin' tablet, he'd had no option but to change his plea to guilty of possessing heroin. His counsel could only throw him on the court's mercy, citing his exemplary service with the British army against Mau Mau terrorists in Kenya, and adding that since being busted he had fought to wean himself off hard drugs and was now 'completely cured'. Again Judge Block deferred sentence until all three defendants had been dealt with, and remanded Fraser in custody also. He and Mick were allowed a brief meeting with their lawyers while Keith, still free on bail, drove at top speed back to Redlands to fetch Mick some clean clothes and creature comforts, including a book on Tibetan philosophy and a jigsaw puzzle. Mick and Fraser were each handcuffed to a police officer, loaded into a white van amid shrieks and camera flashes, and driven off to the grim Victorian prison at Lewes, thirty-eight miles away.

The original, wise plan had been that Marianne should not attend the trial and should stay well out of the media searchlight until it was over. That first day, as Mick stood in the dock, she had taken her son, Nicholas, to the home of the Small Faces' Steve Marriott, accompanied – according to her book, *Faithfull* – by an occasional lesbian lover named Saida. Marianne was taking acid with Marriott and the other Faces when the Stones' driver, Tom Keylock, arrived and told her Mick needed her to be around after all. Keylock drove her to Redlands to meet Michael Cooper and they went on to Lewes Prison together, taking sixty cigarettes, a draughts board, newspapers and fresh fruit. There they found Mick and Robert Fraser sharing a room in the prison hospital. Fraser, an old army man, was stoical, but Mick was in tears. Cooper surreptitiously shot a few pictures – including one of Mick lying on his bed with a view to a future album cover – but a prison officer spotted his camera and confiscated the film.

The next morning, Mick and Fraser were returned to court, once more in handcuffs, to be held in a cell during Keith's trial and brought back before Judge Block for sentencing when it ended. Among the day's press reports, several had questioned the use of 'bracelets' on individuals not accused of violent crime, who were never other than totally co-operative. A spokesman responded lamely that it had been because the Prison Service 'had no orders to do otherwise'. As the police van arrived, a *Daily Sketch* photographer snatched a picture of them together on the back seat, manacled hands raised together to shield their faces from the flash. The image was afterwards turned into a silkscreen print by the artist Richard Hamilton, whose title for it sardonically altered London's 'Swinging' prefix to 'Swingeing', or brutal. Four decades later, *Swingeing London 67* would hang on permanent display at the Tate Gallery, one of the most famous and revealing Pop Art images of that otherwise myth-clouded season.

Keith's trial, in front of a new jury, was to take the best part of two days and generate by far the most lurid headlines – most referring back in some way or another to the unspeaking and now unseen Mick. Keith was accused of 'knowingly permitting' his home to be used for drug taking, a charge not necessarily provable through the traces of cannabis found in various containers around Redlands or even the 'strong, sweet smell' of incense allegedly used to mask its distinctive odour. Instead, the prosecution set out to prove that Keith's houseguests had been palpably under the influence of drugs with his full compliance, if not encouragement. This endeavour naturally focused on the only female among the party, who at the time happened to be wearing nothing but a fur rug.

Marianne had not been charged with any offence, so her name could not be mentioned in court. However, thanks to the extensive coverage of the case before it came to trial, the whole world knew the identity of 'Miss X', as she was now futilely camouflaged. Moreover, thanks to Mick's SOS call, she was not prudently hiding away but seated in open court, listening to herself being dragged through the mud by the Crown's prosecution of Keith without any chance to answer back. So much for Sir Lancelot's chivalrous self-sacrifice to save her from being thrown to the wolves.

A succession of West Sussex police officers, male and female, testified to Marianne's 'merry mood' throughout the raid and how at that moment on the staircase she 'deliberately let the rug slip, disclosing parts of her nude body'. Rather than just a giggly hash smoker, she was represented as a shameless hussy, surprised with eight men in an orgy which had not stopped at drugs. All at once, that rather low-key Sunday-evening scene in Keith's living room was transformed into Britain's juiciest sex scandal since the Profumo Affair in 1963. But even Profumo had not contained incidental detail as sweet. After this second day, a story began circulating that when the police burst in they had found Mick licking a Mars bar lodged in Marianne's vagina. It was pure invention, inspired by the national fascination with Mick's lips and tongue (though, according to Keith, a Mars bar had been in the room to satisfy the craving for sweets that drugs created). Yet it would become rock 'n' roll's most famous legend – the one thing about Mick that almost anyone in the English-speaking world was sure to 'know' – as well as repositioning forevermore the homely chocolate snack whose best-known slogan was 'A Mars a day helps you work, rest, and play.'

At 5 P.M., the court was adjourned again, and Mick had to face his second night in custody with Fraser in the Lewes Prison hospital. No orders to do otherwise still having been given, they were put back into handcuffs.

The next morning, 29 June, brought Keith before the court at last, looking positively Wildean in a black frock-coated suit and high white polo neck. In the Stones' whole career thus far, his speaking voice had been an almost unknown quantity. Now at last the contrast could be savoured between that bony, menacing face and the pleasant, rather educated voice, devoid of any of Mick's class affectations, that issued from it. Equally surprising were his humour and quick-wittedness against witheringly hostile cross-examination which for much of the time put an invisible Mick back in the dock alongside him.

Only now did the mysterious Acid King David 'Schneidermann' enter the backstory as alleged owner of the 'large supply of cannabis' found at Redlands. Keith gave a winningly plausible description of the hangers-on who always beset the Stones to explain why this most casual American acquaintance had joined his weekend houseguests (though, of course, not mentioning what had made Acid King David so very *persona grata*). The court heard how at the time Mick was suing the *News of the World* for untrue drug allegations and how everyone around the Stones now believed Acid King David to have been planted by the paper to give out drugs, then tip off the police, so killing off the libel action. Cross-examining, Malcolm Morris QC asked whether Keith seriously accused the *NoW* of 'a wicked conspiracy . . . to have Indian hemp planted at your house . . . because it did not want to pay libel-damages to Mick Jagger'.

'That is the suggestion,' Keith replied.

Once again, the prosecution strategy for proving that drugs had been used was to suggest a simultaneous sex orgy, with Keith implicitly as ringmaster. At one point, the crushingly supercilious Morris asked whether he wouldn't have expected 'Miss X' to feel embarrassed 'if she had nothing on but a fur rug in the presence of eight men, two of whom were hangers-on and the third a Moroccan servant'. 'We are not old men,' Keith retorted in a genuinely Wildean moment. 'We are not worried about petty morals.'

Judge Block's summing-up was worthy of any periwigged dotard in half-moon spectacles ever created by W. S. Gilbert. Having allowed hours of legally sanctioned smut and innuendo about the defence-less Marianne, generating all those lip-smacking banner headlines, Block now ruled that none of the Miss X evidence was admissible and instructed the jury, in all seriousness, to disregard it. But the genie was out of the bottle or, rather, the Mars bar out of its wrapper. He also came as close as a quarter sessions chairman could – and that was very close – to signalling the verdict he expected the jury to reach. After retiring for just over an hour, they pronounced Keith guilty as charged.

The three defendants were then placed in a row and sentenced in ascending order of celebrity. Robert Fraser received six months' imprisonment and was ordered to pay £200 in costs; Keith received a year with £500 costs and Mick three months with £200 costs. While the other two remained impassive, he crumpled up and clutched his forehead with one hand. 'I just went dead,' he would recall. 'I could think of nothing. It was just like a James Cagney film except everything went black.' The savagery of his sentence caused hysteria among the young women present and was hardly less shocking to police officers involved in the raid, like John Challen. For a first offender with such a borderline drug, the usual penalty would have been a fine or probation. It was plain Judge Block shared the public perception of Mick as the new Antichrist – a view which his immaculate court conduct had done nothing to moderate – and, in that fine old judicial phrase, had determined to 'make an example of him'.

The sentences began from that moment. Mick was allowed a fifteen-minute meeting with a weeping Marianne while the police dealt with crowd-evasion problems that normally fell to Stones roadies. The court building was by now effectively under siege, with a highly vocal, 600-strong crowd massed around its rear entrance. While a decoy police Land Rover inched through this keening, camera-flashing throng, Mick, Keith and Fraser were snapped into handcuffs again, hurried through the front vestibule and put into a squad car, which pulled away without obstruction. Just outside Chichester – where the rejected Summer of Love still sat weeping at the roadside – they transferred to a prison van with a seven-officer crew.

Her Majesty's prison system absorbed Jagger and Richard with a smoothness and efficiency that suggested some forethought. It had been decided that both should do their 'porridge' in London but, like criminal siblings or members of dangerous gangs, in institutions as widely separated as possible. Mick therefore went to Brixton Prison in south London while Keith and Robert Fraser were assigned to Wormwood Scrubs across the Thames in Hammersmith. The two establishments were equally tough but with different characters, to which their newest arrivals seemed to have been matched. The Scrubs historically specialised in more flamboyant types of wrongdoer like the Edwardian con man Horatio Bottomley and Lord Alfred Douglas, the 'slim gilt soul' who landed Oscar Wilde in the dock. Brixton was more political, having over the years confined several notable Irish republicans and British fascists; it also happened to be where Mick's fellow London School of Economics alumnus Bertrand Russell served six months as a conscientious objector during the First World War.

Mick's numerous foes were now enjoying the pleasantest mental pictures of what awaited him and Keith inside: screaming guards, vile food, gang rapes in the showers, above all, the ritual savage shearing of their hated hair. But while there was as yet no idea that they would serve less than their full term, orders appeared to have been given to go easy on them. Though both underwent full induction as prisoners, checking in all their personal possessions, exchanging their names for numbers (Mick's was 7856) and their Carnaby threads for heavy blue serge suits and black shoes, no attempt was made to cut their hair or otherwise molest them. Far from leaping on them in sadistic delight, their fellow inmates proved sympathetic, even respectful. At the Scrubs, Keith was treated like a hero, and offered cigarettes, chocolate, even hash. At Brixton, Mick was allotted a cell to himself, which, he later said, 'wasn't so much worse than a hotel room in Minnesota . . . We had very, very good treatment, though no different from the other prisoners. They all wanted our autographs. The other chaps [*sic*] showed a great interest in the case and wanted to know all the details.'

In the *London Evening Standard*, a Jak cartoon showed him standing on a cell gallery in a convict's arrow suit with a shifty-looking man in dark glasses close behind him. 'I'm his agent,' the man was telling a warder. 'I get 25 per cent of everything.'

THE JUDGEMENT AT Chichester unleashed a storm of protest, mostly but by no means all from Rolling Stones fans or the young. In London, an all-night vigil was held around the Eros statue in Piccadilly Circus to express solidarity with Mick and Keith in their prison cells, while 200 less sedentary souls marched to Fleet Street and shouted insults at the *News of the World* for its supposed role in their downfall. In clubs and discos all over the country, deejays called for moments of silence or played non-stop Stones music. In New York, when the news came through, there were angry demonstrations outside the British consulate. The image of Mick being paraded in manacles like some eighteenth-century horse thief even sparked a brief fashion trend. At a Carnaby Street store named I Was Lord Kitchener's Valet, sets of plastic handcuffs went on sale under a sign saying BE FAITHFULL WITH A PAIR OF JAGGER LINKS.

Melody Maker voiced the outrage of the UK music press with a front-page editorial denouncing the sentences. There was also a surge of sympathy and support from fellow musicians, though hash and hippie woolly-mindedness together produced little practical help. One bright idea that went nowhere was a giant Free the Stones benefit concert whose proceeds would be spent on an 'avalanche of flowers' to bury Judge Block. The most eloquent fraternal gesture came from the Who, the Stones' nearest rivals on the concert circuit since the Beatles' withdrawal. While the trial was in progress, they recorded cover versions of two Jagger–Richard songs, 'The Last Time' and 'Under My Thumb', to be rush-released on their own Track label with all proceeds going to charity. Full-page advertisements in London's two evening papers, the *Standard* and the *News*, explained why: 'The Who consider Mick Jagger and Keith Richard have been treated as scapegoats for the drugs problem and as a protest against the grave sentences imposed on them at Chichester, The Who are issuing today the first of a series of Jagger–Richard songs to keep their work before the public until they are free again to record themselves.'

This was a world where many people over thirty were still indifferent to pop music. Mick and Keith's conviction made it a national topic that the Beatles never quite had, drawing in even upmarket newspapers that previously had managed to ignore the subject. A range of prominent voices from the older, non-rock generation spoke out against Judge Block's justice, some predictable, like the jazz singer George Melly and the libertarian drama critic Ken Tynan, others unexpected, like the playwright John Osborne and the right-wing journalist Jonathan Aitken. Britain's so-called traditional sense of fair play can sometimes be exaggerated, but it was now undoubtedly stirred – on Mick's behalf in particular. Singing a few louche pop songs, neglecting to visit barbers, peeing up garage walls, even enjoying Mars bars from unusual angles clearly did not merit anything like the retribution that had been dealt out to him. A letter writer to *The Times* summed it up by quoting from lines written by the poet A. E. Housman after Oscar Wilde's trial in 1895:

> *Oh, who is that young sinner with the handcuffs on his wrists?*
> *And what has he been after, that they groan and shake their fists?*
> *And wherefore is he wearing such a conscience-stricken air?*
> *Oh, they're taking him to prison for the colour of his hair.*

Once Mick and Keith had been banged up, however, the madness inexplicably began to go into reverse. At the end of the trial, Michael Havers had registered an appeal on their behalf against both conviction and sentence. With unusual speed, a preliminary hearing was scheduled in the High Court on the very next day, 30 June, before Lord Justice Diplock. The full appeal could not be prepared before the current legal term went into a two-month recess, which meant the pair must either be given bail or remain behind bars until September. Just before going into court on 30 June, Havers was told by the prosecution QC, Malcolm Morris, that Morris had 'direct instructions' from the nameless authorities paying his fee not to oppose bail if it were requested. After a twenty-five-minute hearing, this was granted in the sum £7,000 apiece with the proviso that Mick and Keith should not leave the country before their full appeal was heard, and must surrender their passports in the meantime.

By mid-afternoon the 'young sinners' had been sprung from their cells and were back in their normal, or abnormal, clothes with wrists free of all metal restraint, giving a press conference in a Fleet Street pub named the Feathers. The location had been chosen by their publicist, Les Perrin, to symbolise good fellowship with the press corps which had covered the trial; at Perrin's direction, too, their tone was not of Stones-like anti-establishment fury and contempt, but grateful euphoria to be free again. Sipping a vodka and lime (for which the landlord refused to accept payment), Mick said he'd spent some of his time inside 'writing poetry' and that everyone at Brixton had been 'very kind and helpful'.

The next day, Saturday 1 July, The Times's main editorial or first leader was devoted to him. It had been written by the paper's editor, William Rees-Mogg, an erudite, tweedy man seemingly at the opposite extreme of everything the Stones represented. Rees-Mogg's headline was borrowed from the great eighteenth-century satirist Alexander Pope in his 'Epistle to Dr Arbuthnot': 'WHO BREAKS A BUTTERFLY ON A WHEEL?' Subjecting an unimportant or defenceless target to his lethal mockery, Pope meant, was as futile as strapping that most fragile and evanescent of insects to the medieval revolving rack which broke every bone in its victim's body.

Two hundred years later, when young men once again wore shoulder-length hair, frilly cravats, gold-trimmed coats, gaudy waistcoats and buckled shoes, the observation had never been more apposite.

Rees-Mogg observed that a butterfly of modern times, whom he referred to with old-fashioned formality as Mr Jagger, had been pinned to the wheel and ritually dismembered for 'about as mild a drug case as can ever have been brought before the courts'; one for which as a first offender, where no major drugs were involved and there was no question of trafficking, he could normally have expected to get off with probation. 'There are many who take a primitive view of the matter,' the editorial continued. 'They consider that Mr Jagger "got what was coming to him".' They resent the anarchic quality of the Rolling Stones' performances, dislike their songs, dislike their influence on teenagers and broadly suspect them of decadence.

'As a sociological concern, this is reasonable enough, and at an emotional level it is very understandable, but it has nothing whatever to do with the case. One has to ask a different question: has Mr Jagger received the same treatment as he would have received if he had not been a famous figure, with all the criticism and resentment his celebrity has aroused? If a promising undergraduate had come back from a summer visit to Italy with four pep pills in his pocket, would it have been thought right to ruin his career by sending him to prison for three months? Would it also have been thought necessary to display him handcuffed to the public? . . . It should be the particular quality of British justice to ensure that Mr Jagger is treated exactly the same as anyone else, no better and no worse. There must remain a suspicion in this case that Mr Jagger received a more severe sentence than would have been thought proper for any purely anonymous young man.'

In commenting on a case that was still *sub judice*, Rees-Mogg had deliberately put his paper and himself in contempt of court and liable to draconian penalties. But there was no talk of prosecuting or even reprimanding *The Times* for having articulated what every rational person in Britain now felt. And as a result, the process of making amends accelerated still further. Michael Havers was notified that Britain's foremost judge, Lord Chief Justice Parker, had intervened to squeeze Mick and Keith's appeal hearing into his personal division of the High Court before the end of the law term, on 31 July.

Until then, extreme circumspection was vital. And that didn't only mean no more weekend parties at Keith's. The case had become a peg for the growing campaign to have marijuana recognised as less harmful than either nicotine or alcohol and decriminalised. Mick and Keith were naturally in hot demand as figureheads, but — easier for Mick than Keith — could say nothing that might prejudice their appeal. On 24 July *The Times* published a full-page advertisement headed 'The Law Against Marijuana Is Immoral in Principle and Unworkable in Practice, paid for by Paul McCartney'. Its signatories were the four Beatles and Brian Epstein, Jonathan Aitken, George Melly, artist Richard Hamilton, leftist demagogue Tariq Ali, broadcaster David Dimbleby and more than fifty other names from across the arts and media. Two signatures were notably absent — but might as well have been written in fire.

A week later, still in Monterey-strength sunshine, came the most extraordinary of all the days later to be so firmly erased from the Jagger memory bank. Mick and Keith began it at the offices of their accountant, Laurence Myers, which had been besieged by anxious fans since before dawn. It happened that the Stones' fan-club secretary, Shirley Arnold, was to get married a couple of weeks later. Shirley had been one of Mick and Keith's greatest supports through their trial and imprisonment, keeping in constant touch with their distraught mothers and relaying cheerful messages — which no one really believed — not to worry because everything would be fine. In case he should be behind bars again on her wedding day, Mick took the trouble to go to Shirley before leaving for the appeal hearing and wish her happiness. 'I remember I was in tears and he was comforting me, but of course I could see he was nervous. Both of them made out it was no big deal, but I knew they were terrified at the thought of going back to prison.'

Outside the High Court in Fleet Street, crowds were massed as for the start of a Harrods sale. Keith having been smitten by chickenpox, only Mick accompanied their legal team into the tiny courtroom where

Lord Chief Justice Parker sat with two fellow appeal judges. Part of the unreality of the experience was that Britain's most powerful lawmaker should prove as mild-mannered and courteous as the little local beak had been testy and intolerant. Since the Stenamine incontrovertibly counted as unlawful drugs, Mick's conviction was upheld, but his three-month prison sentence was quashed and a conditional discharge for one year was substituted. This meant that if he committed another offence during the next twelve months he would be punished for the pills also.

There followed a mildly spoken homily from the Lord Chief Justice that made Mick hang his shaggy head as no one ever had, or would again. 'You are, whether you like it or not, the idol of a large number of the young in this country . . . Being in that position, you have very grave responsibilities. If you do come to be punished, it is only natural that those responsibilities should carry higher penalties.'

Keith, quarantined in an anteroom, fared even better. The appeal court censured Judge Block for allowing the sub-pornographic detail about Marianne to be recited in court, and found that police testimony about her 'merry mood' and insecure fur rug was insufficient evidence of cannabis smoking. Since Keith could not be convicted of 'knowingly permitting' something not proven to have happened, both his conviction and sentence were overturned. However, for the co-defendant who had shared Mick's handcuffs and seen the nadir of his hopes in Lewes Prison, there was no such VIP fast track or happy outcome. Robert Fraser had appealed against his sentence for possessing heroin but, after suffering the handicap of being tried alongside two Rolling Stones, now found himself completely cut loose from them. Fraser had to stay behind bars until a High Court appearance where no kindly Lord Chief Justice presided; because of the serious nature of the drug, his appeal was rejected and he served his full six-month term in Wormwood Scrubs. Oscar Wilde could have warned him, and many to come after him, about the danger of 'feasting with panthers'.

From here, it all became about Mick. After his High Court appearance, he was joined by Marianne and driven straight to the headquarters of Granada Television in Golden Square. As well as their famous northern soap opera *Coronation Street,* Granada were the makers of British TV's toughest investigative documentary series, *World in Action.* Mainly through the persuasiveness of a young researcher named John Birt – in later years, Director General of the BBC – Mick had agreed to star in a special rush edition devoted to his ordeal.

The opening sequence was a heavily stage-managed press conference, with questioners instructed in advance not to ask if he felt bitter about his treatment. Now dressed in a cream embroidered smock and purple watered-silk trousers, flanked by Allen Klein and Les Perrin, he seemed distinctly woozy – indeed, could hardly pronounce the word *responsibility* when Lord Parker's admonition about his power over young people was quoted back at him. 'How does one . . . exercise it? Perhaps one doesn't ask for responsibility . . . perhaps one is given responsibility when one is pushed into the limelight in this particular sphere. My responsibility is only to myself . . . The amount of baths I take and my personal habits are of no consequence to anyone . . .' Marianne would recall that he'd been liberally dosed with Valium beforehand and was still 'very scared . . . You got the feeling he only had to say one word out of place and he'd have been taken straight back to Brixton Prison.'

Rather than probe into the background of the case (much as that cried out to be done), *World in Action* opted for an uncharacteristically soft format – a discussion between Mick and four representatives of the establishment he had managed to put so hysterically on the defensive. These were the editor of *The Times,* his new champion William Rees-Mogg; the Bishop of Woolwich, Dr John Robinson; a former Labour Home Secretary and Attorney General, Lord Stow Hill; and a leading Jesuit priest, Father Thomas Corbishley. The encounter took place in the Essex garden of the county's Lord Lieutenant, Sir John Ruggles-Brise, surrounded by the kind of security nowadays associated with G8 summits.

Even though it had been set up for a television programme, the scene that would be transmitted to the nation in old-fashioned grainy black-and-white had a surreal quality the most Technicolor acid trip could scarcely have bettered. A month earlier, Mick had been prisoner number 7856, facing the bleakest vista of barred windows, naked lights and 'slopping out' urine pails. Now four distinguished emissaries from the system that had so recently tried to break him were doing obeisance before him, like magi at the feet of some Mod messiah; tacitly apologising on the nation's behalf, acknowledging that his power to communicate with people was infinitely greater than all of theirs put together, and asking in all humility what they might learn from him.

Here in starkest relief was the generation gap which had been endlessly talked and written about since the mid-fifties and which the sixties, for all their revolutionising, had essentially done nothing to change. On the one hand, lounging on a garden chair, looking cool and collected once again, the twenty-four-year-old in his butterfly-wing silks who'd flown into rural Essex by helicopter; on the other, ranged along a bench, four middle-aged men who'd had to slog all the way out through east London by car, thick-suited, five-o'clock-shadowed, and palpably embarrassed and apprehensive.

From all they had read of Mick, *World in Action*'s production team expected him to take ruthless advantage of having the establishment thus at his mercy – possibly to deliver some ringing manifesto to rally the flower children as Wat Tyler had rallied the peasants in Dartford in 1381 – at the very least, to express outrage over what he had endured and the stress it had caused his family. But they had not reckoned with the Jagger facility to adapt to whatever company he was in and take on the accents of those around him. What they got, instead, was the cosiest of chats in which the butterfly, astonishingly, turned out to speak the same language as the lepidopterists. And proved to have no sting whatsoever.

'Mick,' said William Rees-Mogg, sounding more like a bishop than a newspaper editor, 'you are often taken as a symbol of rebellion, and mothers deplore the influence of the Rolling Stones because they think the Rolling Stones are rebellious. Do you think the society you live in is one that you ought to be rebelling against [and] that you are rebelling against it?'

Could this really be what had so terrified everyone – this pleasantly spoken young man with his obvious articulacy and intelligence, yet respectful and unassuming manner? 'Well, obviously we feel that there are things wrong with society. But until recently I haven't been into this kind of discussion because I didn't feel it was my place or think my knowledge was enough to start pontificating on these kinds of subjects . . . I try to keep out of discussions of things like religion or drugs . . . I didn't ever set myself up as a leader in society. But society, really, has pushed one into that position.'

Lord Stow Hill: 'Mr Jagger . . . you appeal to millions of young people. [Cut away to big, charming smile from lips that surely could never have subjected a wholesome and much-loved chocolate bar to such gross mis-application.] What I would like to ask is how you conceive yourself as an influence with them? In your personality, your approach to music and rhythm, and so on, what is the way in which you would like yourself to be understood, by young people especially?'

Mick: 'Just in the very way I started when I was quite young, which was to have as good a time as possible – which most young people do try to do without regard to responsibilities of any sort, social, family or otherwise.'

Before long he was not just taking questions but, to use his own impressive word, pontificating on a variety of sociological issues, rather as he would once have done in a London School of Economics debate . . . the changes in young people's lives brought by the mid-twentieth cen-tury . . . their vastly increased affluence and access to communication . . . the recent race riots in America, which were also helping stir privileged white American teenagers into anarchy . . . Timothy Leary's doctrine of 'turn on, tune in, and drop out' (which, no, he didn't happen to sub-scribe to) . . . the erosion of individual freedom in America and Western Europe . . . state infiltration of the press and broadcasting media . . . the change in the law's role from the protector of liberty to its enemy . . . He seemed to have taken over the chair from William Rees-Mogg, yet with-out raising his voice or delivering a single put-down. Far from laughing at their heavy-handed efforts to comprehend him and his kind, he saw things from their side . . . gave them credit where it was due . . . offered criticism only in the kindliest manner. 'Our parents went through two world wars and a depression. We've had none of that . . . I'm sure you do your best . . . it may be, for your generation.'

Rees-Mogg: 'What are the qualities you think your generation are going to bring forward because quite soon, after all, you are going to be the dominant generation?'

Mick: 'I don't really want to formulate a new code of living or code of morals or anything like that. I don't think anyone in this generation wants to.'

Drugs, naturally, were dealt with in the same abstract sociological manner; perish the thought that those courteous, careful lips might ever have dragged at a joint or sucked acid from a sugar cube. Would he not agree, Lord Stow Hill asked, that some drugs — heroin, for instance — represented 'a crime against society'? 'It's a crime against the law,' he replied. 'I can't see it's any more a crime against society than jumping out of a window.' But shouldn't real crimes against society be punished to suit the case? 'People should be punished for crimes. Not for the fears of society, which may be groundless.'

As in this case, they seemed to have been.

A FEW WEEKS later, the *News of the World* published a brief paragraph announcing that Mick Jagger had dropped his libel action against the paper. There would be no apology for the false allegations, no out-of-court damages or reimbursement of legal costs — Mick was simply throwing in the towel. It was a warning to all celebrities not to seek legal redress for lies printed about them in such wealthy, ruthless scandal sheets, however gross and damaging. Pop music figures in particular, with their extra vulnerability to journalistic dirty tricks and often disorganised managerial and legal back-up, were best advised to grit their teeth and just take it.

The *News of the World* not only won a total victory, saving itself hundreds of thousands of pounds; it had the further satisfaction of moral outrage over Keith's suggestion in court that it had employed Acid King David as an *agent provocateur* and informer to precipitate the Redlands bust. The Sunday after the trial's end, a front-page editorial rebutted what the paper called 'a monstrous charge . . . It was a charge made without a shred of evidence to support it . . . a charge made within the privilege of a court of law . . . which denied us the chance of answering back at the time . . . These outrageous allegations are, of course, totally unfounded. We have had no connection whatsoever with Mr Schneider-mann directly or indirectly, before during or after this case.' The *NoW* took credit for tipping off West Sussex police but, lapsing into sudden vagueness, said it had received the information from 'a reader'.

This claim to have been the mysterious party on the line to Detective Sergeant John Challen at Chichester police headquarters directly contradicted what DS Challen himself had been told when he visited the *News of the World*'s offices immediately after the raid. Likewise, the paper's response to the Acid King David allegation had – unusually for it – a ring of truth. It was famous for using undercover reporters and informants to achieve its exposés. If Acid King David really had been such a paid operative, it would have made much of the fact, devoting a multi-page spread to 'HOW OUR MAN GOT INSIDE STONES SEX 'N' DRUGS DEN'.

There was never any serious attempt by the British police to locate Acid King David, still less bring him back to Britain to stand his trial and resolve the mystery of who and what he really had been. And, beyond a rumour that he might be in Canada, nothing more was ever heard of him. As time passed, the drug charges fell into abeyance, and more and more people who had played a role in Mick's career emerged to give interviews or write books, one might have expected some American publisher's catalogue to announce a forthcoming memoir entitled *I Was the Acid King*. Yet it never happened.

In 2004, a man named David Jove died in Los Angeles, aged sixty-four. Jove was an eccentric figure on the fringes of West Coast punk culture who produced one of the earliest cable shows with his New Wave Theater Group, directed music videos and held fancy-dress happenings at his cave-like studio in Fairfax. His real surname, jettisoned during the late sixties, was Snyderman. He left behind numerous images of himself

on the Internet, surrounded by his New Wave Theater cronies, camouflaged by face paint – but still unmistakably the weekend guest Michael
Cooper had photographed hugging Keith Richard on West Wittering
beach a few hours before the bust. Same short curly hair . . . same sensitive cheekbones, like some actor in art-house movies . . . David Jove was
Acid King David.

One of the few people who ever learned his secret was a British
woman named Maggie Abbott who worked as a film agent in LA – and,
by a strange coincidence, represented Mick in that field for most of the
1970s. She met the eccentric Jove in a professional capacity during the
1980s and the two became friends. Eventually Jove revealed to her that
his real surname was Snyderman and, after swearing her to secrecy, told
her the whole story.

In January 1967 he had been a failed TV actor, drifting around
Europe in the American hippie throng with Swinging London as his
final destination. At Heathrow Airport he had been caught with drugs in
his luggage and expected to be thrown into jail and instantly deported.
Instead, British Customs had handed him over to some 'heavy people'
who hinted they belonged to Britain's internal security service MI5 and
told him there was 'a way out' of his predicament. This was to infiltrate
the Rolling Stones, supply Mick Jagger and Keith Richard with drugs,
and then get them busted. In return, the charges against him would
be dropped and he'd be allowed to leave Britain without any questions
being asked.

To Maggie Abbott he recounted how easy it had been, with his ency-
clopedic knowledge of LSD, to gain entry to Keith's circle and get himself invited down to Redlands with the 'Sunshine' that was meant to
have been the incriminating evidence. Things had gone somewhat awry
when, instead, the West Sussex police raiders had found amphetamines
in Mick's jacket pocket, and also Robert Fraser's heroin. Nonetheless,
the desired end result of busting two Stones had been achieved, and
Snyderman had been able to leave the country with his remaining acid
stash, as promised.

In fact, at Redlands just before the raid, he had come close to giving himself away when – his guard possibly lowered by drugs – he'd started talking enigmatically to Michael Cooper about spying and espionage, 'the James Bond thing . . . the whole CIA bit'. Three decades later in LA he confessed to Maggie Abbott that he'd been recruited by MI5 on behalf of America's Federal Bureau of Investigation, specifically an off-shoot known as COINTELPRO (Counter Intelligence Program) set up by the FBI's director, J. Edgar Hoover, in the 1920s to protect national security and maintain the existing social and political order. For almost forty years, COINTELPRO operated against so-called subversive elements, from Communists and socialists and Soviet spies to the civil rights movement, black radicals, the campaign against the Vietnam War and feminists, unhindered by any normal restraints of democracy or morality. Its methods, for which it would finally be wound up by a Senate investigation in 1971, included illegal surveillance, black propaganda, burglary, forgery, conspiracy and harassment.

By 1967 COINTELPRO had switched its focus to the subversive effect of rock music on America's young, particularly the kind coming from Britain, most particularly the kind played by the Rolling Stones. Getting two Stones busted for drug possession would ensure they were denied visas for any further US tours in the foreseeable future. Britain's security services had been more than happy to assist in the thwarting of these public menaces. And once they were nailed – so Snyderman had been led to understand – the next ones on the hit list would be the Beatles.

Though Snyderman had done everything asked of him, and afterwards been discreet to the point of changing his identity, his reward was what he called 'a lifetime of fear'. For the rest of his days, even after COINTELPRO no longer existed, he half expected those heavy people who'd spirited him out of Britain in 1967 to come after him and make sure he never did blow his cover. Maggie Abbott several times tried to persuade him to go public but dared not press the point too far. He always carried a handgun and was suspected of having murdered an actor named Peter Ivers when Ivers defected from one of his TV shows. Not long after turning into David Jove, he had married a comedienne named Lotus Weinstock, whose brother Joel also discovered his real surname. Jove gave Joel Weinstock a few hints about the Redlands story, but threatened to kill him if he ever breathed a word of it.

When Jove died in 2004, he still had not broken his silence, though by that time two of his principal victims in the Redlands bust, Mick and Marianne, both knew his true identity.

CHAPTER TEN

'Mick Jagger and Fred Engels on Street Fighting'

A ny modern celebrity who had come through such an experience might reasonably be expected to plunge into intensive bouts of therapy or counselling or, at the very least, escape to some remote tropical island for an indefinite period. Yet Mick emerged from it seemingly unscathed in mind as well as body, not needing any rest or recuperation beyond a few days in Ireland with Marianne. As always with him, it was straight on to the next thing: tomorrow, not yesterday. And experiences that might have been expected to sear themselves onto his soul were soon wiped by that famous Jagger amnesia. A few years later, he'd claim to have forgotten even which prison he was in.

No less extraordinary was his seeming lack of any desire to exact vengeance or redress via the many avenues open to him. There was no newspaper interview headed 'My Prison Hell by Mick Jagger'; no round of condemnatory appearances on TV chat shows; no big-buck deal for a book to be rush-released in Britain, America and a dozen other territories to recoup some of the fortune in lawyers' fees he'd had to spend.

At the time this was seen as proper acknowledgement of how lucky he'd been; four decades on, with celebrity whinges and sob stories the stuff of everyday life, it looks like quite amazing restraint.

Musically, his lips remained almost as firmly buttoned. The title of Jagger–Richard's next Stones single, 'We Love You', released in August 1967, seemed as much a satire on hippie values in general as a message of gratitude for their fans' support or sarcastic turning of the other cheek to their late persecutors. Built around an unhippieishly energetic piano riff, it had been recorded before their appeal hearing with John Lennon and Paul McCartney anonymously singing back-up vocals. Despite the introductory sound of a cell door slamming shut, Mick's lyrics were muffled in a kind of baby talk: 'We don't care if you hound we, and love is all around we . . . your uniforms don't fit we . . . We forget the place we're in . . .'

His self-identification with an earlier martyr to British judicial vindictiveness was underlined by a pop video to promote 'We Love You' on television, should he and Keith not be around to do so in person. Shot in colour by Peter Whitehead, this was a parody of the trial of Oscar Wilde, with Mick as Wilde, complete with trademark green carnation buttonhole. Keith was the judge, in a bell-bottom wig with curls made of rolled-up legal documents, while a crop-haired, trouser-suited Marianne played Wilde's nemesis, Lord Alfred Douglas. At one point, a fur pelt was pointedly slapped over the judge's desk; at another, Marianne waved what looked like an outsize spliff; at another, the camera cut away to Brian Jones, sweaty and vacant-eyed, with no relevance to the action beyond his Victorian-length side whiskers.

Released as a single straight after Mick and Keith's successful gig before the Lord Chief Justice, it should have been an instant No. 1, especially when accompanied by the most hotly topical pop video ever made. Instead, the BBC's *Top of the Pops* show banned the video (though it was shown throughout Europe) while the record made only No. 8 in Britain and No. 14 in America as the B-side to 'Dandelion'. Even as tongue-in-cheek hippies, they were evidently too much for many of their fans to take. And there was still, alas, plenty more of that to come.

By no means everybody had applauded the appeal court's decision or been won over by the softly spoken, intelligent butterfly netted on *World in Action*. A poll conducted by the *Daily Mirror* showed that 46 per cent of its readers felt Mick had deserved his sentence and should have served it in full. Judge Leslie Block remained in no doubt that by banging up a pair of Rolling Stones he had performed a public service which feebleness higher up the legal chain had exasperatingly thwarted. In a speech to his fellow Sussex landowners a few months later, Block made humourous play with his and his putative victims' names in a famous line from Shakespeare's *Julius Caesar*, 'You blocks, you stones, you worse than senseless things!' implicitly aimed at his judicial superiors. 'We did our best, your countrymen, my fellow magistrates and I, to cut these Stones down to size,' he told the Sussex landowners apologetically. 'But it was not to be. The Court of Criminal Appeal let them roll free.'

For all Mick's chivalrous self-sacrifice to protect Marianne's reputation, the trial had turned them into Britain's most notorious couple since King Edward VIII and Wallis Simpson thirty years earlier – though even that Constitution-shaking scandal had not featured 'a girl in a fur rug' or a Mars bar. Today, any chocolate manufacturer given such publicity would doubtless rush out a TV commercial slyly hinting at its possibilities beyond mere sustenance between meals ('A Mars bar fills that gap'?). But at the time, Swinging Sixties permissiveness notwithstanding, a deep vein of Puritanism still ran through the British character, and rather than celebrities, Mick and Marianne often found themselves to be pariahs. On 11 August, they took the only break Mick seemed to need, flying to Ireland to spend four days with the brewing heir Desmond Guinness. On their return to Heathrow Airport, they had not arranged to be met by Tom Keylock with a limo, so were forced to use a regular black taxi from the rank. The first two drivers they approached refused to take them.

Marianne had undergone perhaps the greatest image change in pop history, from virginal Lady of Shalott to shameless, druggy vamp who, when not lolling around half naked or submitting to chocolate-and-caramel-flavoured cunnilingus, thought nothing of taking on eight men at a time. After the trial, she received a flood of hate mail from people who had bought 'As Tears Go By' and now felt personally betrayed. *Private Eye* magazine lampooned her as 'Marijuana Faithfull'. Not that she was altogether heartbroken to slough off the goody-goody persona Andrew Oldham had given her. The promising classical actress, so recently a sensitive Irena in Chekhov's *Three Sisters*, now agreed to star in an Anglo-French feature film entitled *The Girl on a Motorcycle* alongside Alain Delon. As every right-thinking Briton knew, only one thing ever happened in French films and only one kind of girl was ever found on a motorcycle.

For Mick, the best therapy was recording with the Stones again after a layoff of almost five months. Back in February they had begun a new album to follow the threadbare *Between the Buttons,* but the spring and early summer had left Jagger and Richard little time to spare for music, and the project had ground almost to a standstill. With the shadow of penal servitude lifted from them both, work restarted in earnest at Olympic Studios. Far from being exhausted or deflated by his recent traumas, Mick was bursting with energy and determination to make up for all the time that had been lost; moreover, he thought he knew exactly how to do it.

On 1 June the Beatles had released the concept album whose evolution Mick and Keith were watching on the eve of the Redlands bust. Rather than the usual random collection of tracks, *Sgt. Pepper's Lonely Hearts Club Band* was presented as a continuous, cohesive performance, saturated with the influences of its makers' Liverpool childhoods along with LSD and psychedelia, and punctuated with canned laughter and applause harking back to the live shows they had lately abandoned. It was hailed as an instant classic, the Summer of Love's apotheosis, which took Lennon and McCartney's songwriting to stratospheric new heights and raised the bar dizzyingly for every band setting out to make an album. The cover was a masterpiece in itself, designed by Peter Blake and showing the Beatles as sateen-suited brass bandsmen amid a collage of Pop Art icons from Tom Mix to Marlon Brando. In the lower right-hand corner was a stuffed doll in a sweater inscribed WELCOME THE

ROLLING STONES – a sentiment Mick interpreted literally. The way for the Stones to bounce back, he told the others, was to make their very own *Sgt. Pepper*.

Unfortunately, Andrew Oldham had different ideas. Despite having hived off the Stones' financial affairs and PR, Oldham was still their record producer, the maestro of mischief who could turn vinyl into dynamite. And after the enforced summer break, he rejoined them at Olympic Studios, ready to pick up where he'd left off. But the old feeling of complicity – the manager who was one of the band and took equal shares of the trouble he stirred up – had vanished long ago. Mick and Keith both felt that in their direst-ever hour of need Oldham had deserted them, floating off to California to have fun with the Monterey festival. (True enough, but he'd also put in place the support system of Allen Klein and Les Perrin which had served them so well.) Most important, the way that Mick had handled himself through the whole crisis was final proof that he had no further need of a Svengali.

There were a few uncomfortable sessions at Olympic, when Mick outlined the *Sgt. Pepper*-y direction in which he felt the Stones should now go and Oldham made his opposition forcefully plain. From then on, the Stones resorted to a kind of industrial go-slow, keeping him waiting for hours, sometimes failing to turn up at all, or wasting hours of expensive studio time by busking old blues numbers as badly as possible. Eventually the desired effect was achieved: Oldham lost patience and his temper and walked out. Later that same evening, he phoned Mick, suggesting they 'call it a day' and that from here on the band should deal solely 'through Allen'.

The split was reported in the following week's *New Musical Express* and described, the way such things always are, as mutually amicable. Mick's accompanying quote paid no tribute to the precocious brilliance that had made the Stones the sullen flipside to the Beatles – not to mention the small matter of inventing him. 'I felt we were practically doing everything ourselves [in the recording studio] anyway. And we [i.e., Oldham and I] just didn't think along the same lines. But I don't want to have a go at Andrew . . . Allen Klein is just a financial scene. We'll really be managing ourselves. We'll be producing our own records, too.'

Rave magazine, for one, was not deceived by that diplomatic gear change to *we*. 'Mick Jagger is out on his own and he knows it. He has no acknowledged manager, no agent and no record producer . . . although the other members of the band have the same freedom of decision and action, it is largely his whims and ideas which decide which way the Stones will roll. He is the king Stone, the man in charge, whether he likes it or not.'

While at work on the new album the band was now producing as well as creating, he spent long hours in the Beatles' company, as if hopeful that some of *Sgt. Pepper*'s magic might rub off. Wearied by success, adulation and consumption, each of the band's three thinking members, John, Paul and George, had begun to be gnawed by a feeling there must be more to life. In August they seemed to find it in the Indian holy man Maharishi Mahesh Yogi and his philosophy of Transcendental Meditation. Mick and Marianne joined them in becoming disciples of the Maharishi and, on August Bank Holiday weekend, accompanied them to an indoctrination session in Bangor, North Wales. During the session, news came from London that Brian Epstein, who once might have managed the Stones along with the Beatles, had been found dead of an accidental drug and alcohol overdose at his Belgravia home, aged only thirty-two.

But while Lennon, McCartney and Harrison embraced the Maharishi unreservedly – the more so in their vulnerable state following Epstein's death – Mick behaved with his usual caution, sidestepping the duty of converts to study for several months at the guru's mountain ashram in India (as all four Beatles later would) and quietly letting his allegiance lapse soon after. He maintained he still felt 'a need for some kind of spirituality that is living' and continued to meditate and read books about Buddhism, sometimes retiring inside a Native American tepee which he had pitched in the Rolling Stones' office, the better to commune with the spiritual world. However, Hindu non-materialism had as little appeal for him as hippiedom's social anarchy and dropping out. He expounded this have-your-hash-cake-and-eat-it philosophy to one interviewer with an image bordering on the surreal: 'You [should] just drop out of those sections of society imposing unfair and restrictive practices on individuals. Someone has to deliver the milk, but it should work on a cooperative basis. I'll deliver the milk for a week . . . I don't mind.' Needless to say, Milkman Mick was a persona that never materialised.

The Beatles and Stones already had a kind of tacit alliance, not only singing on each other's records but sometimes staggering their releases to allow each other a clear run at the charts. In the aftermath of Brian Epstein's death, plans were discussed for a Beatles-Stones merger whereby the two bands would share offices and build a recording studio to be used by them both and also run as a commercial enterprise. A suitable site was earmarked in Camden, north London, and Mick got as far as registering the name 'Mother Earth' for the record label. The scheme was then firmly squashed by Allen Klein, who now had his own agenda concerning the Beatles and saw how such a workers' cooperative could threaten both that and his control over the Stones.

Even the band's staunchest supporters in the music press doubted whether they could survive the double whammy of Mick and Keith's imprisonment and splitting from Andrew Oldham. They had, after all, had a far longer career than anyone could have expected – more than four years! – and were now well into their twenties, past rock's traditional age limit (Bill Wyman would soon be thirty-one). Most of the other British bands who'd come up through the R&B circuit had folded or seen their star players defect to form new ones in the psychedelic mode, like Stevie Winwood with Traffic and Eric Clapton with Cream. Dozens of arresting new collective names had sprung up on both sides of the Atlantic – Pink Floyd, Procol Harum, Moby Grape, the Doors, the Grateful Dead, Canned Heat, Jethro Tull, the Incredible String Band, the Electric Prunes – exploring realms very different from the Stones' simplistic sex-with-a-sneer; all with hair far longer and shaggier than theirs had ever had been; several with the feature which had once made them unique, a charismatic front man who didn't play an instrument.

Most seriously, it was eight months since the Stones had last showed their faces in America: a lifetime to fickle pop fans with such an array of alternatives to choose from. In press interviews, Mick insisted that they'd soon be back on the road, but gave no details beyond a vague promise to schedule some concerts where no admission would be charged. 'The kids,' he said with a twenty-four-year-old's avuncularity, 'ought to be able to groove around and have a nice time for nothing.'

The Stones' comeback as a live act hinged on one question above all: whether, after a drug scandal of such epic dimensions they would ever be allowed back into America to tour. In September they tested the water, flying to New York for the first time in nine months, to meet with Allen Klein and (in new self-producing mode) art-direct a cover for the new album. At JKF Airport they were subjected to stringent baggage and body searches, blameless Bill and Charlie, as always, undifferentiated from the rest. Finally pronounced clean, they were let in, but Mick and Keith were warned that if they applied for US visas in the future the authorities would look at their British court cases in detail, implicitly to see if the Lord Chief Justice had got it right, before reaching a decision.

Mick and Keith of course were not the only reason for this uncertainty. Brian Jones still had to stand trial for the cannabis, cocaine and methedrine found at his flat, with such suspiciously perfect timing, on the day of the others' first court appearance, back in May. For Brian, unlike them, there was no fast track to judge and jury: he had had to wait in suspense through the whole summer, although the media tempests surrounding 'the girl in the fur rug', Acid King David and the Mars bar had largely kept the spotlight off him. Believing himself vulnerable to further police raids at Courtfield Road, he'd sought refuge in a succession of West End hotels, moving on from each one after a few days when he thought the drugs squad had targeted him again, or when the management discovered who he was and evicted him. Determined to stay clean until his return to court, he employed a succession of doctors to dose him with placebos and, for a time, checked into London's most famous private rehab clinic, the Priory.

After losing Anita Pallenberg to Keith, he had enjoyed a measure of revenge by going around with Keith's ex-girlfriend, Linda Keith, although their relationship was purely platonic and 'born of mutual dependency', Linda says now. He had then found a new lover in the model Suki Poitier, former girlfriend of Tara Browne, who had emerged miraculously unscathed from the hara-kiri sports-car crash in which the young Guinness heir died. Suki was loving, soothing and undemanding, but in all other respects a dead ringer for Anita.

On 30 October Brian's jury trial finally took place at the Inner London Sessions in Southwark. It happened that right opposite the court building lived the parents of the Stones' loyal assistant Shirley Arnold. To give Brian sanctuary from the waiting fans, Shirley took him to Mr and Mrs Arnold's flat. As always with older people, his manners were impeccable and he gratefully accepted and demolished a plate of Mrs Arnold's home-made beef stew.

In court, he pleaded guilty to possessing cannabis and permitting its use on his premises, but denied ownership of the cocaine and methedrine. It was said that since being busted he had suffered 'a virtual breakdown' and was now under strict medical supervision as much to preserve his fragile mental state as to stop him reoffending with drugs. The prosecution accepted his not-guilty pleas regarding the cocaine and methedrine, implying official suspicion that they had been planted by the police. On the cannabis charge he received three months' imprisonment, and for permitting its use nine months, both to run concurrently. The *Daily Sketch* criticised the sentences for 'turn[ing] this wretched young man into a martyr . . . as happened in the case of Jagger'. Brian was sent to Wormwood Scrubs – an infinitely more devastating experience for him than prison had been for either Mick or Keith – but then freed on bail pending appeal.

The appeal was heard on 12 December, with Mick present in court to lend moral support. After hearing that Brian was 'potentially suicidal', Lord Chief Justice Parker, sitting with two other law lords, set aside both prison sentences and substituted a £1,000 fine and three years' probation on the condition that he also continued receiving psychiatric treatment. Brian celebrated with an orgy of drink and pills which culminated with him onstage at a club, playing stand-up bass with such violence that eventually it fell to pieces. Two days later he was back in hospital.

On 8 December the Stones' new album was finally released in Britain, appearing in America a day later. It had taken ten months, four more than *Sgt. Pepper's Lonely Hearts Club Band*, and survived pressures the Beatles never had to contend with: not just the trial and imprisonment of its main performers and sole songwriters but also the loss of a manager and producer, equally brilliant and successful as both. The title was *Their Satanic Majesties Request*, a play on the perception of the band as devils incarnate and also the continuing uncertainty over their international travel. Inside old-style black British passports was a message in elaborate copperplate script, addressed to foreign frontier officials with the hauteur of empire days: 'Her Britannic Majesty's Principal Secretary of State for Foreign and Commonwealth Affairs requests and requires in the name of Her Majesty all those whom it may concern to allow the bearer to pass freely without let [obstruction] or hindrance.'

Their Satanic Majesties' aspirations were all too obvious. Its cover — photographed by Michael Cooper, who'd also shot *Sgt. Pepper's* famous pop art collage — showed the five Stones in mystical robes, seated hippie fashion on the ground with Mick in the middle wearing a conical wizard's hat. The image had a shimmery lamination which made their faces (all but Mick's) appear to move when it was tilted. If one peered closer, the four Beatles materialised like ectoplasm, as though in acknowledgement of the wholesale larceny within. For here were all *Pepper's* spontaneous-seeming innovations calculatedly trotted out again — the droning Indian ragas, wheedling Mellotrons, tinkling temple bells and beefy brass bands, the vaudeville sound effects and comic voices (including Mick's at one point rather unwisely demanding 'Where's that joint?'). The difference was in the music.

Of ten tracks, only 'She's a Rainbow', an upbeat, multichrome 'Ruby Tuesday', was a song that could be instantly understood and hummed. The rest were little more than extended electronic doodles, with Mick's voice so distorted and monotonous and strangely muted that often he hardly seemed there at all. 'Sing This All Together', later reprised as 'Sing This All Together (See What Happens)', was a laboured attempt at a hippie campfire chorus featuring more incognito back-up vocals by John Lennon and Paul McCartney which the bell jingling and tambourine bashing unfortunately concealed. 'On with the Show' began with sound effects from a Soho strip club, then turned to a *faux*-posh Mick monologue in the style of the Temperance Seven. '2000 Light Years from Home' had been started in his prison cells in Lewes and Brixton and, with his verbal gifts, might have aimed at Oscar Wilde's *Ballad of Reading Gaol,* if not quite *De Profundis.* Instead, he droned cosmic claptrap about 'freezing deserts' and 'fiery oceans' as if singing through a megaphone with a clothes peg attached to his nose.

The track list did, however, contain a major surprise. One night, punctual, orderly Bill Wyman had arrived at Olympic at the time arranged for the session to find, as so often, no sign of any of the others. While waiting for them to drift in, he had improvised a song on the piano which he titled 'In Another Land'. Steve Marriott of the Small Faces helped him record a tremolo-heavy rough track which, to his surprise, was worked on some more by Mick and Keith, then pronounced good enough to go onto the album. Still more flatteringly, it later became a Stones single in America. But for Bill triumph was to be outweighed by chagrin. First, Mick took him aside and said that, as a quid pro quo for developing 'In Another Land', Jagger and Richard wanted a share of the publishing. Then the news that someone else in the band wrote songs was kept jealously under wraps. On the album credits it was attributed to 'the Rolling Stones'; only on its American release as a single did Bill get an individual credit.

A few weeks earlier, a new and avowedly serious music paper had started in San Francisco, with a name making no bones about its founder-editor Jann Wenner's favourite band. Nonetheless, the fifth issue of *Rolling Stone* was brutally frank about *Their Satanic Majesties Request.* 'Despite moments of unquestionable brilliance,' wrote reviewer Jon Landau, it put 'the status of the Stones in jeopardy . . . With it, [they] abandon their capacity to lead in order to impress the impressionable.

They have been far too influenced by their musical inferiors [*sic*] and the result is an insecure album in which they try too hard to prove they can say something new . . . It is an identity crisis of the first order and one that will have to be resolved . . . if their music is to continue to grow.'

Mainly on the strength of advance orders, the album grossed $2 million in the United States within ten days, outselling the Beatles' *Magical Mystery Tour* and reaching No. 2 there and No. 3 in the UK. But reviewers on both sides of the Atlantic voiced the same disappointment, bafflement and fears that for whatever reason – prison, drugs, hippie virus, Beatle-fixatedness, the non-participation of Andrew Oldham – the Stones had lost it.

Mick professed himself unbothered by the storm of ridicule and reproach. 'It's just an album, not a landmark or a milestone or anything pretentious like that,' he told the *NME*. 'All we have tried to do is make an album we like with some sounds that haven't been done before. It doesn't mean we'll never release any more rock 'n' roll.' He added that the album should be treated as 'a sound experience rather than a song experience' – which was a bit like calling a play a scenery experience rather than a dramatic one – and insisted he was as proud of it as of anything the Stones had ever done.

Not for many decades would he concede that they had been 'out to lunch'. And in any case, the lunch break was soon over.

MICK AND MARIANNE were never comfortable at his Harley House flat with its too-palpable echoes of a previous relationship. After a year, Mick decided to move back to Chelsea, renting a house in Chester Square while he looked around for somewhere to buy. As much as a home for Marianne and himself, he wanted a symbol of just how far he'd come since his squalid flat-sharing days in Edith Grove, and by March 1968 he'd found it.

Back then, just £50,000 secured the freehold of 48 Cheyne Walk, an eighteenth-century town house in the exclusive row whose white walls and ornate black wrought-iron balconies front the Thames Embankment between Chelsea and Albert Bridges. By a long way Chelsea's most prestigious address, 'the Walk' had at one time or another been home to writers Elizabeth Gaskell, Henry James and Dante Gabriel Rossetti, painters J. M. W. Turner and John McNeill Whistler, composer Ralph Vaughan Williams, actor Laurence Olivier and suffragette Sylvia Pankhurst. Piquantly for its first resident rock star, Oscar Wilde had lived at number 34 at the time of his arrest and trial in 1895.

Number 48 dated from 1711 and was a particularly beautiful and unspoiled example of the Queen Anne period, wood-panelled throughout and with many original features like fireplaces and balustrades, though, as customary with even wealthy abodes built at that time, the rooms were rather small and narrow. Part of the attraction for Mick was a substantial summerhouse in the back garden which he could convert into a music and rehearsal room.

The house was redecorated (by society interior designer David Mlinaric) and furnished with an extravagance mostly dictated by Marianne – for these were still days when Mick found it hard to refuse her anything. If he balked at the Regency double bed or the 'Louis XV' bath, allegedly dating from 1770, she would remind him he now resided at one of London's best addresses and had a duty to live up to his position. Hence the chandelier in the front hall for which she persuaded him to pay £6,000. 'Look a' that!' he'd marvel as he opened the door to visitors. 'Six grand for a fuckin' light!'

Occasionally, he'd dig in his heels, making Marianne realise that 'he thought more about money than anyone I ever knew'. Once in Morocco he doggedly refused to buy a white fur rug she'd set her heart on, even though it didn't cost that much. And the concept of investing in artworks was still alien to him. Through his connection with the Robert Fraser Gallery, he heard that a Balthus painting was to be offered for sale at a bargain price by the artist's son. Marianne urged him to make it the basis for an art collection like his canny friend Paul McCartney's, but he refused.

In these first days in their wood-panelled Thames-side retreat he seemed utterly besotted with Marianne. Friends like the director Donald Cammell later recalled 'the sense of sheer possession' when he looked at this 'bird' who was not only stunningly beautiful but classy and intellectual beyond his dreams. They had rows almost from the beginning, usually stemming from Mick's belief – inculcated first by his mother, and hardly challenged by the dominant element of his audience – that all females were put on earth to be his slaves. However, the rows were never as bitter as those with Chrissie Shrimpton used to be, and he usually knew how to defuse them. Even at Harley House, Marianne remembers, his male chauvinism would sometimes make her bolt out of the flat and down the stairs, grabbing up 'a £5 note and a lump of hash' as she went. Mick would run after her and cajole her back by making her laugh.

Marianne continued to expand his mind more than any hallucogen ever had, taking him to the theatre, ballet and foreign-language films; above all, telling him about books. A typical buying spree under her tutelage piled his bedside table with Alfred Lord Tennyson's *Le Morte d'Arthur*, the collected sayings of Confucius, a guide to Jungian philosophy, *The Rubáiyát of Omar Khayyám* and poetry by Yeats, Dylan Thomas and e.e. cummings.

Absorbed in the Stones, and himself, though he was, he took enormous pride in Marianne's apparently blossoming theatrical and movie career. He helped her learn her part as Irina in *The Three Sisters*, reading the roles of the other two sisters, and on opening night sent her an orange tree for her dressing room – much to the annoyance of her co-star Glenda Jackson, who had to share the same cramped space. Throughout the run he would often slip into the rear stalls to catch its last few minutes, and afterwards find a new way of telling her how good she'd been.

He also loved the entrée into the theatre and film world that Marianne gave him, and the especially delectable adulation of stars from those other media whom he himself secretly adulated. One evening, the crowd in their new Moroccan-style Queen Anne living room included both the Hollywood actress Mia Farrow, fresh from starring in *Rosemary's Baby*, and Britain's greatest playwright, Harold Pinter. Despite Pinter's forbidding appearance, he enjoyed pop music and, when a record was put on the hi-fi, got up to enjoy a good bop. An embarrassed Mia Farrow had to explain that 'it isn't cool to dance at Mick's'.

With Marianne's son, Nicholas, now aged two and a half, Mick assumed the role of surrogate father, taking on the job of finding a nanny, so Marianne remembers, 'as if he'd been hiring servants all his life'. He became the same masculine presence to Nicholas that his own father had been to him, authoritative yet untyrannical; establishing routines and boundaries a million miles from rock-star lifestyle; playing football and cricket with the little boy in the back garden; providing such essential pieces of guidance as how to undo his own trousers to pee.

Marianne's mother, Baroness Erisso (who had the same Christian name as Mick's mother, Eva), was delighted by the arrangement – and not solely because of the financial security it brought her daughter. The baroness had never hit it off with her son-in-law, John Dunbar, or understood why Marianne should want to marry a penniless aesthete. Mick handled her perfectly, deploying his quietest voice and most irresistible old-world courtesy, encouraging her to talk about her days as a Max Reinhardt dancer and all the other adventures and misadventures which had brought her to a cramped terrace house in a Reading back street. For Marianne, his meanness over the Balthus was more than wiped out when he bought Baroness Erisso a cottage in the pretty Berkshire village of Aldworth, presenting it to her as a *fait accompli*, so as not to offend her proud nature, and with no strings attached.

He continued to be friendly with John Dunbar, whom these days he often saw in the company of John Lennon. The potentially tricky matter of giving Dunbar regular access to Nicholas was managed good-humouredly and without causing undue distress to the boy, though the handovers sometimes failed to happen as arranged if Mick suddenly decided he wanted to do something *en famille*. Once Dunbar arrived to collect Nicholas only to find that Mick and Marianne had taken him away on holiday without any prior warning. The usually supercool Dunbar was furious, confronting Mick later and calling him 'a ten-cent Beatle'.

As far as Marianne and Mick's friends knew, Chrissie Shrimpton was history, disinvented as utterly as some Russian commissar after a purge. But that wasn't entirely true. Chrissie now lived in Knightsbridge, sharing a flat platonically with the singer George Bean, who had recorded one of Jagger–Richard's earliest songs. Ironically, she had gone on to date Steve Marriott of the Small Faces, the band on which Andrew Oldham had been concentrating since the break-up with the Stones. Marriott was even shorter than Mick – indeed, the contrast with mannequin-height Chrissie was so extreme, she nicknamed him Peter and made him call her Wendy, as in *Peter Pan*.

For some months after Mick dumped her for Marianne, Chrissie says, he would turn up at her flat without warning and want to have sex – something she still found impossible to refuse him. But if they saw each other at a party, he never acknowledged her. And after about a year, the visits ceased.

The Stones now had their own office at 46a Maddox Street, just off Piccadilly, staffed by trusted figures like Shirley Arnold and Ian Stewart, who'd been with them since their blues-club days. The attic rooms had belonged to Lillie Langtry in the 1880s when she was mistress to the future King Edward VII. Visitors used an old-fashioned lift with a polished wood interior, said to have been installed by that portly prince to save himself the effort of climbing the stairs.

Though the set-up was meant to service all five Stones, there was never any doubt as to its chief executive. Mick took positive pleasure in telling Marianne he was 'going to the office', especially relishing the weekly meetings between the band and their various advisers in the specially designated boardroom. Before long, he brought in a curly-haired young American woman named Jo Bergman, who'd previously worked for the Beatles, to be his personal assistant. For his bandmates, it was often galling how he always took priority with the staff, and how his personal expenses, like sending flowers to Marianne during her theatrical stints, were charged to the Stones' collective account.

Until now, Joe and Eva Jagger had preferred to stay mostly apart from his life in London. But the thought of her elder son having an office just a Stone's throw from the Royal Academy, Burlington Arcade and Fortnum & Mason gave the socially conscious Eva huge gratification. She took to coming up from Dartford regularly every week with Keith's mum, Doris, like a pair of tweedy ladies from the shires to visit 46a Maddox Street, go shopping and have lunch at Fortnum's Fountain. Eva had retained her job as a part-time beautician and would bring with her a selection of creams and lipsticks to sell to the office secretaries. 'She'd come around, showing us new products and advising us about our skins,' Shirley Arnold remembers. 'When Mick found out he was furious and put a stop to it immediately.'

Even after Jo Bergman's arrival as his PA, Mick continued to entrust Shirley with tasks of special delicacy, like buying his mother's birthday and Christmas presents if he was away – usually knitwear from the White House on Bond Street – or tactfully suggesting to Keith, as no one else could, that he ought to get his terrible front teeth fixed. One day, she received an SOS from Mick's brother, Chris, who had followed the hippie trail to Nepal and was now stuck in Kathmandu, flat broke. 'Mick read the message, thought for a moment, and then said, "Send him fifty quid".'

Shirley recalls that, despite his supreme authority in the office, he never played 'the boss'. 'I once said something to Mick about how I worked for him. "You don't work for me," he said. "You work *with* me".' And, moody, capricious, petulant, and changeable though he could be, she realised that, unlike Keith – so very unlike Keith – 'he had no dark side'.

Everyone agreed on the Stones' most urgent priority for 1968. They must make an album to bring them back from the electronic limbo into which they had strayed with *Their Satanic Majesties Request*. And even Mick accepted that their attempt to produce themselves had been a disaster and their chance of success depended largely on putting a professional back at the control desk. Rather than some star name with aspirations to be a second Andrew Oldham, they picked Jimmy Miller, a young New Yorker who had produced successful singles for the Spencer Davis Group but was junior enough to accept that his role would be primarily technical. Now that every other band

had a non-instrument-playing vocalist, Mick started to learn the guitar in his garden room at Cheyne Walk, with help from British rock's
acknowledged maestro, Eric Clapton.

The way back from *Satanic Majesties* turned out not to be the long
labour of an album, but was accomplished in a single jump. By Keith's
account, the idea was born at Redlands after he and Mick had been sitting up late and, too drunk or stoned to crawl to bed, crashed out on
adjoining sofas. Early the next morning, they were roused by the sound
of Keith's gardener, Jack Dyer, stumping along the path outside. 'What's
that?' Mick had mumbled. 'Just Jack . . . Jumpin' Jack,' Keith had mumbled back.

Another component was provided by Bill Wyman, that stubbornly
creative second ranker, during rehearsals for the new album when yet
again he found himself waiting around for the others. To pass the time,
he picked out an intro riff on the organ, like the one on 'Satisfaction' but
harder and flatter. When Mick arrived, he liked the riff so much that he
wrote a whole lyric to follow it.

With 'Jumpin' Jack Flash' he didn't only come up with the perfect
antidote to *Their Satanic Majesties'* hippie wooziness. He also hit on
an answer to the problem of being a songwriter who chose to reveal
nothing of himself in his lyrics. This was to create a character he could
assume like a role in a play, one that bore no resemblance to him – or any
other member of the human race – yet was a perfect distillation of his
public self in all its manic energy, sexual ambiguity and sneering cool. If
Keith's gardener and Bill's bass riff were the character's starting point,
it owed most to the British folk legend of Spring-Heeled Jack, a spec-
tral giant with 'a diabolic physiognomy and eyes like red balls of fire',
who could leap over buildings with a single bound. To make the casting
still more perfect, this apparition was said to have 'spoken like a gentleman', worn all-over white leather in a literal jumpsuit, and possessed the
power to make young women 'fall to the ground in fits'.

The song was pure pantomime, Mick at one moment bawling
out a ludicrously apocalyptic life story ('Ah was bawn in a crawss-fire
hurr'cayne . . .'), at the next simpering into bathos ('But it's a-a-awl right

now, in fact it's a gas . . .'). As he could never be bothered to write out fair copies of his lyrics, Shirley Arnold did it from a rough cut of the record. 'When I was given "Jumpin' Jack Flash" it happened to be one of the days when his mum was coming up on her weekly visit,' she recalls. 'I remember copying out "I was raised by a toothless, bearded hag" and thinking, "I hope Mrs. Jagger doesn't see this."'

Added to that was a sound more lustily malevolent even than 'Satisfaction'; naked bass that segued into the full, vicious intro at Mick's cry of 'Watchit!'; the preposterous *King Lear* storm in each verse undercut by a tinkly country guitar descant in the chorus. A promotional colour film clip showed the band with faces daubed in gold and silver, like statues from some ancient Egyptian tomb, while Jumpin' Jack Flash in person cavorted before them, all leering lips and black eyeliner. Fans and pop critics heaved a sigh of relief. The Stones weren't just back to pre-*Satanic Majesties* form, but wilder, wickeder and (though the song itself was actually quite sexless) raunchier than ever.

By 22 June they were at No. 1 in Britain, reaching No. 3 in America a few weeks later. It really did seem to be a-a-awl right now.

AFTER MICK'S *World in Action* appearance, there were further attempts to persuade him to be the voice of his generation. Britain's political parties in the sixties were obsessed by the need to engage with young people and counteract their general apathy and cynicism towards politicians. It was a special preoccupation of Harold Wilson's Labour government, which had come to power with a promise of youthful dynamism but which, behind the Swinging Britain façade, was beset by industrial troubles and financial crises leading to the devaluation of the pound in 1967. With a passion for gimmickry scarcely rivalled by its New Labour successors thirty years later, Wilson's government thought of a seemingly surefire way to attract youth to its banner. In 1968, unofficial overtures were made to see whether Mick would consider standing for Parliament.

The intermediary was Tom Driberg, MP for Barking, former chairman of the Labour Party – and, by coincidence, godfather to Mick's first love, Cleo Sylvestre. For Driberg, however, more than political considerations were in play. A notorious predatory homosexual, he had been repeatedly arrested for cottaging, or soliciting in men's public toilets, but had always been saved from disgrace by his powerful friends in government and Fleet Street.

Mick never had any serious intention of becoming a parliamentary candidate, well knowing how much tedious and thankless work would be involved – and also that Keith would never stand for it. But he was amused by Driberg's overt infatuation and stories of being a Fleet Street gossip columnist in the thirties. The drooling politico and flirtatiously non-committal rock star would meet for lunch at the Gay Hussar, a Hungarian restaurant in Soho (*gay* in its old sense of carefree) where the socialist intelligentsia was wont to gather over cold pike mayonnaise and wild cherry soup.

Eventually Driberg visited 48 Cheyne Walk, as he thought, to reel in this vote-winning catch for his party, accompanied by (also gay) American beat poet Allen Ginsberg. Like all visitors, the cottage-loving MP and the author of *Howl* were invited to join Mick and Marianne seated cross-legged on Moroccan cushions strewn about the eighteenth-century wood floor. But, as Marianne recalls, the sight of Mick's tautened velvet crotch was too much for Driberg, who blurted out, 'What an enormous basket you have!'

By 1968, in any case, politics had ceased to be the exclusive preserve of politicians, and young people needed no PR trickery to get them involved. In reaction to the previous year's carefree Summer of Love, a wave of unrest was engulfing Europe's student population, fuelled equally by moral outrages abroad and material grievances at home. The main catalyst had been Czechoslovakia's short-lived Prague Spring when young Czechs had taken the lead in trying to free their country from Soviet Russian dominance and had been mercilessly crushed. Since then, left-wing student marches and rallies of increasing violence and destructiveness were being reported from West Germany, Holland and, particularly, France under the faltering presidency of wartime leader Charles de Gaulle. For the first time since Russia's Bolshevik coup in 1917, the dread word *revolution* was heard across Europe – now, though, not meaning internal conflagration in a single country but a cross-border forest fire.

Britain's young were as eager as any to obey this clarion call to radicalism. The problem was that they had almost nothing to rise up against, living as they did in a country which adulated youth and, by and large, treated them with extraordinary indulgence. In Britain, the insurrectionary movement was known as the Underground after Europe's Second World War anti-Nazi resistance and London's metro system. Despite these overtones of fighting tyranny and lurking in deep cover, it existed openly and without the least danger, demanding the overthrow of capitalism and worshipping totalitarian Communism while enjoying all the benefits of a democratic consumer society.

In many ways, the Underground reflected the pop music culture that had recently obsessed so many of its members to the exclusion of almost all else. The political factions within it were as numerous as rock bands, with followings as fanatical and mutually hostile as those who once disputed the rival merits of Beatles and Stones. (Are you Anarchist or Workers Revolutionary Party?) It threw up youthful demagogues, notably the Punjab-born Oxford graduate Tariq Ali, with the crowd-swaying charisma of pop stars; it supplied posters of Communist icons like Lenin, Che Guevara and Mao Tse-tung to displace those of Mick Jagger and Scott Walker on bedroom walls; it published newspapers and magazines full of impassioned, not always very coherent polemics that were as avidly read as Top 20 charts used to be. Above all, it worshipped rock stars, if possible even more than had the unthinking teenyboppers of 1963, and numbered the leading ones among its chief figureheads.

Despite the Underground's best efforts, the only outrage which roused youthful passion across all factions and classes was one happening on the far side of the world, and without any British involvement – America's bloody, unwinnable Vietnam War. The biggest anti-war 'demo' yet took place in London on 17 March 1968, when 10,000 people gathered in Trafalgar Square to hear speeches by Tariq Ali and the actress Vanessa Redgrave, then marched on the US embassy in Grosvenor Square, chanting the name of America's arch-demon, North Vietnamese leader Ho Chi Minh. Outside the embassy they were met by a phalanx of police without special riot gear but supplemented by mounted officers. Initial good humour turned into an ugly scrimmage in which dozens on both sides were injured, police horses were ridden directly at demonstrators, and riders dragged from their saddles and trampled on. So Mayfair's posh heartland finally witnessed the Domesday prophecy of Oscar Wilde's Lady Bracknell of 'acts of violence in Grosvenor Square'.

The pop star most likely to have heeded the call to take part was John Lennon, but he and his fellow Beatles were in India, studying with the Maharishi. Mick sidestepped an invitation to march alongside Vanessa Redgrave ('Just didn't feel like it,' he recalled later) but was in Grosvenor Square when the violence erupted, and narrowly escaped the police's cavalry charge. An American demonstrator named Robert Hewson, then studying at Cambridge, recalls seeing him 'standing coolly on the steps of a house in the square, surveying the chaos'.

Keenly aware of the *Zeitgeist* as always, Mick was quite happy to be a hero of the Underground, even though its vision of Britain as a Communist utopia wasn't exactly his. A few days after the Grosvenor Square riot, he did a Q&A session with its leading newspaper, the *International Times*, running about ten times the length of any he'd ever allowed *Disc* or *Melody Maker*. The *IT* did not ask awkward questions about his love life, but allowed him to ramble on unedited for column after column about the history of European civilisation, astronomy and economics. He did, however, put his finger on the difficulty of bringing revolution to a peaceful, phlegmatic society where Grosvenor Square was seen as a one-off aberration. 'We can't be guerrillas . . . We haven't got enough violence, we've no opportunity . . . There's nothing . . . It's a whole drag . . . the army's all over! There's no guerrillas . . . well, there's the Welsh Nationalists. You can go and join them, but what a joke . . . I mean, there's nothing in this country.' Thanks to the Underground press's mania for psychedelic graphics, the text was printed in green on a red background and so almost indecipherable.

Fired up by what he had seen on 17 March, Mick wrote a song for the Stones' album in progress that was recorded under the elliptical title 'Did Everybody Pay Their Dues?', then dropped in favour of a renamed, very different version, based on Martha & the Vandellas' 1964 Motown hit 'Dancing in the Street'. 'Ev'rywhere Ah hear the sound of marchin', chargin' feet, boy,' it began. "Cause summer's here and the time is right for fight-tin' in the street, boy . . .' Months before John Lennon found nerve enough, it went on to utter the word that had every European government in a panic, rhymed and scanned as meticulously as Lennon would later do it: 'Hey . . . think the time is right for palace revo-loo-shun / But where I live the game to play is compromise so-loo-shun.'

In 'Street Fighting Man' he seemed to come down off the fence at long last, declaring solidarity with the Grosvenor Square demonstrators and all other youthful insurgents across Europe, champing at the bit to join them on the streets and exulting in the prospect of violence and destruction. Actually it was just another role: the street-fighting man wasn't Mick, but Tariq Ali, while the 'revo-loo-shun' had a vaguely Arthurian sound in its not very dire threat to 'kill the king and rail at all his servants'. (Even the resourceful Lennon never used the archaic verb to rail, meaning to shout insults.) As in 'Jumpin' Jack Flash', fire-and-brimstone verses alternated with a cop-out chorus, which was about the lyricist but dodged into the third person to justify his non-appearance on the barricades. 'Sleepy London town' just couldn't produce a riot good enough to be worth his while. So what was 'a poor boy' to do, he asked disingenuously, but 'sing in a rock-roll band'?

All these shifting poses and evasions faded into irrelevance in the studio, when Keith provided a rampaging acoustic intro guitar that opened up the most explicit vista of shop windows being smashed and cars torched. The track's title alone was incendiary enough, but world events through that Summer of Non-Love would give it an infamy akin to Nero's lyre recital as Rome burned.

When the final mix was completed in May, Paris's street battles had reached such a pitch that it couldn't be released as a UK single lest this gratuitous further incitement should carry across the Channel like the noise of big guns in World War I. Yet for Britain's Underground, the very existence of a Stones track called 'Street Fighting Man', even with its residual element of fence-sitting man, was propaganda beyond price. Tariq Ali planned a second march on Grosvenor Square for 27 October and, to swell recruitment, asked permission to print the lyrics in his magazine, *Black Dwarf.* The same issue carried an article about Marx's co-founder of communism, Friedrich Engels, whose best-known maxim was 'an ounce of action is worth a ton of thought'. *Black Dwarf*'s cover line read 'MICK JAGGER AND FRED ENGELS ON STREET FIGHTING'.

In any case, something more potentially significant than a mere pop record was to turn Mick into a poster boy for France's new revolutionaries. Late in May, the great film director Jean-Luc Godard, then aged thirty-seven, asked the Stones to appear in an English production, half documentary, half feature, he was about to begin shooting in London. Mick had revered Godard since striped-scarf student days at LSE, and instantly jumped at the chance even though baffled, as all the rest of the band were, by the director's stated aim 'to destroy the idea of Culture [because] Culture is an alibi of Imperialism'. At the beginning of June Godard spent several days at Olympic Studios with a film crew, shooting the evolution of a new song for the album in progress, from first rehearsal to finished track.

This third, and most notorious, of Mick's roles on record in as many months had a long history among the musicians who were still his greatest heroes. Blues had always been known as 'the devil's music' and, indeed, rather revelled in its identification with evil eyes and cloven hooves. The immortal Robert Johnson reputedly owed his talent to a pact with Satan and, as if in corroboration, went on to write 'Me and the Devil Blues' (including the line 'I'm gonna beat my woman till I get satisfied').

But in fact the idea had come to Mick after reading Mikhail Bulgakov's novel *The Master and Margarita,* another in the library of esoteric literature he had acquired through Marianne. One of the few satirists to flourish in Stalin's Russia, Bulgakov depicts the devil as a sophisticated, even sensitive figure, visiting Moscow in the 1930s and being appalled by its stifling bureaucracy and philistinism. The fantasy also has a sequence re-creating what Christians regard as Satan's ultimate triumph, Pontius Pilate's weak-kneed refusal to save Jesus from the Cross. Its climax is a 'Spring Ball' given by the devil, at which 'all the dark celebrities of history' pour out of hell's open gates.

Mick's lyric, originally titled 'The Devil Is My Name', borrowed Bulgakov's device of having Satan introduce himself with silky urbanity as 'a man of wealth and taste', then went on to review all the human catastrophe he had engineered down the centuries, from Pilate's refusal to reprieve Christ through the Bolsheviks' murder of the Russian royal family ('Anastasia screamed in vain') to Nazism, John F. Kennedy's assassination, and the modern age, where 'every cop is a criminal and all the sinners saints'. With an economy that more serious versifiers might have envied, the devil's orchestration of Hitler's mechanised onslaught and the Holocaust was compressed into: 'Rode a tank / Held a general's rank / While the Blitzkrieg raged and the bodies stank.'

What he had written was one of the tiny number of epic pop lyrics, worthy to rank alongside Lennon's 'A Day in the Life' and Dylan's 'Tangled Up in Blue'. But at the time he felt far from confident about taking such a step. 'I knew it was a good song,' he would recall. 'It had its poetic beginning and then it had historical references and then philosophical jottings and so on . . . It's all very well to write that in verse but to make it into a pop song is something different. Especially in England – you're skewered on the altar of pop culture if you become pretentious.'

As the track neared completion under its new title, 'Sympathy for the Devil', with Jean-Luc Godard still filming, a new triumph for the forces of darkness needed to be chalked up. John F. Kennedy's younger brother Robert, now himself a presidential candidate, was assassinated in a kitchen corridor of the Ambassador Hotel, Los Angeles, after a midnight speech which had seemed to set him on course for the White House. Mick accordingly updated the line 'killed Kennedy' to 'killed the

Kennedys'. On the final night of shooting, the hot film lights set the studio's ceiling ablaze and the fire brigade had to be called while producer Jimmy Miller, helped by Bill Wyman, scrambled to rescue the precious tapes. Nor would it be the last time that playing the song seemed to have unpredictable and unpleasant results.

Godard's film turned out to be an unintelligible Marxist-Maoist rant in which the great auteur seemed to forget his own maxim that 'cinema is the truth twenty-four times per second'. There were baffling scenes of American-accented Black Power figures brandishing firearms in what was all too obviously a south London scrapyard, hostages in a newspaper shop being humiliated by children, and – a recurrent motif – young women enduring highly unpleasant acts of persecution and violence. A succession of voice-overs read from Hitler's *Mein Kampf*, droned far-left dogma, irrelevantly pastiched American detective fiction or delivered weighty aphorisms such as 'Orgasm is the only moment when you can't cheat life'.

After viewing the film in rough cut, the producers realised their only hope of putting bums on cinema seats. The documentary scenes of the Stones at Olympic Studios were given equal prominence to the 'fictitious' ones and Godard's title, *One Plus One*, was changed to that of the track they were recording. Whereas Godard had intended to show 'Sympathy for the Devil' as a work still in progress, its finished version in soundtrack now rounded off the film. Godard himself had no idea how drastically his work had been re-edited until its première at the London Film Festival four months later. He was so enraged that he threw a punch at one of the producers in the cinema foyer.

The Stones' sequences, however – Godard evidently believing them to be a political statement needing no elucidation – were shot in a style as simple and straightforward as the rest of the filmy was tricksy, without voice-overs or arty cuts and employing long stretches of real time. *Sympathy for the Devil* the movie thus has enduring fascination as a window on the band in its most turbulent era and the creation of Mick's only masterpiece through the most presumptuous of all his masquerades.

Here he is dressed in a white smock with matching trousers, seated among the studio's hardboard room dividers and dirty teacups – for Olympic resembles nothing so much as a low-grade government office – playing the song over for Keith to his own more than adequate guitar accompaniment. He originally intended 'a sort of Bob Dylan feel', and one early version has a churchy organ motif by session musician Nicky Hopkins. Then Keith suggests playing it to a souped-up samba beat, adding an African drummer, Rocky Dijon. Mick, whose childhood mimic's repertoire always featured lots of animal noises, goes off to practise screeching like a parrot for the intro, to suggest witch doctors and voodoo. There are unkindly lingering shots of Brian Jones, an isolated figure whose part in the song looks minimal, even though off camera he is still bedevilling Mick and Keith's every effort to go straight. Indeed, the FBI hardly needed Acid King David Snyderman to ensure that the Stones never re-entered America, but could simply have left it to Brian. On 20 March he had been questioned by police after an unsuccessful suicide attempt by Linda Keith at his flat while he was out. On 21 May Scotland Yard's drugs squad had busted him again, this time allegedly finding forty-four grains of cannabis inside a ball of brown wool. He was currently on £2,000 bail and waiting trial at Inner London Sessions on that charge plus a further one of breaching his probation order of the previous December.

Shot from behind in his hardboard booth, the one-time instrumental virtuoso merely strums a guitar – often appears only to pretend to strum it. His hair is oddly dark, as if its much-shampooed blondness has drained away along with his golden talent. The only time he's seen leaving his gimcrack cell is to join an improvised vocal group, including both his ex-girlfriend Anita Pallenberg and his current one, Suki Poitier, for the witch-coven chorus of 'woo-woo, woo-woo!' towards the end.

In the course of numerous takes, Mick's voice assumes the character it will have forever afterwards. By now, the Deep South impersonation has become so extreme as to be almost unrecognisable as such, but instead seems the unique dialect of Planet Jagger. Its low is almost Uriah Heep-ishly soft and sibilant: 'Pleeze 'lau me to interdooce mahself

. . . Ah'm a ma-yne of wealth and tay-yeast . . .' Its high is a glottal bel-
low that occasionally creates an entirely new vowel sound: 'Pleezed to
meechu . . . hope you guess mah NOERME!'

Sympathy for the Devil leaves no doubt as to who is now running the
whole diabolic show, and includes a moment that will be repeated many
times over the next forty years in hotel suites, dressing rooms and backstage enclosures across the world. A member of the support staff deferentially sidles up to Mick and murmurs a question in his ear: is it okay
if this happens . . . is he cool with so-and-so doing such and such? He
considers for a moment, then nods.

PART II

THE TYRANNY OF COOL

CHAPTER ELEVEN

'The Baby's Dead, My Lady Said'

The Stones' central role in *Sympathy for the Devil* was a reminder that they had yet to make a feature film of their own and, in particular, that Mick's obvious potential as a screen actor still remained untapped. He was evidently keenly aware of this, and could be quite curt with interviewers who brought up *Only Lovers Left Alive*, the dystopian fantasy in which he was supposed to have co-starred with Keith three years earlier. 'I've forgotten about *Only Lovers Left Alive* and it's about time everyone else did,' he snapped at the *New Musical Express*. 'We'll do a film at the right time, with the right director and in the right way. I want to do something of value, not another pop-stars-on-ice fiasco.'

Actually, finding the right screen vehicle for the Stones and him – or just him – was at the top of Mick's agenda, right up there with getting back on the road in America. One short-lived idea, fired by his interest in Arthurian legend, was a film version of the anonymous fourteenth-century poem *Gawain and the Green Knight* featuring himself as Sir Gawain. The script was to have been co-written with his friend Christopher Gibbs and the budget to have come from the Stones' collective coffers (a decision taken at a Round Table meeting at 46a Maddox Street, of which their two ordinary men-at-arms, Bill and Charlie, were blissfully unaware).

Efforts still continued to get Mick into Anthony Burgess's *A Clockwork Orange*, the rights to which were now owned by American producer Si Litvinoff. The photographer Michael Cooper came up with a script and a plan to shoot the film inexpensively on location around London, but then Litvinoff made a deal with Stanley Kubrick for the version eventually released in 1971 with Malcolm McDowell in the Alex role that seemed so perfect for Mick. Another idea was a screen version of *The Master and Margarita*, the Mikhail Bulgakov novel that had inspired 'Sympathy for the Devil'. He was keen enough to portray Satan for real, especially if Marianne could play opposite him, but no one seemed to know how to make it happen.

It was his older friend, the handsome and sophisticated Donald Cammell, who finally brought him the right film project. As well as a successful portrait painter, Cammell was an accomplished screenwriter with one Hollywood production, *Duffy*, starring James Coburn, already to his credit. Early in 1968, he wrote an original treatment entitled *The Performers* with Mick specifically in mind. The story was of a young Cockney hoodlum named Chas, on the run from his own mob and forced to seek refuge in the house of a reclusive rock star named Turner. The action moved between the sadistic world of Chas's gang boss, Harry Flowers, and the weird mansion where Turner and two live-in girlfriends initiated him into drugs, kinky sex and transvestism.

In late-sixties London, Cammell's mixture of gangsters and rock culture hardly strained credulity. The fearsome Kray twins, Reggie and Ronnie, had run organised crime in the East End for years while simultaneously hobnobbing with showbiz celebrities, politicians, even royalty, and becoming icons of Swinging London through David Bailey's photographs. Ever since Andrew Oldham's Reg the Butcher, the Stones' entourage had included a sprinkling of villains who tended to be both psychotically violent and homosexual.

The most prominent was David Litvinoff, reputedly a former lover of Ronnie Kray, though some said pint-size, hyperactive 'Litz' and paranoid-schizophrenic Ronnie only used to go out picking up boys together. Litvinoff it was, after the Redlands bust, who established that Nicky Cramer wasn't a police informer after beating him to a pulp.

The role of Turner offered Mick that long-sought chance to do something right outside the traditional pop-movie genre – perhaps even of value – and he took the shortest time he ever had, or ever would, to say yes. Cammell then pitched *The Performers* to his agent, Sanford 'Sandy' Lieberson, a London-based American who also represented the Stones for film and TV and had done the deal for them to appear in Jean-Luc Godard's *Sympathy for the Devil* as well as trying to set up *A Clockwork Orange* and *The Master and Margarita* for Mick.

Recognising *The Perfomers* as a hot commercial proposition, Lieberson offered his services as producer and suggested Cammell should direct the film as well as script it. Every major Hollywood studio at this time had a British offshoot, focused mainly on the youth market, and, with Mick's name attached, Lieberson had no difficulty in selling the project to Ken Hyman, UK head of production for Warner Bros–Seven Arts, whose father, Eliot, owned the company. Commercial prospects looked even bonnier when the gifted cinematographer Nicolas Roeg came on board as co-director, and a top young British actor, twenty-nine-year-old James Fox – hitherto best known for upper-class roles like Tony in Joseph Losey's *The Servant* – agreed to go working class and play the fugitive gangster, Chas.

The budget was set at $1.1 million, a more than respectable figure for 1968. Mick was to receive $100,000 for an eleven-week shoot on location in London the following autumn, plus 7.5 per cent of the gross. Included in the fee was a soundtrack by Jagger and Richard which Warner would then release as an album on their eponymous record label. 'That was when I first came into contact with Allen Klein,' Sandy Lieberson recalls. 'His reaction when I told him about the soundtrack and album deal was "Over my dead body." I just told him Mick wanted to do it, so he had no choice but to negotiate. But he was one of the most obnoxious people I ever met.'

First in line, however, came the album intended to restore the Stones' musical credibility after their unhappy detour into *Sgt. Pepper*-land. Having no tours, criminal trials or psychological skirmishes with unwanted managers to distract them, the band had worked quickly and cohesively under producer Jimmy Miller, and the result was scheduled for British release by Decca in July. 'Sympathy for the Devil', its undisputed centrepiece, could have provided a thrillingly attention-grabbing concept for the entire collection, but the Stones had unfortunately queered that particular pitch for themselves with their feeble masquerade as 'Satanic Majesties'. Instead, the album was entitled *Beggars Banquet,* a paradox suggesting Old English legends of kings waiting at table on serfs (Mick's bedtime reading again) as well as the Stones' own reputation as lords of misrule. But the content was as devoid of medieval minstrelsy as of *Their Satanic Majesties'* fey-ness and artifice. As luck would have it, American music had created a new genre which allowed the Stones to return to their roots and yet stay at the cutting edge. Country and western had been as cru-cial as blues in the creation of rock, but previously had always been identified with naff rhinestone cowboys and right-wing rednecks. Now younger bands, interested in their heritage, had spiced it up as country rock, mixing the beat-making weaponry of Fender guitars and Ludwig drums with traditional instruments like violins, mando-lins, slide guitars or dobros; exchanging hippie smocks and amulets for western shirts, buckskin jackets and ten-gallon hats. Bob Dylan's backing musicians, the Band, had recorded an instant classic album, *Music from Big Pink,* exploring diverse forms of folk and hillbilly music, while Dylan himself embraced the form in his *John Wesley Harding* and *Nashville Skyline* albums, the latter with help from country colossus Johnny Cash.

Two young country-rock pioneers had come into the Stones' orbit, initially as fans, then as instructors in the new form. One (fated also to be a victim) was an astoundingly pretty twenty-one-year-old named Gram Parsons, just recruited to the Byrds and about to play a pivotal role on their first country album, *Sweetheart of the Rodeo*. The other was twenty-one-year-old Ryland 'Ry' Cooder, a slide-guitar virtuoso who had previously worked with the blues-man Taj Mahal and Captain Beefheart's Magic Band. When Cooder showed Keith Richard the trick of 'open G' tuning – so that the guitar strings play a G major without any fingering on the fretboard – he little imagined how he was shaping Rolling Stones intros for-ever afterwards.

'Sympathy for the Devil' and 'Street Fighting Man' apart, *Beggars Banquet* thus became a mixture of blues and country rock on which Mick's accent veered back and forth between the Mississippi Delta and the Appalachian Mountains. 'Parachute Woman' brought blues sexual imagery into the jet age ('Parachute Woman . . . la-aynd on me tonight . . .'), while 'Stray Cat Blues' was a leer at schoolgirl Stones groupies ('Ah can see yaw fifteen years old . . . no, Ah don't want yaw ID . . .') which nowadays might bring a knock on the door from the police. Blues purism went a little too far with 'Prodigal Son', a straight copy of 'The Prodigal Son' by the Reverend Robert Wilkins, for which Jagger and Richard took a songwriting credit, believing Reverend Wilkins to be dead. (He was in fact still very much alive, and cut up extremely rough when he found out.) Brian Jones's instrumental virtuosity featured for what would be the last time, notably on slide guitar in a ballad with the horribly ironic title 'No Expectations'. As if feeling some vague premo-nition, Mick's voice took on a melancholy that made it seem suddenly human again: 'Never in mah sweet, short life have I felt . . . lahk this . . . befaw . . .'

His lingering desire to write a populist chant *à la* John Lennon was reflected in 'Salt of the Earth' with its right-on leftist plea for 'the hard-working people . . . the uncounted heads' (as long, of course, as they didn't come too close). He was serious enough about it to fly to Los Angeles with Jimmy Miller to supervise the overdubbing of a full gospel choir. There he met America's hottest new band, the Doors, and, in their classically beautiful lead singer, Jim Morrison, witnessed a performer who took risks he himself would never dare. The previous December, Morrison had become the first rock star to be arrested in mid-show, after telling his audience a policeman had sprayed him with Mace backstage. A year from now, he would be charged with indecent exposure onstage; three years from now, he would be buried in the same Paris cemetery as Molière, Colette and Oscar Wilde, and attracting posthumous fans by the hundred every week. Mick said he found Morrison 'boring'. (To borrow the sixties' most famous riposte, 'He would, wouldn't he?')

The *Beggars Banquet* cover, art-directed by the Stones themselves, once again had nothing to do with either banquets or beggars, and plumbed depths of bad taste unimagined by even Andrew Oldham. It showed the grimy toilet wall of a Los Angeles car-repair shop scrawled with graffiti gibes at President Lyndon Johnson, Mao Tse-tung, Frank Zappa and Bob Dylan, and a subtitle 'Music from Big Brown', parodying the Band's country classic, *Music from Big Pink*, which was Keith's particular contribution. Even though the actual toilet pedestal was barely in shot, both Decca and the Stones' American label, London, pronounced the graffiti offensive and refused to manufacture the cover. The Stones equally flatly refused to consider any alternative one, and in the resulting impasse the album lost its prime summer release slot – a major disappointment to Mick, who'd wanted it to come out on 26 July, his twenty-fifth birthday.

Instead, he could only preview the album to his musician friends at a party at the Vesuvio Club (a venture into legitimacy by Keith's drug dealer, Spanish Tony Sanchez, which was to burn down in mysterious circumstances not long afterwards). Guests including John Lennon and Paul McCartney enjoyed a buffet featuring mescaline punch and a hashish-impregnated birthday cake, then listened to *Beggars Banquet*'s two lead tracks, 'Sympathy for the Devil' and 'Street Fighting Man'. Both were brilliant, the company agreed, but Mick's triumph was spoiled when McCartney slipped the club deejay an advance copy of the Beatles' epically long new single and Hades got elbowed aside by 'Hey Jude'.

London Records were not so squeamish about releasing 'Street

Fighting Man' as the Stones' next American single on 31 August, although the argument for holding it back seemed even stronger than in Europe. Following the assassination of Dr Martin Luther King on 4 April, race riots and vicious official fight-backs had convulsed major cities across the nation all summer. Mick's (qualified) call to the barricades went on sale just days after the infamous Democratic Party convention in Chicago, when not only anti-war protesters but journalists and even delegates were beaten up in full view of TV cameras by Mayor Richard Daley's crash-helmeted police. As a result, 'Street Fighting Man' was banned by hundreds of radio stations, and so failed to make even the US Top 40. That did not stop the coy urban guerrilla from becoming a bigger hero to all the wrong kind of people than he had been since 'Satisfaction'.

By now, it was clear that Brian Jones, with his drunkenness, drugginess and horrible vulnerability to police raids, had become too big a liability to continue with the Stones and that, hampered by such a 'wooden leg' (in Mick's phrase), they could never complete their post-prison and *Satanic Majesties* renaissance by returning to the American tour circuit. Why then not simply fire him, as the Beatles did their original drummer, Pete Best, as the Yardbirds had Jeff Beck, as any top band would have done without compunction to a member who'd become more trouble than he was worth?

The answer is that the other Stones were all essentially nice people who shrank from inflicting such a blow, however necessary for their collective survival. Even the usually selfish, calculating Mick could not forget the passion for the blues that had first brought them together, or that the band had originally been Brian's and, without his initial enthusiasm and drive, would never have got off the ground at all. Thus, long after he had ceased to be a viable member of the line-up, his bandmates did their best to maintain an outward show of unity and – as far as it was possible for spoiled, egocentric young rock gods – to look after him.

He was still awaiting trial for the cannabis allegedly found in his flat on 21 May and also for breaching the probation order made after his previous bust, in December 1967. To reduce the risk of further police raids during these summer months on bail, it was clearly advisable to get him right away from London. Since he had nowhere to go but his parents' home in genteel Cheltenham, he and his girlfriend Suki Poitier were installed at Keith's Sussex cottage, Redlands, with Tom Keylock, the Stones' driver–bodyguard, to keep an eye on him. It was in no sense an exile or banishment; the other Stones would periodically meet up at Redlands for rehearsals, even though Brian was seldom in a condition to do more than woozily strum along. In between, he swilled brandy laced with Mandrax, ill-treated the uncomplaining Suki, and scanned the music papers, terrified of reading that he'd been replaced without the others telling him – by Mick's late guitar tutor Eric Clapton, perhaps, now that Cream were set to disband.

Mick's relief at having Brian out of the way was tempered by moments of concern that surprised even Marianne, the only person to whom as a rule he showed his sensitive, caring side. One day at Cheyne Walk, while casting a hexagram from the *I Ching Book of Changes* – a regular domestic routine in any sixties' pop-star home – she read a prophecy that Brian would suffer 'death by water'. Mick became alarmed, and insisted they both drive down to Redlands at once. But the kindly gesture misfired. Fastidious as ever, he did not fancy the dinner Brian and Suki had cooked, instead going off with Marianne to a local pub. Brian took it as a mortal insult and there was a fist-fight between the pair which ended with Brian jumping into Keith's four-foot-deep pond and Mick hauling him out to the ruination of a pair of new velvet trousers.

On 26 September Mick and Keith both attended Inner London Sessions to support Brian publicly yet again – and see him treated with unexpected clemency. Despite strong evidence that the cannabis had been planted, he was found guilty of possession, but the court decided it had been a lapse from sincere efforts to clean up and he escaped with a £50 fine, plus £105 costs. Afterwards the other two joined him to face the paparazzi with arms protectively draped around his shoulders.

In the wake of this atypical good luck came a musical project that concentrated Brian's mind as the Stones no longer could. On visits to Morocco, Brion Gysin had turned him on to the Master Musicians of

Jajouka, a pipe-and-drum ensemble from a remote village in the Rif Mountains whose playing could induce trances and was even said to possess healing powers. In a resurgence of his old earnest musicological self, Brian planned to record Jajouka's mystic pipers *in situ*, then overdub a rock accompaniment to show the affinity between North Africa's and North America's musical traditions. He had already made two trips to Jajouka with recording equipment, but both times had got too stoned to capture anything usable.

In August, just before his last court appearance, he'd returned with Suki to witness Jajouka's centuries-old Rites of Pan Festival, when a young boy was ritually garbed in the skin of a freshly slaughtered goat. This time, a professional sound engineer had accompanied him, and the Master Musicians were finally in the can. The tapes would later be released as an album, *Brian Jones Plays with the Pipes of Pan at Jajouka*, an early instance of what we now call world music. Twenty-one years later, Mick would follow his footsteps back to Jajouka and (not quite the same thing) co-opt the Master Musicians as session players for a Stones album.

Brian never knew about the *I Ching*'s chillingly accurate death-by-water prophecy, but in the Rif Mountains, watching Jajouka's Rites of Pan, he seemed to receive a different sign of having 'no expectations'. Suki and he were sitting cross-legged in the village square when a white goat was carried past to be sacrificed. It had a strangely familiar-looking blond fringe, and as Brian looked into its terrified eyes, something prompted him to whisper, 'That's *me*!'

MARIANNE WAS FIRST to make it to the big screen, starring opposite French heart-throb Alain Delon in *The Girl on a Motorcycle*. The film's trailer showed her in one-piece black leather and featured a voice-over whose supercharged sexual imagery clearly had someone other than Delon in mind: 'Now you'll know the thrill of wrapping your legs round a tornado of pounding pistons . . . like the Girl on a Motorcycle! She goes as far as she wants, as fast as she wants . . . straddling the potency of a hundred wild horses!' In America the title was changed to *Naked Under Leather*.

It was just how the public had imagined Mick and Marianne's private life ever since Chichester Quarter Sessions and the 'girl in the fur rug' headline: a non-stop high-octane sexual burn-up fuelled by cartons, if not crates, of Mars bars. In fact, Marianne would admit in *Faithfull* that she'd always found sex 'a problem' – as beautiful people not infrequently do – and that within about six months the initial passion between Mick and her had cooled to friendship, 'the kind you get when you've been married a long time and know your partner doesn't expect too much of you'. In bed, more often than not, they would have ramparts of books between them and be reading aloud to each other.

From the earliest stage, her autobiography would say, Marianne knew that Mick was continually unfaithful to her and, like the European aristocrat she was at heart, accepted it as his *droit du seigneur* over virtually every attractive female who crossed his path. 'Getting upset about a little fucking around was unhip and middle class.' Nor did she care if – in her own enigmatic words – he 'slept with men'. She herself had a few one-night stands, though more from a sense of fair play than any sense of rejection or frustration. One she would record was with Stash, Brian's Russian princeling friend and co-bustee, who appealed to her sense of the romantic by climbing up the wisteria outside 48 Cheyne Walk and through her bedroom window while Mick was working in the garden studio with Keith.

The public perception of a drug-saturated couple was even more illusory than their supposedly unbridled sex life. While Mick certainly sampled most of what was available, moderation was his watchword, as in everything else except vanity; despite being around heavy drug users all the time, he himself never took a smidgen too much or lost an iota of precious self-control. Even LSD gave up in despair after finding no inner demons with which to unsettle him. Marianne, by contrast, was both naturally addictive and recklessly adventurous. From hash and acid, she soon progressed to cocaine, which she first encountered at a party with Robert Fraser: six neat white lines for six different guests to snort through a rolled hundred-dollar bill. Unaware of the protocol, Marianne snuffled up all six, one after the other.

Mick thoroughly disapproved of her growing drug intake and did all he could to discourage it – sometimes with anger, occasionally with heartfelt tears. The main sanction he could apply was money, and as a result Marianne also had a brief affair with the drug dealer Spanish Tony, whom she found repulsive but who was generous with freebies.

Drugs for Marianne increasingly became a way of anaesthetising herself against the pressures and ordeals of life with Mick. Not the least of these was his infatuation with aristocrats, 'any silly thing with a title and a castle', most of whom bored her silly. Occasionally she would embarrass him in front of his high-born friends, as at a banquet given by the Earl of Warwick at Warwick Castle when she took five Mandrax tablets by way of hors d'œuvres and passed out into her soup. The ordeals also included visiting Mick's parents, even though they were never other than sweet to her. Rather than risk a repeat of the Warwick Castle incident in front of Joe and Eva, Mick took to going to his parents' home alone, dropping Marianne *en route* at the house of blues musician John Mayall, whose wife, Pamela, he regarded as a good influence. Chrissie Shrimpton would have recognised the controlling nature that even tried to choose suitable friends for her.

But by far the greatest pressure was living with someone who never forgot he was a rock star, who even in their most private moments together behaved as if he was 'starring in an endless film' and 'had to look good all the time for the great director in the sky'. Kind, thoughtful, generous and chivalrous though he still often was, the compulsion to be cool ruled Mick's existence and increasingly hid his nicer side. Worst of all were the moments when they put aside the books and Marianne tried to talk to him about the problems she was having with their relationship. What she came up against then was not so much rock-star cool as an old-fashioned English reserve – Keith was the same – that shied away from any discussion of emotions or feelings. His refusal, or inability, to let her under his shiny superstar shell hurt far worse in the long run than all his playing around. 'I was a victim of cool, of the tyranny of hip,' she would recall. 'It almost killed me.'

Nonetheless, they both considered themselves to be together for keeps. No sooner had they settled in at Cheyne Walk than they began looking for a country house, selflessly assisted, as ever, by Christopher Gibbs. The search was complicated by *grande dame* whims on Marianne's part that Mick still found amusing. If Gibbs found a property to view in, say, Shropshire, she would suggest 'having lunch in Henley on the way'. When he protested that Henley wasn't on the way to Shropshire, she would smile her misty smile and say, 'It *could* be on the way.' So the lunch reservation in Henley would be made, and a car journey that should have taken only three hours would use up a whole day. In any case, nothing Mick saw, however old and beautiful or stunningly contemporary, was ever quite what he was looking for.

Their shared long-term view was confirmed at the beginning of October, when the Rolling Stones office announced Marianne was expecting a baby. By then she was actually five months' pregnant, but thanks to floaty, shapeless hippie couture no one had known but the Stones' inner circle and her mother. She and Mick were agreed in wanting a girl and had already chosen the name Corrina, after the blues song by Taj Mahal ('I wouldn't trade your love for money / honey, you're my warm heart's flame.')

Mick's immediate response on learning the news was to say they should get married. Despite the sixties' vaunted sexual liberation, women who gave birth outside wedlock were still considered social outcasts and their babies stigmatised as illegitimate. In Marianne's case, it could only be seen as the final step in her chosen career as a fallen woman. However, she declined his proposal, joking that after his vociferous mother, 'there couldn't be another Mrs Jagger'.

Pop stars had, of course, been in such situations before but never publicly acknowledged it, let alone seemed quite happy about it, as Mick did. And the moral outcry, no less from those who had previously drooled over stories of fur rugs and Mars bars, was deafening. Though Marianne was technically Catholic, the Anglican Church adopted her for the purpose of denouncing her as a sinner, the Archbishop of Canterbury himself asking his congregation to pray for her. Marianne made no public response – lest a hail of stones in the biblical sense might have greeted it – but on 12 October Mick went onto David Frost's *Frost on Saturday* TV show to answer their accusers.

Pitted against him was Mrs Mary Whitehouse, self-appointed leader of a campaign to clean up 'filth' on television, now also the nation's main lay spokesperson against unmarried cohabitation and parenthood. With her metallic hair, headmistressy northern voice and glinting spectacles, Mrs Whitehouse had a way of crushing opposition rather like Margaret Thatcher a few years later. 'The fact of the matter,' she lectured Mick, 'is that if you're a Christian or a person with faith and you make that [marriage] vow, when difficulties come you have this basic thing you've accepted. You find your way through the difficulties.' His response was a credit to London School of Economics debating tradition, even though the Tyranny of Cool prevented him from admitting he'd wanted to take that vow with Marianne. '*Your* church accepts divorce. It may even accept abortion . . . am I right or wrong? I don't see how you can talk about this bond which is inseparable when the Christian church itself accepts divorce.'

Marianne's sixth month of pregnancy coincided with Mick's shooting of *The Performers*, now retitled *Performance*. Determined to take care of herself as she had not with her first child, Nicholas, she got right away from London and its narcotic temptations, retiring with her mother to a house Mick rented for her in Tuam in the wilds of Ireland's County Galway. He made constant trips out to see her, for her pregnancy was proving a difficult one, and he also needed her input on how to play his first screen role.

In fact, he had got last-minute cold feet over *Performance*, nervous that he mightn't be able to carry off the part of Turner, the reclusive rock star, and that he'd embarrass himself with intellectual friends like Gibbs and Robert Fraser. Since losing the Jagger name meant losing the whole film, producer Sandy Lieberson had Nicolas Roeg film him in a scene ahead of the main shoot, so easing him gently into the process – and making him feel too involved to pull out. Though the scene was just him alone in a room, spray-painting the wall, Lieberson said it proved the camera loved him and he was a natural. So when principal photography began in London in late October, Mick was on set, ready to make what would be the only worthwhile movie of his career.

The other Stones were not to appear in *Performance* or even feature as a band on the soundtrack, which instead featured an impressive array of top American rock names such as Randy Newman, Buffy Sainte-Marie and guitarist Lowell George. Mick himself was there primarily to be an actor, with the thing for which he was best known coming a long way second. Apart from the theme song, 'Memo from Turner', he had only one musical number on-screen, Robert Johnson's 'Come on in My Kitchen', performed with no back-up but his own guitar.

His nervousness in this alien new medium was mitigated by several familiar faces in addition to co-director Donald Cammell. The first choice to play Pherber, the senior of Turner's two live-in girlfriends, had been Hollywood actress Tuesday Weld, whose most compelling credential was having starred opposite Elvis Presley in *Wild in the Country*. Weld flew to London to start work, but then had to drop out when a too-strenuous massage injured her back. Instead, Pherber was played by Anita Pallenberg, who had already made several movies and whose knowledge of rock stars' ways, as Brian's lover before she became Keith's, was second to none. Just before the shoot, Anita, too, became pregnant, but chose to have an abortion rather than lose the role.

To lend authenticity to the homosexually tinged gangland sequences, David Litvinoff, the Stones' pet enforcer, was hired as technical adviser and dialogue coach. Litvinoff's special charge was James Fox, the hitherto posh young actor, now cast as the Cockney protection racketeer Chas. Under Litz's tutelage, Fox learned to speak in the mock-formal banter London thugs use to their victims – which makes them performers in their own right – and toured the East End, meeting several of the

Krays' henchmen and working out at a boxing gym above the Thomas à Becket pub frequented by real-life muscle. For further verisimilitude, the supporting cast included Johnny Shannon, a former fighter, as the pederastic gang boss Harry Flowers, aka Ronnie Kray, and John Bindon, an enforcer for the Krays whose specialty was cutting off people's hands with a machete.

Almost all of the film involving Mick was shot on location, inside Turner's cavernous house. Though Cammell's script placed this in run-down Notting Hill, it actually was in Lowndes Square, Belgravia, conveniently close to Cheyne Walk. The owner was Captain Leonard Plugge, an eccentric Member of Parliament and friend of royalty who had previously used it for private gaming parties. Christopher Gibbs was brought in to create a rock star's lair with Moroccan cushions, candles, mirrors and closets bursting with unisex clothes. All the windows were blacked out, to deter prying fans and heighten the claustrophobic atmosphere.

Sandy Lieberson, it soon transpired, had not merely been schmoozing: Mick really *was* a natural – and, more than that, a director's dream. In his enthusiasm for the project and desire to learn everything possible about the screen actor's craft, his usual rock-star imperiousness, impatience and petulance vanished completely. For all eleven weeks of shooting he reported punctually for work every day, obeyed his co-directors Nic Roeg and Cammell's instructions to the letter, endured the repetitiveness and frequent tedium of film-making without complaint, and to the other cast members and crew came across as the friendliest, funniest, least pretentious of people. 'It was,' Lieberson recalls wistfully, 'a *very* happy shoot.'

According to folklore, Mick constructed his on-screen persona from the velvet-voiced devilment of Brian in happier times and the saturnine menace of Keith. But apart from dyed-black hair, Turner was pure Jagger, from his rouged and mascara'd face to his huge-buckled hipster trousers, alternately challenging, teasing, haughty, moody, or reading out passages from clever books in a cut-glass accent that would not have disgraced the Royal Academy of Dramatic Art. At one point, the rock 'n' roll hermit was actually referred to as 'Old Rubber-lips'. Even Mars bars made a brief appearance, lined up beside the front doorstep having, somewhat implausibly, arrived with the morning milk.

It was just as well that the house's windows were blacked out. One scene required Turner to smoke joints in the bath with Pherber and his other live-in girlfriend, Lucy, played by an androgynous French nineteen-year-old named Michèle Breton, whom Cammell had discovered on a Saint-Tropez beach when she was only thirteen. To begin with, Mick was reluctant to use real joints in the bath scene lest it should spoil his focus, but was soon persuaded otherwise. Indeed, the reek of pot throughout the shoot made art director John Clark recall later: 'You took one breath and you got stoned.' As one of the crew quipped to his colleagues, the drug supply was more reliable than the location catering. 'You want to get a fuckin' joint, they're coming out of your ear'oles. You want a cup of tea, you got no fuckin' chance.'

At its core, *Performance* was a study of Mick's unsettling effect on other males, especially those who considered themselves most unassailably macho. Like so many unsuspecting guests at rock-star parties, Chas was to be fed hallucogenic drugs, then undergo a trip orchestrated by Turner to shred away all his prized masculinity and expose the lurking demon that he might be just as gay as his avenging gang boss. At the climax, cross-dressed in a frilled shirt and curly wig, he became a grotesque parody of Turner, while Mick's Turner metamorphosed into Harry Flowers. The film-makers were banking on the shock value of seeing Mick in an ordinary suit, with his hair scraped back, taking care of business in a manner unthinkable for sixties rock icons (but exactly as he would be doing a short time hence). Here, too, he Cockney-sneered the line that justified the film's title, and would be endlessly replayed on YouTube into the next century: 'The only performance that makes it, that *re-ally* makes it, that makes it all the way, is the one that achieves madness.'

Though Anita was shown teasing and toying with Chas, so much like real-life Anita, the principal seducer clearly was Turner/Mick. A scene in Turner's private recording studio briefly re-created the Stones' front man performing an erotically charged dance with a fluorescent light tube for his mesmerised audience of one. In the film's most memorable *coup de cinéma*, Chas was shown waking up in bed beside Turner. The long-haired figure instantly mounted him and kissed him devouringly. Only when it brushed its hair aside was it revealed to be not Mick but the androgynous Michèle Breton.

There were also troilistic sex scenes between Turner, Pherber and Lucy which would allow millions who had fantasised about Mick in bed to watch him there in hugely magnified form – his little rib cage and hairless flesh; the prodigious lips in profile, gaping open like some scarlet-daubed volcano as Anita's tongue flicked down like forked lightning from above. At these moments the set was closed and Nicolas Roeg filmed in 16mm to give more of a home-made porn-flick feeling. The gusto with which both played their parts gave rise to rumours that, with Marianne safely in County Galway, Mick and Anita actually did have sex on camera. Anita would always deny it, saying that at the time she was 'a one-guy girl' (i.e., faithful to Keith) and that, anyway, Mick 'was the last guy I would do that with'. Even if merely simulation, it was so convincing that, without Mick's knowledge, the outtakes were turned into a half-hour short entitled 'Rehearsal for *Performance*'. And on the internet today one can see still photographs of him during the sequence, lying beside Breton, some with a hand shielding his genitals, some not.

With Brian still at Redlands, Anita and Keith had borrowed Robert Fraser's flat in Mount Street, Mayfair, also a conveniently short distance from the Plugge house. But, like Arthur Miller while his wife Marilyn Monroe was shooting *The Seven-Year Itch*, Keith firmly refused ever to come and watch Anita in front of the camera. He was deeply uneasy about her sex scenes with Mick, even on the assumption these went no further than acting, and almost as put out that Mick should be doing something without him and the rest of the band. He could not stay away completely, however, and would sit outside in his car, sending in anguished notes to Anita – about which, Sandy Lieberson recalls, 'she didn't give a shit'. To Donald Cammell she seemed to be 'teasing Keith about wanting Mick, the way she used to tease Brian about wanting Keith'.

Forty-two years later Keith would claim in his autobiography to have hit back at Mick's supposed affair with Anita by rogering Marianne at 48 Cheyne Walk, escaping through the window – leaving his socks behind – when they heard the sound of Mick's car. But since at the time Marianne was heavily pregnant and away in Ireland, one can only assume he was thinking of their brief fling before she and Mick got together (or alternatively, as with other things in his book, just making it up).

Anyway, a far readier weapon of retaliation was the song he and Mick were committed to write for *Performance*'s soundtrack. He refused to buckle down and work on it, until Mick had – tearfully – to admit defeat to Donald Cammell and suggest hammering out something with Cammell instead. Together they wrote a track entitled 'Memo from Turner', but still did not solve the problem, since Keith was also supposed to play on it, and in the studio resolutely ensured – as only he knew how – that it sounded terrible. Finally he had to be replaced by the young slide-guitar wizard Ry Cooder and the song credited to Mick alone. Apart from its title, 'Memo from Turner' had nothing to do with the story or even London, but was an invocation of 'Noo Awleans on a hot and dusty night' in the spirit of the soundtrack's other American country rockers. Despite lacking Keith, or possibly for that very reason, it would stand as Mick's best-ever solo track.

In the end, *Performance* was less a Mick Jagger vehicle than a Nicolas Roeg one. For it had all the trademarks that would make Roeg one of the most influential directors of the 1970s: the scenes out of sequence, the switches from colour to black-and-white or movie to stills, the distorting close-ups and enigmatic long shots not only recalling European cinematic surrealists like Luis Buñuel but the nightmarish and conspicuously gay paintings of Francis Bacon. It was ahead of *Easy Rider* in using a multi-artist rock-music soundtrack, including an early example of rap, and in celebrating the drug culture;

it was ahead of a whole voyeuristic decade in on-screen eroticism; it was ahead of Michael Caine's *Get Carter* and Clint Eastwood's *Dirty Harry* – and remains way, way ahead of twenty-first-century upstarts like Guy Ritchie – in making violence seem cool. Its future admirers would include directors of the standing of Stanley Kubrick, Bernardo Bertolucci and Martin Scorsese.

And the studio hated it. Warner Bros–Seven Arts' UK head of production, Ken Hyman, had not exactly been expecting a pop-star romp in the style of the Beatles' *Help!* but was horrifed by the first rushes, particularly the joint-smoking bath scene with Mick, Anita and Michèle Breton in which, he complained, 'even the bathwater is dirty'. Work was shut down for three days while Sandy Lieberson persuaded Hyman to let the shoot run its course. Then, when the footage went to be processed, the Humphries Film Laboratories told Lieberson it contravened British pornography laws and, fearing prosecution as an accessory, destroyed the print in front of him. The Technicolor labs proving less sensitive, a second print was made and shown to Ken Hyman. He pronounced it unreleasable as a Hollywood product – a judgement endorsed by his studio-boss father, Eliot – and the film was shelved indefinitely.

One part, however, did receive speedy exposure. The on-set photographs of a naked, tumescent Mick were published in *Oz* magazine, *en route* to the future internet. And 'Rehearsal for *Performance*', the off-cuts from his sex scene with Anita, fell into the hands of Jim Haynes, American co-founder of the Underground porno newspaper *Suck*. Haynes included it in *Suck*'s Wet Dream Film Festival in Amsterdam, where it was voted winner in the One-Night Stand category.

ON 19 NOVEMBER Marianne returned to London from County Galway and checked into a private maternity clinic in St John's Wood. Her condition had been giving increasing cause for concern, so much so that at one point Mick had to take a Harley Street gynaecologist, Dr Victor

Bloom, out to Ireland to examine her. Fears that she might be too anae-
mic to bring the baby to term proved sadly correct: the day after entering
the clinic she suffered a miscarriage.

Marianne, as she would later write, felt 'devastated and guilty . . .
and it took me ages before I could even begin to grapple with my feelings about it'. For Mick, the loss of the baby he so much hoped would
be a little girl named Corrina can have been no less devastating. Yet
he did not allow it to derail him any more than had his trial, national
humiliation and imprisonment a year earlier. Under the Tyranny of
Cool, he showed no emotion to the outside world – and almost none
to the distraught Marianne – simply picking himself up and carrying
on with his superstar life as if nothing could ever be more important.
His only vague hint at heartbreak was a seemingly incongruous line in
'Memo from Turner' (actually recorded some time earlier): 'the baby's
dead, my lady said'.

The end of 1968 allowed little time for sad reflection. Early in December, the Stones' *Beggars Banquet* album was finally released in Britain and
America, having been delayed for four months by the impasse over its
toilet-wall cover artwork. In the end, they had settled for a plain white
front cover with the title in italic script and 'RSVP' in the bottom left-
hand corner, just like all Mick's real-life invitations to the homes of toffs.
Inside was a picture of the band at a banquet table in medieval motley, with Mick biting an apple brandished on the end of Keith's knife.
Unluckily, the Beatles double-disc White Album had just appeared, and
Beggars Banquet attracted criticism for seeming to copy its minimalist
cover design and for the brevity of some tracks. But every critic hailed
it as a magnificent return to form after that previous duff invite, *Their
Satanic Majesties Request*.

The album's UK launch was a banquet-style lunch for the press in
a wood-panelled room at London's super-respectable Kensington Gore
Hotel. All five Stones were present and correct in stripy Dickensian tail-
coats and top hats, and Tudor-style serving wenches with frilled caps,
aprons and low-cut bodices brought round the food. In a further time
shift, to silent-movie slapstick, there followed a custard-pie fight in

which VIP guests like Britain's future ambassador to Washington, Lord Harlech – and even the usually circumspect PR Les Perrin – joined with enthusiasm. Face dripping with white foam, Mick somewhat rashly announced that everyone's dry-cleaning bills should be sent to him. He later wrote a charming letter to the hotel, apologising for the mess.

Yet despite this triumph in the transatlantic album charts, and their determined public show of unity, the Stones had internal problems by now far worse than just Brian Jones. Mick's apparent switch of focus to film acting, and the awkwardness with Keith over his sex scenes with Anita, seemed to have halted the Jagger–Richard partnership in its tracks. During the seven months since their last performance together (a surprise appearance at the *NME*'s annual Pollwinners' Concert), Bill and Charlie had begun to wonder if they still were a band at all. In the continuing absence of any definite tour plans, something was urgently needed to restore a sense of unity and, especially, make Mick and Keith best mates again.

The answer came from *Performance*'s producer, Sandy Lieberson, in his other role as film and television agent for the whole band. Lieberson suggested they should make a one-hour TV Christmas special, thereby in one stroke reaching as many fans as they would by months on the road. The idea had instant appeal to Mick because the previous Christmas the Beatles had appeared in just such a special, *Magical Mystery Tour*, which turned out the most resounding flop of their career. True, the Stones would be accused of following the Beatles yet again, but this could be a first chance to trump them.

Rather than seek finance from the BBC or one of the commercial companies and be subject to interference or censorship, the Stones themselves put up £50,000 for an independent production which could then be syndicated worldwide. To direct, Mick approached Michael Lindsay-Hogg, whom he had known since the *Ready Steady Go!* days and who'd shot the riveting 'Jumpin' Jack Flash' promo (as well as sequences for the Beatles' 'Hey Jude' and 'Revolution'). Together they searched for a theme from the same well of 1950s nostalgia as motor-coach mystery tours. 'I kept doodling circles on a notepad,' Lindsay-Hogg remembers.

'Then it suddenly came to me, "The Rolling Stones' Rock 'n' Roll Circus". I called Mick and said just those seven words, and he got it immediately.'

The idea was as simple and contained as *Magical Mystery Tour*'s had been vague and picaresque. The Stones would perform in the setting of a circus big top which, Mick specified, should not be 'glamorous Ringling Barnum & Bailey but like some tatty little European circus'. Their supporting cast would be other rock acts who were friends or whom they admired, interspersed with circus turns of amusing kitschness. Getting the other musical big names, Lindsay-Hogg remembers, was the easiest part. 'Mick just took out his little address book and called people up. There were no managers or agents involved. They were a community. It made me think of the time in France, when all the Impressionist painters were still friends, before they became corrupted by fame and money.'

In this fraternal spirit, one of Mick's first calls was to Pete Townshend of the Who, the band that had most publicly supported Keith and himself after the Redlands bust. Though the Stones had never seemed much interested in fostering young talent, it was also decided to give a spot to an up-and-coming band. The newly formed Led Zeppelin were rejected in favour of Jethro Tull, wacky folk rockers whose lead singer–flautist, Ian Anderson – sporting hair longer and wilder than any Stone's had ever been – liked to perform standing on one leg like a stork. At Keith's insistence, a spot was reserved for the American bluesman with the most un-American of names, Taj Mahal. To lighten the male atmosphere – and reintroduce another voice long absent from the pop scene – Marianne was also invited to take part.

Another Lindsay-Hogg idea was to feature a one-night-only supergroup made up of stars from other bands in the fashion then just starting. As vocalist he thought of Stevie Winwood and Paul McCartney, but decided the idea would most appeal to John Lennon, especially in view of Lennon's distance from the other Beatles since becoming involved with Yoko Ono. Also in the line-up were Eric Clapton, drummer Mitch Mitchell from the Jimi Hendrix Experience, and Keith on bass guitar, with the Israeli violin virtuoso Ivry Gitlis as a surprise walk-on. Their name – a Lennonesque reference to the grubby raincoats associated with sexual perverts – was the Dirty Mac.

Rehearsals and filming took just two days, 10 and 11 December, on a scaled-down circus set at London's Intertel Studios. To maintain continuity and add a surrealistic touch, the audience wore bright yellow, blue or orange ponchos and floppy-brimmed felt hats. The rock sets were punctuated by clowns, acrobats, a fire-eater and a rather elderly male-and-female trapeze act. There was also to have been a pair of boxing kangaroos, but at the last moment Yoko Ono came to Lindsay-Hogg and told him that if the kangaroos appeared, Lennon wouldn't. Otherwise, the director suffered little interference. 'Allen Klein was hardly in evidence at all,' he remembers. 'If I needed clearance on anything, which usually meant spending more money, I just asked Mick.' Shooting began around noon on 11 December with a grand procession of the cast into the circus ring to the strains of Fučik's 'Entry of the Gladiators'. Mick was ringmaster (a role originally intended for Brigitte Bardot) in scarlet tailcoat and tipped-back top hat, using his most irony-laden Cockney to announce 'sights and sounds and marvels to delight your eyes and ears'. Around him the others Stones in *Beggars Banquet*-y fancy dress mimed playing trumpets and tubas like a second, less amiable *Sgt. Pepper* band. Brian stood out gorgeously in a floor-length blue-and-gold caftan, but his face looked blank and prematurely aged and his once-gleaming eighteen-carat hair was lank and grubby.

Mick had the only real speaking part, a bantering exchange with John Lennon as 'Michael' and 'Winston' in the schmaltzy accents of American chat-show hosts. All four of the other Stones took a turn at introducing the acts, though when the film was eventually released both Brian and Bill's contributions had been cut. Under the band's internal class system, neither Bill's new Swedish girlfriend, Astrid Lundström, nor Shirley Watts was invited to join the audience.

First onstage were Jethro Tull, followed by the Who with a mini-opera entitled 'A Quick One (While He's Away)' whose references to having sex with young girls troubled 1968 ears no more than Mick's

'Stray Cat Blues'. Taj Mahal had been filmed on the previous day, so next in the running order, announced by a reverent-looking Charlie, was 'the lovely Miss Marianne Faithfull'. Seated alone in the sawdust ring, Marianne sang 'Something Better', a Goffin–Mann ballad somewhat like 'As Tears Go By', but with plangent echoes of what had befallen since ('It is absurd to live in a cage / You know there's got to be something better'). Amid the jokey glitter, she was an interlude of loveliness, classiness and pent-up sadness, as out of place in her elegant purple gown as an amethyst in a tub of popcorn.

By the time John Lennon, Eric Clapton and bass-playing Keith were ready for their one-off appearance as the Dirty Mac, it was past 10 P.M. As Lennon sang his apocalyptic 'Yer Blues' from the Beatles' White Album, Michael Lindsay-Hogg noticed a black sack to one side of the stage. When the song ended, Yoko emerged from the sack, joined Lennon at the microphone, and, with his encouragement, began to shriek and ululate just as Ivry Gitlis appeared for the scheduled violin recital. Gitlis played an accompaniment to this 'singing' with as much good grace as he could muster, and Clapton and Keith followed suit. The sequence was later titled 'Whole Lotta Yoko' as if it had been intended all along. Lennon's rock-star pals thus seemed to be saying that, whatever brickbats others might throw, his new love and creative partnership was fine with them.

The French film cameras Lindsay-Hogg was using began to give trouble and, what with one thing and another, weren't ready for the Stones' seven-song finale until almost 2 A.M. 'Keith was in a thoroughly bad temper by that time,' the director recalls. 'The crew had been working for twelve hours, the audience were tired . . . It was going to be up to Mick to hold everything together.'

The set featured the pick of *Beggars Banquet,* 'Sympathy for the Devil', 'Parachute Woman', 'No Expectations' and 'Salt of the Earth', plus 'Jumpin' Jack Flash', the just-written 'You Can't Always Get What You Want' and an old favourite, 'Route 66.' For this return to the spotlight after so long, Mick chose a surprisingly modest outfit of orange hipsters and a skimpy scarlet T-shirt that crept above his navel, plus the full maquillage he had worn in *Performance*. (Even Keith had by now succumbed to the habit, brooding over his guitar with eyes as mascara-thick as some Hollywood silent-movie vamp's.) Thanks to Mick's perfectionism and Lindsay-Hogg's problematic cameras, each song needed several retakes. It took until almost 4 A.M. to get four in the can, among them what would be Brian's last-ever solo with the band, playing slide guitar just as he had on his first-ever one.

'We still had "Sympathy for the Devil" to do – the moment everybody had been looking forward to,' Lindsay-Hogg remembers. 'We did two takes, but one wasn't right for the cameraman and the other wasn't right for the band. By that time, everyone was totally exhausted. Between four-thirty and five, I had a meeting with Mick and Sandy Lieberson, and we discussed breaking there and coming back to finish up the next evening. But we decided it would be too expensive to keep the set in place, and the next evening people would still be tired. So Mick went back to the Stones and told them, "We've got to do it one more time, and it's got to be right."'

Despite his exhaustion, he gave his diabolic Bayeux Tapestry the most extraordinary interpretation it had ever had, or would have, galvanising his sleepy audience awake in their coloured ponchos, daring the temperamental cameras to miss so much as a millisecond, focusing even Brian's beclouded features into a trance of ecstatic approval. By the end, the 'mayne of wealth and taste' had turned into a sacrificial victim, kneeling low before the camera as if for the headman's axe, then tugging off his red T-shirt to reveal that skinny yet well-muscled physique, tattooed across chest and biceps with black-magical faces and designs. 'It was the first time I realised the sheer force of Mick's will when he wanted something to happen,' Lindsay-Hogg says. 'He just *wouldn't* be denied.'

As well as yielding matchless performance footage, the *Rock 'n' Roll Circus* had achieved its object of stabilising Mick and Keith's relationship. Directly afterwards they set off with Anita, Marianne and Nicholas for an extended holiday in Brazil, which Mick had visited with Marianne in the flush of first love a year earlier. They travelled from Lisbon to Rio on a cruise liner whose largely British passengers were ocean voyagers of the old school, playing deck quoits and shuffleboard and dressing for dinner. No one apart from the younger crew members recognised them, and the archaic daily routine of organised games and endless meals proved oddly relaxing.

They spent three weeks travelling around Brazil incognito and seldom recognised, staying in conditions far more spartan than they were accustomed to and smoking industrial amounts of *maconha*, the local grass. The highlight of the trip was a visit to the Mato Grosso, the country's western prairie region, where gauchos herded cattle like movie cowboys – a sight that spurred Jagger–Richard's songwriting into action again. The plan had also been to witness voodoo rites, or macumba, but at the one ceremony they stumbled on, with Nicholas in tow, the locals were not welcoming. Nicholas would remember it as the one time when the grown-ups' being stoned meant having actual stones thrown at them.

But if the boys were all serene again, Marianne still felt 'jangled' by the rumours about Mick and Anita that had reached her from the *Performance* set as well as by her miscarriage. Suffering from a bad throat and elaborately shielded from the sun in 'hats with veils, long dresses that trailed on the ground and high red boots', she struggled around after the others, feeling like 'an apparition with a persistent cough'. As though seeking solace for little lost Corinna, Mick was even more fatherly than usual to Nicholas, carrying him uncomplainingly when he was tired, ensuring he always wore sandals on the beach in case of sharp stones.

Yet Marianne could never banish a suspicion that whatever flame had flared up during *Performance* wasn't yet extinguished, and Mick was still 'continually whispering come-ons into Anita's ear'. In fact, despite the passionate intimacy they had recently shared before the camera, Anita was back to treating him with her old indifference bordering on contempt. Indeed, she showed herself to be Keith's 'one-guy girl' (though not in a way to give Marianne much comfort) by returning from the holiday pregnant again.

Surprisingly, that most uncool of sea voyages to Rio would leave its watermark on Rolling Stones history. Among Mick and Keith's fellow passengers were a middle-aged British couple who realised the pair were celebrities of some kind and quizzed them continually during the ten days afloat, but without ever figuring out who they were or what they did for a living. 'Go on,' the couple used to plead, unavailingly, 'give us a clue . . . just a glimmer.'

In memory of those flummoxed shipmates, Mick christened Keith and himself 'the Glimmer Twins' – a neat enough paradox, considering their strobe-lit lives, but also tacit acknowledgement of being all but joined at the hip.

CHAPTER TWELVE

Some Day My Prince Will Come

Throughout pop music history, most artists who decided to fire a powerful manager and run their own career have landed themselves in the most almighty mess. Lawsuits from their vengeful former protector have crippled them financially for years to come, while the attempt to run their own career has only run it into the ground. Such stories traditionally end with a humiliating admission of defeat and hasty rehire of conventional management to pick up the pieces. The most famous exception the music industry has seen over six decades was Mick's jettisoning of Allen Klein and skilful handling of a resultant financial crisis which made the Beatles' cash troubles look petty by comparison. Yet even for him the victory was not total.

In so many ways, the stocky New Yorker with his greasy cowlick and malodorous pipe had been just what the Stones needed. The $1.25 million advance Klein bludgeoned out of Decca in 1965 had put them into a financial league far above any other British rock band, the Beatles included. It also had transformed the economics of an industry in which record companies were accustomed to calling the shots and even the most celebrated performers accepted miserly royalty rates and dubious accounting practices simply for the honour and glory of being associated with them. From then on, power moved from the labels to the artists.

If the Stones' fame, or ill fame, was mostly generated by Andrew Oldham, Klein had apparently brought wealth on a commensurate scale to them all, regardless of rank within the band. Charlie Watts had moved into a luxurious cottage near Lewes, Sussex, formerly owned by the lawyer and politician Lord Shawcross; a perfect place for autodidact Charlie to tend his collection of American Civil War memorabilia and antique silver and for his wife, Shirley, to indulge her passion for horses. Bill Wyman had gravitated from Penge to a moated fourteenth-century mansion named Gedding Hall, near Bury St Edmunds, Suffolk, which brought the former electrician the feudal rank of lord of the manor. Even Brian, despite palpably having 'no expectations', had been able to pay £30,000 for Cotchford Farm, near Harefield, Sussex, the former home of the author A. A. Milne.

But only Mick so far owned both a town and a country house. The latter was Stargroves, a rambling Gothic pile located in the Berkshire village of East Woodhay, dating back to the sixteenth century and previously owned by an eccentric nobleman named Sir Frederick Carden. Mick had bought it at the same time as 48 Cheyne Walk for a mere £25,000, but both the house and its extensive grounds were in a badly run-down state and many thousands more would have to be spent on renovations. His unofficial estate agent, Christopher Gibbs, advised caution, especially as Mick made an atypically snap decision to buy Stargroves after one late-night visit with a carload of friends and hangers-on including the American writer Terry Southern. But he insisted he'd finally found a place where 'the atmosphere felt right'. Whatever it might cost – and with Marianne around, that promised to be a lot – he was determined to restore the property to its former magnificence.

In terms of opulent houses, flash cars, unlimited clothes and expensive holidays, all five Stones looked as though they must have millions in the bank. Actually, none of them had direct control over his own earnings and none – not even their keen-witted, calculating leader, the one-time economics student – knew exactly how much wealth the band had accumulated and continued to accumulate under Allen Klein's aegis. Instead, a system had evolved, born jointly of young rock stars' impatience with mundane details and Klein's calculated policy of 'keeping the talent happy'. In those pre-credit-card days, when one of them needed money, their office sent a request to Klein's ABKCO organisation in New York. For Mick, this could be as be as large as the purchase price of Stargroves or as small as £50 to help out his brother, Chris, on the Nepal hippie trail. The money was always paid without question, from collective reserves he was encouraged to regard as bottomless.

Klein, in short, had fallen victim to one of the most familiar syndromes in pop. The deals he had made for the Stones that seemed so miraculous when they were young and hungry seemed much less so now that they were famous. The percentage they had gladly granted him then felt uncomfortable now, especially with Mick making most of the decisions. The old rule about familiarity breeding contempt had also come into play. Where once Klein's attention had been entirely focused on them – as during the Redlands drug bust – he now seemed far more concerned with other matters in his empire.

The clearest sign of this was the increasing difficulty in getting money from him. Early in 1969, Keith took the opportunity to buy number 3 Cheyne Walk, a 1717 Queen Anne house, slightly smaller than Mick's at number 48 – but just as elegant and unspoiled – whose former tenants had included a president of the Royal Society, a St Paul's Cathedral organist and the Tory politician Sir Anthony Nutting. To complete the purchase Keith needed £20,000, and the usual request went to across the Atlantic to Klein. But this time there was no immediate pay-out, as there had been for the new homes of Mick, Bill and even Brian. When volleys of phone calls and cablegrams to Klein produced no response, Keith had to send the Stones' driver–bodyguard Tom Keylock across to New York to collect the money, Ronnie Kray style. Only with the hefty Keylock standing over him did Klein finally write out the necessary cheque.

Along with everything else, the Stones relied on Klein for the upkeep of their – far from grandiose – office at 46a Maddox Street. Here, too, the cash flow from New York had become increasingly problematic; there was a mounting stack of unpaid bills, including one from the band's invaluable publicist, Les Perrin, and red-printed final demands from both the London Electricity Board and Post Office Telephones. In his role as managing director, Mick sent Klein a sardonic telex message: 'The phone and electricity will be cut off tomorrow. Also the rent is due. I am having to run the office despite your wishes. If you would like to remedy this, please do so.'

Piquantly, the first serious mutterings about Klein came from the very person who had handed the Stones over to him. Since walking out on the *Satanic Majesties* sessions two years earlier, Andrew Oldham had been in negotiation with Klein for a pay-off reflecting his (actually incalculable) contribution to their success. Klein's well-honed litigation skills were also needed in dealing with Eric Easton, Oldham's original management partner, who was still seeking redress for having been dumped back in 1965. The sometimes farcical Oldham–Easton lawsuit – during which at one point each simultaneously tried to have the other jailed for contempt of court – brought adverse financial consequences for the Stones just when their income was becoming a matter of acute concern to Mick. Pending a settlement with the co-manager they had all but forgotten, $1 million of their record royalties was frozen.

Once the Easton case was resolved, the two cronies who had carved up the Stones between them turned on one another. Oldham started legal proceedings against Klein over the very transaction which had made him seem like the Stones' saviour: their $1.25 million advance from Decca Records in 1965. This, Oldham now claimed, had never gone to its rightful recipients, but had been intercepted by Klein and used 'for his own benefit'. Instead of passing on the money to Nanker Phelge Music, the British-based company set up by Oldham and the Stones, he had paid it into an American-based one named Nanker Phelge *USA*, which he had specially created for the purpose and of which he was president and sole stockholder.

Klein indignantly denied that he'd diverted the band's money into his own coffers by such barefaced sleight of hand. Nanker Phelge USA, he said, existed solely to protect the band's income as far as possible from British income tax. All of them were guaranteed annual payments from the company (in Mick's case, around £50,000) and the residue would go into a 'balloon fund' which ultimately would be shared out among them. Nonetheless, the seeds of doubt had been sown in Mick's mind, and he had hired a firm of London solicitors with no previous connections to either Klein or the Stones to look in detail at the whole financial picture. Ominously, the unanswered calls to ABKCO in New York had included several from the band's accountants, Goodman Myers, asking for the information necessary to complete their individual income-tax returns and urgently requesting £13,000 already owing to the Inland Revenue – as it would turn out, the merest drop in the ocean.

Ten minutes' walk away from the Stones' office, in Savile Row, Mayfair, the Beatles had been taking their own doomed stab at self-management through their Apple organisation, an attempt to combine youth-oriented businesses, like recording and clothes retailing, with hippie openheartedness and openhandedness. Run with an extravagance the very opposite of Mick's regime at Maddox Street, Apple had quickly become a home for charlatans and scroungers and, although partly conceived as a tax write-off, was bleeding the Beatles whiter than the White Album.

Klein, of course, had coveted the Beatles since 1964, when they were under Brian Epstein's seemingly unassailable control, and even bagging their arch-rivals, a year later, had felt no more than second best. His seeming loss of concentration on the Stones during 1968 was largely due to his close monitoring of the chaos at Apple and realisation that the ultimate managerial prize might not have eluded him after all. Not a word of this reached Mick, even though Klein had laid a £1,000 bet with a mutual friend, Mickie Most's wife, Chrissie, that he would have the Beatles by Christmas.

To sort out Apple and fill Epstein's long-empty shoes, Paul McCartney proposed New York attorney Lee Eastman, whose daughter Linda he was on the point of marrying. But John Lennon, encouraged by Yoko, had other ideas. In January, Lennon told *Disc* and *Music Echo's*

Ray Coleman that if Apple continued spending at its present rate the Beatles would be broke in six months; a few days after the story broke, he and Yoko had a secret meeting with Allen Klein at London's Dorchester Hotel. Klein gave the same artful performance to Lennon as he had to Mick four years earlier, showing comprehensive knowledge of Beatles music and promising to make him so rich he could say 'Fuck you, money!' Lennon's response was to place himself unilaterally under Klein's management, then persuade George Harrison and Ringo Starr that this New Yorker was far preferable to McCartney's future father-in-law – thereby creating a rift within the band that would never be healed. Klein's prediction of getting the Beatles by Christmas was only a month out, but Chrissie Most still collected her £1,000.

The news reached Mick at the Stones' office via Michael Lindsay-Hogg, director of the *Rock 'n' Roll Circus*, who had gone on to film the Beatles' strife-torn recording sessions for what would become their *Let It Be* album. More than once over recent years, Mick had extolled Klein's management to Lennon and Paul McCartney and urged them, too, to become ABKCO clients. Now he was so appalled by Lennon's decision that he asked Lindsay-Hogg to 'walk him over' to the Apple building in Savile Row to voice his forebodings first-hand. There he found Klein ensconced at a boardroom table with all four Beatles and – never one for confrontation – left again without unburdening himself. Later he phoned Lennon, warning him against making 'the biggest mistake of your life', but to no avail.

Not that Mick's help was needed in projecting a negative picture of Klein. Virtually unknown to Britain's media while managing the Stones, he was now catapulted into the headlines as a kind of transatlantic cat burglar who had made off with a national treasure second only to the Crown Jewels. By an unhappy chance, he was concurrently in trouble on his home turf for having bought a near-defunct record label named Cameo-Parkway, then talked up its value with fictitious suggestions that major music companies were in a bidding war for it. As a result, dealing in Cameo-Parkway shares had been suspended on the New York Stock Exchange and Klein faced an investigation by the Securities and

Exchange Commission. He had also attracted the notice of the London *Sunday Times*'s famous Insight investigative team, for both the Cameo-Parkway affair and his handling of the Stones' $1.25 million Decca advance. Insight's front-page exposé, headed 'THE TOUGHEST WHEELER-DEALER IN THE POP JUNGLE', accused the Beatles' new manager of duping the Rolling Stones over the American Nanker Phelge company, 'lying like a trooper' and having bad breath into the bargain.

Well before these revelations, Mick had decided that Klein would have to go. But as yet he had no idea when or how that tricky operation might be accomplished. Meantime, he decided to appoint a personal financial adviser who, since his and the Stones' interests were inseparable (if far from equal), would effectively be representing the whole band.

For help in finding such an adviser he turned, as ever, to Christopher Gibbs, whose impressive family tree included a number of bankers and whose education at Eton College had bequeathed contacts far outside the antiques trade. Gibbs consequently could recommend his old Eton chum, thirty-six-year-old Prince Rupert Ludwig Ferdinand zu Loewenstein-Wertheim-Freudenberg, a descendant of Bavaria's elector palatine Friedrich I and a partner in the merchant bank Leopold Joseph. Despite his name and heritage, Prince Rupert looked and spoke like a pure-bred English aristo, was an Oxford graduate in medieval history, and a well-known party-giver and socialite. 'I thought he'd be amused by Mick and Mick would be by him,' Gibbs remembers. 'They met at Cheyne Walk and instantly got on well, even though Rupert knew nothing at all about pop music. They liked many of the same things and the same people – often surprisingly.' It was agreed that Prince Rupert would wait in the wings, conducting a thorough review of the Stones' finances – especially with regard to the looming income-tax question – until such time as an exit strategy from Klein's grip could be devised. Thus did another person of exotic European antecedents come into the Kentish lad's life, following after Giorgio Gomelsky, Alexis Korner, Andrew Loog Oldham, Marianne Faithfull and Anita Pallenberg, but destined to do his wallet more good than all the rest put together.

Klein now spent most of his time in London at Apple with the Beatles, very clearly putting the Stones a long way second but still seemingly unaware that his hold on them might be loosening. In mid-February, he did find time to attend a first viewing of *The Rolling Stones' Rock 'n' Roll Circus*, which Michael Lindsay-Hogg had been editing for the past two months. Lindsay-Hogg felt elated with the various great performances in the film and the atmosphere of good humour and harmony – so unlike the Beatles' *Let It Be* sessions, which he'd gone on to shoot. Never mind that the *Rock 'n' Roll Circus* had missed its intended Christmas television slot. The Stones' seven-song set featuring Mick's sacrificial strip-tease on 'Sympathy for the Devil' – not to mention John and Yoko, Eric Clapton and the Who – would make it hotly saleable all over the world in any season.

But at the screening, doubts began to creep in. Keith felt that the Who's mini-opera, 'A Quick One (While He's Away)', performed at the very start of filming when the audience was fresh, with Pete Townshend's arm windmilling around his guitar and Keith Moon on drums going even more berserk than usual, made them look like the stars of the whole show. By the time the Stones appeared – after all the other acts, at almost 5 A.M. – the audience had been too tired to show proper enthusiasm. In vain did Lindsay-Hogg argue that the band provided an unforgettable climax, with lipstick-and-rouged, half-naked Mick giving the most mesmerising performance of his career. Strangely, Mick himself could not see this, and agreed with Keith: the Who had upstaged them in their own film.

It was agreed that Lindsay-Hogg should shoot extra scenes with the Stones playing on their own in some exotic outdoor location, in front of an audience whose wakefulness could not be doubted. Thinking of an age when circuses meant something more sinister than clowns and candy floss, Mick and Keith flippantly suggested the Colosseum in Rome. Amazingly, this 3,000-year-old monument to spectacle and excess far beyond rock 'n' roll's proved available for rent. Mick formally announced that the Stones were to perform in the arena where gladiators had once fought to the death and Christians been torn apart by lions. However, the story caused a furore in the Rome press, and the permission was hastily withdrawn.

By this time, both Mick and Keith were fast losing interest in the project, while Klein, who had only ever been peripherally involved, was too busy with his number one clients over at Savile Row to push it any further. As a result, *The Rolling Stones Rock 'n' Roll Circus* joined Mick's other recent screen tour de force, *Performance*, on the shelf, where it would stay for the next twenty-seven years.

His climactic performance in the film, tattooed with those weird symbols – 'like a dervish', thought Lindsay-Hogg – heightened speculation among Mick's courtiers that 'Sympathy for the Devil' wasn't just another role, but really did unleash supernatural forces that took possession of him as he sang it. Having so long been regarded as an earthly manifestation of Satan, was he now genuinely becoming one? A preening, pouting Prince of Darkness in counterpoint to the Prince of Enlightenment whom he hoped to entrust with his finances?

Since writing 'Sympathy' he had certainly become keenly interested in satanism and black magic and had amassed a large collection of books on the subject to add to his Cheyne Walk library. His particular interest was Aleister Crowley, aka the Great Beast, who had scandalised Edwardian Britain by openly espousing witchcraft and sorcery and founding a pagan religion called Thelema which flouted every moral code of the time. The Beatles had first resurrected Crowley by putting his bald head and crazed stare into the Pop Art collage on their *Sgt. Pepper* album cover. But in truth he seemed a more likely Stones aficionado with his bisexuality, his heavy drug use, his cult of prototype groupies known as Scarlet Women (a tag often given to Marianne after the Redlands bust) and his motto, in the face of no matter how much outrage or revulsion: 'Do What Thou Wilt.'

Certainly, too, there were people around Mick who could keep his fascination with such things at a boiling point. Donald Cam-

mell's father had been a Scottish druid who'd known Crowley well
and joined in secret rites at the Great Beast's home on the shores of
Loch Ness. Cammell himself, for all his civilised charm, had a dark
side utilised to the full in *Performance*, some scenes of which could
almost have had a cloven hoof working the clapperboard. Closer to
home, Anita Pallenberg was rumored to be a witch – and not only for
the spell she had cast over two, if not three, Stones in succession. She
wore a garlic necklace to ward off vampires and, according to Spanish
Tony Sanchez, would put the evil eye on anyone who displeased her,
using a collection of bones and other relics she kept in a secret drawer
in her bedroom.

After 'Sympathy for the Devil', not to mention *Their Satanic Majesties Request*, it was only a matter of time before Mick would be courted
by Kenneth Anger, America's leading film-maker in the realm of black
magic and the occult. Anger believed himself to be a reincarnation of
Aleister Crowley as well as a magus, or master sorcerer, in his own right,
and had the name Lucifer tattooed on his chest. He was also a homosexual, in whose films satanic imagery alternated with naked young men
undergoing different unpleasant forms of mutilation. He was therefore
not wholly disinterested in proclaiming Mick a channel for occult forces
more powerful and chaotic than any Rolling Stones fan riot of yore.

For the past two years, Anger had been working on a screen epic
entitled *Lucifer Rising*, intended to bring black magic out of the closet,
as it were, and establish him as a serious film-maker in the same league
as Bergman or Buñuel. However, almost all the footage had recently
been stolen by his current lover, a would-be actor and pop singer named
Bobby Beausoleil. With what remained of *Lucifer Rising*, Anger began
putting together a short called *Invocation of My Demon Brother*, for which
Mick agreed to provide a musical score to be played on the newly modish Moog synthesiser.

But there his flirtation with Satan ended. It was clearly dangerous,
as well as fundamentally repugnant to someone with so solid a Church
of England upbringing, and anyway Kenneth Anger had started to be a
bore. So one day, helped by Marianne, Mick carried his entire collection

of magic books into the back garden of 48 Cheyne Walk and made a bonfire of them, thinking that was that.

The rebonding of Mick and Keith was further strengthened as they set about writing a new album that had to maintain the form they had recovered on *Beggars Banquet*. To avoid distractions from their respective old ladies, they went off by themselves to Positano in southern Italy – where, two years earlier, Marianne had awaited those nightly surreptitious phone calls from Mick in London. Now, at the tail end of winter, the town was almost deserted and they could write songs sitting outside cafés in the sunshine, Keith with his guitar, Mick with a harmonica. If anything brought back Keith's old affection, it was realising afresh what a fine harp player his Glimmer Twin was.

Two songs for the new album were already finished, each in its own way a future Jagger–Richard classic. The one they'd started on holiday in Brazil's Mato Grosso, surrounded by cattle and gauchos, had metamorphosed into 'Honky Tonk Women', a lazy-paced sex hymn whose only clue to its origin was the *clop* of a cowbell before Keith's opening riff. Mick's lyrics returned to his usual milieu in the upper part of the Americas, eulogising 'a gin-soaked bar-room queen' in a Tennessee blues capital which his over-Dixified accent strangulated into '*Myemphyssss*'. It went on to make one of rock's first direct references to copulation ('I laid a divorc-ay in Noo Yawk Cit-ay . . .') and the first ever to snot ('She blew mah nose and then she blew mah mahnd').

There was also 'You Can't Always Get What You Want', written and recorded before the release of *Beggars Banquet* and unusual among Jagger compositions in using scenes from his own life: 'a recep-shun', 'a demonstra-shun', even a visit to the Chelsea Drugstore, the newly opened King's Road showpiece that was actually London's first shopping mall. As often in his more reflective mood, it took the form of a sermon, first to a woman ('practised at the art of decep-shun') then to 'Mr Jimmy', aka the Stones' producer Jimmy Miller. It was also his most heartfelt blues performance since 'Time Is on My Side', arranged by Jack Nitzsche and background-vocaled by American soul divas Madeline Bell and Doris Troy. For the irony without which no Jagger pronouncement could ever be complete, the opening chorus was sung by an all-female section of the London Bach Choir.

Elsewhere on the album, Lucifer still seemed to be rising without any serious resistance from Mick. The very title, *Let It Bleed*, was an echo of Aleister Crowley's so-called sex magic, created by intercourse with a Scarlet Woman during her menstruation. 'Midnight Rambler' (conceived in Positano sunshine) was the monologue of a serial rapist and killer, inspired by the Boston Strangler, Albert DeSalvo, yet couched in tones even jokier than 'Jumpin' Jack Flash'. Keith's principal – and stunning – contribution, 'Gimme Shelter', written at the height of his paranoia over Mick and Anita on the *Performance* set, had an apocalyptic menace and anguish ('War! Children! It's just a shot away . . .') that made 'Sympathy for the Devil' seem more like *Tea and Sympathy*. Even the band's respectful nod to their roots, a cover version of Robert Johnson's 'Love in Vain', recalled the first legendary pact between a musician and Mephistopheles, and what fatal consequences resulted.

Along with everything else now on hold in *The Rolling Stones' Rock 'n' Roll Circus* was the heart-tugging performance of 'Something Better' that might have revived Marianne's long-dormant pop career. Such was her notoriety as Head Stone's consort that nowadays many people barely remembered her as a singer – still less that she and Mick had started out as collaborators, with 'As Tears Go By'. Her last single had been 'Is This What I Get for Loving You?' in 1967, a title which the impact of his trial on her had made all too appropriate. As some small payback for literary guidance, he could easily have written her a song or two or worked with her in the studio they had in their garden, but somehow it never happened. Turning his lover into an artistic partner, like John Lennon with Yoko, had no appeal for Mick. He was far too busy keeping the gold-spinning dynamo named Jagger–Richard efficiently turning over.

Then it happened that he came up with a tune for which, uncharacteristically, he could think of no words. He and Marianne were in Rome with Keith and Anita, and when no inspiration came from his Glimmer Twin either, Marianne offered to help, The result was 'Sister Morphine', a cry from a hospital patient to a nurse for a desperately needed shot of painkiller: 'Aw, come on, Sister Morphine, you better make up my bed/'cause you know and I know in the morning I'll be dead . . .' Although the extent of Marianne's contribution has since been disputed (by none more than the man who supposedly 'can't remember anything'), she is adamant that the lyric was all her work, inspired by John Milton's poem 'Lycidas', but with Keith also firmly in mind. Its Crowl-eyesque reference to 'clean white sheets stained red', for instance, came from the Brazilian holiday of the previous December. During the sea voyage to Rio, pregnant Anita had begun to suffer bleeding and received a morphine injection from the ship's doctor – hugely impressing Keith for having made such a score quite legally.

Marianne claimed 'Sister Morphine' as her long-overdue next single, and Mick agreed to produce it in Los Angeles, together with her *Rock 'n' Roll Circus* track, 'Something Better'. He was also now a good enough guitarist to play acoustically on the session, alongside Ry Cooder on slide guitar, Charlie Watts on drums, Bill Wyman on bass and Jack Nitzsche on piano. 'Sister Morphine' came out in Britain as the B-side to 'Something Better' in February 1969, but the record was withdrawn from sale by Decca two days later on the grounds that it glorified hard drugs. Mick protested to Decca's chairman, Sir Edward Lewis, that it portrayed their nightmare *consequences,* but Lewis (possibly still recol-lecting being called 'a fucking old idiot') refused to intervene.

Ironically, when Marianne recorded that croak of seemingly termi-nal morphine addiction, she had not yet tried the drug's more seductive, quick-acting and deadly cousin, heroin. To drive away the clouds that piled above her golden head – darkened now still more by the loss of baby Corrina – she had settled into a mixture of cocaine, pills and alcohol, consciously bingeing on each in reaction to Mick's eternal restraint. She would later say that even getting blind drunk together a few times might have helped break down the wall that now seemed to separate them.

According to her autobiography, getting into heroin was a deliber-ate decision to become genuinely as bad as she had been painted after Redlands and 'Sister Morphine'; a two-fingered retort of 'You ain't seen nothin' yet.' She took her first sniff not in some rock god's joss-reeking den like the *Performance* house, as one might expect, but amid the cheery bottle clink of a Berkshire country pub. It was on a day when she and Mick drove down to see how work was progressing on Stargroves and he had no idea what she had done. 'All the other drugs I had taken were in a quest for sensation,' she would write, 'but this was a cessation of all sensation, an absolute absence of pain.' So, too, for all first-time users, smack does not derange or disorient, but seems to put one in perfect balance with oneself and the whole universe. No subsequent rush will ever match that miraculous first one, although the convert will spend his or her life – literally – in trying to recapture it.

Nor was it necessary to have sex with the pusher Spanish Tony San-chez to continue the experiment. For in a twin Queen Anne house to Mick's at the other end of Cheyne Walk, Keith and Anita were already well advanced on it. Mick at first had no suspicions, since smack is white powder identical to cocaine and snorted in the same way. 'Don't you think you're doing too much of that stuff?' he would sometimes protest mildly, echoing his line to Anita in *Performance:* 'You shoot too much of that shit, Pherber.' Marianne would reply that she was only chipping (using occasionally) and he believed her.

Anyway, he had a new habit of his own, in the one area where he never practised moderation. In September 1968 Britain's three-centuries-old theatre censorship had been abolished and an American show called *Hair* had opened in London's West End, taking advantage of the new freedom to depict anti-Vietnam War propaganda, drug taking, swearing and full-frontal nudity. Among the stars of this 'tribal love-rock musi-cal' was a black American singer–actress with a huge puffball Afro by the name of Marsha Hunt.

Born in Philadelphia, Marsha had studied at the University of California, Berkeley, before coming to London in 1966, aged twenty. Her first career had been as a blues singer around the same club circuit Mick had left not long earlier – often directly in his footsteps, first as a back-up vocalist for Alexis Korner, then with Long John Baldry in a band called Bluesology, whose organist was Reg Dwight, later Elton John. She also lived for several months with John Mayall, whose Bluesbreakers nurtured several young guitar virtuosi, notably Eric Clapton, and whose wife, Pamela, would later be chosen by Mick as a suitable friend for Marianne.

It was the time of the slogan 'Black Is Beautiful', when for the first time black women began appearing on the covers of glossy magazines. Marsha, with her delicate face, enormous curly halo and air of gravitas, became London's incarnation of Black Is Beautiful, featuring on the front of the *Weekend Telegraph Magazine* with a royal crest tattooed across her bare breasts. Leaving the cast of *Hair*, she was signed by Track Records, whose roster included the Who and Jimi Hendrix, and began a relationship with the future glam-rock icon Marc Bolan.

Ever since his platonic love affair with Cleo Sylvestre, Mick had always had a weakness for beautiful young black women. Not long after the *Weekend Telegraph Magazine* cover came out, Marsha was rung up by the Stones' office and asked to appear in a publicity picture for their next single, 'Honky Tonk Women', posing in 'tarty clothes' alongside the whole band. She declined, explaining that she preferred not to look as if she'd 'just been had by all the Rolling Stones'. Mick then called her up in person and, a few nights later, paid a surprise visit to the Bloomsbury flat where she was staying. As she did an amazed double take, he grinned, pointed his finger like a pistol and went 'Bang!' Marsha was not a Stones fan and, in comparison with the elfin Marc Bolan, thought Mick 'not beautiful or even striking'. What won her over, she would recall, was 'his shyness and awkwardness'. They spent the rest of that night just sitting and talking about the blues clubs and characters they both knew so well. She noticed how his voice, slurrily Cockney at first, became softer and genteeler the more he relaxed.

They began an affair in deepest secret but, since Marsha was a fellow recording artist, could also be seen together in public without arousing suspicion – in any case, London still had almost no paparazzi. Mick's name for her, to which surprisingly she did not object, was Miss Fuzzy. He liked it that she didn't go gooey-eyed and weak-kneed in his presence like most females, but had a crisply forthright manner ('butch', he called it) as well as an educated and inquiring mind and a natural classiness.

Best of all, despite all the dope smoking that had gone on in and around *Hair*, she was completely straight. Marsha would later recall him often talking about Marianne's increasing drug use, how much it upset and worried him, and his powerlessness to stop it.

If Marianne's singing career had stalled, her acting one still seemed to be on the rise. In the spring of 1969 she was invited to play Ophelia in Shakespeare's *Hamlet* in a new production by the eminent film and theatre director Tony Richardson. Although married to Vanessa Redgrave, the most adored young British actress of the day, Richardson was bisexual and had an obvious crush on Mick; nonetheless there was no question of Marianne's having been chosen on any basis but merit. Hamlet was to be played by thirty-year-old Nicol Williamson, described by the great drama critic Kenneth Tynan as 'a young contender for the title of best actor in the world', and the top-drawer supporting cast included Anthony Hopkins as Claudius. The play was to have a limited run at the Roundhouse, a converted train shed in Camden Town which had become London's foremost arena for experimental theatre and music; it would also be filmed for cinema release.

The parallels were only too painfully obvious between Marianne and the young woman tormented by the vagaries of the revenge-obsessed Prince of Denmark (who at one point is said to be 'lov'd of the distracted multitude' like some prototype rock star) until finally her sanity unravels and she effectively commits suicide by drowning. And, indeed, the British stage had never seen quite such a haunted and heartbreaking Ophelia, with her death-white complexion and dark-ringed eyes; an incarnation of that dubious style known as heroin chic three decades too early.

It was, unfortunately, not just makeup. To get her through the scene where Ophelia's insanity is revealed, Spanish Tony Sanchez would deliver a nightly heroin jack to Marianne at the theatre. In readiness for the almost inevitable reaction, called 'pulling a whitey', a bucket was positioned in the wings so that she could vomit into it directly as she came offstage. In *Faithfull*, too, she admits to carrying on an affair with Nicol Williamson during the run, and frequently playing Ophelia's anguished scenes of unrequited love with the Prince of Denmark just after having sex with him in her dressing room.

Performance might be languishing in Warner Bros' vaults, but the hearsay accounts of Mick's brilliance in it led Tony Richardson to offer him a second major screen role. Fresh from both critical and commercial success with *The Charge of the Light Brigade,* Richardson was to make a film about Ned Kelly, the nineteenth-century Irish-Australian outlaw, or bushranger, who became a folk hero much like the American West's Jesse James. In preference to the many fine antipodean actors around, he proposed casting Mick as Kelly. Even for so practised a mimic, portraying an Australian desperado in a big-budget action movie represented a huge leap into the unknown; nonetheless, Mick accepted the challenge with none of the agonising that had preceded his Turner self-portrait. Though he would later bitterly regret being talked into *Ned Kelly* by Richardson, at the time it looked like the fast track to film stardom that *Performance* hadn't provided.

Shooting was to begin on location in New South Wales in July, when Mick's schedule was still empty of performing commitments with the Stones. He would also for the first time be acting opposite Marianne, who'd been cast as Kelly's sister, Maggie, a rather less alluring role than Ophelia. She took it mainly in hopes that going away together – far from the political and sexual intrigues of the Stones' court – might somehow revive their relationship.

Since receiving a conditional discharge for his minuscule drug offence two years previously, Mick had had not the smallest brush with the British police. But now suddenly there was evidence of a renewed attempt to break a butterfly on a wheel. One day as he was driving himself down King's Road, he was pulled over and his Rolls given a thorough search for drugs – which, of course, yielded nothing. Then, on the evening of 28 May, the day his role as Ned Kelly was announced, he emerged from 48 Cheyne Walk to go to a recording session and beheld a carload of police led by a contradictorily titled officer named Detective Sergeant Robin Constable.

Marianne was not with Mick (a telling detail about their life by that point) but down in the basement kitchen, talking to Christopher Gibbs. 'On looking from the window,' her official statement would say, 'I saw Mick being held by a lot of men. There was also a woman there. All the men were in plain clothes. I never heard anyone, but saw someone's hand over Mick's mouth . . . I assumed Mick was being attacked by thugs and ran from the kitchen up the stairs to the front door, which I opened. At this, Mick said "Shut the door, you silly twit, it's the police."'

As with the Redlands bust, the police's timing seemed suspiciously perfect, though no tip-off from the *News of the World* or any other scandal sheet was to be alleged this time. Rather, it looked as if a member of the Stones' entourage had been bribed to set up Mick on his own doorstep. Suspicion later fell on the Stones' driver, Tom Keylock, who had many contacts at Scotland Yard and was the only one who knew to the minute when the intended target would be leaving for the studio.

The next day, Mick and Marianne appeared at Great Marlborough Street Magistrates' Court, jointly charged with possession of a lump of cannabis weighing a quarter of a pound, to which they pleaded not guilty. Mick's treatment, however, had none of the hysteria and overkill of 1967. The case was adjourned until 23 June and he was released on £50 bail. That second hearing ended in a further adjournment and continued bail until 29 September, which would allow him to go to Australia and appear in *Ned Kelly* in the meantime.

Thirty-six years later, in 2005, a cache of hitherto confidential documents released by Britain's Public Records Office was found to include the court papers from this second, and last, Jagger drug bust. Among them were claims by Mick that the police had planted 'white powder' (i.e., heroin) at Cheyne Walk, and Detective Sergeant Constable had solicited a bribe for arranging – in a total turnaround of the Redlands episode – that Marianne should take the blame while he walked free.

According to Mick's statement, the find had been made in a cardboard box from Cartier, the jewellers. 'I saw Constable pick up the box. I walked over to him, by which time he opened the box [and] pulled out a folded piece of white paper . . . He said "Ah, ah, we won't have to look much further." He had a little while earlier been asking me where the

LSD was . . . He showed me the paper and I saw that it contained some white powder . . . Constable licked one of his fingers and dipped it in the powder and tasted it. I did the same of my own volition. It had a talcum powder flavour . . . I would not know what heroin tastes like, but the flavour was not bitter.'

DS Constable was then alleged to have said: 'Don't worry, Mick, we can sort it out . . . You plead not guilty and she [Marianne] pleads guilty.' He had asked Mick several times 'How much is it worth to you?' and himself suggested a bribe of 'a thousand', adding 'You can have it back if it doesn't work.' During the charging process at Chelsea Police Station, the police had applied further pressure, reminding him that another drug conviction would probably get him banned from America. On getting home late that night, he had immediately telephoned Michael Havers, his counsel in the Redlands trial, and asked Havers to defend him once again.

In the end, the white powder did not figure in the case, and Mick was charged only with possession of the cannabis. After the second court hearing, on 23 June, he claimed Detective Sergeant Constable privately said to him, 'It's not a quarter-pound piece any more, is it?' – implying that since the raid the police had sold or used some of it. Constable had allegedly hinted that another of his team had planted the cannabis at Cheyne Walk, but told Mick: 'To know that will cost you a big drink [bribe].' Mick had suggested, 'Drop a note through my door,' but the matter had gone no further. Signing the statement that same evening in his solicitor's office, the autographing habit proved too strong and he added a cross for a kiss.

He would ultimately be found guilty and fined £200, with 50 guineas' costs – a very different outcome from his trial in the Summer of Love. The case also illustrated how much his social status had changed since then. Bowing to pressure from several of his friends in high places – including Michael Havers and Tom Driberg, MP – the police conducted an internal inquiry into his bribery allegations, headed by a senior Scotland Yard officer, Commander Robin Huntley. In Huntley's adjudication, Mick was described as 'a very intelligent, shrewd and well-known public figure with many influential friends': different indeed from the 'dirty', 'ugly' Rolling Stone of yore. By contrast, Marianne was clearly considered little more respectable than in the era of fur rugs and Mars bars, and her testimony was dismissed as irrelevant. Thus in the end it came down to Mick's word against the 'astute and experienced' Detective Sergeant Constable, and no further action was taken.

As the last summer of the sixties got under way, it was common knowledge among London's rock elite that the Rolling Stones were now actively seeking a replacement for Brian Jones. Hard though they had tried to hide their 'wooden leg', the still-unfinished *Let It Bleed* sessions made further pretence impossible – as well as reminding them afresh just what they had lost. In something like two months, Brian had managed to stagger into the studio only twice, to play percussion on 'Midnight Rambler' and autoharp on 'You Got the Silver'. The country-rock groove was continuing, helped by a clutch of top American session musicians like saxophonist Bobby Keys, pianist–organists Leon Russell and Al Kooper, and guitarist–mandolinist Ry Cooder. Time was, of course, when Brian could have played all those parts on his head.

There were hopes that his exit could be stage-managed without undue personal trauma or giving offence to the Stones' female-fan following, the majority of whom still adored him. At the time, many star players were walking away from established bands to make more experimental music or join with stars from other bands in so-called supergroups. Brian himself seemed reconciled to leaving, and had several ideas for new projects as both a producer and a performer. But in acknowledgement of his huge past contribution to the Stones – not least founding and naming them – he expected a substantial financial settlement.

A far trickier issue was who should take over Brian's official role of lead guitarist. It would be hard enough finding a player half as brilliant, let alone one who gave off the thrill of danger and mischief he had in his prime. And the Stones' peculiar power structure made the job qualifications far from that simple. In most rock bands, especially since the male-skewed acid and heavy-metal era, the lead guitarist ranked second to the vocalist, if not equal first. But here, with rhythm-guitarist Keith unchallengeable in that place, he would have to accept subordinate status along with Bill and Charlie.

The problem was finally solved by Marsha Hunt – or, rather, by John Mayall, the hard-core blues-band leader with whom Marsha had lived briefly before finding fame in *Hair*. She had kept up friendly relations with Mayall, and so knew that his Bluesbreakers currently featured a twenty-year-old guitar virtuoso named Mick Taylor, who was looking to move on. Marsha passed the news to Mick at one of their secret trysts, and Mick immediately summoned Taylor to an audition. With his unsmiling baby face and girlishly thick hair, the twenty-year-old looked nothing like anyone's idea of a Rolling Stone – still less, anyone's idea of a Mick. But his talent was undeniable, and, more important, he struck up an instant playing rapport with Keith. After contributing riffs to two *Let It Bleed* tracks, 'Live with Me' and 'Country Honk', he was asked to join by Mick for a wage of £150 per week.

So, late in May, the moment arrived for officially giving Brian the boot. Since he rarely visited London any more, the deed would have to be done at his new country house, Cotchford Farm, near Harefield in East Sussex. For a character so addicted to *faux* innocence, it was richly appropriate to be now living in the former home of A. A. Milne, surrounded by mementoes of Milne's famously befuddled bear, Winnie-the-Pooh, and his companions Christopher Robin, Piglet, Eeyore and Tigger. Cotchford was originally to be a love nest shared with the Anita Pallenberg look-alike Suki Poitier, but the previous Christmas Suki had finally tired of Brian's violence and left him. In her place he had installed a twenty-three-year-old blonde Swede named Anna Wohlin.

He had stayed connected to the Stones' office, still treating Shirley Arnold as his personal PA without any objection from managing director Mick. Indeed, Mick remained full of concern for him, though characteristically preferring to conceal it. 'Whenever Brian phoned,' Shirley remembers, 'Mick was always the first one to ask, "How is he?"' The drug bust at Cheyne Walk had deepened this fellow feeling, for Detective Sergeant Robin Constable had also busted Brian a year earlier and then, too, drugs had come to light that the bustee swore he had never seen before. When news came through that Brian was back in the Priory for another drying-out session, Mick immediately arranged for flowers to be sent to him. Even the well-known Jagger parsimony was suspended in the matter of Brian's golden handshake. 'Mick recognised what a huge contribution Brian had made to the band,' Shirley says. 'He wanted the pay-off to be as generous as possible.'

Harefield was only about an hour's drive across Sussex from Redlands, and rather than take the coward's way out and employ a third party – as the Beatles had when ditching their original drummer, Pete Best – Mick and Keith did the firing in person, taking along Charlie Watts in case a mediator should be needed. But the meeting passed off with none of Brian's usual histrionics or hysteria. It was agreed that the press would be told he was leaving by amicable mutual consent, and he would receive a once-for-all payment of £100,000 (well over £1 million by modern values) in addition to the royalties still accruing to him from Stones' recordings. When it was all over, Brian shook hands and wished them good-bye with old-fashioned courtesy: only when their Rolls had turned out of the front drive and disappeared did he run back into the house, lay his head on his kitchen table and weep.

The following day, a press release from Les Perrin's office announced that Brian had left the Stones because of 'musical differences', describing it (in words that would prove somewhat unfortunate) as an 'amicable termination'. A statement from Brian himself explained he had taken the decision because 'I no longer saw eye to eye with the others over the discs we are cutting.' One from Mick added a persuasive note of personal warmth: 'We have decided that it is best for him to be free to follow his own inclinations. We have parted on the best of terms. We continue to be friends and we're certainly going to meet socially in future.'

For London, summer 1969 brought a return of the sunshine that seemed to have saturated it throughout the decade. And on 7 June the predominantly sunny mood of its young was demonstrated as never before by a free rock concert in one of its cherished royal parks.

The chosen space was Hyde Park, the 350 verdant acres bounded by Knightsbridge, Bayswater and Mayfair, whose loudest sound as a rule was the splash of oars on the Serpentine lake or the soapbox orators at Speakers' Corner. The licence had been obtained by a new promotions company named Blackhill Enterprises; its star attraction was Blind Faith, the supergroup lately formed by Eric Clapton and Ginger Baker from Cream, Steve Winwood from Traffic and Rick Grech from Family. A stage was constructed on the wide plateau in the park's northeast corner next to Marble Arch and the spectators sat on the grass or in deckchairs, just yards from grinding traffic. The event attracted an audience of 150,000, by a long way the largest crowd ever formed in London since the end of the Second World War. Despite the competition for good vantage points and the extreme heat – in an era long before people carried their own bottled water – not a single case of violence, drunkenness or dehydration was reported.

Blind Faith had only recently come together, and their set – including a cover version of the Stones' 'Under My Thumb' – scarcely lived up to their hype. But the atmosphere of good humour and togetherness was like no festival's since Monterey. In the VIP area, the show's organiser–compère, Sam Cutler, bumped into Mick, wandering around with Marianne and Nicholas, clearly as enraptured as everyone else. That evening, Cutler went to a concert at the Royal Albert Hall and again encountered Mick, by this time free of Marianne and Nicholas and with Marsha Hunt at his side. He was in high spirits, having realised the perfect way to restart the Stones' live performing career and introduce their new lead guitarist. They, too, would give a free concert in Hyde Park.

As always when Mick made up his mind, events moved rapidly from then on. Blackhill Enterprises were brought in to organise the staging, with Sam Cutler as compère once again. Despite the prevailing atmosphere of hippie altruism, Cutler had to explain to Mick that putting on a free concert was just as expensive as putting on a commercial one. Mick's neat solution was to sell the television rights to the Granada network, which would effectively underwrite the event in return for exclusive access to the Stones and himself, both on- and offstage.

There was also input from Rock Scully, manager to San Francisco's legendary Grateful Dead and a friend of Cutler's, who happened to be passing through London. Scully talked enthusiastically of free festivals in California whose promoters used Hell's Angels bikers to protect the electricity supply by parking their machines next to the generators, so giving the performers an effective but – Scully stressed – unaggressive security screen. Cutler remembers Mick saying he'd like to do a free show in California also, on the same lines.

So the date of the Stones' first live appearance in more than two years was set for 5 July. Their alfresco rebirth in fact would take place only a few streets west of the Soho pubs and clubs where Brian Jones had first slapped them into life. That was the last thing on anyone's mind until, with only two days to go, Brian was found dead in his swimming pool.

HIS DEATH WOULD turn into the pop world's most famous whodunnit. Although an excellent swimmer, he had drowned in a few feet of water, within earshot of his girlfriend, Anna Wohlin, and several houseguests who could easily have come to his aid. Sudden, lonely, inexplicable deaths have been the fate of many other major rock figures; those of Jimi Hendrix, Janis Joplin and Jim Morrison were, indeed, soon to follow in quick succession. But Brian's peculiar blend of brilliance and self-destructiveness – and the fact that the most decadent rock star of his time expired in a garden dedicated to Winnie-the-Pooh – have generated an unparalleled degree of fascination, speculation and Kennedyesque conspiracy theory.

The inquest found his drowning to have been 'misadventure', due to the level of drugs and alcohol in his system and his appalling physical shape for a man of only twenty-seven. But among investigative journalists and broadcasters a suspicion still lingers that he was murdered and a cover-up inside the Stones' camp prevented his killer or killers from being brought to justice. The motive most commonly suggested (albeit without a shred of hard evidence) is that, despite having left the band in seeming amicability, he still posed some threat or knew some dark secret about them which he was threatening to make public.

In the countless articles and documentaries about the case that have appeared since 1969, the Stones have never been accused of direct involvement in either the alleged murder or conspiracy. They receive a large share of blame nonetheless for the seeming callousness with which they had fired him from the band he founded, so sending him off a metaphorical deep end well before he plunged from the real one. Mick is always portrayed as the most selfishly indifferent to his plight, stealing his leadership without a qualm, then, once he was gone, not sparing him a backward glance. As we have already seen and will now again in spades, all this could not be further from the truth.

Brian's final undoing seems not to have been drink or drugs but his pathetic need for friends, all the greater now that he was no longer a Rolling Stone. To carry out renovations at Cotchford Farm, he had hired a local builder named Frank Thorogood, a crony of the Stones' driver, Tom Keylock, who had previously done some work for Keith at Redlands. The misnamed Thorogood took shameless advantage of the situation, dawdling over his construction work while sponging off Brian and living rent-free with a woman friend in a flat above the garage.

Twenty-six years after the event, Thorogood, by that time terminally ill with cancer, made a supposed death-bed confession to Keylock that he'd drowned Brian by accident during some drunken horseplay while they were temporarily alone together in the pool. But there remain puzzling aspects to the case, for instance precisely how many people were at Cotchford Farm at the time, and what happened to the large amount of Brian's possessions and private papers that disappeared immediately afterwards. The Sussex police's investigation – using some of the same officers who busted Mick and Keith in 1967 – was later revealed to have been seriously flawed, and there have been repeated calls for an official re-examination of the evidence, the most recent in 2010.

When Brian died, at around midnight on 2 July, the reconfigured Stones happened to be all together at Olympic Studios, working around the clock to finish off *Let It Bleed*. The news reached them at between 2 and 3 A.M., in telephone calls from their assistant, Shirley Arnold, and their press officer, Les Perrin. The Olympic session was aborted, and the band went home, reconvening later at their Maddox Street office in a state of collective shock. Charlie Watts was weeping, while Mick – as Shirley remembers – wandered distractedly up and down, repeatedly kicking a dog's water bowl on the floor.

The immediate assumption was that the Hyde Park concert in two days' time would be cancelled. But after a chance remark by Charlie, another idea emerged. That afternoon, Mick gave an interview to the London *Evening Standard* and said the concert would go ahead, but now as a tribute to Brian. Afterwards he continued with the busy day as scheduled, premiering 'Honky Tonk Women' on the BBC's *Top of the Pops* show, then going on to a 'white ball' at the country home of Prince Rupert Loewenstein, at which the guests included the Queen's sister, Princess Margaret.

His comments to the media about Brian were gracious and heartfelt (in contrast with Paul McCartney and George Harrison's flip responses to John Lennon's death, eleven years later): 'I just say my prayers for him. I hope he becomes blessed, I hope he is finding peace . . . Brian will be at the concert. I mean, he'll be there. I don't believe in Western bereavement. You know, I can't suddenly drape a long black veil and walk the hills . . . I want to make it so that Brian's send-off from the world is filled with as much happiness as possible.' The Oscar Wilde line, however, came from the Who's Pete Townshend: 'It's a normal day for Brian. Like, he died every day, you know.'

Given the length of the Stones' lay-off, and the changes in rock tastes and presentation in the meantime, there was no knowing how many people would turn out to see them in Hyde Park. Brian's many loyal fans might well refuse to accept Mick Taylor in his place and, despite the tribute theme, could boycott the event in their thousands. Even Mick felt nervous about how he would go over, and didn't anticipate a crowd anywhere near Blind Faith's 150,000 the previous month.

He spent the forty-eight hours leading up to Saturday 5 July, compiling a fourteen-song playlist with Keith and rehearsing the band in what would be the first-ever stage versions of most. For convenience, they used the Beatles' basement recording studio at 3 Savile Row, with John and Yoko running their world peace campaign on the floor above. Three floors higher was Allen Klein, preoccupied with Beatle problems to the exclusion of all else and still unaware that the Stones were no longer in his pocket.

The weather continued to be glorious, but London's unusually high pollen count gave Mick a bout of hay fever, something he had not suffered since his schooldays, which developed into full-blown laryngitis. On the following Monday, he was due to fly to Australia to begin filming *Ned Kelly*, having just heard that his still-unresolved drug case would not prevent him from travelling. The film-makers were starting to fear rock-star unreliability and hinting at legal action if he did not arrive on the set on time, fit and ready for work. Even so, there was no question of the show being called off.

What he wore onstage clearly was of critical importance. By 1969, rock stars performed in hippie clothes as colourless and shapeless as their fans', but this gig, more than any before, demanded some sartorial splash on his part. He first asked the couturier Ossie Clark to make him a snakeskin suit, but realised it would be too purgatorially hot. Then at the Mister Fish boutique he found a white cotton suit whose ruffle-fronted, puffy-sleeved, flounce-skirted jacket looked feminine even beyond the gender-blurring modes of the day. It had been made for the American cabaret star Sammy Davis Jr, but Mick borrowed it for the Hyde Park show, trying it out first on Princess Margaret and the other posh guests at Prince Rupert's white ball (where only Marianne had defied the dress code by wearing top-to-toe black). The Fish outfit was light and summery and also fitted the new, solemn mood, white in many cultures signifying bereavement.

By early Saturday morning, it had become clear that Blind Faith's concert had been the merest sideshow and that around 250,000 people were gathering in Hyde Park to welcome back the Stones. Blackhill Enterprises had provided a workmanlike stage well over six feet high, with a canopy and a thirty-foot scaffolding tower to house some of the extra speakers needed for so vast an open-air auditorium. Obedient to Mick's wish for a natural look in keeping with the surroundings, potted palm trees decorated the stage, with a colour blow-up of the *Beggars Banquet* album gatefold group picture as a backcloth. On Mick's orders, too, there was no backstage VIP enclosure. The Stones would wait in a suite at the Londonderry Hotel, at the Apsley House end of Park Lane, and when their moment came they would be delivered to the stage by armoured truck.

The other innovation – copied from Californian festivals as detailed by the Grateful Dead's Rock Scully – was to recruit fifty Hell's Angels as stage-front security. The purpose was to show that, despite recent flower-power detours, the Stones remained as edgy as ever; outlaws of rock, guarded by black-leather-clad, dangerous motorbike outlaws of the road. These British Angels, however, bore only a superficial resemblance to their genuinely ferocious and much-feared American counterparts – in fact, were not an official chapter of the international Angels brotherhood. Though adorned with the regulation tattoos, metal studs, Nazi helmets and swastikas, they were a weedy-looking bunch whose only payment for acting as stewards was to be a free cup of tea each.

Otherwise, the question of security hardly arose. Hyde Park had its own substantial police station, including mounted and dog-handling sections, which stayed on full alert but would be exercised hardly at all. In the whole day, there were just twelve arrests for minor offences, a handful of knives were confiscated, and 400 people had to be treated for heat exhaustion.

The Stones were preceded by a string of not too threatening support acts: King Crimson, Family, Screw, the Battered Ornaments, the Third Ear Band and, for old times' sake, Alexis Korner's latest blues band, New Church. In the absence of a VIP enclosure, special guests sat on either side of the stage or in the scaffolding tower. Among them were Paul McCartney with his new wife, Linda, and Eric Clapton with his new girlfriend, Alice Ormsby-Gore (Mick's penchant for the upper classes had proved catching). Marianne and Nicholas drove with Mick to the Stones' base camp at the Londonderry, then were ushered to front seats on the right side of the stage. Marianne's hair was still cropped short for her role as Ophelia; in her own words, she 'looked like death . . . dope sick, coming off smack, anorexic, pale, sickly and covered in spots'. On the tower she could see a figure with an enormous Afro, dressed in a skimpy suit of white buckskin. Mick had been unable to resist having Marsha Hunt there, too.

Everyone in the grass-sprawling multitude, it is safe to say, had wondered how he would present himself to them after all this time. None could have guessed it would be in a white garment which, despite matching bell-bottom trousers, resembled nothing so much as a little girl's white frilly party dress, set off by a metal-studded leather dog collar and full makeup. Still less could they have imagined that, having greeted them with a Dixie Mama-ish 'Well, a-a-a-aw-RIGHT!' the ruched and beflounced figure would go to the rear of the stage and return with seemingly the least relevant object at this moment – a small hardback book.

'Okay . . . now listen, will you cool it for a minute?' he instructed rather than requested, as if he were suddenly his father, Joe, taking some huge, torpid gym class. "Cause I really would like to say something for Brian . . . about how we feel about him just goin' when we didn't expect it.' The 'something' was a reading from *Adonais,* Percy Bysshe Shelley's 1821 poem about the death of John Keats – no brief quote but two hefty stanzas, declaimed in serious, level tones from which all traces of slurry Cockney and camp Dixie had miraculously vanished:

Peace, peace! he is not dead, he doth not sleep –
He hath awakened from the dream of life –

'Tis we, who lost in stormy visions, keep
With phantoms an unprofitable strife,
And in mad trance, strike with our spirit's knife
Invulnerable nothings! – We decay
Like corpses in a charnel; fear and grief
Convulse us and consume us day by day,
And cold hopes swarm like worms within our living clay . . .

The One remains, the many change and pass;
Heaven's light forever shines, Earth's shadows fly;
Life, like a dome of many-coloured glass,
Stains the white radiance of Eternity,
Until Death tramples it to fragments. – Die!
If thou wouldst be with that which thou dost seek!

Nor did the poetic mood end there. On the stage was a stack of brown cardboard boxes containing 2,500 white butterflies, which, as Shelley's words died away, were shaken out into the crowd. These symbols of Brian now more than Mick – who more thoroughly broken on a wheel? – had been purchased for £300 and permission to release them obtained from the Royal Parks authority on condition that they were all sterilised and included no leaf-munching cabbage whites (they were in fact mainly cabbage whites). The heat had caused many to expire inside their boxes, but a goodly number fluttered free to ravage gardens throughout the neighbourhood.

The Stones' opening number was 'I'm Yours and I'm Hers' by the albino Texan Johnny Winter, which had been a particular favourite of Brian's but was hardly the most tactful choice on Mick's part with Marianne and Marsha both looking on. And from the first notes of even this straight-ahead heavy-metal rocker, the band's underpreparedness was painfully obvious. Keith and Mick Taylor's guitars, so harmonious at first meeting, turned into a pair of pneumatic drills fighting a grudge match to the death. Charlie's drumming and Bill's bass each seemed to have melted into jelly. Only Mick's frilly white figure seemed fully awake and on the beat, walking the invisible Travelator he had stolen from James Brown all those years ago, singing into two globular hand microphones taped together. 'The *tempo!*' he kept hissing over his shoulder at Keith. 'Get the *tempo* together!'

But the fluffs, lurches and whistles of feedback could not have mattered less. All that concerned the assembled quarter million was that the Rolling Stones were back, reborn on that golden afternoon next to Bayswater Road as surely as the Beatles had come to an end on their chill Mayfair rooftop five months earlier. Mick Jagger was back, somehow more sex-soaked and shocking with his white dolly dress and poetry book than ever in his career before; the unchallenged simultaneous king and queen of rock.

There was one great difference, however, from live shows three years before. The Stones' music seemed to have lost its old power to unleash violence and mayhem. 'Satisfaction', 'Jumpin' Jack Flash', even 'Street Fighting Man' thundered out in turn, yet brought no shadow to the sea of happy faces and waving arms, and dwindled away among the treetops and Park Lane hotels. The stage's six-foot-plus height kept it mostly free of the female invaders whom Mick once had to dodge like on-heat meteor showers. Occasionally, a lone figure would manage the ascent via the shoulders of friends, then be instantly collared and carried, squirming, into the palm-fronded wings. This was done by the band's own minders rather than the Hell's Angels, who remained below the stage throughout. A confidential police report later called them 'totally ineffective' as stewards and a threat to no one.

For the first time, too – discounting that now-buried *Rock 'n' Roll Circus* moment – Mick's performance featured an element of striptease. The frilly dress was torn off and thrown aside after about half an hour, soon followed by the metal-studded dog collar, leaving only a skimpy violet T-shirt and white bell-bottoms, with a constant wink of bare midriff between. The strangely intimate space in the eye of that vast crowd became an arena for showmanship (if *man* is the right middle-of-word) that no Jagger audience had ever witnessed before. Sometimes he rolled and writhed on the stage as though actually in the grip of 'Midnight

Rambler''s rapist-killer, sometimes punished it with his belt; at one barely believable moment, he knelt with the double hand mike rearing between his thighs, leaned forward, spread his hair over it, and seemed to fulfil the ultimate narcissist fantasy of sucking himself off.

The finale was an eighteen-minute version of 'Sympathy for the Devil', backed by a troupe of African tribal drummers in full costume – even this darkest of all his masquerades seemingly purged of all malignity by sunshine and good vibes. At its end, the 'mayne of wealth and taste' showed masterly crowd control yet again, winding things up like a parent mollifying over-tired children: 'Aaw-*right*... We gotta go ... We 'ad a good time ... We 'ad a *good* time ...'

While the heat-drunk 250,000 dispersed, as peaceably as they had assembled, the five tons of rubbish strewn on the grass was picked up by an army of volunteers (rewarded with a copy of 'Honky Tonk Women' apiece), leaving the park tidier than after a normal Saturday.

CHAPTER THIRTEEN

The Balls of a Lion

The following Monday morning, with his usual unstoppable energy, Mick flew to Australia with Marianne to begin shooting *Ned Kelly*. They had no sooner reached Sydney than she became the second of his lovers (Chrissie Shrimpton had been the first, in 1966) to try to kill herself.

As Marianne would later recall, several factors had brought her to this extremity: her feeling of isolation in her life with Mick, the side effects of drugs she was taking, the shock of Brian Jones's death, the humiliation of sharing the stage with Marsha Hunt in Hyde Park (and knowing Mick had had a tryst with Marsha that same evening under cover of a Chuck Berry–Who concert at the Royal Albert Hall). Nor had it helped to be playing Ophelia in *Hamlet* and driven to the point of suicide night after night by another charismatic but unreachable swain, 'lov'd of the distracted multitude'.

The tipping point came after they had checked into the Chevron Hilton hotel, overlooking Sydney Harbour. While Mick was asleep, Marianne looked into the dressing-table mirror and thought she saw Brian's face looking back at her. She wanted to jump from the fourteenth-storey window, but found it painted shut, so instead she swallowed 150 Tuinal barbiturate tablets, enough to kill three people, washing them down with sips of room-service hot chocolate.

Mick awoke just in time to get her to St Vincent's Hospital, where doctors managed to flush out the barbiturates before they could cause brain damage. The police naturally had to be involved and – with memories of fur rugs and Mars bars still fresh – initially treated the episode as a drug orgy gone wrong. Rather than a Samaritan, Mick found himself briefly a suspect, undergoing hard-faced questioning about where Marianne had got the huge stash of Tuinals and whether he had had any part in feeding them to her.

A couple of hours later, he was holding a packed press conference for media from all over Australia, greeting them with a raucous Cockney 'Ma-a-awnin!' as if he hadn't a care in the world. Director Tony Richardson apologised for their slight lateness, explaining that Marianne had 'collapsed' as a result of the long flight from Britain. Mick showed no anxiety to be anywhere else as he declared that he took his role as Ned Kelly with total seriousness – though he hoped it would also be fun – and joked about the 'incestuous relationship' he would have with Marianne in the role of Kelly's sister.

It was a different story later, when the exact nature of her collapse became known and St Vincent's was besieged by the same media pack Mick had charmed that morning, but no longer playing by the same civilised rules. When one photographer sneaked through security and into her room, Mick had to be physically restrained by his PR, Les Perrin. Marianne would have seen no Tyranny of Cool in the enraged figure struggling in Perrin's arms and shouting, 'I'll get him . . . I'll get him!'

Though the doctors had saved Marianne's life, she remained in a coma for six days, seemingly beyond all medical efforts to revive her. Her mother, Baroness Erisso, flew from Britain to be at her bedside, and, fearing all hope was gone, summoned a Catholic priest to administer the last rites.

For Marianne, the time passed in a vivid dream of meeting and talking to Brian Jones in some transit area between life and death. In her clear recollection of the encounter, Brian made no reference to having been murdered, but was just faintly perplexed at finding himself no longer alive. Two days into the coma, on 10 July, his funeral took place in his genteel home town of Cheltenham. There were 500, mainly distraught female, mourners, and the floral tributes included an outsize wreath 'from Mick and Marianne with love'. The officiating clergy asked the congregation to pray for the lifeless-seeming young woman on the other side of the world along with the Rolling Stone about to gather infinite moss.

Eventually, as Marianne recalls, she heard three voices calling her into the land of the living once more – her mother's, her son Nicholas's, and Mick's. When she opened her eyes, Mick was at her bedside, holding her hand (although, pragmatic as ever, he had managed to start some filming in between hospital vigils). 'You've come back,' were his first words. 'Wild horses wouldn't drag me away,' she weakly replied.

When she became stronger, her mother had her moved to the more tranquil surroundings of a hospital run by nuns. ('Get thee to a nunnery,' Hamlet cruelly tells Ophelia at the height of her psychological torment.) Mick returned to the *Ned Kelly* set, where Marianne's role as Kelly's sister Maggie had been taken over by the Australian actress Diane Craig. He remained full of anxiety about her and wrote to her constantly from the location: 'beautiful letters', as she would recall, 'full of remorse, asking for forgiveness'.

The film was mainly shot around Birdwood in New South Wales, where Mick's mother, Eva, had been born and spent her first two years before coming to Kent. It had caused much controversy in the Australian press, not only because a Pommie pop singer had been chosen to play a national folk hero, but because Kelly's actual field of operation had been the neighbouring state of Victoria.

During the shoot, Mick lived on a small farm near Palarang, some thirty miles from Canberra, sharing the one-time overseer's modest quarters with Tony Richardson and producer Neil Hartley. July in New South Wales is the coldest month of the year, and much of the action took place out of doors, taxing all Mick's secret reserves of athleticism and stamina. The production did not have the same good feeling as *Performance* and, going on from Marianne's suicide attempt, suffered so much ill luck one might have thought 'Sympathy for the Devil' had been ritually sung on its first day. There was recurrent illness among the cast and crew, some of the costumes were destroyed in a fire, and Mark McManus, playing Kelly's henchman Joe Byrne, narrowly escaped serious injury when a cart in which he was riding accidentally tipped over. Then, in the second week, Mick squeezed the trigger of a prop pistol and it backfired, causing quite a severe burn to his right hand. Despite being in some pain and able to use the hand only with difficulty, he insisted on continuing work.

While keeping up the flow of letters to Marianne, he also wrote constantly to Marsha – 'laughing, sad, pensive, deep, observant, touching' missives, she would later call them, including an especially sweet and supportive one just before her appearance at the Isle of Wight pop festival headlined by Bob Dylan. Another, written on Sunday 20 July, the day of the first moon landing, was headed 'Sunday the Moon'. For a time, his bandaged right hand couldn't hold a pen, so he wrote to Marsha with his left.

Despite the dawn-to-dusk days on the set, and the need to learn lines for the next day, he still had to keep turning out material for the Stones. He'd brought a notebook for jotting down lyric ideas that he kept near at all times, and a new electric guitar that proved useful in coaxing his injured right hand back to full flexibility. One day, sitting by himself in the chill New South Wales landscape and thinking about Marsha, he sketched out a lyric with the notably un-pensive provisional title of 'Black Pussy'. This changed to the not much less dubious 'Brown Sugar', a synonym both for interracial sex – specifically in the Mars bar area – and dun-coloured street heroin. Its familiar 'Noo Awleans' setting also featured nineteenth-century slave markets, the casual rape of young female slaves by their white traffickers, youths losing their virginity, and mothers with strings of toyboys. Even at that time of barely articulated feminism and zero political correctness, he was slightly surprised by his own apparent urge to use 'all the nasty subjects in one go'.

From time to time, celebrity friends of director Tony Richardson would visit the set and stay at the house Richardson and Mick were sharing. These included the author and poet Christopher Isherwood, then sixty-five, who had travelled all the way from California with his thirty-years-younger lover Don Bachardy. The eminent author of *Goodbye to Berlin* and bosom friend of W. H. Auden expected to meet a brash, butch rock star, but instead got Mick in serious film-making mode – that is, at his most winning. '[He] is very pale, quiet, good-tempered, full of fun, ugly-beautiful . . . almost entirely without vanity,' Isherwood's collected diaries record. 'He hardly ever refers to his career or himself . . . you might be with him for hours and not know what it is he does. Also, he seems equally capable of group fun, clowning, entertaining, getting along with other people, and of entering into a serious one-to-one conversation with anyone who wants to. He talked seriously but not at all pretentiously about Jung and about India . . . and religion in general. He also seems tolerant and not bitchy.'

During Isherwood's visit, Tony Richardson received word that a gang of students from Canberra University were headed for Palarang, intending to kidnap Mick and demand a thousand dollars ransom for charity. The kidnappers never materialised, but ten local policemen kept an all-night watch in the kitchen unaware that the house's occupants were smoking pot in the adjacent sitting room. A couple of days later, Marianne was released from her nunnery and rejoined Mick, which for Isherwood made their shared quarters 'the most fascinatingly wicked house in Australia'.

After what they had both been through in Sydney, wickedness was the last thing on Mick and Marianne's minds. The Australian trip that was supposed to bring them closer together ended a month later when Marianne flew to Switzerland, at his unstinted expense, for psychiatric treatment. There she found a woman doctor who grasped her situation and genuinely did help her. But at no point along this world-circumnavigating trail of misery did anyone suggest she should stop doing drugs.

Also now in Mick's notebook were the lyrics for a new Jagger–Richard song, inspired by Marianne's wan little joke on being recalled to life, that 'Wild horses couldn't keep me away.' It was the first real love song he had ever written, not at all tyrannically cool in its confession of guilt mixed with helplessness, and declaration that he was still there for her: 'I watched you suffer a dull, aching pain / Now you decided to show me the same / No sweeping exit or offstage lines / Could make me feel bitter or treat you unkind.'

He had been back in London only a few days when his car was broken into and a few small items disappeared, including the notebook with the 'Wild Horses' lyrics, which, as usual, he had not bothered to memorise. Rather than go to the probably unsympathetic and unhelpful police, he had Les Perrin plant a few newspaper diary stories that if the notebook were returned a reward would be paid and no questions asked. Within hours, an anonymous male caller rang Shirley Arnold at the Stones' office to say he had the book but wanted £50 for it. 'When I told Mick, he said, "I'll give him thirty,"' Shirley recalls. 'However precious it was to him, he still tried to beat the price down. And the bloke agreed to thirty.'

It was arranged that Shirley would meet the caller in the concourse at Waterloo station, hand over the money and receive the notebook. She felt extremely nervous about dealing with someone possibly unpleasant or even dangerous all on her own but never thought of objecting, such was the devotion Mick inspired. Only as the hand-over took place did she realise she hadn't been sent alone after all: Mick's new young driver, Alan Dunn, was standing near, keeping an eye on her.

With Britain now thoroughly Rolling Stones-conscious once again, the time had come for the second, even more crucial stage in Mick's plan for their renaissance. The review of their finances by Prince Rupert Loewenstein was now complete, and made far from happy reading. Prince Rupert's urgent recommendation was that they get back to America on tour as soon as possible, ideally before the year's end. Mick agreed and, moreover, was determined that the earnings from such a tour should not fall into the same black hole that other group receipts these past several years appeared to have done. In other words, Allen Klein must have no part in it.

While Mick was in Australia, Keith had confronted Klein in London – taking along the Hyde Park compère, Sam Cutler, for support – and told him he was fired. But, as everyone knew, it wasn't as simple as that. Instead, Mick and Prince Rupert came up with a plan to loosen Klein's grip by degrees rather than try to machete his hand off at the wrist. His nephew Ron Schneider had worked for his ABKCO organisation since before he signed the Stones and was popular with all of them. Schneider in fact had recently quit ABKCO, tired of Klein's control freakery, and was looking to start in management on his own. At this opportune moment Mick rang him from the *Ned Kelly* location and asked him to organise the Stones' first US tour in more than three years, beginning early in November.

When Schneider told his uncle about the offer, he recalls, Klein 'went ballistic' but was too deeply enmeshed in Beatles problems to trample on it with the ferocity he once would have done. His only stipulation was that the tour must be run out of ABKCO's New York office, which Schneider did for a short time before quietly transferring operations to his home in Riverdale. Amazingly, Klein even agreed to the creation of a company called Stone Productions, jointly administered by Schneider and Prince Rupert, into which all the tour earnings would be paid.

Schneider's initial approaches produced an overwhelmingly positive response from major concert venues across America, including New York's Madison Square Garden and the Los Angeles Forum. The problem was that putting together a tour on the necessary scale required major finance, and with around $1million of their royalties still frozen by the Oldham–Eric Easton litigation, the Stones' collective bank account was virtually empty. The one small advance of $15,000 offered by the William Morris organisation would not have paid Keith's back-stage bar tab. Schneider's solution was to approach each venue individually and make a deal for 75 per cent of the gate, with 50 per cent of the projected total payable upfront.

There was another major stumbling block – one that Brian had created for so long but was now, ironically, down to Mick. His cannabis bust the previous May made it doubtful, to say the least, that the US Immigration Service would grant him a visa. John Lennon at the time had a similar 'crime of moral turpitude' on his record and was being denied entry for a much shorter visit that included no public performances. But while Lennon took every opportunity to rail against American imperialism, Mick these days was careful never to say anything that might make the US government consider him a threat. Luckily, too, the Stones' contacts included an official in the consular department of the US embassy in Grosvenor Square, where he had once demonstrated against the Vietnam War. In exchange for sweeteners that included an all-expenses-paid holiday in the South of France, this friendly insider made sure his visa went through.

The final months of the sixties had turned into a climactic celebration of rock music's seemingly limitless benign power and the ability of its young audience to gather together peaceably in huge numbers. There had already been Blind Faith and the Stones in Hyde Park and Bob Dylan on the Isle of Wight. Then, for three days in mid-August, a record 500,000 gathered on a dairy farm near Woodstock, New York, to watch thirty-two acts, including the Grateful Dead, Crosby, Stills and Nash, Jefferson Airplane, the Who and Jimi Hendrix; this double-Hyde Park multitude not basking in sun like their British cousins, but lashed by humid rain and floundering in mud, yet just as euphoric, mutually supportive and devoid of any urge to destruction or violence.

However, there were growing signs that this sunny, smiley counterculture possessed a dark and threatening underside. Just prior to Woodstock, the leader of a California hippie commune, a failed songwriter named Charles Manson, had turned his young male and female disciples loose on a murder spree suggested by a Beatles song, 'Helter Skelter'. In two nights Manson's so-called family had randomly slaughtered seven people, including film actress Sharon Tate, eight-months-pregnant wife of the director Roman Polanski, and had scrawled pop-song references on the walls of their luxury homes with their blood. It later emerged that one of the killers told one of the victims he was 'the Devil, here to do the Devil's work'.

The devil's work was also currently being celebrated in a new film, *Invocation of My Demon Brother*, directed by Kenneth Anger (whose former lover Bobby Beausoleil had gone on to join the Manson Family) and with a Moog synthesiser score by Mick Jagger, that best-known of all modern apologists for Satan. To underline the connection Mick thought he had severed months ago, Anger's images of naked young men in pagan crucifixions were intercut with glimpses of a white-flounced figure onstage in Hyde Park.

If the Stones in the person of Mick carefully abstained from all comment that might threaten to destabilise American society, no such restraint governed the publication that had borrowed their name. *Rolling Stone* had evolved into a radical political paper as much as a music one, and had recently dubbed 1969 'the Year of the American Revolution'. Many credulous souls – especially in the world's credulity centre, California – presumed *Rolling Stone* spoke directly for the Stones and so believed their impending arrival would ignite that revolution; if aided by the dark forces seemingly now at their command, so much the better.

The US embassy official who issued Mick's visa in London might have paused had he or she seen a pamphlet already circulating in Oakland. 'Greetings and welcome Rolling Stones,' it said, 'our comrades in the desperate battle against the maniacs who hold power. The revolutionary youth of the world hears your music and is inspired to even more deadly acts . . . the bastards hear us playing you on our little transistor radios and know they will not escape the blood and fire of the anarchist revolution . . . Comrades, you will return to this country when it is free from the tyranny of the state and you will play your splendid music in factories run by the workers, in the domes of emptied city halls, on the rubble of police stations, under the hanging corpses of priests, under a million red flags waving over a million

anarchist communities . . . ROLLING STONES, THE YOUTH OF
CALIFORNIA HEARS YOUR MESSAGE! LONG LIVE THE REV-
OLUTION!!!'

ON 27 OCTOBER Mick announced the tour's twenty-eight-show
itinerary to a packed press conference at Los Angeles's Beverly Wilshire
Hotel. He had been in LA for three weeks already with Ron Schneider,
preparing for the Stones' biggest assault on American sensibilities since
The Ed Sullivan Show in 1964. Their *Let It Bleed* album was to be released
to coincide with the start of the tour, along with a compilation of golden
oldies, *Through the Past Darkly* (whose cover commemorated Brian Jones's
last-ever photo shoot with the band) and a special fourteen-track promo
album for radio stations.

In contrast with hit-or-miss trans-America journeys in the past –
remember those redneck state fairs and performing seals! – every detail
of the tour had been meticulously organised, using the best profession-
als available but with the Stones (i.e., Mick) in overall control. For the
first time, they were to have their own sound and lighting systems and
special stage decoration, including carpet, all directed by 'Chip' Monck,
who had played the same role at the Monterey and Woodstock festivals,
and also emceed Woodstock. Rather than perform behind barriers of
glowering local police, as in the old days, they would have their own
stage security force composed of detectives moonlighting from the New
York Police Department narcotics squad. Through Ron Schneider and
their new company, Stone Productions, they would control the sale of
programmes, T-shirts and other merchandise. There was also a specially
designed poster of a nude Pre-Raphaelite-looking girl with the now-
familiar Jagger aura of raunch and refinement.

Acknowledging the band's own main creative inspiration – something that no one made them do – the main support acts were to be
black artists: bluesman B. B. King and Ike and Tina Turner, with Chuck
Berry replacing the Turners for the Dallas show. As if Mick hadn't spent

enough time on camera recently, the tour was to be filmed by America's noted documentary-making brothers Albert and David Maysles, whose fly-on-the-wall record of the Beatles' first US visit in 1964 had captured pop at its most amiable and innocent.

Mindful of the Stones' creaky Hyde Park performance, Mick insisted they should have two full weeks of rehearsal in LA before starting out. The original idea was for the band to live together in a house on Oriole Drive, but, as always, its officers and other ranks quickly divided. Mick and Keith moved into the Laurel Canyon home of Stephen Stills from Crosby, Stills, Nash (and now Young), while Charlie stayed on at Oriole Drive with his wife, Shirley, and small daughter, Serafina, and Bill and his girlfriend, Astrid, moved to a hotel. Mick Taylor and Sam Cutler accompanied the Glimmer Twins to Laurel Canyon, Cutler because he was essential to the tour planning and Taylor so that the senior Mick could keep a fatherly eye on him.

The Stills house – once the home of Brazilian movie star Carmen Miranda – came equipped with three young women: a pair of twins known as the Dynamic Duo, and an ethereal blonde named Angel, whose sole function was to sit around looking stunning, read tarot cards (not very accurately, it would prove), and give what Sam Cutler diplomatically remembers as 'back rubs'. Gram Parsons lent his roadie Phil Kaufman to act as major domo and general fixer, and the moon-lighting NYPD cops mounted permanent guard outside. Though the location was supposedly top secret, the odd intruder still attempted to climb through Mick's bedroom window shrieking her own version of Carmen Miranda's 'I-yi-yi-I like you very much!'

Cutler had expected life with Mick and Keith to be non-stop parties and orgies, but to his surprise both behaved 'like . . . English gentlemen . . . at a sedate country hotel'. Mick remained totally focused on the tour ahead, 'the general of the rock 'n' roll army', overseeing every logistical detail, however small, and every cent in expenditure; his most frequent query was 'Are we *paying* for that?' And even though housemates with his emcee and newest band member, he remained a being apart. 'He was never *not* Mick Jagger,'

Cutler remembers. 'Even if he came downstairs in his pajamas, he was always onstage.'

Whipping the Stones into good enough shape for the LA Forum and Madison Square Garden, however, threatened to be too much even for him. Rehearsals initially took place at the Laurel Canyon house, but only Charlie ever turned up on time and the playing continued to be ramshackle. Finally, in exasperation, Mick changed the venue to a sound-stage at Warner Bros film studios in Burbank. To simulate actual concert conditions, Chip Monck rigged the sound and lighting and decorated the stage just as it would be on the road.

Once the tour pre-production had been sorted and the band were playing with something closer to efficiency, Mick sent for Marianne. Despite her psychiatric treatment in Switzerland and months of supposed recuperation in London, she remained as ghost-pale as dead Ophelia adrift on the 'weeping river'. Her autobiography describes how carefully she was prepped so that the reunion would not be too upsetting a surprise for Mick. Phil Kaufman met her at the airport and escorted her not to Laurel Canyon but to a bungalow in the Hollywood Hills, where she was put on an intensive regime of fruit juice, vitamins and massage, still without any communication from Mick. 'When I had recovered, I was wrapped up in a bow and returned to him.'

According to Marianne, he wanted her to go with him on the tour, but she refused, sensing that their relationship was doomed either way. In what would be one of their last public appearances together, they visited a Hollywood club whose darkness was packed with stars from music, movies and TV. When Mick walked in, the place suddenly went as quiet as a church.

The tour kicked off with a sold-out show at Colorado State University's Fort Collins Sports Arena on 7 November. Faced with 9,000 howling Colorado students, Sam Cutler introduced the Stones as 'the world's greatest rock 'n' roll band', the title they would hold against all comers forever after – even though, Chuck Berry material apart, they never played classic rock 'n' roll music. At the time, such self-aggrandisement seemed risky for a band returning to the homeland of rock 'n' roll after three years off-road and still noticeably out of practice. Mick, in particular, resisted what he initially saw as a sacrifice of dignity rather than a masterstroke of pre-emptive branding. 'It was a stupid epithet . . . like we were a circus act,' he would recall, strangely for the late ringmaster of a 'rock 'n' roll circus.' 'I used to say [to Cutler], "*Plee-ase* don't use that. It's too embarrassing."'

For America, he had wisely not packed the white flouncy dress, but instead put together a look that mixed androgeny with irony: a scoop-necked black T-shirt and stud-seamed trousers, set off by his bondage dog collar and belt and a trailing pink chiffon scarf, the kind that gar-roted the great Edwardian dancer Isadora Duncan when it entangled with the wheels of her open Bugatti. Tipped back on his head was an outsize red, white and blue top hat, as worn by America's Uncle Sam.

Far more than their palmy Hyde Park gazebo, Fort Collins Sports Arena's giant stage revealed the strange contradiction in the Stones' new line-up. Until then, there had essentially been two kinds of rock band: those from the fifties and early sixties who jigged around and enjoyed themselves like the Lovin' Spoonful or Freddie and the Dreamers, and the modern kind, like Pink Floyd and Soft Machine, who conjured forth their vast electronic symphonies and cacophonies without seeming to move a muscle.

Yet here were both elements together; a front man who never stayed still – tossing his hair and pink scarf, inflating and deflating his outsize lips, pumping his elbows like a small boy playing trains – while his side-men competed with one another in studied lack of motion or expression. Keith, once so smiley and jiggy, now had a brooding menace, only intensified by thick-caked mascara. Curly-haired, child-faced Mick Tay-lor, eyes downcast on his guitar fretboard, might have been some shy Victorian girl embroidering a pious sentiment on a sampler. Bill Wyman had never moved or cracked a smile anyway. Only Charlie, in his nest of smashed cymbals, showed any animation, even if it never got as far as his sad turtle face.

In contrast with the twenty-odd minutes of yore, their performance now lasted a stupendous one hour, fifteen minutes. Most bands who'd come up earlier in the decade despised their early hits and refused to play them live. But the supposedly supercool, unsentimental Stones did oldies without even having to be asked. Their set thus ranged from the sunny good times of 'Little Queenie' and 'Carol' to the dark places of 'Sympathy for the Devil', 'Gimme Shelter' from the soon-to-be released *Let It Bleed,* and, climactically, 'Midnight Rambler', when Chip Monck drenched the stage in blood-red light and Mick beat it senseless with his dominatrix's belt. Mephistopheles, rape and murder then melted into hippie benevolence. 'We're gonna kiss you good-bye,' were his farewell words, 'and leave you to kiss each other good-bye.' And the 9,000 dispersed as peaceably as if Hyde Park had come to the Rocky Mountains.

The real test of America's welcome was the tour's second gig, two nights at the 18,000-capacity Los Angeles Forum, where advance ticket sales of $260,000 had broken the Beatles' box-office record from any venue. California was the epicentre of 'serious' rock, to be witnessed as well as listened to with studious earnestness. As Mick stood ready to chug out into Chip Monck's cross-hatched spotlight beams, a Forum official warned him, 'Don't expect them to scream.'

But at first sight of an ironically tilted Uncle Sam topper and trailing pink scarf, they screamed as dementedly as if rock's past six cerebral years had never been. Screaming gave way to a wholly new kind of approbation in 'Street Fighting Man', when they stood and punched air in time with the 'marchin', chawgin' feet – BOY!' Among the newspaper critics present was Albert Goldman, in later years the most malevolent of rock biographers. Goldman's *New York Times* review, written in a caricature German accent ('Ja, mein kamerads, *dot's* right . . .') likened the show to a Nazi rally at Nuremburg and characterized Mick as 'the Leader', exhorting his latter-day storm troopers to mass masturbation. In LA he also taped a performance of 'Honky Tonk Women' for *The Ed Sullivan Show,* which was transmitted without an edit mark from the censors who'd once thrown up their hands at 'Let's Spend the Night Together'.

Being on the road in America proved much the same as three years before, only bigger, louder and grosser. There were still the same glowering cops, drab grey-brick dressing rooms, and anonymous hotel and motel bedrooms. There was still the same avalanche of young women with un-British white teeth and peachy complexions, out to sleep with Mick Jagger and ready to do the same with any of the road crew who might facilitate it. Competition among groupies had grown so intense that some resorted to novel methods to attract their quarries' attention. The most famous was Cynthia Plaster-Caster, who memorialised every top-echelon rock star she bedded by making a cast of his erect penis, using a substance usually employed for dental moulds. Her subjects included Jimi Hendrix, Eric Burdon and Wayne Kramer of MC5 but – despite frequent invitations – never Mick. In later life, Cynthia would recognise female emancipation by making casts of breasts also, and, still later, run for mayor of Chicago.

Before the Dallas show, Ron Schneider was approached by a young blonde woman who introduced herself as 'the Butter Queen' and said her handbag contained a pound and a half of butter which she wanted to spread over Mick's nude body, then lick off. Any other Stone would do equally well, she said, but time was short, as she had to collect her young son from school. Sam Cutler excused them *en bloc* by saying they were all vegans, unable to tolerate animal products even in poultice form, so she had to be content with buttering up a few roadies.

At New York's Madison Square Garden, two nights in a row, capacity audiences of 18,200 screamed as instantly and unanimously as at the LA Forum. There was also a guest appearance by Janis Joplin, white rock's nearest reincarnation of Bessie Smith, who was to follow the Brian Jones path and die of heroin and alcohol abuse at the same age, twenty-seven, less than a year later. So sure was Mick of his crowd control that he positively invited stage boarders, switching back to lascivious Cockney again: 'I think I bust a button on my trahsers. I 'ope they don't fall down. You don't want my trahsers to fall down now, do yah?'

When he sang 'Live with Me', a smacked-out and sozzled Janis yelled: 'You don't have the balls!'

Later, he was stopped on the street by a grey-haired, grandmotherly woman who said she had a photograph she wanted to show him. It proved to be of herself, lying on a bed, naked, with legs spread wide. When Mick showed distaste, the vintage vamp grabbed his hair and pulled him to the ground. Two or three of the NYPD minders had to work quite hard to disentangle them.

Provocativeness onstage gave way to extreme circumspection at press conferences whenever tricky political questions came up. On 15 November the so-called Moratorium Rally brought 250,000 marchers to Washington, DC, for the biggest-ever protest against the Vietnam War. To TV interviewers in Australia, Mick had not hesitated to call the war 'awful and wrong', but now all references to the subject were fobbed off with smiling *faux*-Cockney banter. What sympathy did he have to offer America in the continuing trauma of seeing its air force bomb straw huts and its young men brought home in body bags? 'Just get over it as soon as you can.' Did the Stones have a message for the revolutionary young who regarded them as leaders? 'We're with you . . . right be'ind you.'

Those who tried to involve him more directly in the 'Year of the American Revolution' got equally short shrift. In Chicago, his backstage visitors included Abbie Hoffman, leader of the Youth International Party, or Yippies, and one of the Chicago Eight awaiting trial for conspiracy and incitement to riot following the '68 Democratic Party convention. Hoffman asked Mick to help fund his defence, but met the usual Jagger equivocation. 'He didn't say yes and he didn't say no,' the perplexed Yippie said later. In Oakland, California, militant Black Panthers demanded a pledge of personal allegiance from Mick, citing his past sympathy for black radicalism and the fact that black acts were on the tour. No such pledge being forthcoming, security had to be stepped up, for black performers as much as white. Though protected by armed bodyguards, Ike and Tina Turner still did not feel safe and took to carrying their own handguns.

The tour saw the birth of another Stones tradition, unwittingly based on the old vaudeville axiom 'Make 'em laugh, make 'em cry... but above all, make 'em *wait*.' Shows took to starting half an hour late, then an hour, and eventually two. The pop-festival era, in any case, had accustomed audiences to long inter-set vigils caused by shambolic staging and the performers' Mediterranean disregard of time. For the Stones' audiences, this tardiness was not the slackness or slight it might appear, but part of the fuck-you attitude that made the World's Greatest Rock 'n' Roll Band so ineffably exciting and enviable. The waiting masses were quite happy to imagine them delayed by some great party, which they would eventually condescend to bring onstage and share.

It was a habit that soon brought Mick into conflict with America's foremost rock promoter, Bill Graham. As operator of two legendary San Francisco music venues, the Fillmore and Winterland, and New York's Fillmore East, the famously volatile Graham had considered himself a natural choice to mastermind the whole Stones tour, but had been allotted only a few West Coast dates. He was mortally offended that such a plum should have gone to a newcomer like Ron Schneider, resentful of the sums he had to pay Schneider up front; above all, disgusted by what he saw (even if neither side concerned did) as the Stones' contempt for their paying customers.

Mick did not encounter Bill Graham until the double-show night Graham presented at the Alameda County Coliseum in Oakland. There was, fortunately, no incursion by the Black Panthers, but backstage conditions were more than usually bleak and during the first of the two shows the in-house equipment repeatedly malfunctioned. Afterwards Graham got into a furious row with Schneider and Sam Cutler, then burst into the Stones' dressing room, shouting that he'd cancel the second house. Mick – who was applying cosmetics at that moment – put aside Dixie and Cockney to greet him with the stinging offhandedness of some English theatrical *grande dame*: 'Didn't I speak to you on the phone once? You were rude to me. I can't stand people who shout on the phone. It shows the most appalling manners.' He then turned back to the mirror and went on with his *maquillage*.

His imperviousness to the allure of Cynthia Plaster-Caster and the Butter Queen, of course, had nothing to do with being faithful to Marianne. With his penchant for beautiful black women, he had taken an instant shine to Claudia Lennear, a back-up singer with the Ike and Tina Turner Revue who was not only stunning but blessed with a voice almost the equal of Tina's. Claudia was seen with Mick constantly offstage, despite a warning from Tina that the philandering, wife-beating Ike Turner also had designs on her. It was some consolation for being apart from Marsha Hunt, who had gone to Denmark to make a feature film – and would shortly become the first black woman ever on the cover of American *Vogue*. Back in London, meanwhile, Marianne received regular phone calls and letters from Mick, saying how much he loved and missed her and giving her little tasks so that she'd still feel included in his life, like scouring the Chelsea Antiques Market for the belt with which he lashed the stage in 'Midnight Rambler'.

While Mick felt free to indulge in any amount of midnight ramblings on the road, it never crossed his mind that Marianne might do the same. But when the tour reached Dallas, he learned that she was having an open affair with the Italian photographer Mario Schifano. To add yet another twist to the Mick–Keith sexual labyrinth, Schifano was a former boyfriend of Anita Pallenberg; indeed, Marianne would always suspect Mick-unfriendly Anita of setting her up with Schifano by asking her to let him crash at Cheyne Walk when he was visiting London. The UK press reported that they'd decamped to Rome together, taking Nicholas with them, and quoted Marianne as calling Schifano her 'Prince Charming'.

Such a thing would be a terrible blow to any young man's pride, let alone one accustomed to appear nightly in front of thousands of shrieking females to whom he was the most fanciable thing on two legs. Even so, the Tyranny of Cool – not to mention economics – exerted an iron grip. There was no question of interrupting the tour and returning to London to find out whether Marianne was serious or merely trying to get his attention. That night, at University Coliseum in Auburn, Alabama, the top-hatted, pink-scarfed, head-tossing, either-way sex god appeared onstage as per programme.

The Stones' last official tour gig (for $100,000) was the West Palm Beach Music and Arts Festival at West Palm Beach International Raceway on 30 November, headlining a bill that included Jefferson Airplane, Janis Joplin, Sly and the Family Stone, the Byrds, Johnny Winter, King Crimson and Grand Funk Railroad. The event was atrociously organised, with insufficient catering, sanitary and medical arrangments for the 40,000 crowd; there were 130 reported drug overdoses and a teenage boy died after being accidentally run over by a truck. The Stones didn't go onstage until 4 A.M. on 1 December, eight hours behind schedule, by which time it was so cold that spectators had chopped up many of the 300 portable toilets for firewood and Keith had to play swathed in a blanket. Even so, the vibe remained miraculously good.

Before returning to Britain in unquestionable triumph, they were to appear at a second festival – for free, like Hyde Park – at which conditions promised to be far superior to West Palm Beach Raceway's. While arrangements for this were finalised, the band had a recording date at Muscle Shoals Sound Studios in Sheffield, Alabama, following in the footsteps of great soul artists like Aretha Franklin and the Staple Singers. There, galvanised by his recent second spoonful, Mick finished off 'Brown Sugar' at top speed, writing one verse per page of a yellow legal pad. He also handed 'Wild Horses' to Keith, who was feeling some of the same pain of separation from his new baby son, Marlon.

There were some communication difficulties with the Muscle Shoals studio crew, whose Alabama accents the Stones sometimes found impossible to understand despite long conditioning to Jagger Dixie-speak. The Alabamans in turn were frequently baffled by the whiskey-and dope-slurred tones in which Keith now addressed the world. To avoid misunderstandings, Mick would repeat everything his Glimmer Twin said, like instantaneous translation at the UN.

The two nailed 'Brown Sugar' and 'Wild Horses' on the last night in just two takes per track, sharing a microphone and swigging from the same bottle of bourbon. Afterwards – as he had at every previous session – Mick destroyed all the outtakes so there could be no bootleg versions.

IT IS THE darkest of all rock legends: how at a Rolling Stones concert at Altamont, California, in December 1969, an inoffensive audience member was stabbed to death by Hell's Angels while, a few feet away, Mick Jagger sang 'Sympathy for the Devil', as usual not giving a fuck. And how the magic decade which the Beatles had defined with melody, charm and laughter was seen off by him and his band amid violence, chaos and callousness. Almost everything in the legend is untrue, especially the part about Mick's attitude. In fact, the horrible Altamont episode only came to pass because he *did* give a fuck.

While the tour had delighted its audiences without exception, it had created a backwash of resentment among promoters like Bill Graham, who'd been forced to dance to the Stones' tune, and media commentators to whom Mick seemed altogether too pleased with himself. To both camps, he was probably at his most insufferable at a press conference in New York's Rainbow Room on 25 November, when a matronly woman journalist quoted his so-wicked 1965 hit to ask if he was more 'satisfied' by America now. 'D' you mean foinancial-*ay*?' he replied in his best mixture of Cockney barrow boy and college debater. 'Sexual-*ay*? Philosophic-*lay*?'

Among these disgruntled promoters and disapproving journalists, one complaint recurred time and again: that ticket prices for Stones shows throughout the tour had been set at an extortionately high level. The *San Francisco Chronicle* columnist Ralph J. Gleason – who happened also to be a founding editor of *Rolling Stone* – made it into a positive crusade, repeatedly asking just how much money the band needed to squirrel away to 'Merrie England' and suggesting that, despite this supposed avalanche of dollars, their black supporting acts were being shamefully underpaid.

In reality, despite the Stones' urgent need of capital, top seat prices at prime venues like the Los Angeles Forum were $8.50, just a dollar more than to see Mick's arch-rival Jim Morrison with the Doors. In planning the tour, Mick had insisted on proscenium shows, where the whole audience got a frontal view, even though in-the-round venues could sell as many as 25 per cent more tickets. While raking in $260,000 from the Forum, he'd accepted just $35,000 for the gig at Alabama's Auburn University. And Ike and Tina Turner and B. B. King, far from being exploited, were receiving their biggest career boost in years.

Clear as Mick's conscience was, Gleason's constant harping had started to get to him. 'We aren't doing this for money,' he told another media levee at the LA Beverly Wilshire, with what can only be called breathtaking disingenuousness. 'We just wanted to play in America and have a lot of fun. We're not really into that sort of economic scene. I mean, you're either gonna sing and all that crap or you're gonna be an economist. We're sorry people can't afford to come. We don't know that this tour is more expensive. You'll have to tell us.'

In the tour's closing stages, however, a chance came along to answer Ralph J. Gleason and all those other accusations of greed and exploitativeness. Six days after the Stones' last official gig, California was to have its own Woodstock-style free festival, aimed at equalling, or surpassing, the original four months previously, but this time, in truer hippie style, organised by the musicians themselves. The idea had come from the Grateful Dead, supported by Woodstock co-headliners Jefferson Airplane, Carlos Santana and Crosby, Stills, Nash and Young. The one-day event would take place on 6 December in San Francisco's Golden Gate Park, an easily accessible public space with all the facilities for large crowds that Woodstock had so sorely lacked.

Mick had always regretted not being at Woodstock and, even before his alfresco Hyde Park triumph, had talked about such a Californian festival, as had Keith, with the Grateful Dead's manager, Rock Scully. Performing for free at this 'Woodstock West' would not only be one in the eye for Gleason but a thank-you to all the American fans who had taken him to their bosoms, or whatever, once again. It would also provide a climax to the film which Albert and David Maysles had been shooting throughout the tour. Such was Mick's enthusiasm that, while the Stones recorded at Muscle Shoals, key members of their tour team were sent to help put together the event from the Dead's communal house in Marin County. Not only the Dead but all the West Coast bands involved hugely revered the Stones and regarded them as the event's *pièce de résistance*. Even so, it was never seen as a Rolling Stones concert, but as a multi-act show in which the Stones would give the climactic closing performance. With sunny Hyde Park memories still lingering, Mick expressed the hope that it would continue to 'set a standard of how one can behave in large gatherings'.

The Grateful Dead's initial planning was quickly revealed to be wholly inadequate. Golden Gate Park had been announced as the festival venue without anyone first ascertaining whether it was available. When belated approaches were made to San Francisco's parks department, the necessary permit was granted but then revoked because a football game was due to be played there on the same day. An alternative site then materialised in a car-racing track, Sears Point Raceway, in the Sonoma Mountains, whose setting formed a perfect natural amphitheatre. The Stones' production chief, Chip Monck, was immediately dispatched to build a stage which, since it would nestle against a mountainside and command a steep downward slope, needed to be only about three feet high.

Sears Point had been officially announced as the festival venue when another problem arose. The raceway was owned by a Los Angeles film company, which suddenly added a rider to its original easygoing terms, claiming distribution rights to any film made of the festival. Failing that, a $1 million fee would have to be paid with a further $1 million lodged in escrow against site damage. By ill luck, the company also included the promoters of the Stones' LA Forum shows, who were still smarting from the 75 per cent of gate receipts they'd had to hand over, so there was no possibility of negotiation. As a result, forty-eight hours before the festival's scheduled start, with thousands of spectators already *en route*, Sears Point Raceway had to be scratched.

Losing faith in the Grateful Dead's organisational powers, Mick hired a flamboyant LA lawyer, Mel Belli – known as 'the King of Torts' and most recently seen in the Manson trial – to conduct the seemingly hopeless search for yet another site. And, miraculously, the world of Californian automotive sport again provided one. This was Altamont Raceway, a stock-car track near Livermore, eighty miles from San Francisco and sixty from Sears Point. The owner, Dick Carter, offered it gratis, provided the festival truly was free, $5,000 was paid for clearing up afterwards and a $1 million insurance policy taken out against site damage. Chip Monck and his crew dismantled the stage they'd built at Sears Point and worked through the night to reassemble it at Altamont, while radio stations and the stop press column in that week's *Rolling Stone* announced the venue change to the festival-goers in transit. The idea of what *RS* termed an 'instant Woodstock' gained further momentum when the promoter of the original New York marvel, Michael Lang, was brought in to advise on the logistical complications involved. The only Cassandra voice came from Lang's fellow entrepreneur Bill Graham, seemingly puckered with sour grapes: 'They'll never do it . . . it could explode in their faces.'

Graham knew, if no one else did, that all that Sears Point and Altamont had in common was being called a raceway. While the former was a well-run, well-patronised place of family entertainment, the latter was a run-down resort of mainly rowdy young males which for years had been hovering near bankruptcy, hence its owner's eagerness to attract high-grade rock performers there. Whereas Sears Point's steep slope would have made a perfect auditorium, provided good sightlines for hundreds of yards around, and given Chip Monck's concert stage an unassailable height, Altamont was almost totally flat. But there was no time for Monck to raise the level of the three-foot-high structure he was reassembling.

Least promising of all was the neighbourhood. The hippies trekking out from San Francisco to Livermore would find themselves in the mainly working-class, redneck East Bay area, where long hair was still greeted by howls of 'faggot' and fusillades of fist-crushed empty beer cans. It also was the territory of the Oakland Hell's Angels, the most feared and lawless of their kind in California.

By the afternoon of Friday 5 December a crowd of Woodstock proportions, or very nearly, was collecting at Altamont Raceway. One hundred thousand people had already claimed the area nearest the stage, and thousands more were arriving every hour in endless parallel columns, bearing tents, bedrolls, cooking utensils and musical instruments, like some medieval peasant army. Parking arrangements were shambolic: the nearest place cars could be left was a stretch of unfinished freeway eight miles off. Everyone but artists and VIPs (who used helicopters) had to foot-slog it down neglected access roads or, dangerously, along a railway line.

The muddy meadows of Woodstock would have seemed Elysian by contrast with these bleak, treeless flats, barely warmed by Northern California's pallid winter sun. Altamont was, indeed, the only festival site ever to need cleaning up *before* the event, being littered with the hulks of cars wrecked in its regular demolition derbies and carpeted with a foot-crunching layer of metal fragments and broken glass. The catering, toilet and first-aid facilities that had been shipped in over the past frantic twenty-four hours clearly were nowhere near sufficient. But festival-going hippies by now had some of the same spirit as Londoners during the Second World War Blitz, and the vibe initially seemed excellent.

In the early hours of Saturday, the Stones arrived by chopper from San Francisco, accompanied by key members of their entourage (and, as usual, a Maysles brothers film crew) for a first inspection of the stage. Unfortunately, the darkness prevented Mick, or anyone else, from realising the implications of its minimal height. Later, wearing a pink satin cape and matching Bonnie and Clyde cap, he talked to some of the audience as they shivered in their bedrolls, passing from campfire to campfire rather like King Harry before the battle of Agincourt in Shake-speare's *Henry V:* 'a little touch of Jagger in the night'. Someone offered him a joint and – having asked for the camera to be switched off – he accepted it and took a hit.

The vibe changed drastically the next morning with the arrival of the Hell's Angels. Though this was Oakland Angels country, they made up a virtual convention from chapters throughout California, the 'Frisco, the San Bernadino, the San Jose: some fifty riders in all, mounted on 850-cc Harley-Davidsons, each in a black leather jacket with a pale horseshoe-shaped insignia across the back; some with an equally tough-looking girlfriend clinging on behind; all bearing as much resemblance to Hyde Park's pimply *faux* Nazis as white lightning does to orange Fanta. With the convoy of gleaming, jouncing high-handlebar 'hogs' came a yellow school bus, loaded to the gunwales with their private store of beer and rotgut wine.

The Angels' recruitment as stewards is always held up as Altamont's crowning folly – and the ultimate manifestation of Mick's rock-star van-ity and arrogance. Actually, it had been planned by the Grateful Dead, abetted by chic radicals like Emmett Grogan, well before the Stones' involvement, and did possess a glimmer of sense. Since security staff and even police could not handle the Angels, it was safest to include them in the organisation, give them a privileged stage-front view, and cast them flatteringly as a Praetorian guard to the Stones. Previous fes-tivals had found them a deterrent to violence if they were allowed to park near the stage-side generators, so protecting the electricity supply along with the performers. There had never been any serious trouble with them before.

At noon, with the crowd now close to 300,000, emcee Sam Cutler announced 'Santana, the first band in the biggest party of 1969!' With the first elegiac notes of Carlos Santana's guitar, violence began erupt-ing all around the stage-front area between two immediately recogni-sable factions in that overwhelmingly white assembly. One consisted of hippies, male and female, breaking into the jerky lone gyrations music always awoke in them; the others were redneck youths, attacking any long-haired, wavy-sleeved dancer in reach, male or female, with pool cues that seemed to have been issued from some invisible quartermaster's store. Both factions were already out of their heads, the rednecks on booze and amphetamines, their victims on various types of bad acid that made many strip naked and almost offer themselves to the flailing cues. According to Cutler, the assailants were not fully fledged Angels but would-be recruits, hoping to make their bones by breaking a few hippie ones. The attacks went on in full view of the performers, uninhibited by snapping press cameras or the Maysles brothers' several film crews. There was not a security man, let alone a police officer, in sight.

The three-foot-high stage left the musicians horribly vulnerable. Angels stepped on and off it as they pleased, sometimes commandeering the MC's microphone to make their own private announcements or simply utter obscenities. The school bus had been parked a few feet away and a row of Angels stood on its roof, enjoying the grandstand view and occasionally lobbing an empty beer can or bottle at the performers. As a tactful way to remove this nuisance, Ron Schneider bought the entire beer supply for $500, then gave it back on condition its containers were no longer used as missiles (hence the legend the Angels were paid $500 worth of beer).

During Jefferson Airplane's set, vocalist Marty Balin saw a particularly nasty assault going on directly below him. He jumped down to intervene and a vicious blow to the face knocked him unconscious. When fellow vocalist Grace Slick – who had previously told Mick the Angels were 'really good' – ventured a cringingly polite protest, one of them seized the mic and roared, 'Fuck you!' Panic spread among the other bands scheduled to precede the Stones. Crosby, Stills, Nash and Young rushed through their set, then bolted for their escape helicopter. The Grateful Dead, who had conceived the event in a haze of hippie idealism, took one look at the crowd and left without playing a note. Only the ethereally pretty Gram Parsons gave a value show with his Flying Burrito Brothers and was brave enough to stick around afterwards to watch the headliners.

The Stones returned in the late afternoon and, there being no back-stage VIP area, had to walk the fifty yards from the helipad through the crowd milling around the nearby first-aid tent. Their private security force of NYPD cops had all taken fright and melted away; their only remaining protector was a huge black man named Tony Fuches, who earlier on had hit somebody so hard that his right wrist was now bound in a splint. As the band threaded their way among the punters, a wild-eyed boy lurched up to Mick and clouted him in the face, screaming 'I hate you, you fucker!' Mick shrugged the incident off, however, and ordered Fuches not to harm the boy. The only dressing room was a shabby trailer, with Hell's Angels posted all around it. If any Stone wanted to venture outside, he had to do so inside a phalanx of Angels.

Mick had originally planned to go onstage at sunset. But, rather than declining slowly in a crimson-flushed sky, the sun hurriedly popped out of sight, almost as if foreseeing what bad things were to come. Hence the legend that he deliberately waited for darkness, to give maximum effect to his entry and also goad and tantalise his audience beyond endurance. In fact, the delay was largely caused by the Angels, who now occupied the stage in such number that there was no room for any performers. With perilous plain speaking, Sam Cutler announced that the Stones wouldn't start until everyone got off. One of the few police officers in evidence came to Mick and offered a convoy of squad cars to give him safe passage back to San Francisco after the show, but mindful of his hippie cred, he refused to 'go out that way'.

The stage remained clear only for as long as it took the Stones to take up position and wan cheers to echo back from the 300,000 in outer darkness. By halfway through their opening number, 'Jumpin' Jack Flash', it was again choked with cracked black leather jackets and pale horseshoe-shaped insignia. 'Who was up there?' Sam Cutler echoes sardonically in retrospect. 'Who *wasn't*?' Normally, Hell's Angels were Stones fanatics second to none, but tonight Mick's pink cape, pink-and-black harlequin blouse, yellow crushed-velvet trousers and burgundy suede knee boots seemed to have aroused their deepest ire.

In these impossible conditions, he tried to do his usual show, pumping his satin-winged arms and boogieing determinedly up and back, from time to time asking the Angels on either side to 'give me some room, fellers . . . *please?*' A further contingent had taken up position below the stage, straddling their bikes and facing the crowd, their pale horseshoe-imprinted backs resembling the shells of poisonous beetles. Smoke from fires that had been lit against the sharp evening chill mingled with Chip Monck's red stage light to create a hellish effect long before Satan was formally invoked. Most of the crowd that heaved chest-high against the stage were having a good time even so, grooving to the music, making peace signs, offering up draggled flowers, taking photographs – something ferociously forbidden at later rock concerts – oblivious to the whirligigs of violence among them. Near the front was a conspicious figure, one of the very few black spectators among 300,000: a lanky young man in a pale green Beau Brummel suit and a dark fedora.

Dazzled as Mick was by the lights in his eyes and the high of performing, he took some time to realise anything was seriously wrong. 'There's so many of you,' he observed woozily before going into 'Carol', that good-natured old Chuck Berry favourite. 'Be cool at the front there. Keep still, keep together. Don't push around.'

'Sympathy for the Devil' was third on the playlist, as throughout the tour. With the first sound of its demented samba beat, a sudden forward surge by the stage-front Angels made the entire crowd retreat several yards. Mick shouted to Keith to stop playing and harangued the invisible troublemakers in flawless hippie-speak, clearly confident that his Hyde Park crowd magic would work again here: 'Hey, people . . . brothers and *sisters* . . . C'mon! Cool *out*! . . . Who's fighting and why? Why are we *fighting*? We don't want to fight, come *on*!' Believing he'd sorted the problem, he couldn't resist adding a little white lie to get them back on the Lucifer kick again: 'Something funny *always* happens when we start that number.'

He started it again, and managed to reach the end despite distractions that few other star vocalists can ever have faced. At one point, a large and ferocious-looking Alsatian dog wandered across the stage in front of him; at another, a naked, crazed girl in his sight line was set on and obliterated by five pale horseshoes; at yet another, a huge, bearded Angel in a Quakerish broad-brimmed hat stopped him singing to speak at length into his ear. The closing chorus of the devil anthem instead became part of his plea for calm: 'Oh yeah . . . awl right . . . ever'body got to cool out . . .' Then, almost in synch with Keith's final chord, there was another whirligig, and another casualty, a bearded white boy, was lowered to the ground in front of the stage, whether by his assailants or his rescuers it was impossible to tell.

Mick's tone by now lacked any trace of the arrogance that had put so many backs up. 'San Francisco,' he pleaded in no accent but that of Wilmington, Kent, 'this could be the most beautiful night. Don't fuck it up. All I can do is ask you, *beg* you, to keep it together. It's within your power.' In the interest of cooling out, he asked everyone to sit down, a ploy his teacher dad would have approved. The next song was 'Under My Thumb', possibly the most arrogant thing he'd ever put on record, but now softened down almost to a lullaby. A few feet away, a greasy-bearded Angel in the grip of God-knew-what junk narcotic clutched his head and glared upwards, with lips grimacing in time like some homicidal mime artist. Once again, the jeering last chorus became hopefully emollient: 'Baby, it's awl right . . . I pray that it's awl right . . .'

The music died away into stillness which for a moment gave hope that prayer had been heard. Then, before there was even time for applause, a gap in the crowd suddenly opened up twenty feet or so away to Mick's right. At its centre was the young black man in the dandyish pale green suit who'd earlier been standing quietly near the stage. Now he was struggling violently with a young white woman in a cream-coloured crocheted waistcoat and brandishing something aloft in his right hand. In an instant he was yanked aside and obliterated by horseshoe-imprinted black leather. It all happened so fast that even the Maysles-team cameraman who caught it on film barely saw it happen.

The stage dissolved into chaos. Keith ran forward, pointed out into the darkness, and shouted that the Stones were 'splitting, man, if those cats don't stop beating up everyone in sight'. Someone shouted back that there was 'a guy out there with a gun and he's shooting at the stage'. But for the present no one thought the incident any worse than others during the day. At Mick's appeal over the PA, one of the few doctors in attendance went to the spot and the crowd made way to let him through. A senior Angel in a lion's-mane headdress commandeered the microphone, ordering his colleagues to behave and assuring those whom they had terrorised that 'No one wants to hassle anyone.'

Nonetheless, the obvious course for Sam Cutler as emcee was to stop the show. Mick was clearly in danger, if not from gunmen in the crowd, then from two or three particular Angels who had kept murderous glares fixed on him throughout the evening. His once-zealous security seemed to have dwindled away, leaving only the small derringer pistol in Cutler's jeans pocket. In addition, the pilot of his helicopter feared the Angels might wreck it and was threatening not to stick around much longer. But Mick insisted on continuing.

The green-suited young black man was named Meredith Hunter, and despite his willowy height and street-smart air he was only eighteen years old. He had been stabbed in the neck with a seven-inch knife by a Hell's Angel wearing the horseshoe of the Oakland chapter after a scuffle in which Hunter pulled a handgun from inside his *faux*-Regency coat. Other Angels had then weighed in, smashing him over the head with a trash can and kicking him as he lay on the ground. Hundreds of people had been standing nearby, listening to 'Under My Thumb', but only his seventeen-year-old white girlfriend had attempted to come to his aid. While the Stones' set continued – 'Little Queenie', 'Midnight Rambler', 'Brown Sugar', even, amazingly, 'Street Fighting Man' – Hunter was receiving emergency treatment on the ground, then being carried, by Sam Cutler among others, to the stars' helipad, behind the stage, to be flown to the nearest ER. Before the chopper lifted off he was dead.

The Stones were due to leave America the next day, 6 December, having already extended their tour time by a week. Since none of the band had even seen the attack on Hunter, there was no attempt by the police to detain them. Sam Cutler offered to stay behind and answer any official queries, having been assured that his expenses would be sent to him along with his fee for emceeing the whole tour (never mind thinking up 'the world's greatest rock 'n' roll band'). He is still awaiting the cheque.

The benign tradition of rock festivals was by now so well established that the media at first could not imagine this one being any different. The following Monday's *San Francisco Chronicle* hailed Altamont as a brilliant success, only slightly marred by the stabbing of Meredith Hunter and the accidental deaths of three other male spectators (two accidentally run over by a car as they lay in sleeping bags, the third drowned in an irrigation ditch). Back in Britain in the run-up to Christmas – all the more frenetic for also being the run-up to a new decade – Fleet Street reported yet another triumph for peaceful youth power to set alongside Woodstock, Bob Dylan on the Isle of Wight and, of course, the Stones in Hyde Park. Exhausted and harrowed, even the usually honest, outspoken Keith was not in a mood to argue, telling reporters at Heathrow that Altamont had been 'basically well organised, but people were tired and a few tempers got frayed'.

It was only over the next week that the full, grisly story of the festival began to be pieced together. Audience members by the hundreds phoned in to San Francisco music radio stations, like KSAN, to complain about the lack of proper facilities, the unchecked circulation of bad drugs and the numerous other acts of random, unprovoked violence by the Hell's Angels that had preceded Hunter's knifing. In the process, those who had conceived the event – the Grateful Dead and their radical pals like Emmett Grogan – were forgotten. Multi-act Altamont turned into a Rolling Stones concert for which they, and in particular Mick, bore the whole blame.

For the *Chronicle's* Ralph J. Gleason, this attempt to give something back to their fans had damaged the spirit of rock far worse than the 'greed' for which he had previously condemned them. Altamont, wrote Gleason, symbolised 'the end of rock's innocence, a warning that the vast amount of energy contained in the music and its immense worldwide audience had elements of danger . . . And it seemed significant that all this was presided over [sic] by the greatest live performer in rock history, Mick Jagger.'

'Jagger's performing style is a form of aggression,' wrote *The New Yorker*'s Pauline Kael. 'Not just against the straight world but against his own young audience, and this appeals to them because it proves he hasn't sold out and gone soft. But when all this aggression is released, who can handle it?' There was even a dig from David Crosby of Crosby, Stills, Nash and Young, who had seen plenty of violence during their own set and had fled while the going was good: 'The major mistake was taking what was essentially a party and turning it into an ego game . . . I think [the Stones] have an exaggerated view of their own importance, especially the two leaders.'

Most damning of all was the magazine whose *raison d'être* had once been to celebrate the band now in the pillory. In a 20,000-word reconstruction of the day's events, published five weeks later, *Rolling Stone* described Altamont as 'the product of diabolical egotism, hype, ineptitude, money, manipulation and, at base, a fundmental lack of concern for humanity' – all implicitly emanating from Mick. As evidence of the Stones' stone-heartedness, *RS* pointed to their hasty departure the day afterwards – and the fact that not a word of apology or even condolence had subsequently been sent to Meredith Hunter's family. A subsequent call-in from Mick to radio KSAN, lamenting that San Francisco hadn't been the 'groovy scene' he expected, hardly helped his case. 'Some display – however restrained – of compassion hardly seems too much to expect,' was *Rolling Stone*'s very reasonable conclusion. 'A man died before their eyes. Do they give a shit? Yes or no?'

Promoter Bill Graham was equally specific in his condemnation, and gave vent to it with the uninhibitedness of a man who never expected to work with Mick again: 'I ask you what right you had, Mr Jagger . . . in going through with this free festival. And you couldn't tell me you didn't know the way it would come off. What right do you have to leave the way you did, thanking everyone for a wonderful time and the Angels for helping out? What did he leave behind throughout the country? Every gig he was late. Every fucking gig he made the promoter and the people bleed. What right does this god have to descend on this country this way? But you know what is a great tragedy to me? That cunt is a great entertainer.'

Today, however – despite that long-outstanding IOU – Sam Cutler remembers Jagger the pro rather than the poseur, the orange satin butterfly who, with guns and knives breaking out in his audience and Hell's Angels looking murder at him from either side, refused to disappoint the peaceful majority and went on to finish his set. 'He showed massive, *massive* courage at that terrible moment,' Cutler says. 'To have stayed on that stage and carried on performing needed the balls of a lion, and I take my hat off to him.'

CHAPTER FOURTEEN

'As Lethal as Last Week's Lettuce'

From the public backlash over Altamont, Mick turned somewhat belatedly to the personal problem of his errant girlfriend
and the Italian photographer who'd had the nerve to run
off with her. Marianne and Mario Schifano were now back from their
Roman holiday and spending Christmas at the thatched cottage in Aldworth, Berkshire, that Mick had given Marianne's mother. He found out
where they were, drove there alone, and confronted Schifano; after what
Marianne describes as 'operatic' scenes between the rival males, she
went to bed with Mick while her erstwhile Prince Charming took the
living-room couch. The next day she sent Schifano packing and accompanied Mick back to Cheyne Walk.

As she would write in *Faithfull*, it was the last thing she wanted to
do, knowing in her heart that their relationship was over – and sensing
Mick knew, too, but couldn't stand the thought of any woman dumping
him. And he wooed her back with the skill of any Latin Prince Charming, swearing he loved her alone and that everything from here on
would be different. The clincher was the Stones' elegiac country version
of 'Wild Horses', that phrase from her Ophelia suicide bed which Mick's

plaintive (indeed, rather whiny) vocal had transformed into a seeming pledge of undying devotion and faith in their future together. While Marianne listened to the finished mix, he knelt in front of her, holding her hands and gazing into her eyes, his full, reddened lips tracing the words: 'Wawld hors-es, couldn't drag me er-way / Wawld, wawld hors-es, we'll ride them serm-day . . .' How could she not melt?

There was another, less selfish incentive for believing 'Wild Horses' and trying to carry on at Cheyne Walk. The affair with Schifano had shown Marianne just how much her five-year-old son, Nicholas, loved and needed Mick, effectively his father since toddlerhood. When Schifano presented her with a sable fur coat, Nicholas waited until the grown-ups' backs were turned, then purloined the coat and, in a gesture of loyalty to Mick, flung it onto an open fire. Even this not-overly-attentive mother realised that for Nicholas to lose Mick a second time, and permanently, could have a devastating effect on him.

One of the biggest British hit singles of early 1970 was Blue Mink's 'Melting Pot', a plea for worldwide love and racial harmony whose lyrics included a respectful nod to 'Mick and Lady Faithfull'. With the public still refusing to recognise John Lennon's marriage to Yoko Ono or Paul McCartney's to Linda Eastman – and discounting Sonny and Cher – this seemed the only love affair in pop to have weathered the craziness of the past decade and stand a chance of maturing in the brand-new one.

In reality, Mick and Lady Faithfull teetered on the edge of their own particular melting pot, each lacking the resolution to jump or push the other. In a strange – though far milder – reprise of 1967, they returned to court together for the conclusion of their outstanding cannabis-possession case; Mick was fined a token £200 and Marianne was acquitted. They were back on the front pages a few weeks later, when Nicholas's father, John Dunbar, finally divorced Marianne on the grounds of adultery, citing Mick as corespondent ('MARIANNE WASN'T FAITHFUL,' the headlines exulted). For most couples, it would have been a moment of liberation, allowing them to legalise their love at long last in church or registry office. But Mick these days never mentioned marriage, nor did Marianne expect him to. Despite his protestations, she knew wild horses hadn't been able to keep him away from Marsha Hunt, never mind the innumerable other willing mounts always on offer.

The most melancholy reminder of what might have been was Stargroves, the Gothic mansion near Newbury where Mick had once planned to live the life of a country squire. His enthusiasm for the house had waned as he discovered just how much he'd have to spend to restore it and carry out Marianne's grandiose plans for the sixty-acre grounds. As a result, it was still gloomy and univiting, with many rooms still unusable and no central heating. Mick had spent no more than a couple of nights there with Marianne, then moved his parents in as caretakers, succeeded after a time by his brother, Chris, and Chris's American girl-friend, Vivienne Zarvis. A young man named Maldwyn Thomas, who used to cut Mick's hair at Vidal Sassoon, acted as caretaker (sharing the gatekeeper's cottage, for a time, with Brian's former girlfriend Suki Poitier).

Far more than Mick's domestic arrangements was bound for the melting pot. Prince Rupert Loewenstein's investigations into the Stones' financial affairs had uncovered a devastating fact: that throughout the bumper-earning era with Allen Klein, they had not paid a penny in British income tax. The liberal cash advances Klein had been wont to dole out counted as loans, on which tax could be deferred until they were repaid. The aim had been to provide the band with money to live on while spreading their income to avoid the worst impact of the 90-per cent-plus top tax rate which the Labour governments of the sixties had imposed. At the outset, the Inland Revenue had not formulated rules to deal with such a situation, but now they had. Once the Stones parted from Klein, all the deferred tax would fall due in one horrific lump. Even from Bill Wyman, in the far lower-earning second rank, the sum demanded was £160,000, equal to about £2 million nowadays.

Mick, that supposedly beady-eyed economics student, was caught just as unawares as his bandmates. 'I just didn't think about taxes,' he would admit. 'So after working for seven years, I discovered that noth-ing had been paid and I owed a fortune.' Such a fortune, indeed, that all his earnings from the '69 American tour might be gobbled up, yet still not clear his debt. Prince Rupert advised that there was one way not to go broke, though it would involve major disruption to a band that had already been disrupted more than enough. If they were domiciled out-side Britain during the tax year 1971–2, their 1969–70 income, includ-ing that from the US tour, would escape the Revenue's clutches.

The last ingredient to be thrown into the melting pot was vinyl. For at the same time as making the final break from Klein, Mick intended to jettison the UK record label on which the Stones had spent those seven years. Their contract with Decca was due to expire in July 1970, and there was not the slightest chance of its being renewed. Despite the millions Decca had earned from Stones records, relations between them had always been strained. And, after the band's recent spectacu-lar renaissance, every major label on both sides of the Atlantic could be expected to offer them deals that made Decca's once-stupendous $1.25 million advance look like small change.

Already well ahead of the pack was America's Atlantic label in the person of its president, Ahmet Ertegun. Forty-seven-year-old Ertegun had the same mixture of exotic, upper-class foreignness and earthy musical taste as every other important catalyst in Mick's career thus far. Born in Istanbul, the son of a former Turkish ambassador to Washing-ton, he had fallen in love with American jazz and blues as a schoolboy and started Atlantic with a fellow college student in 1947. Aided by the brilliant producer Jerry Wexler, he had brought black music into the commercial mainstream with signings like Ruth Brown, Aretha Frank-lin, the Coasters, Otis Redding and, most famously, Ray Charles. Since 1966 he had also been collecting white British rock acts: Led Zeppelin, Yes and – bizarrely – Screaming Lord Sutch.

Ertegun had made his pitch to the Stones in masterly fashion, strik-ing up an instant rapport with Prince Rupert Loewenstein and recog-nising that the only real point at issue was Mick – or, as Prince Rupert discreetly referred to him, 'the Artiste'. On top of Ertegun's immacu-late musical credentials, he and his interior-designer wife, Mica, were dedicated socialites with access to the top strata of New York society (in many ways more exclusive than London's), which Mick had never quite been able to infiltrate. If all that wasn't sufficient Jagger bait, he also had a passion for sport, especially football, and was shortly to co-found the New York Cosmos, one of the most successful teams in the North American Soccer League.

Although the Stones were still theoretically up for grabs to the highest-bidding label, Ahmet Ertegun had become the acknowledged front-runner by the end of the '69 American tour. Ertegun had arranged their recording session at Muscle Shoals, just before Altamont, and 'Wild Horses' and 'Brown Sugar' – those almost schizophrenic manifestations of Mick's current love life – were earmarked as the basis of their first album on Atlantic.

From the beginning of discussions with Ertegun, Mick made clear that the Stones were no longer willing to be just names in a record company's catalogue, subject to interference and censorship from weak-kneed executives as they had been with Decca all these years. Instead, they wanted their own label, like the Beatles' Apple but with none of the same extravagance and waste. The label would be under Atlantic's umbrella, using its production and distribution facilities, but with total creative independence.

The new label's prospective boss, Marshall Chess, was even more a piece of dream casting than Ahmet Ertegun. Marshall's father and uncle, Leonard and Phil, had founded Chess Records, the Chicago label which had nurtured all the Stones' greatest musical heroes, from Muddy Waters to Chuck Berry. As a teenager working in Chess's mailroom, Marshall used to deal with the orders for Muddy and Chuck albums from a blues-fixated schoolboy named Mike Jagger in far-off Dartford, Kent. The two had finally met in 1964, when Andrew Oldham brought the Stones to Chess to record 'It's All Over Now'. Indeed, that breakthrough session only took place because Marshall persuaded his father to let an upstart young white British band in among the mature black masters.

After Leonard's death in 1969, Marshall had not inherited Chess as he'd expected to, or received a sufficient legacy from his father to set up his own label. Hearing that the Stones were nearing a breaking point with Decca, he rang Mick from America to see if there was any possibility of working together again. Mick's US visa being temporarily suspended (because of the recent cannabis case), Marshall had to fly to London to continue the discussion. 'I met Mick at Cheyne Walk,' he recalls. 'In the room where we met, there was a long table against the wall with about a hundred albums on it, a lot of them blues. Mick put on 'Black Snake Blues' and was dancing to it while we talked.'

Mick then took him along to 3 Cheyne Walk for a reunion with Keith, who was tinkering at a psychedelic piano with Gram Parsons. 'They told me they were signing with Ahmet Ertegun at Atlantic and they were going to have their own label inside Atlantic, that they'd like for me to run. Ahmet was an old friend of my father's — he'd even been at my Bar Mitzvah — so that was another close link we had. But then I didn't get any follow-through from Mick, until in the end I had to play games and say I needed to know in two weeks because I was considering other offers. At the eleventh hour of the last day of the second week, I got a Western Union telegram, asking me to head up Rolling Stones Records.'

The final album for Decca could be provided without effort – a selection of live performances from the '69 American tour, entitled *Get Yer Ya-Ya's Out!* [a line from a Blind Boy Fuller song] *The Rolling Stones in Concert.* However, this left the band still owing Decca one further Jagger–Richard song, which the label doggedly insisted it must have. Mick and Keith accordingly went into the studio and recorded a track to be played at the final meeting with Decca's elderly chairman, Sir Edward Lewis. It was entitled 'Cocksucker Blues' and featured Mick in the character of a boy prostitute extolling fellatio and buggery ('Where can Ah get mah cock sucked? / Where can I get mah ass fucked?') and mentioning sex aids including policemen's truncheons and pigs. Needless to say, no release date was set.

As all these imminent plans and strategies for Mick took shape, Marianne felt with increasing certainty that there was no place in them for her. On the contrary, she knew that both Prince Rupert and Ahmet Ertegun regarded her the main obstacle to their fulfilment. She had already announced that she didn't want to leave Britain and join whatever expatriate commune the Stones might set up. And in Ertegun's courtship dance with Mick, the Atlantic boss had made one thing brutally clear. If he signed the band, he could not risk his investment being jeopardised by any further trouble over drugs. One day at Cheyne Walk, she overheard them discussing this very subject; Ertegun saying she was 'out of control' and he needed 'some guarantee that the whole deal isn't going to be blown by Marianne'.

The knowledge, she admits, sent her still further out of control in her drug use and compulsion to embarrass and undermine Mick in front of the two rather proper gentlemen who promised rescue from his financial predicament. Yet he still resisted their barely coded exhortations to get rid of her, and remained endlessly patient and forgiving. 'I put him through such hell,' she would recall. 'I made all the trouble. And through all this, he really acted practically like a saint.'

Past pain was stirred up for them both with the release of *Ned Kelly* on 24 June – but for Mick, unluckily, the pain did not end there. On the face of it, the film had every chance of continuing the run of Tony Richardson directorial successes after *Tom Jones* and *The Charge of the Light Brigade*. The story of Kelly, a well-meaning young man forced into outlawry (sound familiar?), had antipodean echoes of *Butch Cassidy and the Sundance Kid*, a recent box-office smash for Paul Newman and Robert Redford. Although Mick had excelled at portraying himself in *Performance*, he was clearly not an instinctive screen actor like Elvis Presley or John Lennon and, moreover, had opted to play Kelly with a peculiarly strained, unconvincing Irish brogue. In the action sequences, by contrast, the supposedly effete and pampered rock star was impressively at ease and independent of stand-ins, whether brawling with prison warders, sprinting across country, horseback riding, winning a bush hop-step-and-jump contest or ending a bare-knuckle fight by whirling his larger opponent around on his shoulders. It was all stylishly shot, authentically in period, not badly written and, at 106 minutes, hardly an endurance test.

Mick, however, loathed the finished film, was appalled by how he looked and sounded in it, and refused to attend its London première. The next morning, the British press echoed his sentiments a thousandfold. For most critics, the sight of rock's foremost sex god wearing a wide-brimmed Australian slouch hat, his famous lips weighed down by a bushy chin beard, was too intrinsically absurd for his acting to be judged with any objectivity. Others were mystified that he performed only one song on-screen, a traditional Irish-Australian ballad called 'The Wild Colonial Boy', while the soundtrack consisted of songs written by Shel Silverstein and sung by American country star Waylon Jennings. Still others felt cheated because in his one, very brief, scene in bed with a young woman, both were fully clothed. Greatest ridicule was reserved for his Irish accent and for the homemade armour Kelly puts on to combat seemingly the entire State of Victoria police force. One reviewer wrote that in this *Butch Cassidy*-inspired climax, encased in his crude helmet and breastplate, Mick resembled 'a cut-price sardine'; another rated him 'as lethal as last week's lettuce'.

Any hope that his worshippers among the Stones' following would confound the critics was soon dashed. *Ned Kelly* failed dismally at both the British and American box office, though it did moderately well in Australia. There, too, his association with the Kelly legend would be seen as a benefit rather than an outrage: the breastplate in which he'd seemed so ridiculously sardine-like (with the initials '*M.J.*' scratched inside) was later put on permanent display at the City Library in Queanbeyan, New South Wales.

ON 30 JULY 30 Les Perrin's office issued a press release announcing that the Rolling Stones had terminated their professional relationship with Allen Klein and would no longer be recording on Decca or its US affiliate, London. Whereas Decca had long realised the end was nigh, Klein appeared taken by surprise when the dismissal letter was hand-delivered to him at the Beatles' Apple house. Just a month previously, he had told *Variety* magazine of his plan to give the Stones exactly what Ahmet Ertegun was promising: their own record label under the umbrella of a major American one.

If Klein received a shock, there was one in store for Mick even nastier than the discovery of the unpaid taxes. It now emerged that there could not be a clean break with Klein, since he owned the copyrights to everything the Stones had recorded on Decca/London since 1965. The agreement they had originally signed with Andrew Oldham had vested all rights to their master recordings with him. Oldham had then sold the rights *en bloc* to Klein, at a moment when Decca was also seeking to acquire them. That meant the manager Mick had jettisoned so skilfully owned all his greatest moments on record: 'The Last Time', *Aftermath*, 'Satisfaction', 'Jumpin' Jack Flash', *Let It Bleed*, 'Sympathy for the Devil' ... *everything.*

A couple of weeks after the Stones left Klein and Decca, Marianne left Mick. This time, no other man was involved: she waited until he went away on a European tour, then packed a small suitcase and took Nicholas back to her mother's. Mick pursued her again and pleaded for them to try again, but she managed to stand firm.

Coming down to earth after their four years together was a scary business: she now had no singing career to fall back on, no money to speak of, a child to care for, and a ravenous drug habit to feed. As with Chrissie Shrimpton before her, there was no question of claiming a substantial part of Mick's fortune for the many ways she had enriched his life as well as complicated it. However, he did not try to take back the cottage at Aldworth that was now her main refuge, so she did not end up either homeless or penniless. (Both states were to come, but entirely through her own efforts.)

Her first boyfriend after Mick was his total opposite in every way: a lanky Irish peer named 'Paddy' Rossmore, whose 'monkish, spiritual' habits had powerful appeal after the rock-star lifestyle and who, above all, answered her need for someone to talk to. Lord Rossmore also paid for her to see a Harley Street specialist to wean her off the mixture of barbiturates and alcohol she was substituting for smack. The pair went so far as to announce their engagement – even though both at the time were living with their mothers – but called it off before any matrimonial plans could be made. So harrowed was Rossmore by what he'd learned about drug addiction and its treatment (or in Marianne's case, mistreatment) that he went on to found a rehab centre in Ireland.

Even after the Rossmore interlude, Mick continued to bombard Marianne with letters and phone calls, pleading with her to come back to him. Her final dissuasion was to destroy her own beauty, mutilating her once-golden hair into a raggedy crop and gaining more than three stone in weight. Unaware of the change in her appearance, Mick asked her to come and see him at Cheyne Walk. When she walked through the front door, she saw his jaw drop and knew the stratagem had worked. 'He finally realised I wasn't on the market any more,' she would remember. 'I never got another phone-call or letter from him.'

It was the first time in six years that Mick had been without a permanent live-in girlfriend and he, too, seemed to find difficulty in adjusting. For one thing, his love of nightlife temporarily vanished: at the Stones' office, he would give Shirley Arnold a £1 note and ask her to go out and buy two lamb chops and some vegetables for his Italian housekeeper, Bruna Girardi, to cook as his dinner that evening. Even at 1970 pre-decimal prices, £1 did not cover both meat and vegetables; rather than risk his annoyance by requesting three or four extra shillings, Shirley would draw it from the office petty cash.

Initially, there seemed a natural candidate on hand to take Marianne's place. Marsha Hunt, his so-called Miss Fuzzy, had been Mick's semi-public lover for almost a year and, with her dignity, drug-free lifestyle and uninvolvement in Stones internal politics, was not seen as any kind of threat by his financial advisers. After Marianne's departure, Marsha moved into 48 Cheyne Walk for a couple of weeks, at a time when Chris Jagger and his girlfriend, Vivienne, also happened to be visiting. Marsha saw how the change in his domestic circumstances seemed to have depressed Mick, but felt 'he missed the child [Nicholas] and the dog more than the woman ... He was very insecure, and needed the stability of a child.'

By Marsha's account, they were at Mr Chow's restaurant in Knightsbridge one evening when Mick suddenly suggested they should have a

TOP
Bianca on the road with Mick. She hated and feared his entourage, calling it 'the Nazi state'.

—

MIDDLE
Mick with Lou Reed and David Bowie. His relationship with Bowie provoked endless gossip.

—

BOTTOM
Mick marries Bianca in St Tropez. He said he never wanted it to be 'a circus'.

SOME OF MICK'S WOMEN

Opposite page, clockwise from top left: Marianne Faithfull, who expanded his mind more than LSD did but collapsed under the Tyranny of Cool; Cleo Sylvestre, the north London schoolgirl who was his first love; Marsha Hunt, the mother of his first daughter, Karis; L'Wren Scott, a 'high fashion Goliath' to Mick's David; Bianca, at one of her less elegant moments; Carla Bruni, who went on to be France's First Lady. This page: Mick and Chrissie, still happy, in a photo-booth; Jerry Hall (seen here with previous beau Bryan Ferry); Anita Pallenberg in an unusually docile pose.

ONSTAGE MOMENTS
IN VARIOUS STAGES
OF UNDRESS, SHARING
THE MIKE WITH KEITH,
WOODY, TINA TURNER
AND AMY WINEHOUSE.

TOP LEFT
Get the suit: Mick and Bianca at Jade's wedding to deejay Adrian Fillary in 2012

—

BOTTOM LEFT
Low-key Dad: with Jerry and two of their children (on the right) at a school sports-day.

TOP CENTRE
With father Joe and daughters Karis (on the left) and Elizabeth (right) after being knighted for 'services to music' in 2002.

—

BOTTOM CENTRE
With Luciana Morad and their son, Lucas.

TOP RIGHT
Putting on a brave face at Bill Wyman's wedding to Mandy Smith.

—

BOTTOM RIGHT
On the beach with Jerry after the Balinese wedding whose legitimacy he would challenge once she'd borne him four children.

Mick and Keith, aka 'the Glimmer Twins', rock music's longest-lived performing and songwriting partnership. But it has not been without its squalls. 'When are you going to stop bitching about Mick?' a journalist once asked Keith. 'Ask the bitch,' he replied.

baby together. She knew how much he longed to be a father – the more so since Marianne had miscarried their daughter, Corrina, while Anita had given Keith a son, Marlon. It was a very sixties rock-god proposition, Marsha recalls, designed not to interfere with his forthcoming tax exile or his image as world's number one stud. She would stay in London and have the baby while Mick played the role of absent father, flying them out regularly for visits in whatever tax haven he might end up. He made everything sound so plausible, and heartfelt, that she was unable to refuse.

She became pregnant almost immediately and, fearing Mick might have changed his mind, offered to have an abortion. But he insisted she should have the baby and that everything would be as he'd outlined. He said he wanted a boy, whom he proposed naming Midnight Dream (poor child) and sending to Britain's most exclusive school, Eton College. There was no suggestion of marriage, on Marsha's part any more than Mick's; as she often said, she could never marry any man who didn't get up until two in the afternoon.

She managed to hide her pregnancy for several months while still accepting music and modelling gigs – including a nude photo shoot for *Club International* magazine. And when the news finally did emerge, Mick's involvement was never made public. One newspaper sniffed out the story but was dissuaded from running it by threats of legal action from Marsha and an expert PR smoke screen from Les Perrin. In private, Mick continued to be a model of tenderness and solicitude, although she was puzzled that when his parents came to tea at Cheyne Walk during her stay he didn't tell them they were soon to be grandparents.

Even now that Marsha was carrying his child, she did not expect him to be monogamous, and he fully justified her lack of expectation. All that summer – including before Marianne's final exit – an unending stream of young women passed through 48 Cheyne Walk, some staying just a single night, or less, others lasting as long as a weekend, one or two later finding their way onto the largely female staff, led by Jo Bergman, who ministered to Mick's every practical need. They tended to be American, usually Californian, aged around twenty-two, with a free and breezy attitude to sex that British girls had yet to learn.

Bedding such beautiful nobodies from thousands of miles away was a typically judicious policy on his part, being less likely to attract the attention of the press, not to mention other bedfellows waiting in line. By an unwritten code, American groupies talked about their conquests only to one another, and there was as yet almost no kiss-and-tell market to tempt them. Not until decades later – by that time substantial matrons in superannuated hippie tea gowns – would they gurglingly recall their time as 'Mick's Girls' to tabloid newspapers or TV documentaries.

Perhaps the most famous, at least in retrospect, was Pamela Ann Millar – later Des Barres – a misleadingly angelic-looking twenty-one-year-old with a chin dimple to rival Kirk Douglas's. 'Miss Pamela' was already famous on the LA rock scene as a former lover of the Doors' Jim Morrison and a member of Frank Zappa's non-musical groupie girl band, the GTOs. When she first met Mick, on the Stones' '69 American tour, she was dating Led Zeppelin's Jimmy Page, but Mick enticed her away with tittle-tattle about Page's infidelity: a mind-boggling instance of pot traducing kettle. The result was 'a fabulous fling' with 'the most thrilling, naughty, sexy man I ever met'. In after-years, the gurgling matron would describe how his lips left hickeys (love bites) all down her thigh, which she later showed off to friends as the groupie equivalent of a Victoria Cross.

The following summer, her American boyfriend came to London to manage the Granny Takes a Trip boutique on King's Road, and on an impulse she decided to follow him. When she walked into the shop, she heard a shout of 'Miss Pamela!' and saw Mick there, trying on clothes. A second fabulous fling ensued, conducted at Cheyne Walk or the flat of her boyfriend – who quickly discovered what was going on but made no attempt to stop it; indeed, regarded it almost as a compliment. One day when Mick turned up, Pamela was in the bath and answered the front door naked to find him standing there with Charlie Watts. With old-fashioned propriety, he clapped a hand over Charlie's eyes.

Cheyne Walk's temporary tenants were not exclusively female. Also quartered there during these first post-Marianne weeks was the Texan sax player Bobby Keys, one of the outer ring of musicians henceforward to appear onstage with the five Stones. Keys had met them on their first

American tour, in 1964, when he was part of Bobby Vee's mohair-suited backing band. Bumping into him at an LA studio five years later, Mick had invited him to solo on a *Let It Bleed* track, prophetically named 'Live with Me'. Together with trumpet and trombone player Jim Price, he now composed the horn section Mick wanted for the first Atlantic album and for the Stones' return to touring Europe in August and September.

The stocky, hilarious Keys, a teenage friend of the great Buddy Holly, palled more naturally with Keith (they had been born on the same day of the same month in the same year) but esteemed Mick as 'a world-class harmonica player, the equal of any black guy I ever heard,' and 'the best country singer in rock 'n' roll'. He was even so a little apprehensive when Mick invited him to crash at Cheyne Walk while working on the album. Like many others around the Stones, he suspected Mick might be partly gay or bisexual, and had to suffer a good deal of ribbing from his fellow unequivocal 'straights'. 'People said, "Ah, you're gonna live at Jagger's . . . guess you'll be sleepin' with one eye open." I thought, "What am I gonna do if he makes a move on me? If I hit him, there goes the gig."'

Of course, no such awkwardness ever arose. It was a harmonious, low-key couple of months, hinting at Mick's loneliness at the time and his need for society more amusing than dreamy-eyed Californian nymphets. The domestic ménage consisted of his housekeeper, Bruna (whom even the ebullient Keys found intimidating), and his driver, Alan Dunn, whom he would periodically instruct to dress in full Edwardian chauffeur's uniform with jodhpurs and peaked cap. When the housemates weren't in the studio or out at clubs, they played chess, listened to music in the garden studio, or Mick held forth about vintage wines or the poems of Shelley and Keats. 'I sure learned a lot from that ol' boy,' Keys remembers. When a female visitor appeared, he would be 'a tactful Texan' and make himself scarce.

One day, Mick even persuaded him to attend a cricket Test match at the Oval ground, largely by telling him that alcohol was available there all day during games. Keys's wife happened to be in London and wanted him to go shopping that afternoon, but he fibbed that the Stones needed him in the studio. He hadn't bargained for the fact that all three British TV channels gave saturation coverage to Test matches, and Mick's appearance among the spectators, however unobtrusive (as it always was), would be bound to attract the cameras. 'So while I'm supposed to be workin' my ass off, she sees me on TV, drinkin' beer and tryin' to understand the goddammed game of cricket.' Hardly one's usual idea of being led astray by Mick Jagger.

For a time, just like *Performance*'s Turner, he had two live-in female companions, albeit in this case both Californian rather than French and polyglot Danish. The first to be installed, a bubble-haired blonde named Janice Kenner, had found herself alone with Mick in the back of his car and received a well-tried Jagger line: 'Do you like waking up in the city or the country?' Replying 'the country', she had been spirited away to Stargroves, there acquitting herself well enough to be asked to wake up in the city with him as well. Soon afterward, he also brought home Catherine James, a solemn-looking twenty-two-year-old who had taken the same roundabout car ride via Berkshire. The two coexisted at Cheyne Walk without rancour, each fixing on a distinct role for herself: Catherine was Mick's girlfriend while Janice was his cook, but available for the occasional 'romp'. In fact, their easy relationship rather irked Mick, who preferred the women around him to be at loggerheads for his attention. One day, to their bemusement, he got them to plaster each other with strawberries and whipped cream like a polite English garden-party version of mud wrestlng.

Mick's re-creation of Turner's domestic set-up was to prove strangely prophetic. For, having lain on the shelf for more than a year, *Performance* suddenly became a live project again. The Hollywood studio that had bankrolled it, Warner Bros—Seven Arts, had meantime been sold to the giant Kinney Corporation and acquired a new chairman, Ted Ashley. Looking over his inventory, Ashley was surprised to find a film starring Mick Jagger on which the previous owners had spent more than a million dollars but which had been junked after just one viewing of its first cut, early in 1969. Mick's name was far hotter in America now than when that decision had been made, so Ted Ashley decided to send *Performance* out into the world.

A sneak public preview of the original cut was held at a small cinema in Santa Monica, attended by Warner's new high command, the film's producer, Sandy Lieberson, and its writer–co-director Donald Cammell. The scenes of bloody gangland violence and deviant rock-star sex caused palpable shock and disgust and, Lieberson recalls, 'people walked out in droves'. Ashley ordered Cammell to do an extensive re-edit, paring down the long preamble featuring the young hoodlum, Chas, and his cronies – so reducing the bloodshed – and making Chas's interplay with Turner the crux of the story. Far from welcoming this expansion of his role, Mick was outraged by the changes and dilutions, and joined Cammell in a letter of protest to Ashley that both knew in advance would be futile: 'This film is about the perverted love affair between Homo Sapiens and Lady Violence. It is necessarily horrifying, paradoxical, absurd. To make such a film means accepting that the subject is loaded with every taboo in the book . . . If [it] does not upset audiences, it is nothing.'

Performance opened in the United States in August 1970, and was both a box-office and critical disaster. *Time* magazine's Richard Schickel called it 'the most completely worthless film I have seen since I began reviewing'. Decades would need to pass before a poll of directors and critics rated it number twenty-eight in the list of all-time cinema greats, and *Film Comment* magazine voted Mick's Turner 'best ever performance by a musician in a feature film'. For the cinema historian David Thomson, it is 'not anywhere near as good as the stories that surround it', but essential viewing 'if you ever doubt the tempest of repressed sexuality and pretension in the English soul'.

Nor were those stories yet at an end, for in after-years the film seemed to cast a malevolent spell over almost all its leading players. The most visible casualty was James Fox, who had taken the role of Chas as Britain's leading young screen actor, with a seemingly boundless career in front of him. Chas's gender-bending sexual games with Turner/Mick helped trigger a profound psychological crisis for Fox, further heightened by the death of his theatrical-agent father, Robin (who had not wanted him to accept the part and had asked Sandy Lieberson to keep a paternal eye on him). After the shoot, Fox disappeared to South America for several months, then abandoned his career at its zenith to join a fundamentalist Christian sect called the Navigators, not returning to the screen for more than a decade.

Anita Pallenberg – whom Turner chides for 'shoot[ing] too much of that shit, Pherber' – was soon to live out the line with Keith, falling into heroin addiction that would ravage her perfect face and body as cruelly as quicklime. Michèle Breton, the androgynous nineteen-year-old for whom appearing in a sex threesome with Mick Jagger should have been the autoroute to stardom, instead vanished into total obscurity. Not long after his stint as 'dialogue coach', the hyperactive, hyperviolent David 'Litz' Litvinoff mysteriously committed suicide.

The darkest shadow fell over writer–director Donald Cammell, who until then had seemed to lead a charmed life. Despite his extraordinary cinematic vision, Cammell wrote and directed only three more films over the next twenty years, each as visually and sexually daring as *Performance*, and each even more drastically diluted and recut by nervous producers. After the third, *Wild Side*, suffered this same fate, the once-charming, easygoing Cammell sank into paranoid depression, carrying a handgun with him everywhere and sleeping with it under his pillow. In April 1996 he used it to kill himself with the same 'execution-style' single shot to the head, learned from his East End gangster friends, that Chas uses to dispatch the tormenting Turner at the end of *Peformance*. It was later reported that he'd positioned a mirror so as to be able to watch his own death throes. Truly, in the words he'd written for Mick, 'the only performance that makes it . . . all the way is the one that achieves madness'.

As usual, Mick seemed to be the only one to have come through the experience unscathed – but even for him, *Performance* was to turn into a kind of curse. After that extraordinary first screen performance, people would endlessly ask, how come he never managed to do it again?

AROUND THE FIFTH month of Marsha Hunt's pregnancy, she began to sense a change in Mick's attitude to their parenthood pact. Where once he could hardly wait for her to bear his child, so she would later write, he now seemed to take a step back; where once he had been all tenderness and positivity, he now 'vacillated between approval and disapproval ... It alerted me ... that he was already forgetting the baby had been his idea.'

They still remained on close enough terms for Mick to suggest Marsha should join him in Paris during the Stones' European tour, even though by then she would be seven months' pregnant and the secret would be bound to get out. She declined the invitation but – with no diminution of supportiveness on her side at least – told him to phone her whenever he wanted to talk.

As further proof of his rather lonely state, he also asked 'Miss Pamela' on the tour (she decided to return to her boyfriend, however) and took along one of Cheyne Walk's two resident houris, his 'cook' Janice Kenner. The other, Catherine James, was dismissed as she lay in bed, with a farewell kiss and instructions to lock up the house before returning home to California.

The Stones' first appearances in Europe since before Mick and Keith's trial in 1967 featured their largest-ever retinue, sixty-five people, and a custom-built stage set and lights. As always, the support act was a revered blues figure, in this case guitarist Buddy Guy with a band including harmonica virtuoso Junior Wells to keep the headliners' own harp player on his mettle. At a press conference before the opening show, in Malmö, Sweden, on 30 August, Mick announced that the tour would not make any money, but was a gesture of appreciation to European fans for their loyalty over the past three years. (He would later say the band had earned just $1,000 each.) Asked about *Ned Kelly*, he snapped, 'It isn't worth seeing.'

Europe repaid the favour with displays of Mick-mania as extreme as any back in dear old revolutionary 1967 (though, after the close-up horror of Altamont, they could not but seem slightly anticlimactic). In West Berlin, street battles between fans and riot police left sixty-three officers injured. In Milan, a crowd of 2,000 attempted to storm the already full-to-capacity Palazzo dello Sport; only by a miracle were people not trampled or crushed to death. At Paris's Palais des Sports, about a dozen young women jumped onstage around Mick and stripped off their tops in unison, like some synchronised Olympic event, to reveal a common absence of bras. 'Normally, that wouldn't have bothered me too much,' sax player Bobby Keys remembers. 'But I'd flown in my mom from Albuquerque, New Mexico, to see the show, so she'd know how good her little boy was doin'. So I'm standin' there, these beautiful young chicks shakin' their tits in my face, knowin' Mom's watchin' – and *dyin'* by the minute.'

Meanwhile, the Stones' final Decca album, the live *Get Yer Ya-Ya's Out!*, had reached number one in Britain and six in America, belatedly rousing the label into efforts to win them back. Emissaries from Decca hurried to Paris to see whether, even at this late stage, Mick could be persuaded not to defect to Atlantic. A helpful gesture, Mick's people suggested, would be for them to pay the band's bill at the George V hotel. Decca's men eagerly agreed, not realising that the George V still allowed guests to make purchases at expensive stores on the nearby Champs-Elysées and charge them to their hotel account. The result was a shopping spree at Cartier for Mick and the boys, a hotel bill of tens of thousands of dollars, and an end to any further overtures on Decca's part.

Despite the availability of cook Janice to, in her words, 'calm him down' after each night's show (implicitly by means of something other than a warm milk pudding), Mick still seemed unhappy without a permanent relationship and was frequently overheard on the telephone to Marsha, albeit talking about himself rather than the progress of her pregnancy. One night, he called her to say he'd been feeling lonely but had met 'someone named Bianca who was from Nicaragua' and whom he intended to see again in Italy.

The meeting had been on 21 September, at an extravagant after-show party at the George V for which Decca Records would find themselves paying. Ahmet Ertegun, now Mick's goateed shadow, had brought along an old friend, the French pop mogul Eddie Barclay. With the fifty-year-old Barclay was his twenty-five-year-old former girlfriend, Bianca Pérez-Mora Macias. Also present when Ertegun introduced Bianca to Mick was Donald Cammell, still at this time a creature of geniality and light. 'You two are going to have such a great romance,' Cammell told them. 'You were made for each other.'

The most impressive woman ever to enter Mick's life – if not quite for the reasons he first thought – had grown up in Managua, capital city of Central America's largest, richest and least stable nation. Bianca's father was a wealthy commodities dealer, and her family on both sides had provided diplomats for various key posts in the Nicaraguan foreign service. When her father's business failed, her parents separated and her powerhouse mother, Dora, supported her and her brother, Carlos, by running a small restaurant in Managua. Though nominally a republic, Nicaragua was ruled by the Somoza family, a thuggish dynasty that held on to power for forty years by systematically murdering or intimidating all opposition. Dora was a fierce and fearless activist against the regime, and from the earliest age her daughter and son accompanied her on marches and demonstrations and were likewise marked down as enemies of the state. Bianca showed strong academic gifts and at the age of seventeen was offered a scholarship by the French government to study at the Institute of Political Science in Paris. Dora made her go, thinking she'd be safer out of the country.

Bianca and Paris *were* made for each other. With her remarkable beauty went an elegance that had little to do with sixties dolly fashion, and a faint air of mystery somewhat recalling the girl in the Peter Sarstedt song who 'talk[s] like Marlene Dietrich and dance[s] like Zizi Jeanmaire', whose 'clothes are all made by Balmain' and has 'diamonds and pearls in [her] hair'. While still in her teens, she became the girlfriend of Michael Caine, then as glamorous as any rock star for films such as *The Ipcress File*. Caine brought her to London and showed her off in many places where she might have crossed paths with Mick, but somehow never did. She later complained that 'unkind, superficial' Caine 'kept me like I was his geisha'. She hadn't seen nuthin' yet.

After Michael Caine came an almost five-year relationship with Eddie Barclay, a former bandleader who had built up his eponymous record label with a mixture of French artists like Charles Aznavour and Jacques Brel and imported American jazz and blues. Though twice her age, and gnomically unattractive, Barclay provided the security Bianca needed. His extravagance and openhandedness were legendary, especially in Saint-Tropez, the high-fashion Riviera resort in which he spent most of every summer. There he wafted around the narrow streets in a white Rolls-Royce, gave 'white parties' frequented by the cream of the international jet set, and block-booked a huge table every day at the exclusive 55 beach club, paying for dozens of meals and bottles of wine whether he used the table or not.

Legend has it that Mick fell for Bianca because she looked exactly like him. It has become a modern myth of Narcissus: the world's most lusted-after creature, entranced by the thought of making love to himself. In fact, the two did not really resemble each other, apart from both being slight and fine-boned, with the same air of not belonging to the noisy, taller crowd around them. What Mick saw was a young woman as intriguing as she was beautiful – so different from all those bland Californians – virtually offered to him on a canapé tray just when he was seeking a new relationship. For Bianca, after years with a middle-aged father figure, Mick's primary attraction was not being a world superstar, or being incredibly wealthy, or even being incredibly sexy, but simply being *young*. As to so many females on first meeting, he seemed 'shy, vulnerable and human' – though he rather spoiled this impression by mischievously pulling off Eddie Barclay's toupee.

So smitten was he that all his usual secretiveness went out of the window. When the tour moved on to Italy, Bianca flew to join him in Rome and was met at the airport by his personal limo. In this birthplace of paparazzi, the story soon got out, unleashing harassment so extreme that Mick punched a photographer, was hauled before a judge, and fined the equivalent of $1,200. After the tour's final concert in Amsterdam on 9 October he returned to Britain with Bianca openly at his side, joking to reporters at Heathrow Airport that they were 'just good friends' while Bianca took refuge in a ferocious, but still beautiful, frown. 'I have no name,' was her answer to all questions. 'I do not speak English.'

From that night on, 48 Cheyne Walk had a new chatelaine. When recent tenants like Miss Pamela or Catherine James telephoned and asked to speak to Mick, a stern Latin-inflected voice would reply that he was unavailable. 'Cook' Janice Kenner remained on the staff, but with duties now strictly confined to the kitchen.

Bianca's impact on the Rolling Stones was not far short of Yoko Ono's when John Lennon first unloosed her on the Beatles. Whatever Mick's previous sexual or social digressions, his primary concern had always been keeping the Stones on track and pushing them ever forward. Now, suddenly, here was something that interested him more. The repercussions were felt, not only within the band itself but all down the pyramid of individuals whose livelihoods depended on proving their indispensability to him on a daily, sometimes hourly, basis.

Not that Bianca – unlike Yoko – sought to exert any influence whatsoever. Whereas all Mick's previous women, to some or other degree, had belonged to the pop music world, she was a total outsider. Even the Parisienne Holly Golightly in the Peter Sarstedt song kept Rolling Stones records in 'a fancy apartment on the Boulevard Saint-Michel'. But, despite years with France's best-known record boss, Bianca knew nothing about rock – indeed, regarded it and its practitioners as rather childish. For Mick, at the beginning, that was part of her irresistible allure.

With Yoko, of course, the opinions of all three other Beatles had counted, whereas with Bianca, Mick was concerned with only one Stone, his fellow Glimmer Twin. Keith initially considered her just 'some bimbo', and resignedly prepared for Mick to take another furlough into the society columns. Though he found Bianca aloof and humourless, he was constitutionally incapable of being nasty in the way George Harrison, for example, was to Yoko. A far more dangerous foe emerged in Anita, until now the reigning beauty among the Stones' harem wives. While feigning a sisterly welcome, Anita whispered and intrigued against Bianca behind her back, even getting the drug dealer Spanish Tony Sanchez to pursue a rumour that she'd been born a man and undergone a sex-change operation.

Thanks to a strict Catholic upbringing in Nicaragua, Bianca was a conventional, even rather straitlaced young woman, and the discovery of the sexual free-for-all around the Stones came as a profound shock to her. Before very long, too, she heard about the swathe Anita had cut through the band, and the still-active rumour that being Brian's old lady first, and now Keith's, was all part of a long-term plan to end up with Mick. The other persistent whisper to trouble her was that Mick's sovereignty in the band conferred a kind of *droit du seigneur*; throughout their time together Bianca would believe he had 'fucked all the other Stones' wives except Charlie's'.

As things turned out, Mick and Bianca spent much of their first months together at the country house he had bought to share with Marianne but, until now, had used mainly as a chat-up line ('Do you like waking up in the town or the country?') to his Californian handmaidens. Just before the decision to become tax-exiled nomads, the Stones had acquired a custom-built mobile sixteen-track recording studio housed inside a large truck painted the anonymous khaki of a bird-watcher's hide. They were now using this Mighty Mobile to complete *Sticky Fingers*, the first album for their own Rolling Stones record label. Stargroves was the handiest place to park the vehicle and hook it up to a power supply. The Gothic pile therefore suddenly had to provide accommodation for the Stones, their staff and technicians, plus visiting session musicians like the organist Billy Preston. As most of the house was still unfurnished, Marshall Chess used a company that supplied décor for film sets to assemble a dozen instant bedrooms.

In his capacity as head of Rolling Stones Records, Chess became *de facto* executive producer on *Sticky Fingers*, operating the same tough regimen as Chess Studios in the old Chicago days, when the house rule used to be 'three tunes in three hours'. But even he could not always keep Mick's eye on (or rather off) the ball. Bianca had no concept of the iron rule that when the Stones were recording, their old ladies waited patiently for as long as it took. She would come into the studio, give Mick a smouldering glance, and he would break off work and disappear with her, sometimes for days.

After years in musty limbo, Stargroves suddenly boomed with electric noise and echoed with pot-fumed laughter. Its decidedly Edgar Allan Poe atmosphere even brought a brief resurgence of sympathy with the devil. Film-maker Kenneth Anger had at long last raised sufficient funds to make his black magic epic *Lucifer Rising* (with music written by some-time Manson disciple Bobby Beausoleil in the California prison where he was now serving a life sentence). Unable to persuade Mick to play Lucifer, Anger had cast Chris Jagger instead, with Donald Cammell as Osiris and Marianne Faithfull as Lilith. Keith still found Anger amusing, if Mick did not: while setting up the production, he was a frequent occupant of Star-groves' *ad hoc* bedrooms, and even sketched ideas for visuals on its stone floors. 'That was a crazy time,' Marshall Chess recalls. 'I'd be woken in the middle of the night by someone banging on a piano, and the next morning there'd be all these weird occult drawings all over the floor.'

On 4 November Marsha Hunt gave birth to a daughter she named Karis. She went through the whole process alone, checking herself into the grim Victorian St Mary's Hospital, Paddington, and avoiding all questions about Karis's father, though the baby's remarkably full lips provided a clue. Towards the end of her pregnancy, Marsha had been seriously short of money, having had to give up performing, and been unable to extract the royalties she was owed from her record label, Track. Finally, she had no alternative but to ask Mick – who, she knew, was now living with Bianca – for financial help. As she would recall, he sent £200 with a note saying 'I know I haven't done right by you,' or words to that effect, and also lent her a ring of his that she liked. What a miserly chill there is in that word *lent*.

After Karis was born, the signals from Mick initially seemed encour-aging. Marsha received a congratulatory telegram and a bouquet of red roses from him, and he dispatched Bruna, the Cheyne Walk house-keeper, to prepare her flat for her return from the hospital. Some time passed, however, before he could slip away from Bianca and pay Marsha and Karis a visit. He was accompanied by his driver, Alan Dunn, and was 'cordial and charming'. Marsha would recall, but seemed 'in a hurry to be somewhere else'. Soon afterwards Bruna was recalled to Cheyne Walk.

He did not reappear for another ten days. By now, Marsha's tolerance was exhausted, and she railed at him for his neglect, holding baby Karis in her arms. Mick responded that 'he had never loved me, and I was mad to think he had'. He added that, if he chose, he could take the baby away from her. Marsha's spirited answer was that she'd 'blow his brains out' if he tried.

For Marsha, there was thus an unpleasant double meaning in the title of Mick's third film that year, *Gimme Shelter*, when it premièred in Britain a month later. And the Maysles brothers' colour documentary of the Stones' return to America, and its gruesome climax at Altamont, seemed to reflect everything she now felt about Mick's irresponsibility and uncaringness. The Maysles had continued filming as a twenty-two-year-old Hell's Angel wannabe named Alan Passaro, identified mainly through their concert footage, had gone on trial in Oakland for the murder of the black teenager, Meredith Hunter. Passaro pleaded self-defence, claiming that Hunter had actually fired the handgun he was seen waving. *Gimme Shelter* was central to the prosecution's case, but during the trial its seemingly irrefutable eyewitness evidence began to crumble. Outtakes from the film seemed to show Hunter previously taunting a group of Angels, and an orange flash coming from his weapon just before he was felled. The jury concluded that anyone who pulled a gun around Hell's Angels, especially if he was black, deserved everything he got, and Passaro was acquitted.

Gimme Shelter showed Mick in the most unflattering possible light, a puny orange-satin harlequin at first oblivious of the nightmare around him, then powerless to affect it. His departure from Altamont Raceway looked most ignominious of all, sweat-soaked and visibly traumatised, crammed with thirteen other people into a helicopter bubble designed for eight. There was no mention of his 'balls of a lion' for going onstage at all, let alone staying as long as he had. As usual, he was too cool to tell the real story, or allow it to be told, so once again the world thought the worst of him.

ON 4 JANUARY 1971 *Performance* opened in London with a charity première at the Warner Cinema, Leicester Square. Mick had asked that the proceeds be donated to Release, the hippie charity which – largely inspired by his and Keith's ordeal in 1967 – provided legal representation to young people arrested for drug possession. The Warner organisation had at first thrown up their hands in fresh horror, but capitulated when Mick threatened to boycott the event unless his wishes were respected. His support, in fact, came as a godsend to Release's founder, Caroline Coon, who was struggling against heavy odds to keep the service going. London's foremost Beautiful People flocked to buy expensive tickets, with the promise of joining Mick at the pre-show reception and the party afterwards.

However, despite his enthusiasm for Release and his desire to cause Warners maximum discomfiture, his attendance at the première was never seriously on the cards. He had long ago lost interest in the film or any pride in his playing of Turner; more to the point, Bianca would hardly relish his steamy on-screen sex scenes with Anita Pallenberg and frolics in the bath with Anita and Michèle Breton.

On the night, an expectant crowd of literary and media celebrities gathered at the Warner West End, among them the famous drama critic and libertarian Kenneth Tynan and the editor of *Oz* magazine, Richard Neville. Anita turned up, accompanied – surprisingly – by Keith, but as the minutes ticked away to showtime there was no sign of Mick. Finally, an angry deputation, led by Tynan's wife, Kathleen, surrounded Caroline Coon, shouting that they'd been conned, if not Cooned. The celebs received assurances that Mick was flying in from Paris to join them and were persuaded to watch the film, then go to Tramp for dinner – on him – and he'd catch up with them later. But he never did. The explanation was that his flight had been delayed by fog.

Under the UK's lingering film-censorship code, *Performance* received an adults-only 'X' certificate which consigned it to the realm of cheap horror and skin flicks, limited its showings outside London and ensured that thousands of youthful Mick fans could not legally see it. His one song from the soundtrack, 'Memo from Turner', had been released as a single the previous October, but had reached only No. 32. His best screen performance and best solo track thus came and went together.

The deal with Atlantic had by now been hammered out between Prince Rupert and Ahmet Ertegun. Marshall Chess remembers Ertegun repeatedly mopping his perspiring bald pate with a handkerchief during the final negotiations, as well he might. The Stones were to deliver four albums over six years and receive a royalty of one dollar on every copy sold – the highest rate ever paid to a recording act. The albums would be released under the imprimatur of Rolling Stones Records, with cover artwork as well as content dictated solely by the band. Rather than a lump sum shared out among them, Atlantic's advance was to be a budget to cover the making of each album. Mick and Keith had originally wanted other artists on the label – distributing Jimi Hendrix's label was one possibility – but Atlantic's funding proved only enough to maintain the Stones.

It was Chess who suggested the label should have a logo that instantly identified it without need of any printed name. The idea occurred to him while he was driving through Holland to meet the Stones in Amsterdam and passed the wordless but universally recognised scallop-shaped symbol of the Shell Oil company. That inspired the notion of branding Rolling Stones Records, and all ancillary merchandise, with Mick's lips and tongue – the most blatant declaration yet of who was both the star and the boss. Various designs were submitted by leading graphic artists, including one of a tongue with a pill on it, but none seemed quite right. Finally, a Royal College of Art student named John Pasche came up with the garish red, slurping, slavering winner. For creating what would become rock's most famous piece of corporate identity (ultimately representing wealth almost comparable with Shell Oil's), Pasche was paid £50, with a later top-up of £200.

Early March brought the Stones' first British tour in four and a half years. At its opening press conference, Mick revealed that the band would be emigrating to France a month from now, and this was a formal farewell to their UK fans. Because no Briton must ever be seen to avoid tax, even by perfectly legal means, their PR man, Les Perrin, tried to dress up the decision as a purely aesthetic and cultural one, in line with Mick's well-known dedication to self-improvement. 'It's not a case of

running away from the tax man,' Perrin said with reeking disingenuousness. 'The Stones like France tremendously.'

No other British band had ever gone abroad like this in the footsteps of literary celebrities like W. Somerset Maugham and Graham
Greene. Some commentators initially suspected it might also be a device
for quietly breaking up the Stones rather than letting them take their
chances against younger competition in the already teeming new pop
decade. Just a month earlier, the Beatles' long disintegration had finally
come into the open with Paul McCartney's application to the British
High Court to wind up their business partnership. One interviewer
reminded Mick how often John Lennon had accused the Stones of copying the Beatles, and asked whether that applied even now. 'Nah, we're
not breaking up,' he answered. 'And if we did we wouldn't be as bitchy
as them . . . We'll remain a functioning group, a touring group, a *happy*
group.' The *Daily Telegraph* suggested that over the years they could have
earned as much as £83 million. Mick took a whole-page advertisement
to dismiss the figure as 'ludicrous'.

Prior to this UK farewell tour, Keith had made the first of what would
be numerous attempts to overcome his heroin addiction. For all his
gypsy-rebel air, he remained a shy, rather insecure character for whom
drugs were a hiding place from the pressures of fame, and heroin the
best one of all. (In later life, he would observe that Mick had an equally
powerful addiction to flattery, 'which is very like junk', but never made
the slightest attempt to clean up from that.) Over the previous year, his
dependence had grown steadily more serious, encouraged not only by
Anita but by his angelic-looking country-rock crony Gram Parsons, to
the point where Mick's PA Jo Bergman had seriously wondered whether
he'd survive the 1970 European tour.

Widely read Mick knew that when heroin threatened to destroy
the great American writer William S. Burroughs, author of *Naked
Lunch,* he had sought help from a British doctor named John Dent,
who reduced the usual horrific withdrawal symptoms by means of an
electronic box attached to the patient's head. Dr Dent had since died,
but the treatment, known as apomorphine aversion therapy, was still

practised by his former nurse, a brisk matron known as Smitty. Keith submitted to Smitty's ministrations at 3 Cheyne Walk in company with Gram Parsons, both sharing one bed like small boys in a boarding school sick bay. After putting them through five days of almost continual vomiting and incontinence, their nurse pronounced them cured.

The tour revisited most of the Stones' old northern package-tour haunts, like Coventry, Manchester and Newcastle-on-Tyne. They were almost the last survivors of those innocent days and, despite the gigantic loss of innocence they represented, met with screams as blissfully infantile as ever. To conserve resources for the coming months abroad, inter-show travel was by ordinary domestic flights or the purgatorial nationalised rail network. Bianca accompanied Mick, who already looked more than a little French in his floppy blue cap and grey suede maxicoat. He had spoken the language reasonably well since his school days, and now practised constantly with the fluent Bianca. Journeys between gigs were whiled away with games of backgammon, at which Bianca proved remarkably adept, while still unbending little to their fellow players. Marshall Chess, from whom she won a small fortune, grumbled that 'she even gambles in a foreign language'.

The final farewell gig was a nostalgic return to Soho's Marquee Club, which had given the Stones their first break as an interval band, fronted by 'R&B singer Mick Jagger', in the matelot-striped summer of 1962. But the return was not a happy one. At the moment they were due to start, Keith – whom the prospect of emigration seemed to be stressing almost as much as going cold turkey – was still at Redlands, sixty miles away. He did not arrive until two hours later, in a filthy mood, leaving his Bentley parked on a double yellow line and stomping into the Marquee barefoot. Unluckily, the club was still run by Harold Pendleton, whose hostility to the beginner Stones for being 'too rock 'n' roll' Keith, in particular, had never forgotten or forgiven. The performance was to be filmed for American TV – to make up for their non-appearance in the States that year – and to gain maximum publicity Pendleton wanted them to play in front of a large neon sign saying MARQUEE CLUB. There

was a furious row which ended with Keith swinging
leton's head.

On 30 March 30 the band bade their friends in Britis.
sonal farewell with a party at the super-respectable Skindles
the Thames at Maidenhead, attended by John Lennon and Yoko
(soon to go into exile themselves), Eric Clapton, and Roger Daltrey fro.
the Who. At 2 A.M., the party was still in full swing, and after numerous complaints from other guests about its deafening music, the hotel
abruptly cut off the power supply. An inebriated Mick picked up a table
and hurled it through a plate-glass window.

Just before the start of the new British tax year, he and Bianca left
London for Paris. Amazingly, Marsha Hunt still had not revealed the
identity of Karis's father or sought any further financial help from Mick,
merely telling him he was free to see the baby whenever he wanted.
According to Marsha, he seemed to have an attack of conscience just
before he departed, and asked for Karis to be brought to see him. A meeting was duly arranged, but when Karis arrived she was accompanied
only by her nanny. Marsha did not attend, nor did she seize this golden
opportunity for putting pressure on Mick afterwards. The opportunity
was still more golden, had she but known: Bianca was three months'
pregnant.

On 7 April the Stones reconvened in Cannes on the French Riviera
to sign the agreement with Atlantic's parent company, Kinney Services – who concidentally now owned Warner Studios and, therefore,
Performance. In the second week of the month, Atlantic released their
début single on Rolling Stones Records, breaking the immemorial
two-title formula with 'Brown Sugar', 'Bitch' and a live track, 'Let It
Rock'. Hard on its heels came the *Sticky Fingers* album with a cover
conceived by Andy Warhol – a blue-denim-clad male crotch with a
real zip fastener up its front. The zip unzipped to reveal white Y-fronts,
an exposure somehow far more shocking than naked genitalia would
have been.

The new Stone Age kicked off with a landslide victory: *Sticky Fingers*
at No. 1 in the United States and UK and 'Brown Sugar', No. 1 and No. 2,

respectively. Disgruntled Decca tried to cash in by releasing a compilation of old Stones tracks (that is, with copyrights all owned by Allen Klein). Mick placed full-page advertisements in the music press, warning fans that it was sub-standard.

On 10 May he telephoned his London office from Saint-Tropez and told Shirley Arnold that he was to marry Bianca there two days later. He gave Shirley a list of seventy people he wanted invited and asked her to charter an airliner to fly them out at his expense. 'But don't tell them I'm getting married,' he added.

CHAPTER FIFTEEN

Friendship with Benefits

Mick's secretiveness about the marriage indicated that it was to be a private affair, solemnised in some tasteful, tranquil place which no intrusive camera lens could penetrate. Up to the last minute, he kept the secret from everyone but the trusted associates whose organisational help he needed, not telling even his fellow Stones until twenty-four hours beforehand. The media had their suspicions, particularly when he was spotted collecting two matching gold rings from a Parisian jeweller, but his spokesman, Les Perrin, firmly denied any wedding was in the wind, as did a frowning Bianca. He seemed determined to stop the event becoming, as he put it, 'a circus'.

If you wish to marry quietly, of course, the place not to do it is the Côte d'Azur's most glamorous resort at the height of the spring season, surrounded by dozens of your internationally famous chums. Mick's Saint-Tropez nuptials in fact were the first celebrity wedding as we have since come to know them through magazines like *Hello!* and *OK!*, where the whole world effectively gets invited. The only difference in today's version is the pre-selling of exclusive photographic access and the sponsorship deals which usually pay for the whole occasion and leave a tidy profit over. Perhaps the ultimate example was to come in 2000, when the wedding of British TV personality Anthea Turner helped promote a new chocolate bar. Now, if the Mars company had been on the ball in 1971 . . .

This veritable stampede to the altar after just eight months was entirely Mick's idea. Bianca, as she later said, felt nowhere near ready for such a commitment and did not think her pregnancy ought to be a factor. Indeed, she told him she was quite prepared to flout her Catholic upbringing and have the baby out of wedlock. 'As far as marriage was concerned, I was frightened of the whole idea,' she said later. 'It's Mick who is the bourgeois sort . . . He insisted on having a proper ceremony and becoming man and wife in the conventional sense.'

He certainly was doing it strictly by the book – or, rather, *le livre*. In traditional French style, there was to be a formal civil marriage in Saint-Tropez's town hall followed by a service in the pretty hilltop chapel of St Anne. For the latter to be allowed, protestant Mick had to receive instruction in the Catholic faith from a Jesuit priest, Father Lucien Baud, during which it emerged that the feast day of Saint Anne happened also to be his birthday. Father Baud was pleasantly surprised by his intelligence, knowledge and receptiveness.

Despite the cloak of secrecy, British photographers began staking out Saint-Tropez several days before the wedding. Among them was a Paris-based freelancer named Reg Lancaster, who happened to have done some early shots of the Stones in their pub R&B days. Though initially hostile to these advance skirmishers, Mick ended up joining them to watch TV coverage of the soccer cup final between Arsenal and Liverpool being played back home in Britain. The game went to extra time, in which Arsenal beat Liverpool 2–1, but the French transmission cut off before this vital last segment. 'Mick was an Arsenal fanatic,' Lancaster recalls. 'He went bananas when he couldn't find out the score.'

On 12 May a chartered Viscount airliner arrived in Nice, bringing the seventy wedding guests Shirley Arnold had rounded up at forty-eight hours' notice. They included two Beatles, Paul McCartney and Ringo Starr (still barely on speaking terms after the recent High Court action); Eric Clapton and his girlfriend, Alice Ormsby-Gore; the Queen's photographer-cousin Lord Litchfield; the designer Ossie Clark and the Faces' guitarist Ronnie Wood. Pot freely circulated throughout the flight, much to the consternation of Les Perrin's wife, Janey, who had to bully the worst offenders into hiding their stashes before touchdown.

Nor was this the only contraband undetected by Nice Airport's *douaniers*. Also on the guest list was socialite and amateur racing-car driver Tommy Weber, whose wife, Susan 'Puss' Coriat, heiress to the Maple furniture fortune, was an acquaintance of Anita's. Being currently back in rehab, Puss could not make the wedding, but Tommy had brought their two sons, eight-year-old Jake and six-year-old Charley, to act as pageboys. Thirty-nine years later, Jake Weber would allege that their true role had been as drug-carrying mules. Taped to his bare body under his shirt, each small boy carried half a kilo of cocaine, Jake's a wedding gift from Keith to Mick. The bridegroom was suffering more nerves than he let on, and had earlier told Spanish Tony Sanchez – so Sanchez later claimed – 'A guy needs a little C-O-K-E to get him through his wedding day.'

The wedding's operations centre was the famous Hôtel Byblos, just off Saint-Tropez's main square, Place des Lices. Mick had flown in his parents ahead of the main group but somehow forgotten to book accommodation for their two-night stay. 'I had to get on to him to get them rooms at the Byblos,' Shirley recalls. 'And for Les Perrin, his wife Janey, and myself.'

The tiny, whitewashed town was by now a heaving mass of photographers and television crews even more aggressively competitive than in the days when Brigitte Bardot used to pose in striped bikinis on its beach. The wedding would, indeed, be a circus – in its original Roman sense of sacrificial victims and baying, pitiless mob – and several times hover perilously close to being abandoned altogether.

The first such moment came early in the day when Bianca was faced with the marriage contract prescribed by French law, stating whether Mick's property and hers were to be held in common or separately in case of divorce. 'Pre-nups' had yet to become a standard feature of wealthy celebrity marriage, and to Bianca it seemed a cold-blooded transaction, implying that she was only interested in Mick's money. She became upset and pleaded with him to call the whole thing off. His response – a thumbscrew turn from the Tyranny of Cool – was 'Are you trying to make a fool of me in front of all these people?'

The civil ceremony at the town hall was scheduled for 4 P.M. and was to be conducted by the mayor, Marius Estezan. The film director Roger Vadim and Bianca's actress friend Nathalie Delon acted as witnesses. The only other Stone to have been invited here and to the religious service was Keith, although Ahmet Ertegun, Marshall Chess and even sax player Bobby Keys were present. Keith, wearing the field-grey tunic of a Second World War Nazi officer, was not recognised by the gendarme at the door and barred from entry. There was a furious altercation which ended with him throwing 'a large piece of metal' at the officer. Only strenuous PR from Les Perrin allowed him to take his seat with Anita and Marlon rather than getting beaten and thrown into the Saint-Tropez lock-up.

To give the proceedings some semblance of dignity, Perrin had decreed that only four photographers should be allowed into the hall. But as French civil marriages are open to the public, it had proved impossible to stop something like 100 other cameras from pushing in. After a twenty-minute delay, word was brought to Mayor Estezan, wearing his official tricolour cummerbund, that Mick and Bianca would not appear unless he cleared the room of photographers. The mayor refused, backed up by the senior police officer present, and told Les Perrin he'd give them just ten more minutes. Perrin relayed the message to Mick, who retorted that, in that case, the ceremony was off. Perrin's reply, overheard by his wife, Janey, was the terse, paternal one that generally defused such petulance: 'Don't be silly . . . Don't be *silly.*'

At 4:50, almost an hour late, the couple finally made their entrance. Bianca was a figure both virginally pure and stunningly chic in a low-cut, tailored white jacket that gave no hint of her condition, set off by a matching floppy-brimmed hat with a veil and gloves. Mick looked somewhat less classy in an *eau de nil* Tommy Nutter three-piece suit and open-necked floral shirt. With 100 photographers pushing, scuffling and sometimes coming to blows around them, they finally reached the two chairs arranged in front of the mayor. With unwavering poise, but clearly upset, Bianca sat down, raised her veil and pulled off her gloves while Mick hovered solicitously over her, remonstrating with the nearest snappers in both English and French. 'I don't think we can do it in front of all these people . . .' he was heard to say again. However, enough calm was regained for Mayor Estezan to solemnise the marriage, albeit without much geniality. When the newlyweds signed the register afterwards, they found themselves on the same page as Bianca's ex-lover, Eddie Barclay, who had married the fifth of his eventual nine wives at the town hall not long previously.

The onward journey to St Anne's chapel for the religious ceremony involved a steep uphill climb on foot, hemmed in by photographers, gaping onlookers and a posse of jeering local students. Mick held Bianca's hand and – just like during the Redlands trial in 1967 – Les Perrin held his. Arriving at the chapel, they found its front door had been locked to keep out gate-crashers, and Mick had to hammer loudly for admittance. British royalty in the person of Lord Lichfield gave the bride away, and the service, again entirely in French, was conducted by Mick's late theological tutor, Father Lucien Baud, whose address made approving reference to their talks together: 'You have told me that youth seeks happiness and a certain ideal and faith . . . I think you are seeking it, too, and I hope it arrives today with your marriage.' This part of the day, at least, had some beauty and spirituality, even if Mick and Bianca exchanged vows and rings with the proprietorial Ahmet Ertegun almost breathing down their necks. The organist played Bach's 'Wedding March' and, at Bianca's request, the theme from 1970s weepie blockbuster *Love Story*. Not in the least cool, of course, but it still pleased Mick to let her have her way.

The reception, in a private room at the Café des Arts, was attended by 200 guests, with Bill Wyman, Charlie Watts and Mick Taylor and their consorts, Astrid, Shirley and Rose, finally included, and the Queen's

cousin taking photographs. Bianca exchanged her virginal white for a
slinky couture gown and jewelled turban – once again eclipsing every
other female around – and she and Mick made a point of thanking Shirley Arnold for delivering their British guests there. The party went on
until 4.30 A.M. Bianca retired early, apparently not in the best spirits, but
Joe and Eva Jagger hung in, not yet having had a chance to give their son
his wedding present. The room had a small stage, on which Mick needed
little persuasion to get up and perform, backed by Bobby Keys, Stephen
Stills and soul diva Doris Troy, though not the Stones other ranks or
Keith, who had passed out on the floor. Next day, the new Mr and Mrs
Jagger boarded a seventy-five-foot luxury yacht, the *Romeang*, for a ten-
day honeymoon cruise off the French and Italian Riviera: coincidentally
the scene of Mick's first idyll with Marianne Faithfull.

There was, of course, no *Hello!* in 1971, but Fleet Street did its best
to fill the gap, even *The Times* publishing a front-page report headed
'MICK WEDS IN HIPPIE CHAOS'. *Oz* magazine's editor, Richard Neville, who
had been at the wedding, penned a long editorial voicing the disgust
of Britain's Underground to see their former Street Fighting Man thus
absorbed into the international jet set. 'Jagger has firmly repudiated the
possibilities of a counterculture of which his music is a part,' thundered
his ungrateful guest. 'Street-Fighting Man found Satisfaction in every
pitiable cliché of la dolce capitalism . . . The Jagger myth, epitomising
multilevel protest for nearly a decade, finally exploded with the champagne corks.' *Private Eye*'s next cover was a photograph of Mayor Estezan
asking Bianca in a speech bubble 'ARE YOU TAKING THE MICK?'

There was even a comment from Bianca's ex-boyfriend Michael
Caine to add to the tiny store of public knowledge about her – and hint
that domestic life for the Jaggers might not be all perfect harmony: 'I
was with Bianca for quite a long time. We enjoyed the relationship very
much, and I was a bit upset about her marrying Mick . . . She'll argue
about everything until you feel you're going mad. I bet they're fighting
like cats and dogs already.' He wasn't far wrong.

No public response, however, came from the long-term partner Mick
had finished with less than a year earlier; Marianne had already sunk

too far out of sight. She had not heard the wedding was imminent and knew nothing about it until she came up to London from Berkshire for one of the regular Valium injections with which she was now trying to fight her heroin habit. Arriving at Paddington station to catch her train home, she saw 'MICK WEDS BIANCA' all over the evening papers. The shock made her forget her train and head for the station bar to add three vodka martinis to the Valium already inside her. Shortly afterwards the police were called to a nearby Indian restaurant, where she had passed out into a plate of curry. She was taken to Paddington Green Police Headquarters and locked up overnight.

Not until her release the next morning did her captors finally realise she was, or had been, somebody. Paddington Green HQ was an ultra-modern complex only recently opened, and when Marianne emerged from her cell she was deferentially asked to sign the visitors' book. The only other name in it so far was that of the home secretary, Reginald Maudling, who'd performed the opening ceremony. Inscribing a shaky signature after Maudling's was the nearest she would be to celebrity for a long time to come.

THE PROVENÇAL HOME originally selected for Mick and his bride was a villa called Nellcôte on the craggy heights above Villefranche harbour. Formerly owned by the shipping magnate Alexandre Bordes, it was more palace than villa, fronted by heavy iron gates and surrounded by a double tier of Romanesque columns. Within was a maze of interconnecting Art Nouveau salons with parquet floors, mirrored doors, marble fireplaces and chandeliers. Acres of exotic gardens led down to a private beach and jetty. But Mick thought it all too showy, not to mention too public, so poor Nellcôte was assigned to Keith instead.

For tax-exile rock stars, there was an abundant choice of accommodation along the Azure Coast, long colonised by wealthy British and Americans, with its opulent coastal villas and apartment blocks and hinterland of medieval mountain villages. And all the lesser Stones were quickly settled: Bill and Mick Taylor in Grasse, Charlie (whose sensitive soul shrank from Côte d'Azur glitz) at Arles, Vincent Van Gogh's old home in the Vaucluse, far away to the north-west.

Mick, as usual, took the longest to decide, staying on at the Byblos, then moving to an even more luxurious hotel, Bastide du Roy in Aix, as his chief PA, Jo Bergman, continued the hunt. His eventual choice was at Biot, just outside Antibes, a secluded property owned by the Prince de Polignac, uncle of Monaco's ruler, Prince Rainier. It had a tradition of being let to composers and musicians but always hitherto in the classical sphere, and de Polignac was initially reluctant to entrust it to the most infamous name in pop. He would later say that Mick and Bianca were the best tenants he ever had.

Strangely, after having been so resentful about moving to France, the one who settled into the new life most quickly and contentedly was Keith. In his cliff-top Art Nouveau palace he became like a gypsy reincarnation of Dick Diver in F. Scott Fitzgerald's *Tender Is the Night*, presiding over a huge and constantly changing circle of friends and hangers-on, British, American and French. The house's population was seldom fewer than twenty – including sundry small children like the former cocaine mules Jake and Charley Weber – splashing in the pool, sunning themselves on the balustraded terraces and taking perilous rides with Keith round Villefranche harbour in the speedboat he named *Mandrax 2*. So many sat down to the regular gourmet meals that the kitchen had to be enlarged, at a cost that made Prince Rupert Loewenstein mop his noble brow. In time, even people-hungry Anita wearied of the incessant party and banquet, complaining, 'Why does no one ever say good-bye?' Finally, one day, the revels became too much for Keith also, and he and Anita fled to Mick Taylor's house in Grasse for some peace and quiet.

Mick and Bianca's house at Biot, by contrast, was pristinely neat and wrapped in deep quiet, broken only when Mick played a blues record from the large collection he'd had shipped over or practised on the drum kit he kept in the living room. With the property came a resident housekeeper, a wizened little Italian woman named Madame Villa, whose initial *froideur* was quickly melted by the Jagger charm. It all seemed a long way from Nellcôte, the more so as few of Keith's multitudinous house-guests ever found their way there. One exception was a young British falconer who had turned up at Nellcôte carrying a baby eagle in his pocket (which Nice Airport security no more detected than Jake and Charley Weber's cargo of cocaine). Mick invited him to train falcons in the garden at Biot, and liked to sit and watch – rather different exercises with birds than the Prince de Polignac had feared. 'It was very restful,' he would recall. '[Life] wasn't mad, really, for me, to be honest.' The staff who ministered to both Glimmer Twins all felt that, while Keith had made himself completely at home on the Côte d'Azur, Mick always remained a transient.

The plan was not for the Stones to sit around in sun-soaked idleness but to get straight on with recording their second Atlantic album, using the cache of Jagger–Richard songs written over the previous two years, which the pair had carefully kept out of Allen Klein's clutches. Their producer, Jimmy Miller, and engineer, Andy Johns, were poised to commute from London, while the horn section of Bobby Keys and Jim Price had loyally followed them to France and were living in rented houses in Villefranche. Recording studios around Nice and Cannes were scouted, but none proved suitable. It was then that Keith came up with the idea which would give him his one and only era as Chief Stone. Nellcôte had a labyrinthine cellar, reputedly used to interrogate prisoners during the villa's occupation by senior Nazi officers in the Second World War. Why not make the album down there?

Led by the Stones' resourceful roadie Ian Stewart, their back-up team made the transformation speedily enough for recording to start less than a month after Mick's wedding. Electric cables were run into the cellar and rough wooden partitions erected to screen the musicians from each other, though little could be done to moderate its dank smell and torture-chamber heat. The control room was the Mighty Mobile studio-in-a-truck, parked outside. The electricity supply proved erratic and there were frequent power cuts until Stu found an answer that would have brought mass deportation quicker than any drug, had it ever come to light: One side of Nellcôte's garden overlooked the electrified railway line to Monaco in one direction and Nice in the other. Stu managed to tap into the power lines, so obtaining an unlimited free supply courtesy of France's national rail network, SNCF.

This being Keith's house, recording sessions took place in what became known as Keith Time. He would rise around 4 P.M., then spend several hours hanging out with his innumerable houseguests, or alone in his room with just a needle for company. Not until well past 10 P.M., as a rule, would he pick up his guitars from the parquet floor and lurch downstairs, the back-up musicians assemble in their sweltering wooden stalls and the juice from French railways start flowing. It being Keith's house, too, the tracks tended to start out as instrumentals which could ramble on for hours as he sought the right killer riff for each. Mick, an onlooker recalls, 'would play a little harp, then start yelling a few things'.

Such lethargy and lack of structure was repugnant to the orderly, focused Mick. 'I didn't have a very good time,' he remembered. 'It was this communal thing, where you don't know if you're recording or living or having dinner . . . and too many hangers-on.' As Keith later summed up their essential difference: 'Mick likes knowing what he's going to do tomorrow. Me, I'm just happy to wake up and see who's hanging around. Mick's rock, I'm roll.'

For all Mick's distaste for the Nellcôte bacchanal, he remained strangely possessive where Keith was concerned, and was hostile, as only Mick knew how, to anyone who occupied too much of his Glimmer Twin's attention. This chiefly meant the beautiful young country rocker Gram Parsons, who paid an extended visit with his soon-to-be wife, Gretchen. Keith and Gram would spend hours together, strumming old Everly Brothers songs and making vague plans for Gram to sign with Rolling Stones Records. While Mick was equally drawn to Gram's musical talent, his silent, sinuous ill will towards his unknowing rival was likened by another houseguest to 'a tarantula'. Keith would later talk of his 'weird possessiveness . . . I [had] the feeling Mick thought I belonged to him.'

Côte d'Azur sun shone uninterruptedly all summer, and there were ample ways for the sports-mad Mick to work off his abundant excess energy. He began playing tennis obsessively – though, to his annoyance, chain-smoking, booze-swilling junkie Keith could still best him on the court. When an expatriate Englishwoman named June Shelley joined the Jagger support squad, she received a typically demanding assignment: Mick wanted a Harley-Davidson motorcycle and *had* to have it that same afternoon. Locating a Harley proved impossible, but she found Hondas of almost equal power to be available in Nice. Mick and Bobby Keys bought one each and rode them home to Mick's house in Biot (Keys wrecking his a couple of days later). Many times afterwards June would learn that 'the words *no* or *it can't be done* weren't in Mick's vocabulary. "What do you mean we can't get a piano tuner at three in the morning? We need the piano tuned."'

As the ogling court around him could not fail to observe, strains were already evident in Mick's brand-new marriage. Bianca disliked the sprawling, smoky, drugged-out scene at Nellcôte even more than he did, went there only for short periods under sufferance, and always returned seething about something Anita had done or said. As the first glow began to fade, they had frequent rows – the public kind Mick most hated – in which Bianca revealed a volatile temper and pugilistic ways that he hadn't experienced since Chrissie Shrimpton. 'I've seen her whop him round the ear a few times,' Bobby Keys remembers. 'Let me rephrase that 'fore I get my ass chewed off. I've seen her give him a few slaps.'

Bianca's pregnancy was proving difficult, and she'd made clear she wanted the baby to be born in Paris when the time came, in late October. She began to spend time there, establishing a base at the chic L'Hôtel, in the rue des Beaux Arts, where Oscar Wilde had died (uttering the immortal last words 'Either that wallpaper goes or I do'). Mick would join her whenever he could get away from recording sessions at Nellcôte. Still optimistic about his screen career, he was currently in talks with *Performance*'s producer, Sandy Lieberson, about a film version of Michael McClure's play *The Sermons of Jean Harlow and the Curses of Billy the Kid*.

Lieberson paid several visits to the Biot house, but never saw Bianca there. Increasingly on Friday nights, Keith would tell the Nellcôte cellar crew with a scowl that Mick wouldn't be joining them because he'd 'pissed off to Paris again'.

On 21 October, at the city's Belvedere Nursing Home, Bianca was safely delivered of a six-pound baby girl. Mick announced to waiting reporters that his daughter was 'very precious and quite, quite perfect' and would be named Jade Sheena Jezebel. 'Why Jade?' a girlfriend was to ask him some years later. 'Her eyes were so green,' he replied.

For almost six months, Keith nurtured the comfortable belief that the Côte d'Azur's laid-back attitudes extended to hard drugs. Thanks to Nurse Smitty, he was clean when he first arrived in France but, after a go-karting accident, had been prescribed a course of painkilling morphine injections which put him straight back on smack again. And, as always, there were plenty of people around to keep him there. His cook at Nellcôte, an unsavoury-looking character known as Fat Jacques, kept a constant supply of a superior grade coming via contacts in Marseille. When small boys were no longer available as mules, Spanish Tony Sanchez brought cocaine for Keith from London hidden inside a toy piano that was a gift for his son, Marlon. One day while Keith was out in the *Mandrax 2*, sailors on an American aircraft carrier threw him down a big bag of weed. When John Lennon paid him a visit, after coming to Nice for an art exhibition, Mick and the other Stones saw nothing of their old friend and fan. Lennon spent forty-five minutes closeted with Keith upstairs and then left, vomiting on the hall carpet by way of farewell.

In fact, the Nice *gendarmerie* had Nellcôte under close surveillance and were simply waiting for their moment to pounce. This came when daylight robbers strolled into the house and made off with most of Keith's guitar collection and two of Bobby Keys's saxophones. The police apparently believed the robbers to be Marseille drug dealers whose bills hadn't been paid. Keith was forbidden to leave France pending an appearance before an examining magistrate to answer charges as yet unspecified but, so he was warned, likely to include heroin dealing and running organised prostitution. Thanks to Prince Rupert's contacts, the more extreme counts were not pursued, and Keith received permission to travel abroad on the condition that he continued paying the hefty rent for Nellcôte.

Away from the Côte d'Azur, the old pecking order was restored. When the Stones moved to Los Angeles to finish off the new album, Mick took charge once more, driving the unfinished tracks to a conclusion and adding star session musicians like Billy Preston and Dr John. Keith, anyway, had other pressing problems to deal with. In his absence, the French police had belatedly raided Nellcôte and come up with incriminating evidence that made the Redlands bust in 1967 seem laughable. His American visa was about to expire and, thanks to the audible media clamour from France, was unlikely to be extended.

Like Marianne Faithfull a couple of years earlier – and just as erroneously – he decided the country where he would be most likely to get clean for good was Switzerland. June Shelley, who went with him, later reported he'd almost died in an ambulance *en route* to the clinic. In April 1972, while he was still undergoing treatment, Anita gave birth to their second child, a baby daughter, in the maternity clinic down the road. Whatever happened, it seemed, the Glimmer Twins just couldn't stop competing.

That May, a year of legal action by the Stones against Allen Klein seemed to reach a conclusive settlement. While the band were shaking the dust of Britain from their wedgy boot heels, their American lawyers had filed suit against Klein in the New York State Supreme Court, charging that during his tenure as their manager he had used $29 million of their earnings 'for his own profit and benefit'. It was in America, too, that Mick planned to challenge Klein's ownership of all the band's record copyrights between 1963 and 1970. The contention was that young, naïve musicians had been suckered of what was rightfully theirs by a cunning, amoral entrepreneur.

Neither strand of litigation, however, brought the desired results. On the copyright issue, American courts would take the view that Klein had bought them legitimately from the Stones' first manager, Andrew Oldham, and that, however young and naïve, the Stones had always known those copyrights were vested in Oldham, not them. Under American law, very little overturns the sacred principle that a deal is a deal. And the $29 million lawsuit came to a stop when Klein's lawyers offered $2 million 'in settlement of all outstanding difficulties'. The negotiations were partly conducted by Klein's nephew, Ron Schneider, who tape-recorded his separate discussions with his uncle and Mick. At one moment Mick could be heard expressing willingness to talk to Klein personally, because 'this whole thing has gotten to be a drag'. Klein was heard saying rather wistfully, 'I think Mick Jagger still *likes* me.'

In mid-May, the Nellcôte basement tapes were released as a double album, *Exile on Main St.* Apart from the word *exile*, it gave no hint of the circumstances in which it had been recorded, and conveyed not the slightest flavour of France. Keith's guitar dominated the Stones' now-familiar post-sixties mix of stripped-down rock, hard-core blues and hillbilly ballads. Only here and there did a track title accidentally refer to the band's Riviera lifestyle or the ramshackle recording process – 'Tumbling Dice' and 'Casino Boogie', for instance, to Monaco's gambling joints; 'Loving Cup' to Keith's profligate hospitality; 'Ventilator Blues' to that stifling cellar studio; 'Stop Breaking Down' and 'Shine a Light' to the wavery power supply; 'All Down the Line' to the unwitting contribution of the French national railways. From bilingual Francophile Mick, however, came not even the most oblique mention of his new surroundings, his new wife or new baby. Whatever emotions were inside, his voice remained firmly stuck on Planet Jagger, with its make-believe honky-tonks and whorehouses and its capital, Noo Awleans.

Exile did not so much overstep the limits of pop-lyric decency as pole-vault far beyond them, abounding with previously forbidden words like *shit, fucking, cunt,* even *nigger,* and naming one track (for no obvious reason) 'Turd on the Run'. Also included was Jagger and Richard's first specific protest song, 'Sweet Black Angel', about the trial of the American Black Power activist Angela Davis. The track also became the B-side to the album's advance single, 'Tumbling Dice', which reached number five in the UK and seven in America. It says much about how times had changed since 'Let's Spend the Night

Together' that scarcely a demurring voice was heard in the press and censorship problems on radio were minimal.

The album received mixed reviews, even the good ones sounding vaguely disapproving. 'There are songs that are better and there are songs that are worse,' wrote Lenny Kaye in *Rolling Stone*, 'and others you'll probably lift the [gramophone] needle for when time is due.' But, he concluded, 'the great Stones album of their mature period is yet to come'. For the same magazine's Robert Christgau, it was 'a fagged-out masterpiece which explores new depths of recording-studio murk, burying Jagger's voice under layers of cynicism, angst and ennui'. Over time, most of the critics would eat their words, and *Exile on Main St.* would be seen as the Stones' supreme achievement on record – though Mick himself never seemed that keen on it.

'It's very rock 'n' roll, you know. I didn't want it to be like that. I'm the more experimental person in the group, you see. I mean, I'm very bored with rock 'n' roll. Everyone knows what their roots are, but you've got to explore everything. You've got to explore the sky.'

To PROMOTE *Exile* in its most important market, there was to be an American tour in June and July, the band's first shows there since Altamont. Since Keith was still trying to get straight in Switzerland, pre-tour rehearsals had to take place in a small cinema in Montreux on the shores of Lake Geneva. It was when the band returned to Los Angeles to do publicity for the album and continue limbering up that the Pisces Apple lady joined Mick's entourage.

Chris O'Dell was a lissome Arizonan with tumbling hair and a wide, warm smile who managed to become an insider at the two most exclusive courts in rock. She started out working at the Beatles' Apple company – hence her nickname – becoming especially close to George and Ringo and their not over-happy wives. She was also a friend of fellow American Janice Kenner, Mick's 'cook' during his final bachelor days, and would occasionally drop by 48 Cheyne Walk to hang out with the

two of them. Janice's ambiguous role in Mick's household taught Chris
that any attractive young woman he employed might be called on for no-
strings sex – an arrangement later known as friendship with benefits.

Being trusted by the Beatles was an automatic passport to being
trusted by the Stones. As the band prepared for their 1972 American
tour, Chris O'Dell became assistant to Marshall Chess, who immediately gave her the job of finding Mick and Keith homes to rent in LA
For Mick, she came up with 414 St. Pierre Road, Bel Air, an H-shaped
pink stucco mansion on a 6.5-acre estate built by press baron William
Randolph Hearst for his movie-star mistress Marion Davies and since
used as a hideaway by Howard Hughes and a honeymoon retreat by
Jack and Jackie Kennedy. The house had twenty-nine bedrooms, a
ballroom, an enormous library and three pools, and looked over pink
Italian gardens which had lately featured in the gruesome horse's head
scene in *The Godfather*. Mick loved the property and lost no time in
installing Bianca, six-month-old Jade and her English nanny. Though
still technically working for Marshall Chess, Chris effectively became
his personal assistant.

In her time with the Beatles, Chris learned that looking after super-
colossal rock stars was a great deal easier if you got along with their
wives. 'Each morning,' she remembers, 'my first call would be to Bianca
to see what she needed doing, before I contacted Mick and found out
the hundred and one things he needed doing.' Bianca she felt to be 'a
spoiled girl' who showed little of Mick's appreciativeness when some
near-impossible whim was gratified. And, as in France, she didn't like
Mick to spend too much time at Keith and Anita's house on Stone Canyon Drive, a few minutes' drive away. 'Bianca wasn't the type to just
go hang out. It always seemed that her relationship with Mick had an
element of rivalry. When they came into a room, each looking fabulous,
they seemed to be competing to get everyone's attention.'

The house was also planning headquarters for the forthcoming tour,
and dozens of people tracked through it each day, seeking Mick's permission for something or other. Yet he still found time for fatherhood.
'I remember him in the kitchen with Jade, totally wrapped up in her,'

Chris O'Dell says. Rock superstars tend not to bother much with baby care, but after Jade's birth he had gone to Sally, her English nanny, and requested lessons in bottle-feeding and nappy-changing.

America in 1972 was no more stable a society than in the expiring sixties. The year was to bring a presidential election in which the voting age would be lowered from twenty-one to eighteen. Republican incumbent Richard M. Nixon – the most paranoid character ever to occupy the White House – feared being ousted from office by a massive youth vote, substantially whipped up by British pop stars. John Lennon, now in exile with Yoko in New York, had become deeply involved in extreme-left politics and as a result was under surveillance by the Federal Bureau of Investigation as well as threat of expulsion by the immigration authorities. Nixon's paranoia was assiduously fed by the FBI's director, J. Edgar Hoover, a ferocious reactionary whose secret penchant for wearing girls' dresses even frillier than Mick Jagger's none yet suspected.

The Bureau had regarded Mick as an anti-American subversive since 1967 when its collusion with British MI5 in the Acid King David affair had led to his trial, imprisonment and consequent exile from the United States for two years afterwards. He still had a fat FBI file, noting such threats to its internal security as his vague murmurs of support for the Black Panthers and the *Exile on Main St.* track dedicated to Angela Davis. According to a former FBI operative, 'J. Edgar Hoover hated Jagger probably more than any other pop-cultural figure of his generation.'

Gunfire still echoed through the land with terrible promiscuity. The shock had barely subsided of the Kent State University massacre when Ohio National Guardsmen had killed four students and wounded nine during a peaceful demonstration against the US invasion of Cambodia. Then on 16 May 1972 George Wallace, the segregationalist governor of Alabama, now running for president, was shot five times at a political rally and paralysed for life. One balmy evening in Los Angeles, Mick buzzed down his limo window to chat with some girls convulsed with pre-tour excitement. 'Oh, Mick,' breathed one, 'aren't you afraid of getting shot?' He reflected a moment, then gave an unwontedly straight answer: 'Yeah . . . I am.'

Above all there were fears that the Hell's Angels might be planning revenge against the Stones for leaving them to take the flak, as they saw it, after Altamont. 'The band were all very scared,' recalls Marshall Chess, 'Mick especially. Every time we came out of somewhere late at night, we'd always be careful to look both ways.' As a result, security was tighter than on any tour before. Key members of the entourage, including Chess, provided themselves with handguns and Mick himself bought two .38 Police Specials. Chip Monck's stage crew all had to have *bona fide* union cards, lest some disguised Angel should beg a casual job with the team, then re-enact Meredith Hunter's murder on Mick or Keith in mid-set. The pair were assigned two formidable-looking black bodyguards with open white shirt collars as big as snowy shawls. According to an insider who prefers not to identified, these guardians did not just keep watch outside the Glimmer Twins' hotel suites: 'They were with them *in* their bedrooms. *All night.*'

No more was the Stones' progress through America to be reported merely by the drones of the music press. For this tour, the nation's most prestigious general-interest magazines sought backstage passes, competing with one another in the literary heavyweights they assigned to the story. The *Saturday Review* nominated William S. Burroughs, the countercultural colossus whose heroin cure Keith had so recently, and futilely, tried. When the *Review* could not meet Burroughs's price, his place was taken by Terry Southern, author of screen classics like *Dr Strangelove* and *Easy Rider,* who had previously served a spell as writer-in-residence at the Beatles' Apple house.

Rolling Stone trumped even Burroughs by commissioning Truman Capote, perhaps America's greatest prose artist of the post-war era. Though best known for his harrowing non-fiction novel *In Cold Blood,* Capote had written an earlier, hilarious account of a black operatic company touring Soviet Russia, and had always hankered to do something else in the same vein. As a hopeful added attraction for Mick, he had a huge circle of famous friends in both show business and New York's 400. Equally at home with high and low life, he seemed an inspired choice to chronicle the rise of a once-scruffy rock band to stratospheric chic.

The tiny, falsetto-voiced Capote as a rule had an uncanny ability to charm his subjects and elicit the most revealing confidences. Unfortunately, he considered himself as big a star as Mick, if not more of one, and their first meeting, at a pre-tour party, was not promising. 'He told me he was going to do the tour for the money,' Mick was to recall. 'When he told me how much [Rolling Stone] offered, I said, "I'm sure that's not enough and besides . . . we don't want you."'

An equally disinguished roster of tour photographers was headed by Robert Frank, whose black-and-white studies of American rural life in the 1960s had earned him comparisons with Walker Evans. Forty-seven-year-old Frank was along in the role of film-maker, shooting a documentary intended to erase Gimme Shelter's ugly memories. Highly esteemed by both Glimmer Twins, he was to be allowed total access, working entirely in home-movie-ish Super 8; in addition, the Stones would be given cameras to film their own first-person sequences.

Bianca did not accompany the tour. Mick ruled that she should stay behind in LA with baby Jade, joining him on the road for just a couple of brief visits. 'I find it very difficult to travel with anyone on tour,' he explained. 'Bianca's easier than some people, but I just have to be on my own.' According to Jade's English nanny – the second incumbent in the job – Bianca reacted with fury but had to accept the decision. Her one small revenge arose from their habit of wearing the same clothes. Mick had borrowed a scarf of hers, without her knowledge, to take with him. When his bags were all packed, Bianca demanded the return of the scarf and made him rummage through every one until he found it.

For most of the journey, the band and their entourage were to fly in a luxurious private DC-5 decorated with the logo of Rolling Stones Records and consequently nicknamed the Lapping Tongue. A current spate of aircraft hijackings and terrorist incidents at airports heightened the general paranoia. When the tour kicked off in Canada on 3 June, the Lapping Tongue was denied permission to land at Vancouver Airport because of an inadequately prepared flight plan. Marshall Chess managed to contact the prime minister, Pierre Trudeau, but even Trudeau could not help – something which may later have given him a twinge of satisfaction. Instead, the band had to land in Washington State and cross the Canadian border by road.

Some press commentators had wondered whether a rock idol soon to reach the remarkable age of twenty-nine could still draw crowds, especially with the charts now full of pubescent acts like the Osmonds and the Jackson 5 (both of which starred actual children). All such doubts were laid to rest that night at Vancouver's Pacific Coliseum, when 2,000 fans who had been unable to get tickets stormed the front entrance, thirty security staff were injured and a relief column of Royal Canadian Northwest Mounted Police had to be summoned to restore order.

The Stones' *de rigueur* black support act likewise seemed almost a child by comparison – especially with thirty-five-year-old Bill Wyman. Rather than hard-core bluesmen, they had the blind Motown prodigy formerly known as Little Stevie Wonder, whose harmonica playing was as brilliant as his singing and songwriting – never mind his piano, guitar and drum playing – and whose live show with a red-hot soul band named Wonderlove included a killer cover of 'Satisfaction'. It's to Mick's credit that he wasn't uptight about facing such competition, but consciously set out to blow it outta sight. For once in Stevie's life, he had to bow to a superior showman.

Gone were the butterfly capes and jokey Uncle Sam topper of 1969. This time around, Mick took the stage in a selection of velour Ossie Clark jumpsuits, purple, pink, lavender or turquoise, fringed or covered with stars, that gaped open almost to his navel. In every arena, on his orders, the first eighteen rows were kept free of VIPs and photographers so his public could see he really was still as wand-slim as Donny Osmond, still as irrepressibly hyperactive as little Michael Jackson. He also liked an unobstructed view of his audiences and their responses, these days so different from the screamy, straightforward little girls of yore. During one show when he accidently cut his lip on the hand microphone, he saw a respectable-looking middle-aged man at stage front deliberately bite down on his own lip until it gushed blood. While lashing the stage with his belt in 'Midnight Rambler', he'd be aware of male figures below him mutely begging for similar flagellation or grinding lighted cigarettes into their open palms.

Near the top of the tour schedule, as if to get it over with, was the return to San Francisco, to face the lingering Altamont fallout and the clearest danger from Hell's Angel avengers. If that wasn't enough, the Stones' two shows at Winterland were promoted by Bill Graham, who had last been heard from publicly calling Mick a 'cunt'. Mick, however, forestalled any awkwardness by walking straight up to Graham, extending a hand, and saying ' 'Ello, Bill, 'ow are you?' Graham graciously took this as an apology, even admitting that three years earlier he hadn't been 'the nicest person'.

A seventy-five-strong police cordon around Winterland and enhanced security at the Miyako Hotel ensured that none of the Oakland Angels' threatened bloody reprisals ever came to pass. But the Altamont issue was still far from dead. As the band took their seats on their plane prior to take-off for LA, a young woman in hot pants talked her way aboard and thrust a sheaf of legal papers relating to the festival under Mick's nose. Seconds later she staggered down the aircraft steps, screaming that 'that son of a bitch' – Keith – had hit her and thrown her off, hurling her summonses after her. No one on the Lapping Tongue regarded this as other than perfectly right and proper as well as hilarious.

Chris O'Dell, who had joined the tour at Mick's insistence (after hand-delivering his stage outfits) became aware of two separate groups in the thirty-strong road company. On one hand, clustered around Mick, were the workers – like tour manager Peter Rudge, Marshall Chess, Ian Stewart, Jo Bergman and Alan Dunn – who dealt with the thousand and one problems arising from every show, every movement to a new city and sojourn in a new, beleaguered, resentful franchise hotel, and who lived in a permanent state of stress, insomnia and indigestion. On the other hand, clustered around Keith were the players, like Bobby Keys, who would remember this as 'the ultimate, fuck-you, don't-give-a-shit Stones tour . . . one hell of a whopper of a good time'.

Mick maintained his authority with the skill of a regimental colonel who occasionally joins his junior officers for horseplay in the mess. It was on this tour that fitness training became part of his daily routine, usually in a two- or three-mile run which he would do again, treadmill-style, before his audience each night. 'The thing for me [was] to stay as straight as possible,' he explained. 'Not that I wouldn't take a beer or get a bit drunk, but I never went onstage loaded . . . Never once. How could I?' On the short stretches of the journey when Bianca joined him, he was every inch the attentive husband, dutifully staying away from Keith's room, pointing out quaint Americana to her from the back of their limo, hovering protectively over her in their reserved seats at the front of the Lapping Tongue. But once she had gone, the first rule of rock tours, 'it doesn't count on the road', came back into play and he reverted to bachelorhood without a beat.

When the tour reached Chicago – right after Minneapolis, where the police attacked fans with tear gas while Mick sang 'I'm Jumpin' Jack Flash, it's a gas gas gas' – every hotel in the downtown area turned out to be booked solid by business conventions. Fortunately, hospitality was available gratis from Chicago's famous son Hugh M. Hefner, the founder of *Playboy* magazine, who still made his home in the city.

Between shows at the International Amphitheatre on 19 and 20 June, the Stones and their inner circle stayed at Hefner's fabled Playboy Mansion, whose front doorbell bore the Latin motto *Si Non Oscillas, Non Tintinnare* (If You Don't Swing, Don't Ring). As well as food, liquor and gambling around the clock, Hefner provided an unlimited supply of Bunnies, the pneumatic pin-ups who adorned his magazine's centrefolds. His rock-biz guests proved to swing rather too much, and Hefner retreated to his eight-foot-diameter circular rotating, vibrating bed while – in the words of an American guest – 'people screwed everywhere'. In the carnal mêlée, a Bunny who was scheduled to pose for a centrefold ended up covered with cuts and bruises and couldn't go before a camera for ten days afterwards.

Mick's glance, however, passed over these buxom Flopsies, Mopsies and Cottontails to settle on Bobbie Arnstein, a slender thirty-one-year-old, somewhat like the French film star Anouk Aimée, who worked as Hefner's personal assistant. Bobbie in fact was a tragic character, later convicted for drug possession, given a suspended fifteen-year prison term and found dead in a seedy hotel from a barbiturates overdose. She also suffered from an eating disorder which, at the height of the revelry with the Stones, caused her to retire to her room and order *three* three-course meals from the Mansion's twenty-four-hour kitchen. She was halfway through the feast when she answered a tap on her door and beheld Mick, clad in nothing but a pair of white leather trousers.

Bobbie was not averse to yielding to his advances but, having just consumed a hunk of ripe Brie cheese, was embarrassed about her ammoniac breath. As they grappled, Mick trying to plant a kiss and Bobbie to avert her head, he lost his balance and sat down heavily on a chair where she'd parked her next course, a slice of Black Forest gâteau. Not even Mick Jagger could keep desire aflame with chocolate, cream and black cherries plastered over his white leather trouser seat.

Truman Capote joined the tour in Kansas City, appropriately enough since his non-fiction masterpiece *In Cold Blood*, about the random murder of a rancher's family, was set in Kansas. With him, Capote had brought one of his New York society friends, Princess Lee Radziwill, the interior-designer younger sister of Jacqueline Onassis. She was the most distinguished fan yet seen in the Stones' dressing room, though Keith practised determined lèse-majesté by addressing her as 'Princess Radish', sometimes adding 'you old tart' for good measure.

Capote received VIP treatment given to no other embedded reporter, travelling in the Lapping Tongue and the best limos, watching the show from a privileged place in the wings. But relations between Mick and him grew no warmer. It did not help that the great author was apt to call the Stones 'the Beatles' and made no secret of considering their leader 'a scared little boy, very much off his turf'. 'Truman never seemed to be taking the story seriously,' Chris O'Dell recalls. 'He had this mocking attitude toward everyone.' Finally Keith retaliated with one of the heavy-handed practical jokes often born of after-show carousing: in a parody of the Clutter family's slaughter in *In Cold Blood*, Capote's hotel room door was daubed with tomato ketchup.

Capote never turned in his *Rolling Stone* article, complaining the tour hadn't been as interesting as he expected. (Instead, Andy Warhol interviewed him about why it hadn't 'excited his imagination'.) Capote's subsequent comments about Mick around the TV chat shows were waspish but not wholly unobservant: '[There's] no correlation at all between a Jagger and a Sinatra . . . [Mick] has no talent save for a kind of fly-eyed wonder . . . That unisex thing is a no-sex thing. Believe me, he's about as sexy as a pissing toad . . . He could, I suppose, be a businessman. He has that facility of being able to focus in on the receipts in the midst of "Midnight Rambler" while he's beating away with that whip.'

SOME WAY INTO the tour, much to her surprise, Chris O'Dell found herself sleeping with Mick. Like his arrangement with her friend Janice Kenner at Cheyne Walk, it was an occasional, spur-of-the-moment thing that had no effect on their daytime employer–employee relationship – 'friendship with benefits' in other words. 'I never took it seriously or thought. "I'm the one he's chosen,"' Chris recalls. 'We'd come back to the hotel some nights and Mick would say, "Why don't we go to the room?" He was fun, charming, and had a lovely twinkle, and there was never any awkwardness afterward. It was like when you were a kid and you and some little boy would play together in a sandbox. Every so often, Mick and I would go play in the sandbox.

'It also had partly to do with trust. People on that level of fame can't trust many people, so, rather than sleep with a stranger and risk being betrayed, they often end up in bed with people who are really their friends. I'd seen that before, with George Harrison and Maureen Starkey. I was sitting at the kitchen table when George said, "Ringo . . . I'm in love with your wife."'

She felt no pangs of guilt either when Bianca rejoined the tour for another spell, wearing a jaunty little Panama hat. There had been no love lost between them since Bianca had unjustly accused Chris of stealing some jewellery that vanished from the Hearst mansion in Bel Air. 'I didn't feel any guilt because I knew what was going on with Mick didn't mean anything,' Chris says. 'He was sleeping with other women at the same time, and I think Bianca realised it. I got the feeling they'd decided on an open marriage.'

The Stones' Washington, DC, concert happened to be on the Fourth of July. Mick considered taking the stage in a George Washington-style wig, breeches and buckled shoes but was persuaded that, with the present jumpy state of American law enforcement, it might not be the best idea. Jumpy law enforcement instead struck in the quiet little Anglophile state of Rhode Island. As the band passed through Warwick Airport, *en route* to play the Boston Garden, Keith swung his shoulder bag at an intrusive photographer and was promptly arrested. In the shouting match that followed, Mick, Marshall Chess, Keith's bodyguard, and the film-maker Robert Frank were also collared, thrown into a police van, taken downtown and locked up. The mayor of Boston, Kevin White, personally had to arrange bail so that the evening's performance could go ahead. Even the brusque police camera that took Mick's post-arrest mug shot could not help flattering him.

The tour ended in New York with four sold-out shows over three nights at Madison Square Garden. Still nervous of Hell's Angel action, the Stones checked into the Sherry-Netherland hotel under aliases different from those they'd been using at Holiday Inns and such out in the sticks. Mick and Bianca (who occupied President Nixon's usual suite) were 'Mr and Mrs Shelley', Bill Wyman and Astrid were 'Lord and Lady Gedding' and Keith was 'Count Ziggenpuss'. They were also advised not to use room service in case someone tried to poison the food.

Feeling the real danger was past, Marshall Chess went to the East River and thankfully threw in his handgun. Unknown to Chess, the Angels' New York chapter had been phoning tour manager Peter Rudge for weeks past and now demanded a sit-down meeting, which, with Madison Square Garden imminent, Rudge felt it wisest to grant. Claiming that Altamont had left their California brothers $60,000 out of pocket, the New York Angels proposed the Stones should make amends with a concert promoted by them. Rudge was playing them along until the band could get safely out of the country.

The final concert at the Garden was on 26 July, Mick's twenty-ninth birthday. Among the audience was the cream of Manhattan society: Princess Lee Radziwill, Lady 'Slim' Keith, Oscar and Françoise de la Renta, Winston and C. Z. Guest, as well as Andy Warhol, Truman Capote, the great playwright Tennessee Williams, and the film star Zsa Zsa Gabor. To mark the occasion, Chip Monck had wanted to put a live elephant onstage and release 500 live chickens into the auditorium, much as white butterflies had been unloosed in Hyde Park, but the Garden's spoilsport management vetoed both schemes. Instead, recalling *Beggars Banquet* days, Mick and the band pelted each other with custard pies and the 17,000 present sang 'Happy Birthday to You', conducted by Stevie Wonder.

Afterwards came a lavish birthday party thrown by Ahmet Ertegun on the roof of the St Regis Hotel, with live music from the Count Basie Orchestra. At the big circular top table, Mick talked business with Ertegun while an unsuspecting Bianca chatted to Chris O'Dell beside her. Warhol went around taking Polaroids, showing particular interest when one of his Factory protégées, Jerry Miller, popped out of the giant birthday cake wearing nothing but a few tactfully hung tassels. Cocaine and joints openly circulated, among rockers and socialites alike. Later, Mick broke off from discussing grosses and percentages for an impromptu jam with Stevie Wonder and Muddy Waters, the guest who still probably thrilled him most. It was all a little too much for the society columnist Harriet Van Horne. 'I thought of all the ancients who would have been perfectly at home at such a Bacchanale as Jagger's birthday party,' she wrote. 'Nero . . . Caligula . . . the Marquis de Sade. I also thought of *A Clockwork Orange* and the Manson Family.'

BY SEPTEMBER, MICK was back in London and living at 48 Cheyne Walk again. With a Stones Far East tour planned for early 1973 and a European one straight afterwards, the perennial question – Would he still be singing 'Satisfaction' when he was thirty? – no longer needed asking. But soon after returning to 'dear old England' he announced he'd retire from the band when he reached thirty-three. 'That's the time when a man has to do something else. I can't say what it will definitely be . . . but it won't be in show business. I don't want to be a rock 'n' roll singer all my life . . . I couldn't bear to end up as an Elvis Presley and sing in Las Vegas with all those housewives and old ladies coming in with their handbags.'

To his London staff, too, it seemed that the shine was wearing off Mick's marriage rather quickly. When Shirley Arnold left the Stones' employ after nine years' devoted service, he and Bianca turned up at her farewell party separately, each bearing a different gift for her – respectively a topaz pendant and some perfume – and then began bickering about which was the official leaving present. However, Mick was just as charming and appreciative to Shirley as ever, and Bianca no less so.

By late November, he was off on his own again when the Stones reconvened to start a new album at Dynamic Studios in Jamaica. The choice of venue was dictated by Keith's ever-widening notoriety as a drug user: apart from Switzerland – which he was already starting to find insufferably bland – no other country but Jamaica would grant him a visa. Mick, besides, was determined the follow-up to *Exile on Main St.* should not be just 'another collection of rock songs', and hoped the birthplace of reggae would give the band a new direction. A secondary attraction was that, thanks to its colonial past, the island was as cricket-obsessed as Britain, so he'd be able to watch the game in midwinter to his heart's content.

The album, eventually released as *Goats Head Soup,* was the Stones' last involving Jimmy Miller. Despite having overseen every one of the band's hits since 'Jumpin' Jack Flash' in 1968, Miller had never received official recognition as their producer, or been able to persuade Mick to up his original modest percentage. Being treated like a tradesman, hired and rehired from album to album, was the least of Miller's problems. Thanks to spending all that time around Keith, he now had a drug problem just as serious but without the same wealth, or prodigious constitution, to deal with it.

Working at Dynamic, with Jamaican and Guyanese musicians and Chinese engineer Mikey Chung, gave the band a shot in the arm in the positive sense. But Jimmy Miller noticed how the normally focused and disciplined Mick could be discombobulated by phone calls from Bianca in London. One evening when she called, he was in the midst of working on a vocal track that had the Jamaican sidemen and Mikey Chung all beaming in admiration. But when he returned to the studio after talking to her, the vocal was ruined.

Recording was interrupted on 2 December when the Nice police issued warrants for the arrest of Keith and Anita on heroin-possession charges and Mick and the other three Stones were called back to the Côte d'Azur to give statements before a magistrate. Mick revisited his former rented home in Biot, where the housekeeper, Madame Villa, pressed a suit for him to wear at the hearing. On 4 December he issued a statement saying that he, Bill, Charlie and Mick Taylor had not been charged or even arrested in connection with heroin and that 'at no time did we hold drug parties in our houses'.

Returning to Bianca and Jade at Cheyne Walk, he found the pre-Christmas atmosphere turned to superfreeze by a new American hit single, Carly Simon's 'You're So Vain'. It was a song for the feminist ego, a satirical out-of-love letter to a narcissistic paramour who wore his hat 'strategically dipped below one eye' and never took his adoring gaze from his reflection in the mirror. The seeming detailed portrait of Mick, than whom no more strategic hat-dipper or greater mirror-worshipper walked the earth, became still more pointed in its second chorus ('You're so vain, you probably think this song is about you') when his muffled but still unmistakable tones chimed in on backing vocals.

The daughter of Richard Simon, co-founder of New York publishers Simon & Schuster, Carly was the first noticeably high-class girl to make a career in American pop. Mick had met her early in 1972 through the Beatles' former Apple protégé James Taylor, whom she was soon to marry. Some months afterwards, while she was in London recording 'You're So Vain' backed by Harry Nilsson, Mick had happened to drop by the studio and had joined in, apparently seeing nothing objectionable about the lyric. Recognising a vocal chemistry between the other two, Nilsson had good-naturedly bowed out.

The line in the song with least appeal to Bianca – dwelled on, as it seemed, by Carly's chewy voice – was 'You had me several years ago.' Various other prominent lotharios, notably Warren Beatty, would be cited as its inspiration, and the songwriter herself always coquettishly refused to name names. But Bianca, at least, never had any doubts. She would later admit that, of all the women in Mick's past, that perpetually self-renewing realm, Carly Simon caused her the worst insecurity.

Such domestic upheavals faded from importance when, on 23 December, a powerful earthquake struck Bianca's home city of Managua, Nicaragua, killing 5,000 people, injuring 20,000, and destroying 80 per cent of the buildings. Both her long-separated parents had still been living in Managua, but frantic phone calls from Cheyne Walk throughout Christmas Eve and Christmas Day failed to locate either of them. On 26 December Mick called Les Perrin with one of the tasks that always had to be dealt with instantly, national holiday or not. This time, what he wanted *now* was not a Harley-Davidson but an airlift of emergency supplies to Nicaragua.

In the end, he took much of the initiative, chartering a private aircraft for Bianca and himself to reach Managua in the shortest possible time, with one brief stop-off at Kingston, Jamaica, to pick up a cargo of medicines including anti-typhoid serum. Once there, he faced up unflinchingly to the death, devastation and squalor, multiplying his usual attention span by millions as Bianca followed one unsuccessful lead after another as to her parents' whereabouts, vanishing from media view so completely, in fact, that some British papers reported him lost. Finally, on New Year's Eve, both his in-laws were located, safe and well, in Nicaragua's unscathed second city of León.

The moment when rock musicians ceased merely to be bywords for selfishness and self-indulgence, and began to use their vast power for humanitarian ends, is generally agreed to have been George Harrison's Concert for Bangladesh in 1971. But Mick, that seeming paragon of self-ishness, was not far behind. Directly after he returned from Nicaragua,

he mobilised the Stones to give a benefit concert for Managua's earthquake victims in a brief window of opportunity before setting off on
their Far East tour. The concert took place on 18 January 1973 at the
Los Angeles Forum, with Santana and Cheech and Chong as support
acts, and raised $350,000 for America's contribution to the Nicaragua
relief effort. In addition, Mick donated a jacket and Keith a guitar to be
auctioned by an LA radio station and Mick contributed a further sum,
reportedly $150,000, out of his own pocket.

As some cynics remarked, the concert had enormous PR value for
the band in the eyes of the American government; it was also a way for
him to keep showing Bianca he wasn't *so* vain. Still, this was Mick at his
best – soon to be followed, as is often the way of stars, by Mick at his
worst.

CHAPTER SIXTEEN

The Glamour Twins

For two years, Marsha Hunt had concealed the fact that she'd borne Mick Jagger a daughter named Karis. Even more amazingly, she had demanded no hefty regular maintenance payments from Mick as the price of her silence. All that mattered to Marsha, she would later explain, was that he acknowledged being Karis's father and seemed to want to keep seeing her. With idealism perhaps possible only in a sixties person, Marsha trusted him to do right by their child in the end.

Being married to Bianca and about to become a father for a second time did not initially seem to change Mick's attitude towards Karis. He had promised she would visit him when he moved to France, and proved as good as his word; in the summer of 1971, not long after his wedding, he invited Marsha to bring her out to the Stones' Provençal enclave.

When they arrived, however, Marsha learned they were not to stay with Mick and Bianca at Biot but with Mick Taylor and his wife, Rose, in Grasse; the equivalent of being boarded out with the domestic staff. Marsha was invited to the Biot house only once, for a dinner at which Mick and Bianca spent most of the meal conversing together in French, though well aware that she couldn't understand a word. After that, Mick saw Karis just once more, for about an hour. As they said good-bye, Marsha, to her embarrassment, had to ask him for £200 to settle bills awaiting her back in London.

For the most part, she supported Karis and herself with singing and modelling work, although now somewhat less of a celebrity than when she'd starred in *Hair.* Only in times of dire need would she seek financial help from Mick, through the Stones' London office. She seldom asked for more than a couple of hundred pounds and always received it immediately. When Bianca gave birth to Jade in 1971, Mick at first seemed keen that his two daughters should get to know each other. He invited Marsha to bring Karis to 48 Cheyne Walk and photographed her in the garden with Jade on her lap while Karis played nearby.

In the summer of 1972, as the Stones prepared to tour America, Marsha was offered some gigs in West Germany, fronting a band called 22. She wanted to take Karis along and asked Mick for £600 to pay for a nanny to travel with them, which, as usual, was sent without question. One evening in a German café, Karis upset a glass of hot tea over herself, suffering burns to her arm, leg and chest. Marsha rushed her to a local American military hospital for emergency treatment, then telephoned across the Atlantic to Mick, who, as she later recalled, was greatly concerned and immediately offered help. It was agreed that Marsha should get Karis back to the UK as quickly as possible and Mick would pay for her stay in a private clinic.

Her burns were serious enough to keep her in the clinic for ten days. Marsha slept in her room, going away only once, to do a singing gig in Wales for some badly needed cash. The bill for Karis's treatment was £75, but the promised payment from Mick never came. Marsha had to do a midnight flit from the clinic, racked with guilt after the kindness she'd received there. But when she met Mick later in London, he made light of the money's non-arrival, saying she probably would have used it 'to buy shoes'. At this, Marsha's previous forbearance, tact and trust in his better nature evaporated and she got herself a lawyer.

Compared with the $4 million which the Stones' 1972 American tour had been forecast to earn, her aspirations were modest – a £25,000 trust fund, payable when Karis left school some sixteen years into the future. She hoped Mick would agree without litigation, but the young lawyer she consulted took the precaution of going before a magistrate and obtaining a paternity order, or summons to an alleged father to attend court. The plan was that Marsha should meet Mick on his own and ask for the trust fund; only if he refused would the paternity order be served.

The rendezvous was the Albert Memorial in Hyde Park, just across the road from the Royal Albert Hall. Mick turned up alone, as Marsha had asked, and they sat on the seat at the base of the monument while her lawyer waited, unseen, at the foot of the steps down to the park. If Mick's response was negative, Marsha had to signal the lawyer by shaking her head. After a few moments she gave the signal and her lawyer approached. 'Are you Mick Jagger?' he asked – an unnecessary question since he was an ardent Stones fan. 'Oo wants to know?' was the surly response. He handed the paternity order to Mick, who took one look, snarled 'Fuck off!' and tore it up.

In subsequent negotiations between lawyers, Mick's side initially offered a £20,000 trust fund for Karis, then revised it downward to £17,000. Out-of-court paternity settlements at that time were relatively small and the barrister Marsha consulted thought she should accept. Following the Albert Memorial sting, relations with Mick recovered sufficiently for her and Karis to be invited back to Cheyne Walk for Jade's first birthday party. But almost six months after she'd agreed to the reduced trust fund, there was still no sign of its being set up. This was because, contrary to all Mick's previous behaviour towards Karis – never mind the values with which he'd been brought up, and still largely maintained – he now intended to deny that he was her father.

In June 1973 Marsha launched the paternity suit at Marylebone Magistrates' Court, just a short walk from Mick's old home, Harley House. He himself was not present at the hearing. His lawyer said that the claim was 'not admitted' and there was 'discussion between the parties as to the merit of these allegations'.

As a result, the story appeared in the British press, with Marsha's previous dignity and discretion now weighing against her. Having kept her involvement with Mick secret for so long, she looked like an opportunistic gold digger suddenly coming out of the woodwork to destabilise his brand-new marriage. Mick remained studiedly flippant, implying it was just a publicity stunt to promote Marsha's latest record. His lawyers, meanwhile, fought a stonewalling campaign, asking for adjournments and blood tests. The whole affair shocked close associates like Shirley Arnold, who had seen his previous acceptance of Karis. 'I told him he should admit she was his and that if anyone asked me, I'd say she was,' Shirley recalls. 'But he just didn't want to hear it.'

After two further hearings, Marsha received a new out-of-court offer: £500 per year and a £10,000 trust fund, on condition her lawyer signed a document saying that Mick was not Karis's father and the settlement was being made simply to avoid embarrassing publicity. The lawyer considered it the best deal she was likely to get, so Marsha told him to sign.

NINETEEN SEVENTY-THREE WAS the year when Mick started to turn respectable – or, rather, when the reluctant rebel invented by Andrew Loog Oldham finally disappeared like the illusion it had always been, and a thoroughly self-controlled, calculating and conformist rebel materialised instead.

In May, the former perceived threat to US homeland security – and FBI mark – became the first pop star to receive an official honour in Washington. The Stones' benefit concert for Nicaragua's earthquake victims had raised $787,500 and Mick was invited to hand over the cheque personally to its recipients, the government-endorsed Pan American Development Foundation. 'Not only Mick,' gushed the usually measured *Washington Post*, 'but the newest superstar of the family, Bianca Jagger, his wife and twin in sullen-lipped looks.'

Assembled for the presentation ceremony were a bevy of Latin American ambassadors and US senators, including New York's liberal Republican senator Jacob Javits, whose help Bianca had enlisted to protect the relief funds from Nicaragua's sticky-fingered president, Anastasio Somoza. But even such an occasion could not get Mick to turn up on time. 'All we have to do now,' quipped Javits as the canapés went round yet again and diplomatic small talk faltered, 'is wait for Hamlet.'

This Hamlet eschewed his 'sable suit' for a blue-and-white-striped blazer with a yellow rose in its lapel, while his saturnine Ophelia wore a green Ossie Clark coat with matching straw hat and sequined shoes. In recognition of what was, by any measure, a magnificent humanitarian effort, they were jointly presented with a golden key (though the other Stones did not receive so much as a thank you for participating in the benefit concert).

Just four months earlier, before the band's Far East tour, Mick had been denied a Japanese visa because of his drug record and also faced a short-lived ban from Australia. After the Washington ceremony, he would never again be classed as a subversive in America or be declared *persona non grata* anywhere, excepting the city's snobby Sans Souci restaurant where he went later that same day, his gold key to DC in his pocket, only to be turned away for not wearing a tie.

At the outset of her marriage, in her unsmiling – and so not very sympathetic – way, Bianca had said she wished to be known as something more than just a rock star's trophy wife. 'I am a person in my own right,' she told one interviewer. 'Mick's accomplishments and achievements are his. Nothing to do with me. I must achieve on my own. He's a musician and I am not. The people who surround the Stones bathe in the reflected light. I refuse to.'

Nowadays, with such beauty and stylishness added to the Jagger name, she would have gone straight to the top of the celebrity A-list and found more than enough autonomy there. One can easily imagine her filling page after page of *Vogue,* both English and French, dominating party spreads in the *Tatler,* showing *Hello!* or *House & Garden* around her latest Tuscan villa, joining the judges on *American Idol,* shaking out her shiny hair in TV shampoo ads, or using that sumptuous scowl to drive home the sales pitch for L'Oréal cosmetics: 'Because you're worth it!'

But in the Britain of 1973, what we now call celebrity culture was in its infancy. There were as yet no gossip columns except faintly parodic specimens in mass-circulation newspapers; no supermodels, no reality-TV stars, no billionaire soccer players' wives, no fashionistas, no red carpets for anyone but the Queen. Celebrity rested on tangible achievement, like starring in films – or fronting a rock band – and the phenomenon of being famous for being famous was still largely unknown. So Bianca, cast for celebrity culture but detonated too early, was something of a loose cannon.

If anything, she was a prototype supermodel, albeit not tall and unnaturally skinny enough for the professional catwalk and rather too much of an original, for she had her own highly distinctive style combining 1930s Parisian elegance with a dash of the dominatrix. Her severe-sexy gowns, tailored suits and little pillbox hats with veils were the opposite extreme from from *faux*-naïve sixties dollybird-ism, and started a noticeable trend. After she appeared in a fashion show for Oxfam at the Grosvenor House wearing a two-tone curly wig and flourishing a silver-topped cane, London's only walking-stick dealer, James Smith & Son, recorded their first-ever female clients.

It was the dawn of the age of meaningless awards, and Bianca was given a shelfload – like 'Woman of the Year Hat Award 1972' – usually in hopes that Mick would accompany her to the ceremony. Her tacturnity with the press led one magazine to dub her 'Today's Garbo', while another reported (from sources undisclosed) that 'she wears no underwear and her nipples are shaped like rosebuds'. Despite Britain's deep-seated suspicion of foreign names, there was a surge in baby girls called Bianca. With a public profile this high, it would have made sense to create a Bianca Jagger brand of something or other. But in the Jagger household, needless to say, there was room for only one brand.

At the beginning, it amused Mick to be married to a fashion icon (a phrase not yet coined) and, within reason, share his limelight with her. Under Bianca's influence, he became even fussier about his own wardrobe, adopting several of her ideas, like the silver-topped cane tucked under his arm when he tardily greeted the ambassadors and senators in Washington. The pair began to do fashion shoots together and, in January 1973, were jointly voted onto the world's 'best-dressed' list by 2,000 international fashion editors and experts. A few weeks later, London's *Sunday Times Magazine* had them photographed on the roof of the Biba store in Kensington by the aged Leni Riefenstahl, whose film *Triumph of the Will* eulogised Hitler's 1934 Nazi Party rally at Nuremberg. The American critic Albert Goldman, who compared Rolling Stones concerts to the Nuremberg rally and Mick to 'the Leader', sure would have loved that one.

The couple posing in Biba's Roof Garden, she with her frilly Scarlett O'Hara gown and parasol, he in his bright ochre suit, seemed to embody a perfect rock 'n' roll fairy tale. But the reality was very different. Mick would later say their marriage had been 'good only for the first year' and thereafter became a matter of pretending in public with less and less conviction. Bianca's estimate would be even briefer.

As far as his band and closest associates were concerned, she remained an outsider, alternately mistrusted and mocked. Keith resented her for spiriting his ever-fickle Glimmer Twin away to a glitzy world, populated by couturiers and continental movie stars, where nobody had ever heard of Blind Boy Fuller or open-G tuning. Anita Pallenberg resented her for being so beautiful and stylish and standoffish – all the more now that Anita's own once-heavenly face was coarsened by heroin, her once-eighteen-carat crop hung lank and colourless and her once-fascinatingly husky voice had become a croak. Bill Wyman and Mick Taylor and their respective partners were never unpleasant but kept their distance, as befitted Stones second-rankers. Surprisingly, however, Charlie Watts turned out to be a friend. Bianca found Charlie's genuineness a blessed respite from the sycophancy that surrounded Mick – and also believed his wife to be the only one in the Stones' inner circle Mick had never screwed.

Even the generally tolerant, good-hearted people who worked for Mick in London found it hard to warm to Bianca, and thus easy to think the worst of her. She was seen as a ruthless gold digger only out for his money (no one knowing about the pre-nup she had been handed on her wedding morning) and interested only in herself (everyone forgetting her work for the Nicaraguan earthquake victims). Inevitably, too, she was suspected of being behind Mick's decision to deny paternity of Karis Hunt. It stood to reason: why would a mother want any other child to share in the inheritance that would come to her own?

While Mick was in the studio, or otherwise engaged, the task of keeping Bianca amused would fall to PR Les Perrin's wife, Janey. Usually this meant putting her in the back of a chauffeur-driven car with a wad of £20 notes and sending her off shopping on Bond Street or Knightsbridge. There were endless problems with the chauffeurs, from whom Bianca seemed to expect almost servile deference. One was sent away simply for failing to tip his cap. A hire-car company which the Stones office had used for years refused to accept any more bookings because of her. Janey Perrin came to dread the phone calls complaining that yet another driver had been lacking in respect and that Bianca – as she pronouced it with her faint Hispanic lilt – was 'peesed off'.

Despite her supposed intriguing against Karis on Jade's behalf, she was seen as an indifferent mother who chafed at being stuck at home while Mick gallivanted around as he pleased. At some moments she would seem devoted to Jade, delighting in buying clothes for her and dressing her up; at others, she'd leave her with the nanny, or Mick's parents, and disappear to the shops and Ricci Burns's hair salon in Chelsea. For a time, Jade shared a nanny with Mick and Rose Taylor's daughter Chloe, who was the same age. Despite working for both famous Micks at once, the young woman earned a minuscule amount and, in revenge, would allow the little girls to play with their daddies' Gold Discs in the bath.

Once there had been no doubting Bianca's power to bring Mick to heel. During the *Exile on Main St.* sessions, when he used to travel up from the Côte d'Azur to join her in Paris, he'd sometimes find she wasn't awaiting him at L'Hôtel and had gone missing just like Chrissie Shrimpton used to ten years earlier. As once with Chrissie, he'd have the embarrassment of ringing round her friends to ask help in finding her. While he was away recording in Jamaica, Bianca expressed her boredom and annoyance by getting her luxuriant black hair cut as short as a boy's. Marianne Faithfull had done the same in '69, but whereas Marianne's mutinous crop produced an eerie resemblance to Brian Jones, Bianca's turned her temporarily into a true mirror image of Mick – which, a former employee recalls, 'he loved'.

Such wiles had long since lost their efficacy. Mick and Bianca might share a bed, but outside the boudoir she was now just one of the crowd who daily competed for his attention. She had come to detest the elaborate web of Mick's advisers and assistants with whom she had to negotiate to reach him: 'the Nazi state', she privately called it, subliminally influenced perhaps by that photo shoot with Leni Riefenstahl. There was also a new stinginess and seeming lack of concern for her that had marred even his impressiveness over the Nicaraguan earthquake. When he left Managua for the Stones' Far East tour, Bianca stayed on to help the relief effort, living in a rented house for which he promised to pay. The rent did not arrive and she had to waste hours on disrupted phone lines trying to get through to Ahmet Ertegun's office in New York before the problem was finally sorted out.

Her declaration of complete separateness from the Stones ('I have nothing to do with them!') came less from hauteur than fear, as she later admitted. She was terrified of being drawn too deeply into a world whose pressures and excesses could, and frequently did, kill people. And terrified not only for herself. As a mother, she might not be perfect, but in comparison with Keith and Anita's two small children, Marlon and Dandelion, Jade's life was a model of normality.

Keith now lived part of the time in Jamaica, attracted by the music, the ganja – and, he would later claim, the chance to learn to fight properly with the knife he had always carried. In March, while coming down from the Stones' Far East tour at his Ocho Rios beach house, he had a major bust-up with Anita over what he thought her unseemly involvement with some local Rastafarians. He stormed out and flew back to London alone, whereupon Anita was busted for cannabis possession and thrown into a horrific Jamaican jail, leaving the two children alone until neighbours realised their plight and took them in.

On 26 June 26 the London *Evening Standard* splashed 'ROLLING STONE RICHARD – GUN, DRUGS CHARGES' after Keith and Anita were raided back

at 3 Cheyne Walk and heroin, cannabis, Mandrax, two unlicensed firearms and a quantity of ammunition came to light, generating twenty-
five charges in total. (Interestingly, no attempt was made to widen the
search to Mick's house, just a few doors away. As if some word had been
quietly passed from Washington, DC, he would never again be turned
over by the British police.)

Hard and soft drugs and industrial quantities of alcohol and cigarettes were no longer the only hazards with which the Richard children
had to live. In July, Keith's Sussex cottage, Redlands, the scene of his
martyrdom with Mick in 1967, was gutted by fire. Four-year-old Marlon
having raised the alarm, it was assumed one of his drug-sozzled parents
had nodded out with a lighted cigarette, though Keith claimed a mouse
had caused the conflagration by nibbling through some electrical wires.
In October, he celebrated lenient court treatment for the June bust (a
£250 fine for him, a year's conditional discharge for Anita) with a party
in his suite at the Londonderry Hotel. While the grown-ups partied,
fire broke out in the bedroom where Marlon lay asleep, the whole floor
had to be evacuated and Keith was banned from the hotel for life. Once
again, he denied anyone had fallen asleep while smoking and blamed
faulty electrics.

At four, Marlon was already his father's keeper, ever watchful for
the police raid or the cigarette burning into the bedspread. And loving
mother though Anita was, her childcare left something to be desired.
Marlon would sometimes be looked after by Bianca and Mick – who,
characteristically, was always kind to him. Once when Bianca tried to
take off his socks, she found he'd been wearing them so long that they
were welded to his feet.

What her detractors never realised was that Bianca's Egyptian-cat
aloofness masked a conventional, even straitlaced person for whom life
with Mick proved an endlessly unfolding catalogue of disillusionment.
She hated the impermanence of their existence, which, thanks to his
tax situation, was a constant shuttle between America, France, Britain
and Ireland, never settling longer than a few weeks anywhere. He was a
fugitive from income-tax authorities as much as Keith ever was from the

law, haunted by dread of breaching his non-resident status – especially in Britain, where the tax man was believed to be all-knowing and all-seeing. Bianca would later recall an illicit stay at Cheyne Walk when they had to crouch down when passing windows so as not to be seen, and generally act 'like squatters'.

Then there were the other women. It had been only weeks after her marriage, when still pregnant with Jade, that Bianca had learned about Marsha Hunt and Karis. Her assertion that she didn't care about Mick's long-concealed love child, or Marsha's paternity suit, convinced no one who really knew her. Then there were all the other women she later found out about – and the still-greater number she never did. A faint consolation, as she told the *Sunday Times,* was that 'Mick sleeps with many women, but rarely has affairs with them. They are all trying to use him . . . nobodies trying to become somebodies.'

One such infidelity that Bianca never discovered she certainly would have given a damn about. Just weeks after she met him he'd had a brief final fling with her predecessor, Marianne Faithfull. It was the time of the *Sticky Fingers* album, which coincidentally included Mick's version of 'Sister Morphine', the song marking Marianne's final surrender to heroin.

By this point, pop's former Virgin Mary literally had nothing left to lose; her addiction had destroyed her singing and acting career, eaten up her money, deprived her of custody of her son, Nicholas, and driven her mother, the once-indefatigable Baroness Erisso, to attempt suicide. During a detox attempt in a private clinic, she'd had two of her front teeth knocked out by a male nurse after getting a friend to smuggle her in some smack. Her nadir was spending some months as a street addict in St Anne's Court, a grubby Soho alley with the same name as the Saint-Tropez chapel where Mick and Bianca had married.

One day, she left her West End junkie friends for a nostalgic stroll down Chelsea's King's Road and, outside the Granny Takes a Trip boutique, chanced to bump into Mick. As she would recall, he greeted her as if they'd last seen each other yesterday, kissed her, then began fondling her in a manner clearly indicating that all her attempts to make herself unattractive still had not quite succeeded. The manager of Granny Takes a Trip let them borrow a room above the shop, where they had sex without speaking a word, then kissed and went their separate ways.

Marianne's led to yet another attempt to clean up – this time at, of all places, Bexley Hospital, near Dartford, Kent, where the schoolboy Mike Jagger had worked as a porter during his summer holidays.

THE NEWEST FAD in British pop was glam rock; the sound was a pastiche of 1950s rock 'n' roll and the style was essentially what Mick had been doing for four or five years already. Bands whose heterosexuality could never be doubted put on effete, glittery clothes, teased their hair into streaky pompadours and slathered their faces in makeup. Glam rock made huge teenybop idols of several artists who had enjoyed only marginal success in the sixties, like Rod Stewart, Elton John and Marsha Hunt's other old flame, Marc Bolan. But the one with the most obvious designs on Mick's throne was David Bowie.

Born David Jones in 1947, Bowie shared Mick's Kentish roots, having been raised in Bromley first, then in still-less-compelling Beckenham. After a one-off hit single, 'Space Oddity', in 1969, he had developed into a performer whose high-art influences, and sky-high camp, did not prevent him acquiring a female following as frantic as Mick's had ever been. While Mick's stage persona had always been a fiction, Bowie went the further step of creating an actual alter ego, a spiky-haired, white-faced, platform-booted space alien named Ziggy Stardust who had fallen to earth and become a rock star.

Though no one looking at Ziggy's blend of vaudeville and sci-fi would have guessed it, Bowie had to a great extent modelled himself on Mick. He used a stage name half in homage to the American frontier knife and half to Jagger; he recorded at Olympic Studios because of their historic connection with the Stones; he had even been photographed in a Mr Fish frilly dress reminiscent of Mick's in Hyde Park. While most of

his songs came from their own weird, genderless world, the odd one –
like 'The Jean Genie' on his *Aladdin Sane* album – had blazing guitar riffs
and an unequivocal sexual challenge that suggested he would always
have preferred to be fronting the Stones. More than one UK music journalist had dubbed him 'Mick Jagger's heir'.

For all Ziggy Stardust's huge success, Bowie quickly tired of his
imposture and in July 1973, after a sold-out concert at London's Hammersmith Odeon, announced he was killing Ziggy off. Mick was at the
show and, at the Café Royal party afterwards, transfixed a room full of
celebs, including Barbra Streisand and Ringo Starr, by kissing Bowie
full on the lips.

Despite his mega-campness, Bowie was married to a young American woman previously known as Angie Barnett who had played a crucial part in his rise. Both were self-proclaimed bisexuals, their marriage
was a famously open one, and before long Mick was rumoured to be
having an affair with each of them simultaneously. Certainly, Bowie's
admiration seemed to border on infatuation. *Melody Maker*'s New York
correspondent, Michael Watts, recalls him spending an evening rhap-
sodising about Mick and showing every sign of being 'totally in love
with him'.

To facilitate the supposed *ménage à trois*, the Bowies had a flat on Oak-
ley Street, Chelsea, just a short distance from Cheyne Walk. Though no
hard evidence of Mick's involvement with either Mr or Mrs Bowie ever
emerged, Angie claimed to have once returned home from America early
one morning to find him sharing a bed with David. Bowie, through
his lawyer, said all suggestions of a sexual relationship were 'absolute
fantasy', while Mick dismissed them as 'total rubbish'. However, the
pair did not exactly discourage such speculation; a snapshot survives of
them cuddled up together suggestively on a couch.

Mick may have been rather more concerned with monitoring his
biggest rival since Jimi Hendrix. Bowie, indeed, had formally thrown
down the gauntlet, declaring that Rudi Valentino, his post-Ziggy Stardust alter ego, was 'the next Mick Jagger'. Mick's keenness to hang
out with him had a slight whiff of the old Mafia proverb 'keep your

friends close and your enemies closer'. This could sometimes backfire: when Bowie came to a Stones concert in Newcastle, Mick suffered the novel experience of losing his audience's attention mid-song. Glancing round, he realised the front rows had sighted Bowie's carrot-haired figure in the wings.

The next Stones album, *Goats Head Soup* (released 31 August in the UK, 12 September in the United States), showed glam rock firmly taking hold. Goat's-head soup, or Manish water, is a Jamaican delicacy, and an inner sleeve to the album showed an eyeless ram's head immersed in broth, looking more like the ingredients for a satanic rite than supper. The front cover was a David Bailey shot of Mick's face through a gauzy veil, his scarlet lips parted in coquettish surprise somewhat recalling Marilyn Monroe in *The Seven Year Itch* when the subway breeze blows up her dress.

The single from the album was a ballad called 'Angie', sung with a whispery pathos that did not distort the name so much as stretch it on a rack: 'Ayn-jeh . . . *Ay-y-y-n-n-jeh* . . .' Mick was generally thought to be serenading Mrs David Bowie, but actually the song was by Keith, written for his daughter, Dandelion, to whom the Swiss maternity clinic had given the local saint's name Angela. Ahmet Ertegun had qualms about releasing such an untypical Stones product, but was overruled, and the single immediately went to No. 1 in America, though only No. 5 in Britain.

A battle Ertegun did win was over Mick's song 'Starfucker', aimed at a type of female he knew so well and including a line about 'giving head to Steve McQueen'. The title had to be changed to 'Star Star' and the 'giving head' reference cleared in advance with McQueen (who, of course, was hugely flattered). During the composition process, Chris O'Dell had been surprised to get a phone call from Mick, whom she had not seen since they'd enjoyed friendship with benefits a year previously. With the enthusiasm he never showed in public, he sang 'Starfucker' to her down the line and also gave her to understand he was still hanging out with Carly Simon.

Goats Head Soup likewise topped the album charts – ultimately going triple platinum (three-million-plus copies) in America – but pleased the critics hardly more than *Exile on Main St.* had done. In *Creem* magazine, Lester Bangs wrote there was 'a sadness about the Stones now because they amount to such an enormous "so what?"' For Thomas Erlewine, it marked the end of 'the greatest winning streak in rock history . . . where the Stones' image began to eclipse their accomplishments as Mick ascended to jet-setting celebrity and Keith sank into addiction . . . It's possible to hear them moving in both directions on *Goats Head Soup*, at times in the same song.'

September brought a tour to promote the album in Britain and Europe, with Mick noticeably cracking down on on-road bad behaviour. The main casualty was saxophonist Bobby Keys, hitherto Keith's most faithful partner in crime. Bobby had already blotted his copybook during the Far East tour when a syringe slid out of one of his saxes as the band went through airport security in Hawaii. On 17 October he failed to show up for the penultimate European gig, at Brussels' Forêt Nationale, being otherwise engaged with a Belgian girl in a bathtub full of champagne. Mick summarily fired him and, despite all Keith's pleas, remained implacable.

Bobby therefore sadly missed the first viewing of Robert Franks's documentary on the '72 American tour, whose title employed one of his favourite expressions: it was called *Cocksucker Blues*. The name came from Mick's pornographic blues song about rent boys and sex with pigs which the Stones had recorded as an up-yours gesture to Decca Records when they defected to Atlantic. Though he had written and sung 'Cocksucker Blues' purely as a joke, it had since found its way into circulation and, performed by a different vocalist, even featured in an off-Broadway show, *The Trials of Oz*, about *Oz* magazine's prosecution under British obscenity laws. Rolling Stones Records' boss, Marshall Chess, also planned to put Mick's original version on an album of X-rated music, featuring various other prominent artists. The Stones' sometime session pianist Dr John had already turned in a contribution entitled 'How Much Pussy Can You Eat?'

Cocksucker Blues, the documentary, followed on from Dr John. If there wasn't much rock 'n' roll (Robert Frank being too much of an artist merely to film a band onstage), there were drugs and sex in superabundance. Shooting some colour but largely black-and-white – what the American novelist Don DeLillo would later call 'a washed blue light, corruptive and ruinous' – Frank had used his access-all-areas and his force of camera-operating insiders to the full. There were scenes of people unself-consciously snorting cocaine, smoking and passing joints, and a heart-chilling one of a young girl in a hotel room mainlining heroin. A naked groupie lay on a bed with wide-open legs, fondling herself appreciatively while a male voice-over enthused about her 'snatch'. Other unclad females lounged around, exchanging banal small talk, like goods on a supermarket shelf.

Most of the action involved minor figures in the road company, although an early vignette showed Mick slipping a hand inside his sateen trousers and appearing to masturbate (surely an unnecessary act for him if anyone). Caught up in the most depraved scene, an in-flight orgy aboard the Lapping Tongue, he made obvious efforts to distance himself. The culmination was the stripping naked of a nineteen-year-old groupie by a burly middle-aged roadie, who then twirled her aloft and buried his face in her crotch. As it was happening, Mick boogied down the aisle with Mick Taylor, shaking a rattle in Latin rhythm and chortling that the 'show' deserved an Oscar.

Just as unsparing was Frank's record of life on the road in America: the raw concrete backstage areas and monotonous hotel suites, the endless packing and unpacking, the card games on unmade beds, the massed liquor bottles, the overloaded ashtrays, the despoiled room-service trolleys, the endless, bored wandering back and forth between interconnected rooms, the monolithic black bodyguards stationed in corridors day and night for fear of avenging Hell's Angels. One backstage sequence showed a stoned-to-the-gills Keith squatting on a metal bench and mumbling incoherently while Ahmet Ertegun, immaculately blazered as always, did his best to murmur agreement in suitable places. There was also the beyond-*Spinal Tap* moment in Denver when Keith and Bobby Keys staged an example of rock-star naughtiness for the camera, heaving a TV set from their hotel room window onto some garbage cans seven or eight floors below, then doubling up in rather contrived hysterics.

Frank had even been given access to Mick and Bianca's suite at the New York Sherry-Netherland before the wrap-up shows at Madison Square Garden. Although it was Mick's birthday, the immense brocaded space was wrapped in silence, its only other occupant Mick's super-discreet driver-assistant, Alan Dunn, folding and packing jumpsuits. Bianca, appropriately all in white, flitted to and fro, scarcely uttering a word. At one point she volunteered that she'd like to go to Elaine's restaurant, whose owner kept a communal table for favourite star clients like Woody Allen. But Mick — still oh so quietly — thought not: 'terrible food, terrible people, terrible woman'.

Marshall Chess, the film's producer, showed it to the Stones while they were working at Musicland studios in Munich on a new album that would become *It's Only Rock & Roll*. Seeing what was only their kind of rock 'n' roll in such minute detail, as Chess recalls, 'left them all in shock'. However, there was clearly no question of the worldwide cinema release that had been intended. Warner Bros, the financiers of *Performance*, had first refusal on distribution. But even in the new Hollywood of the 1970s, where nudity and four-letter words had become the norm, no mainstream company would tolerate a production called *Cocksucker Blues*, or dare to market this one, whatever its title. Not the least problem was the film-maker's failure to obtain signed releases from most of the people shown in compromising situations. 'When you're having sex or shooting up,' Marshall Chess says, 'you're not going to want to sign a release.'

Mick congratulated Robert Frank on a brilliant piece of work, but said that if it were released he'd never be able to show his face in America again. So *Cocksucker Blues* was put on the shelf alongside *The Rolling Stones Rock 'n' Roll Circus*. Instead, a crew from John Lennon's Butterfly film company cobbled together a straightforward record of the '72 tour, using stage footage from the Fort Worth and Houston concerts and blamelessly entitled *Ladies and Gentlemen: The Rolling Stones*.

Those who spent lengthy periods with the Stones tended never to be quite the same afterwards, and Robert Frank was no exception. Having months of arduous work thrown away was just the start of the bad luck that *Cocksucker Blues* brought Frank. His daughter, Andrea, and his young assistant, Danny Seymour (who appeared in the credits as 'Junkie Soundman'), were both to die suddenly soon afterwards.

IN THE JANUARY 1974 issue of American *Viva* magazine, Bianca dropped the first public hint that she and Mick had begun seriously to drift apart. She was being interviewed for a cover story on Rock Royalty (a status conferred not only on her and Mick but also on Carly Simon and James Taylor). 'Perhaps Mick isn't attracted to me anymore,' *Viva* quoted her as saying. 'When I first met him, I knew who he was. But not now . . . All I need is to find a human being who is truthful. It's so sad when I discover that someone I care for isn't truthful . . . I can't forgive lies. Lies are offensive to the intelligence.'

Here was a very different Bianca from that frowning, uncommunicative clotheshorse; here was an uncertain, vulnerable young woman who admitted the situation frightened her, especially 'when I look at Jade. My parents were divorced and I remember how painful it was to be a child divided between two loves.' Interviewed in the same magazine, Mick played down any idea of a serious rift, merely saying he was 'not in the least domesticated' and, more revealingly, 'I try not to hang around my family any more than I have to.'

Under Prince Rupert Loewenstein's strategy, 1974 was a year empty of Stones tours. Keith spent much of it in Switzerland, attempting yet another cure (the one in which, according to folklore, all his drug-infused blood was pumped away and a fresh supply substituted). As a result, Switzerland once more became the band's command centre. There were frequent business meetings – attended, one participant recalls, by 'about twenty lawyers' – when Prince Rupert and Mick hammered out plans for touring America, Latin America and the Far East in '75 and '76, this time definitely without any fly-on-the-wall film-makers tagging along.

Rather than hang around his family, Mick also was often in Los Angeles, hanging out with the only fellow musician to whom he ever deferred. A few months earlier, John Lennon had split from Yoko in New York and moved to the West Coast for the riotous interlude he later called his Lost Weekend. High on the agenda was sex, which Lennon felt had come his way in insufficient quantity while he was a Beatle and which had latterly begun to pall with Yoko. As he often said, he aspired to be like Mick, sitting in the bar at New York's Plaza Hotel, waiting to be picked up by some stunning woman, then retiring with her to one of the hotel's suites.

Lennon desperately wanted the green card that would allow him permanent residency in America, but was continually threatened with deportation by the Immigration and Naturalization Service because of his history with drugs and radical politics. Mick, by now thoroughly *persona grata* in Washington, could easily have obtained a green card, but never would because it would make him liable to US income tax.

Hard though Lennon tried to be dissolute, he spent much of his Lost Weekend in the recording studio with trusted British cronies like Ringo Starr, Elton John – and Mick. In one session at the Record Plant West, he produced Mick singing Willie Dixon's 'Too Many Cooks (Spoil the Soup)' with Al Kooper on keyboards, Jesse Ed Davis – who'd appeared in the Stones' *Rock 'n' Roll Circus* – on guitar, and Jack Bruce from Cream, and the Ealing Blues Club, on bass. When Lennon returned to New York (though not yet to Yoko), Mick joined him at the Record Plant East to work on the Dixon track some more and also visited him and his girl-friend, May Pang, at their apartment on East Fifty-second Street.

It's Only Rock & Roll, released in October 1974, was the first Stones album produced by Mick and Keith under their Glimmer Twins pseud-onym. The initial plan had been a mixture of live performance extracts from the '73 European tour and soul standards like the Temptations' 'Ain't Too Proud to Beg'. But the ever-fecund Twins soon switched to doing their own new material, albeit working separately more often than together. The album cover was by the Belgian painter Guy Peellaert, whose lushly airbrushed portraits of record idols from Hank Williams to Eddie Cochran had made him the Rubens of glam rock. Peellaert depicted the Stones walking through what seemed to be a Parliament chamber full of Pre-Raphaelite young women and little girls, seemingly immune to their outstretched bare arms.

The title track, released as 'It's Only Rock & Roll (But I Like It)', felt exactly right for glam rock's prevailing mood of pastiche and *faux naïveté*. Nonetheless, it failed to make the American Top 10 and only just scraped it in Britain. Its sound was not in the least glam but the rough-edged mixture as usual, with Mick mouthing some sarcastic cal-ligrapher–hara-kiri guff about sticking a pen in his heart and bleeding all over the stage. What perplexed the punters was a colour video of the band who had once abhorred matching uniforms, now all dressed in white Victorian sailor suits and playing in a tent that gradually filled with foam. The foam proved only too plentiful, rising relentlessly to above head height, so that by the time the five rockin' sailor boys finished their performance they appeared to be trapped inside a washing machine in mid-cycle. It seemed the very last message Mick's fans wanted to hear from him at this point was 'Hello, sailor!'

Mick Taylor looked least comfortable in his prissy white suit with soap bubbles brushing his nose, and in December he handed in his resignation. In five years he had contributed enormously to the Stones while stoically accepting his paradoxical role as soloist overshadowed by chord player, resigned to being the Mick people thought of a long way second, following the others into exile despite having no tax problems and uncomplainingly sharing the fall-out from Keith's drug problems. Yet he still remained just a salaried employee, confined to the same NCOs' barracks as Bill and Charlie.

Taylor had ambitions as a songwriter, but all his attempts to realise them had been crushed by the Glimmer Twins juggernaut. During the making of *It's Only Rock & Roll*, so he complained, he'd made major con-tributions to several songs, but received no credit. At heart, he was a live-action bluesman who preferred blasting out a riff in seconds to working on it for weeks in the studio. And to the bluesman who thought he'd joined a blues band, Mick's recent foray into glam rock was the final straw.

On a personal level, too, five years had taken their toll. Taylor had arrived in 1969 as a non-smoking vegetarian; now he was a heroin user on a scale not far behind Keith. A wake-up call (as no one yet said) had come in September 1973, when Keith's acolyte, the beautiful Gram Parsons, died of a smack overdose. Always in Taylor's mind, too, was the fate of his predecessor in the lead-guitar spot, Brian Jones. He would later call himself 'the only lead guitarist to have left the Stones and lived'.

The story to the media was that he wanted a change of scene. From Keith he received a warmly appreciative telegram but from Mick merely a catty epigram when asked about the problem of replacing him: 'No doubt we can find a brilliant six-foot-three blond guitarist who can do his own makeup.' That was just the Tyranny of Cool speaking; actually Mick thought Taylor's delicate single-string playing the perfect counterpoint to Keith's rhythm lead, and tried hard to persuade him not to leave. The final attempt was at a party given by impresario Robert Stigwood. 'Mick talked to Taylor a long while that night, with Eric Clapton reeling around dead drunk in the background,' Marshall Chess recalls. 'But it was no use.'

With hindsight it seemed that Taylor's good friend, twenty-seven-year-old Ronnie Wood, affectionately known throughout the business as Woody, was (as no one yet said) a shoo-in to take his place. Woody had known the Stones since the Ealing Blues Club days, when his older brother Art used to sing with Blues Incorporated. He was now lead guitarist with Rod Stewart's band the Faces, who, despite being glam-rock idols, were just as macho as the Stones and their main rivals in both the UK and the United States. Prior to Woody's arrival, the Faces had been the Small Faces, the act on which Andrew Oldham had mainly focused after parting from the Stones in 1967.

Woody's own face, bony and long-nosed, somewhat like an amiable anteater, seemed a natural fit with Mick and Keith; indeed, he already had a strong working relationship with each of them. His

Victorian mansion, The Wick, on Richmond Hill – where he lived with his wife, Krissie, a former groupie said to have slept with both John Lennon and George Harrison – was a popular party zone for musicians of every stripe. Keith was a frequent visitor and, during a period of turmoil with Anita, had spent some months as the Woods' houseguest. As a result, intensive police surveillance had been placed on the house and one raid conducted, though its only find was Krissie Wood in bed with a female companion.

The Wick had a basement recording studio where Woody was sporadically at work on a solo album between gigging with Rod Stewart and the Faces. Mick liked to hang out there, and had been some little assistance with the album, particularly a track called 'I Can Feel the Fire'. On a later visit, Woody helped him tape the basis of 'It's Only Rock & Roll' with the two of them on guitar and David Bowie doing back-up vocals (inaudible on the released version). Assistance of that scale would normally earn a co-writing credit, but Mick had a better idea: he would leave Woody's name off 'It's Only Rock & Roll' and, in return, ask no credit for his help on 'I Can Feel the Fire'. This doubtful bargain was a further foretaste of working with the Glimmer Twins.

But for now Woody was in a hugely successful band whose concert and recording commitments stretched years ahead; moreover, Rod Stewart was an old blues-club friend whom Mick and Keith hesitated to antagonise by stealing his key sideman. So when the Stones returned to Munich in December 1974 to start the album that would become *Black and Blue*, auditions for a new lead guitar were held at the same time. The chance of becoming a Stone brought most of the current guitar gods winging to Musicland Studios, as tremulous with nerves as any modern *X Factor* hopefuls, among them Eric Clapton, Jeff Beck, Muscle Shoals' virtuoso Wayne Perkins and former Canned Heat member Harvey 'the Snake' Mandel. Each had to play a number with the band that was also put on tape: the best takes were then thriftily put aside to be slotted into the album in progress.

The two finalists were Clapton and Steve Marriott, the latter of whom had fronted the Small Faces when Andrew Oldham tried to turn them into the new Rolling Stones, then gone on to co-found Humble Pie. Recruiting Marriott would be fraught with potential embarrassment, since he had dated Chrissie Shrimpton immediately after Mick dumped her. Sooner or later it would be bound to come out how Chrissie could only endure a boyfriend even shorter than Mick by calling him Peter, after Peter Pan, and making him call her Wendy. As a powerful vocalist with a huge female following, he would also be a major threat to Mick's limelight. Eric Clapton, on the other hand, was a sublime instrumentalist and a friend, but currently had drug and alcohol issues all too reminiscent of Brian Jones's. So the Glimmer Twins turned back to Ronnie Wood.

To lessen the feeling of larceny from Rod and the Faces, the Stones were said only to be borrowing Woody for their next American tour, in the early summer of 1975. And, like Mick Taylor, he would be just a salaried employee. When Mick handed him his contract, the cheery soul signed it without reading it.

Woody was to make his half-début in a show more extravagant than anything previously offered the Stones' American public. It would start with a giant metal flower whose (bulletproof) petals opened to reveal the band playing inside. Mid-way through, a forty-foot inflatable phallus would come thrusting from rear stage and Mick would sit astride it to sing 'Star Star'. All this capital investment was suddenly put in jeopardy, however, when US Immigration denied Keith a visa as a result of his recent drug headlines in Britain and France. Mick appealed for help to the American ambassador in London, Walter Annenberg, and thanks to their combined clout with Washington the visa was granted.

As a rehearsal space for the Stones, and to 'hang around his family' for a spell, Mick rented Andy Warhol's summer home in Montauk on the eastern tip of Long Island. The oceanfront house had several Warhol-esque touches, like shelves full of books reversed to show only white pages. Though original Warhols crowded the walls and were stacked dozens deep in spare rooms and passages, the place had no special protection; indeed, its doors were usually left unlocked. Mick imported heavy security for the Stones' warm-up sessions, which he doubled before the arrival of 'my baby' as he called three-year-old Jade. So that her education wouldn't be too disrupted, he also enrolled her in the local hippie-progressive Little Red School House.

The band rehearsed in a cottage on the grounds, making a din that echoed across the peninsula. While Woody's guitar meshed in with Keith's – a virtually instantaneous process, as it proved – Warhol pottered around in his peroxide-blond toupee and took endless Polaroid pictures, blissfully unconscious that in *Cocksucker Blues* Mick referred to him as 'a fuckin' voyeur'. Warhol was a notoriously poor conversationalist (as a rule saying little beyond 'Really? Oh!' and 'Oh, really?'), but Jade, already a precocious charmer, roused him to eloquence that her father certainly never had. 'I love Mick and Bianca, but Jade's more my speed,' he was to recall. 'I taught her how to color and she taught me how to play Monopoly . . . Mick got jealous. He said I was a bad influence because I gave her champagne.'

The next-door property belonged to ABC-TV talk-show host Dick Cavett, who had done a celebrated live transmission from the Stones' Madison Square Garden concert in 1972. With a low hill screening him from the Warhol house, Cavett was not disturbed by the Stones' rehearsals, and became aware of their presence only when young women began crossing his private beach in search of Mick. 'Some I saw were naked, with their pubic hair dyed green,' he recalls. 'And there were four with heads shaved as bald as eggs camping in my woods.'

Also at rehearsals was twenty-five-year-old Annie Leibovitz, a photographer with a remarkable knack for catching rock dignitaries in the most unguarded situations, yet not damaging their *amour propre*. She had covered the '72 tour for *Rolling Stone* in a junior capacity, but Mick had spotted her qualities and asked her to join this one in effect as his personal photographer. At first she tried to be as unintrusive as possible, but then realised that 'what might have seemed like a nuisance to him became a source of comfort . . . to know I was somewhere nearby . . . I remember him saying I should tell him if I wanted him to be at a specific place on the stage at any point in the show, but . . . I couldn't think of anything for him to do that he wasn't doing already.'

One day, while leaving a restaurant in Montauk, he mistook a plate-glass window for a door and shattered the pane with his forearm, making a seven-inch gash that needed twenty-four stitches. As he showed off the gory wound later, Annie Leibovitz unslung her camera and began snapping it in black-and-white. Mick at first demurred but then changed his mind and told her to continue – this time in colour.

CHAPTER SEVENTEEN

'Old Wild Men, Waiting for Miracles'

Mick's failure to become the major screen actor *Performance* had promised was not for want of trying. And most of that trying was done by his long-time English film agent, Maggie Abbott. Abbott had known him socially in London since the mid-sixties and worked for the Stones' film agents, Creative Management Associates, with Sandy Lieberson, who went on to produce *Performance*. Mick's screen début as the teasing, reclusive Turner had profoundly impressed her, but she thought *Ned Kelly* an ill-advised follow-up and had vainly tried to talk him out of it. As a result, he trusted her judgement and showed her a professional loyalty he did to precious few others. During the 1970s, Maggie Abbott would bring him some twenty-five film projects, offering diverse acting challenges and the chance to work with directors of the calibre of John Boorman, Steven Spielberg and Franco Zeffirelli; several more came from other quarters, including the Andy Warhol circle.

His interest was often aroused, sometimes turning into enthusiasm, occasionally into actual commitment. Yet thanks to indecision, conflicting obligations with the Stones or – most frequently – last-minute attacks of cold feet, he ended up not doing a single one.

Predictably, a high proportion had a musical theme. In 1973, when plans were first mooted to film the Who's rock opera *Tommy*, Mick was considered for the name role, then invited to play the Acid Queen. He decided he didn't want to be 'in the Who's movie' – hadn't they upstaged him in *his* movie, *The Rolling Stones Rock 'n' Roll Circus?* – so Tina Turner got the part instead. Around the same time he was approached to star in a biopic of his blues hero Robert Johnson, who died aged only twenty-seven having reputedly made a pact with the devil, but that one never got as far as a pact with an agent either. There was more progress with *Blame It on the Night*, the story of a rock star getting to know his estranged son, which Maggie Abbott was to co-produce. Mick was initially interested, especially when producer Gene Taft offered him a co-credit for 'original story' if he would provide material from his own direct experience of rock stardom. He changed his mind, however, on realising that the estranged parent–child theme had uncomfortable parallels with himself and his daughter Karis. When the film finally came out in 1984, 'Michael Philip Jagger' was still co-credited for the story.

Another field to generate numerous offers – one increasingly dominant in seventies cinema – was science fiction and fantasy. Mick could have co-starred with Sean Connery and Charlotte Rampling in John Boorman's *Zardoz* (1974) about an apocalyptic future world ruled by a cult known as the Exterminators, whose sub-Orwellian god preaches a somewhat anti-Jaggerian doctrine: 'The penis is evil. The gun is good.' He could have co-starred with Malcolm McDowell in Nicholas Meyer's *Time After Time* (1979), in which the Victorian visionary H. G. Wells uses his Time Machine to pursue mass murderer Jack the Ripper into the twentieth century. (David Warner ended up with the role Maggie Abbott had wanted for him.) He could have played the lead in *Stranger in a Strange Land*, about a young man raised by Martians readjusting to earth, or in *Kalki*, adapted from Gore Vidal's 1978 novel about the leader of a drug-selling religious cult bent on world domination. Mick had several meetings with the putative director, Hal Ashby, in Malibu, and even visited India to scout locations before the project withered. Perhaps the biggest missed plum was the *The Man Who Fell to Earth* (1976) directed by *Performance*'s Nicolas Roeg. When Abbott suggested Mick to play the visiting extraterrestrial, Roeg objected that he was 'too strong' and someone more frail and ethereal was needed. So the role went to David Bowie.

Mick's oft-expressed desire to portray a character totally unlike himself and outside his world brought further juicy possibilities. He could have been in yet another remake of Hollywood's favourite parable, *A Star Is Born*, playing the screen idol who (in a nice twist on his real-life situation) becomes eclipsed by a more talented wife. He could have played opposite Charlotte Rampling in *I Never Promised You a Rose Garden* (1977), adapted from Joanne Greenberg's novel about a schizophrenic girl and the 'angel–devil character' she creates inside her head. One of the nearest misses was *Nothing Like the Sun*, adapted from the novel by Anthony (*A Clockwork Orange*) Burgess, which would have cast Mick as the young William Shakespeare. Negotiations got as far as a deal letter from Warner Bros (despite their unhappy history with *Performance*) when he decided to pull out. He was also briefly tempted by *The Moderns*, a story of writers in 1920s Paris, and *Inside Moves*, charting the friendship between a disabled young man and a baseball-playing bartender, which was eventually released, starring John Savage and David Morse, in 1980. He turned down the role of Rooster in *Annie*, and was turned down for those of Mozart in *Amadeus* and Dr Frank N. Furter in *The Rocky Horror Picture Show*.

Maggie Abbott had moved from London to Los Angeles in 1975, first working at the Paul Kohner Agency, then for independent producer Dan Melnick, later with Melnick as an executive at Columbia Pictures, and finally as a producer in her own right, with Mick remaining her client throughout. She soon realised that most senior Hollywood figures still had no understanding of rock music and thus no idea of the potential cinema audience he could command. So when the Stones played the LA Forum on their '75 tour – the one where Mick bestrode a forty-foot rubber phallus, so cock as much as rock – she had 200 free tickets distributed to studio executives and major movers and shakers. They also received backstage passes to the VIP Forum Club to enjoy lavish hospitality and Mick at his most charming. 'It was fun to watch them being seduced,' Abbott recalls, though actually the process was merely cock-teasing.

Her main problem was always Mick's incessant, all-consuming life with the Stones; first, getting him to make time to read a script, then – even trickier – persuading him to meet its putative producers and/or backers. Often on these occasions, Abbott recalls, the latter could barely hide their disappointment. 'They're expecting to meet some kind of god, and here's this person who's tiny, skinny, knock-kneed and pigeon-toed. But whoever I introduced him to instantly fell in love with him – producers, directors, film crews, children, old people . . . *everyone.*'

Like many before her, she noticed how Mick would adopt an accent to suit the company, one minute broad Cockney, the next an almost parodied poshness she called his 'brine trisers' (posh pronunciation of 'brown trousers') accent. And also how, when they were out together in public, he could make himself unnoticeable to the point of invisibility. 'Then when we got somewhere he didn't mind being recognised he'd completely change . . . the walk, the gestures, you could spot him a mile off.'

After a time, it occurred to Abbott that he'd feel more committed to a film project, and so less likely to bale out at the eleventh hour, if he also had a hand in producing it. In 1977, she persuaded her boss at Columbia, Dan Melnick, to okay an 'ultimate rock-concert movie', of which Mick would be both star and executive producer, rounding up other rock legends including the reunited Beatles to appear alongside him. Mick flew in from New York to discuss the project and Melnick and Abbott gave him a tour of the studios followed by lunch in the boardroom. As talks continued later at Melnick's home, the name of Steven Spielberg – just then finishing up *Close Encounters of the Third Kind* for Columbia – was mentioned as a possible director. 'Dan telephoned Spielberg and asked him to come over, without mentioning who he had with him,' Maggie Abbott recalls. 'When Spielberg walked in and saw Mick Jagger, he fell on his knees and started salaaming.'

Much as Spielberg worshipped Mick, he had conflicting commitments (mainly to become the richest movie mogul in Hollywood history), so, instead, approaches were made to, among others, the great Italian director Franco Zeffirelli. There was one meeting with Zeffirelli which convinced Maggie Abbott of Mick's potential as a producer: 'All the time Franco was talking, Mick was working out the box-office revenues and percentages like lightning in his head.' But nothing came of that one either.

As well as the projects listed, Abbott recalls, 'there was a steady flow of interest, be it scripts, treatments, ideas or adaptations, but they were often flights of fancy and a lot of people were simply turned on by the idea and image of Mick Jagger'. From time to time, too, there would be an approach from Donald Cammell to renew the partnership that had worked so spectacularly in *Performance*. But Cammell's later film projects became increasingly bizarre and difficult to finance, and he never again managed to land the Turner prize. 'Donald was very persistent,' Maggie Abbott says, 'and got cross with me sometimes when I couldn't deliver Mick.' Outside Hollywood, there were various attempts to team Mick with Bianca for something more than just fashion shoots. One short-lived idea was for him to write a stage musical in which she would star, despite having no noticeable vocal ability, with backing from Andy Warhol. Another was for Warhol's protégé Paul Morrissey to film André Gide's *Caves of the Vatican* with Mick and Bianca playing brother and sister. As things turned out, their only joint appearance on-screen would be in *All You Need Is Cash* (1978), a made-for-TV satire on the Beatles written and co-directed by Eric Idle from *Monty Python's Flying Circus*. The cast was recruited jointly from the *Python* team and America's *Saturday Night Live* show, and featured two genuine Beatles, George Harrison and Paul McCartney. Bianca played Martini, the wife of McCartney's character, Dirk McQuickly, while Mick appeared as himself.

For a time, Bianca looked like film-star material in her own right, and seemed eager to be viewed as such. In 1975, she accepted the co-lead in Ray Connolly's screen adaptation of his novel *Trick or Treat*, to be co-produced by *Performance*'s Sandy Lieberson with David Puttnam and directed by the eminent Michael Apted. Connolly was a well-known pop music columnist whose first essay into scriptwriting, *That'll Be the*

Day, an exercise in rock 'n' roll nostalgia featuring Ringo Starr, had been turned into a box-office hit by Lieberson and Puttnam. *Trick or Treat* was in a rather different genre, the story of two lesbian lovers who decide they want a baby. Bianca's role as one of the women involved a nude scene, to which she did not initially object.

Shooting began in Rome, but was quickly thrown off course by her unreliability, erratic moods and Mick-size tantrums over things like the size of the toilet in her trailer. Mainly at her instigation, Ray Connolly's script went through repeated rewrites and rethinks to the point that his usually abundant curly hair began to fall out. And when the time came for her nude scene, she hid under a bedsheet. The Rome shoot was abandoned and, shortly afterwards, so was the whole production, with losses of £500,000. For Connolly, no longer having to work with Bianca was literally a tonic: his hair started growing again.

During their Roman holiday, however, he caught a fleeting glimpse of the earthier character beneath the couture *grande dame* and scriptwriter's nightmare. Late one night on the Via Veneto, Bianca suddenly needed to pee, but no toilet was at hand. So, squatting behind a parked car, she hitched up her designer frock and did it in the gutter. Unlike the similar incident involving Mick at a London petrol station exactly ten years earlier, nobody came along and hauled her into court.

EARLY IN 1976, Mick acquired a permanent New York base, purchasing a two-storey brownstone house on West Eighty-sixth Street, the heart of the city's wealthy Upper West Side. The property was given an expensive total refurbishment by Andy Warhol's pet designer, Jed Johnson, but still had somewhat the same anonymous feel as the hotel suites it was meant to replace. The emptiness of Mick's refrigerator became a standing joke among his visitors, who would go in search of a late-night snack and find only, as Keith later recalled, 'a bottle of beer and half a tomato'. He finally got the point when his friend the *Saturday Night Live* comedian John Belushi turned up dressed in an apartment-house porter's peaked cap and frock coat, with a delivery of twelve cartons of gefilte fish.

This New York *pied-à-terre* served to increase the distance between him and Bianca, who remained based in London when she wasn't off with her couture friends in Paris or defoliating hapless screenwriters in Rome. The couple were by now seen together only seldom, and generally in an obvious state of massive mutual disenchantment. One paparazzo picture of them in a nightclub showed Mick all over Charlotte Rampling, his almost-co-star in *Zardoz*, while on his other side Bianca had fallen asleep.

The only reason they stayed together – showing what old-fashioned scruples ruled each shallow-seeming egomaniac – was their child. Jade was now aged four and attending an expensive private school, Garden House, in Sloane Square. Bianca attracted further criticism from the Mick camp (ludicrous though it may seem now) by trying to keep Jade on a healthy diet and limit her sugar intake. She was served a special stodge-free school lunch, and her teachers were under strict orders not to give her puddings or sweets, though the rule proved unenforceable: bloodhounds hunting escaped convicts through mangrove swamps are not more relentless than five-year-olds in pursuit of sugar.

In class, Jade was said to be often noisy and disruptive, her father's daughter in other words, but – also like him – she could be winningly sweet and vulnerable. With Mick not always around to screen them, there were continuing problems with nannies. Classes at Garden House ended at around four, but sometimes Jade would still be waiting to be collected at six or even later.

Mick adored her as much as ever, and was as good a father as any peripatetic, tax-avoiding rock superstar could be. When he was in London, he would pick her up from school each afternoon; still a teacher's son at heart, he took a close interest in her lessons and quizzed the Garden House staff about her progress. When a nervous music teacher had to confess that Jade showed no sign of singing ability, Mick burst out laughing and said, 'She gets that from her mother.'

His parents were the other reason for preserving the façade of his marriage. Joe and Eva Jagger both doted on Jade, especially Joe, that for-mer domestic martinet. 'He lets Jade get away with anything,' Mick told friends in amazement. 'If it had been me or Chris when we were small, we'd have got a wallop or a task to do as a punishment.'

Most songwriters in a bad marital situation would be unable to pre-vent it from seeping into their work – but not this one. The Stones' new album, *Black and Blue*, released in April 1976, had all the band's usual macho swagger with an unpleasant added hint of domestic violence. In Los Angeles, a giant billboard on Sunset Boulevard showed the model Anita Miller made up to appear covered with bruises after an encounter with Mick. 'I'm Black and Blue from the Rolling Stones,' said the cap-tion, 'and I Love It.' A feminist group, Women Against Violence, lodged a protest and the image was scrapped. Mick riposted that 'a lot of girls are into that [i.e. enjoy being beaten up by men]'. Nowadays, whole careers are scuppered by less.

The album's lead single, 'Fool to Cry', momentarily raised expecta-tions he was about to get personal at long last. For although the real-life Mick could and frequently did dissolve into tears, the lip-curling Head Stone had never before admitted such weakness. It was a 'Wild Horses' – slow ballad with a melancholy, confiding feel, spoken more than sung, its first verse a poignant picture of a weary man with a small daughter on his knee, smoothing his brow and asking, 'Daddy, what's wrong?' But by the second verse he was with a woman who 'live [rather than "lives"] in the paw part o' town', making 'lerve serm-tahms . . . so fahn', safely back on Planet Jagger.

As the Stones prepared for that year's UK and European tour to promote *Black and Blue*, any suggestion of vulnerability on his part produced a strong reaction (luckily without any further feminist back-lash): 'It's not like I'm on tour and I'm the Lonely Rock Star. Forget it. It doesn't apply to me . . . There's no reason to have women on tour unless they've got a job to do. The only other reason is to fuck. Oth-erwise they get bored . . . they just sit around and moan. It would be different if they did everything for you, like answer the phone, make the breakfast, look after your clothes and your packing, see if the car was ready – and fuck. Sort of a combination of what Alan Dunn [his driver] does and a beautiful chick.'

Ronnie Wood had become a full member of the band (though still only on salary) with the break-up of Rod Stewart's Faces in December 1975. So far as Keith was concerned, Woody had more than qualified for admittance during his loan-out for the previous summer's American tour. Driving through Arkansas together, the pair had been caught with a car full of coke, grass, mescaline and peyote as well as a consignment of local liquor in the trunk and Keith's constant companion, a lethal-looking hunting knife. Thanks to a crafty lawyer, a drunk judge and a youthful crowd chanting 'Free Keith!' outside the courthouse, he had somehow escaped with a $162.50 parking ticket.

Even more than for Mick, the '76 European tour offered Keith a welcome escape from difficult domestic circumstances. Heroin's chalk-faced dream by now possessed Anita and him so completely that they said little to each other around the house but 'Has it arrived yet?' Not content with wiping out Anita's beauty, smack had made her prone to fits of violence and delusion when she would take apart entire hotel rooms looking for the stash she imagined to be hidden there. Yet she had become pregnant again and, in March, bore Keith a son whom they named Tara. He went back on the road in late April nonetheless, taking his elder son, Marlon, the six-year-old minder he now could not do without.

With Keith, increasingly, the effect of his prodigious daily drug intake was nodding out at the most inopportune moments. During the tour's UK leg, he fell asleep at the wheel of his car on the M1 and crashed, fortunately without injury to himself or anyone else. Police who attended the scene searched the vehicle and he was charged with possessing cocaine and LSD. One night in West Germany, he even fell asleep onstage, during the new spot where Mick ceased cavorting to sing 'Fool to Cry' at the electric piano.

Against all advice, Keith insisted on driving himself across Europe, with Marlon as his navigator, prodding him whenever his ragged head drooped, warning him if a frontier was approaching so that he could take a quick hit, then throw away his stash. On many nights as showtime loomed, he would be deep in catatonic slumber from which his burliest assistants were afraid to rouse him, knowing his uncertain temper at such moments and that he kept a handgun under his pillow. Only Marlon could perform the task without risk to life and limb.

The boy forced to play father figure to his zonked-out dad would never forget how fatherly – in his own word, 'nurturing' – Mick often was to him on the tour. Back at their hotel after the Hamburg show, with Keith unconscious again and no prospect of supper, he wandered into Mick's room. Asked whether he'd like a hamburger, he replied that he'd never had one. 'You've *got* to have a hamburger in Hamburg,' Mick told him, and immediately rang down to room service.

In Paris, the Stones were booked for four straight nights, 4–7 June, at Les Abattoirs. On 6 June, as Keith prepared to go onstage, he learned that his son Tara had died of respiratory failure – cot death, as it would come to be called – aged just two and a half months. He insisted on doing that evening's show and finishing the tour without making his loss public. If a Rolling Stone's life has ever seemed enviable, think of being onstage with that kind of pain and remorse inside and Mick singing 'Daddy, you're a fool to cry . . .'

The tour's British leg culminated with six sold-out nights at London's Earls Court arena (extended from three after one million ticket applications). Among the fellow artists who came to pay court in Mick's dressing room was Bryan Ferry, singer with the glam-rock band Roxy Music, accompanied by his nineteen-year-old fiancée, the American fashion model Jerry Hall. Jerry's first impression of Mick was most people's, that he was much smaller than she'd expected, all the more noticeably so from her own commanding height of six feet. The audience lasted somewhat longer than most, then Mick suggested to Bryan Ferry that the three of them go out to dinner.

*

THE WOMAN WHO would come nearest to pinning the butterfly down was born Jerry Faye Hall, one of female twins, in Gonzales, Texas, and raised in the blue-collar Dallas suburb of Mesquite. Her truck-driver father was an inveterate gambler who once lost the family home in a poker game. He was also an alcoholic and a domestic tyrant whose five daughters all frequently had to stay home from school to conceal the bruises on their legs from lashes with his belt. Eventually, Jerry's twin sister, Terry, pulled a gun on him and threatened to kill him if the maltreatment continued. Despite these experiences, Jerry always refused to classify herself as an abused child or hold a grudge against her father. 'In our town,' she would recall nonchalantly, 'a lot of the kids were beat up.'

She was raised in the great outdoors, learning to ride as second nature, watching cowboys round up and castrate steers, and spending summers on her grandmother's chicken farm, where the old lady would roust her and her sisters out of bed each morning with a stick, shouting 'We're gonna can preserves!' In contrast to her loutish father, her mother instilled ladylike southern-belle ways, insisting that she gulp down a full meal before going out on dates with boys so that, like Scarlett O'Hara in *Gone With the Wind*, she didn't 'eat in front o' no gennelman'.

By her early teens, she had risen to full height, with a mass of gleaming, genuine blonde hair and a smile that could stop traffic. She had already decided on a modelling career, but the nearest Mesquite could offer was a job at the local Dairy Queen (from which she was soon fired for giving away too many milkshakes and orders of french fries). Her aim was simple: 'I want to marry a millionaire so I can have caviar any time of the day or night and take nice long champagne baths.' The only way of achieving it was to become a modern-day Texas Ranger.

At the age of sixteen, she was awarded $800 in compensation for medical negligence during a routine procedure on her sinuses. Showing herself every bit as much a gambler as her father, she spent the whole sum on a trip to France. A fashion agent spotted her sunbathing on the beach in Saint-Tropez, the scene of her future love's matrimonial 'circus' in 1971; as a result, she began to get modelling jobs in Paris, for a time sharing an apartment with a black woman of equally Amazonian proportions, the singer Grace Jones. One day at La Coupole brasserie, she was asked to join the table of France's two most eminent writers, Jean-Paul Sartre and Simone de Beauvoir. As she later recalled, they were 'fascinated' that she knew their works on existentialism and 'wanted to understand nothingness and being'; they also 'love[d] also to hear me talk stuff about rodeos'.

In 1975, Bryan Ferry saw her picture in *Vogue* and asked her to appear on the cover of Roxy Music's new album, *Siren*. Ferry at the time was the epitome of glam-rock pastiche chic with his slicked-down hair, tailored suits, white shirts and ties – everything the Rolling Stones were once thought to have stamped out. For Roxy's *Siren* album – a UK No. 1 – Jerry impersonated the mythical seductresses who lured mariners to their doom, lying half-naked on a rock with her gold tresses hidden under seaweed-coloured curls. After the shoot, she began an affair with Ferry, moving into his house in Holland Park, west London, and accepting his proposal of marriage.

Although the era of sickly, stick-like supermodels was yet to come, Jerry's slightly horsey beauty and air of glowing health made her stand out from as well as tower over all her catwalk competitors. She earned an unprecedented $1,000 per day, enough to buy herself a 200-acre ranch back in Lone Oak, Texas. In Britain, her lips became as well known as her face after a Revlon lipstick ad put them on the sides of London buses (something the nation's most famous mouth hadn't achieved). In 1976, she appeared with Ferry in the video for his solo single 'Let's Stick Together', clad in tiger print split to the waist and uttering zestful rebel yells. The single was a hit, but its title proved sadly ironic.

Even before she met Mick, in fact, the engagement to Bryan Ferry had been going downhill. Despite a working-class background in County Durham, Ferry affected the airs of an English squire together with those of a poet; he liked his six-foot blonde siren to wear tweeds and sit decorously while everyone fluttered around him. Jerry preferred partying, raucous laughter and leg wrestling, a Texan barroom sport at which she was remarkably adept.

Ferry initially had no suspicions on that June evening in 1976 when he accepted the invitation for them both to have dinner with Mick. Afterwards, still believing himself Mick's main object of interest, he suggested they all return to his house in Holland Park. On the car journey, Jerry later recalled, Mick pressed his knee hard against hers, causing her to feel 'an electric sensation'. When they arrived, she went to make tea and he offered to help, 'jumping around, joking . . . and spilling things', much to the distress of the house-proud Ferry. Mick had also somehow or other invited several additional people to join them, so ruining Ferry's hoped-for quiet chat about the problems of being pop idols together.

In one version of the story Jerry has often told, Mick would follow her every time she went into the kitchen and Ferry would suspiciously follow them both. In another, Mick chased her around a table-tennis table until Ferry came and chased him off. Eventually, freaked out by all the hyperactivity and mess, Ferry sullenly retired to bed. By Jerry's account, Mick tried to kiss her, but she wouldn't let him. However, as Mick later told a friend, she gave him an unequivocal come-on: 'He said Jerry was wearing stockings with suspenders, which she kept flashing at him.'

Afterwards he would often phone Ferry and leave cheery messages like 'Hi Bryan, let's go out again . . . ,' but his calls were not returned. 'I'm never going out with him again,' Ferry told Jerry. 'All he did was ogle you.'

The end of the European tour in July made it necessary for Mick to hang around his family again. He and Bianca went to the Olympic Games in Montreal – getting tickets at short notice being, of course, no problem for him – to see the Cuban sprinter Alberto Juantorena win two gold medals. Afterwards they took Jade for a second stay at Andy Warhol's beach house in Montauk, where Mick celebrated his thirty-third birthday.

To mitigate the uneasiness with Bianca, there was a stream of celebrity houseguests, including John Lennon and Yoko Ono (now reconciled), Eric Clapton, David Bowie and Warren Beatty. As during Mick's previous tenancy, his visitors sometimes unwittingly wandered onto the adjoining property of talk-show host Dick Cavett. One morning, Cavett bumped into Jackie Onassis, widow of both President John F. Kennedy and the Greek shipping tycoon Aristotle Onassis, walking alone on the shore.

Cavett came to know Mick and Bianca well in this twilight of their marriage – and to be as smitten by Jade as Warhol had been the previous year. 'She was the cutest thing, and Bianca used to dress her up so beautifully in little pant suits and bow ties. And, God, was she bright – and funny! I remember I was driving her and Bianca in the car one day, the thing wouldn't start, and I said, "Oh, shit!" I apologised for the bad language, and in this beautiful British accent Jade said, "You needn't concern yourself. I'm quite accustomed to hearing it."'

An intellectual and bibliophile, Cavett discovered literary depths in Mick that he had never revealed in their chat-show encounters. 'One evening, my wife and I had Bianca and him over for drinks. As they left, I said what a pleasure it had been to have them in our house. "In *our* house . . ." Mick repeated, which I realised afterward was a quotation from *Macbeth*.' Another night, they went to a Japanese restaurant in Manhattan. 'When the young boy waiting on us recognised Mick, he just slid down the wall and onto the floor.'

Towards the end of the Jaggers' stay, Cavett left his property for a while. 'I used to lend my house to my secretary, Doris, every summer, and so she got to know Mick and Bianca as well. She later told me that they'd called round one evening, stayed a while, and been very dignified, but she suspected they'd been drinking. "What made you think that?" I asked her. "Because," she said, "Bianca was reading the *New York Times* upside down."'

A visit by Mick's parents unfortunately coincided with the reported approach of a hurricane named Belle. It had mostly blown itself out by the time it reached Long Island, but produced one curious manifestation directly in front of the Warhol and Cavett properties. A giant wave came in but didn't break, staying there in suspense like a ten-foot-high green wall. For the rock star who wanted out of his marriage but feared the consequences, in both publicity and monetary terms, it was a perfect marine metaphor: the wave had to break but, please God, not just yet.

In August, the Stones returned to Britain to headline a pop festival in the rolling grounds of a stately Hertfordshire home, Knebworth House, their first festival since Altamont. The intended lead act was the hottest new glam-rock band, Queen (a name that would have been unthinkable in the sixties, even when Mick was at his queeniest). Queen was quickly dropped, however, when the Stones offered to appear for relatively modest money. Much more important to Mick was proving he was still on top and able to see off any competition.

But Knebworth did not turn out well. For the first time, the fact that the Stones were advancing into their thirties became an issue in the British media, which still regarded the cut-off point for rock musicians as around twenty-five. Much gleeful play was made with the fact that one of their supporting acts, 10cc, had a song called 'Wild Old Men' with lines cruelly apposite to this near-pensioner status: 'Old men of rock 'n' roll come bearing music . . . where are they now? . . . they are over the hill . . . but they're still gonna play on dead strings and old drums . . . wild old men, waiting for miracles.'

The age question received further exposure when Keith gave an interview complaining about Mick's continued flirtation with glam rock. 'Mick's got to stop slapping paint all over his face to that absurd Japanese theatre degree. [He's] getting older and he's got to find a way to mature if he's gonna do what he does. He's got to get in front of that fuckin' mike and SING!' Mick might have retorted that taking so many drugs that you crash your car and your six-year-old son goes supperless did not show great maturity either. But he said nothing, a policy to be wisely maintained throughout every Keith diatribe to come.

Unlike Altamont, the Knebworth festival was primarily a Stones event, with a red stage modelled on Mick's mouth and extended tongue, and *Beggars Banquet*-style jugglers and clowns to entertain the 200,000-strong crowd between sets. But the tongue-shaped apron had the effect of pushing the spectators back even farther than usual, and few wanted to leave their hard-won places on the grass to watch jugglers or clowns. After memorable sets by Todd Rundgren's Utopia and

Lynyrd Skynyrd, there was a four-hour wait as adjustments were made and remade to the Stones' lighting effects. Their eventual performance was described by *The Times* as 'a shambling parody'.

Knebworth marked Les Perrin's final appearance as the Stones' and Mick's PR man. Perrin had contracted hepatitis on the '73 Far East tour, then suffered a stroke from which he'd never fully recovered. The old chain-smoking Fleet Street hand had devoted ten years to his unruly clients, steering them through disasters that could have annihilated them, like the Redlands bust and Brian Jones's death; sharing their notoriety to the extent of suffering police harassment and bugged telephones; talking straight to Mick as no one else but his own father ever dared to; more than once pulling him back from self-harm with a paternal 'Don't be *silly*.' Such was the essential decency of the Stones' organisation that no one liked to fire Les Perrin, even though former music journalist Keith Altham had already been lined up to replace him. On the day of the festival, Mick reversed all usual PR–client protocol by ordering a chauffeur-driven car to bring Perrin and his wife to Knebworth, arranging the best seats in the VIP enclosure and ordering him simply to enjoy the show and not think of doing any work.

One other Knebworth festival vignette is, in its way, just as poignant. A television crew packing up to return to London was amazed to be approached by Bianca Jagger and asked for a lift in their van. On the journey she proved herself utterly unlike the disdainful diva of the fashion prints, friendly and unpretentious as well as touchingly grateful for the ride.

How she came to be left out of Mick's motorcade was never explained. But the fact that his wife had to hitch home, while his PR rode in chauffeured comfort, spoke volumes.

BIANCA, THOUGH, WAS to have a *Star Is Born* moment when she really did outshine Mick. In April 1977, entrepreneurs Steve Rubell and Ian Schrager opened a discotheque for New York's *demi-monde* that they intended to be as exclusive as the city's most historic college alumni club. Their premises being the former CBS TV and radio studios at 254 West Fifty-fourth Street, Rubell and Schrager named the new venture Studio 54.

Steve Rubell, the front man of the duo, personally selected Studio 54's clientele as if holding auditions for a Broadway show. Every night, several hundred exotically dressed people would congregate outside, all striving to persuade Rubell they were beautiful, fashionable or interesting enough to be granted entry. In pursuit of what he called 'the right mix', he would split up married couples, boys and girls on dates, or family members, lifting the red rope barrier for wives, brothers or mothers while their husbands, sisters and daughters remained miserably in outer darkness.

Certain people, of course, were not subjected to this sieving process: the artist Andy Warhol; the screen goddess Elizabeth Taylor; the writers Truman Capote and William S. Burroughs; the actors Jack Nicholson, Elliott Gould, Ryan O'Neal and Helmut Berger; the couturier Halston; the *Cabaret* star Liza Minnelli; the shoe designer Manolo Blahnik; the *Vogue* magazine eminence Diana Vreeland; the record mogul Ahmet Ertegun; the ballet dancer Mikhail Baryshnikov; the recently-turned-solo pop star Michael Jackson; the Hollywood *ingénue* Brooke Shields; the models Verushka and Jerry Hall; and the increasingly free-agent wife of the world's number one rock god, Bianca Jagger.

Bianca, in fact, had first put Studio 54 on the map. For her thirty-second birthday on 2 May her friend Halston persuaded Steve Rubell to open the club on a Monday night, when it was normally closed, so he could throw her a surprise party. During the evening, a white horse paraded around the dance floor led by a man wearing only white gloves. Bianca, in her off-the-shoulder scarlet dress, leaped onto the horse's back for a couple of circuits, led by the naked and notably well-hung groom.

Thereafter, she became known as the Queen Bee of Studio 54. She would be there several nights a week, seeing off all pretenders to the title with her endlessly varied outfits and the way she wore them, holding court on the sofas around the dance floor or in the

VIPs-only basement – a different person in every way from the frost-bound fashion plate who'd spent the past five and a half years in Mick's shadow.

Paradoxically, Studio 54 was more decadent than anything which used to offend her around Mick. The dancers – many naked, or almost so – gyrated to Donna Summer's orgasmic disco anthems beneath a giant effigy of the Man in the Moon being fed cocaine on an animated spoon. The usual cabaret was a drag chorus line, nude but for glittery headdresses and thongs. Drugs of every kind were scored and guzzled more blatantly than the worst scenes in *Cocksucker Blues*. Waiters and busboys wore only tiny shorts and bow ties and many were available for sex with women or men, charging a top rate of $300 for the service known as 'going all around the world'. All this in the city which had once thrown up its hands in horror at the Rolling Stones' long hair.

Most nights, Bianca's escort would be Andy Warhol, whose usual crippling shyness vanished with the realisation that Studio 54 harboured even more human freakery than his own Factory (and also that he could pick up thousands of dollars in portrait commissions during a single evening). Warhol was an ideal date, being sexually unthreatening and happy to endure the longest, latest hours without complaint, though many suspected him of whispering about Mick's infidelities into Bianca's ear. She was seen dancing as no one thought she ever could – sometimes with her legs wrapped round her partner's waist – and on the couches beside the dance floor canoodling variously with Ryan O'Neal, Elliott Gould and Helmut Berger. The gossip columns insinuated that she'd had affairs with all three. Good for her, the public thought, after what she must have had to put up with.

The most bizarre of these supposed liaisons came about through Bianca's involvement with Warhol's *Interview* magazine, which allowed art and show-business celebrities to ramble on about themselves, unedited, for thousands of words at a stretch. One night, ringing the changes at the El Morocco club, she shared a table with the octogenarian Duchess of Windsor (who for some reason believed herself aboard the liner *QE2*) and President Gerald Ford's twenty-five-year-old son, Jack. As a result it was arranged Bianca should interview Ford Jr at the White House, with Warhol along to take photographs. These included a shot of her and the president's son together in Abraham Lincoln's old bedroom, as the papers reported breathlessly, 'with his hands resting on her waist'.

However much Mick might be lionised at Studio 54, it was always Bianca's territory and he just a visitor (once even forced to pay a $6 entrance fee by the genial but implacable door manager, Haoui Montaug). Occasionally the two would be seen there together; at her thirty-second birthday party, for instance, where they sat and held hands. At other times, they arrived separately without greeting or even appearing to notice each other. One night, at a star-studded gala for Elizabeth Taylor, their respective entourages came in through different doors and passed on the dance floor as gloweringly wordless as Sharks and Jets.

London in this same era was gripped by a very different kind of music from silkily orchestrated disco, a look very different from Studio 54's naked carnival. The sunshiny optimism it had enshrined in the 1960s was now but an unreal memory. Whereas British youth back then had been a privileged, cosseted elite, their 1977 counterparts could look forward only to unemployment, urban decay and hyperinflation, which successive Labour governments seemed powerless to check. Whereas pop acts then had been groundbreaking rebels, most nowadays produced either long, pretentious quasi-classical symphonies (Yes; Rick Wakeman; Emerson, Lake & Palmer) or facetious sub-vaudeville (Showaddywaddy, the Brotherhood of Man, the Wurzels). And punk, the music and the fashion, was the result.

Though New York had inspired something called punk rock early in the seventies, this was a very British version in its anger and nihilism as well as its strong satiric streak. UK punk was rebellion in the form of self-torture, its uniform the kind of bondage garments previously worn only in private by sadomasochistic fetishists, its jewellery chains, rings, metal studs and outsize safety pins piercing the tenderest parts of the body and face. Punk was in fact the same blast of energy through a somnolent youth culture and pop scene that the Rolling Stones had been a decade and a half earlier. Its defining band, the Sex Pistols, exactly followed the Stones' footsteps to becoming a national scandal. Their manager, Malcolm McLaren, a worthy heir to Andrew Oldham, took a comprehensively untalented boy named John Lydon, gave him spiky hair and a torn T-shirt, renamed him Johnny Rotten after his decaying teeth, and turned him into a modern Mick Jagger, with an equally talentless boy dubbed Sid Vicious counterpointing him as a contemporary Keith. The Sex Pistols behaved as the 'wicked' Stones of yore could never have done, spitting at their audiences, insulting the Queen and using four-letter words on teatime television. Whereas parents had once considered Mick the Antichrist, Johnny Rotten's best-known song announced he actually was (a notion every bit as absurd).

With the coming of the Sex Pistols, the Stones found themselves regarded even more as irrelevant old buffers. Johnny Rotten called them 'dinosaurs' and opined that Mick 'should have retired in 1965'. Mick affected elder-statesmanly amusement, aligning himself with the Pistols' main target: 'I'm along with the Queen, you know, one of the best thing's England's got . . .' He accused the Pistols of selling out their fuck-'em-all principles by appearing on BBC TV's *Top of the Pops* and the cover of *Rolling Stone* (just as the Stones had before them, amid the same accusations of selling out). He said he liked the punks' energy, but not their attitude and certainly not their clothes. Whatever the new street fashion, he vowed that no one would ever catch him in a torn T-shirt.

Despite the punk uprising, the Stones' fan base seemed to be holding as steady in Britain as in America. *Black and Blue* and 'Fool to Cry' had reached No. 1 and No. 6 respectively, and their forthcoming double live album, *Love You Live*, was expected to sell two million, well up there with the current adult-oriented rock giants, Fleetwood Mac. In February they signed a four-album contract with WEA in America and EMI in the rest of the world. Mick was quick to dampen speculation that the deal was worth $14 million. 'None of us is really concerned with making money . . . I just try to make the best music I can.' Try as they might, no one could see his nose increasing in length.

And rock's dinosaurs could still show punk's squeaking pterodactyl chicks a thing or two. That same month, the Stones convened in Toronto to record further tracks for *Love You Live* incognito at a small club named the El Mocambo. They lacked only Keith, whom British magistrates had recently fined for possessing cocaine in a crashed car on the M1. Belatedly flying out with Anita and Marlon, he took a heavy-duty dose of smack on the aircraft as a means of keeping going after five days without sleep. At the Toronto airport, the spoon he'd used was found on Anita, who was promptly arrested and taken into custody.

Unknown to Keith, a package of 'stuff' he'd sent ahead had been intercepted by Canada's Royal Northwest Mounted Police. Later that day, a squad of Mounties disguised as room-service waiters raided his suite at the Harbour Castle hotel. As an economy measure, there were no bodyguards outside the door, and he himself had gone off into another of his profound sleeps, so it was left to little Marlon to deal with the raiders. An ounce of heroin was found in the suite, enough to warrant a charge of trafficking. By law, Keith had to be awake to be charged. It took the Mounties forty-five minutes to rouse him.

Although Keith clearly had no intention of trafficking heroin to anyone but himself, the police would not reduce the charge, which carried a penalty of up to seven years' imprisonment. Suddenly, a low-key private jaunt had turned into the Stones' worst public catastrophe since the Redlands bust. All Mick's years of careful nurturing and planning were thrown into jeopardy because his Glimmer Twin did not possess a glimmering of common sense.

He might have been expected to react with cold fury as well as distancing himself from the trouble scene as rapidly as possibly. Not so, according to Keith's memoirs: 'Mick looked after me with great sweetness, never complaining. He ran things, he did the work and marshalled the forces that saved me. Mick looked after me like a brother.' And not only Mick: the immediate, urgent problem was Keith's need of another fix with no stash left. It was Bill Wyman, that least-regarded but most kind-hearted Stone, who, at great personal risk, went out and scored for him.

Marooned in the Harbour Castle hotel, awaiting legal developments, the band hardly had need of further lurid publicity. It arrived nonetheless in the shape of Margaret Trudeau, twenty-eight-year-old wife of Canada's fifty-seven-year-old prime minister, Pierre Trudeau. Notoriously fun loving and indiscreet, Madam Trudeau had hotfooted it to the Harbour Castle when the Stones checked in, and was subsequently sighted in their bedroom corridor clad in a bathrobe. Inevitably, her name was linked to Mick's (a turnaround, indeed, from seven years earlier when John Lennon had met her husband to discuss world peace), though it was actually Ronnie Wood, according to his 2007 memoir, *Ronnie*, who enjoyed a brief dalliance with her.

Mid-way through the Keith emergency, Mick had to fly down to New York to see Jade, who was there with her mother and had fallen ill. Margaret Trudeau was reported to have followed him and – to her prime-minister husband's further embarrassment – was sighted among the near-naked throng at Studio 54.

Pending Keith's trial in Canada, his lawyer managed to get him a visa to enter America with Anita for treatment of their heroin addiction. He underwent the treatment in New Jersey and also carried on his smack habit, buying children's doctor-and-nurse outfits from FAO Schwarz's toy shop in New York and using the plastic toy syringes. There seemed little hope of avoiding a hefty prison sentence for trafficking, maybe as much as five years, and even Mick seemed to acknowledge the Stones might soon need a new rhythm guitarist if they didn't fall apart completely: 'We can't wait five years,' he said. 'Five years from now we won't be touring at all, just a few lounges.'

IN MAY 1977 Bryan Ferry began a world tour with Roxy Music. Disinclined to stay in purdah at Ferry's London house, Jerry Hall flew to New York and, a few evenings later, found herself at a dinner party seated between Warren Beatty and Mick, whom she hadn't seen since his tea-making performance a year earlier. Since then, his name had been linked with the singer Linda Ronstadt and the brewing heiress Sabrina Guinness, and he'd been carrying on a secret affair in California with a twenty-five-year-old British model-turned-photographer named Carinthia West.

The dinner party turned into an unashamed contest between Mick and Warren Beatty as to who could get off with Jerry. But for her, despite Beatty's legendary power as a seducer, there could be only one outcome. She left with Mick to go to Studio 54, where Bianca happened not to be holding court that night, then accompanied him back to his house on West Eighty-sixth Street, where the coast was also conveniently clear, to share another cup of tea.

Afterwards, in Jerry's words, Mick 'laid siege' to her, bombarding her with flowers and arranging to be seated next to her at other dinner parties. When she objected that he was married, he said he hadn't lived with Bianca for a year. Jerry agreed to an affair but imposed a strict time limit, saying she must go back to Bryan Ferry when he returned from his tour at the end of the summer. Knowing the Stones' reputation, she also refused to date anyone who used drugs. Mick admitted that in the sixties he'd taken LSD 'every day for a year' and that, while nowhere near Keith's level, he did occasionally smoke heroin. 'Go away,' Jerry told him, 'and don't come back until you're straight.' He obeyed.

They saw each other regularly in New York over the next four months, taking care to go nowhere they might be spotted by the paparazzi. After her prim, introverted fiancé, Jerry found Mick a refreshing change; unlike Ferry, he made no attempt to curb her yee-haw high spirits and thought her prowess at leg wrestling hilarious. They had not been dating long when Jerry's truck-driver father, John, died suddenly. Mick, she would recall, was 'kind and supportive' as she tried to comfort her mother and four sisters. He also showed his usual generosity in the first flush of romance, giving her a pair of antique diamond hoop earrings for her twenty-first birthday in July.

At the summer's end, they said good-bye, as per arrangement, and the next day Jerry rejoined Bryan Ferry, who still knew nothing of what had gone on while he was away. He seemed overjoyed to see her, giving her an emerald bracelet for the twenty-first birthday he'd missed, so Jerry decided to try to forget Mick and make a fresh start with him. In pursuit of this, she and Ferry moved to Los Angeles, where, a few weeks later, they happened to have dinner with the Stones' business adviser,

Prince Rupert Loewenstein. While Ferry was out of the room, Prince Rupert slipped her Mick's telephone number. She rang Mick the next day, and he told her he missed her and begged to see her again. They arranged to meet in Paris, where Jerry was appearing in some fashion shows. After the shows, they decided to go to Morocco, that old Rolling Stones bolt-hole. Jerry called Ferry and told him she had further modelling work there.

When they arrived, the airline had lost their baggage, so they had to buy Moroccan djellabas, voluminous gowns with hoods that provided a perfect disguise. They hired a car and spent several days just driving around in their obscuring monkish robes and matching kohl eyeliner, with the radio on full blast. At night they stayed in small hotels where the rooms were lit only by candles and perfumed by bowls of roses. Sometimes there was an open fire and Mick would sit beside it, singing and playing guitar.

At a restaurant in Agadir, Jerry ran into a fashion-editor friend who was on a shoot with a team of models and lent her and Mick some clothes to replace those lost by the airline. When she next telephoned Ferry, he accused her of lying, saying he'd read about Mick and her in the papers. The fashion team must have talked. Ferry offered to take her back, but she knew he 'wasn't the forgiving type' – and, anyway, she believed, he had been having an affair of his own on tour in Japan. In fact, he was furious at having been treated like such a fool and even talked about beating Mick up until friends pointed out Mick's considerably higher level of physical fitness. He contented himself with not letting Jerry have the clothes and possessions she kept at his house, including a book called *The Mists of Avalon* she'd left on the bedside table. He was later to make an album called *Avalon*, but didn't speak to her again for years.

Mick rented an apartment in Paris beside Notre Dame Cathedral and moved in there with Jerry. 'We made love four times a day, ripping each other's clothes off [and] never got bored or disagreed,' she would recall. Yet as late as September 1977 he was still firmly denying his marriage to Bianca was all over now. 'We are still living together and in love with each other. I haven't got the seven-year itch. In fact I didn't know we'd been married for seven years [actually six and a half] until I read it in the newspapers . . . We spend six months of the year together. We take it just as it comes.'

In May 1978, when they'd been married seven years to the month, Bianca filed for divorce on the grounds of irreconcilable differences, subsequently amended to adultery. Though Mick had hardly wanted the marriage to continue, he hated being thus pre-empted and took instant retaliatory measures, shutting down her charge accounts with couturiers, hairdressers and department stores. He also made 48 Cheyne Walk uninhabitable for her by having all the furniture removed, telling Jade it had gone away to be repaired. All the clothes from the closets were packed into wardrobe-size cardboard cartons – Bianca's Ossie Clark and Halston dresses and Jade's little velvet-collared coats jumbled up with Mick's old satin shirts and buckskin jackets – and stored in a south London warehouse where they would still be mouldering together a decade later.

THE STONES' 1978 album, *Some Girls*, could hardly have been better named considering the girls of different generations who were currently complicating Mick's life. And try as he always did to keep his songs autobiography-free, the odd bit of relevance would keep creeping in. The disco-influenced 'Miss You' was plainly inspired by the recent Jerry situation, even if his falsetto vocal sounded closer than ever to Mammy in *Gone With the Wind* ('Dying to meet you', for instance, became 'Da-a-A-A'n-a-*meechu!*') and the protestation 'Ah've bin sleepin' awl alone' rang as true as a rubber spittoon. 'Beast of Burden', with its rhetorical 'Am I rich enough?', seemed to look forward gloomily to paying alimony to Bianca. Most topically, the title track might have been his belated answer to a five-year-old paternity allegation: 'Some girls give me cheeldrun . . . Ah never asked them faw.' For the Marsha Hunt problem had resurfaced again.

Not that Marsha was any more covetous of Mick's fortune or anxious to portray herself as a victim now than in 1973, when she'd launched paternity proceedings against him in London. After drawn-out delaying tactics by his lawyers, she had accepted the extremely modest out-of-court settlement of £41.67 per month to support their daughter, Karis. By her account, she then had to wait until January 1975 for the first payment. To supplement it she had had to work literally around the clock, presenting programmes on London's Capital Radio, doing cabaret gigs and making an album for a German record company at Munich's Musicland Studios – where she might easily have bumped into Mick but, luckily for him, never did.

In 1977, she moved from London to Los Angeles with Karis, now aged seven, in hopes of promoting her album. It happened that during her brief screen-acting career in Britain she'd become friendly with Mick's film agent, Maggie Abbott. As well as trying to shoehorn him into movies and discovering who had betrayed him in the Redlands bust, Abbott now became a bridge between him and his unacknowledged first-born.

Karis had grown into a sparklingly intelligent as well as beautiful child and had been recommended to a special school in LA by the Gifted Children's Association, where she was receiving adulatory reports from all her teachers. Maggie Abbott felt certain she would captivate Mick – all the more so now that Bianca was no longer around – and resolved to arrange a meeting between them. When he next passed through LA, this time accompanied by Jerry, Abbott sent him photographs of Karis and a full account of her progress at school, adding, 'If she's not your daughter, I'm the Queen of Sheba.'

Mick suggested that Karis should spend an afternoon with him at his hotel, L'Ermitage, in Beverly Hills. The meeting was a great success, in no small measure thanks to Jerry, who showed no insecurity at meeting a love child from his past but was 'sweetness itself', according to Maggie Abbott. Marsha spoke to Mick afterwards and mentioned how keeping Karis at the gifted children's school was taking almost everything she earned. He gave her the telephone number and false name he was currently using but, as she would recall, 'It was back to the old routine, spending money I didn't have trying to contact him.'

Marsha's efforts to make a career in LA were not successful, and in a few months she was reduced to applying for welfare as a single mother unsupported by her child's father. However, the application form required her to give the name of the absent father, who then in theory would be pursued for maintenance by the government. Writing 'Mick Jagger' in the space provided was clearly unfeasible, so Marsha decided her only option was to turn to lawyers again. She agonised about putting Karis through such an ordeal, and did so only after explaining the situation to the wise little seven-year-old and receiving her blessing. How quickly these rock 'n' roll children had to grow up.

To represent her, Marsha chose a flamboyant LA lawyer named Marvin Mitchelson, who specialised in winning substantial 'palimony' settlements for the discarded long-term girlfriends of American showbiz stars. Mitchelson's first act was to fly to London to examine – and dismiss as irrelevant – the paper she had signed three years earlier, absolving Mick of being Karis's father in return for that modest out-of-court settlement. Within a few days, Mitchelson had served Mick with legal papers and was in a California court, successfully applying for Mick's share of the box office from two recent Rolling Stones concerts in Anaheim to be frozen pending a final judgement.

Coincidentally, at this same time Mitchelson acquired a second client who'd borne Mick a daughter. Bianca had initiated her divorce action in London but then realised that if it were held in California the state's community-property law would give her a right to half of everything Mick owned. She, too, therefore consulted Mitchelson, showing him the French pre-nuptial agreement which she'd reluctantly signed on her wedding morning in Saint-Tropez. Mitchelson had no doubt it could be overturned, and opined that Mick's presence in LA was frequent enough for him to be legitimately sued for divorce there.

For Marsha, Mitchelson and the California courts between them finally obtained a measure of satisfaction. After her previous experience, she wanted no further truck with out-of-court settlements, and the case was heard in January 1979. Mick's paternity of Karis was confirmed and he was ordered to pay $1,500 per month in maintenance. According to

Marsha, no lump sum was involved, nor were the payments made ret-roactive.

But for Bianca there was to be no California Gold Rush. She had, rather naïvely, expected that if her divorce action moved to LA, it would be handled in the same low-key manner it had been in London. How-ever, Mitchelson lost no time in announcing that she was seeking $12.5 million, or half Mick's estimated earnings during their marriage. As an interim measure, she wanted $13,400 per month in living expenses, which broke down as $4,000 for rent, $2,000 for clothes, $2,000 for transport, $1,500 for chauffeur, nanny, and live-in maid, $1,500 for food, $1,000 for entertainment, $500 for travel, $500 for incidentals, $300 for telephone, $200 for laundry and cleaning and $200 for utilities.

Early in February, Mitchelson went before the California Supe-rior Court to make the case that Mick was so often in Los Angeles he should be considered a *de facto* resident. A written deposition by Bianca – with potential to cause him problems beyond the court – said that during their entire married life 'he and I literally lived out of suitcases in a nomadic journey from one place to another in his quest to avoid income tax'. She alleged that on some visits to his London house they had crawled around on their hands and knees to avoid anyone seeing that they were back in Britain. Likewise 'on numerous occasions [Mick] told me he had to keep secret the fact that he was making recordings in Los Angeles so as not to be forced to pay United States income tax'.

Mitchelson instanced a particular two-week visit Mick had paid to California with Jerry as one such illicit working trip. In fact, as his film agent Maggie Abbott could confirm, it had simply been to discuss yet another movie he never made, *The Moderns*. Nonetheless, Judge Harry Shafer ruled California had jurisdiction to hear the divorce and ordered Mick to pay Bianca $12,000 in temporary support, $2,500 for medi-cal treatment (she had injured her knee in a roller-skating accident) and $35,000 against her legal expenses.

Mick's response was to launch a cross-petition in London, complain-ing of Bianca's 'unreasonable conduct', which turned into a tug-of-war beween the British and American legal systems as to where the divorce proceedings should take place, or rather, continue. When the hearing opened in July, Marvin Mitchelson flew over to present his arguments on behalf of California with customary force and flamboyance. But he proved no match for Mick, who put on a virtuoso performance before the judge, Sir Michael Eastham. 'He charmed the pants off the judge,' recalls one of the lawyers present. 'And when he spoke, he put himself into the legal world as if he'd spent his whole life in it.'

Sir Michael having found against Bianca, she took the case to the court of appeal, where it was heard on 17 October. Wearing a black trouser suit and a red polo-neck sweater, she sat taking notes as her counsel, Robert Johnson (not the legendary blues singer), pleaded that the highest settlement she could expect in Britain would be $1 million, a grossly inequitable share of Mick's estimated $21.5 million net worth. But the three appeal judges ruled that her claims for a California divorce 'could not be weaker' and the action must continue in London. Afterwards Bianca once again proved herself rather different from the usual frowning Sphinx by asking reporters outside the court if anyone had a cigarette.

The precise amount of her settlement was not fixed until November 1980 and was never made public, though her counsel's estimated figure of $1 million apparently erred on the side of pessimism; Jerry would later say it took 'most of what [Mick] had' at that point. Even so, compared with pay-outs in future superstar divorces, and the amounts he was destined to earn, it would soon seem like small change.

Nor was that the only way in which he got off lightly. A rock star's ex-wife in Bianca's situation might have been expected to remedy the alimony shortfall by signing a lucrative contract to write a tell-all autobiography, then to make a round of chat-show appearances whose damage to her former spouse would more than counterbalance the money he'd saved. But Bianca wrote no book and spilled no beans – then or ever. And, bitter though she felt about the divorce, its final residue was sadness, for she'd genuinely cared for Mick and believed he had for her. A few years later, she would reflect they had never really stood a chance from the moment he decided to get married in Saint-Tropez in the presence of half the world's media. Or, as Bianca expressed it, 'My marriage ended on my wedding day.'

Mick, for his part, expressed neither regret nor remorse, only the Tyranny of Cool rampant: 'I only did it [got married] for something to do . . . I've never been madly, deeply in love with anyone. I'm not an emotional person.'

That came as a surprise to many people, not least his former fiancée, Chrissie Shrimpton. From their years together in the mid-sixties, Chrissie knew how very emotional he could often be, and possessed a thick bundle of love letters from him to prove it. Now married, with two small children, she no longer had any connection with the pop or fashion world, but lived quietly in south London and was studying for a sociology degree. By so doing, she hoped to rationalise that unreal era when not only her boyfriend, her elder sister Jean, and Jean's boyfriend, David Bailey, but almost everyone else she knew had suddenly become world famous.

Since being dumped so ruthlessly by Mick in 1966, Chrissie had barely looked at his old love letters. But when his divorce – and declaration that he'd 'never been madly, deeply in love' – hit the headlines, she mentioned the cache to a female journalist she happened to meet in a restaurant. The journalist urged her to sell it to a Sunday newspaper without delay, but Chrissie, as she recalls, was 'far too proud' to let thousands of strangers pore over her love life. The cat was now out of the lavender bag, however, and soon afterwards, while driving to her sociology class, she heard on the radio that Mick intended to start legal action against her. The material in a letter, even a love letter, belongs to the sender not the recipient, and to publish them without the writer's permission is breach of copyright.

Chrissie was panic-stricken, but had no way of contacting Mick to ask him to call off his lawyers. All she could do was talk to David Bailey, the one member of that old Swinging London elite who remained close to him. Bailey warned that things were about to get 'very nasty' and advised that the only way of placating Mick was to send him back all the letters. She did so, not realising that although he might own their content, the paper and envelopes were her property.

IN OCTOBER 1978 Keith Richard finally went on trial in Toronto for trafficking heroin into Canada. He'd spent much of the previous summer sharing a house in Woodstock, New York, with Mick and Jerry, and undergoing another bout of black box electric treatment for his addiction before reappearing in court. Helped by Jerry, Mick looked after the couch-bound, sweating, hallucinating sufferer, bringing him meals, reattaching the electrodes when they fell off his head, celebrating his every small step back to sensibility and self-respect like shaving or taking a bath. Jerry realised he was on the road to recovery when he went outside and started throwing knives at trees.

The draconian punishment which had hung over Keith for eighteen months did not materialise after all. The court was swayed to mercy by his apparently conscientious efforts to kick his habit (luckily, no one had found out about the bulk purchase of toy syringes from FAO Schwarz). And for once the Stones' aura of depravity worked to his advantage. The Canadian government was anxious to play down the embarrassing aftermath to the Harbour Castle hotel bust, when Prime Minister Pierre Trudeau's wife, Margaret, had been sighted there in a bathrobe for a rumoured assignation with Mick. To spare the PM any further embarrassment, it had been decided to deal with the case as quickly and quietly as possible.

Keith was found guilty on the trafficking charge, but sentenced only to probation. There was an additional penalty for the Stones as a whole, innocent NCOs as much as officers. As part of his defence, the judge had heard the touching story of a blind Canadian girl who would turn up unescorted at Stones gigs all over North America, and to whom the wicked smackhead had often been kind. In a final expiation of his offence, the band was ordered to give two concerts from which all receipts would go to the Canadian National Institute for the Blind.

These duly took place at the Oshawa Civic Auditorium, Ontario, on 22 April 1979, emceed by John Belushi. The opening set featured Keith in an *ad hoc* band called the New Barbarians, put together by Ronnie Wood and featuring another penitent hell-raiser, Bobby Keys, on tenor sax. Then the original barbarian came prancing out to join them, looking more the part than ever.

So much for that elder-statesman-like vow never to join the punk rockers. Mick was wearing a torn T-shirt, loosely held together with duct tape.

CHAPTER EIGHTEEN

Sweet Smell of Success

The Rolling Stones' 1981–2 world tour marked their twentieth anniversary as a band. Mick would still be singing 'Satisfaction' at pushing forty – although using that phrase to him risked awakening the pedant who always lurked inside the rock god. 'I'm not "pushing forty",' he corrected one BBC interviewer stiffly. 'I was only thirty-eight a few months ago.'

The turn of the decade had already brought what would be his last serious shot at the movies, in Werner Herzog's *Fitzcarraldo*. The eminent German director had first met him years before through Anita Pallenberg and considered him 'a great actor . . . something I feel the world has not yet seen'. In 1980, Herzog began production of a screen epic based on the nineteenth-century Peruvian rubber tycoon Carlos Fitzcarrald, whose exploits included building a La Scala-scale opera house in the remote mountain city of Iquitos. The American actor Jason Robards was cast in the name role with Mick as his simpleton sidekick, Wilbur. And this time, despite ample excuse, there was no eleventh-hour case of Jagger cold feet.

The film reconstructed Fitzcarraldo's battle with the Peruvian wild, culminating in the haulage of a full-size ocean-going ship through the rainforests by manpower alone. Since Herzog disdained the use of special effects or models, this meant months away on location in and around Iquitos. Conditions were harsh, with only the most basic accommodations and sanitation and unreliable telephone links with the outside world. There was unremitting sticky heat and the threat of wild animals and poisonous insects; if all that wasn't enough, a local nomadic tribe declared war on the unit, killing one of its Peruvian employees with bows and arrows and wounding several others.

As both times previously when he'd committed to a film, Mick turned without a beat from rock god to team player, getting on well with everyone from co-stars to clapper boys, never complaining of the hardships. A car had been provided for him, but, as Herzog would recall, he used it mostly to chauffeur other unit members around. He stuck it out for months, getting away only for occasional weekends with Jerry back in New York. Then, with 40 per cent of the picture shot, Jason Robards fell ill with dysentery, returned to America for treatment, and was ordered not to continue filming by his doctors. As Herzog pondered how to overcome this catastrophe, Mick also had to leave to begin rehearsing for the Stones' tour. Rather than replace him, the director dropped his Wilbur character and reshot the entire film from the beginning with Klaus Kinski in the title role. 'Losing Mick,' Herzog later recalled, 'was the biggest loss I have ever experienced as a film director.'

Ahead of the tour came a new album punkishly entitled *Tattoo You,* its cover a shot of Mick's face embroidered like Queequeg the cannibal harpooneer in *Moby-Dick.* His year-long involvement with *Fitzcarraldo* having left no time for songwriting: *Tattoo You* was just a set of outtakes, some recorded as long ago as 1972, spruced up with new vocals and overdubs. It spent nine weeks at No. 1 on the American charts, reached No. 2 in Britain, and ultimately achieved enough worldwide sales to go platinum three times over. Its lead single, 'Start Me Up' (dating from 1977) turned into the Stones' biggest since 'Tumbling Dice'. After the disco flourishes and introspective, even melancholy note of their late-seventies output ('Miss You', 'Emotional Rescue', 'Waiting on a Friend'), this went right back to basics with a growly guitar riff and unregenerate three-chord beat. Despite pushing forty, Mick could still sing like an adolescent with only one thing on his mind.

Earlier in 1981, the American journalist Landon Y. Jones had identified a new demographic, the baby boomers, destined to wield even more economic power in the eighties, and beyond, than teenagers in the sixties. Baby boomers were those same teenagers, the fruit of the post-war copulation surge, now grown to maturity, affluence, even authority, but still unwilling to relinquish the youth had that been so golden and the music that had largely made it so. A Rolling Stones single admitting a need for jump leads ('Start me up . . . I'll never stop . . .') and a tour admitting to a twentieth anniversary saw the baby boomers first come into their own.

When tickets went on sale for the tour's opening American leg, the lines that instantly formed included professional men and women in their mid-thirties, wearing the preppy business clothes that had replaced caftans and headbands. In the New York area, there were 3.5 million applications for 100,000 seats. A powerful indicator of the new market was the introduction of commercial sponsorship, hugely multiplying the traditional ancillary income from 'Lapping Tongue' posters and T-shirts. A bidding war among half a dozen brands identified with this or that aspect of baby-boomer lifestyle had been won by the Jôvan perfumery corporation, which as a result would have its name on the face of every ticket sold. In all, the tour was said to be worth an unprecedented $40 million.

The band reconvened to rehearse at a recording-studio-cum-farm in rural Massachusetts, at that time vivid with the glories of a New England autumn. Despite his recent strenuous months in Peru, Mick considered himself hopelessly out of condition and began an intensive programme of weight training, karate, squash and daily seven-mile runs, in addition to overseeing the tour's security arrangements and Kabuki-esque stage design, and conferring with Prince Rupert Loewenstein. After a couple of weeks, he was down to just nine stone and a waist measurement of twenty-seven inches.

As an extra warm-up, the band gave a surprise performance at a small club called Sir Morgan's Cave in the neighbouring town of Worcester. Three hundred tickets for a one-night-only appearance by 'Blue Sunday and the Cockroaches' had been issued to listeners of a local radio station in strict secrecy, but a rival station got wind of the plot and leaked that the Stones were coming. On the night, 4,000 people besieged Sir Morgan's Cave, which averted a riot only by throwing open all its doors. Next day, a string of other Massachusetts towns issued hasty ordinances to prevent any similar surprises being visited on them. The tour could thus begin with headlines juxtaposing 'STONES', as so many times before, with 'RIOT' and 'BAN': not the fragrance of Jôvan perfume but a White Lightning reek of their old danger and lawlessness.

The first show was on 25 September, at Philadephia's 100,000-capacity John F. Kennedy Stadium. Clouds of party balloons nodding above the stage could not disguise the tension in the humid, hot-doggy air. It was only nine months since John Lennon had been gunned down by Mark David Chapman outside the Dakota building, virtually next door to Mick's present New York address, 123 Central Park West. There was palpable, and by no means illogical, fear that yet again Jagger might follow in Lennon's footsteps.

The murder had shaken Mick to the core, however hard the Tyranny of Cool might try to conceal it. Lennon had been one of his very few long-term friends and one of the still-fewer professional rivals he unreservedly admired. When Lennon first settled in America, they had often socialised, even made music together on occasion. But with the birth of his son Sean in 1975, Lennon had retreated inside the Dakota, devoting himself to child care, giving over his business affairs to Yoko Ono and severing contact with even his oldest music cronies. Mick, as a result, had found himself in the – for him – highly unusual position of wanting to see someone but having his every friendly overture rebuffed.

From his sitting-room window he could see the Gothic rooftops of Lennon's home, and would sometimes act out the part of a spurned girlfriend: '[John's] right over there. Does he ever call me? Does he ever go out? No. Changes his phone number about every ten minutes. I've given up . . .' But there was no disguising how much this apparent indifference really hurt. Once or twice, he put aside the Tyranny of Cool sufficiently to leave Lennon a note with his own current phone number at the Dakota concierges' desk, but no response ever came. He little suspected that, despite having ostensibly retired from music, Lennon still followed his every move almost as closely as Paul McCartney's, and felt vaguely envious of his partying across town at Studio 54.

Mick's life had been threatened many times over the years, of course, but always by those whom, consciously or unconsciously, he'd goaded to hatred: cuckolded boyfriends, disgruntled promoters, disrespected Hell's Angels. The terrible difference was that Lennon had been murdered by someone professing to love him. Now, as millions across America screamed welcome back to the Stones, any one of them might be a potential assassin.

Consequently, the security – which in the modern world meant *insecurity* – was at a level never known in live rock before. Hundreds of police and Highway Patrol officers guarded the approaches to each venue and fussed to and fro overhead in helicopters. As well as the Stones' regular, populous protection team, a force of local stewards was recruited at each stop, uniformed in yellow T-shirts and stationed along the stage front to glare ferociously at the paying customers and meet any breach of bounds, however accidental or innocent, with mass, unrestrained force.

The most conspicuous of these mercenaries was a genuine giant, seven feet tall at least, clad in jogging clothes and a baseball cap lettered TULSA POLICE, who guarded the VIP enclosure at JFK Stadium with an expression suggesting he would not merely deter unauthorised intruders but pop them into his mouth and crunch them up, chanting 'Fee Fi Fo Fum!' Among Mick's personal Praetorian guard was a squat Chinese gentleman in a baby-blue tracksuit, identified as Dr Daniel Pai, grand master or White Dragon of the Pai-Lun martial-arts order. Dangling from one sleeve the doctor carried a small fan with a sharp metal edge. The implication was that it could simultaneously create a cooling breeze and take someone's head off.

Draconian restrictions were also placed on the press and broadcast media, who for the most part found themselves penned in the bleachers far behind the stage and unable to see the performance at all. Photographers and camera crews were allowed to shoot Mick in action only for a couple of minutes each, all under strict supervision and from the same fixed seventy-degree upward angle. If any attempted to depart from this or loiter when ordered to vacate their position, a man named Jerry Pompili would touch their camera with a long metal instrument like a cattle prod, instantly destroying the film inside.

The tour's second most important figure was the Stones' director of security, Jim Callaghan, a man in every way unlike his British prime-ministerial namesake, from his pugilist's face to his crumpled, pale green, dragon-embroidered caftan. But even Callaghan's power was limited to saying no. In that whole giant, paranoid travelling circus, only one person had absolute power to say yes.

That person was to be seen during the ritual couple of hours' delay before each show jogging up and down the special warm-up area set aside for him backstage, seemingly oblivious to the ebb and flow of VIP guests and Keith and Woody's relentless merrymaking. In his stage wardrobe, butterfly-wing feyness had been replaced by the severely practical and uncompromisingly masculine – American football player's breeches, bulk-purchased on New York's Canal Street at $15 per pair, together with protective knee pads, a low-key coloured T-shirt and shoes suitable for extended roadwork. Limbering and psyching himself up to face yet another eighty or a hundred thousand people did not prevent his being approached by a constant stream of subordinates, from Jim Callaghan downwards, all seeking that unique, definitive 'yes'. Sometimes he would accompany Callaghan on a quick inspection of the stage and the area immediately in front of it, where another Mark David Chapman might conceivably lurk. No one in the expectant multitude even noticed, let alone recognised, the diminutive figure with a camouflage hat pulled down low over its eyes.

On this tour, his stage act was no longer notable for its outrageousness but for its athleticism. For more than two hours he was all over the giant stage, slaloming in and out among his static bandmates, prancing along each of the forty-yard aprons in turn, climbing the scaffolding and hanging off by an arm and leg or skidding onto his padded knees like a football player scoring a touchdown. There were no brief retirements into the wings for a restorative drag of something or other, no quieter interludes seated on a stool that a man pushing forty might be expected to need – no pauses at all except to introduce the other four, toss out a deeper-than-Dixie 'A-a-w-*right*!', or swig from a plastic bottle of Evian water. The one-time epitome of decadence and self-indulgence now looked all about simplicity and clean living.

Starting with 'Under My Thumb', he delivered most of the Stones' golden oldies, a man pushing forty using the same voice, acting out the same charade, he had as an eighteen-year-old. And even on humid, balloon-filled, onion-smelly afternoons in Philadelphia or Orlando, those oldies still stirred up all the wickedness of their innocent hey-day – the 'nana-nana-nana-nana-na' prelude to 'Let's Spend the Night Together', for instance, getting much more reaction than 'Start Me Up's' 'you make a dead man come'. Only towards the end did he look more like the old over-the-top Jagger, using a cherry-picker crane to be swung out above his audience and sing 'Jumpin' Jack Flash' while pelting them with long-stemmed red carnations.

With memories of Altamont never far away, the after-show escape was a military exercise, set in motion while the Stones still had an hour of playing time left. After the final encore, they boarded four identical yellow vans and were removed while any tardy assassin was distracted by a $12,000 fireworks display. Thanks to radio microphones, Mick could continue goading the crowds with cries of 'A-a-aw-*right*!' while already halfway back to his hotel.

At press conferences he was his usual regally bland self, tossing out the occasional well-honed epigram ('Touring's like sex. You may enjoy it but you don't wanna do it all the time.'), studiously avoiding all political controversy, like Britain's war with Argentina in the Falkland Islands ('None of my business'), and, in a literal sound bite, talking about 'the diamond'. This was no thumping rock for Jerry Hall such as Richard

Burton might have given Elizabeth Taylor, but a tiny chip set into his upper right incisor tooth. The story went that he'd first tried a tiny emerald in the tooth, but people had mistaken it for a speck of spinach. Journalist after journalist requested to view the minuscule sparkler up close and were willingly indulged; at last, he'd found a way of opening his mouth and literally not saying anything.

The tour's British leg ended with a giant open-air show at Roundhay Park, Leeds, on 25 July 1982. It seemed the climax to a triumphant comeback, proof that the Stones could go rolling on through the eighties, still as free of moss as Mick's upper incisor was of suspected spinach. In fact, having created this template for a mega-earning future, they were not to tour again until 1989, or record together between 1985 and the decade's end.

At Roundhay Park, the backstage amenities that had to be laid on for them included a Japanese water garden with a stream, a bridge, a waterfall and koi carp. The very sun umbrellas in this inner sanctum had to say 'Welcome the Rolling Stones' in Japanese, even though no one present would be able to translate it. The show was emceed by Andy Kershaw, an outspoken BBC radio deejay who had little time for pointless superstar whims. Kershaw therefore recruited an expert in Japanese calligraphy from Leeds University to inscribe another message around the parasols. 'Fuck the Rolling Stones,' it said.

Which, prophetically enough, their singer was almost to do with his long-delayed attempt to go solo.

JERRY DID NOT bring a breath of fresh air into Mick's life so much as a gale. Visitors to his hotel room on the morning after a show usually found a twilit mess of rumpled sheets, strewn papers and books, and dirty breakfast dishes. These days, Jerry was often to be found there, exquisitely dressed, Dairy Queen-fresh, and, as like as not, chortling with laughter. One journalist arriving for an interview was surprised when she thrust a small whirring object into his hand: Mick's electric shaver. 'Neither of us can get it to switch off,' she explained. 'Would you have a try?' What price now the Tyranny of Cool?

Jerry dealt with the Machiavellian politics around Mick by simply disregarding them. Texan down-home charm is always hard to resist, but especially so when accompanied by spectacular blonde beauty, six feet high. One of her earliest triumphs was winning over Prince Rupert Loewenstein, whose view of Mick's paramours tended to be governed by their potential impact on his finances. Jerry nicknamed the assiduous Loewenstein 'Rupie the Groupie' and soon had him eating out of her hand.

Her exuberance and easygoingness, after Bianca's reserve and super-touchiness, were only part of the tonic for Mick. There was also the fact – especially relevant in the aftermath of divorcing Bianca – that her supermodel career had made her independently wealthy; she couldn't possibly just be after his money. Indeed, when he told her how he dreaded the effort of getting back into shape for the '81 tour, she said he needn't if he didn't want to: she was rich enough to support them both.

He did want to, of course – couldn't live without it – so Jerry uncomplainingly became part of a rock 'n' roll lifestyle that made Bryan Ferry's look pale indeed. Since the Toronto bust, every customs authority in the world had the Stones logged on computer, and the sight of any one of them automatically triggered maximum alert. One Christmas Eve, Mick and Jerry landed in Hong Kong for what was supposed to be a romantic break together in a luxury hotel. The immigration official took one look at their passports, pressed a button, and they were instantly surrounded by armed police with obviously itchy trigger fingers. Drug-free as Jerry had always been, she found herself receiving the same sort of treatment when travelling alone on her modelling assignments; for the computer, her affiliation with the Rolling Stones was enough.

The press had always liked her, and as Mick's 'lady,' it liked her even more – something that, one day, would stand her in good stead. She unfailingly provided wonderful copy with that extravagant yet entirely natural Southern accent (so unlike the one Mick used) and her willingness to discuss their sex life, apparently without any repercussions from him. 'Ah do all that stuff to liven up the bedroom,' she confided to one British magazine, making it sound like bucking broncos and lariats. 'You know ... suspenders and all that.'

Fortunately, the member of the Stones' inner circle who might have dimmed even Jerry's sunny smile was no longer a force to be reckoned with. Keith had finally split from Anita, realising he had no hope of staying off heroin while she was around, and that her urge to self-destruct was beyond his power to check. The final breaking point came at a house they were renting in Salem, Massachusetts, when a seventeen-year-old gardener named Scott Cantrell, rumoured to be Anita's lover, shot himself dead on her bed with one of Keith's guns, apparently as a result of playing Russian roulette. Adding to an already unsurpassed store of rock-kid experiences, little Marlon Richards was in the house when it happened. Salem's connection with a notorious seventeenth-century witch-hunt reawakened the old rumours about Anita being a witch and prompted tabloid stories that she and her hapless toy-boy had been involved in a local coven. For Keith, the once-bewitching, brainy blonde had become 'like Hitler ... trying to take everything down with her'.

In 1979, after one or two inconclusive affairs (the baddest Stone being not that highly sexed as well as essentially monogamous), he had met a twenty-three-year-old American fashion model named Patti Hansen, recently the face of Calvin Klein on giant billboards in New York's Times Square. He had pursued her with all the ardour of his romantic nature, bombarding her with love letters, some written in his own blood. Patti, surprisingly, had not turned tail and bolted, and the two were now permanently together. With upbeat natures as well as *Vogue* covers in common, Patti and Jerry became friends and allies – closer, in fact, than their respective Glimmer Twins would soon be.

Despite having come out so much on top in his divorce, Mick still seemed to harbour great resentment towards Bianca, describing her as difficult and 'devious', and rejecting any idea that they might ever become friends. It particularly irked him that she intended to continue using his surname, even though claiming it had brought her nothing but unhappiness. He had no doubt she intended to exploit it to the full to make up the shortfall in her alimony.

Still, a veneer of civility had to be maintained for the sake of their daughter. Mick received regular access to Jade – an area in which Bianca could *really* have been difficult or devious if she'd chosen – and remained as loving and attentive a father as ever. Jade joined him for some of the '81 American tour, watching from the wings with the restive air of any ten-year-old visiting Dad at work.

Jerry handled her unofficial stepmother's role with the same aplomb as she did everything else. During the stop in Orlando, to play the Tangerine Bowl, she left off her makeup, scraped her hair into a ponytail and took Jade and a group of other tour children off to spend the day at Disney World. Mick admitted that he'd have liked to go with them, but couldn't face the kerfuffle that would result. 'I *do* enjoy a good Big Dipper,' he added almost wistfully as he jogged up and down in his football player's breeches, preparatory to facing the next 80,000.

As things turned out, the uses to which Bianca put the Jagger name were not to distress Mick by earning her piles of money, or encroach on his territory in any way. For a time, she pursued her screen-acting career, appearing in one or two minor roles but scarcely justifying Andy Warhol's view of her as a modern Greta Garbo. Then, in 1979, she returned to her native Nicaragua as part of a Red Cross delegation looking at the country's reconstruction since the 1972 earthquake. Despite the aid that had been poured into it – not least via Mick and the Stones – it remained one of Latin America's worst poverty black spots, and the grip of the corrupt Somoza family as secure as ever.

From that moment Bianca's life – hitherto about little but clothes and finding wealthy men to protect her – changed completely. Studio 54 lost its queen and the people of her own and neighbouring countries, similarly oppressed by poverty and vicious despots, found a passionate, selfless advocate.

In 1981, while Mick was gearing up for his American comeback, Bianca went to Honduras with a party of US congressional delegates to observe the plight of refugees streaming over the border from civil-war-torn El Salvador. As they watched, a Salvadoran death squad armed with M16 rifles rounded up a group of forty refugees and marched them away. Bianca and the other delegates followed the squad and shouted that only killing them, too, would stop them telling what they'd seen. As a result, the captives were released.

Her international profile was raised still further when Nicaragua's Somoza clan was finally overthrown by the revolutionary FSLN Party, or Sandinistas, and the US government – fearing the spread of communism in Latin America – began lending covert support to a right-wing counter-revolutionary alliance known as the Contras. Bianca took part in lobbying against this policy and was a leading voice in the subsequent furore, when the Reagan administration was discovered to have secretly sold arms to Iran, its supposed arch-enemy, to fund the Contras. So the world finally did see a Jagger getting involved in politics and speaking out fearlessly.

JOHN LENNON'S ASSASSINATION did not sour New York for Mick and certainly did not make the city feel too dangerous for him to continue to have a home there. But getting together with Jerry awakened the first serious interest he'd ever shown in accumulating property. By the early eighties he was spending equal amounts of time in two different overseas locales, each in its own way satisfying his insatiable thirst for social status.

The first was France's Loire Valley, a region famous for its wines and the historic châteaux that give their names to the most exclusive vineyards. In the tiny village of Pocé-sur-Cisse, near Amboise, he bought a château named La Fourchette (the Fork) dating from 1710 – the same year as his old house in Chelsea – and once owned by the Duc de Choiseul, finance minister to King Louis XVI. Quite small, as châteaux went, La Fourchette was surrounded by fruit trees somewhat reminiscent of Mick's native Kent. History buff that he was, he discovered that, unlike

many smaller Loire châteaux, it had not been built for a rich nobleman's mistress; interestingly, too, it lacked a back staircase, suggesting
its eighteenth-century occupants had kept no live-in servants. With it
came a private chapel that could be converted into a recording studio.
The property was utterly secluded and peaceful (save for the grunt of
the wild boars bred on a neighbouring farm), yet Paris was still within
easy reach, and from nearby Tours an air taxi could whisk him across to
London in only seventy minutes.

The quiet of Pocé-sur-Cisse was not disturbed by its new rock-star
seigneur. While at La Fourchette Mick kept the lowest of profiles, driving
around in an old Opel estate or a modest Nissan Micra, training for his
tours on the poplar-lined back roads to Tours. Workers in local fields
and vineyards grew accustomed to the sight of him shadow-boxing,
karate-chopping or – an essential pre-show exercise – running backwards at high speed. Impressively to the French, his houseguests were
not just family and music friends but eminent cultural figures like John
Richardson, the art critic and biographer of Picasso. Richardson was full
of admiration for the classic walled garden which Mick commissioned
the society landscape designer Alvida Lees-Milne to lay out. He later
recalled long, leisurely meals at 'big trestle tables under the chestnut
trees . . . the children having buns, the adults smoking joints . . .' There
were also spectacular cross-dressing parties, for which Mick particularly
enjoyed borrowing the more extravagant items from Jerry's wardrobe.

Like Keith, his preferred holiday destination had long been the West
Indies, though on a more rarefied level than Jamaica's ganja belt. Since
1970 he had been paying regular visits to Mustique, a tiny island in the
Grenadines owned by a British aristocrat, the Honourable Colin Ten-
nant (aka the third Baron Glenconnor) and a favourite retreat of the
Queen's divorced sister, Princess Margaret. Other wealthy and titled
people had homes on the island, and applicants to join its charmed circle
were vetted as strictly as at any old-school Pall Mall Club. Trust Mick
to zero in on the one place in Britain's former empire where its upper
classes still ruled triumphant.

He had holidayed on Mustique while still with Bianca (as Jerry had with Bryan Ferry), and in that era – more than welcome, of course, to the ruling elite – had bought a small property which initially was not much more than a shack on the beach. This he now set about developing into a Japanese-themed six-bedroom villa with extensive grounds that included a koi fishpond and a series of pavilions connected by a walkway. The house was named Stargroves, after the Gothic folly in Berkshire he'd bought for Marianne Faithfull back in the sixties (and which, to Jerry's relief, he'd finally sold). The Mustique Stargroves was to have a somewhat happier history, though it, too, would end up being for rent.

Despite all the changes that Jerry brought to Mick's life, one thing remained unalterably the same. It inspired a lugubrious *bon mot* from one of his on-the-road press officers, a man often required to smuggle some casual companion out of his hotel suite before journalists could be let in. 'Does Mick play around?' the PR said with a hollow laugh. 'Does Dolly Parton sleep on her back?'

For the rock star pushing forty, teenagers continued to have irresistible appeal. Around the time of the aptly named *Some Girls* album, he began dating a seventeen-year-old he had met, with Jerry by his side, at one of Ahmet Ertegun's glittering parties. As well as belonging to a distinguished aristocratic and literary family – an irresistible combination for Mick – she was beautiful and highly intelligent, with a wicked sense of humour and a cynicism about the rock world that came as a refreshing change from goggle-eyed worship. She still lived at the family home in Kensington, where one evening her older sister answered the phone to someone calling himself Mick Jagger. 'Yes, and I'm the Queen of Sheba,' her sister replied.

She dated Mick over the next five years on a casual, irregular basis and with the full knowledge of her family, to whom he was known as 'Michael J' ('Isn't he a bit *old*?' queried her grandfather, a distinguished and high-profile member of the House of Lords). Because of her famous family, Mick took unusual care to keep the relationship a secret; in London, their dates would usually be to see some high-brow film like

Luis Buñuel's *The Discreet Charm of the Bourgeoisie* at an art-house cinema where no one gave him a second glance unless he wanted them to. And Jerry never suspected a thing.

He was equally chary of letting her into the Stones' social circle, mainly because Keith's girlfriend, Patti Hansen, and Charlie's wife, Shirley, were both so staunchly fond of Jerry. The only exception was one night in 1980 when the band and their womenfolk – all but Jerry – went to a cinema in Tottenham Court Road to watch the heavyweight title fight between Muhammad Ali and Larry Holmes projected on a big screen. Mick prepared the seventeen-year-old for her first meeting with the other Glimmer Twin by explaining in a rather protective tone that Keith was 'lovely but very shy'. During the evening Shirley Watts acted as a kind of den mother, taking her aside and impressing on her that she must never, ever talk about her current adventure to the newspapers. But Patti – dressed all in red leather – was tight-lipped and pointedly inquired, 'Where's Jerry?' Silly girl to try to outbitch Mick. 'She's doing fashion shows,' he replied, 'the same as *you* should be.'

The day inevitably came when Jerry got wise and Michael's erstwhile cinema date found herself listening to an outraged Texan voice down the telephone line repeating 'Ah thought you were mah *fraynd* . . .' 'But Jerry,' she replied with impressive quick-wittedness, 'I'm not nearly as beautiful as you are. Why would Mick ever want to have an affair with *me*?' There was a short silence, then Jerry said, 'Maybe you got a point,' and put the phone down.

Even after that, the relationship continued its casual course, with Jerry seemingly fully aware but unable to do anything – at least to Mick. Some time afterwards the seventeen-year-old kept a tryst with him at the Savoy Hotel, where she arrived to find him reading a book of poetry. A few days later, at a society wedding, she – literally – ran into Jerry. 'We were coming down a narrow garden path from opposite directions, Jerry in a sleek black velvet dress, I in a fuchsia satin Scarlett O'Hara numero. She narrowed her huge almond eyes, swept me off the path into the bushes, and said, "*Sooo* sorry!"'

Such tactics grew increasingly necessary as Mick's dalliances became more and more blatant. In 1982, he and Jerry were staying at the Carlyle Hotel in New York while their new town house on West Eighty-first Street was being refurbished. As they ate in the restaurant, lovely young women kept coming up to Mick, offering telephone numbers which he would often accept. Or Jerry would answer the phone in their suite and hear the person at the other end hastily hang up. When strange rings and earrings began turning up in their bed, she decided enough was enough, and moved out. She and Mick went on seeing each other, but he seemed to enjoy flaunting his infidelities and their cradle-snatching element, once explaining he was late because he'd been 'out with some eighteen-year-old débutante'.

While still with Bryan Ferry, Jerry had met the international horse-racing tycoon Robert Sangster. At forty-six, Sangster was almost twice her age, but a dynamic, charming character as well as an authority on her greatest passion after couture. Hearing that she'd split from Mick, he got back in touch and invited her to go with him to the Kentucky horse sales. They later met up again in Los Angeles, but stayed in different hotels. By this point, according to Jerry, she'd decided there could be no future in their relationship, and, strange earrings in the bed or not, the only man she wanted was Mick.

But events were moving far ahead of her. In Paris, where he'd gone to record with the Stones, Mick saw newspaper pictures of her with Sangster at the Kentucky horse sales. Almost neck and neck came a *People* magazine cover story of exotically mixed metaphor: 'MICK AND JERRY SPLIT! A Scandal Brews as Jerry Gallops off with a Millionaire Horseman'. Jerry was quoted as saying that Sangster 'could buy Mick ten times over'.

Mick had been publicly cuckolded like this only once before, when Marianne Faithfull had bolted with Mario Schifano thirteen years earlier. In the celebrity-conscious eighties – and to a man pushing forty – the humiliation was infinitely worse. He instantly got on the phone to Jerry in LA, saying he'd been stupid and selfish and begging for another chance. (Sangster later described overhearing him on an extension, crying 'like a big baby'.) He persuaded her to come to Paris, where he was actually waiting to meet her at the airport. A few days later they returned together to New York, where, after more mutually tearful scenes, Mick finally came up with the lyric she wanted to hear: 'We're going to get married, we're going to have babies, and we're going to be so happy.'

As the first woman to bring a major rock star to heel, never mind this particular one, Jerry became something of a heroine. She received many letters from other women, applauding her determination, and saw her stock with the British press rise even higher. A *Daily Mail* cartoon showed Mick departing on tour carrying a long, padlocked wooden crate that evidently contained his beloved. 'I've promised Jerry I won't mess around any more,' he was telling reporters, 'and she's not going to either.'

Not long afterwards she and Mick were in a restaurant when yet another lovely young thing came up, leaned over him and offered her telephone number. Jerry gave her an almighty kick on the shin under the table while never slackening by a millimetre that big, sunshiny Texan smile.

CHAPTER NINETEEN

The Diary of a Nobody

Back in the sixties, paranoid Brian Jones was always accusing his fellow Stones of ganging up on him. As the eighties went on, it really would happen to Mick; the difference was that he didn't care.

His Glimmer Twin made little secret of finding him unbearable these days. The Stones' *Emotional Rescue* album in 1980 had contained an acrid ballad called 'All About You', written and sung by Keith as a footnote to life with Anita. But one line seemed to point to an equally wearisome relationship that had no end in sight: 'So sick and tired hanging around with jerks like you.'

The sorest point with Keith was Mick's need always to look youthful and with-it, and the consequent threat to the Stones' integrity as hard-core country bluesmen. With his fortieth birthday looming, Mick still made a beeline for every trendy new club, from New York's Limelight to London's Blitz, to hang out with young hit-makers like Paul Young and Duran Duran, in the same jade-green shirts, shoulder-padded jackets and sheaf-cut hair. At their concerts, too, he would often be in the front row, studying their vocal tics and body language to see what he might appropriate. It mystified Keith that such a mighty original tried to copy kids who'd almost all started out as would-be Mick Jaggers.

In New York, the craze was rap or hip-hop: black music as simple and formulaic as the blues, which replaced melody with a hard, unadorned beat and singing with the recitation of belligerent doggerel verse. Rap's real artistic creation was break-dancing, for single males only, usually performed on the street, which demanded extreme gymnastic agility and drew crowds wherever it was demonstrated. Skilled break-dancers created complex routines that went from splits to Cossack-style crouch kicking and spinning like a top on one shoulder or even their heads.

Mick, of course, took an immediate interest in rap and paid several anonymous visits to the clubs where it could be heard. Here, the live attractions were no longer bands, as in his young days, but 'scratch' deejays who manipulated the vinyl discs on their turntables so that the rasp of the needle, once anguish to any music lover, became an exciting augmentation to the beat. He claimed to have tried break-dancing, even spinning on his head, for which he paid with symptoms like a severe hangover the next day. To Keith, however, *rap* still only meant something he'd spent the last few years dodging.

Now clean and in possession of his full senses for the first time in years, he was discovering just how tight Mick's grip on the Stones had become while he was out of it. Despite those brotherly ministrations in Woodstock, he felt that on one level Mick had been happy for him to be a junkie, as it stopped him interfering too much in band business. Now, at conferences with Prince Rupert, he became increasingly aware of Mick's voice saying 'Oh, shut up, Keith.'

On the *Tattoo You* tour he had received virtually equal recognition with Mick, not only for his peerless riffs but also for what one writer called his wasted elegance – henceforth the aim of any boy who picked up a solid-body guitar. These days, he did almost as many interviews as Mick, revealing a humour and honesty very different from his Glimmer Twin's bland equivocations. In contrast with Mick's studied Cockney, the previously taciturn 'Human Riff' turned out to speak with the faint staginess of some boozy old repertory actor. His recent decision to drop the stage name Andrew Oldham had wished on him in 1963 and go back to being Keith Richards with an *s* seemed further proof of how genuine and comfortable with himself he was.

Yet behind the scenes he'd had constant battles with Mick and ended up losing most of them. He complained that he'd wanted to call their surprise hit album plain *Tattoo* but Mick had surreptitiously added the 'You', and that his objections to the tour's pastel-Kabuki stage design had been similarly ignored. He fulminated against 'plastic Jagger' after Mick started employing a movement coach to choreograph what used to come naturally. Most of all he hated the finale when Mick had himself swung out above the crowd in the cherry-picker crane to scatter carnations during 'Jumpin' Jack Flash'. Keith called it 'a fucking sideshow' and one night sabotaged it by hijacking the cherry-picker to play an extended guitar solo.

Ronnie Wood had become Keith's soul mate, drinking, drugging and gun-pulling at practically the same level, and the pair began poking fun at Mick behind his back like schoolboys while teacher is writing on the blackboard. After Keith discovered the existence of a historical novelist called Brenda Jagger, they nicknamed Mick 'Brenda', which also was *Private Eye* magazine's name for the Queen. Keith also began alluding to him as 'Beef Curtains', male slang for the lips of the vagina. He, in turn, mocked Keith for an unadventurous old stick-in-the-mud and characterised the Stones as 'a bunch of pensioners'.

The arguing and backbiting continued through the summer of 1983 as the band worked on their next album, *Undercover*, at the Pathé-Marconi Studios in Paris. Its lead single, 'Undercover of the Night', was written entirely by Mick and evoked his recent time in Peru (and Bianca's new vocation) with references to 'one hundred thousand *disparus* [disappeared] lost in the jails of South America' and 'death camps back in the jungle'. The video for this most overtly political Stones track since 'Street Fighting Man' was directed by Julien Temple, who had made his name with the Sex Pistols' feature film *The Great Rock 'n' Roll Swindle*.

Temple's 'Undercover of the Night' video had a convoluted story line featuring Mick in the dual role of a rock star kidnapped by South

American terrorists and a moustached Fitzcarraldo-like tycoon in a white suit and Panama hat. All in all, it seemed more a vehicle for his unrealised screen-acting ambitions than a showcase for the Stones, whose ensemble performing moments came and went so quickly as to be almost subliminal. At the end, his rock-star character was shot in the head by a death squad just like the one Bianca had recently helped to thwart in Honduras. Even though only pantomime, the scene proved too strong for the BBC's *Top of the Pops*, so Mick celebrated his fortieth year by having another single banned.

For Julien Temple, the filming was an experience that made the Sex Pistols seem almost a rest cure by comparison. One day in the men's room of the George V Hotel in Paris, Keith shoved the young director up against a wall and held a sword stick to his throat. It was Keith's way of saying he didn't think he was seen in the video enough.

Mick was making one concession, at least, to advancing years. In late 1982 it had been announced he was working on his autobiography. The lucky publisher was to be the London house of Weidenfeld & Nicolson, whose co-founder and chairman, George Weidenfeld, was famous for the lavish sums he paid his authors, the star-studded parties he threw and the publicity his titles tended to attract. Weidenfeld lived in Cheyne Walk, Chelsea, a few doors from Mick's old home, and enjoyed a reputation in the literary world similar to Mick's in the rock one, under his (self-bestowed) nickname 'the Nijinsky of Cunnilingus'.

Weidenfeld inevitably knew his fellow émigré and party-giver Prince Rupert Loewenstein (the two portly, white-tonsured figures almost looked like Tweedledum and Tweedledee) and offered a pre-emptive deal munificent even by his standards. Mick would be paid an advance against royalties of £1 million. The book would be put together from tape-recorded interviews by a ghostwriter whom he himself was allowed to choose.

Ghosting someone else's book may not be the most prestigious literary work, but is a craft nonetheless. Unfortunately, when Mick's people began casting around for likely candidates, their first port of call was not the lists of reliable, sometimes brilliant ghostwriters kept by every publisher. Mick declared that he didn't want 'some hack' but a literary name, young and interesting enough not to bore him during their hours closeted together. It happened that *Granta* magazine had just published its choice of 'the Best of Young British Novelists', a twenty-strong list including Martin Amis, Salman Rushdie, Julian Barnes, Ian McEwan, Kazuo Ishiguro – and this author. So the search for his amanuensis began there.

Among the Young British Novelists selected to audition was twenty-nine-year-old Adam Mars-Jones, whose short-story collection *Lantern Lectures* had won the 1982 Somerset Maugham Award. Mars-Jones was instructed to go to London's Savoy Hotel, where Mick was registered under the name 'Mr Philips'. In one of the hotel's best suites, a barefoot Mr Philips was watching cricket on television with only Charlie Watts and a single young female PA for company. He was, as so often, disarmingly informal, squatting down on the floor next to Mars-Jones and asking suggestions for the dream England cricket side he and Charlie were compiling.

For tips on how to handle the situation – not knowing anyone personally acquainted with his prospective collaborator – Mars-Jones had consulted the eminent critic and literary editor John Gross. In Gross's view, it was vital not to suggest that writing an autobiography meant Mick's career was over or in decline. Accordingly, Mars-Jones had coined for himself the job description of 'word engineer' rather than the mausoleumy 'ghost'. Mick turned out to have read *Lantern Lectures* and also to have been skimming the memoirs of Charles Chaplin (another small man, and notorious sexual athlete, who became globally famous) as a possible model for his own narrative. Mars-Jones asked him how good his memory was, but received a rather non-committal reply.

Their discussion was interrupted by the arrival of Ian Botham, the most famous English cricketer of the 1980s, otherwise known as Beefy for his almost Rolling Stone unruliness on and off the field. Beef Curtains treated Beefy with huge respect, and literature gave way to cricket talk, in particular the question of whether England players were banned from having sex before important matches. At one point Mick referred

to Charlie as 'my drummer', but Charlie seemed not to care, merely protesting jocularly, 'Hey, you're *my* singer.'

Adam Mars-Jones did not get the job of Mick's word engineer. He
believes he disqualified himself when Mick handed him a joint after taking a puff and he didn't savour the smoke for long enough, so showing
himself uncool beyond redemption. Nor did anyone else from the Best
of Young British Novelists land the gig. Instead, Mick chose a journalist,
John Ryle, deputy literary editor of the *Sunday Times*. Ryle had no track
record in writing about rock, but was young, cultivated and – a crucial
consideration – extremely pretty.

The book's editor was to be Weidenfeld & Nicolson's recently
appointed deputy chairman, Michael O'Mara. Giving the task to such a
senior figure was proof of the loving care and attention George Weidenfeld had promised Prince Rupert. Weidenfeld himself, as was his habit,
remained apart from the editorial nitty-gritty, often absentmindedly
referring to Mick as 'Michael' and calling O'Mara 'Mick'.

Mick having shifted his base back to New York, the book had to be
put together there. John Ryle was installed at the Barclay Intercontinental Hotel in midtown Manhattan, and his subject would come to
his room for tape-recorded interviews which were then sent back to
Weidenfeld in London to be transcribed. Meanwhile the prospect of
Mick Jagger's story in his own words continued to generate worldwide
expectation. O'Mara sold the North American rights for £1.5 million
– instantly earning back Weidenfeld's whopping advance plus 50 per
cent – and made a string of lucrative deals with publishers in other territories.

His euphoria waned on reading the first transcripts of Ryle's interviews with Mick. Rather than the expected white-hot revelations, they
were full of stuff about Dartford in the 1950s, the cinemas he used to
patronise and film stars he used to like. And to O'Mara the conversation
seemed altogether too unfocused and laid-back for an urgent million-
dollar project; as he recalls, 'I got a feeling that the ashtrays were full.'

There was no lack of effort on the ghostwriter and the publishers'
part and even, up to a point, the subject's. Ryle diligently interviewed

Mick's parents, his brother Chris and other figures from his inner coterie. Mick sent out personal letters to a number of people from his past (some of whom believed they'd been totally forgotten by him) asking them to talk to Ryle. They included his old girlfriend, the former Chrissie Shrimpton, who'd last heard from him via lawyers a few years earlier after it had been (falsely) reported that she intended to publish his old love letters.

The main problem was that after the Stones' career got going Mick was unable to recall almost any dates and possessed no diaries or letters from which a narrative could be constructed. To jog his memory, the *New York Times*'s rock critic and Rolling Stone specialist Robert Palmer was hired as a supplementary interviewer. A personal letter also went to Bill Wyman, who had kept a detailed diary and preserved almost every piece of paper relating to the band's career since its earliest days. In a respectful tone Bill was hardly used to, Mick asked him to talk to John Ryle, adding, 'You can say what you like.' A handwritten footnote asked for access to his archive to fill in the book's many yawning chronological gaps. But Bill had no particular reason to want to help Mick, and in any case was planning to write his own autobiography, so sent back a brusque refusal.

Whatever was tried, nothing seemed able to flesh out the taped interviews flowing from the Barclay Intercontinental across the Atlantic to Weidenfeld & Nicolson. The only fleshing out was in the ghostwriter, who, after months of living on room service at Mick's expense, had lost his formerly lissome, boyish appearance. Michael O'Mara had a few meetings with the interviewee but was never able to communicate his growing anxiety.

Despite being a year Mick's junior, he felt he was dealing with 'an eighteen-year-old'. Sometimes he would land in New York, phone Mick at home and be told to come right over. When he arrived, Jerry, by now heavily pregnant, would open the door and tell him Mick was out. 'I'd sit around and wait for him, trying to make conversation with Jerry, but he never came. I had the strong feeling he was hiding upstairs all the time. When I did manage to talk to him, he'd just tell me not to worry, the book would be fine. He just seemed to think the right words would arrange themselves on the page like magic. But Jerry seemed to realise already something was going badly wrong.'

Finally, after something like nine months, a complete manuscript was submitted. Unlike the ghostwriter by now, it was curiously slim, weighing in at around 80,000 words, half the normal size of a block-buster biography. And it exceeded O'Mara's worst fears. Mick had not only failed to tell all, he came across as not much less bland and evasive than in his press conferences. Towering figures from his past were dismissed in throwaway lines – Marianne Faithfull, for instance as 'a girl I used to know' or words to that effect. And sex, as O'Mara recalls, 'didn't get a look-in . . . It wasn't just dull, it was heart-stoppingly dull. I thought we should call it *The Diary of a Nobody*.'

He made an appointment to see Mick, anticipating the most awkward moment of his career. But for once the eternal eighteen-year-old was wholly adult and pragmatic. 'This isn't working, is it?' Mick said before they had even sat down.

George Weidenfeld was mortified to lose such a prize, and various ideas for saving it were suggested (including O'Mara's brief notion of marketing it as unexpectedly 'subtle'). But Mick's interest in the project, perhaps never great, had waned, and there were now other, more urgent forms of self-expression on his agenda. So the £1 million contract was cancelled and the first instalment already paid by Weidenfeld had to be returned. As O'Mara recalls, it took some time and effort to get the cheque from Prince Rupert.

ON 26 JULY 1983 that dreaded fortieth birthday finally arrived. The many media salutations included one in *The Times* by Pete Townshend, currently on sabbatical from the Who and working for publishers Faber & Faber under the aegis of Mick's old London School of Economics classmate, Matthew Evans. With tongue only slightly in cheek, Townshend paid tribute to 'a complete exhibitionist . . . a name dropper . . .

whose beauty is its owner's greatest joy . . . who will still be beautiful when he's 50 [and whose] talent will still be as strong at 50'.

The difference between Mick and other rock stars – indeed, stars of any kind – was pithily summed up by this most intelligent of his contemporaries, John Lennon apart. 'His ambition,' wrote Townshend, 'is not dependent on his youth, his songwriting is not dependent on his own suffering and his desire to be popular and loved not dependent on his personal insecurity . . . Jagger was into rock 'n' roll before me but, unlike me, he still lives for it.'

Townshend was wrong about the insecurity, however: it always lurked inside Mick the performer, if not the person, and was never stronger than in his forty-first year. After a decade of seeking a young band worthy to be the next Beatles, the music industry had been stormed from left field by the little boy who used to front Motown's putative black Beatles, the Jackson 5. Michael Jackson's *Thriller* album was on its way to becoming the biggest-selling of all time, generating seven top ten hits from its nine tracks and winning eight Grammy Awards. Jackson had in effect become a black, one-man Beatles, just as his loucher rival, Prince, had become a black, one-man Rolling Stones. But it was primarily as a dancer of stunning inventiveness, mixing elements of punk, hip-hop, *Rocky Horror* and moonwalking astronaut that he'd seized the throne as pop's number one thriller from its twenty-year incumbent. And to cap it all, he had to be called Michael.

That August, the Stones parted from Atlantic Records and signed a deal with the American CBS label, guaranteeing them $24 million for four albums. Mick also signed a separate deal to make three solo albums. CBS's top brass had convinced him that on his own he could be as big as Michael Jackson, and were promising a huge advertisement and promotion budget to help it to happen.

The other Stones knew nothing about the solo-albums deal until Mick announced he'd be starting the first after the release of *Undercover*. 'The Rolling Stones cannot be, at my age and after all these years, the only thing in my life,' he said. 'I certainly have earned the right to express myself in another way.' It was hardly new for someone

in a famous band, or even in the Stones, to make a solo album; Bill
Wyman had already released three. But the underhand way the deal
was done (so reminiscent of Brian Jones) put everyone's back up. In
later years, Keith would describe it as 'a betrayal' and the starting
point of the bitterest, most nearly fatal internecine war between the
Glimmer Twins.

For now, however, no further shots were fired, and by December
relations between the two had stabilised sufficiently for Mick to be best
man when Keith married Patti Hansen in Mexico on his own, unprob-
lematic fortieth birthday. It was from a very different, wholly unexpected
quarter that the first serious anti-Mick eruption would come.

Since the Stones began, Charlie Watts had never shown the least
egotism or temperament, accepting his place in the second rank with
almost Zen-like stoicism, absorbing his undeserved equal share of all
the trouble and notoriety without complaint, staying faithful to his wife,
Shirley, in the face of all temptation, injecting a note of common sense,
humour or humanity when the madness threatened to become overwhelming, staying friends with all the others and helping them to stay
friends – in every way fitting the definition of the ideal drummer as 'the
cement that holds the band together'.

For some years past, in fact, Keith's riffs had been the cement and
Charlie the only drummer in rock whose job was to follow the rhythm
guitarist. Despite all the wealth and celebrity, he still regarded joining
the band as a disastrous wrong turning in his life; while grinding out the
same juvenile backbeat in giant open-air arenas, he secretly pined to be
playing jazz with kindred spirits in some smoky little Soho club. It was
said of him that wherever in the world he found himself with the Stones
he always longed to catch the next plane home.

Of all the band, he was the one Mick respected most, treated best
and listened to with the most attention. When Adam Mars-Jones auditioned to be Mick's word engineer, Charlie had been the only other
Stone sitting in, and Mars-Jones had sensed that he needed to be won
over every bit as much as the biographee. And this esteem appeared fully
reciprocated. During Mars-Jones's visit, a courier had delivered Charlie's

housewarming present to Mick for his new French château, a small oil painting of a horse. Mick had at first been flippant, putting on a joke Jerry-Texan accent ('Oh, Ah'm so tickled! . . . Ah'm so *grateful*!'), but had changed his tune when he learned the painting was worth £15,000.

Latterly, however, after all those years of self-containment and self-control, drink and drugs had started to catch up with Charlie. And after years of unsullied monogamy amid the others' orgies, his marriage to Shirley was also showing signs of strain. It was against this background that his seemingly infinite tolerance of Mick finally ran out.

Towards the end of 1984, the Stones met in Amsterdam, now the centre of the business structure Prince Rupert had built around them. Mick had a bridge-building evening out with Keith, for which he borrowed the jacket Keith had worn to marry Patti. When they returned to the hotel, everyone gathered in Mick's suite, except Charlie. Mick picked up the phone, dialled Charlie's room and made the same quip he had in front of Adam Mars-Jones at the Savoy, on that occasion without giving offence: 'Where's my drummer?'

After a lengthy interval, there was a knock at the door and Charlie entered, dressed with extreme dapperness, even for him, and smelling strongly of cologne. He walked up to the seated Mick, hauled him to his feet by his (or, rather, Keith's) jacket lapels, and hit him so hard that he toppled into a platter of smoked-salmon sandwiches. 'Don't ever call me "your" drummer again,' Charlie growled; 'You're *my* fuckin singer,' then exited before Mick had time to say a word.

When Mick had recovered his equilibrium, he tried to laugh off the incident, saying that Charlie had been drunk and, in his generally confused state nowadays, hadn't known what he was doing. This diagnosis seemed confirmed a few minutes later when Charlie rang down to say he was returning. 'He's coming to apologise,' Mick announced. Instead, Charlie walked in and walloped him again, 'Just so you don't forget.'

★

MICK'S DÉBUT SOLO album, *She's the Boss*, mustered formidable resources, as CBS had promised. To help him produce it, he had two of the best young American talents, Bill Laswell and Nile Rodgers. Pete Townshend was wooed away from reading manuscripts at Faber & Faber to join an immense roster of star session musicians including guitar maestro Jeff Beck and jazz-rock organist Herbie Hancock. Two of the tracks, 'Just Another Night' and 'Lucky in Love', were co-credited to Mick and Carlos Alomar, the Puerto Rican composer–guitarist best known for his work with David Bowie.

Apart from the *Performance* soundtrack album, backing Carly Simon and messing around with John Lennon, it was the first time Mick had ever recorded away from the Stones. Yet what should have been a liberating experience had a tentative, almost nervous atmosphere, one former CBS executive recalls, 'as if he didn't feel he had the same rock 'n' roll credentials as Keith'.

Early in 1985, the Stones reconvened in Paris to begin a new album with the gloriously appropriate title *Dirty Work*. Keith had had time to brood about Mick's dirty work with CBS, and turned up with a fistful of new songs whose titles seemed to make his feelings menacingly clear: 'Had It with You', 'One Hit (To the Body)', 'Fight'. The atmosphere in the studio was so bad that both Charlie and Bill stayed away for extended periods. But it proved a boon for Ronnie Wood; there was so little good Jagger–Richards material available that Woody snuck an unprecedented four of his songs into the playlist.

She's the Boss was released in February, preceded by the Jagger–Alomar song 'Just Another Night'. With the single came a video of Mick in a club with a gorgeous young black woman (strangely like Marsha Hunt ten years earlier), being cajoled by her into performing and wowing her with his utter brilliance. In an echo of that recent, so much less than routine night in Amsterdam (at least, the admissible part), he borrowed a glittery jacket, grabbed a guitar and was transformed into an eerie replica of Keith.

'Just Another Night' was a strong commercial single and the album as a whole an impressive effort, as it could hardly fail to be with such talented auxiliaries. Keith was privately scathing at the time and later, in his autobiography, compared it to Hitler's *Mein Kampf:* 'Everybody has a copy but no one listened to it.' Actually, the single made No. 1 on the US mainstream rock chart and No. 12 on the US pop chart, while the second Jagger–Alomar collaboration, 'Lucky in Love', reached the Top 40. Following the old adage 'Where there's a hit there's a writ,' a Jamaican reggae singer named Patrick Alley came forward to claim – unsuccessfully – that 'Just Another Night' had plagiarised a composition by him. That was something else the Führer never experienced.

Mick's defection from the Stones seemed to trigger a general exodus in that summer of 1985. Bill put together a band called Willie and the Poor Boys to raise funds for research into multiple sclerosis, whose victims included the former Faces bass player Ronnie Lane. Charlie and Woody both joined the line-up, along with Led Zeppelin's Jimmy Page, and a successful album and tour resulted. Charlie was also playing regularly in a boogie-woogie instrumental band called Rocket 88 with Ian Stewart and Mick's old Ealing Club mentor, Alexis Korner.

On 13 July the foremost names in British and American pop, past and present, came together for Live Aid, a mammoth fund-raising concert for victims of the famine then devastating Ethiopia. Two simultaneous televised shows, one from London's Wembley, the other from Philadelphia's JFK Stadium, presented an extraordinary line-up including Paul McCartney, David Bowie, the Who, Queen, Madonna, U2, Status Quo, Phil Collins, Duran Duran, Alison Moyet and Bob Dylan. The Stones were asked to take part, but declined on the grounds they were 'no longer a band'.

Instead, Mick went on alone at JFK Stadium, making his first live appearance since the *Tattoo You* tour and his first ever as a solo. His five-song allotment included two duets with Tina Turner, that most vital of his early role models, the second an extended, raunchy 'It's Only Rock & Roll' which revived whispers of a long-ago affair between them, especially at the end when he pulled her dress off. Keith appeared in the next, and climactic, segment, backing Bob Dylan on acoustic guitar with Woody. Live Aid's worldwide audience of 1.9 billion was thus privy to the vast gulf now yawning between the Glimmer Twins. Mick in his trainers and blue T-shirt – still showing that schoolgirlie flash of bare midriff – looked youthful and current, while tattered, emaciated, cigarette-drooping Keith was the Stone Age unrepentant.

As well as benefiting Ethiopia's famine victims by around £150 million and giving pop a new aura of nobility, Live Aid raised Mick's solo career another notch. Part of the day's programme was a video of David Bowie and him performing the old Martha & the Vandellas' hit 'Dancing in the Street', the inspiration for 'Street Fighting Man'. The duet was meant to have figured in the live concert with one of them in London and the other in Philly, but technical problems proved insurmountable. So it had been filmed in advance in London's Docklands, the two encountering each other at night with no one else around in what inevitably somewhat resembled a gay tryst.

Bowie, in a long camouflage overcoat, looked the more stylish, although Mick worked his still-tiny butt off, trumpeting his lips ('Cawlin' awl aroun' the world . . .') and dilating his eyes as ferociously as a Maori warrior. Halfway through, just to show who was still the coolest and who still didn't give a fuck, he picked a canned drink off the ground and sipped from it. The resulting single spent four weeks at No. 1 in the UK and the video was one of that year's most popular on MTV.

December brought a temporary armistice within the Stones when Ian Stewart died suddenly of a heart attack, aged forty-seven. Stu undoubtedly *was* the cement that held the band together: since being dropped from the line-up by Andrew Oldham for looking too normal, he had been their indefatigable roadie, driver, protector and impartial friend. Latterly, he had rejoined them onstage as back-up pianist – the square-jawed family man from Surrey a match for the bluesiest black Chicagoan – but his musical taste and uncompromising standards had always kept the others on their toes. 'Stu was the guy we tried to please,' Mick said, meaning every word.

On 23 February 1986 the band took the stage together for the first time in four years to pay tribute to Stu at the 100 Club on London's

Oxford Street, just along from the old Marquee. Playing blues covers with long-time friends like Pete Townshend and Eric Clapton rekindled a glimmer, if only a faint one, between the sundered twins. A further show of unity was required two days later when the Stones received a lifetime achievement award at the Grammys. Mick voiced their appreciation of this 'great honour' even though, like writing an autobiography, it implied one's best days were past.

Hostilities were resumed on a far more vicious scale later in the year over Mick's second solo album, and transparent self-definition, *Primitive Cool*. Buoyed by the success of *She's the Boss*, he had only one co-producer, Keith Diamond, rather than the previous two, and dropped the itinerant cast of thousands in the studio, instead relying mainly on guitarists Jeff Beck and Dave Stewart (no relation to Stu) from the Eurythmics. The album was recorded mainly in New York with supplementary sessions in Holland and Barbados – the latter the scene of a traumatic adventure for Jerry. Arriving at Grantley Adams Airport to collect some sweaters she'd had air-freighted from America, she was arrested and charged with possessing twenty pounds of marijuana. It proved to be a mix-up by customs; Jerry's name had been put on the wrong incoming consignment and she was soon pronounced innocent and freed. But for Mick, it was all a highly unpleasant dose of *déjà vu*.

Primitive Cool looked like a calculated affront to Keith, not just in subtext-heavy track titles like 'Kow Tow' and 'Shoot Off Your Mouth' (Lennon and McCartney at war had been just beginners at this game) but also the serial flaunting of a rival guitar hero like Jeff Beck. Even more galling was Mick's unabashed focus on his own interests at the expense of his band's. A new Stones album, *Dirty Work*, was due in March 1986. Mick refused to go on the road to promote it because he planned a solo tour when *Primitive Cool* came out the following year.

Even Charlie, not one given to hyperbole, felt this 'folded up twenty-five years of the Rolling Stones'. Keith's fury and contempt waxed even greater when it emerged that Mick was recruiting a stage band – including a lead guitarist who would be expected to do Keith-like moves – and that the solo tour would still feature around twenty Stones songs.

To any journalist who'd listen, he excoriated 'Disco Boy Jagger's little jerk-off band', threatening that if Mick really did take the stage with other musicians, 'I'll slit his fuckin' throat.' Mick called the Stones 'a millstone' around his neck and said that, much as he 'loved' Keith, working with him had become impossible. 'When are you two going to stop bitching at each other?' one interviewer asked Keith. 'Ask the bitch,' he replied.

With that, the other Stones seemed to roll off in different directions as if from a snooker cannon shot. Mick went ahead and recruited a new tour band, dubbing them the Brothers of Sodom, even though they included female backing vocalists. Keith released his own solo album, *Talk Is Cheap* (including another jab at Mick entitled 'You Don't Move Me'), then formed his own breakaway band, the X-pensive Winos, and made a film with his abiding musical hero, Chuck Berry. Ronnie Wood toured with Bo Diddley and became the front man for a short-lived Miami bar named Woody's on the Beach. Bill Wyman turned to writing film music and embarked on his autobiography, using the extensive archive he'd withheld from Mick and with a seasoned music journalist, Ray Coleman, as ghostwriter. Charlie found his way back to jazz at last by forming a big band called the Charlie Watts Orchestra.

And after all that, *Primitive Cool* was a flop, reaching only No. 26 in the UK and No. 41 in America, while its lead single, 'Let's Work', barely scraped *Billboard*'s Top 40. It sent Mick into an atypically subdued and reclusive mood where he took to draping himself in concealing scarves, as one friend recalls, 'like the Elephant Man'. And as a result, the solo tour had to narrow its scope, leaving out both America and Europe and going only to Japan and Australia.

In Sydney, he was visited backstage by Maggie Abbott, the British film agent who had tried so long and hard to get his movie career going. Subsequently no one else had fared any better: since *Fitzcarraldo* his only screen appearances had been an American TV series called *Faerie Tale Theatre*, not totally miscast as the Emperor of Cathay in 'The Nightingale'.

But Abbott now had a story to tell that would have made any film producer salivate. After Mick ceased to be her client she had run across an LA video maker named David Jove, an egocentric character who at the same time appeared concerned never to become too famous. They had become friends and finally Jove had told her a secret he had harboured for fifteen years. His real name was David Snyderman, aka 'Acid King David'; he was the mysterious figure behind Mick and Keith's drug bust, trial and imprisonment in 1967.

Over time, Abbott had learned the whole story: how Snyderman had been recruited by the FBI in cahoots with MI5 to get Mick and Keith busted as a means of keeping the Stones permanently out of America; how he'd infiltrated himself into the weekend party at Redlands in the guise of an acid dealer with an irresistible new variety; how, after tipping off the Sussex police to swoop, he'd been spirited out of Britain by his FBI–MI5 handlers and done his best to disappear completely thereafter, settling on the West Coast and changing his surname to Jove; how he'd kept his head down all these years, resisting all temptation to cash in on rock's most famous legend; but how, even so, he lived in fear that his former FBI handlers might one day come after him and seal his lips permanently.

From her years in London, Maggie Abbott also knew the third and perhaps most grievously wounded victim of the Redlands affair, Marianne Faithfull. Marianne had by now returned from the nadir of heroin addiction to re-establish a career in music and win respect as one of its most unlikely survivors. The two women had kept in touch, and in 1985, while Marianne was on a trip to LA, Abbott had introduced her to David Jove. Marianne was clearly uncomfortable during the meeting and afterwards confirmed to Abbott that he was 'Mr X . . . the guy at Redlands, the guy who set us up'.

One might have expected the revelation to fascinate Mick, penetrating even the famous Jagger amnesia with memories of the 'Summer of Love', from his cell in Brixton Prison via the mythical Mars bar to his summit meeting with the establishment. What a chapter for that recently aborted autobiography! One might have expected at least mild curiosity about the person responsible for the worst fright of his life. But he showed no interest in Maggie Abbott's story, and cut her off before she could get started, merely saying he was 'cool' about what had happened and it was 'all in the past now'.

EARLY IN 1988 Ronnie Wood took on the role of peacemaker and persuaded Mick and Keith to talk on the telephone. Then on 18 May a business meeting at the Savoy Hotel in London put all five Stones in the same room for the first time in almost two years.

With Woody as intermediary, the Glimmer Twins agreed to meet up on their own in the West Indies and try to thrash out their differences. Mick didn't want to do it in Jamaica and Keith refused to go to Mustique, so they chose the neutral ground of Eddie Grant's recording studios in Barbados. It was a meeting every bit as crucial as that first encounter between an economics student and a scruffy beatnik at Dartford railway station in 1961. Keith had no great hopes, warning his family he might be back home in hours rather than days. But as soon as the two got together, the baggage of the past twenty-seven years seemed to fall away; they began quoting each other from their recent public war of words and were soon both roaring with laughter.

In January 1989 the Rolling Stones were inducted into America's Rock and Roll Hall of Fame along with Mick Taylor, Woody's predecessor on lead guitar. Although neither Bill nor Charlie attended the ceremony, it was clear the Stones were a band once again, with that errant soloist firmly back in the fold. Mick had never sounded more sincere as he said what a privilege it had been to work with them and how proud he was of the songs he'd written with Keith. In a rare revisitation of the past, he paid tribute to Ian Stewart and, going even further back, acknowledged Brian Jones's 'marvellous' musicianship. Keith's speech likewise proclaimed reconciliation, albeit less coherently and naming Mick only second in the order of his thanks, after the guitar maker Leo Fender. In the first, and probably last, mention of Jean Cocteau ever made at a music awards ceremony, Mick quoted the artist's comment that 'Americans are funny people. First you shock them, then they put you in a museum.'

So it was that in August the Stones picked up where they'd left off seven years earlier with a new album, *Steel Wheels*, and a year-long world tour already guaranteed to smash the earnings record they'd set in 1982. A young and largely untried Canadian named Michael Cohl had won out over their long-time promoter Bill Graham with a strategy for reaching still deeper into Baby Boomer pockets. The main corporate sponsor would be brewing conglomerate Anheuser-Busch, makers of Budweiser beer, for around $10 million. 'Lapping Tongue' merchandise like T-shirts and bomber jackets would not only be sold at concert venues but through a string of major department stores. The whole operation was projected to cost between $70 and $90 million. In place of the customary *Rolling Stone* spread, Mick and Keith appeared on the cover of *Forbes* magazine, the American business tycoons' bible. Bill Graham – who had once publicly called Mick 'that cunt' – lamented that losing them to Cohl, and Budweiser, was 'like seeing my favourite lover become a whore'.

THE FIRST PART of Mick's promise to Jerry when she came back to him in 1982 had been amply fulfilled. In March 1984 she'd given birth to a daughter, his third. Eschewing wacky rock 'n' roll names, they had chosen the classically simple Elizabeth, followed – at the suggestion of Mick's second daughter, Jade – by the more colourful Scarlett. The baby was baptised into the Church of England in an ultra-traditional ceremony at St Mary Abbot's, Kensington, wearing a robe and cap by David and Elizabeth Emanuel, who had designed Princess Diana's wedding dress. Jerry's mother came from Texas to be present, and Karis, Mick's daughter by Marsha Hunt, was also invited.

Nine months later, Jerry was found to be pregnant with twins. At five months one of the twins died and she suffered a blood clot where the other's placenta connected to her uterus. Lying in bed, weak and grief-stricken, she watched Mick on TV at the Live Aid concert, tearing off Tina Turner's dress. The rest of her pregnancy she spent at a rented house in upstate New York, mainly kept company by her stepdaughter Karis while Mick was recording in the city. On 28 August 1985 the surviving twin, a boy, was born at Lenox Hill Hospital, New York, and christened James Leroy Augustin. Jack Nicholson and Anjelica Huston were his godparents and the christening photographs (St Mary Abbots, Kensington, again) were taken by David Bailey.

Yet the second part of the promise continued to be delayed. 'I'm not gonna get married,' Mick had told the media while Jerry was pregnant with Elizabeth. 'Not right now. I *may* get married. But not right now.' Perhaps understandably, after his experience with Bianca, he saw matrimony as no more than 'legalistic contractual claptrap'.

For a time, Jerry tried not to exert undue pressure. Her first autobiography, *Tall Tales,* published – without any objection from him – in 1985, ended with the cliffhanger still unresolved. 'I still want to marry Mick. But I'm not nagging him about it. All I really care about is our happiness and our bab[ies].' For her birthday, right after Elizabeth's christening, she'd asked for an antique silver tea-kettle with a view to accumulating heirlooms for the baby, but instead Mick had given her an antique Cartier diamond-and-lapis-lazuli ring – 'not a wedding ring', she conceded, 'but the next best thing'.

Since then, they had become the world's most famous nearly married couple. 'We've definitely set a date,' Jerry announced in 1987. But by the time of her Barbados airport ordeal the following year that date had receded again. Now, whenever journalists brought up 'the M word', she responded as if to some rodeo audience impatient for her to rope that steer: 'Golly, I'm tryin'. Would y'all quit rubbin' it *in?*'

In what looked very much like a Plan B, she had refocused on her career, launching her own swimwear line and capitalising on her continuing popularity in Britain. Beef Curtains begat beef extract when she appeared in a series of TV commercials for Bovril, a drink not previously identified with glamour or couture. Now it had Jerry in a slinky black-and-white frock and broad-brimmed hat, sashaying through a gym full of sweaty hunks to deliver the line 'Are you a Bovril Body? Ah know *Ah* am.' Still, whenever they went to Mustique she packed a wedding dress, hoping some warm Caribbean night would inspire Mick to pop the question and they'd have a romantic ceremony on their own stretch of Macaroni Beach.

Once the *Steel Wheels* tour was rolling, however, Jerry began to give up hope. Reports kept coming back that Mick was playing around again and, specifically, that he'd stolen Eric Clapton's girlfriend, the Italian-born supermodel Carla Bruni. His mother had been kind and supportive throughout both Jerry's pregnancies and made no secret of her longing for Mick to legalise things and 'give Elizabeth and James a name', as it was still called. As a result, Jerry hoped Eva might back her up in telling Mick his behaviour was unacceptable – but any attempt to raise the subject with either of his parents met with a blank wall.

Jerry went off to Italy to make a film (for which she learned to speak Italian), then took the children to stay with friends in Tuscany, more or less resigned to being a single mother. But Mick kept phoning her, telling that he loved her and that he'd changed, and finally asking her to marry him in Bali. She believed him and accepted.

When the tour ended, they went on an extended trip to Nepal, Bhutan and Thailand, accompanied by the two children, a nanny, a tutor, Mick's assistant, Alan Dunn, and twenty-six pieces of baggage. The last stop was Bali, where they were married on 21 November 1990. All the arrangements had been made by Mick, without any reference to his bride-to-be. The ceremony was performed by a Hindu holy man in the beachside hut of a wood-carver named Amir Rabik. Mick and Jerry both wore traditional Balinese dress, Elizabeth and James acted as bridesmaid and pageboy respectively, and Alan Dunn was best man. Unbeknownst to Jerry, the proceedings also signified their conversion to Hinduism. The next day, Mick flew on to Japan to receive an award, while Jerry, the children and most of the twenty-six bags returned to London.

One of the few people Mick let in on the secret was the Englishwoman he'd dated when she was only seventeen. They had remained friendly, and she'd even been to stay at his French château, La Fourchette. One night when she retired to her room, Mick popped out of the wardrobe, evidently 'on for it', but she managed to get rid of the *seigneur* without damaging his *amour propre*.

Now he phoned and told her about the ceremony in Bali, somehow not sounding as if it had been the most magical experience of his life. And when she offered congratulations and said how happy Jerry must be, his response was even more puzzling. 'I'm not *really* married,' he said. Remembering how Jerry had hopefully toted her wedding dress around all these years – and forgetting being vengefully barged into the bushes by her – the forthright young woman gave him a brisk telling off.

'God, you're so nice about Jerry,' Mick replied. 'And she's so awful about you.'

CHAPTER TWENTY

Wandering Spirit

So the ephemeral music played by those naughty boys in the early 1960s proved to be among the more durable things in life. And the naughtiest boy, for whom a maximum career of six months had been predicted, was to find himself still churning it out to undiminished acclaim in middle age and beyond. As Mick approached fifty, the burning question of his twenties no longer even arose: he would *never* be too old to go on singing 'Satisfaction'.

It is the nature of veteran rock stars – and what their public expects, even demands of them – to remain stuck in perpetual adolescence. They are everlasting teenagers, not only in their clothes, hair and speech but also their ruthless pursuit of self-gratification and inability to deal with uncomfortable or boring realities. Whenever something disagreeable needs doing, they always have someone to do it for them. As the ultimate veteran rock star, Mick became the ultimate case of such arrested development. For all his great intelligence and sophistication, he continued living essentially the same life and inhabiting the same mind space that he had aged nineteen.

When Harold Nicolson wrote the official biography of King George

V, a major narrative problem was that after passing sixty the king did almost nothing but shoot pheasants and stick postage stamps into albums. Similarly, from his fifth to his sixth decade Mick was basically to have only two occupations. The first was tending the international corporation known as the Rolling Stones. And, like George V, the second involved sticking something in – although not stamps into an album.

THE STONES ENTERED their fourth decade riding as high as ever. A joint readers' and critics' poll in *Rolling Stone* at the end of 1990 saw them beat off all competition, past as well as present; they won 'Band of the Year', 'Album of the Year' for *Steel Wheels* and 'Tour of the Year', while a vote on the greatest rock singles of all time put 'Satisfaction' at number one.

In 1991 came the (mostly) live album *Flashpoint*, featuring a track more overtly political than anything ever sung by the so-called street-fighting man back in the radical sixties. America and Britain had recently sent forces into Kuwait to crush an invasion by Iraq's president Saddam Hussein – a despot whom the British government had supported for years as a bulwark against Iran. 'Highwire' was an unambigous rant by Mick against the international arms dealers who stood to win however this First Gulf War turned out ('we got no pride, don't care whose boots we lick . . .'). It did better in the UK than anything from *Steel Wheels*, also giving him the satisfaction of yet another BBC ban.

More interestingly, *Flashpoint* also contained his one and only acknowledgement of a condition that showed no sign of abating. 'Sex Drive' was modeled on James Brown's 'Get Up (I Feel Like Being a) Sex Machine', but with an added tinge of the confessional ('Ah got this secks dra-aive . . . drivin' me ma-ayd . . .'). The video showed Mick actually lying on a therapist's couch while visions of scantily clad females whirled around him, finally turning into an engulfment of the real thing. But the listening therapist was played by Charlie Watts, and Charlie's enigmatic smile held no condemnation.

The question was to be raised many times over the next few years: how could someone otherwise so intelligent, fastidious and careful of his public image continually cheat on his wife so recklessly and publicly? How, indeed, could he have gone back to cheating on her with hardly a beat after solemnising their relationship in that wood-carver's hut in Bali?

The answer was Eternal Teenager Syndrome. After three decades as a rock god, Mick inhabited a separate universe in which the normal rules of morality did not apply and inconvenient facts never needed to be faced, least of all about his own advancing years. Almost every female he met, of whatever age, still flung herself at him, not minding – not even noticing – the deep-grooved face that now went with the school-girlish torso and the mythic lips. It all could have been managed without giving pain to Jerry, as he was constantly away from home, either working with the Stones or avoiding tax, and surrounded by people as practised at hiding his dalliances as the courtiers of Louis XIV. Yet he could be almost crazily incautious, less like a teenager than some defiant small boy who, while smashing a window or pulling the cat's tail, believes that grown-ups simply can't see him.

Jerry was fully aware of how quick he'd been to return to his old ways, but, with two children now to consider, did her best to put a brave face on it. When tabloids tattled about Mick and the New York socialite Gwen Rivers or Mick and the singer Nadine Expert or Mick and the model Lisa Barbuscia, who'd appeared in the 'Sex Drive' video, Jerry laughed it off as meaningless or quoted homespun cattle-ranch wisdom: 'Let 'em stray and they'll always come back again.' However, Carla Bruni was something much more serious.

Mick had first met her on the UK leg of the *Steel Wheels* tour, which in Europe changed its name to the *Urban Jungle* tour. At the time she was dating Eric Clapton, with whom she came backstage after the Stones' Wembley show. Knowing his friend's predatory ways – which had once even threatened his relationship with his wife, Pattie Boyd – Clapton took Mick aside and pleaded, 'Not this one, *please*, Mick. I think I'm in love.' But the law of the Urban Jungle was inexorable.

Not that Carla Bruni was anyone's idea of helpless prey. Born in Italy but raised in France, she was heiress to the Italian SEAT car-tyre fortune and, at only twenty-two, had become France's top supermodel, sought after by every fashion house from Dior and Chanel to Versace and Lacroix. Long, dark hair aside, there was something of Anita Pallenberg in her rangy elegance, sculpted cheekbones and the fascination she exerted over powerful men, particularly in the lower height range. Before Eric Clapton, she had had a string of prominent lovers including Crown Prince Dmitri of Yugoslavia. A decade later, when she had risen far above rock stars and minor European royalty, one of many unofficial French biographers would call her 'a female Don Juan'.

The thought of being supplanted by a sister supermodel – especially one more than a decade younger – finally drove Jerry to confront Mick. Not least of her concerns was that the HIV epidemic, long thought to be confined to male homosexuals, now struck down promiscuous heteros also. Mick angrily denied the affair, as Carla already had to the French media, and stormed out of their temporary UK home in Barnes, southwest London. But then a few weeks later they were seen having lunch together in Barbados, clearly back on the most affectionate terms. After they left the restaurant, a fellow customer picked up a piece of paper from their table which seemed to be a written apology – from Jerry to Mick. 'I want you to have your freedom,' it read in part, 'and I won't mind if you fuck other girls.' Shortly afterwards Jerry became pregnant for a third time.

The conscientious, far-sighted father within the errant husband had decided his three latest children should be educated in England. Accordingly, in mid-1991, he paid £2.5 million for Downe House, a twenty-six-room Georgian mansion on Richmond Hill, once owned by the dramatist Richard Brinsley Sheridan (whose most famous play, aptly enough, is *The School for Scandal*). The house had magnificent views of the River Thames and adjoined Richmond's famous royal park with its free-ranging deer. Not far away was the Station Hotel, where Andrew Oldham had happened on the Stones in 1963 and an artless boy Trilby met his Svengali. Pete Townshend lived up the hill in Ronnie Wood's old house, The Wick, while Woody himself now owned a mock-Tudor hunting lodge (with its own fully equipped pub) on the other side of Richmond Park.

Though Downe House was intended as a permanent base for Jerry, Elizabeth, James and the new baby who would soon join them, Mick's endlessly complex tax situation meant he could spend only limited time there each year. On his visits, it always took him a while to come down from his other life of touring, recording and teenager-ing. Then he was happy enough to be a family man, walking dogs through Richmond Park and taking his turn in supervising his seven- and six-year-old. A visitor remembers him vainly trying to keep order as Elizabeth and James created a post-bedtime ruckus – the voice of 'Get Off of My Cloud' and 'Midnight Rambler' bawling upstairs 'Stop that fuckin' *noise!*'

He was a good cook, more patient and painstaking in the kitchen than anywhere else except music, and might spend a whole afternoon cycling from shop to shop to find every last correct ingredient for a Japanese recipe that appealed to him. Jerry had no such aptitude, but approached cookery in the same cheery spirit as everything else, donning a novelty apron her sisters had given her. Inspired by the Stones' *Sticky Fingers* album cover, it had a zip-up panel from which a fabric penis popped out. This was symbolic on two levels, the less obvious being Jerry's ability to cock up even simple child dishes like scrambled eggs and pasta. As a result, her son, James, took to cooking as a small boy and before long was skilled enough to be entrusted with the family's Christmas lunch.

Mick happened to be home for part of Jerry's pregnancy, and was loving and attentive throughout. To add to the reassuring atmosphere, Carla Bruni seemed to have transferred her attention to the New York property tycoon Donald Trump. Each night in bed, Jerry later recalled, 'I would put my foot next to Mick's big, warm foot and feel so much love and happiness and peace. And in the morning I would wake up to [him] bringing me a cup of tea.'

One might imagine that no man of forty-eight in his right mind would risk jeopardising such a set-up. But nothing could restrain the

Eternal Teenager, or stop the willy jumping out of the apron. Mick had continued seeing Carla and somehow getting away with it, even when he invited her to his French château after Jerry and the children had returned to London.

In January 1992 Jerry gave birth to a second daughter, Georgia May Ayeesha. The next day, Mick flew to Thailand for an apparent tryst with Carla in the luxury resort of Phuket (not, alas, pronounced 'Fuck it', but 'Foo-ket'). Press reports said they were sharing a villa at the Amanpuri Hotel, where Mick was registered under the Thai-sounding name of 'Something'.

Jerry launched a vigorous counter-offensive, telephoning Carla to deliver several colourful Texan variations on the theme 'Leave mah man alone,' then using the glossy magazines to send out a message of unbroken conjugal bliss. *Hello!* photographed her with Elizabeth, James and the new baby on Mustique, while to France's *Voici* magazine she expressed the hope she'd still be making love to Mick when she was ninety. '[It's] the best way for me to keep my figure. That is why I hate those times when Mick is far from me. But when we are back together, we make up for lost time, believe me.' On one modelling assignment, she actually came face-to-face with the alleged man rustler. 'Why cain't you leave mah husband alone?' she hollered across a room full of top designers and fashion journalists, among whom the strongest permissible passion as a rule was the air kiss. 'Tell him to leave *me* alone,' Carla shouted back.

Jerry kept up her brave face for several months more, shining and smiling at Mick's side even on occasions when her non-participation could most have embarrassed him. She was with him, for instance, in May 1992 when Karis, his daughter by Marsha Hunt, graduated from Yale University. Once he had tried to dodge paternity of Karis; now he was as proud a dad as any other present, videoing every possible angle of the brilliant as well as beautiful young woman in her scholar's gown and mortarboard.

Jerry was there for him, too, in July, when – far sooner than he had expected or wished – the Eternal Teenager found himself a grandfather. Jade, his daughter by Bianca, had turned into a bit of a hippie, leaving her conventional English boarding school to study art history in Florence, then deciding to be a painter. At age nineteen she had became pregnant by twenty-two-year-old Piers Jackson, also an aspiring painter, who showed little sign of being able to keep a Jagger daughter in the style to which she was accustomed. The baby girl, just six months younger than her grandpa's latest daughter, was named Assisi Lola. Jerry got along as well with Jade as with Karis and, in addition, had built bridges between Bianca and Mick and Marsha and Mick. Without her, the whole event could have been fraught with embarrassment; as it was, only she had to be embarrassed.

In her struggle to hold on to Mick, she even persuaded him to make the 'Sex Drive' video come true, at least a little bit, by accompanying her to a marriage guidance counsellor. But without cameras to play to, the Tyranny of Cool quickly proved impermeable. 'These things don't really work unless both of you are absolutely committed,' Jerry was forced to concede. 'Mick's never going to change.'

Finally, she came clean to the *Daily Mail*'s showbiz columnist, Baz Bamigboye: 'We are separated and I suppose we'll get a divorce. I'm in too much pain to go on any longer . . . It's unforgivable what happened and I don't think there's any hope for us any more.' To *McCall*'s magazine she added: 'There's nothing more humiliating than loving him so much that you forgive the infidelities. But I've always hoped that he'd outgrow these things and it won't happen again.'

For the first time ever, the threatened end of one of Mick's relationships caused dismay throughout his circle. Even Keith was moved to say something not about Keith or the finer points of blues playing: 'If [he and Jerry] split up, it will be a real shame. I hope the man comes to his senses . . . you know, the old black book bit. Kicking fifty, it's a bit much . . . a bit manic.'

Shortly afterwards, the man seemed to do just that. He telephoned Jerry and asked her to meet him in Dallas. Three days later they had lunch together very publicly in a Dallas hotel to let everyone know they were all right again. Only this time, no letter of apology from Jerry came to light afterwards.

✳

BEFORE THE WATERSHED of Mick's fiftieth birthday, there were spasmodic attempts to revive the film career that had stalled with *Performance* and *Ned Kelly* more than twenty years earlier. He himself had never really stopped trying, though latterly his thoughts had run more on a screen partnership with David Bowie, who'd taken the role he refused in *The Man Who Fell to Earth* (and was now his neighbour on Mustique).

The pair put themselves up for two expensive Hollywood buddy movies, *Dirty Rotten Scoundrels* and *Ishtar,* but in the first lost out to Michael Caine and Steve Martin and in the second to Dustin Hoffman and Warren Beatty – luckily, since *Ishtar* proved a spectacular turkey. When plans were announced to film Tom Wolfe's sprawling New York novel *The Bonfire of the Vanities,* Mick fancied the role of the sleazy British journalist, a breed he knew only too well, but in the end the part was rewritten for an American and given to Bruce Willis.

In 1992 the name 'Mick Jagger' was finally seen on a film poster again, though he was soon to wish it hadn't. *Freejack* was set in a future America where ailing rich people could have their brains transplanted into healthy bodies and young victims were hunted down for the purpose by so-called bonejackers. Mick was approached to play the ruthless 'Bonejacker' Vacendak at short notice, happened to have a few spare weeks before starting a new solo album, so gave the firm yes that so many producers had sought, and then didn't have time to chicken out. It was ironic that, having turned down dozens of prestigious and challenging roles, he should end up in exactly the kind of science-fiction dross he'd repeatedly sidestepped throughout the seventies – 'not Philip K. Dick', as one critic wrote, 'more Philip K. Dildo'. Especially short shrift was given to 'Jagger in sci-fi leather riot gear, looking extremely silly' as a character patently too young for him.

In a TV interview to promote the film, he let slip that, while on location in Atlanta, he'd made the rounds of the city's strip clubs with his twenty-nine-year-old co-star, Emilio Estevez. How did that square with his image as a family man? he was asked. The phrase seemed positively distasteful: 'You can have five kids without being "a family man."' But he had the grace to apologise, in case any of them were watching.

Nineteen ninety-three brought his third solo album, the making of which involved further prolonged absences of his big, warm foot from the marital bed. Learning the lessons of his eighties solo efforts, he stuck to a mainly soul/country/gospel formula and and brought no celebrity helpers into the studio other than Billy Preston, jazz saxophonist Courtney Pine, Lenny Kravitz for one vocal, and Flea from the Red Hot Chili Peppers playing bass. The album sold two million copies and earned a gold disc in America, though its title, *Wandering Spirit*, was something of a misnomer. Jerry, for one, might have argued that his spirit was not the bit of him that tended to wander. And that year's real wandering spirit turned out to be Bill Wyman, who resigned from the Stones aged fifty-six.

At the beginning, back in 1962, it wasn't Bill the others wanted so much as his impressive spare amp. The chemistry between them hadn't been right then, and had never come right since. In the Stones' class-bound hierarchy, 'Mister Formica' (as Andrew Oldham nicknamed him) had always been a figure of faint fun, snobbishly derided for his neatness and punctuality, for being so much older than the rest of them, for having a wife and child when they were still single, and coming from the joke south London suburb of Penge. Even now, thirty-one years on, it was said of him (and by him) that he'd never really joined the band.

Electric-bass playing is not high art, but good rock bassists are rare and worth their weight in gold to any band. Paul McCartney was one such, Bill Wyman another. The Stones' killer sound derived just as much, if less obviously, from the bass guitar Bill held at that odd, near-vertical angle as from Keith's riffs. Yet Bill had never been made to feel indispensable. Other Stones frequently doubled on bass – Mick Taylor on 'Tumbling Dice', Woody on 'Emotional Rescue' and 'Fight', Keith on tracks as far back as 'Let's Spend the Night Together' in 1966.

While Bill's exterior life as a Stone mainly consisted of sharing blame for what Mick or Keith got up to, his interior one bristled with reminders of how much less important he was than either of them. If Mick wanted to go to the Olympic Games at impossibly short notice (no problem), there would be half a dozen acolytes eager to make the call; if Bill wanted to (problem), the assignment would bounce around the office like a game of pass-the-parcel. When Bill wanted studio time booked to work on a solo track, everyone would be far too busy trying to find Keith a new cook.

But by far his greatest grievance was over money. Publicly he maintained that the Stones' collective income was distributed in scrupulously equal portions, with Charlie and himself receiving no less as NCOs than the officer class of Mick and Keith. He certainly looked the perfect pop plutocrat with his Suffolk stately home, Gedding Hall, and his villa in Provence, next door to the great artist Marc Chagall (each location the farthest conceivable from Penge). In reality, his income as a founder-member of the world's highest-earning band was but a fraction of what was generally supposed – so much so that for long stretches he'd been forced to live on bank overdrafts.

A huge slice of the earnings, of course, went to Mick and Keith as songwriters, but even that did not seem enough for them – or, at any rate, for Mick. When Bill had written 'In Another Land' for the *Satanic Majesties* album, he'd been pressured to hand over a share of the publishing to Jagger–Richard and, as a result, had never had a song on a Stones album since. Likewise, his contributions to major Jagger–Richard tracks had received no gratitude, let alone recompense. Coming up with the classic riff for 'Jumpin' Jack Flash', for example, might have brought a co-writing credit from more generous, democratic colleagues. With Mick and Keith, especially Mick, it wasn't even worth asking.

Bill had thought of quitting the band at the same time as Mick Taylor, but had hung on, a disgusted but impotent spectator as Keith almost wrecked it in the seventies and Mick almost did in the eighties. To Bill, the distinction was that, however suicidal Keith's behaviour, he was always wholeheartedly for the Stones, whereas Mick was only ever for Mick. Ronnie Wood's arrival made life in the ranks a little pleasanter for Bill but did nothing to correct the vast internal imbalance. Woody was a practised and prolific songwriter but (in a reprise of the 'In Another

Land' situation) was expected to split the publishing on his compositions for the Stones with Jagger–Richard. Why should you put up with
it? Bill often asked him. Happy-go-lucky Woody didn't want a fight and,
anyway, regarded the honour of having a song on a Stones album as
worth more than any royalties.

The joke on his denigrators in the band was that quiet, unflamboy-
ant Bill Wyman had turned into the best known of them all – Mick
apart – both as a solo musician and as a personality. More than that,
he had succeeded in the very areas where Mick had most conspicuously failed. He was not just the first Stone to release a solo album,
but the only one ever to have a UK Top 20 single, 'Si Si Je Suis un
Rock Star'. He'd written the music for the 1981 film *Green Ice*, winning
considerably more acclaim than Mick's only movie-scoring effort, for
Invocation of My Demon Brother. He had published a successfully ghostwritten autobiography, *Stone Alone*, a bestseller in 1990. Even in the
area of priapism he now ranked alongside Mick, claiming to have the
names and addresses of 1,000 different women he'd slept with stored
on his computer.

Here, indeed, he had generated a scandal surpassing any of Mick's.
In 1984, at the age of forty-eight, he'd begun dating a thirteen-year-
old London schoolgirl named Mandy Smith – purely platonically, so
he later maintained, and with the full consent of her mother. The relationship had been exposed by the *News of the World* and consequently
investigated by the Director of Public Prosecutions, giving Britain's
tabloids their yummiest feast since the Year of the Mars Bar: 'BILL
TAKES A TEENAGE LOVER'; 'MANDY'S WAGES OF SIN'; 'WYMAN TO FACE THE
MUSIC'; and when the DPP decided to take no action, 'LET OFF FOR SEX-
PROBE STONE'.

The Mick-eclipsing headlines had continued until the decade's end:
first with fifty-two-year-old Bill's lavish wedding to eighteen-year-old
Mandy in June 1989; then with the eating disorder that struck the bride,
reducing her weight to five and a half stone; then with the couple's speedy
divorce, having spent barely a week of married life together; finally with
the Gilbert and Sullivan plot-twist when Bill's twenty-seven-year-old

son, Stephen, became engaged to Mandy's mother, Patsy, transforming Bill's recent mother-in-law into his prospective daughter-in-law.

The Mandy episode was a grievous misjudgement on Bill's part – Eternal Teenager Syndrome at its most distasteful – and he lost no time in admitting as much. It still would always rankle with him that none of his bandmates ever offered a word in his support, publicly or privately. Keith might have felt especially motivated to stick his head above the parapet, as Bill had done for him in 1977 by scoring desperately needed smack for him in Toronto. But Keith's sole comment, inaccurate as well as unhelpful, was that '[Bill] only thinks with his dick'. Mick was appalled by the whole affair, as behoved the father of two then eighteen-year-old daughters, although not much delving into history was needed to find him dating a seventeen-year-old, never mind singing 'Stray Cat Blues' ('Ah can see that yaw fifteen years old / No, Ah don' want yaw ID').

Mick had always hated any of the other Stones to intrude on his social life, and now Bill, of all people, was starting to do it. Sometimes they would both separately be invited to concerts in aid of the Prince of Wales's Prince's Trust charity, attended by the gorgeous, pop-loving Princess Diana. Mick's face, one onlooker recalls, would 'turn grey' whenever he arrived in the VIPs' box to find Bill already there, chatting with the royals.

Occasionally it was convenient to pretend they were mates and equals. If Bill was in a restaurant having dinner with friends, Mick would join his table accompanied by a large entourage, order the most expensive champagne, then leave before the whopping bill arrived. Then again Bill would request a one-to-one meeting with him to discuss some aspect of Stones business and be told he was too busy. Bill's ghostwriter, Ray Coleman, witnessed more than one such brush-off. Even for Coleman, with his long experience of rock-star egomania, it was 'unimaginable that the bass guitarist in the Stones rings the vocalist and is told he hasn't got time to see him'.

The iron had finally entered Bill's soul with the *Steel Wheels* tour of 1989–90, which supposedly ended the warfare within the Stones and netted $260 million, almost three times the original estimate. After the tour ended, he told friends that the accountants had earned more than Charlie and himself put together.

His resignation in 1993 astonished the music business. In November 1991 the Stones had signed with a new label, Virgin – the least appropriate trademark they could have found – for their largest advance yet, $25 million; they were now lining up a world tour to promote their first Virgin album, *Voodoo Lounge*. As with *Steel Wheels*, the whole operation had been contracted out to the young Canadian Michael Cohl and his company, TNA (short for The Next Adventure). Cohl was already certain of breaking the *Steel Wheels* tour's record with new revenue streams from sponsorship, merchandising, TV rights and luxury 'skyboxes' to end the long tradition of purgatorial discomfort at rock gigs, at least for those who could afford them. In short, it looked as if Bill was walking away from a gold mine.

His thirty years' service with the Stones were not marked by any farewell ceremony or even public tribute. 'Bass-playing can't be all that difficult,' Mick commented. 'If necessary, I'll do it myself.' Keith sent a fax saying 'No one leaves this band except in a wooden box,' implying he had the box at the ready and the wherewithal to put the defector there. But in the media he contented himself with calling Bill 'too wrinkly' to stay with the band. That was rich, coming from Keith; in any case, Bill was the only one of them to have remained virtually wrinkle-free.

No attempt was made to find a new Stone to play bass on the *Voodoo Lounge* tour. Instead, the job went to American Darryl Jones, a fine musician who had once backed Miles Davis, but who, like Mick Taylor and Woody, would merely be a salaried employee.

Leaving the band was not the end of Bill Wyman, as many predicted, but, in many ways, the making of him. Just before his final tour, he had opened a Tex-Mex restaurant named Sticky Fingers after the Stones' 1971 album and decorated with memorabilia of their career from the archive he'd had the small satisfaction of withholding from Mick. His original plan had been a chain of restaurants named Rolling Stones, but Prince Rupert had warned that his sticky-fingered ex-bandmates would require 90 per cent of the take. Just this one establishment, in Kensington, west London, was soon making him more per month than he'd ever earned with them.

A man of many enthusiasms outside music, he never became one of the industry's numerous professional victims and whingers, or revealed his feelings about his former CO except on the odd private occasion. One such was when he happened to bump into Mick's long-ago fiancée, the former Chrissie Shrimpton, accompanied by her daughter, Bonnie. 'Your mother was lovely,' he told Bonnie, 'and [Mick] treated her like shit . . . and all his girlfriends like shit . . . and all of us like shit.'

IN 1997 FORTY-THREE-YEAR-OLD Tony Blair became Britain's youngest prime minister since 1812, leading a Labour Party rebranded, and supposedly rejuvenated, as New Labour. Blair had sung and played lead guitar with a student rock band in the early seventies, and had been swept to his landslide victory over John Major's Conservatives on a tide of triumphalist pop music, notably D:Ream's 'Things Can Only Get Better'. His cabinet and closest advisers were mostly around his age, with the same history of shoulder-length locks, crushed-velvet flares, and bopping to 'Brown Sugar' and 'Honky Tonk Women'. As had already happened in America with President Bill Clinton, political as well as economic power passed to the baby boomers.

With Blair – or, rather, the boomer advertising men behind him – came the concept of Cool Britannia, when New Labour Britain in the late nineties was portrayed as experiencing the same upsurge of youthful creative energy and national pride it had under Old Labour during the mid-sixties. The sixties were back, and destined never really to go away again: in clothes, hair, design and décor, in iconoclastic young artists (widely seen as 'the new rock 'n' roll'); above all, in a stream of bands wearing high-button suits and mop-top haircuts, singing in their true accents rather than Jaggeresque *faux*-American ones and generically known as Britpop. There was even an echo of that mythical mid-sixties rivalry between the Beatles and the Stones, albeit in inverted form, with lovable southerners Blur versus uncouth northerners Oasis.

For Old Labour's Harold Wilson, thirty years earlier, battening on to youth culture, as represented by the Beatles, had been just a cynical ploy to woo the youth vote. But Blair was a besotted rock fan for whom being prime minister offered a heaven-sent chance to hang out with the superhero of his adolescence. So, after warming up at a few Cool Britannia parties at Number 10 with Ultravox's Midge Ure and Oasis's Noel Gallagher, he sought a meeting with Mick Jagger. It proved an object lesson in Mick's power to reduce the most alpha of boomer males to jelly.

The encounter took place at a private dinner, hosted by Blair's friend the novelist Robert Harris. Also present were Jerry (standing by her man yet again); Blair's wife, Cherie; Harris's wife, Gill; and Blair's Machiavellian chief image maker, Peter Mandelson. Recalling the evening in his autobiography two decades later, Mandelson described Mick as 'intelligent and politically astute' – precisely the conclusion of Old Labour's Tom Driberg circa 1968. As Mandelson went on to chronicle mercilessly, Blair remained prime ministerial during the meal, but 'afterwards . . . summoned his courage and went up to Mick. Looking him straight in the eye, he said, "I want to say how much you've always meant to me." For a moment, I thought he might ask for an autograph.'

Mick was now fifty-four, but his sex drive remained stuck in overdrive and his pursuit of women young enough to be his daughters was as embarrassment-free and reckless of consequences as ever. Lately, his public dalliances had built up into a positive surge. A twenty-six-year-old, six-foot one-inch Czech model named Jana Rajlich was caught on camera wrapped in a towel and peering out of his bungalow at the Beverly Hills Hotel as if checking whether the coast was clear. *Pulp Fiction* star Uma Thurman was observed being snogged by the famous lips (eternal teenager!) in an LA club named the Viper Room. A twenty-two-year-old British model named Nicole Kruk claimed to have slept with him in Japan, leaving his hotel suite in the nick of time as Jerry was on her way up in the lift. That summer, Jerry again decided she'd had enough and consulted the eminent British divorce lawyer Anthony Julius. However, Mick once again managed to dissuade her, and as if to cement their *rapprochement* she became pregnant for the fourth time.

In August, he left Jerry planning nursery décor and rejoined the Stones in New York, where, coincidentally, they had to make a video for a track called 'Anybody Seen My Baby?' from their next album, *Bridges to Babylon*. The decidedly non-nursery story line called for a young stripper to catch Mick's eye in a sleazy club, then be pursued by him through the New York traffic in her underwear.

To play the stripper, he wanted twenty-two-year-old Angelina Jolie, one day to be among his enraptured audience at the BAFTA Awards but in 1997 the most beautiful among Hollywood's rising actresses – and also, by some way, the wildest. The daughter of Jon (*Midnight Cowboy*) Voight, she was already on her first husband, the young British actor Jonny Lee Miller, and known for a lifestyle with more than a touch of Rolling Stone. At her wedding to Miller, for example, she walked down the aisle wearing black rubber pants and a white shirt on which her bridegroom's name was written in blood.

Jolie initially turned down the role in the 'Anybody Seen My Baby?' video, having more important film work in hand. But she was talked into it by her mother, Marcheline, an avid Jagger worshipper since the early seventies. Her bravura performance in shedding her clothes and blonde wig, then weaving through midtown traffic in a bra and knickers, drove all thoughts of six-foot Czech models, even Uma Thurman, from Mick's mind. His being five years older than her father, of course, meant nothing.

However, according to Jolie's biographer, Andrew Morton, the wooing of this real-life Angie was very different from any that had gone before. Now Mick was the infatuated follower and Jolie the flighty superstar, as hard to pin down as the butterfly of rock had ever been. Seemingly unimpressed by his vast fame and mystique, as Morton recounts, she was the first of his girlfriends ever to treat him 'like shit'.

Their relationship lasted around two years, apparently without ever getting back to Jerry and abetted by Jolie's mother, Marcheline, as a way of living out her own long-ago Mick dreams. Marcheline's ultimate plan, according to Morton, was that Mick should divorce Jerry and marry Angelina, and then she would move in with them.

Though Mick never showed any sign of wanting to go that far, he was clearly smitten far beyond reach of the Tyranny of Cool. When Jolie failed to return his phone calls – as she usually did – he would leave long, pleading messages at the number she'd given him, not realising it was actually her mother's. Marcheline would gloat over the messages at length, sometimes inviting friends in to share them. Despite her cavalier treatment of Mick, Morton writes, Jolie became drawn into Marcheline's matrimonial fantasy, once telling her mother he'd actually proposed to her. She also announced a plan to adopt a special-needs child whom she would name 'Mick Jagger'.

Jerry had a different bone to pick with Mick: he had been seen with Carla Bruni again. And this time the show of public unity she usually kept up began to waver. At a dinner party at Elton John's, fellow guests noticed how many furious glances she directed across the table at Mick. He responded by getting drunker than people usually saw him, then joining Elton, pop's other most famous eternal teenager, in an impromptu duet.

On 23 September the Stones set off on their *Bridges to Babylon* world tour, destined to extend over almost three years rather than the scheduled one, playing to 4.5 million people in North America, Japan, South America and Europe, and grossing $390 million. As well as Darryl Jones on bass again, they had six auxiliary musicians, including Bobby Keys, and three back-up vocalists. The show began with an explosion of fireworks from which Keith emerged, playing the intro to that recently voted greatest rock single of all time, 'Satisfaction'. It also had an intimacy and proactiveness never previously associated with Mick. Audiences could take part in an advance Web vote for songs they wanted to hear, and halfway through each set the band crossed a cantilevered bridge to continue playing on a 'B stage' like a tiny boxing ring 150 feet out into the crowd. Back in the UK, where Stones foreign tours had once caused paroxyms of vicarious repulsion and humiliation, New Labour's Home Secretary Robin Cook expressed hopes of enlisting them among Cool Britannia's 'Ambassadors of British Excellence'.

In London, Jerry was going through her pregnancy alone, feeling 'neglected, fat and unloved', but with Texan chutzpah undiminished. During her eighth month, she sat for a nude portrait by the great Lucian Freud, seventy-four-year-old grandson of Sigmund and a man whose reputation as a pursuer of much younger women and begetter of children was right up there with Mick's. During their thrice-weekly sessions, the supposedly misogynistic Freud showed a surprisingly kind and chivalrous side, making her feel like the most beautiful woman in creation, suggesting frequent breaks for delicious meals, and trading literary quotations, Lord Rochester from him, Edgar Allan Poe from her.

Freud later admiringly spoke of Jerry's 'spiritedness' and the 'physical intelligence', or ease within her own body, she still had as an eight-month-pregnant mum no less than did the new mega-supermodel, Kate Moss. As a rule, he depicted his female sitters as repellent blubbery heaps, but his reclining Jerry, with 'lump' and flowing gold hair, had an atypical radiance.

The portrait was finished by 9 December, when she gave birth to Mick's second son, Gabriel – an archangel to chase away any lingering shades of Lucifer. Mick was not present, having a pressing previous engagement to sing 'Sympathy for the Devil' in Atlanta, and did not see the baby until a week later. Jerry's first visitor in the hospital was the smitten Lucian Freud, loaded down with boxes of flowering narcissi.

In a few days, Mick was off again to rejoin the Stones – but this time there would be no chivalrous Lucian Freud to fall back on. Freud was at work on a second nude portrait of Jerry, now breast-feeding Gabriel. When a bout of flu made her cancel three sittings in a row, he was furious, painting over Jerry's half-finished figure and substituting one of his male assistant breast-feeding the baby in her place. He then wrote her a note telling her what he'd done and enclosing a nude sketch of her with fluids spouting from every orifice. Lucian Freud could make even rock 'n' roll paranoia look tame. Jerry was initally devastated but soon forgave him, deciding that 'all the best people are a bit mad'.

On the *Bridges to Babylon* tour, according to Andrew Morton, Mick was still in hot pursuit of Angelina Jolie. Early in 1998, as the tour headed for South America, he asked her to join him in Brazil, but she declined – had she not, much future trouble, possibly even his marriage, might have been saved. Before the Stones' show at Rio de Janeiro's Praça da Apoteose stadium on 11 April, an overwhelming Web vote demanded 'Like a Rolling Stone', Bob Dylan's unwitting tribute (though Mick now claimed it had been written for them). And who should come out to join Mick for the vocal, looking almost amiable, but Dylan himself.

In May, while the Stones rested up for the tour's final European and UK leg, it was announced that Keith Richards had fallen off a ladder at his home in rural Connecticut and broken three ribs. Preconceptions of a characteristic drug- or booze-fuelled prank were exploded when the ladder turned out to have been in Keith's private library and the fall caused by overbalancing as he reached for a volume on Leonardo da Vinci, with collateral damage from a shower of heavy *Encyclopedia Britannica*. As a result, the opening concert in Berlin had to be put back by a month, four more in France and Spain were cancelled and one in Italy was postponed.

British fans, meanwhile, had learned that the Stones would not be coming in August as planned, and that they had Tony Blair's supposedly rock 'n' roll-loving New Labour regime to thank. Blair's Chancellor of the Exchequer, Gordon Brown, had recently abolished an income-tax loophole for UK citizens based abroad which allowed them a certain number of working days in the country each year without affecting their non-domiciled status. The measure had been backdated to March, wiping out the arrangements Mick, Woody and Charlie had made in advance with the Inland Revenue (Keith had dual US citizenship through his marriage and so was not affected). Rather than face an extra collective tax bill of around £10 million, the band called off their scheduled performances in Edinburgh, Sheffield and London.

There was an outcry in the British media against this seeming cavalier treatment of the audience who should have meant most to them. In fact, the new rule did not only affect the three Stones but other non-doms among their 270-strong road crew – although a third assistant roadie clearly stood to lose somewhat less. Mick had no wish to disappoint the British fans, and went to unusual diplomatic lengths to reach a compromise with the government, offering a charity concert in exchange for a temporary waiver of the tax penalty, even taking over the *Independent*'s 'Right of Reply' column to put out his side of the story. But all that he'd always meant to Tony Blair proved to signify nothing. A treasury spokesman whose surly tone contrasted sharply with Mick's conciliatory one (even Whitehall pen-pushers now considering themselves 'the new rock 'n' roll') replied that no exceptions could be made and declined to be 'lectured by millionaire tax-exiles'.

BY THIS POINT in 1998, the tour had landed Mick with a somewhat larger problem. The previous March, after Angelina Jolie refused to join him in Rio de Janeiro, he had consoled himself with a twenty-nine-year-old Brazilian model named Luciana Morad. She now alleged they had gone on to have an affair stretching over eight months, and as a result she was pregnant with his child. A New York-based lawyer had filed a paternity suit on her behalf and was reportedly claiming £5 million for the future child's maintenance.

Luciana Morad was the breaking point for Jerry. Until then she had resigned herself to a one-sided open marriage, but the deal had always been no children. In January 1999, tired of 'other women tryin' to knock the door down', she filed for divorce in Britain on grounds of Mick's 'repeated adultery'. To represent her, she hired barrister Sandra Davis, who had helped secure Princess Diana's £17 million divorce settlement from the Prince of Wales. Mick's response was to claim the wedding ceremony he and Jerry had gone through in Bali had no legal validity (which he'd told at least one friend at the time); therefore a divorce action was inappropriate and a spousal financial settlement even more so.

He seemed hell-bent on verifying every legend of his arrogance, self-ishness and meanness, first disappointing a quarter of a million British baby boomers to save income tax; now trying to short-change the woman who'd been a superlative wife to him for eight years and borne him four children. In the vigorous new climate of British feminism – self-styled Girl Power – Jumpin' Jack Flash's sexual mystique seemed to evaporate; suddenly he looked like any other pathetic old roué trying to recapture his youth by pursuing women half his age. The headlines were more virulent than any since 1967: 'IT'S ALL OVER NOW FOR MICK AND JERRY'; 'NO LONGER UNDER HIS THUMB'; 'MAYBE THE LAST TIME FOR SKINFLINT STONE'; 'NO SATISFACTION FOR JUMPIN' JACK STASH'.

Not until June 1999, when Jerry's divorce action and Luciana Morad's paternity suit were both well advanced, did tax conditions allow the *Bridges to Babylon* tour to reach Britain. The hiatus after the main European segment had been filled by a short extra American tour with premium-price tickets and a different name, No Security – which, in those condom-conscious times, Mick had cause to regret about his fling with Morad.

Everyone who remembered the old Mick Jagger was amazed by the charm offensive he launched to dispel the bad vibes of the previous year and win younger Britons over to the Stones. His masterstroke was an extended appearance on Channel 4's riotous youth show *TFI Friday*, casting himself as an avuncular guide to his band's inner workings rather like his father, Joe, had once been to canoeing and rock climbing. *TFI Friday*'s presenter, Chris Evans, was given unprecedented access to him in the run-up to the two London concerts, at Shepherd's Bush Empire and Wembley Stadium. The programme included a backstage tour personally conducted by Mick in faultless Estuary English ('Yeh, it's quih a loh of sho-yoos if you think abouh ih.' Translation: Yes, it's quite a lot of shows if you think about it.) and a short lecture on the importance of projection. Evans was even allowed to tease him a little, laying out Polaroid pictures of various road-crew members and offering a $50 prize if he could name every one. He could.

The bridge building was completed before two audiences of 88,000 at Wembley on 11 and 12 June. At both shows, the dominant female element were no longer mindless Mick-lovers as of old, but standard-bearers for Girl Power, drinking beer from the bottle, swearing as lustily as any male and ready to give a deafening collective raspberry to any hint of Neanderthal sexism from the stage.

As a first disarming gesture, the performances started closer to on time than any Stones shows in recorded memory. There was barely half an hour's wait before the four of them appeared on a giant video screen loping along like the gang from *Reservoir Dogs*, eerily unchanged save that every line had been removed from their faces, leaving the blank white ovals of Marcel Marceau mimes. And from Mick came no traditional mocking Dixie-Mama greeting of 'A-a-aw*right*!' but a formal apology in his best BAFTA accent: 'I'm sorry it's taken so long. We really appreciate your waiting. And we're going to work our arses off to make up for it.'

After more than two years almost continuously on the road all over the world, a band of such antiquity might have been expected to show exhaustion, carelessness and terminal boredom. Yet those two Wembley shows were among the best the Stones had ever given. There was a special symbolism in the moment when they crossed the cantilevered bridge to the tiny B-stage to play old favourites like 'Route 66' in the round. Millionaire tax exiles turned into bluesmen once again, still as true to the music as ever after all these years, and close to their home crowd in a way they hadn't been since nights at the Marquee or the Richmond Crawdaddy Club.

As for Mick, from the moment he shed his sparkly jade frock coat to reveal a turquoise crop top – still with a flash of bare midriff – he proved yet again that whatever new rock gods might come along, none could ever be more than his apprentice. And Planet Jagger cast as potent a spell as ever. By the end of the first hour, he was no longer a fifty-six-year-old grandfather being divorced by his more popular wife and embarrassingly sued for paternity of an unborn Brazilian baby. He was the eternal teenager whose sex drive was a modern wonder of the world. Each day, his audience wondered if he'd dare sing the suddenly relevant

'Some Girls', and in one show he did, giving almost defiant emphasis to 'Some gurls give me cheeldrun . . . Ah never aysked them for . . .'

The laughter that rippled through Wembley Stadium came as readily from females as males and held no whisper of reproach.

IN AUGUST, MATTERS with Jerry were resolved by a brief hearing in London's High Court. Two experts in Indonesian matrimonial law were summoned to pronounce on Mick's claim that the Hindu marriage he'd orchestrated in Bali in 1990 had had no legal validity, therefore he could not properly be sued for divorce. Both experts opined that, because the ceremony in the wood-carver's hut had not been ratified by any civil proceedings, its legality might indeed be open to question.

Unlike the endings of all Mick's previous relationships, however, he did not use his get-out-of-jail card to the full. There were his four children with Jerry to consider; he also feared that attempting to fob her off with some Bianca-sized pittance would bring a tell-all autobiography down on his head. It was therefore announced that their marriage had been annulled 'by mutual agreement' and Jerry would receive an undisclosed financial settlement (reportedly a £4.5 million lump sum plus £100,000 per year maintenance and £25,000 for each of the children until the age of twenty-five). In a first for any of his outgoing women, she described his provision as 'very, very generous'.

They had remained good friends before the High Court action, and afterwards their relationship seemed unharmed. Jerry took the children off to her new house in the South of France, where, it happened, Mick's collaborator and her friend Dave Stewart was to marry the photographer Anoushka Fisz. Mick came to the wedding, then spent the night in Jerry's guest room.

Luciana Morad had by now given birth to a son whom she named Lucas Maurice Morad Jagger. Blood tests, taken on Mick's insistence, established that he was the child's father, bringing the grand total of his offspring to seven, and Luciana was awarded $6,000 per month in maintenance. She expressed the hope that Lucas would share the educational opportunities of Mick's other children and have his name put down for Eton College.

The news about the incriminating blood tests reached Mick while he was staying with Jerry in France. Next morning he went on his way, accompanied by a British film crew who were making a documentary about him. 'I waved good-bye and thought how lucky I was that I didn't care what he got up to any more,' Jerry would recall. 'It was no longer my problem.'

They no longer shared a bed, but otherwise, the Marriage That Never Was appeared to turn seamlessly into the Break-up That Never Was. Having initially moved out of Downe House, Mick took a flat next door and, during his tax-exempt trips back to Britain, was constantly around, seeing the children and presiding over meals. Being relieved of his marital obligations to Jerry seemed to have an almost magical effect: he treated her almost like a suitor again, phoning her several times a day, sending her surprise bouquets of flowers. One evening, Ronnie Wood came across Richmond Park for dinner at Downe House with his second wife, Jo, a refreshing new voice of sanity in the Stones' seraglio (and a good influence on Woody he would later foolishly let go). Seeing how comfortable Mick and Jerry were together sent Jo Wood into peals of laughter. 'Mick said, "Wossamatter with you?"' she recalled. 'I said, "You two get on far better now than when you were married."'

Jerry, for her part, became something of a national heroine as proof that a wife annulled by a rock megastar in her mid-thirties could still have a life, and then some. Over the next few months she appeared on the cover of Hello!, became the face of Thierry Mugler perfume, was appointed a contributing editor of Tatler magazine, joined the judging panel of the Whitbread literary awards, began studying for an Open University degree and announced plans to sell replicas of her engagement ring from Mick on the TV shopping channel QVC.

In the summer of 2000 she made her West End acting début when she replaced Kathleen Turner as Mrs Robinson in The Graduate, which, unlike the famous screen version with Anne Bancroft, involved a nude scene to follow those in Lucian Freud's studio. Mick was there on her opening night (just as he'd been on Marianne Faithfull's at the Royal Court back in the sixties) and even offered to babysit Gabriel during the play's run. 'He's wonderfully kind and supportive,' Jerry told an interviewer on Radio 4's *Woman's Hour* – adding, in the most loving way, 'He just isn't very much of a husband.'

CHAPTER TWENTY-ONE

God Gave Me Everything

In March 2000 Joe and Eva Jagger attended the opening of the Mick Jagger Arts Centre at Dartford Grammar School – an alma mater now proud to acknowledge an even more distinguished ex-pupil than the nineteenth-century colonial hero Sir Henry Havelock. The £2.25 million complex had received a £1.7 million grant from the National Lottery and Mick had made up the balance, despite having little cause to thank Dartford Grammar for the artistic, still less musical, grounding he'd received there. The inauguration ceremony was perfomed by him jointly with the Duke of Kent, and Jerry was again loyally on hand to help steer her former parents-in-law around the centre's two luxuriously appointed performance spaces, recording studio, rehearsal rooms, bar and art gallery. At the suggestion of one of the students, Mick wrote 'I was here' on a wall (something which would have been rewarded with a beating when he was fourteen) so that it could be preserved for posterity.

Two months later, at Parkside Hospital, Wimbledon, Eva died of heart failure after a short illness, aged eighty-seven. The following December she and Joe would have celebrated their diamond wedding anniversary after sixty years of marriage. Mick was at the Cannes Film Festival, but flew home immediately to be with his father. The funeral, at St Andrew's Church, Ham (Surrey), was attended by Jerry and her four children, Bianca and Jade, and the three other Stones. The service included a performance by Mick and his brother, Chris, of the Carter Family spiritual 'Will the Circle Be Unbroken?'

All Eva's dreams of social advancement and more had been fulfilled by her elder son – though, sadly, she did not live to experience the ultimate one. Yet she had never allowed Mick to overshadow the younger sibling who, in their childhood, had often seemed her favourite. Chris Jagger had tried his hand as a recording artist in the seventies and again in the nineties, both times without much success; he had also variously been an actor, a waiter, a decorator, a journalist, a broadcaster and a vendor of Christmas trees. In latter years he'd fronted various amateur blues and Cajun bands, playing venues like pubs and village halls, seldom to audiences of more than a few dozen. Eva was loyally attending such a gig when a woman recognised her as Mick's mother and gushed, 'I *love* your son.' 'Which one?' Eva asked firmly.

Joe Jagger, that one-time wiry gymnast, was now a frail eighty-eight-year-old, lost without his partner of almost sixty years. The same attentive son as ever, Mick ensured that Joe was comforted by seeing plenty of his grandchildren; he joined the family holidays to France and Mustique that continued as usual after Mick and Jerry's annulment, and also went with them to see Mick's oldest daughter, Karis, marry Jonathan Weston at the Treasure Island resort in San Francisco Bay.

Now that Mick had no more reason to hide his affairs from Jerry, he paradoxically began showing more discretion than he ever had while they were together. During his quite lengthy relationship with twenty-three-year-old Sophie Dahl, six-foot supermodel granddaughter of author Roald – and a former school friend of Charlie Watts's daughter – the two managed never to be photographed together (proving that any celeb can be invisible who *genuinely* wants to). When they went to a restaurant, the limo would drop Sophie first, then circle the block before depositing Mick. There was equally little trace of his reported fascination with the television presenter Amanda de Cadenet, who, at twenty-nine, seemed on the old side for him.

The paparazzi had better luck when he met up with Luciana Morad in London for a first look at the baby boy whose paternity he'd finally been forced to acknowledge. He was photographed wheeling Lucas Maurice Morad Jagger through Hyde Park in a buggy and, despite all the humiliating legal and medical process that had gone before, seeming not at all unhappy about this seventh addition to his brood. Journalists who managed a close look at the infant reported lips of a volume as conclusive as any DNA test.

It was the height of the so-called dot-com boom, when instant fortunes were to be made by companies providing services and commodities to the internet. Mick's friend and Mustique neighbour David Bowie had been in the vanguard with BowieNet, a vanity internet service provider dealing mainly in Bowie's numerous (terrible) paintings, drawings and prints. Mick similarly channelled a private passion into Jagged Internetworks, which beamed major international cricket matches over the net and soon acquired an impressive catalogue of exclusive rights, notably to the Champions Trophy in the United Arab Emirates.

The other concurrent boom was in the work of Cool Britannia's young British artists, as epitomised by Damien Hirst and Tracey Emin, who had become the latest claimants to be 'the new rock 'n' roll'. (And certainly, both Hirst's sculpture of a dead shark immersed in formaldehyde and Emin's installation of an unmade, garbage-strewn double bed might easily have been found in some hotel room lately occupied by Keith Richards.) The market was virtually owned by the former advertising man Charles Saatchi. Mick became a close friend of Saatchi's, invested in one of his companies, and, since Saatchi controlled demand as well as supply, had access to tips on which pieces to buy before their value skyrocketed.

This diversification into fields away from music also brought fulfilment of Maggie Abbott's idea back in the seventies that Mick would make as good a film producer as star. He set up his own production company, Jagged Films, and immediately announced two major projects, a biopic of the poet Dylan Thomas and an adaptation of Robert Harris's bestselling World War II novel, *Enigma* (which really should have been the title of that stillborn Jagger autobiography). One early choice as *Enigma*'s male lead was Jonny Lee Miller, at the time still married to Angelina Jolie. According to Jolie's biographer, Andrew Morton, it was largely a ruse to keep Mick in contact with this most elusive of his lady-loves.

Jagged Films' other début production was a television documentary about Mick to promote a new solo album, his fourth, in 2001. His choice as director was thirty-three-year-old Kevin Macdonald, who'd made a film about *Performance*'s scriptwriter Donald Cammell and gone on to win an Oscar for *One Day in September*, about the massacre of Israeli athletes by Palestinian terrorists at the 1972 Olympics. Knowing Mick's troubled history with documentaries like *The Rolling Stones Rock 'n' Roll Circus* and *Cocksucker Blues*, Macdonald was initially dubious; however, a TV tie-in with Britain's Channel 4 and an album release made it unlikely this one would join those vetoed classics on the shelf. Some parts were to be filmed by Macdonald, others by Mick himself with a tiny digital camera and a recorder in his pocket. Needless to say, the boss of Jagged Films would enjoy total editorial control.

Macdonald followed Mick around for much of 2001, just before the official end of his marriage to Jerry. Braced for an unreliable, temperamental superstar, the director found his subject 'amazingly open, generous with his time, always good company . . . and very sweet'. The main problem was keeping up with someone almost thirty years his senior. Having travelled together from London to New York on the latest available flight, Macdonald would be fit for nothing but a meal and an early night, but Mick would be ready to go straight out to meetings, dinners and parties.

Off camera, his innate conservatism often showed itself. 'A lot of the time he seemed no different from someone you'd meet in a golf club in Hampshire,' Macdonald recalls. 'But whenever he walked into a recording studio, it was as if he was inhabited by a different spirit. He just changed into a blues singer from Mississippi. Most of all, I was struck by

how much he still loved being Mick Jagger – that after forty years of partying and enjoying oneself, that kind of thing could still be of interest.'

On the mild, sunny morning of 11 September, two commercial air-
liners hijacked by Al Qaeda terrorists flew into the twin towers of New
York's World Trade Center, reducing them and thousands of their innocent occupants with horrific speed to a mound of dust. Mick happened
not to be in the city at the time, but his sixteen-year-old daughter, Elizabeth, was staying only a few blocks away from the inferno. It took a day
of frantic telephoning by her father and mother in London to establish
that she was safe.

Five weeks later, Mick and Keith took part in the all-star Concert for
New York staged by Paul McCartney at Madison Square Garden for the
families of 9/11 victims and to honour the police officers and firefighters
who died in the towers' collapse. The Glimmer Twins' two contributions
were 'Miss You', with its sad new dimension to 'sleepin' awl alone', and
'Salt of the Earth' from *Beggars Banquet*. They had always wanted the
song to have an anthemic John Lennon quality, and now, suddenly, it
did.

Inevitably all this rather overshadowed the première of Jagged Films'
Enigma in the presence of another notably dodgy husband, HRH the
Prince of Wales, on 24 September. Set in Britain in 1943 – coincidentally
Mick's birth year – the film revolved around the cryptographers at
Bletchley Park, Buckinghamshire, who broke the German naval code
known as Enigma, so ensuring Hitler's eventual defeat. The director
was Michael Apted (who'd had the arduous experience of working with
Bianca on *Trick or Treat* in the seventies) and the script was by one of
Britain's foremost playwrights, Sir Tom Stoppard. As well as producing,
Mick played a cameo role as an RAF officer and also lent the Enigma
coding and decoding machine he personally owned to the film's properties department.

Enigma was criticised for trivialising the Bletchley Park story by leaving out Alan Turing, the gay mathematical genius who was most instrumental in cracking Enigma, to create love interest between Kate Winslet
and leading man Dougray Scott. But, mainly thanks to Winslet's pres-

ence, it did moderately well at the box office. During filming, Mick had been exactly the hands-on presence Maggie Abbott had envisaged years before, paying visits to the cast and crew on location and joining in an anguished debate about rewriting the ending. He was also tireless in promoting it, even appearing on the cover of *Saga*, a magazine previously associated with retirement cruises and walking frames.

He could hardly be criticised for under-productivity. In November came the fourth Jagger solo album, *Goddess in the Doorway*, accompanied by Jagged Films' promotional TV documentary, *Being Mick* (subtitled *You Would If You Could*). But it was not quite the film which director Kevin Macdonald thought he'd been making in that year of extraordinary access. He'd been making *cinema verité* where what his subject actually wanted was a fairy tale. Everything awkward or spiky or adult had to be trimmed out so that being Mick would seem an existence as sunny and carefree as a teenager's.

In the approved cut, therefore, here were screaming crowds, police barriers, red carpets and young female TV reporters, nearly swooning at the sight of him. Here he was taking his daughter Elizabeth to Elton John's White Tie and Tiara charity summer garden party to mingle with the likes of Hugh Grant and the *Enigma* female lead, Kate Winslet. Here he was working with reverential young record producers, eerie throwbacks to the sixties with their long hair, straggly moustaches and lumberjack shirts. Here he was in Cologne, watching U2's Bono record a vocal for his album track 'Joy', receiving an emotional hug from his guest vocalist, being quizzed over a salad lunch about just *how* he and Keith had managed to write all those Stones songs, and being as uninformative as ever. ('Dunno . . . we just wrote 'em.') Here he was reading an article on the restructuring of European finance in-flight to Miami to make another album track, 'God Gave Me Everything', at Lenny Kravitz's house, a low-rise mansion with an all-through décor of burst-artery crimson.

Many private, even intimate scenes were left in, most without the faintest icy breath of the Tyranny of Cool. Here he was giving a thoroughly relaxed, jolly party with Jerry at Downe House at the time they were supposedly separated. Here he was playing with his toddler son Gabriel, unable to stop a tiny forefinger being jammed unphotogenically up a nostril; here fitting Elizabeth and her little sister, Georgia, with earphones before their début as his back-up chorus; here giving an appreciative Georgia his 'war voice', like the clipped commentary in a 1940s newsreel: ' . . . gled to be beck with their mothers and fathers, reunited after giving Hitler a biff on the nose'. Here he was, baseball-capped, taking part in the fathers' race at Georgia's school sports, watching Test cricket with his brother, Chris, and on Mustique with his father discussing long-ago athletic events in Dartford. Here he was on the phone to Karis, talking about her mother Marsha's new career as a novelist; here voting in the 2001 General Election ('Name, please?' 'Michael Jagger'); here in a study lined with leather-bound volumes like some lawyer's office in a John Grisham story; here at Jerry's house in France for Dave Stewart's wedding, just before she waved him and the film crew off, thankful that he wasn't her problem any more.

But neither of the two main strands in his life – what one might call the King George V elements – made it into the film. Apart from a frolicksome appearance by Woody at the Downe House party, there was no interaction with the other Stones. And although spectacular young women, including Sophie Dahl, had milled around Mick all through the filming, his only female companions on-screen were beautiful, widelipped daughters in various sizes. The one reference to this absent component came when his daughter Jade was arranging to meet him with a date (his not hers) yet to be decided. 'Nobody younger than me, please,' Jade said half jokingly – but only half.

There were a few close-to-introspective moments, as when he recalled toying with the idea of schoolteaching as a career and reflected that he'd used its essential quality in his very different profession: 'If your father and grandfather were teachers, you can't help telling other people what to do.' He said he lived the life he did for fear of turning 'just an old fart' and that he had 'a bohemian, artistic attitude to love and marriage'.

Being Mick was picked up in America by ABC and shown at peak time during the Thanksgiving holiday. Although generally panned in the media as 'vanity TV' and 'pure *Hello!* TV', it won a huge audience there, as it had on C4 in the UK, and left most of its audience liking Mick more, if still not remotely understanding him.

Goddess in the Doorway fared less well despite all manner of promising ingredients. Several of the album's tracks had been co-written by Mick and his young producer, Matt Clifford, and there was studio back-up from Pete Townshend, Lenny Kravitz, Bono and the Haitian hip-hop star Wyclef Jean. Townshend praised the content for sounding nothing like the Stones, but in fact, 'God Gave Me Everything', recorded at Kravitz's blood-red Miami mansion – with lyrics dashed off by Mick just before the session – was like a premium Stones track of the early seventies as well as his best solo performance since 'Memo from Turner'. *Goddess in the Doorway* received a five-star 'instant classic' rating from *Rolling Stone's* editor in chief, Jann Wenner, but failed to chart significantly in either America or Britain. There hasn't been another Mick Jagger album since.

12 July 2002 was the fortieth anniversary of the Stones' début at the Soho Marquee Club, when 'R&B vocalist Mick Jagger' in his off-the-shoulder matelot-striped sweater had first edged uncertainly into the spotlight. The amazing milestone was marked by a compilation double album called *Forty Licks* – a sly pun on guitar soloing and that ever-active Lapping Tongue – which for the first time combined Stones tracks in their ownership with the pre-1971 catalogue still controlled by their former manager, Allen Klein. For, despite periodic ligitation by Mick, Klein's grip on all-time Jagger–Richard classics like 'The Last Time' and 'Get Off of My Cloud' and '19th Nervous Breakdown' and 'Paint It Black' and 'Jumpin' Jack Flash' and 'Satisfaction' had proved more unbreakable than any Enigma code.

There was also a year-long *Licks* world tour, sponsored by the online financial corporation E*TRADE and featuring the artiest stage set to date. Jeff Koons, the American artist famous for his stainless-steel balloon animals, contributed a graphic, and an animated video showed a naked young woman astride the Lapping Tongue, then being lapped to oblivion by it. Where once the most serious health hazard on Stones world tours had been diarrhoea and gonorrhoea, now there was severe acute respiratory syndrome (SARS), a pandemic impartially affecting East and West which had put the band's rehearsal base of Toronto into virtual isolation. They took part in the Molson Canadian Rocks for Toronto Concert to raise funds for the stricken city, and later made their first-ever appearance in Hong Kong as another morale booster for a SARS emergency zone.

On the tour's American leg, a Texas billionaire paid them $7 million to play for 500 people at a private party. And the personal gifts always showered on Mick included one of special significance. At the Wiltern Theater, Los Angeles, he was joined onstage by Solomon Burke, the blues legend whose 'Everybody Needs Somebody to Love' used to be the Stones' favourite show opener. Now weighing 400lb, Burke had to be helped from the wings, wrapped in his trademark regal cloak. In the finale he took off the cloak and draped it around Mick, as if he were handing on the mantle of R&B's supreme monarch. The honour took Mick by surprise, and the heavy cloak almost knocked him over.

Nor was the Stones' fortieth Britain's only significant anniversary that summer. It was fifty years since the Queen's accession to the throne after the death of her father, George VI. And in addition to the expected round of royal visits and banquets, showing how immeasurably times had changed, there was a marathon pop concert in the grounds of Buckingham Palace, opening with Brian May from Queen standing on the palace roof to play 'God Save the Queen' on electric guitar.

The Stones could not join Paul McCartney, Cliff Richard and Brian Wilson at this royal command rave-up as they were in Toronto, rehearsing for their *Licks* tour. But after the live concert was over and Buckingham Palace glimmered in a garish blue *son et lumière*, what was its mega-volume overture? First, that pioneering fuzz-box riff, less guitar than diabolic pipe organ: 'Duh-duh duh-duh-*duh* da-duh-duh . . .' Then that much-loved, unlovable voice in sarcastically soft register, those prodigious lips remoulding every syllable: 'Ah cain't git no-o . . . Sa-tis-*fack*-shern . . .'

All the British parents who had fulminated about 'obscenity' back in 1965 little thought they were listening to an alternative National Anthem.

IN THE QUEEN's Golden Jubilee Birthday Honours, announced some weeks previously (and actually compiled by the Blair government), Mick had been given a knighthood for services to music. Ever since Harold Wilson had cannily made the Beatles Members of the Most Excellent Order of the British Empire thirty-seven years earlier, successive administrations, Tory and Labour, had sought popularity by showering gongs among entertainers. But as almost every other name in the pop super-echelon had received knighthoods – Cliff Richard, Paul McCartney, Elton John, Bob Geldof – Mick had always noticeably been passed over. With George Harrison now deceased, the only one behind him in the line was Ringo Starr.

Accustomed as the British were to the debasement of the honours system, enough of his old notoriety lingered for the award to produce widespread disgust. One might almost have been back in 1965, with outraged colonels and civil servants returning their MBEs to protest against the Beatles'. Such an accolade seemed disproportionate for a career apparently lacking the necessary charitable good works – indeed, exclusively given over to egotism, selfishness and greed. He had in fact been associated with numerous charity events, from the Nicaraguan earthquake appeal to the recent SARS benefit concerts, but, thanks to the Tyranny of Cool, had never drawn public notice to them. Thus, few disagreed with the acid observation of Charles Mosley from the honours system's bible, *Burke's Peerage and Baronetage*: 'He should go in for a bit of charity. What about unwed mothers?'

The outrage of old military men in the shires was nothing, however, to that of Keith Richards, for whom Mick's acceptance of a knighthood was a betrayal of everything the Stones had always stood for. In public, Keith complained of conduct unbecoming a one-time lefty LSE student, adding that it was 'ludicrous to take one of those gongs from the establishment when they did their very best to throw us in jail'. In private, he admitted feeling such 'cold cold rage at [his former Twin's] blind stupidity' that he almost pulled out of the *Licks* tour. '[Mick] said, "Tony Blair is insisting that I accept this." I said, "You can always say no." . . . But quite honestly, Mick's fucked up so many times, what's another fuck-up?' Lest Downing Street be considering him for the royal sword touch, he added that he 'wouldn't let that family near me with a sharp stick, let alone a sword'.

Interviewing the now Sir Mick for BBC2's *Newsnight* programme, Robin Denselow cautiously mentioned that Keith was 'not happy' about the honour.

'He's not a happy person,' Sir Mick replied.

September 2002 found him back on the screen again, almost forty years after *Performance*. In *The Man from Elysian Fields* he played Luther Fox, boss of the upmarket Elysian Fields escort agency – one service that, in real life, he'd never needed. Despite a strong cast including James Coburn, Anjelica Huston, and Andy Garcia, and being called 'a work of elegance' by America's hardest-to-please critic, Roger Ebert, the film did poorly in its home market and went straight to video in Britain. The suave Luther seemed an awkward fit for Sir Mick, though it did give him two lines with powerful personal resonance. One was 'I've been blessed to live a life without boundaries'; the other, 'You're lucky to have a wife and children; don't let their love slip through your fingers.'

On a fashion shoot the previous year, he had met the American fashion stylist and designer L'Wren Scott. At thirty-four, she was twenty-three years his junior, and at six foot three the tallest woman ever to excite his ardour. Thanks to the internal punctuation mark that gave her first name the appearance of a French noun (suggesting the tiniest of birds), she was known among couture colleagues as the Apostrophe. Even though in her company Sir Mick was reduced to the size of a semicolon, they'd begun dating.

L'Wren had started life as Luann Bambrough, one of three adopted children of a Mormon insurance salesman living near Salt Lake City. In her teens (like Jerry Hall before her) she had escaped to Paris to become a model; her first name duly Frenchified, she then moved back to LA. to work as a stylist for the fashion photographer Herb Ritts, superintending the wardrobe and hair of stars like Ellen Barkin, Sarah Jessica Parker and Julianne Moore. A marriage to a London property developer had ended shortly before she met Sir Mick.

They began to be photographed everywhere together, L'Wren tactfully dipping at the knees to reduce the disparity in their height. The joke, in fact, became not how small he was but how unreasonably tall *she* was. And in a remarkably brief time the girlfriends as young as daughters, or younger, faded from contention. It really seemed that the Apostrophe had brought his wandering spirit to a full stop. Speaking from near Salt Lake City, her adoptive mother, Lula (not L'Ula), commented: 'L'Wren is very independent and would not take any nonsense from anyone, no matter how famous they were. It does not surprise me at all that she's tamed Mick. She is very much her own woman and it would be my guess that that is why Mick likes her.'

In 2005 they were still together, like a high-fashion David and Goliath, at Hollywood's Golden Globes. Sir Mick picked up the Best Original Song award for 'Old Habits Die Hard', written with Dave Stewart and featured in the remake of *Alfie*. In his acceptance speech he thanked L'Wren for not wearing heels that night.

The past few years had brought a steep decline in record sales thanks to free music downloads on personal computers and the competitive allure of DVDs and video games. Where once rock tours were seen as promotional campaigns for new albums, they were now every major act's main source of income. And such was the weight of baby-boomer nostalgia that legendary bands who'd split up in acrimony decades before now found themselves offered fortunes for reunion tours – an experience Pink Floyd's David Gilmour likened to 'sleeping with your ex-wife'.

But none of these reunited old stagers, from Floyd to the Monkees, could compete with the Stones on the road, any more than could contemporary superbands like the Kaiser Chiefs, Franz Ferdinand, the Backstreet Boys or the Foo Fighters. The world tour around their album *A Bigger Bang*, between 2005 and 2007, broke their own record to become the world's highest grossing yet at $558 million, with input from three different commercial sponsors, Tommy Hilfiger menswear, Sprint communications and Castrol oil. Following the formula of the past three decades, mammoth shows alternated with more intimate ones in clubs or theatres, where the now-sixty-plus Sir Mick would still be bombarded with invitations from compliant young women in the form of notes, flowers or the occasional flying bra.

On 18 February 2006, in a free concert on Copacabana Beach, Rio de Janeiro, they played to a crowd three times as big as Woodstock's, an estimated 1.5 million. When no deaths were reported, it could be said that the ghost of Altamont had been laid to rest. Two months later they made their first-ever appearance in the People's Republic of China (originally planned for the 2003 *Licks* tour but cancelled because of the SARS outbreak). At the government's request, 'Brown Sugar', 'Honky Tonk Women' and 'Beast of Burden' were omitted from their show as too sexually suggestive, though the last-named seemed more suggestive of their audience's predicament under communism.

In October, two nights at one of their smaller venues, New York's Beacon Theater, became a cinema documentary, *Shine a Light*, named after a song from *Exile on Main St.* and directed by Martin Scorsese. Since releasing *Mean Streets* with its Stones-heavy soundtrack in 1973, Scorsese genuinely had made cinema 'the new rock 'n' roll'; his keenness now to capture them in the flesh conferred huge prestige, as even Sir Mick and the Tyranny of Cool freely acknowledged. More pertinently, *The Last Waltz*, Scorsese's documentary about the Band's farewell concert in 1976, still stood as the best live-performance film ever.

The Beacon Theater shows were a benefit for former President Bill Clinton's foundation and were introduced by the man whose saxophone playing and sexual antics in the White House had given even the US presidency a claim on being 'the new rock 'n' roll'. Among the first-night audience were his wife, Hillary, now a member of the Senate, and the former president of Poland, Aleksander Kwaśniewski. Beforehand, all the Stones, Keith included, lined up for a simpering meet-and-greet that would have sickened their young outlaw selves to the soul.

Sixty-three-year-old Sir Mick's performance was unchanged from when he was twenty-three – same tossing hair, staring eyes and letter-box lips; same jacket shrugged halfway down his arms like a rebellious schoolboy; same stripperish bottom wiggling with fingers locked behind head; same flashes of girlish bare midriff. Donning a guitar, he duetted with Jack White, from Stones sound-alike band the White Stripes, on 'Loving Cup', making White's enunciation seem almost BBC-perfect by comparison ('Goo me a liddle dranke . . . and Ah fawl down drernke'); then came a predictably sexy shimmy with Christina Aguilera on 'Live with Me', then a version of 'Champagne & Reefer' with Buddy Guy, showing the many who did not realise that no white man (except Brian Jones) ever played blues harmonica better.

In common with Scorsese's classic 1976 rockumentary, *Shine a Light*, featured the director as a character, Sir Mick's new best friend 'Marty', alternately charming and irascible (as when, with only hours to show-time, he still hadn't been told which songs the Stones would be play-ing). The resulting film had characteristic Scorsese energy and drama, yet came nowhere near *The Last Waltz*. That had been about a still-young band breaking up at the peak of their form; this was about one just a few steps ahead of the taxidermist.

For all its cash and kudos, the *Bigger Bang* tour proved to be jinxed like none since 1969. In April 2006, during a break in Fiji, Keith decided to climb a coconut tree and fell off it onto the beach, landing on his head and knocking himself unconscious. He was rushed to New Zealand for medi-cal treatment, reported as a brain scan; in fact, he had sustained serious head injuries and a team of top surgeons only just managed to save his life.

A tragic reprise of the incident took place on 29 October, during the filming of *Shine a Light*, when Ahmet Ertegun, the Stones' old label boss at Atlantic and still Sir Mick's good friend, fell and knocked himself out in a backstage hospitality area. He never regained consciousness, and died a few weeks later, aged eighty-three.

Then, on 11 November, Joe Jagger died of pneumonia, aged ninety-three. He had been in hospital since suffering a fall a few weeks earlier, and his son had only just returned to America after a flying visit back to Surrey to see him. The news of his death came as the Stones were about to play a sold-out show at the MGM Grand Hotel in Las Vegas. The performance went ahead as scheduled, and Sir Mick made no reference to his loss from the stage.

The slight, quiet, sinewy man with hardly a hair on his head had shaped the shaggy superstar more lastingly than the world ever knew. If Sir Mick felt respect for precious little else, he always had huge respect for Joe, the richer-than-Croesus rock god admiring as well as wondering at his father's steadfast altruism. In 1981, when the Stones were on their first mega-money US tour, Joe had been in the country at the same time, giving a series of lectures in his tireless crusade to persuade young people to lead clean lives. 'Physical training from the Renaissance to the present day', his son was fond of quoting with almost paternal pride. There was real affection between them, too, in an understated British way: whatever the pressures of being Mick, the superstar could always make time to tramp the wet Welsh Marches on one of the hiking tours Joe so much enjoyed. His funeral took place at St Mary's College Chapel, Twickenham, on 28 November, in the presence of three Sir Mick exes who had all adored him: Marsha, Bianca and Jerry.

The tour ended with a gig perhaps not as lucrative as others but one triumphantly demonstrating the Stones' continued power over the young of their homeland. On 10 June 2007 they headlined at the Isle of Wight Festival, their first appearance on the island since they'd played at a repertory theatre there in 1964 with Brian and Bill, and the scenery from the current production (including french windows) as a backcloth. Forty-three years on, they proved as big a draw as any of the hot young twenty-first-century bands on offer, from Snow Patrol to Muse. Their set included an appearance by Amy Winehouse, the eeriest sixties throwback yet, with her black-caked eyes and outsize beehive hairdo, though her self-destructive drinking and drugging were pure mid-seventies Keith Richards. The honour of singing with Sir Mick seemingly helped her hold it together for once; their duet on the Temptations' 'Ain't Too Proud to Beg' was the festival's acknowledged highlight.

In January 2008, Carla Bruni, that explosive figure from Sir Mick's past, secretly married another diminutive, powerful individual, France's president Nicolas Sarkozy; so, rather than the man from Elysian Fields, she ended up with the one from the Elysée Palace. One commentator of an anagramatic turn of mind wondered if from now on 'Elysée' should be pronounced 'Easy lay'.

OVER THE PAST twenty years, Keith Richards's appearance has become increasingly bizarre. Whereas advancing age has etched Sir Mick's face into Mount Rushmore stone, it has given Keith's the horrific fluidity of a gurner, those competitive grimace makers peculiar to England's north country. When he smiles, and his features seem to dissolve like some old-fashioned movie special effect of Dr Jekyll turning into Mr Hyde, one feels a genuine need to cover small children's eyes. He has also taken to doing strange things with his hair, twisting it into dreadlocks tipped with metal objects resembling clothes pegs or tying it up in none-too-hygienic-looking bandannas.

Yet all those decades of suicidal drug abuse have left him essentially unscathed, a tribute to a constitution rivalled only by Winston Churchill. (Sad that so many who tried to emulate him, from Gram Parsons to Amy Winehouse, were not similarly armoured.) He claims to be still off heroin and not to have used cocaine since nose-diving from that coconut tree in Fiji, though his voice, and in particular his thoroughly scary laugh, still sound like a thousand unemptied ashtrays made audible. 'Nice to be here,' he tells the audience in his solo spot in every Stones show. 'Hey, it's nice to be *anywhere*, y'know.' Or sometimes: 'Nice to see you. Hey, it's nice to see *anyone*, y'know.'

That special timbre – less rock guitar hero than boozy, sentimental old repertory actor – has now also endeared him at second hand to a worldwide cinema audience. In the first *Pirates of the Caribbean* film in 2003, Johnny Depp borrowed it – adding a touch of cartoon skunk Pepé Le Pew – for his character, Captain Jack Sparrow. Knowing Keith's reputation, Depp wondered if he might find himself slammed up against a wall with a sword stick at his throat. But Keith was hugely amused, and in the third film of the series played a cameo role as Sparrow's father, Captain Edward Teague (his beaten-up pirate hat, thick black beard and dangling crucifix earrings striking a relatively normal note for him).

As Captain Teague prepared to go before the camera for the first time, a journalist asked if any advice had come from that seasoned film actor Sir Mick. 'He's the last person I'd ask in the world,' Keith replied. Since the *Pirates* franchise shows no sign of ending, Sir Mick will have to keep watching his Glimmer Twin make the splash on-screen that has eluded him for more than forty years.

May 2010 brought a reissue of the Stones' 1972 album *Exile on Main St.* with ten previously unreleased tracks. Critically panned on its original appearance, it was now hailed as one of the all-time-great rock albums and in its new form became the band's first UK/US No. 1 since *Voodoo Lounge.* With it came a documentary, *Stones in Exile,* recounting the escape from the British tax man to France and the album's evolution in Keith's basement at Villa Nellcôte. When it was premièred at the Cannes Film Festival, a line began to form two hours before the screening. Sir Mick was there to introduce it, supported by L'Wren (once again tactfully *sans* heels). His self-deprecating humour about old times with the Stones, in both English and fluent French, delighted his audience. '[In] the early seventies,' he said, 'we were young, good-looking and stupid. Now we're just stupid.'

The problem with recapturing the revelry at Nellcôte was that almost none of it had been filmed. *Stones in Exile* therefore consisted mainly of black-and-white still photographs, almost all by the young Frenchman Dominique Tarle. As a further oddity, several of those interviewed about their part in making *Exile on Main St.* appeared only as voice-overs, as if they were ashamed to show the physical ravages of their decadent youth. Its British transmission on BBC2 included a brief sofa chat between Sir

Mick and the BBC's arts supremo Alan Yentob. Sir Mick yielded to a little sentiment, saying it was 'kinda nice' when people came up and told him which Stones concerts had been milestones in their lives. Unfortunately, after half a century moulded by the Tyranny of Cool, his face just didn't have an expression to go with 'kinda nice'.

Movie acting was not the only area where Keith finally trumped his Glimmer Twin. Following his début as Captain Edward Teague, he trousered a reported $7 million advance for his autobiography. The ghostwriter was James Fox – not the actor who went off the deep end after appearing in *Performance* but a former *Sunday Times* journalist (like Sir Mick's former ghostwriter, John Ryle) and author of *White Mischief,* an investigation into the Happy Valley murder in 1940s Kenya. Keith's infinitesimal attention span, lassitude and new passion for burying himself in his library promised Fox an even more difficult task than Ryle had faced with the Jagger memoirs in 1983; nevertheless, a manuscript was completed, pronounced fascinating, and published in October 2010 as *Life.*

In a handwritten message on the back of the book, Keith assured his readers that it was 'all true' and that he remembered 'everything'. Actually, most of the 547-page narrative passed in a woozy haze, specific only about blues music, guitars and epic drug-abuse. But on one subject he was utterly specific: his seeming total alienation from the onetime teenage soul mate he now called 'Brenda'. 'I used to love Mick,' he wrote, 'but I haven't been to his dressing-room in twenty years. Sometimes I think "I miss my friend." I wonder "Where did he go?"'

His friend was portrayed as an egomaniacal megalomaniac and impossible diva and snob who treated all women abominably and usually left them to cry on his, Keith's, shoulder. *Goddess in the Doorway,* his friend's most recent (and probably best) solo album, was wittily renamed 'Dog Shit in the Doorway'. The *coup de grâce* came in the section about his friend's relationship with Marianne Faithfull in the late sixties. 'Marianne . . . had no fun with Mick's tiny todger. I know he's got an enormous pair of balls, but it doesn't quite fill the bill.'

Strange vocabulary apart – *todger* being a children's word, more commonly used by little girls – this hardly sounded like the worldly-wise old soul of rock 'n' roll *Life* sought to portray. It certainly was not a complaint ever heard from a vast number of, er, consumers over the years; in any case, it was extraordinarily catty and irrelevant. The book's editors urged Keith to cut it, but he refused. Sir Mick, he claimed, had read the proofs and asked for only one cut – about his use of a voice coach. Sir Mick himself emulated royalty once again and made no public comment. His one consolation was that when *Life* became a bestseller, his todger had been of material assistance.

The size of Keith's advance, if not the desire to answer back, led several publishers to wonder whether Sir Mick might at last be ready to write the autobiography he had aborted in 1983. However, something promising to be almost as hot was already on its way: Jerry Hall had been paid £500,000 of a £1 million advance from a major UK house to continue the life story broken off in her 1985 memoir, *Tall Tales*. The project was to some extent therapeutic: as her friends knew, Jerry had been much less buoyant than she seemed after the end of her marriage, and had since felt depressed, even agoraphobic. Despite that purportedly 'very, very generous' annulment pay-off, she told friends she also needed the money.

She started out writing the book herself, but after a time her publishers persuaded her to work with a ghost. The rumour in the book trade was that her narrative about her life with Sir Mick had plenty of human warmth, but the ghost was needed to put in more sex. In fact, there was more than enough sex: the ghost was needed to put in more human warmth. The book was complete and ready to go into production one Friday afternoon, with Jerry still gung ho about getting it all off her chest; the following Monday she cancelled the whole project. There could not but be suspicion that, assiduous as ever in covering his tracks, Sir Mick had bought her off.

The whole £500,000 advance was returned to the publisher. And numerous women all over the world must have breathed a sigh of relief, not least France's first lady, Carla Bruni-Sarkozy, who that summer accompanied her titchy spouse to Britain to meet the new prime minister, David Cameron, and was widely admired for her elegance. Jerry subsequently contracted with another publisher, but this time just for a coffee-table book entitled *My Life in Pictures*. Its minimal text, however, still gave a full summary of Sir Mick's post-1985 infidelities, at one point describing him as 'a ruthless sexual predator'.

NO LONGER PERHAPS. L'Wren Scott started her own couture label in 2006 and has since risen to considerable heights, professionally speaking, with creations like the headmistress dress, what *Vogue* called 'calf-corseting gladiator pumps', and the $12,000 Lula bags, named after her mother, which, she says 'open and close with a kind of "woosh", like the first time you ride in a nice car and go "Wow!"' (When the bags were launched, one British columnist noted drily that the Jagger wallet was not famed for opening with a woosh, though it might close with one.) Sir Mick is usually at her shows, video camera poised, not meaning to siphon off all the attention but always doing so as (*Vogue* again) he 'bounces around in a violet blazer and sneakers'.

True to her mother's prophecy, L'Wren has apparently seen off all rivals for his attention, even weaning him away from his long-time, super-efficient PA, Miranda Guinness. As a result, the Apostrophe has a new nickname – 'the Loin-Tamer'. But despite the impressive diamond ring she now sports, there seems no prospect of the first Lady Jagger. After they had been together nine years, he described her to a London *Times* interviewer as someone he was 'sort of seeing' while L'Wren herself says only that they're 'kind of dating'.

The most compelling proof of the real person behind the Jagger mask comes from his seven children with four different mothers. Rock stars' offspring frequently end up loathing their fathers, or at best treating them with weary tolerance, but all Sir Mick's plainly adore him. Despite their widely different ages and ethnic ingredients, they get on well together, indeed regard one another as real sisters and brothers –

something that couldn't happen if he didn't give each of them the same love, attention and status. In this regard, at least, the Eternal Teenager has thoroughly grown up.

After presenting him with a second granddaughter, Amba Isis, in 1995, Jade found fame with stones of a rather different kind. She started her own design company, Jade Inc., when she was twenty-four, and in 1996 became creative director of Garrard's, jewellers to the British Royal Family for 160 years, waking up its staid showcases, rather like Dad once did the Top 10, with her chain-mail underwear, diamond-encrusted revolver and skull pendants, and 'devil-themed' trinkets. She has since launched the Jade Jezebel Jagger line of clothes, redesigned the classic Guerlain perfume bottle and devised a flying lounge for the low-cost Spanish airline Vueling. Now married to deejay Dan Williams, she lives unostentatiously in north London.

Jade's mother, Bianca, is unrecognisable as the white-clad sacrifice who unhappily married a rock star in Saint-Tropez in 1971. For more than thirty years she has worked tirelessly for humanitarian causes, through her own Bianca Jagger Human Rights Foundation, as a good-will ambassador for the Council of Europe, a trustee of the Amazon Charitable Trust and a council member of Amnesty International USA. The numerous honours she has received include the Right Livelihood Award presented by the Swedish parliament 'for outstanding vision and work on behalf of the planet and its people' and regarded as 'the alternative Nobel Prize'; the United Nations Earth Day International Award; the Amnesty International USA Media Spotlight Award for Leadership; the World Citizenship Award from the Nuclear Age Peace Foundation; the World Achievement Award (presented to her by Mikhail Gorbachev); and two honorary doctorates. In her mid-sixties, it is still Bianca rather than Jade who turns every head as they come into the Ivy restaurant in London. There are many around Sir Mick who believe she remains the one real love of his life. Himself excepted, of course.

Both his daughters with Jerry Hall grew up to be models after their mother. Elizabeth, the elder, looks like Jerry, but the younger,

known as Georgia May, looks like Brigitte Bardot, the French sex kitten who was every British schoolboy's fantasy in the 1950s, from her
long blonde hair and enormous eyes to the little gap in her front teeth.
When she was twelve, and first experimenting with lipstick, her father
looked at her in horror one day and said, 'Are you wearing make-up?
You're wearing more make-up than I am!' At sixteen she was signed
up by Tori Edwards, the model agent who represented her mother and
sister, and in no time was the face of Versace and Rimmel and on the
cover of *Vogue*. Indeed, Sir Mick became worried that her career was
moving too fast, and insisted she call a temporary halt to study for her
A-level exams.

In 2010 Georgia May posed topless in an advertisement for Hudson
Jeans; the following year Elizabeth appeared on the cover of *Playboy*. She
had first been approached to do so in 2005 when she was twenty-one,
but her father – that one-time reveller at the Playboy Mansion – was so
shocked by the idea that she refused. (Jerry, of course, had done *Playboy*
back in the eighties, when Lizzie was a baby.) Georgia May is the more
rock 'n' roll of the two sisters, often seen in the Richmond pub the Roe-
buck throwing back cocktails with noisy groups of friends by whom she
likes to be addressed as 'Jagger'. But, as she recently told *Tatler* magazine, she never forgets the first principle inculcated by her mother, that
eternal Southern belle: 'Always smile, be nice and gracious to everyone
. . . and never show your bum.'

His oldest son, James, is the only one of his children to become
a musician, following the rocky path already trodden by Julian and
Sean Lennon and Jakob Dylan. James maintains he was never under
any paternal pressure to start singing or playing guitar, though being
dubbed 'Jimi' as a baby by Tina Turner was probably pressure enough.
After leaving school, he turned down a university place at Loughborough
to turn professional with a band named Turbogeist, but, as of 2011, they
still did not have a record deal and James was living in a 'dodgy' part
of north London where the cookery skills he picked up as a child were
much appreciated by his girlfriend and mates. He recently admitted that
his father hadn't yet been to a Turbogeist gig. 'Dad once joked about

coming along, but I joked that he couldn't because there'd be too many teenage girls there.'

Karis went into film and television production, and recently directed her mother, Marsha Hunt, in a one-woman show based on Marsha's novel *Joy*. Lucas, Sir Mick's twelve-year-old son with Luciana Morad, lives in Brazil with his mother – now a leading TV presenter – but sees his father on a regular one-to-one basis, for instance joining him in South Africa to watch the 2010 football World Cup. All in all, it is a brood of which Captain von Trapp himself could be proud. To be sure, as Jade says, 'My dad likes to get us all together from time to time, line us up, and make sure we're all in check.'

HE STILL TURNS up continually in the papers or on YouTube, that new spy hole for voyeurs, slipping out of the rear entrances of clubs as discreetly as three or four security point men can make him; arriving at the Oscars ceremony, where he will probably now never pick up a statuette; making a surprise appearance in brother Chris's church-hall blues band as a quid pro quo for Chris's occasional help with song lyrics; or hanging out with the co-founder of Microsoft and one of the world's richest men, Paul Allen.

All sorts of figures in public life, unconnected with rock 'n' roll, have a personal, invariably fond anecdote about him: Sir Mick the cricket fanatic, charming a private box full of gruff old Panama hats at a Lord's Test match; Sir Mick the wine connoisseur, ordering a pipe, or sixty cases, of 1977 vintage port (the year of Elvis Presley's death) directly from the makers in Portugal; Sir Mick the history buff, authoritatively pronouncing TV historian Simon Schama 'a bit spotty on the High Middle Ages'; Sir Mick the supposed mega-amnesiac, meeting would-be Tory MP Annunziata Rees-Mogg, daughter of former *Times* editor William, and gratefully recalling how her father saved his career back in 1967; Sir Mick the stickler for etiquette, who insists that all his homes contain a copy of *Mrs Beeton's Household Management*, the Victorian domestic manual, with its definitive rules on table placements, flower arrangement and the correct way to clean silverware.

His legacy is all around us . . . in the endless debate about the sexualisation of pop music that started with Elvis but went into overdrive with 'Satisfaction' and has latterly focused on female performers from Madonna to Lady Gaga and Rihanna . . . in the *faux*-Cockney accent now used by young people from every background in every region of Britain . . . in the very latest hot new boy band, slouched on a sofa and taking the piss out of the media, thinking they're the first ones ever to do it.

American rappers the Black Eyed Peas commemorate him in 'The Time (Dirty Bit)', which, since its release in 2010, has scored 10 million hits on YouTube: 'All these girls, they like my swagger / They callin' me Mick Jagger . . .' In June 2011, Maroon 5's tribute song, 'Moves Like Jagger', featuring Christina Aguilera ('Take me by the tongue / And I'll let you know . . . I've got the moves like Jagger') became an international smash, giving the band their first *Billboard* Top 10 hit since 2007 and Aguilera her first since 2008. At the same time there's still nothing cooler than vintage Stones. When supermodel 'Cocaine Kate' Moss – who has almost single-handedly made modelling 'the new rock 'n' roll' – married guitarist Jamie Hince, the couple drove away from the ceremony in a vintage Rolls-Royce with 'Gimme Shelter' blasting from the stereo.

Moves like Jagger's these days percolate into the most unlikely places, for example the Welsh old-age home where – in a wonderful example of modern institutional care and sensitivity – residents were given a tambourine to shake if they needed to call for assistance. 'These people are pensioners,' commented one justifiably outraged relative, 'not Mick Jagger.' Nor can we forget the modern craze among otherwise rational women for having their lips artificially pumped up to the bolstery proportions God gave him naturally. That mouth, which was once unique to Mick and certain species of tropical fish, is now smeared across female countenances in every capitalist society on earth. (Hardly 'Moves Like Jagger', though, for being fitted with one of these perma-pouts leaves a face virtually incapable of movement.)

Since 1989, the Rolling Stones have earned an estimated £2 billion gross from records, song rights, merchandising, touring and sponsorship, while the Lapping Tongue brand appears on around fifty products, including a range of lingerie by Agent Provocateur. Mick's mouth, *The New Yorker* recently noted, is 'a brand as recognizable on the corporate landscape as McDonald's golden arches'. Over the same period, Jagger–Richard songs are calculated to have earned in excess of $56 million, a significant tranche of this from the computer industry. Microsoft paid $4 million to use 'Start Me Up' to launch its Windows 95 software, and Apple an undisclosed but hardly lesser sum for 'She's a Rainbow' to market coloured Macs.

All of this flows into a nest of companies, based in Holland for its advantageous tax rules, with low-key names like Promopub, Promotone and Musidor; at the top, rather like some blue-chip law firm, is a partnership comprising Sir Mick, Keith, Charlie and Ronnie. America's *Fortune* magazine recently tried to discover if every partner received an equal share, but, after extensive quizzing of their financial advisers, had to report that 'no one will go there'.

On the *Sunday Times* 2011 Rich List, Sir Mick stood at number eight in the entertainers' category with an estimated £190 million, just behind Elton John and just ahead of Sting. Yet 'Stargroves', his house on Mustique, is available for rent during part of each year. According to the rental agent, the place is left just as it was during his occupancy, with family pictures and possessions still on view. Sir Mick personally vets each application and automatically excludes rock stars because of the mess they make.

Under his personal trainer, the famous Norwegian Torje Eike, he maintains as strenuous a fitness regime as ever, with daily running, swimming, cycling, gym work, yoga and Pilates. He drinks a great deal less than formerly, and exercises those once omnivorous lips on a sensible diet of wholegrain bread, rice, beans, pasta, chicken and fish. He also takes numerous supplements, vitamins A, C, D and E as well as B complexes, cod liver oil, ginseng and ginkgo biloba. In an age when even celebrity chefs beat a path to the plastic surgeon's door, he rather impressively sticks to the face he was born with, relying instead on anti-ageing creams and moisturisers – including the £350-per-bottle Crème de la Mer – to soften the Mount Rushmore gullies and crevasses. In other words, the show goes on.

Rumours about a new Rolling Stones tour began circulating in 2010 and strengthened the following year when U2 broke *A Bigger Bang's* $558 million record. In 2011 there was talk of the Stones headlining at the Glastonbury Festival, the last major gap in their CV (although Chris Jagger has appeared on a fringe stage there with his band Atcha, loyally cheered on by nieces Elizabeth and Georgia May and nephew James, but almost no one else). Media opinion was that with the Stones' fiftieth anniversary coming in 2012, Sir Mick would have to end his quarrel with 'the Human Riff' – or should that now be 'Rift'? – over *Life* and take the Stones out for a final farewell withdrawal from the biggest cash point in the universe.

Then it emerged that Sir Mick had put together another breakaway band, named SuperHeavy, and comprising his friend Dave Stewart, the Bollywood composer–producer A. R. Rahman, Bob Marley's son Damian and the serendipitously named chanteuse Joss Stone. For two years past, in conditions of MI5-like secrecy, they had been working on a début album with a no-expenses-spared rehearsal and recording sched-ule in LA, Jamaica, Greece, Italy, India and Miami, and aboard Micro-soft chief Paul Allen's mega-yacht. It was a project, or journey as people said nowadays, of possibly even greater symbolism for Sir Mick than his earlier solo albums. To preview SuperHeavy, he chose the *Mail on Sunday's Live* magazine for its young audience on the borderline of music and fashion. Yet even here, his young female interviewer reported that getting anything quotable out of him was 'like trying to grasp mercury'.

SuperHeavy's eponymous début album and a single, 'Miracle Worker', appeared in September 2011, two months before a re-release of the Stones' 1978 *Some Girls* album. The single, said the *Guardian*, was 'not all that bad – pop-reggae brightened by an agreeably preposterous Jagger performance, so OTT you can hear the spittle flying from his lips . . . To his credit, Jagger doesn't entirely dominate the proceedings, although – as when he provided backing vocals on Carly Simon's 'You're So Vain' – you're somehow always very aware Mick Jagger is in the room.'

As July 2012 approached – the fiftieth anniversary of the first-ever Rolling Stones gig, at Soho's Marquee club – it was revealed that Sir Mick and Keith had got together in New York and were on speaking terms again. Sir Mick conceded that Keith might have felt left out of running the band during the eighties and, if so, it had been 'a pity'. Whether Keith in turn apologised for the todger reference was not recorded.

Speculation about a commemorative tour or show was heightened still further after Keith invited Bill Wyman and Mick Taylor to a jam session, seemingly prefiguring some onstage reunion of all surviving Stones past and present. To buy more time, the official anniversary date was set for January 2013, marking Charlie Watts's final, reluctant absorption into the line-up. But Sir Mick continued to keep his lips firmly sealed and to enforce the same order on the band's second rank. When Ronnie Wood innocently observed in earshot of a journalist that a reunion gig might be nice, he was hauled up before the CO and ordered to write a letter of apology to Keith and Charlie. As it was, the 12 July anniversary was marked by a brief photo-op with the band, posing against a mock-up of the old Marquee façade.

Nowadays it is a rare interviewer whose memory stretches even halfway back through Sir Mick's career. In a recent Q and A with his old ally *The Times*, he was asked whether the fiftieth anniversary tempted him to write an autobiography as Keith had done. The interviewer had no idea that he'd already had a shot at it almost thirty years earlier, and he himself thought it not worth mentioning. His answer headlined the page: 'I DON'T WANT TO RUMMAGE THROUGH MY PAST.'

In fact, he had recently announced yet another return to the cinema screen which, indirectly, would revisit his past's most lurid and terrifying episode. He was both to produce and star in a film called *Tabloid*, portraying a media mogul based on Rupert Murdoch, owner of the Sunday tabloid *News of the World* which in 1967 – before Murdoch acquired it – had set out to destroy him. The pre-Murdoch *News of the World* had, of course, been deeply implicated in the establishment dirty tricks that led to Sir Mick's trial, public pillorying and imprisonment, and so nearly broke a butterfly on a wheel. Now the paper was gone, shut down by Murdoch in the wake of the phone-hacking scandal, and the indestructible 'butterfly' was to morph into a tabloid tycoon. The wheel had come full circle indeed.

WE STARTED THIS rummage through his past at the BAFTA awards in 2009. Let us end it with his appearance at the 2011 Grammy Awards, watched by new sensations like Justin Bieber and Katy Perry, young enough to be his grandchildren.

His performance was a tribute to Solomon Burke, the 400 lb bluesman who had recently died after losing all mobility (but continuing to sing right to the very end, seated on a throne). In 2002 Burke had passed on the mantle of blues sovereignty to Sir Mick by wrapping him in a cloak; now Mick emerged from a rather smaller one to sing Burke's classic 'Everybody Needs Somebody to Love', that long-ago show opener for the wild young Stones of suburban Surrey.

In his sixty-eighth year, the turquoise-jacketed torso was still as slight and hyperactive as ever, the hair as modishly cut and unrelievedly brown, the stomach as awesomely flat, the eyes as starey and the lips as trumpety, the voice still beamed straight from Planet Jagger: 'Ever-baw-deah . . . wawnts some-baw-deah . . . someone to lerve . . . someone to ke-ass . . .' Another innocent vowel was murdered as he stood before the rapturous kindergarten, stabbing a forefinger by turns at the front stalls, the back stalls, the balcony and the gods: 'Ah need youw, youw, *youw*! . . . an' Ah need youw, youw, *youw*!'

Though the accent might be as fake as ever, he'd never sung truer words.

POSTSCRIPT

Scene: the crowded, sweltering carriage of a London tube train at rush hour on the Northern Line. Just after Camden Town, the connecting door from the next carriage – a means of access shunned by all normal people – is violently wrenched open and a busker appears. He's in his late thirties, with the lank-haired, grimy-bearded sixties-hippie look common to buskers old or young; around his neck hangs a steel-strung Spanish guitar lacquered black and festooned in dingy red ribbons. Although busking has been legalised at tube stations, there remain a maverick breed who work the trains, usually emitting horrible sounds, and not much more welcome than muggers or pickpockets. So now everyone down this section of the carriage hastily looks the other way; hands move instinctively to protect bags and wallets; ears brace themselves to be offended.

But this isn't the usual cacophonous nuisance; he's positively charming as he offers a deal – 'a song for twenty pence'. 'Here's one I wrote with Mick Jagger,' he says, then starts to beat out chords which even on a crap Spanish guitar, after half a century, have lost none of their wicked joy: 'Duh-duh duh-duh-*duh* da-duh-duh . . .' And even in this most unpromising of arenas, their effect is the same as always. Spirits suddenly lift; fingers begin to tap on armrests; bums to shift on seats; lips, of whatever nationality, to follow the master's:

'Ah cain't *git* no . . . Sa-tis-*fack*-shern!'

A few months later, BBC Radio 4 celebrates its long-running

Desert Island Discs programme by asking its audience rather than the usual celebrities to choose eight pieces of music they would choose to take with them if cast away on that theoretical desert island. As a trailer, a random selection of voices is heard on the air, saying which piece would top their list. One sound bite comes from a typical conservative-sounding R4 listener, a woman whose crisply authoritarian tones might belong to a duchess, a private school headmistress, a judge or perhaps a former director of MI5.

So what record, above all, would she depend on to brighten her solitude whenever she played it? Mozart . . . Beethoven . . . Elizabethan plainsong? 'Mick Jagger's "Satisfaction",' replies this voice of the establishment, 'because it's the story of my life.'

Such is stardom.

Index